SUNDAYS AND SEASONS
YEAR A 2020

Sundays and Seasons
2020, Year A
Guide to Worship Planning

The Sundays and Seasons family of resources

Sundays and Seasons: Preaching, 2020, Year A (978-1-5064-4968-5)

Worship Planning Calendar, 2020, Year A (978-1-5064-4965-4)

Words for Worship, 2020, Year A (978-1-5064-4971-5)

Calendar of Word and Season 2020 (978-1-5064-4969-2)

Church Year Calendar, 2020, Year A (978-1-5064-4966-1)

Church Year Calendar, 2020, Year A PDF (978-1-5064-4967-8)

Bread for the Day: Daily Bible Readings and Prayers 2020 (978-1-5064-4970-8)

sundaysandseasons.com

preludemusicplanner.org

Acknowledgments

Copyright © 2019 Augsburg Fortress. All rights reserved. Except as noted herein and for brief quotations in critical articles or reviews, no part of this book may be reproduced in any manner without prior written permission from the publisher. Write to: Permissions, Augsburg Fortress, Box 1209, Minneapolis, MN 55440-1209.

Unless otherwise indicated, scripture quotations are from the New Revised Standard Version Bible © 1989 Division of Christian Education of the National Council of the Churches of Christ in the United States of America. Used by permission. All rights reserved.

Revised Common Lectionary © 1992 Consultation on Common Texts. Used by permission.

The prayers of intercession (printed in each Sunday/festival section) may be reproduced for onetime, non-sale use, provided copies are for local use only and the following copyright notice appears: From *Sundays and Seasons*, copyright © 2019 Augsburg Fortress.

Evangelical Lutheran Worship (Augsburg Fortress, 2006): various prayers.

Evangelical Lutheran Worship Occasional Services for the Assembly (Augsburg Fortress, 2009): Various prayers.

"Thanksgiving at the Table: Remembering the Women" used by permission of the Evangelical Lutheran Church in America..

Annual and seasonal materials

Preaching Matthew in Year A: Mary Hinkle Shore

More Than a Warm-up for Easter Day: The Easter Vigil as Culmination: Craig Mueller

Thanksgiving at the Table: Remembering the Women: Gail Ramshaw

Preparing for the Season: Craig Mueller, Miriam Schmidt, Julie Grindle, Sonja Batalden (Advent, Christmas, Time after Epiphany); Paul Hoffman, Kevin Shock, Chad Fothergill, Jean Ely Grube (Lent, Three Days, Easter); Timothy J. Keyl, Elaine Ramshaw, Ryan K. Hostler, Shelly Satran (Summer, Autumn, November)

Seasonal Worship Texts: Jessica Davis (Advent); Mary Shaima (Christmas); Jonathan Niketh (Time after Epiphany); Joel Neubauer (Lent); Tracey Breashears Schultz (Easter); Justin Lind-Ayres (Summer); Kyle Schiefelbein-Guerrero (Autumn); Jay C. Mitchell (November)

Seasonal Rites: Rhoda Schuler (Advent Wreath); Elizabeth Rawlings (Advent Midweek Series); John Jahr (Lessons and Carols for Epiphany); Paul Hoffman (Lenten Midweek Series); Gail Ramshaw ("The Jews" in John's Passion); John Roberts (Vigil of Easter: Creation); Imogen Rhodenhiser (Blessing of a Community Garden); Sarah Stadler (Summer Blessings and Prayers); Jennifer Ohman-Rodriguez (Blessing and Prayer for Seminarians); Joanne Engquist (Blessing of Animals); David Mennicke (Remembering the Saints)

Weekly materials

Prayers of Intercession: Rebecca Ajer Frantz, Jason Bense, Melissa Bills, Elle Dowd, Andy Evenson, Erica Gibson-Even, Meghan Johnston Aelabouni, Lydia Posselt, Jim Rowe, Will Storm, Michael Tassler

Ideas for the Day: Darla DeFrance, Marie Duquette, Melody Eastman, Francisco Herrera, Derek Hoven, Jennifer Shimota Krushas, Kurt Lammi, Rebecca Liberty, Becca Middeke-Conlin, Joel Nau, Katya Ouchakof, Alex Raabe, Keith Spencer, Will Storm, Paul Walters, Sara Yoos

Connections with Creation: Siri C. Erickson, Scott Kershner, Leah D. Schade

Let the Children Come: Betsy Hoium, Jennifer Ohman-Rodriguez, Claire Schoepp, Mark Spitzack

Music materials

Assembly Song: Scott Weidler (hymns), Cheryl Dieter (psalmody), Andrew Donaldson (global), Justin Rimbo and Hilary Ritchie (praise/contemporary)

Music for the Day: Omaldo Perez (choral), Sarah Hawbecker and Mark Spitzack (children's choir), Nathan Proctor (keyboard/instrumental), Jane Irvine (handbell)

Art and design

Cover art: Christina Saj

Interior art: Gertrud Mueller Nelson

Cover design: Laurie Ingram

Interior design: Alisha Lofgren

Development staff

Jennifer Baker-Trinity, Suzanne Burke, Martin A. Seltz

Project management

Julie O'Brien

Manufactured in the U.S.A.

978-1-5064-4964-7

Introduction

Advent

Christmas

Time after Epiphany

Lent

The Three Days

Easter

Time after Pentecost — Summer

Time after Pentecost — Autumn

Time after Pentecost — November

Index of Seasonal Rites

Lectionary Conversion Chart

Time after Pentecost, Year A, 2020

If today is . . .	. . . it falls within this date range.	The "lectionary" number assigned to this date range in *Evangelical Lutheran Worship* is . . .	. . . which is equivalent to "proper ___" in other printed lectionaries.	In 2020, this Sunday is the "___ Sunday after Pentecost."
Sunday, June 14	Sunday between June 12 & 18 (if after Holy Trinity)	Lectionary 11	6	2nd
Sunday, June 21	Sunday between June 19 & 25 (if after Holy Trinity)	Lectionary 12	7	3rd
Sunday, June 28	Sunday between June 26 & July 2	Lectionary 13	8	4th
Sunday, July 5	Sunday between July 3 & 9	Lectionary 14	9	5th
Sunday, July 12	Sunday between July 10 & 16	Lectionary 15	10	6th
Sunday, July 19	Sunday between July 17 & 23	Lectionary 16	11	7th
Sunday, July 26	Sunday between July 24 & 30	Lectionary 17	12	8th
Sunday, August 2	Sunday between July 31 & Aug 6	Lectionary 18	13	9th
Sunday, August 9	Sunday between Aug 7 & 13	Lectionary 19	14	10th
Sunday, August 16	Sunday between Aug 14 & 20	Lectionary 20	15	11th
Sunday, August 23	Sunday between Aug 21 & 27	Lectionary 21	16	12th
Sunday, August 30	Sunday between Aug 28 & Sept 3	Lectionary 22	17	13th
Sunday, September 6	Sunday between Sept 4 & 10	Lectionary 23	18	14th
Sunday, September 13	Sunday between Sept 11 & 17	Lectionary 24	19	15th
Sunday, September 20	Sunday between Sept 18 & 24	Lectionary 25	20	16th
Sunday, September 27	Sunday between Sept 25 & Oct 1	Lectionary 26	21	17th
Sunday, October 4	Sunday between Oct 2 & 8	Lectionary 27	22	18th
Sunday, October 11	Sunday between Oct 9 & 15	Lectionary 28	23	19th
Sunday, October 18	Sunday between Oct 16 & 22	Lectionary 29	24	20th
Sunday, October 25	Sunday between Oct 23 & 29	Lectionary 30	25	21st
Sunday, November 1	Sunday between Oct 30 & Nov 5	Lectionary 31	26	22nd
Sunday, November 8	Sunday between Nov 6 & 12	Lectionary 32	27	23rd
Sunday, November 15	Sunday between Nov 13 & 19	Lectionary 33	28	24th
Christ the King, Nov 22	Sunday between Nov 20 & 26	Lectionary 34	29	Last

Lectionary Color Chart
Year C, 2019

Advent

Dec 1	First Sunday of Advent	Blue
Dec 8	Second Sunday of Advent	Blue
Dec 15	Third Sunday of Advent	Blue
Dec 22	Fourth Sunday of Advent	Blue

Christmas

Dec 24/25	Nativity of Our Lord	White
Dec 29	First Sunday of Christmas	White
Jan 5	Second Sunday of Christmas	White
Jan 6	Epiphany of Our Lord	White

Time after Epiphany

Jan 12	Baptism of Our Lord	White
Jan 19	Second Sunday after Epiphany	Green
Jan 26	Third Sunday after Epiphany	Green
Feb 2	Presentation of Our Lord	White
Feb 2	Fourth Sunday after Epiphany	Green
Feb 9	Fifth Sunday after Epiphany	Green
Feb 16	Sixth Sunday after Epiphany	Green
Feb 23	Transfiguration of Our Lord	White

Lent

Feb 26	Ash Wednesday	Purple
Mar 1	First Sunday in Lent	Purple
Mar 8	Second Sunday in Lent	Purple
Mar 15	Third Sunday in Lent	Purple
Mar 22	Fourth Sunday in Lent	Purple
Mar 29	Fifth Sunday in Lent	Purple
Apr 5	Sunday of the Passion	Scarlet/Purple
Apr 6	Monday in Holy Week	Scarlet/Purple
Apr 7	Tuesday in Holy Week	Scarlet/Purple
Apr 8	Wednesday in Holy Week	Scarlet/Purple

Three Days

Apr 9	Maundy Thursday	Scarlet/White
Apr 10	Good Friday	None
Apr 11/12	Resurrection of Our Lord	White/Gold

Easter

Apr 19	Second Sunday of Easter	White
Apr 26	Third Sunday of Easter	White
May 3	Fourth Sunday of Easter	White
May 10	Fifth Sunday of Easter	White
May 17	Sixth Sunday of Easter	White
May 21	Ascension of Our Lord	White
May 24	Seventh Sunday of Easter	White
May 31	Day of Pentecost	Red

Time after Pentecost

June 7	The Holy Trinity	White
June 14	Lectionary 11	Green
June 21	Lectionary 12	Green
June 28	Lectionary 13	Green
July 5	Lectionary 14	Green
July 12	Lectionary 15	Green
July 19	Lectionary 16	Green
July 26	Lectionary 17	Green
Aug 2	Lectionary 18	Green
Aug 9	Lectionary 19	Green
Aug 16	Lectionary 20	Green
Aug 23	Lectionary 21	Green
Aug 30	Lectionary 22	Green
Sept 6	Lectionary 23	Green
Sept 13	Lectionary 24	Green
Sept 20	Lectionary 25	Green
Sept 27	Lectionary 26	Green
Oct 4	Lectionary 27	Green
Oct 11	Lectionary 28	Green
Oct 12	Day of Thanksgiving (Canada)	Green
Oct 18	Lectionary 29	Green
Oct 25	Reformation Sunday	Red
Oct 25	Lectionary 30	Green
Nov 1	All Saints Day	White
Nov 1	Lectionary 31	Green
Nov 8	Lectionary 32	Green
Nov 15	Lectionary 33	Green
Nov 22	Christ the King (Lect. 34)	White/Green
Nov 26	Day of Thanksgiving (USA)	Green

Introduction

Welcome to the 2020 edition

For twenty-five years, *Sundays and Seasons* has been a trusted worship planning resource, guiding the church's leaders as they prepare for worship in their communities. Whether you are encountering *Sundays and Seasons* for the very first time or it has been essential for you for many years, you are welcome here! As it has been from the beginning, the Sundays and Seasons family of resources continues to support week-by-week planning for Lutherans with content and ideas shaped by the Revised Common Lectionary, the church year, and the assembly gathered around word and sacrament. Its robust family of resources includes the online planning tool, sundaysandseasons.com.

Since 2015 we have also published *Sundays and Seasons: Preaching*, an annual print resource that encourages and provides help for lectionary preaching, taking into account all the readings for the day, in addition to the rest of the service and the day itself in the church year. For each day, someone writing from the perspective of a scholar addresses the question, "What would I want my pastor to know about these readings, this day, in approaching the sermon-writing task?" And a practicing preacher—a different one for each day—provides ideas for ways to craft a sermon that compellingly confronts the worshiping assembly with law and gospel in the vital Lutheran tradition.

New in 2020

In addition to the many dimensions of *Sundays and Seasons* you have come to depend on, the 2020 edition introduces three new features. In 2020 the Evangelical Lutheran Church in America celebrates the fiftieth anniversary of women's ordination. You will find "Remembering the Women," a thanksgiving at the table rich with references to biblical women on page 18. As other resources celebrating this anniversary will become available after this volume has gone to press, we encourage you to seek out materials being developed by the ELCA and Women of the ELCA in 2020. Second, the seasonal introductions this year were written by teams of writers, each author attentive to a specific area: preaching, intercessory prayer, assembly song, or worship space. This collaboration allowed for more focused ideas and reflection on these dimensions of worship. Finally, each Sunday and festival in the church year includes a section titled "Connections with Creation." This new section attends to how the lectionary, the church year, and the weekly gathering around word and sacrament inform our awareness and care of creation.

With the whole church

This resource would not exist without the creative talents of many people across the church. Pastors, musicians, deacons, members of worship committees and altar guilds, seminary professors, and visual artists contribute their wisdom and ideas. They work full-time, part-time, or are volunteers in their churches. They serve large and small congregations and campus ministries in rural areas, small towns, cities, and suburbs in the United States, Canada, and abroad. They come from various cultural contexts and with different approaches to worship in word and sacrament. Over the past twenty-five years literally hundreds of people have contributed to *Sundays and Seasons*. Here's this year's group.

Visual art

Gertrud Mueller Nelson (interior art) grew up in St. Paul, Minnesota. She is an illustrator, author, speaker, and designer. Montessori, the domestic church, and Jung's psychology are often subjects of her lectures and writing. She has written and/ or illustrated thirteen books including the best seller *To Dance with God* (Paulist Press, 1986). Best of all, she is the Oma of three grandchildren. Gertrud lives in San Diego. **Christina Saj** (cover art) has had a longtime fascination with spiritual objects and universal symbols. Using their formal and structural elements as a departure point, she creates paintings in which the symbols can be recognized and reinvented so they may reflect the character of the time in which they were created. Christina lives and works in Cedar Grove, New Jersey. www.christinasaj.com.

Annual and seasonal materials

Sonja Batalden (Advent/Christmas/Time after Epiphany worship space) is a nurse midwife working in a community clinic in St. Paul, Minnesota. She also loves to bring community and worship to life through creative communal art. **Tracey Breashears Schultz** (Easter texts) is bishop's associate for candidacy, call, education, and leadership in the Texas-Louisiana Gulf Coast Synod. She lives with her husband Chris in the Houston Heights. **Jessica Davis** (Advent texts) is a Christian educator and chaplain for #decolonizeLutheranism. She lives in the Philadelphia area and received her MA in religion from the Lutheran Seminary at Philadelphia. **Joanne Engquist** (Blessing of Animals) is lead pastor at Gethsemane Lutheran in Seattle. She gratefully serves in ministries that extend hospitality to the stranger, feed the hungry, and deepen both trust in God and love for others. **Chad Fothergill** (Lent/Three Days/Easter assembly song) is a church musician and musicologist based in Birmingham, Alabama. **Julie Grindle** (Advent/Christmas/Time after Epiphany assembly song) is a lifelong church musician. She serves as director of music ministries at St. Mark's Lutheran in Baldwinsville, New York, and is the outgoing president of the Association of Lutheran Church Musicians. **Jean Ely Grube** (Lent/Three Days/Easter worship space) leads the arts and environment team at St. Paul's Lutheran in Dallas, Pennsylvania. She serves on the worship team of the Northeast Pennsylvania Synod. **Paul Hoffman** (Lent/Three Days/Easter preaching; Lenten midweek series) of Seattle is the author of *Faith Forming Faith* and is called by the Northwest Washington Synod as a writer and teacher. **Ryan K. Hostler** (Summer/Autumn/November assembly song) is an ELCA deacon and serves as the minister of music and worship at Our Savior in Vero Beach, Florida. His simple but profound calling is nurturing the song of the church. **Mary Hinkle Shore** (Preaching Matthew) is pastor of Lutheran Church of the Good Shepherd in Brevard, North Carolina. **John Jahr** (Lessons and Carols for Epiphany) is director of music and organist at Good Shepherd Lutheran in Raleigh, North Carolina. **Timothy J. Keyl** (Summer/Autumn/November preaching) is pastor at Bethesda Lutheran in New Haven, Connecticut, and is director of the Lutheran Studies Program at Yale Divinity School. **Justin Lind-Ayres** (Summer texts) is pastor to Luther Seminary and Augsburg University in the Twin Cities and author of *Is That Poop on My Arm? Parenting While Christian* (Fortress Press, 2018). **David Mennicke** (Remembering the Saints) has been director of choral studies at Concordia University in St. Paul since 1989 and of the senior and men's choirs at Bethlehem Lutheran in Minneapolis since 1996. **Jay C. Mitchell** (November texts) is a baptized child of God serving as pastor of Christ Ascension in Philadelphia. Self-professed liturgi-geek and firm proclaimer of radical-welcome, Jay loves connecting worship with what happens outside the doors. **Craig Mueller** (Easter Vigil as Culmination; Advent/Christmas/Time after Epiphany preaching) is pastor of Holy Trinity Lutheran in Chicago and is interested in the intersection of liturgy, preaching, virtuality, and outreach to the millennial generation. **Joel Neubauer** (Lent texts) is pastor of St. Mark Lutheran in Yorktown, Virginia. **Jonathan Niketh** (Time after Epiphany texts) has served as pastor of First Lutheran in Lynn, Massachusetts, since 2008 and is chair of the New England Synod's worship and music committee.

Jennifer Ohman-Rodriguez (Blessing for Seminarians) is a writer and early child development specialist. She is also pursuing a master of divinity degree at Luther Seminary in St. Paul. **Elaine Ramshaw** (Summer/Autumn/November intercessory prayer) teaches pastoral care online for several different seminaries, meets with individuals for spiritual wayfinding, works at an art cinema, and gives out comic books at Halloween. **Gail Ramshaw** (Remembering the Women; "The Jews" in John's Passion), a Lutheran laywoman, studies and crafts liturgical language from her home outside of Washington, D.C. **Elizabeth Rawlings** (Advent midweek series) is pastor at the Sanctuary, the Lutheran Episcopal campus ministry to the University of Washington and co-founder/co-conspirator at Disrupt Worship Project. **Imogen Rhodenhiser** (Blessing of a Community Garden) serves at Christ Church, Bloomfield Hills, Michigan. She is an avid runner, reader, and singer who delights in her spouse, their baby son, and their German shepherd mix, Vivian. **John Roberts** (script for the Vigil of Easter) recently retired after 41 years in pastoral ministry in California, Pennsylvania, Michigan, and metro Chicago. He has a lifelong interest in the arts and has brought those who are gifted in the arts to worship and the liturgy. **Shelly Satran** (Summer/Autumn/November worship space) is senior pastor at Faith Lutheran in Glen Ellyn, Illinois. **Kyle Schiefelbein-Guerrero** (Autumn texts) is director of digital learning and lecturer at Graduate Theological Union, senior adjunct faculty at Pacific Lutheran Theological Seminary, and a member of St. Mark's Lutheran in San Francisco. **Miriam Schmidt** (Advent/Christmas/Time after Epiphany intercessory prayer) serves as pastor/priest of All Saints in Big Sky, a shared ministry of the Episcopal and Lutheran (ELCA) churches in Big Sky, Montana. **Mary Shaima** (Christmas texts) is a candidate for word and sacrament ministry who is passionate about worship that is both reverent and relevant. Her other passion is snow skiing. **Rhoda Schuler** (Advent wreath) teaches theology at Concordia University, St. Paul, serves as pro bono liturgist at Jehovah Lutheran, and became a liturgy geek as an undergraduate at Valparaiso University. **Kevin Shock** (Lent/Three Days/Easter intercessory prayer) loves to serve God's people at St. Mark Lutheran, Pleasant Gap, Pennsylvania, and animals at Centre County PAWS, where his spouse, Lisa Bahr, works. **Sarah Stadler** (summer blessings and prayers) serves as pastor at Grace Lutheran in downtown Phoenix, Arizona, where they try to practice liturgy in such a way that everyone understands that liturgy is truly the work of the people.

Prayers of intercession

Rebecca Ajer Frantz serves as pastor at St. John's Evangelical Lutheran in Littlestown, Pennsylvania. She lives in nearby Gettysburg with her historian husband. **Jason Bense** serves as pastor of Lutheran Church of Our Redeemer and Gethsemane Lutheran, a two-point parish in Sacramento,

California. **Melissa Bills** is associate pastor of First Lutheran in Decorah, Iowa. **Elle Dowd** (she/her/hers) is a bi-furious seminarian at the Lutheran School of Theology at Chicago with deep gratitude to the places that taught her the most about justice and liberation: Sierra Leone and Ferguson. **Andy Evenson** serves as pastor of Christ Lutheran in Lake Elmo, Minnesota. He enjoys being a husband and father, as well as working on cars, fishing, and running. **Erica Gibson-Even** shares pastoral ministry at Christ Lutheran in Valparaiso, Indiana. These days she's pleased to have kids willing to enjoy nerdy books, games, and shows as a family. **Meghan Johnston Aelabouni** is an ELCA pastor studying full-time for her doctorate. She and her family live in Fort Collins, Colorado. **Lydia Posselt** serves Family of God Lutheran in Buckingham, Pennsylvania. In her free time she enjoys writing, traveling, reading novels, spoiling her two cats, and watching too much Netflix. **Jim Rowe** lives in Denton, Texas. He is a chaplain at a retirement and nursing community and a triathlon coach. He has served congregations in Michigan, Connecticut, and New York. **Will Storm** is a Lutheran pastor living in Saint Charles, Missouri. In his free time he enjoys the Sunday crossword with his wife, Erin, and walks with his dog, Moe. **Michael Tassler** is pastor of Grace Lutheran in Colorado Springs, where, if you don't like the weather—can't imagine why—just wait 15 minutes!

Ideas for the day

Darla DeFrance is the founding pastor of Columbia City Church of Hope, a new ELCA congregation in Seattle, Washington. She lives in the neighborhood with her family. **Marie Duquette** is pastor of King of Kings Lutheran in Ann Arbor, Michigan. Pastor **Melody Eastman** serves Grace Lutheran in Glen Ellyn, Illinois. She also enjoys hiking, biking, and playing bodhrán and penny whistle at local trad Irish music sessions. **Francisco Herrera** writes theology and music, travels too much, wants to cook for you, and is SO DONE with being a PhD student. Email him at chicago.polyglot@gmail.com for kicks. Pastor **Derek Hoven** serves Salem Lutheran in Orlando, where he seeks to unleash people to share their gifts in the gospel with their community and the world. Pastor **Jennifer Shimota Krushas** serves the world God loves alongside the people of Emmanuel Lutheran in High Point, North Carolina. She is not at all convinced that supermarket aisles aren't really karaoke stages. **Kurt Lammi** is the pastor at St. Paul Lutheran on Dog Leg Road in Dayton, Ohio. His writing has also appeared in *Living Lutheran* and *Christ in Our Home*. **Rebecca Liberty** has served in congregations and campus ministries in the western United States and Maine. She is the director of the Wilson Center for Spiritual Exploration and Multifaith Dialogue at the University of Maine in Orono. **Becca Middeke-Conlin** is the pastor of St. Paul's on the south side of Easton, Pennsylvania. She cohosts a podcast called Lit Liturgy on creative worship planning. **Joel Nau** is pastor of St. Paul Lutheran in Winterset,

Iowa. **Katya Ouchakof** is pastor of Lake Edge Lutheran in Madison, Wisconsin. She enjoys canoeing, knitting, Star Wars, the Bible, and her family. **Alex Raabe** is pastor of the spunky Oceanside Lutheran in Oceanside, New York. He loves creative worship, thuribles, cream soda, and believes that Christ calls us to love the world madly. **Keith Spencer** serves Trinity Lutheran in Pembroke Pines, Florida, as pastor, bread baker, and butterfly gardener. He is married to Piper and father to Christian, Thomas, and Luke. Photography is his passion. **Will Storm** (see prayers of intercession). **Paul Walters** is a Lutheran pastor serving in Troy, Michigan. He is husband and the father of three boys. Sir Paul is a Knight of Sufferlandria and a Moth Story Slam winner. **Sara Yoos** is a pastor at Holy Cross Lutheran in Menomonee Falls, Wisconsin. She and her husband, Rev. Drew Yoos, have lived in five different states in the past five years.

Connections with Creation

Siri C. Erickson is chaplain of the college at Gustavus Adolphus in St. Peter, Minnesota, and director of the Gustavus Academy for Faith, Science, and Ethics. **Scott Kershner** is an ELCA pastor serving as university chaplain at Susquehanna University, an ELCA-affiliated institution in central Pennsylvania. **Leah D. Schade** teaches preaching and worship at Lexington Theological Seminary, Kentucky. She earned both her MDiv and PhD degrees from the Lutheran Theological Seminary at Philadelphia (now United Lutheran Seminary) and is the author of *Creation-Crisis Preaching: Ecology, Theology, and the Pulpit*.

Let the Children Come

Betsy Hoium is associate pastor for faith formation at Prince of Peace Lutheran in Roseville, Minnesota. **Jennifer Ohman-Rodriguez** (see annual and seasonal materials). Deaconess **Claire Schoepp** serves at Luther Memorial Church of Chicago where her desk is always piled high with markers, baskets, children's books, and sticky notes. Stop by for chocolate. **Mark Spitzack** is director of music at Olivet Congregational (UCC) in St. Paul and coordinator of perinatal and pediatric support projects for the University of Minnesota Masonic Children's Hospital.

Music suggestions

Cheryl Dieter (psalmody) is business manager for the Association of Lutheran Church Musicians. **Andrew Donaldson** (global) was coeditor of *The Book of Praise* for the Presbyterian Church in Canada and worked as worship consultant to the World Council of Churches in Geneva. He has given workshops on global song in many parts of the world, including Korea, Lebanon, Hungary, and Scotland. He and his wife Wendy live in Toronto, Canada. **Sarah Hawbecker** (children's choir) has served Lutheran Church of the Redeemer in Atlanta as organist and director of music for children and youth since 1996. Her greatest joy is watching her choir "kids" grow up and keep making music. **Jane Irvine** (handbell) has degrees in music education with 30 years' experience in the classroom. She rings with the Mid Ohio Valley Ringers and served as the handbell clinician for the 2018 Augsburg Fortress summer music clinic in Columbus, Ohio. **Omaldo Perez** (choral) suffers from a chronic condition known as "Cantoritis." The good people of Zoar Lutheran in Perrysburg, Ohio, do the best they can knowing his case is terminal. **Nathan Proctor** (keyboard/instrumental) is organist and director of worship, music, and arts at St. John's Lutheran in Northfield, Minnesota. He holds degrees in church music and organ performance from St. Olaf College and Indiana University. Nathan is an active clinician, writer, and hymn festival leader. **Justin Rimbo** (praise/contemporary) is a deacon serving as the minister of worship at Living Springs Lutheran in Columbia, South Carolina. He loves his wife Angie, their kids Owen and Zoe, and their dog. **Hilary Ritchie** (praise/contemporary) is from St. Paul. She is the minister of worship and the arts at Hope Church in Richfield, Minnesota. **Mark Spitzack** (children's choir) is director of music at Olivet Congregational (UCC) in St. Paul. **Scott Weidler** (hymns) is musician at St. Stephen's Anglican Church and First Lutheran, both in Toronto. For 21 years he was program director for worship and music of the ELCA.

Special thanks to our summer 2018 editorial intern **Green Bouzard** for her many contributions to this volume. Green is a freelance musician, editor, and Lutheran Christian living, creating, and dreaming in Minneapolis. She also has the privilege to work day-to-day at Augsburg University. Green wrote some new day introductions and also reviewed and refreshed the entire set of day and reading introductions for year A—a huge task! She also provided editorial assistance with the prayers of intercession, ideas for the day, connections with creation, and let the children come content sets.

You make it happen

Sundays and Seasons continues to be a collaborative endeavor each year. In our editorial conversations here at Augsburg Fortress we regularly evaluate the scope, format, and quality of the content provided in these pages. Your feedback—collected from you firsthand at events around this church, from postings in various forms of social media, from phone calls and emails to our sales and service representatives, and from surveys—helps us make decisions about how to adjust content so it is even more helpful. You, dear partners in ministry, make this resource happen. We welcome your ideas for future content, your suggestions for potential contributors (maybe you!), and your constructive feedback. Thank you for the trust you place in the changing roster of contributors who offer their time and talent to the whole church through *Sundays and Seasons*. Even more, thank you for the many and various ways in which you care for the Sunday assembly and its worship of the triune God.

—Jennifer Baker-Trinity and Suzanne Burke, editors

Preaching Matthew in Year A

Matthew holds together things we find easy to separate:

1. Story and speech
2. Israel and the nations
3. Grace and obedience
4. Heaven and earth

These moments of dynamic tension offer a way into the gospel as a whole.

Story and speech

Matthew was almost certainly written after Mark by an author who had a copy of the gospel of Mark and copied both its content and form. To tell the story of Jesus' ministry, Matthew follows Mark's story line closely: Jesus is baptized by John and tempted by the devil in Judea, after which all of his ministry happens in and around Galilee until he travels to Jerusalem, where he encounters resistance from Jewish authorities and a death sentence from the Roman governor, Pilate. He is crucified and dies. After the sabbath, women arrive at the tomb intending to anoint his corpse, but they are told by a messenger that he is risen. This is Mark's story, which both Matthew and Luke follow and to which they both add additional material.

Most of the material that Matthew adds to Mark appears in five long speeches from Jesus. Five times Matthew writes "When Jesus had finished saying these things . . . ," using identical Greek phrasing in each case. These five statements conclude the Sermon on the Mount at 7:28, a speech sending out the disciples at 11:1, a collection of parables at 13:53, a chapter on resolving conflict and practicing forgiveness at 19:1, and two chapters on the topic of faithful waiting for the unveiling of a new age at 26:1. Jack Dean Kingsbury points out that the rhetorical effect of these speeches is that "the implied reader, in hearing Jesus deliver his great speeches, is made to sense that he or she, along with the crowds or disciples in the story, is being directly addressed by him."[1] The speeches give the story a "you are there" quality.

Israel and the nations

In the very first verse of Matthew we hear three titles for Jesus, each of which connects to his Jewish identity and to the hopes of Israel for a decisive demonstration of God's action on their behalf. Jesus is Messiah (or anointed one): in ancient Israel, prophets, priests, and kings were anointed as a sign of having been chosen by God to lead God's people. Jesus is also "son of David," a title that associates him with a great king of Israel. "Son of David" is often the way people who seek healing in the gospel will address Jesus, which may be Matthew's way of highlighting that healing of the body and wholeness/peace/shalom within body politic are related to each other. Finally, Jesus is "son of Abraham," a point that Matthew's genealogy will reinforce.

Beyond titles, this gospel tells the story of Jesus in a way that identifies him with Israel's history and its hopes. The baby is to be called Jesus, meaning "Yahweh saves," because "he will save his people from their sins" (1:21). His infancy reprises that of Moses: he is a baby under threat from a tyrant, narrowly escaping death and growing up to deliver his people. The wilderness is a place of temptation and provision for him, as it was for Israel. He reinterprets the law ("you have heard it said . . . but I say to you") and calls people to righteousness. Also, throughout the gospel, Matthew interprets the events he narrates as a fulfillment of Israel's scriptures. In Jesus, the words of scripture are coming true; they are coming to life.

Jesus is Israel's hope and the hope of the nations. As early as Matthew's genealogy for Jesus, and throughout the gospel as a whole, the nations (or gentiles) are in view as people to whom and through whom God's blessing extends. The four women in the genealogy (Tamar, Rahab, Ruth, and "the wife of Uriah") are all foreign to Israel. Listing these women by name points out that the God of Israel has always been working across the boundaries of Israel. In addition, non-Jewish people (the magi) are among the first to pay homage to Jesus. Stories borrowed from Mark of healing offered to gentiles continue the theme that the ministry of Jesus extends beyond ethnic boundaries. Finally, the last words of the risen Jesus to his Jewish disciples are a commission to make disciples of *all* nations, thus further extending his teaching. Jesus is the Jewish Messiah, in whom all the nations of the earth will be blessed.

Grace and obedience

The word "hypocrite/s" is used seventeen times in the New Testament: once in Mark, three times in Luke, and fourteen times in Matthew. Throughout Matthew's gospel, we read of the need for words and actions to be in sync. John urges those coming for

---

1 Jack Dean Kingsbury, *Matthew as Story*, 2nd ed. (Fortress Press, 1988), 111.

baptism to "bear fruit worthy of repentance" (3:8). Jesus concludes the Sermon on the Mount by contrasting the wise who hear his words and act on them with the foolish who hear his words and do not act on them (cf. 7:24-29).

At times in the gospel, faithful practice is actually more important than any words spoken. In the parable of the two sons, Jesus wants to know which one did the will of his father (cf. 21:28-32). The parable of the sheep and the goats addresses the judgment of the nations. ("Nations" here presumably points to those who are outside Israel and outside the community to which the gospel is addressed.) In the parable, reward is based not on what people have said or intended but simply on what they have done for "the least of these who are members of my family" (cf. 25:31-46). The commission Jesus gives to the disciples at the end of the gospel commands them to teach others to obey "everything that I have commanded" (28:20). Jesus is a teacher in Matthew, and he expects those who come after him to obey his teaching. One can almost hear James in the background, "Be doers of the word, and not merely hearers who deceive themselves" (James 1:22).

From this perspective, it is easy to see why Jesus is so often in conflict with the scribes and Pharisees. Jesus embodies faithfulness to God in word and deed; he calls others to the same faithfulness, and he gives the disciples a prayer that explicitly asks God to bring about the circumstances in which God's will is done and God's kingdom comes "on earth as it is in heaven" (cf. 6:9-13). The scribes are apparently uninterested in meeting one born "king of the Jews" even though they know from their command of scripture where to find him (cf. 2:1-12)! And the Pharisees "do not practice what they teach" (23:2-3). The problem is not that the scribes and Pharisees are moralistic while Jesus is calling people to freedom. The problem is that the scribes and Pharisees are hypocritical while Jesus is calling people to words and deeds that are aligned with God's will.

The question for preachers is how to inspire this alignment of words and deeds. How may we call hearers to "justice and mercy and faith" (cf. 23:23) without lapsing into moralism? In other words, where is *grace* in the Gospel of Matthew, and how is it related to the obedience that constitutes discipleship?

Grace is in the appearance of "God with us" and in the assurance of the angel in Joseph's dream that the baby will "save his people from their sins." Grace is in the statements of Jesus, borrowed from Mark 2:17 and 10:45, that he came "to call not the righteous but sinners" (9:13) and "to give his life a ransom for many" (20:28). Grace flows through Jesus' promise that in times of conflict within the community, "Where two or three are gathered in my name, I am there among them" (18:20).

Moralism asks, "What must I do (or think, or speak, or feel)?" The preacher working with a text in Matthew can avoid preaching moralism by asking, "Where is 'God with us' in this text?" "How is Jesus seeking and saving the lost *here*?" "How is

this text related to God bringing about God's will on earth as it is in heaven?" Answers to questions like these invariably make God the subject of some verbs. Asking such questions will lead preachers to ways that God is empowering the very obedience to which God calls us.

Heaven and earth

In Mark, Jesus announces, "The kingdom of God has come near; repent, and believe in the good news" (1:15). In Matthew, Jesus announces, "Repent, for the kingdom of heaven has come near" (4:17). Almost every time Matthew wants to speak of the reality Mark calls "the kingdom of God," he changes the language to "kingdom of heaven." Why? We think Matthew writes as a Jew who is concerned to keep the second (or in some numbering systems, the third) commandment, "You shall not make wrongful use of the name of the LORD your God" (Exodus 20:7). He wants to refer to the kingdom without needing to say "God" or the Holy One's name.

For Matthew, then, the kingdom of heaven is not "the place you go to when you die" but rather the time and place where God's will is done perfectly. Matthew's distinction between heaven and earth is spatial (the heavens in biblical texts are *above* the earth), yet this spatial distinction is getting at the same reality that theologians point to with the temporal distinction of "now and not yet." In the person and work of Jesus, the time (not yet) and place (heaven) where God's will is lived in its fullness is breaking into this time (now) and place (earth).

Of course, heaven is not yet fully present, which begs the question of what to do in the meantime. Matthew's answer is to pray for God's kingdom and will to be fully present (cf. 6:9-13) and to live as if it were. Part of the way Matthew tries to inspire faithful waiting is to warn readers away from infidelity with a picture of judgment that includes "outer darkness," a phrase unique to Matthew, and "weeping and gnashing of teeth" (cf. Psalm 112:10). This phrase appears only in Luke and Matthew, with Luke using it once and Matthew using it six times.

Why does Matthew feel it necessary to paint such a vivid picture of the horror of life apart from the divine presence? Often scholars speculate that as a result of their proclamation of Jesus, the evangelist and his first readers had been cast out of positions of importance or cast away from their community. Imagining that justice would eventually be served upon their enemies helped them endure present hardship. In this respect, Matthew's proclamation of judgment is not that different from Mark's words that "many who are first will be last, and the last will be first" (10:31) or Luke's report that Mary sang of the powerful being brought down and the lowly lifted up (cf. 1:52).

Whether Matthew's community is buoyed by the thought of someone else's judgment, these texts serve at least one other function. Judgment texts warn readers away from disaster. While modern readers may question whether there is any place or time that is void of God's love and light, it was clear to New Testament writers that such a place/time existed and was to be avoided at all costs! Think of the horror with which you might watch a child about to wander out into traffic. No! Such a thing should never be! This is the feeling that references to "weeping and gnashing of teeth" mean to inspire.

Put in positive terms, readers are to identify with the "faithful and wise slave" (24:45) who spends the time between "now" and "not yet" providing for the other slaves, and who is at work when the master arrives. As the community hearing this gospel embodies that faithfulness and wisdom, they will have avoided outer darkness in the future, *and* something equally important is happening in the present. They are letting their share of the divine light shine here and now. They are the city set on a hill that cannot be hid (cf. 5:14-16). Looking at them, others can see—even before it arrives in its fullness—that the kingdom of heaven has come near.

Mary Hinkle Shore
Lutheran Church of the Good Shepherd
Brevard, North Carolina

More Than a Warm-up for Easter Day:
The Easter Vigil as Culmination

We live for this night. These are words by Carlos Santiago, the first Caribbean-born lay person beatified by the Roman Catholic Church. Though Carlos faced his own "dark night of the soul" in the form of cancer, he loved the Easter Vigil and found great meaning in the paschal mystery of Jesus' death and resurrection.

Those who are unfamiliar with the Easter Vigil may assume that it is too long, too late, too boring, or yet another addition to an already busy Holy Week. The Easter Vigil may seem like an optional warm-up for Easter Day, but it is actually the culmination of Holy Week. The Three Days include the historical, ecumenical, and catholic liturgies for Maundy Thursday, Good Friday, and the Easter Vigil. To skip the Easter Vigil is to miss experiencing the many meanings of resurrection as expressed in the diverse service of readings, and to miss the important connection of baptismal initiation to the Easter feast. This brief essay is written for those who have not experienced an Easter Vigil or are looking for practical ways to build congregational support and participation.

This is the night. The Easter Vigil opens with strong, evocative language that declares the Easter Vigil as the center and apex of the baptismal life: "This is the night in which, in ancient times, you delivered our forebears, the children of Israel, and led them, dry-shod, through the sea. . . . This is the night in which, breaking the chains of death, Christ arises from hell in triumph" (*ELW Leaders Edition*, pp. 646–647).

In the early centuries of the church, before there was a church year and Easter Day services as we know them, the Easter Vigil was the annual, unitive celebration of Jesus' death and resurrection in one service. It was most often held as an all-night vigil, but the essentials then and now remain the same: a service of light around the paschal candle; readings from the Hebrew scriptures as pictures of resurrection; adult baptisms by immersion; and eucharist.

In the past several decades churches of many denominations have restored the Easter Vigil to its rightful place as the "queen of feasts." A growing number of worshipers would add their voices to the conviction: *we live for this night.* Not only does the Vigil celebrate the essence of our faith—Christ crucified and risen—it is a rich, multisensory liturgy that expresses in word, sacrament, narrative, and symbol the very meaning of our baptismal life in Christ.

Because the Easter Vigil has many moving parts, it deserves careful and detailed planning, and all the creativity and resources a congregation can muster. It is never too early for musicians, pastors, and worship leaders to dream, envision, and plan for the service. It will take effort, diligence, and determination to make the Easter Vigil the high point of a congregation's year. The hoped-for result will be the renewal and transformation of the community and thus loyal and faithful worshipers who invite others to the service the following year. For additional planning help, see *Worship Guidebook for Lent and the Three Days* (Augsburg Fortress, 2009) and *Music Sourcebook for Lent and the Three Days* (Augsburg Fortress, 2010).

Obstacles

Before we move to some specific strategies for implementation, let's consider some resistance to the service that may arise from staff or other members of a faith community.

It's too late. When the Easter Vigil was first reintroduced several decades ago, many congregations employed the late Christmas Eve service as a model. Sometimes the service was scheduled so it would end after midnight. If twelve readings were included and the full liturgy enacted, the service could last up to three hours. Set in the context of multiple Holy Week liturgies and a full slate of Easter morning services the following day, this approach rarely drew large crowds. Rather, it became a service for the most devout, a far cry from the Vigil as the very heart of a congregation's life together.

Ideally, the Vigil begins at sunset. Due to daylight saving time, the time of sunset for a late April Easter Vigil may be close to 8:00 p.m. in some places. If a congregation wants to build support for the Vigil from families (the Vigil can become the favorite service of the year for children as well) and others who are unable to stay up late on the busiest church week of the year, they may want to consider beginning the service at 7:00 or 7:30 p.m. Though it will be light outside some years and in some locations, this decision may be one of several compromises that need to be made.

It's too long. As attention spans decrease in our technological age, it is important to take this concern seriously. A three-hour service will be loved—or endured, as the case may be—by a small group of the most liturgically astute. Some congregations truncate the service to about an hour with an abbreviated service of light, a few readings, baptism or affirmation of baptism, and eucharist.

However, it is also possible with careful planning to do a rather complete Easter Vigil in two hours. It sounds like a long time, but the service moves quickly, especially if we are willing to enter a sense of timelessness and if the liturgy is multisensory, participatory, and fun (more on that below). A two-hour maximum may feel appropriate for many communities. With this in mind, careful attention needs to be paid to the number and lengths of readings and responses. In some communities the service of light and readings may take place in another space/s in the church building. This movement from space to space provides another change of pace that builds variety and momentum during the liturgy.

It's too dark. For many, a sunrise service is more in line with their expectations for Easter than a service in the dark. The ancient, all-night vigil is a new concept for many. The image of the large paschal candle carried into a darkened church is a striking symbol of the resurrection of Christ that shatters sin and death. In fact, the liturgy is a juxtaposition of opposites: darkness and light, bondage and freedom, sin and grace, death and resurrection. Though the liturgy begins in darkness, the return of light, music, and joyful Easter alleluias is a moving and profound part of the Vigil in many places.

Strategies for success and renewal

Involve many people. Since many people have not experienced an Easter Vigil, an important beginning point is getting them there, especially the first year. The more roles and the more people involved, the better the turnout. If the experience is joyful and transformative, these people will then invite others and say to them: "you don't want to miss this."

Find as many roles for people as you can come up with. Involve many worship assistants. Find a way to have one or more choirs sing. This may mean making compromises with musical leadership at other Holy Week services, but the Vigil should take priority. Ask your best readers to present the readings, sometimes using more than one person or even a small cast of characters to illustrate a reading. Plan ways to involve children and families with the readings or in other ways. Invite others to carry in the Easter flowers during the canticle of praise when the lights are turned on. Find volunteers to serve as ministers of hospitality. Recruit a group of people to coordinate a festive and elegant reception.

Schedule baptisms, confirmation, reception of new members. In the early church the Easter Vigil was the preeminent time for adult initiation through baptism. If you have adults preparing for baptism, this is the night to consider immersion. Some churches use a large, decorated horse trough as a baptismal pool! If you make the Vigil the time for other baptismal services (affirmation of baptism/confirmation and welcoming new members), the attendance naturally grows and the congregation begins to understand the importance of this service.

Have a lavish reception. Break the Lenten fast with festive food and drink. Have members sign up to bring appetizers or desserts, which is another way to bring people to the service. This is not the occasion for a bag of chips on the table. Go all out and make this the social event of your congregational life. If the Easter Vigil liturgy is the apex of the year, the reception should match it.

Have fun. For some, liturgy can seem like a serious endeavor. By using humor in some of the readings and a variety of styles of music, the Vigil will become a treasure that members will look forward to each year. Use the various talents in your congregation and think of the readings as storytelling, not simply reciting texts stoically. Design a Vigil that fits your local context. For example, make connections with justice, such as connecting freedom in the Exodus reading with liberation movements today, or connecting the flood reading with environmental concerns.

Plan early and get the word out. There are too many details and too many people to coordinate to begin planning the Vigil just a few weeks before the service. Form a task force that meets in the fall or right after Christmas. Involve all the staff and leaders in orchestrating the details. Work early on creative ways to present the readings. Publicize the service well. Have a special forum or a class on the various rituals, readings, and symbolism of the Vigil. Use Vigil themes and readings as part of Lenten midweek services. Make sure the pastor emphasizes the Vigil in sermons and announcements. If all the congregation's energy has gone into other Holy Week services, and especially Easter Day, gradually find a way to rebalance the week with the Vigil at the center and make compromises as needed. You may find that your Easter Day service is still packed with guests who are not regularly at worship while those attending the Vigil will be those most active in the worship life of your community. Some members may attend on both Saturday evening and Sunday morning, but others may only attend the Vigil. It is a paradigm shift but comes with many gifts and blessings.

Testimonies. Finally, have people tell what the Vigil means to them in special newsletter articles or in other avenues. Gradually, your community will be able to say with Carlos Santiago: we live for this night.

Craig Mueller
Holy Trinity Lutheran, Chicago

Thanksgiving at the Table: Remembering the Women

In 2020 the ELCA marks the fiftieth anniversary of the ordination of women. For this celebration the following thanksgiving at the table was commissioned by the ELCA for use in worship at its 2019 Churchwide Assembly.

This thanksgiving at the table (eucharistic prayer) includes an optional sung refrain quoting the Magnificat, the song of Mary (Luke 1:46). This may be led in a number of ways. The presider may chant on a single tone with the assembly responding on a single tone. A setting found in the service music portion of Evangelical Lutheran Worship *could be used (#234-235). A new tune could also be composed.*

All praise to you, glorious God of grace.
Throughout the ages you have blessed us
with foremothers of the faith.
With Sarah, we bless you for your gift of life. *Gen. 18:12*
With Ruth, we praise you for family and food. *Ruth 4:13*
With Miriam, we celebrate our escape from the foe. *Exod. 15:21*
Remembering Deborah,
we honor the words of your prophets. *Judges 4:4-5*
Remembering the woman at the well,
we laud you for living water. *John 4:29*
Remembering Junia, we thank you for those
who minister among your people. *Rom. 16:7*
One with the daughter of Jairus,
we wake to life in you. *Mark 5:41-42*

With Mary, we magnify your name:
My soul proclaims the greatness of the Lord,
my spirit rejoices in God my Savior. *Luke 1:46*

Remembering Martha and Mary,
we join Jesus at this meal. *Luke 10:38-39*
Living, he healed the bleeding woman; *Mark 5:29*
dying, he cared for his mother; *John 19:26-27*
risen, he sent Mary Magdalene in mission. *John 20:14-18*

On the night before he died,
he took bread, and gave thanks,
broke it, and gave it to his disciples, saying:
Take and eat; this is my body, given for you.
Do this for the remembrance of me.

Again, after supper, he took the cup, gave thanks,
and gave it for all to drink, saying:
This cup is the new covenant in my blood,
shed for you and for all people for the forgiveness of sin.
Do this for the remembrance of me.

With Mary, again we magnify your name:
My soul proclaims the greatness of the Lord,
my spirit rejoices in God my Savior.

Mighty God of mercy,
as you heard the prayers of Hannah,
so now hear us. *1 Sam. 1:27*
Send your Spirit on this bread and wine,
that sharing the body and blood of Christ
we become his body in the world.
Send your Spirit on this assembly, that like Phoebe,
we serve one another with zeal. *Rom. 16:1*
Send your Spirit on the church, that like Anna,
we tell others of your mercy. *Luke 2:38*
Send your Spirit into our hearts, that like Dorcas,
we care for the poor and needy. *Acts 9:40-41*

With Mary, once more we magnify your name:
My soul proclaims the greatness of the Lord,
my spirit rejoices in God my Savior.

All praise to you, powerful God of peace.
We adore you, our God,
Father, Son, and Holy Spirit,
you who mother and feed and comfort us,
today, tomorrow, and forever.
Amen.

Gail Ramshaw
Liturgical scholar

Advent

Preparing for Advent

Preaching

Preachers love Advent. Preparations for Christmas often stir up a combination of anticipation, anxiety, and excitement. The fact that the days are becoming colder and darker in many places brings other connections. Yet, Advent is the season that most honestly names and acknowledges our human condition of longing, waiting, and restlessness. Advent is usually seen in relation to Christmas, and though it is the time of year when listeners face the most distractions due to the many things on their minds and hearts, preachers have the unique role of being spiritual guides, providing time and space for reflection on key spiritual themes.

The texts of Advent can easily lead us into two traps: one in the past and one in the future. The prophecies in the Hebrew scriptures can cause us to pretend that we are waiting for Jesus to be born as he was two thousand years ago. The apocalyptic texts on the first Sunday of Advent can propel us into a distant future, wondering if and when Christ will come again to bring justice and peace to our earth. Though in many ways we are still waiting for the Messiah to come (again), and we need a healthy eschatology that trusts in God's promised future, liturgical preachers invite us to wake up to Christ's presence among us here and now. The Sunday assembly is the place we learn to recognize the Lord's coming week after week, but from there we go to behold anew this Advent coming in the events of everyday life—whether in the news or in our personal circumstances; whether frightening, confusing, or mundane.

The first Sunday of Advent is a particularly opportune time to speak of mindfulness and living in the present, even as the apocalyptic texts seem to name the end of the world at some time in the future. Year A is unique in that two of the passages (Matthew and Romans) speak of watching and waiting. In our age of instant gratification, the spiritual connections are many. Preachers might note the contemporary draw to yoga, meditation, and other spiritual practices that lead to an awareness of the present moment.

The human theme of longing resonates with all of us to some extent. We are always wishing we could delay aging, go back to a certain time in our lives and relive it, or live in an unrealistic ideal situation. In most cases, we fail to embrace fully the present and *what is*.

Images offer concrete ways to organize a preacher's reflection on Advent and daily life, and year A offers a plethora of riches: the peaceable kingdom (Isaiah 11 on Advent 2); the desert rejoicing and blossoming (Isaiah 35 on Advent 3); a farmer waiting in patience for crops to grow (James 5 on Advent 3); Emmanuel as God-with-us, even in the humble story of an unwed mother (Matthew 1 on Advent 4).

Advent puts before us this great mystery: *we wait for what we already have.* Preachers serve as spiritual directors, in a sense, inviting hearers to behold anew Christ coming again and again, Sunday after Sunday, day after day, not only in word and meal, but in the sacramentality of everyday life. There are abundant images to help preachers proclaim a word that has deep resonance with what it means to be human.

Intercessory Prayer

Advent is a short season of waiting in darkness and longing for the light; thoughtful repentance and pregnant expectation; remembering, savoring, and hoping for God's coming. How might your assembly's prayers be subtly—or startlingly—shifted over four Sundays so the assembly might "awake" through their interceding?

Silence: Silence remains a challenging aspect of prayer for many North American Lutheran assemblies. We are not like those gnarled desert fathers and mothers who willingly stripped themselves of words and images in their quest to pray. Instead, we are uneasy with silence. We do not know how to wait within it. We forget that silence is not empty but full. And perhaps it is silence's fullness that challenges us. In silence, we might actually hear God speak, which—if we are anything like anyone in the Bible—would scare the dickens out of us.

What if in Advent we incorporated more silence into our interceding? We could omit any spoken assembly response to the prayers, advising the assisting minister to count to 30—or 50—following each petition. Or we could further limit the words we use, crafting short petitions—*For the church. For the earth. For those at war. For our town. For the children in our community. For those who are dying*—but in between those petitions allow silence to grow and take shape in the worship space, waking us up to a new way to pray.

Preparing the assembly for such silence will be necessary. This could be done in the worship folder, or orally by the pastor before worship.

Music: While some assemblies may be used to praying the intercessions with a musical refrain or with instrumental music providing an aural layer behind spoken petitions, this practice may be new to others. A line from an Advent hymn could form the assembly response to each petition (see the assembly song suggestions later in this introduction). Or an Advent hymn that will be sung this season could be played by an instrumentalist softly throughout the intercessions, coloring how the assembly conveys to God "our lament, our hope, and our thanksgiving" (*Principles for Worship*, Application L-16B). Music behind or throughout the intercessions may serve to wake us up and help us intercede for a needy world.

Gesture: Another assembly might "awake" to intercessions if its members are asked to join in a bodily movement or gesture during the prayers. This approach must be introduced with care, as mandating how to pray—*Pray this way!*—will not help anyone actually pray. But perhaps the pastor, or prayer leader, or a collection of the assembly's children could invite those gathered to pray during Advent using their bodies. This could be as simple as an invitation to kneel. Or the assembly could be invited to lift their hands and pray in orans. Or the assembly could be asked to turn to the four directions as petitions are made toward north, south, east, and west. People, places, and events associated with those directions could be named in prayer petitions.

Our bodies can easily be forgotten as we pray, but certainly—and all of the people in your assemblies who go to yoga classes know this—our bodies can aid our praying. Our bodies, after all, are who we are. It is in, with, and under those bodies that we intercede for the bodies in our world.

Assembly Song

Advent has so many themes to explore, it can be overwhelming: longing, hoping, repenting, expecting; nighttime and the dawn of the new day; freedom and justice. How can this short season be meaningful without being overwhelming?

As you choose assembly song, fight the urge to schedule every hymn in the book, even though each is wonderful in its own way. Instead, read the lections; consider the direction the preacher is heading; examine your local context; and then look to the world and ask yourself: For these four weeks, what words can we sing that will bring new meaning to these themes? What songs can reshape our thinking so that we don't just sing about justice, for example, but learn how God wants us to be the embodiment of justice in our place and time?

"Canticle of the Turning" (ELW 723) has a powerful refrain for this new church year. While the stanzas of the hymn highlight different facets of the season, the refrain is easy to come back to week after week. It can be powerful as a sung response during the intercessions, and the stanzas can be used as a basis for those spoken intercessions. You could use stanza 1 as the gospel acclamation and stanza 4 as the response to the gospel. The hymn could also be used as the offering song or just prior to communion, as the assembly considers that the "hungry poor shall weep no more, for the food they can never earn" (stanza 3). Always ask yourself, How does singing the words (perhaps multiple times) change us and help us embody the good news?

The beauty of this hymn (and others mentioned later) is that it can be sung and retained by the youngest to the oldest. It invites a sprightly tempo that can be accompanied by piano, organ, a rip-roaring fiddle, or, with some creativity, Orff instruments.

Another hymn that can be used in multiple ways is "Come now, O Prince of peace" (ELW 247). Its language fits liturgically as an Advent processional, sung as the procession enters and then encircles the assembly ("make us one body"); a Kyrie ("reconcile your people/all nations"); or an offering song, leading to the unity of eating the meal together. The Korean text is also provided, offering a chance for a soloist—a child, perhaps—to sing the hymn in its original language, uniting us with Christians all over the world. It can be accompanied with piano, organ, or bells, or left unaccompanied for a more haunting sound. You could also experiment with an aleatoric setting: with the help of the choir, have the assembly start singing stanza 4 at their own tempo as the procession reaches them, and then as they finish the stanza, have them hold the last note until all are done—an embodiment of unity.

Finally, consider hymns that can be used liturgically—you could select stanzas of "O come, O come, Emmanuel" (ELW 257) as an acclamation, in place of the Lamb of God, or as a call to worship. "Wait for the Lord" (ELW 262) could be sung as a response to intercessory prayer, with the ending pitches hummed underneath the intercessions. And "He came down" (ELW 253) can be sung joyously in full four-part harmony, swaying gently, while the Advent wreath is lighted.

Worship Space

Not only does Advent mark the beginning of a new liturgical year, but it also opens this unfolding arc of the celebration of the incarnation from Advent through Christmas and into Epiphany. This new season offers us the opportunity to create a clean or refreshed canvas for our worship space. Advent is a pregnant time of waiting and watching. In some ways, we are invited into this fertile and growing darkness of Advent's womb, full of expectation for the unfolding of God's incarnation among us. Much as a pregnant woman tends to her health and environment in a new way when she is nurturing a child growing in her body, Advent affords a time to take stock and look anew at our worship space. How does it create room in our communal life for the ongoing incarnation of God among us? This can happen in big and small ways. How can you change your space to make room for a new thing to happen there?

Here are some guiding questions to help you reflect on your space:

- Are there pieces of art or fixtures that could be moved or removed for the season to create space for either emptiness or a new thing? The defined period of Advent can be a perfect time to experiment with removing something for a short time to create a change.
- Could changing the orientation of assembly seating, the area for proclamation of the word, or the feasting table open up new ways to engage the space?

How can we reflect this growing and rich darkness among us as a space that can give birth to something new? Here are a few thoughts to spark ideas:

- Many churches use an Advent wreath during this season. Is there a way your community might *embody* the Advent wreath? For example, you could ask worshipers of different ages to process with the candle(s) each Sunday, circulate through the worship space, and then set the candle(s) in place. The procession grows as the season unfolds.
- Blue is a rich and beautiful color. Does your space allow you to simply hang blue fabric in a new place? Can it hang from the ceiling or cover a wall that does not usually change with the seasons to visually open up possibility? Could you cut the fabric into four pieces or have four different shades of blue, hanging a new piece/shade each week to create an unfolding in the worship space that mirrors the anticipation and growing depth of the season?
- Can blue fabric or paper be used to create "rivers of living water" (John 4:14; 7:38; Rev. 22:1) that may give rise to a "tree of life" (Rev. 22:2) to flower in the wilderness (Isa. 35:1-2)?
- Is that tree of life a simple birch branch or a tree cut from nearby woods, or is it a bare evergreen Christmas tree awaiting incarnation, highlighted by a blue backdrop?
- What can you do in your space to visually hold the Advent season in its beauty, growing darkness, and simplicity to create a space apart from the way our society prepares for Christmas with hectic days leading up to December 24?

A pregnant woman has the unique opportunity and invitation to take a step back and take stock of herself and her environment. How is she preparing herself and her community to welcome this new child? In a similar way, worship planners can take a step back and take stock. What are the critical pieces to reevaluate or change so there is healthy space to welcome new life?

Seasonal Checklist

- Order candles and greens for the Advent wreath, or ask members of the congregation to make or donate these items. Consider a smaller, table-sized wreath for gatherings outside the principal worship space.
- Recruit volunteers of all ages to help prepare the worship space for Advent.
- Use the gathering song rubric in *Evangelical Lutheran Worship* to help you plan your Advent liturgy: "The time of gathering song may be brief or extended, and may include one or more of the following: hymns; psalms; a Kyrie; a canticle of praise" (p. 98). This carefully crafted instruction invites flexibility and creativity in the liturgy. If lighting an Advent wreath is the only thing you do that is unique to the season, let this invitation tap into new possibilities.
- Work with children's and family ministries to prepare resources that support household prayer.
- Encourage the use of the O Antiphons (versified in "O come, O come, Emmanuel," ELW 257) at home from Tuesday, December 17, until Monday, December 23. Sing the entire hymn on the fourth Sunday of Advent.
- Schedule time after the fourth Sunday of Advent to prepare the worship space for Christmas liturgies.

Worship Texts for Advent

Confession and Forgiveness

All may make the sign of the cross, the sign that is marked at baptism, as the presiding minister begins.

Blessed be the holy Trinity, ✛ one God,
the parent who rouses us from slumber,
the shepherd who gathers us on the holy mountain,
the deliverer who sets us free.
Amen.

Let us come before the living God in confession.

Silence is kept for reflection.

As we wait and watch for the promised day of salvation,
we open our hearts to you, O God.
Search us and know us.
Reveal all that we keep inside.
To you, O God, we confess our sins,
known and unknown.
Forgive us, renew us,
and lead us in your ways of justice and peace.
Make us reflections of the radiant love
of your beloved Son, Jesus Christ. Amen.

Beloved children of the Most High,
you are gathered before the righteous judge
who has mercy on all.
Splash exuberantly in the waters of baptism,
where sin is washed away in the river of life.
Dwell peacefully in the loving arms
of the one who nurtures all creation.
Go forth boldly in the assurance that your sins are forgiven
in the name of the one who is coming and is already here,
✛ Jesus Christ, our Savior.
Amen.

Offering Prayer

Giver of every good thing,
we set before you the gifts that you have already given
to sustain our lives and to share with others.
Help us to be good stewards of the earth and all that is in it,
and let our lives be a testimony to the abundant feast
you prepare for all who hunger.
Amen.

Invitation to Communion

Come now with joy to Emmanuel's table.
Feast at the banquet of hope and love.

Prayer after Communion

God of abundance,
we give you thanks that in this holy meal
you have invited us to feast with you and one another.
May the taste of your love remain with us,
and may our words and our work in your name
invite others into your bountiful grace.
Send us from your table to proclaim your presence,
even as we await the glorious coming of Christ our Savior.
Amen.

Blessing

May God, who gathers us in love,
lead you in pathways of righteousness and justice.

May God, who knows us more deeply than we know ourselves,
lead you in pathways of forgiveness and freedom.

May God, who fills us with good things,
lead you in pathways of equity and abundance.

The blessing of the holy Trinity, ✛ one God,
be upon you and remain with you forever.
Amen.

Dismissal

Go in peace. Christ is with you.
Thanks be to God.

Seasonal Rites for Advent

The Advent Wreath

One of the best-known customs for the season is the Advent wreath. The wreath and winter candle-lighting in the midst of growing darkness strengthen some of the Advent images found in the Bible. The unbroken circle of greens is clearly an image of everlasting life, a victory wreath, the crown of Christ, or the wheel of time itself. Christians use the wreath as a sign that Christ reaches into our time to lead us to the light of everlasting life. The four candles mark the progress of the four weeks of Advent and the growth of light. Sometimes the wreath is embellished with natural dried flowers or fruit. Its evergreen branches lead the household and the congregation to the evergreen Christmas tree. In many homes, the family gathers for prayers around the wreath.

First Week of Advent

Use this blessing when lighting the first candle.

Blessed are you, God of Jacob, for you promise to transform weapons of war into implements of planting and harvest and to teach us your way of peace; you promise that our night of sin is far gone and that your day of salvation is dawning.

As we light the first candle on this wreath, wake us from our sleep, wrap us in your light, empower us to live honorably, and guide us along your path of peace.

O house of Jacob, come,
let us walk in the light of the Lord. Amen.

Second Week of Advent

Use this blessing when lighting the first two candles.

Blessed are you, God of hope, for you promise to bring forth a shoot from the stump of Jesse who will bring justice to the poor, who will deliver the needy and crush the oppressor, who will stand as a signal of hope for all people.

As we light these candles, turn our wills to bear the fruit of repentance, transform our hearts to live in justice and harmony with one another, and fix our eyes on the root of Jesse, Jesus Christ, the hope of all nations.

O people of hope, come,
let us rejoice in the faithfulness of the Lord. Amen.

Third Week of Advent

Use this blessing when lighting three candles.

Blessed are you, God of might and majesty, for you promise to make the desert rejoice and blossom, to watch over the strangers, and to set the prisoners free.

As we light these candles, satisfy our hunger with your good gifts, open our eyes to the great things you have done for us, and fill us with patience until the coming of the Lord Jesus.

O ransomed people of the Lord, come,
let us travel on God's holy way
and enter into Zion with singing. Amen.

Fourth Week of Advent

Use this blessing when lighting all four candles.

Blessed are you, God of hosts, for you promised to send a son, Emmanuel, who brought your presence among us; and you promise through your Son Jesus to save us from our sin.

As we light these candles, turn again to us in mercy; strengthen our faith in the word spoken by your prophets; restore us and give us life that we may be saved.

O house of David, come,
let us rejoice, for the Son of God, Emmanuel,
comes to be with us. Amen.

Preparing in Christ's Presence
An Advent Midweek Series

This midweek worship series provides services of prayer, readings, and song around the themes of "Do Less," "Wonder," and "Hope." Each service offers times for silent reflection as well as opportunities for conversation and reflection using various activities as suggested.

Week 1: Do Less

Focus Question: What can you let go of or erase from your to-do list in order to be more present with Christ this Advent?

Begin worship each week with two minutes of silence marked by a bell or singing bowl. If possible, lead the congregation through conscious breathing. A ringing of the bell marks the end of the silence.

Invocation

In the name of the ✝ triune God in whose presence we wait,
the Holy Parent, fulfilling the promise,
the Holy Child, waiting to be born,
the Holy Spirit, illumining the way.
Amen.

Opening Dialogue

In the hustle and bustle, in the kitchens and malls,
it is hard to feel still.
Our to-do lists are long;
it is hard to be present.
We are called to stillness;
we long to be still.
What can you let go of, that you might rest?
What can we not do, that we might be present with Christ?

Song

Come and fill our hearts ELW 528
Dearest Jesus, at your word ELW 520
Arndt, John/David Gungor/Lisa Gungor/Matt Gungor.
   "Breathe" from CCLI.
We are waiting for Jesus MSB2 S543

Readings

Psalm 46
Luke 10:38-42
"Today," a poem by Mary Oliver (from *A Thousand Mornings: Poems*, New York: Penguin, 2012).

Reflection/Open Space

You may choose to enter into silent reflection or engage in one or more of the group activities suggested. If your context allows, more than one of these activities could take place simultaneously. Depending on the size of your group, you may gather in pairs or small groups to discuss what can be let go of this season and/or where you can find times to be still. These pairs/small groups can be accountability partners for Advent, checking in with one another over the course of the season.

This activity requires having stones and permanent markers available. Invite worshipers to write on the stones the things that are weighing them down this season. They could then come forward and drop them in a bucket or a pot. The pot could contain a plant so that something will then grow out of what was let go. Meditative music could accompany this action.

The ringing of a bell can gather the assembly back together for song and prayer.

Song

Give me Jesus ELW 770
Day by day ELW 790
Be still and know SP 2

Prayer

Ever-present God, in this time when busy-ness is exalted and it seems there is so much to do, keep our focus on you. May we let go of those things that add stress or distract us so that we may sit in your splendor, even for a moment, and be present to that which gives us life. In the name of your Son, Jesus, for whom we wait expectantly.
Amen.

That we are able to let go of things we do not need to carry and be present as we wait for Christ's return,
we pray to you, O God.

That we are freed to both give and receive during this
Advent season,
we pray to you, O God.
That we see holiness in the small things,
we pray to you, O God.
That through the stresses of this season we may live in and live
out your love and grace,
we pray to you, O God.
We lift up our prayers to you, O Lord.
Amen.

Blessing

God, whose presence grants you stillness,
Christ, whose peace helps you wait,
Holy Spirit, whose fire illumines your way,
✝ bless and keep you always.
Amen.

Song

Lord, dismiss us with your blessing ELW 545
He came down ELW 253
To a waiting world MSB2 S530

Dismissal

Go in peace. Be present with Christ.
Thanks be to God.

A greeting of peace may be shared by all.

Week 2: Experience Wonder

Focus Question: How can we experience wonder for God's
works and be fed by wonder in the midst of this busy season?

Invocation

In the name of the ✝ triune God in whose presence we wait,
the Holy Parent, fulfilling the promise,
the Holy Child, waiting to be born,
the Holy Spirit, illumining the way.
Amen.

Opening Dialogue

In the rush of the season,
we forget to look up.
Stars sparkle in the sky;
we do not pause to see.
Weighed down by life's troubles,
we lose the wonder of this season.
How do we reclaim wonder and awe
as we wait for Christ's coming?

Song

You are holy ELW 525
Beautiful Savior ELW 838
Come, light of lights SC 11

Readings

Job 37:14-24
Matthew 8:23-27
"The Birth of Wonder," a poem by Madeline L'Engle (from
        WinterSong: Christmas Readings, Vancouver: Regent,
        2003).

Reflection/Open Space

*You may choose to enter into silent reflection or engage in one
or more of the group activities suggested. If your context allows,
more than one of these activities could take place simultaneously.*
If screens are available in your worship space, invite people to
collect images throughout the week that inspire wonder along
with a short statement from the person on why/how it creates
wonder. Show each image for a minute (depending on how many
images you get). If the person who shared it is there, invite them
to share about the image(s) selected. Create space for conversation about the images and about what inspires wonder.

Invite those gathered to form small groups. Groups can
reflect and share about what inspires wonder, how long it has
been since they have felt wonder, and what steps they can take
to experience wonder this Advent. Reflection could be done
orally or through drawing or coloring.

*The ringing of a bell can gather the assembly back together for
song and prayer.*

Song

How marvelous God's greatness   ELW 830
He comes to us as one unknown   ELW 737
For the beauty of the earth   ELW 879

Prayer

Wondrous God, cultivate in us a sense of awe and curiosity.
Inspire us by your work in this world and in our lives. In the
name of your Son, Jesus, for whom we wait expectantly.
Amen.

That we see the world through the eyes of a child,
 in wonder, awe and hope,
we pray to you, O Lord.
That we find inspiration and joy everywhere we look,
we pray to you, O Lord.
That we marvel in your creation, around and within us,
we pray to you, O Lord.
We lift our prayers to you, gracious God.
Amen.

Blessing

God, whose creation fills you with wonder,
Christ, whose love fills you with awe,
the Holy Spirit, whose power inspires you,
+bless and keep you always.
Amen.

Song

Signs and wonders   ELW 672
Joy to the world   ELW 267
Stir up your power   MSB2 S547, SP 39

Dismissal

Go in peace. Be filled with wonder.
Thanks be to God.

A greeting of peace may be shared by all.

Week 3: Hold on to Hope

Focus Question: How can we hold on to hope in the midst of
the world's troubles?

Invocation

In the name of the + triune God in whose presence we wait,
the Holy Parent, fulfilling the promise,
the Holy Child, waiting to be born,
the Holy Spirit, illumining the way.
Amen.

Opening Dialogue

In a world of shadows,
we seek illumination.
As we wait in night,
we look for sunrise.
Surrounded by fear,
we hold fast to God's promise.
We wait with hope for Christ's return,
for the dawn of peace and justice.

Song

Wait for the Lord   ELW 262
Come, thou long-expected Jesus   ELW 254
For God, my soul waits in silence   SP 11

Readings

Isaiah 58:9-14
Revelation 21:1-6
"Still I Rise," a poem by Maya Angelou (from *And Still I Rise: A
   Book of Poems*, New York: Random House, 1978).

Reflection/Open Space

*You may choose to enter into silent reflection or engage in one
or more of the group activities suggested. If your context allows,
more than one of these activities could take place simultaneously.*
If screens are available in your worship space, invite people to
collect images throughout the week before worship that inspire
hope along with a short statement from the person on why/
how it gives them hope. Show each image for a minute (depending on how many images you get). If the person who shared it
is present, invite them to share about the image(s) selected.
Create space for conversation about the images and about what
inspires hope.

Invite those gathered to form small groups. Groups can reflect and share about what gives them hope and/or what tools they use to hold on to hope when they need it most. If people are willing, share with the whole group.

This activity requires packets of seeds and peat pots/seed pots/seed starter plugs, potting soil, and small strips of paper. Invite worshipers to write down a hope on a paper strip and plant it with the seed/peat pot and water it throughout the season. (Herb seeds that can grow indoors would work well.)

The ringing of a bell can gather the assembly back together for song and prayer.

Song

All earth is hopeful ELW 266
O God, our help in ages past ELW 632
Though the earth shall change SP 42

Prayer

God of light and darkness, in this season of short days and long nights, help us remember that you are always with us. Give us strength to work for your kingdom, living in hope as we wait for Christ to come again. In the name of your Son, Jesus, for whom we wait expectantly.
Amen.

That we keep our eyes on you through tumult and strife,
we pray to you, O Lord.
That we remember your promises,
we pray to you, O Lord.
That we work while we hold on to grace,
we pray to you, O Lord.
That we hold fast to the hope of Christ's return,
we pray to you, O Lord.
We lift our prayers to you, O Lord.
Amen.

Blessing

God, whose covenant calls you to act,
Christ, whose love leads you by grace,
the Holy Spirit, whose wisdom points you toward hope,
+ bless and keep you always.
Amen.

Song

Canticle of the Turning ELW 723
Abide, O dearest Jesus ELW 539
Only you, O God SP 31

Dismissal

Go in peace. Hold fast to hope.
Thanks be to God.

A greeting of peace may be shared by all.

December 1, 2019
First Sunday of Advent

The new church year begins with a wake-up call: Christ is coming soon! In today's readings both Paul and Jesus challenge us to wake from sleep, for we know neither the day nor hour of the Lord's coming. Isaiah proclaims the day when God will gather all people on the holy mountain and there will be no more war or suffering. Though we vigilantly watch for the promised day of salvation, we wait for what we already have: Christ comes among us this day as the word and meal that strengthens our faith in the promises of God.

Prayer of the Day

Stir up your power, Lord Christ, and come. By your merciful protection save us from the threatening dangers of our sins, and enlighten our walk in the way of your salvation, for you live and reign with the Father and the Holy Spirit, one God, now and forever.

Gospel Acclamation

Alleluia. Show us your steadfast love, O Lord, and grant us your salvation. *Alleluia.* (Ps. 85:7)

Readings and Psalm

Isaiah 2:1-5

The visionary message presented in this reading focuses on a future day when God establishes a universal reign of peace. Divine decisions will make war obsolete, and the worshiping community responds: "Let us walk in the light of that Lord now!"

Psalm 122

I was glad when they said to me, "Let us go to the house of the Lord." (Ps. 122:1)

Romans 13:11-14

Paul compares the advent of Christ to the coming of dawn. We live our lives today in light of Christ's coming in the future.

Matthew 24:36-44

Jesus describes his second coming as a sudden, turbulent event that will bring about deep change to our normal, day-to-day lives. Therefore, he urges people to stay awake, be aware, and wait expectantly, because the Son of Man will come unannounced.

Preface   Advent

Color   Blue

Prayers of Intercession

The prayers are prepared locally for each occasion. The following examples may be adapted or used as appropriate.

Keeping awake as we watch for Christ, let us pray for the church, the world, and all in need.

A brief silence.

Not knowing the day or hour of your coming, O Lord, the church cries to you. Strengthen the church in the land of Jesus' birth. Wherever Christians gather, empower them to proclaim love and defy the powers of sin and evil. Hear us, O God.

Your mercy is great.

Not knowing the day or hour of your coming, O Lord, your creation cries to you. Sustain the balance of all living things. Protect the earth from drought, bitter cold, eroding coastlines, and fires and floods, that the earth may flourish. Hear us, O God.

Your mercy is great.

Not knowing the day or hour of your coming, O Lord, the nations cry to you. Bring justice to the marginalized, courage to peacemakers, wisdom to leaders, and hope to generations who have only known conflict, oppression, or poverty. Hear us, O God.

Your mercy is great.

Not knowing the day or hour of your coming, O Lord, your people cry to you. Comfort those separated from loved ones by distance, estrangement, or loss. Help us as we care for others and rely on others' care. (*We pray especially for . . .*). Hear us, O God.

Your mercy is great.

Not knowing the day or hour of your coming, O Lord, this congregation (*or place of ministry*) cries to you. Guide our worship, service, and outreach, that our hearts and hands may be opened in generosity toward others. Hear us, O God.

Your mercy is great.

Here other intercessions may be offered.

Not knowing the day or hour of your coming, O Lord, we remember those whose days on earth have ended, who live now in your eternal love (*especially*). Remind us of their faithful witness, that their example might inspire our daily living. Hear us, O God.

Your mercy is great.

You hear the cries of our hearts, O Lord. Fill us with hopeful expectation, that in each day and hour we may love and serve our neighbors, in Jesus' name.
Amen.

Ideas for the Day

- Paperless singing lends itself well to the season of Advent; the easy melodies and repeated refrains support the themes of simplicity and focus. A sung refrain works particularly well with a litany or prayers as part of the rite for lighting the Advent wreath. Claire Cloninger's Advent hymn "While We Are Waiting, Come" (Word Music, 1986) is well suited to this style of music. Searching for the title of the song at the YouTube channel Music that Makes Community will lead to a video of MMC executive director Paul Vasile demonstrating how to teach and lead this song for congregational singing without using any printed materials.

- The texts this day may make us mindful of how unready we are for the inbreaking of God. In this season we often feel overwhelmed with busyness and what Sharon Daloz Parks calls *cumber*—an old word that refers to the accumulation of goods and the buying of more that can weigh us down and make it difficult to perceive God's presence ("Household Economics" in *Practicing Our Faith*, Dorothy Bass, ed. [San Francisco: John Wiley & Sons, 2010]). Worshipers may want to choose an intentional practice of making themselves ready for Christ by releasing cumber—daily (or weekly) selecting an item to purge from their home while meditating on the call to desire Christ above all things. The congregation might set up a station to collect items that could be donated to a resale shop or agency serving refugees.

- Stephen Bouman, former executive director of the Domestic Mission Unit of the ELCA, has often spoken of flipping societal walls on their sides to create tables for community—an idea that brings to mind the transformative image from Isaiah of turning swords into plowshares. Bouman's book *The Mission Table: Renewing Congregations and Community* (Augsburg Fortress, 2013) provides congregations with a framework (including suggestions for guided conversation) for actively and practically engaging mission for the sake of the kind of restored community Isaiah envisions. Bouman centers his approach in the understanding that the church's missional work flows out from the table of the eucharist.

Connections with Creation

The gospel for today describes a time of environmental calamity—floods sweeping away all life. The warning from Jesus, as well as from Paul in Romans, is to "wake up" and prepare for the inevitable destruction. We are not to be caught off guard, lulled by distractions or sinful behavior. On this first Sunday of Advent, consider exploring what it means for the church to be prepared for the growing environmental calamities as our planet warms. How can we help others wake up to the effects of climate disruption, while reaching out to vulnerable communities that have been ravaged by floods, fires, drought, and rising sea levels? Churches can become like those mountains in the passage from Isaiah, established as strongholds to offer a place of refuge.

Let the Children Come

The first Sunday of Advent provides an opportunity to remind children that a new church year begins today. Create a large black-and-white pie chart (the bigger, the better) with the seasons and holy days outlined in black. Prepare matching colored paper or fabric wedges to affix to the chart. Add a new colored "pie piece" at the start of each new season, or invite the children to help you assemble the entire color wheel during a children's message or in Sunday school. Consider making it out of sturdy cardstock, laminating the pie pieces, and attaching hook and loop fasteners so the wheel can be used and handled repeatedly and frequently. Like the Advent wreath, the circular calendar helps children to visualize the cyclical and eternal nature of the Christian life.

Assembly Song

Music Sourcebook for All Saints through Transfiguration (MSB2) *includes a variety of musical options for Advent, Christmas, and the Time after Epiphany.*

Gathering

Come, thou long-expected Jesus ELW 254, LBW 30
O Lord, how shall I meet you ELW 241, LBW 23
Savior of the nations, come ELW 263, LBW 28

Psalmody and Acclamations

Feeley, Ephrem. "I Rejoiced." SATB, cant, assembly, kybd. GIA G-9627.
Hobby, Robert A. "Psalm 122" from PWA.
Long, Larry J. "Psalm 122" from PSCY.
(GA) Haas, David. "Advent/Christmas Gospel Acclamation." Cant, 2 pt, kybd, opt gtr, 2 C inst. OCP 97089.

Hymn of the Day

Awake! Awake, and greet the new morn ELW 242, WOV 633
    REJOICE, REJOICE
My Lord, what a morning ELW 438, WOV 627, TFF 40
    BURLEIGH
Wake, awake, for night is flying ELW 436, LLC 276, LBW 31
    WACHET AUF

Offering

He came down   ELW 253, TFF 37, LS 4

Let all mortal flesh keep silence   ELW 490, sts. 1-2; LBW 198, sts. 1-2

Communion

Creator of the stars of night   ELW 245, LBW 323

Each winter as the year grows older   ELW 252, WOV 628

Soul, adorn yourself with gladness/Vengo a ti, Jesús amado   ELW 488/489, LLC 388, LBW 224

Sending

Rejoice, rejoice, believers   ELW 244, LBW 25

Soon and very soon   ELW 439, WOV 744, TFF 38, W&P 128, LS 2

Additional Assembly Songs

O heavenly Word, eternal Light   H82 64

For you, O Lord, my soul in stillness waits   GTG 89

We are awaiting the coming   MSB2 S536

⊕ Anon., as taught by Mrs. Lovisa N. Muykiya, Namibia. "Alle nasies/All You Nations" from *Hosanna! Ecumenical Songs for Justice and Peace*. SATB. WCC Publications 9782825416679.

⊕ Sosa, Pablo. "Este momento en punto/This Is the Moment" from *Este es el Día*. U, pno, gtr. GIA G-7021.

☼ Boyd, Aaron/Andrew McCann/Ian Jordan/Peter Comfort/ Peter Kernoghan/Richard Bleakley. "God of This City" from CCLI.

☼ Cantelon, Ben/Luke Hellebronth/Nick Herbert. "Ready for You" from CCLI.

☼ Grace, Ben/Michael Coia. "Advent of Our God (All Glory)" from *Advent*. thecalendaryears.com.

☼ Leonard, David/Leslie Jordan/Don Chaffer. "Wake Up" from CCLI.

☼ Ligertwood, Brooke. "Soon" from CCLI.

☼ Tomlin, Chris/Jason Ingram/Jess Cates. "Even So Come" from CCLI.

Music for the Day
Choral

℗ Brockman, Frederick Gustav. "We Wait for God." SATB, pno. AFP 9781506456959.

℗ Miller, Aaron David. "O Lord, How Shall I Meet You" from *The New Gloria Deo: Music for Small Choirs*. 2 pt mxd, pno. AFP 9780806698403.

O'Brien, Francis Patrick. "Awake, O Sleeper." SATB, kybd, fl, tpt. GIA G-5488.

℗ Schmoltze, Ron. "Each Winter as the Year Grows Older." SAB, org or pno. AFP 9781506425788.

Children's Choir

℗ ♫ Bach, J. S. "Zion Hears the Watchmen Singing" from *Bach for All Seasons Choirbook*. U, kybd. AFP 9780800658540.

℗ Hopson, Hal H. "Prepare Ye the Way" from *ChildrenSing in Worship*, vol. 3. U/2 pt, kybd. AFP 9781451462548.

℗ Shute, Linda Cable. "Stir Up Your Power" from *Augsburg Easy Choirbook*, vol. 1. 2 pt, kybd, fl, opt assembly. AFP 9780800676025.

Keyboard / Instrumental

℗ ♫ Diemer, Emma Lou. "Wachet auf" from *Augsburg Organ Library: Advent*. Org. AFP 9780800658953.

℗ Keesecker, Thomas. "Creator of the Stars of Night" from *The Quiet Center: Piano Music for Advent and Christmas*. Pno. MSM 15-843.

♫ Miller, Aaron David. "Chorale Prelude on Rejoice, Rejoice" from *Bayoubüchlein: New Chorale Preludes, AGO Houston 2016*. Org. SEL 160-616.

℗ ♫ Organ, Anne Krentz. "My Lord, What a Morning" from *Piano Reflections on Advent Tunes*. Pno. AFP 9781451462647.

Handbell

♫ Eithun, Sandra. "My Lord, What a Morning." 3-5 oct, L2+. AGEHR AG35285.

♫ Mazzatenta, Michael. "Wake, Awake, for Night Is Flying." 3-5 oct, L2. SF201997.

℗ Moklebust, Cathy. "Rejoice, Rejoice" from *Celebrate the Seasons*. L2+. 2-3 oct, CG CGB785. 3-5 oct, CGB786.

Tuesday, December 3
Francis Xavier, missionary to Asia, died 1552

Francis Xavier (sayv-yehr) was born in the Basque region of northern Spain. Francis's native Basque language is unrelated to any other, and Francis admitted that learning languages was difficult for him. Despite this obstacle he became a missionary to India, Southeast Asia, Japan, and the Philippines. At each point he learned the local language and, like Martin Luther, wrote catechisms for the instruction of new converts. Another obstacle Francis overcame to accomplish his mission work was a propensity to seasickness. All his travels to the Far East were by boat. Together with Ignatius Loyola and five others, Francis formed the Society of Jesus (Jesuits). Francis spoke out against the Spanish and Portuguese colonists when he discovered their oppression of the indigenous people to whom he was sent as a missionary.

⊕ = global song   ♫ = relates to hymn of the day
☼ = praise song   ℗ = available in Prelude Music Planner

Wednesday, December 4
John of Damascus, theologian and hymnwriter, died around 749

Born to a wealthy family in Damascus and well educated, John left a career in finance and government to become a monk in an abbey near Jerusalem. He wrote many hymns as well as theological works. Foremost among the latter is a work called *The Fount of Wisdom*, which touches on philosophy, heresy, and the orthodox faith. This summary of patristic theology remained influential for centuries.

Friday, December 6
Nicholas, Bishop of Myra, died around 342

Though Nicholas is one of the church's most beloved saints, little is known about his life. In the fourth century he was a bishop in what is now Turkey. Legends that surround Nicholas tell of his love for God and neighbor, especially the poor. One famous story tells of Nicholas secretly giving bags of gold to the three daughters of a father who was going to sell them into prostitution because he could not provide dowries for them. Nicholas has become a symbol of anonymous gift giving.

Saturday, December 7
Ambrose, Bishop of Milan, died 397

Ambrose was a governor of northern Italy and a catechumen when he was elected bishop of Milan. He was baptized, ordained, and consecrated a bishop within one week's time. While bishop he gave away his wealth and lived in simplicity. He was a famous preacher and is largely responsible for the conversion of Augustine. He is also well known for writing hymns. On one occasion, Ambrose led people in a hymn he wrote while the church in which they were secluded was threatened by attack from Gothic soldiers. The soldiers turned away, unwilling to attack a congregation that was singing a hymn. Ambrose is credited with authorship of three hymns in *Evangelical Lutheran Worship*, including "Savior of the nations, come" (ELW 263).

December 8, 2019
Second Sunday of Advent

At the heart of our Advent preparation stands John the Baptist, who calls us to repent and make a new beginning. As the darkness increases we turn toward the approaching light of Christ. For Christians he is the root of Jesse, the righteous judge who welcomes all, especially the poor and meek of the earth. We wait with hope for that day when the wolf will dwell with the lamb, and there will no more hurt or destruction. From the Lord's table we are sent in the spirit of John the Baptist to proclaim that in Christ the kingdom of God has come near.

Prayer of the Day

Stir up our hearts, Lord God, to prepare the way of your only Son. By his coming nurture our growth as people of repentance and peace; through Jesus Christ, our Savior and Lord, who lives and reigns with you and the Holy Spirit, one God, now and forever.

Gospel Acclamation

Alleluia. Prepare the way of the Lord. All flesh shall see the salvation of God. *Alleluia.* (Luke 3:4, 6)

Readings and Psalm
Isaiah 11:1-10

Isaiah describes the coming of a future, ideal ruler who will renew David's royal line (the stump of Jesse). Gifted by the spirit of God, this ruler will reign with perfect justice. Enmity and danger will be restored to harmony and peaceful coexistence.

Psalm 72:1-7, 18-19

May the righteous flourish; let there be an abundance of peace. (Ps. 72:7)

Romans 15:4-13

God's promise to include Gentiles within the circle of God's blessed people has been fulfilled in Jesus Christ. Christians live out their unity by welcoming and encouraging each other just as Christ has welcomed them into God's family.

Matthew 3:1-12

Just before Jesus begins his public ministry, John the Baptist appears, calling people to mend their ways and speaking of a powerful one who is to come.

Preface   Advent

Color   Blue

Prayers of Intercession

The prayers are prepared locally for each occasion. The following examples may be adapted or used as appropriate.

Keeping awake as we watch for Christ, let us pray for the church, the world, and all in need.

A brief silence.

God of promise, your reign has come near. Call your people to the way of repentance and inspire your church to bear fruit in the world through acts of faithful service. Lord, in your mercy,
hear our prayer.

God of creation, we pray for the wolf and the lamb, the lion and the calf, and all species whose lives are intertwined. Repair and preserve ecosystems (*here local examples may be named*), that all life on earth may be sustained. Lord, in your mercy,
hear our prayer.

God of the nations, teach those with power and privilege to serve the vulnerable. Give to all leaders wisdom and understanding, counsel and might, and a heart of compassion for the world you so love. Lord, in your mercy,
hear our prayer.

God of the poor, set tables of abundance in all places where hands are empty, where stomachs ache with hunger, and where hearts and minds suffer pain. Feed and heal all who are in need. Lord, in your mercy,
hear our prayer.

God of hope, renew in your people all joy and peace in believing, especially those facing anxiety, depression, or alienation. Guide this community of faith to welcome one another, just as Christ has welcomed us. Lord, in your mercy,
hear our prayer.

Here other intercessions may be offered.

God of eternal life, you promise to take away our sin and gather us in your care forever. We give thanks for those who now rest from their labors on earth, freed from pain and the power of death (*especially*). Lord, in your mercy,
hear our prayer.

You hear the cries of our hearts, O Lord. Fill us with hopeful expectation, that in each day and hour we may love and serve our neighbors, in Jesus' name.
Amen.

Ideas for the Day

- Repentance, even though it is good and good for us, doesn't always feel good, and it is rarely simple. In her book *Plan B: Further Thoughts on Faith* (New York: Riverhead Books, 2005), author Anne Lamott describes a time when members of her congregation struggled with misunderstanding and hurt around issues of race and expectations. She recounts a phone call in which she was confronted after speaking words she didn't mean to say. While neither party enjoyed the conversation, they kept talking, working toward reconciliation. Even so, the tension was not fully relieved by the end of the call. Lamott reflects on her sense of God and herself after her attempt to practice repentance: "I sat on the couch, astonished. God must see me as so many people at once: beloved, nuts, luminous, full of shadow" (p. 76).

- Sometimes our repentance is nothing more than our attempt to avoid punishment, whether it's getting sent to the principal's office or to hell. Other times our repentance is the realization that we truly wish we had not done what we did, and we pray we never do it again. We often follow repentance with confession and the question "Will you forgive me?" This can easily become a request that the person we have wronged let go of their hurt so we can feel better. Repenting and confessing without asking for forgiveness can be extraordinarily hard—but it signals that our primary concern is not our feelings of guilt or shame, but the well-being of the other. It might be interesting to keep the confession of sin during Advent but refrain from immediately asking God's forgiveness—an exercise in emphasizing God's will for restoration rather than our desire to escape condemnation.

- Consider placing on or near the baptismal font a basket or some other beautiful container filled with small stones. Next to the container place a pile of cards with the words "God is able from these stones to raise up children to Abraham" (Matt. 3:9). Invite worshipers to take a stone home with them, place it near their Advent wreath or wherever they pray, and reflect through the season on how God continues, in baptism, to raise them up from hardness of heart to a life that bears fruit worthy of repentance.

Connections with Creation

Mountains, sun, moon, rain falling on grass, showers watering the earth—God has authority over all aspects of creation. This puts human efforts to dominate nature in perspective. As much as we have attempted to gain mastery over land, water, animals, and insects, our hubris has often done more harm than good. What are the "stumps" that have resulted from this battle with nature? A quick internet search turns up heartbreaking images of entire forests in the Amazon cut to their roots. Yet indigenous communities, environmental groups, scientists, and a growing number of young people are working to protect existing forests and replant clear-cut regions. How can your congregation support these "shoots" rising up with new life? Christians can carry out the work of making peace with creation. "They will not hurt or destroy on all my holy mountain" (Isa. 11:9), because they will recognize that the earth is, indeed, full of the knowledge of the Lord.

Let the Children Come

The peaceable kingdom was a favorite subject for Quaker minister and painter Edward Hicks, who created at least sixty-two paintings of this messianic prophecy. Check your local library to see if they have art prints or art books of Hicks's work, and bring a poster or coffee table book that illustrates the comforting and vivid prophecies of Isaiah in today's Old Testament reading. You may also print two of Hicks's peaceable kingdom paintings, which are in the public domain, at the websites for the National Gallery of Art (nga.gov) and the Metropolitan Museum of Art (metmuseum.org). Display the artwork on a beautiful small table or stand where the assembly will see it as they enter the worship space. Children will readily take in the comforting concept of ordinarily discordant animals living together in friendship in God's promised new world.

Assembly Song
Gathering

Blessed be the God of Israel ELW 250, ELW 552, WOV 725, W&P 20

Fling wide the door ELW 259, LBW 32

The King shall come ELW 260, LS 5, LBW 33

Psalmody and Acclamations

Haas, David. "In the Time of God (Psalm 72)." Choir, cant, assembly, kybd, gt, opt hb, 2 C inst. GIA G-5657.

Mayernik, Luke. "Second Sunday of Advent A" from 5GP.

Mummert, Mark. "Psalm 72," Refrain 2, from PSCY.

(GA) Haas, David. "Advent/Christmas Gospel Acclamation." Cant, 2 pt, kybd, opt gtr, 2 C inst. OCP 97089.

Hymn of the Day

Comfort, comfort now my people ELW 256, LBW 29
FREU DICH SEHR

He came down ELW 253, TFF 37, LS 4 *HE CAME DOWN*

On Jordan's bank the Baptist's cry ELW 249, LBW 36
PUER NOBIS

Offering

Come now, O Prince of peace ELW 247, LS 13

Let all mortal flesh keep silence ELW 490, sts. 1-2; LBW 198, sts. 1-2

Communion

Lo, how a rose e'er blooming ELW 272, LBW 58

The King shall come ELW 260, LS 5, LBW 33

Wait for the Lord ELW 262

Sending

Hark! A thrilling voice is sounding! ELW 246, LBW 37

O day of peace ELW 711, WOV 762

Additional Assembly Songs

Blessed be the King whose coming H82 74

Let us prepare MSB2 S545

We wait the peaceful kingdom GTG 378

⊕ Central Moluccas traditional melody, adapt. Christian Isaak Tamaela. "We Wait" from *Hosanna! Ecumenical Songs for Justice and Peace.* SATB. WCC Publications 9782825416679.

⊕ Mulrain, George. "Animal Choir" from *Put Your Arms around the World.* U, pno. GBGMusik 9781933663166.

☼ Bridges, Michael/George Baum. "Sign" from *Pronto.* speedwood.com.

☼ Church of the Beloved. "What Happens When God Comes Close" from *Adventus.* cotb.bandcamp.com.

☼ Marshall, Eric J. "Come to Us, O Lord," from CCLI.

☼ Oakes, Flo Paris/Katy Bowser/Sandra McCracken. "Isaiah 11" from *Waiting Songs.* rainforroots.bandcamp.com.

☼ Rand, Hannah/Lenora Rand/Gary Rand. "Waiting for You" from *Waiting: Advent & Christmas.* themany1.bandcamp.com.

☼ Riddle, Jeremy. "Prepare the Way of the Lord" from CCLI.

Music for the Day
Choral

P ♫ Culloton, Michael. "Comfort, Comfort Now My People." SSAA, fl, opt perc. GAL 1.3489.

King, Betty Jackson. "I Want God's Heaven to Be Mine" from *The Oxford Book of Spirituals.* SATB, a cap, sop or tenor solo. OXF 9780193863040.

P Rives, Vell. "O Savior of Our Fallen Race." SAB, kybd. AFP 9781506447414.

P Shaw, Timothy. "Come, Thou Long-Expected Jesus" from *The Augsburg Choirbook for Advent, Christmas, and Epiphany.* 2 pt mxd, kybd. AFP 9780800678586.

Children's Choir

P Hopson, Hal H. "Now Hear the Glad Tidings." U, kybd. AFP 9781506456805.

P Keesecker, Thomas. "Hail to the Lord's Anointed" from *The New Gloria Deo,* vol. 2. 2 pt, pno, opt 2nd kybd/gtr. AFP 9781451424133.

P Schalk, Carl. "A Carol for Advent." U, kybd, fl. SEL 405-156.

Keyboard / Instrumental

P ♫ Coman, Ellen. "Comfort, Comfort, Now My People" from *Dance to the Lord: Piano Settings.* Pno. AFP 9781506426426.

Hobby, Robert A. "Prepare the Royal Highway" from *Three Advent Preludes.* Org. MSM 10-019.

P ♫ Hovland, Egil. "Freu dich sehr" from *Augsburg Organ Library: Advent.* Org. AFP 9780800658953.

P Raabe, Nancy M. "Rejoice, Rejoice, Believers and Come Now, O Prince of Peace" from *Grace & Peace, Volume 7: Hymn Portraits for the Christmas Cycle.* Pno. AFP 9781451499124.

⊕ = global song ♫ = relates to hymn of the day
☼ = praise song P = available in Prelude Music Planner

Handbell

♫ Moklebust, Cathy. "Comfort, Comfort." 3-5 oct hb, opt 3-5 oct hc, fl, fc, tamb, drm, L4. CG CGB856. Full score, CGB855.
Phillips, Judy. "Advent Fantasy." 3-6 oct hb, opt 2 oct hc, perc, L3. CG CGB751.

♫ Tucker, Sondra. "Scherzino on Puer nobis." 3-5 oct hb, opt 2 oct hc, L2. LOR 20/2068L.

Friday, December 13
Lucy, martyr, died 304

Lucy was a young Christian of Sicily who was martyred during the persecutions under Emperor Diocletian. Apparently she had decided to devote her life to God and her possessions to the poor. Beyond that, however, little is known for certain about Lucy. However, her celebration became particularly important in Sweden and Norway, perhaps because the feast of Lucia (the name means "light") originally fell on the shortest day of the year. A tradition arose of a girl in the household, wearing a crown of candles, bringing saffron rolls to her family early in the morning on the day of Lucia.

Saturday, December 14
John of the Cross, renewer of the church, died 1591

John was a monk of the Carmelite religious order who met Teresa of Avila when she was working to reform the Carmelite Order and return it to a stricter observance of its rules. He followed Teresa's lead and encouraged others to follow her reform. He was imprisoned when he encountered opposition to the reform. His writings, like Teresa's, reflect a deep interest in mystical thought and meditation. In one of John's poems, "The Spiritual Canticle," he cried, "Oh, that my griefs would end! Come, grant me thy fruition full and free!"

December 15, 2019
Third Sunday of Advent

A note of joyful expectation marks today's worship. Isaiah announces that the desert shall rejoice and blossom, and Jesus points to the unexpected and transforming signs of God's reign. We wait with patience for the coming of the Lord, even as we rejoice at his presence among us this day: in word and holy supper, in church and in our homes, in silent reflection and in works of justice and love. We pray that God would open our eyes and ears to the wonders of Christ's advent among us.

Prayer of the Day

Stir up the wills of all who look to you, Lord God, and strengthen our faith in your coming, that, transformed by grace, we may walk in your way; through Jesus Christ, our Savior and Lord, who lives and reigns with you and the Holy Spirit, one God, now and forever.

Gospel Acclamation

Alleluia. I am sending my messenger before you, who will prepare your way before you. *Alleluia.* (Matt. 11:10)

Readings and Psalm
Isaiah 35:1-10

The prophet describes the return from the Babylonian captivity as a joyous procession to Zion. God's coming reign will bring a renewal of creation in which health and wholeness will be restored. There is no need for fear, for God is coming to save.

Psalm 146:5-10

The LORD lifts up those who are bowed down. (Ps. 146:8)

or Luke 1:46b-55

My spirit rejoices in God my Savior. (Luke 1:47)

James 5:7-10

In anticipation of the Lord's coming, Christians are called upon to cultivate patience rather than discontent.

Matthew 11:2-11

John the Baptist expects the Messiah to bring God's judgment upon the earth (Matt. 3:11-12). From a prison cell, he wonders whether Jesus is the one who will do this. Jesus' response indicates that God's reign is indeed being fulfilled already through healing and restoration.

Preface   Advent

Color   Blue

♫ = relates to hymn of the day
P = available in Prelude Music Planner

Prayers of Intercession

The prayers are prepared locally for each occasion. The following examples may be adapted or used as appropriate.

Keeping awake as we watch for Christ, let us pray for the church, the world, and all in need.

A brief silence.

Holy God, we rejoice that your promises take on flesh in Jesus. Grant patience to your church awaiting the fulfillment of your reign of justice and peace. Restore in us the hope that we are called to proclaim to the world. Hear us, O God.

Your mercy is great.

Life-giving God, we rejoice that you coax flowers from the desert and water from the wilderness. Send rain to parched fields and sun to flooded plains. Nurture all that lies sleeping under frozen ground. Hear us, O God.

Your mercy is great.

Almighty God, we rejoice in your authority as Prince of peace. Deliver us from those who wield power through unjust and oppressive ways. Raise up prophets to speak your truth in this and every nation. Hear us, O God.

Your mercy is great.

Gracious God, we rejoice that you dwell in human bodies. Renew signs of your joyful presence in people of all shapes, sizes, ages, and abilities. (*We pray especially for . . .*) Empower all to embrace their callings and the gifts of your Spirit. Hear us, O God.

Your mercy is great.

Generous God, we rejoice that you create us to praise you. Strengthen the voices and hands of all who prepare to celebrate Christ's birth with music, dancing, and proclamation, in worship and in the community. Hear us, O God.

Your mercy is great.

Here other intercessions may be offered.

Eternal God, we rejoice that all who die in Christ are raised to new life. We thank you for the lives of those who have prepared the way for us and have now joined the great cloud of witnesses (*especially*). Hear us, O God.

Your mercy is great.

You hear the cries of our hearts, O Lord. Fill us with hopeful expectation, that in each day and hour we may love and serve our neighbors, in Jesus' name.

Amen.

Ideas for the Day

- For what do we hope in this Advent season and, more importantly, for whom? The question John asks from prison is common to generations of Jesus' followers: how do we discern the Savior's presence when Jesus' work can be so different from our expectations? In a sermon on Matthew 11 entitled "The Gift of Disillusionment," Barbara Brown Taylor says, "Blessed are those who do not let the Messiah they are expecting blind them to the Messiah who is standing right in front of them" (*God in Pain: Teaching Sermons on Suffering* [Nashville: Abingdon Press, 1998]).

- Multiple images from today's readings and the season suggest movement. Jesus makes the lame to "leap like a deer," as Isaiah envisions. The Magnificat describes how Jesus will turn the world we know upside down. The desert bursts into bloom, and God's people travel the Holy Way. Advent calls to repentance invite us to "turn around." In worship, explore one or more of these movements physically. You could invite one or a few dancers to portray one of the readings or invite the assembly into some simple movements suggested by repentance. Or you could pair movement with music, such as "Canticle of the Turning" (ELW 723). This website describes many possibilities for dance and other movement in worship: spiritmovesomega .weebly.com/carla-de-sola.

- "Be patient," James encourages (5:7), but this is difficult whenever we, like John, feel arrested, imprisoned, or doubtful. In our Advent waiting, we practice spiritual habits that can help us through any time we await God's revealing, hope, and healing. On this day, help people "strengthen [their] hearts" (James 5:8) for times of waiting. Give people a chance to list or share things for which they are grateful—a practice that aligns well with the traditional theme of joy on the third Sunday of Advent. Or, following the inspiration of David Lose, highlight specific opportunities for your congregation to use times of waiting to prepare for Christ's coming: "Because we believe Christ is coming to bring healing, peace, justice, and hope, we act *now* to make our congregations and communities, our country and world more healthy, more peaceful, more just, and more hopeful." Find his blog post, "Advent 3A: John's Blue Christmas," posted December 6, 2016, at davidlose.net.

Connections with Creation

Great reversals of injustice are announced in today's readings. This good news of reversal is not only for human beings but for the earth itself. The Bible reminds us that the health and well-being of people, and the health and well-being of creation, are integrally related. Isaiah describes desert places "rejoicing" with the appearance of the crocus. This little purple flower is among the first to announce that spring is coming. Even for those in the depths of dark, cold winters at this time of year, the knowledge of crocus bulbs lying just beneath the surface of the soil can be a welcome reminder of hope. As Mary carries a tiny body of hope within her womb, we too can remind those huddling in cold darkness that God's justice will break forth like "streams in the desert" (Isa. 35:6).

Let the Children Come

By the third grade, many children are able to read a Bible passage clearly and meaningfully. Today's poetic reading from Isaiah, with its short, straightforward lines, may be just right for a young person to proclaim to the assembly. The reading's many images will capture the attention of children: a desert in bloom, God's glory and majesty, strengthened hearts, sight and hearing restored, burning sand and thirsty ground becoming a pool of water, and more. In the midst of it all is a royal path to God's kingdom, almost like Dorothy's yellow brick road but without the fearsome ravenous beasts. Children need the same practice adults need before reading publicly. In addition, they might need a stool and a good microphone. Teach them how to introduce the reading and to allow silence for reflection following the reading. Instruct them to close with the phrase "The word of the Lord" so the assembly, including the children, can respond "Thanks be to God."

Assembly Song
Gathering

Awake! Awake, and greet the new morn ELW 242, WOV 633
Hark, the glad sound! ELW 239, LBW 35
Prepare the royal highway ELW 264, LS 7, LBW 26

Psalmody and Acclamations

Bedford, Michael. "Psalm 146" from *ChildrenSing Psalms*. U, kybd, 3 hb.
Burkhardt, Michael. "Psalm 146" from *Psalms for the Church Year*. U or 3 pt canon, a cap. MSM 80-708.
Gelineau, Joseph. "Psalm 146" from ACYG.
(GA) Haas, David. "Advent/Christmas Gospel Acclamation." Cant, 2 pt, kybd, opt gtr, 2 C inst. OCP 97089.

Hymn of the Day

All earth is hopeful/Toda la tierra ELW 266, WOV 629, TFF 47
TODA LA TIERRA
Light dawns on a weary world ELW 726 TEMPLE OF PEACE
There's a voice in the wilderness ELW 255 ASCENSION

Offering

Come now, O Prince of peace ELW 247, LS 13
He came down ELW 253, TFF 37, LS 4

Communion

As the dark awaits the dawn ELW 261, OBS 46
Let all mortal flesh keep silence ELW 490, LBW 198
Lost in the night ELW 243, LBW 394

Sending

On Jordan's bank the Baptist's cry ELW 249, LBW 249
People, look east ELW 248, WOV 626, LS 11

Additional Assembly Songs

I will rejoice TFF 271
Stir up your power ASG 38
To a Waiting World MSB2 S530
⊕ Casaldaliga, Pedro/Luiz A. Passos. "O povo de Deus/The People of God" from *Hosanna! Ecumenical Songs for Justice and Peace*. WCC Publications 9782825416679.
⊕ Perez, Bernardo Maria/Francisco F. Feliciano. "Who Will Set Us Free?" from *Sound the Bamboo*. GIA G-6830.
☼ Anderson, Jared. "Prepare the Way" from CCLI.
☼ Egan, Jon. "I Am Free" from CCLI.
☼ Emerson, Sarah. "What Joy (Psalm 146)" from CCLI.
☼ Olson, Larry. "Messiah" from *To Be Alive*. dakotaroadmusic .com.
☼ Tomlin, Chris/Daniel Carson. "My Soul Magnifies the Lord" from CCLI.
☼ Wickham, Phil. "Messiah" from CCLI.

Music for the Day
Choral

P Campbell, Jonathan. "Prepare the Royal Highway" from *Wade in the Water: Easy Choral Music for All Ages*. 2 pt mxd, kybd, C inst. AFP 9780800678616.
♫ Rowan, William/arr. Bradley Ellingboe. "Light Dawns on a Weary World." SATB, pno, opt assembly. GIA G-9369.
♫ Taulé, Alberto/arr. Jerry Gunderson. "Toda la tierra/All Earth Is Waiting." SSA, pno. CPH 983233.
Vulpius, Melchior. "Seihe, ich sende meinen Engel (Behold, I Send to You My Angel)." SATB, opt kybd. PRE 31241612.

Children's Choir

P Hopson, Hal H. "Good News Is in the Air." U, kybd. AFP 9780800664077.
P Kemp, Helen. "Magnificat" from *Magnificat and Nunc Dimittis*. U, pno, C inst, hc, hb. CG CGA954.
P ♫ Phillips, Craig. "There's a Voice in the Wilderness Crying." 2 pt, kybd. SEL 422-903.

Keyboard / Instrumental

♫ Cherwien, David. "Light Dawns on a Weary World" from *We Sing of God: Hymn Settings for Organ*. Org. AFP 9780806698052.
P ♫ Hansen, Sherri. "Light Dawns on a Weary World" from *Piano Weavings*, vol. 2. Pno. AFP 9781506413723.
P Hokanson, Margrethe. "Haf trones lampa färdig" from *Augsburg Organ Library: Advent, Series II*. Org. AFP 9781506448077.
P Kim, Marianne. "Canticle of the Turning" from *My Soul Proclaims: Piano Meditations for Worship*. Pno. AFP 9781451499131.

⊕ = global song ♫ = relates to hymn of the day
☼ = praise song P = available in Prelude Music Planner

Handbell

Afdahl, Lee. "Advent Medley." 5-6 oct, L3. FTT 20472.

Mazzatenta, Michael. "Prepare the Way, O Zion." 2-3 oct, L2-. GIA G-7443.

Page, Anna Laura. "Prepare the Royal Highway" from *Glory in the Highest*. 12-16 bells, opt pno, L2 and 2+. CG CGB1082.

Friday, December 20
Katharina von Bora Luther, renewer of the church, died 1552

Born to an impoverished nobleman, Katharina (Katie) was five when her mother died, and she was sent to live in a convent. She later took vows as a nun, but around age twenty-four she and several other nuns who were influenced by the writings of Martin Luther left the convent. Six children were born to Katie and Martin. Though initially Luther felt little affection for Katie, she proved herself a gifted household manager and became a trusted partner. She was so influential that Luther took to calling her "my lord Katie."

December 22, 2019
Fourth Sunday of Advent

Today Isaiah prophesies that a young woman will bear a son and name him Emmanuel. The gospel is Matthew's account of the annunciation and birth of the one named Emmanuel, God-with-us. During these final days of Advent we pray, "O come, O come, Emmanuel," a beloved hymn based on the O Antiphons, ancient prayers appointed for the seven days preceding Christmas. On this final Sunday of Advent we prepare to celebrate the birth of the one born to save us from the power of sin and death.

Prayer of the Day

Stir up your power, Lord Christ, and come. With your abundant grace and might, free us from the sin that hinders our faith, that eagerly we may receive your promises, for you live and reign with the Father and the Holy Spirit, one God, now and forever.

Gospel Acclamation

Alleluia. The virgin shall conceive and bear a son, and they shall name him Emmanuel. *Alleluia.* (Matt. 1:23)

Readings and Psalm
Isaiah 7:10-16

An Israelite and Aramean military coalition presented a serious threat to King Ahaz of Judah. In response, Ahaz decided to secure his throne and kingdom by seeking Assyrian help. Isaiah reminds Ahaz that human attempts to establish security will fail. The prophet gives the sign that is the only source of true safety: Immanuel, God is with us!

Psalm 80:1-7, 17-19

Let your face shine upon us, and we shall be saved. (Ps. 80:7)

Romans 1:1-7

Most of the Christians in Rome do not know Paul. In this letter's opening he introduces himself as an apostle divinely appointed to spread God's gospel. The gospel's content is the promised coming of Christ, and Paul's mission is to bring about the obedience of faith among all nations, including his Roman audience.

Matthew 1:18-25

Matthew's story of Jesus' birth focuses on the role of Joseph, who adopts the divinely-begotten child into the family of David and obediently gives him the name Jesus, which means "God saves."

Preface   Advent

Color   Blue

Prayers of Intercession

The prayers are prepared locally for each occasion. The following examples may be adapted or used as appropriate.

Keeping awake as we watch for Christ, let us pray for the church, the world, and all in need.

A brief silence.

Hear your church, O God, as we pray for all who belong to Jesus Christ. Where the church is scorned, preserve it; where the church is privileged, grant it humility. Lord, in your mercy, **hear our prayer.**

Hear your earth, O God, as we pray for its healing and care. Protect the grapevine and the mighty cedar, the mountains and seas and all that is in them. Give life, that all life may call on your name. Lord, in your mercy,
hear our prayer.

Hear the nations, O God, as we pray for those who hold power and authority over people and lands. Help those who create and uphold good laws and those working to reform what is unjust, that the world might better reflect your grace. Lord, in your mercy,
hear our prayer.

Hear those in need, O God, as we pray for all who face uncertainty: refugees and immigrants, those who are imprisoned, and those without work, housing, food, or health care. Bring good news to all in need of hope. Lord, in your mercy,
hear our prayer.

Hear this community of faith, O God, as we pray for families and friends who gather in this season, for travelers and hosts, and for those who will work or serve others this Christmas. Let the peace of Emmanuel, God-with-us, shine in every heart. Lord, in your mercy,
hear our prayer.

Here other intercessions may be offered.

Hear all who mourn, O God, as we remember the lives of our beloved dead. Encourage the living to learn from our ancestors in faith as we follow your call. Lord, in your mercy,
hear our prayer.

You hear the cries of our hearts, O Lord. Fill us with hopeful expectation, that in each day and hour we may love and serve our neighbors, in Jesus' name.
Amen.

Ideas for the Day

- Matthew's account of the annunciation and birth of Jesus is unique in its focus on Joseph. His role of adoptive father and protector will become especially poignant when, guided by another dream, Joseph leads the family in fleeing to Egypt after Jesus is born (Matt. 2:13-15). To explore his role of sheltering the vulnerable young Jesus, show a clip from the film *March of the Penguins* (Warner Brothers, 2005). Father penguins are entrusted with the eggs' warmth and safety, a role that requires devotion and determination in the extreme Antarctic environment. You can find the trailer and several clips on YouTube. Help worshipers picture themselves in the place of Joseph, devoted and determined even amid uncertainty. Imagine what it might mean for the church to shelter and protect the most vulnerable, in whom we meet Jesus.

- In a dream, Joseph encounters an angel who leads him toward God's will. Invite worshipers to consider the varied means by which they discover God's will, including dreams as well as intellect or emotions. For individuals or communities in discernment, you could offer discernment resources from the Society of Jesus (the Jesuits, a Catholic order in the tradition of St. Ignatius of Loyola, for whom discernment is a particular focus). The website ignatian resources.com/discernment is one place to start. Discernment involves the Advent work of watching and listening carefully for the presence of Christ. You could strengthen the connection to Joseph's dream with the song "Child of Our Dreams" (Marty Haugen, *Night of Silence: Music for Advent and Christmas*, GIA Publications, 1987).

- Matthew gives us two names for the one we await: Emmanuel, "God is with us" (1:23), and Jesus, "he will save his people from their sins" (1:21). The Bible offers many additional names by which Christ is known. Reflection on the multiple ways they help us recognize Jesus' coming could be a focus of this day or the whole Advent season. Do an online search for "Advent names of Jesus" to find inspiration, instructions, and devotionals for an Advent activity based on the names of Jesus. For example, each day, people could add a paper chain link, hang a Christmas ornament, and/or meditate on a Bible verse with one of the names.

Connections with Creation

As we prepare for the birth of the Christ child, this Sunday is an ideal time to remember that the health of mothers and babies is directly impacted by the environment in which they live. We celebrate—and some even venerate—the image of Mary pregnant, full of grace as she carries Jesus within her womb. But does this translate to our care for pregnant women today? Do we have enough regard for women and their unborn children to remove the threat of toxins in their air and water? Do we provide them with adequate healthcare, regardless of their economic status? Proclaiming that Jesus is Emmanuel—God-with-us—means that we must honor his birth by honoring and protecting those who are preparing to give birth in our own time. As we work to create a healthy environment, we will also help create healthy babies!

Let the Children Come

Smaller congregations struggle to get enough children together to rehearse a Christmas pageant, and by December 24, some families have already left town to visit relatives. If there is a Sunday morning in Advent that lends itself to a small pageant, it might be this one, with Luke's nativity story presented in a nutshell—a sneak peek at things to come. Keep it simple and contemplative. Use 10–15 minutes on the previous Sundays of Advent to teach children a few scripture verses and hymn stanzas, such as the two-stanza "Lo, how a rose e'er blooming" (ELW 272), which conveys the prophecy, mystery, and quiet joy of late Advent and has only two different melodic lines to learn.

Following worship, children and others could be invited to stay to prepare the worship space for Christmas. Greens or poinsettias could be brought in and the white paraments made ready.

Assembly Song
Gathering

Canticle of the Turning ELW 723, W&P 26, GS2 46

O come, O come, Emmanuel ELW 257, LLC 281, LS 10, LBW 34

Savior of the nations, come ELW 263, LBW 28

Psalmody and Acclamations

O hear our cry, O Lord/Psalm 80 GTG 355

Haugen, Marty. "Lord, Make Us Turn to You." SATB, cant, assembly, kybd, gtr. GIA G-2884.

Horman, John, D. "Psalm 80" from *ChildrenSing Psalms*. U, kybd.

Jenkins, Stephen. "An Advent Psalm." SATB, assembly, org, opt U or cant. MSM 80-003.

(GA) Haas, David. "Advent/Christmas Gospel Acclamation." Cant, 2 pt, kybd, opt gtr, 2 C inst. OCP 97089.

Hymn of the Day

Peace came to earth ELW 285, WOV 641 *SCHNEIDER*

The angel Gabriel from heaven came ELW 265, WOV 632 *GABRIEL'S MESSAGE*

Unexpected and mysterious ELW 258 *ST. HELENA*

Offering

He came down ELW 253, TFF 37, LS 4

Let all mortal flesh keep silence ELW 490, sts. 1-2; LBW 198, sts. 1-2

Communion

Each winter as the year grows older ELW 252, WOV 628

My soul proclaims your greatness ELW 251, WOV 730

Wait for the Lord ELW 262

Sending

Joy to the world ELW 267, LS 24, LBW 39

My soul does magnify the Lord ELW 882, TFF 168

Additional Assembly Songs

María, pobre María/Oh, Mary, gentle poor Mary LLC 310

To a maid whose name was Mary GTG 98

Ye who claim the faith of Jesus H82 268

⊕ Blantyre melody, adapt. Tom Colvin. "That Boy-Child of Mary" from *Fill Us with Your Love*. HOP 431.

⊕ Monteiro, Simei. "Um menino/A Child" from *Halle, Halle: We Sing the World Round*. CG CGC42.

☼ Booth, Tom. "Lord, Let Your Face Shine upon Us" from *Spirit & Song 2*, vol 6. ocp.org.

☼ Houge, Nate. "Be with Us Now" from *Storm Home: A Collection of Music from Humble Walk Artists-in-Residence*. humblewalk.bandcamp.com.

☼ Kendrick, Graham/Martin Chalk. "Adore" from CCLI.

☼ Morant, Jason. "Immanuel" from *Oh Light*. theliturgists.com.

☼ Torwalt, Bryan/Katie Torwalt. "God with Us" from CCLI.

☼ Walker-Smith, Kim/Ran Jackson/Ricky Jackson. "Love Has a Name" from CCLI.

Music for the Day
Choral

P Fowler, Andrew. "O Come, O Come, Emmanuel." SATB, pno, fl. AFP 9781506456829.

P Herman, David. "Maria Walks Amid the Thorn" from *The Augsburg Choirbook for Advent, Christmas, and Epiphany*. SA, org, fl. AFP 9780800678586.

P McIntyre, John Samuel. "The Hills Are Bare at Bethlehem." SAB, org, opt. fl or vln. AFP 9781506447506.

Shephard, Richard. "Song of Mary" from *The New Oxford Easy Anthem Book*. SATB, org. OXF 9780193533189.

Children's Choir

Farnell, Laura. "Unto Us a Child Is Born." U/2 pt, pno, opt C inst. CG CGA1414.

P McNair, Anne/William McNair. "An Angel Brought the News to Mary" from *ChildrenSing at Christmas*. U/solo or 2 pt, pno. AFP 9781451499025.

P Patterson, Mark. "Let Every Heart Prepare a Throne." U, pno. CG CGA1320.

Keyboard / Instrumental

Fedak, Alfred V. "Divinum mysterium" from *Divinum mysterium*. Org. SEL 160-513.

P ♫ Manz, Paul. "The Angel Gabriel from Heaven Came" from *Six Advent Improvisations*. Org. MSM 10-002.

P Organ, Anne Krentz. "As the Dark Awaits the Dawn" from *Piano Reflections on Advent Tunes*. Pno. AFP 9781451462647.

P ♫ Raabe, Nancy M. "St. Helena" from *Grace & Peace, Volume 6: Songs of Heaven*. Pno. AFP 9781451479621.

Handbell

Gramann, Fred. "Change Ring Prelude on Divinum mysterium." 3-6 oct, L3+. LOR 20/1239L.

P Hopson, Hal. "Advent Carol." 3-5 oct, L2. CG CGB154.

♫ Wissinger, Kath. "The Angel Gabriel." 2-5 oct, opt solo inst, bell tree, pno, vcs. L2. Rings True Music RE8017AB.

⊕ = global song   ♫ = relates to hymn of the day
☼ = praise song   P = available in Prelude Music Planner

Christmas

Preparing for Christmas

Preaching

Though Christmas is a season, the majority of worshipers will only be present on Christmas Eve when the gospel is Luke 2 and images of the nativity proliferate. How important to make sure that the deep spiritual and theological truth of the incarnation—the Word dwelling among us here and now—is held up as well, not only on Christmas Day and the Sundays following but on Christmas Eve itself.

In any case, if the preacher only uses images and themes from Luke 2 without making connections to what the incarnation means for daily life, the assembly will miss out on one of the great spiritual truths of our faith—that all creation and all of our lives are filled with divine presence. Some theologians call this *deep incarnation*, which broadens the scope of the term beyond Jesus to all persons and, indeed, to the vast expanse of the universe.

Many congregations will not have a Christmas Day liturgy, or if they do, it will be sparsely attended. In addition, though John 1 is assigned on the second Sunday of Christmas, which is observed in 2020 (other years there is only one Sunday after Christmas), a growing number of assemblies will mark the Epiphany of Our Lord on this day. There are several ways to make sure worshipers hear John 1. Consider reading both Luke and John at the principal liturgy on Christmas Eve, locating one of the readings during the gathering rite—such as is done on Palm Sunday/Sunday of the Passion—perhaps accompanied by candles and the singing of "Silent night." The other is to include the opening Christmas dialogue from the service of light in Evening Prayer (*ELW*, p. 310) at the beginning of the liturgy. This gives the preacher the opportunity to bring in material from John 1 if it will not be used at another occasion during the Christmas season.

It is easy to sentimentalize Christmas, yet the harrowing account of the slaughter of the holy innocents on the first Sunday of Christmas (and observed as the feast of the Holy Innocents, Martyrs on December 28, the day before) allows preachers to make connections to the unjust suffering of the innocent through the ages and our harsh human experience of evil, loss, and grief. Yet the good news is proclaimed: Christ is born for you, in this time, in this place, in these circumstances, in this pain and anguish, in these questions.

In other words, the preacher helps us consider what becomes incarnate at Christmas. Surely, with all our senses we experience the divine presence in the liturgy and especially in the body and blood of Christ received at the table. For us, the incarnation is not a past event but something happening in our midst. As with Advent, we are called to continually "awake" and see the salvation at hand.

The mystery never ceases to surprise and catch us off guard: in manger and cross, God's hidden and vulnerable presence is revealed to us, as Martin Luther reminds us. From there the preacher gives concrete examples in which justice, love, joy, and freedom are revealed in the very human circumstances of daily life.

Intercessory Prayer

Christmas is a season of celebrating unexpected good tidings of great joy—the holy child shining in the darkness, the Word incarnate full of grace and truth. But underneath these Christmas themes is a reality of emotional extremes. For some people in our assemblies, Christmas is one of the most special and beloved times of the year. For others, it is a time of deep pain and wakened memories of loss, exclusion, or familial brokenness. These contradictory sentiments may even be felt by the very same person.

In addition, in this calendar year the season of Christmas lasts for two Sundays after many of our worshipers have already packed away the Christmas decorations and rolled up the strings of lights. We get two whole Sundays to mark Christmas, and even if you choose to celebrate Epiphany on January 5, you will be telling what many understand to be part of the Christmas story. How do the tidings remain good, worth lifting up and soaking in, for two Sundays after Christmas Eve and Christmas Day? And how do these incarnation tidings inform our praying for the world?

Incarnation: Who prays?

One way that our praying might be incarnated during the four different services (at least) in the Christmas season is in the people who lead the intercessions. If an assisting minister normally leads the intercessory prayers in the assembly, what if someone else—someone unexpected—led those prayers: children, or youth, or the very old in our assemblies, or those with a disability who have never been asked to lead? Families representing the diversity of your local assembly might be asked to lead the intercessions together. A pastor or assisting minister might give them a template of pre-prepared intercessions (see the weekly suggestions in this volume) but encourage them to add to or develop those prayers. An adult could lead the petitions; a small child could call out "Lord, in your mercy . . ."

Ponder in your preparation for this season: Who has never been asked to lead the prayers of intercession? Who would be surprised by the request? How might one new voice and body (or a handful) help the assembly intercede for the world in what can be so joyful and so sorrowful a time of year?

Unexpected: Where is the prayer leader?

Part of the mystery of the incarnation is its unexpectedness—how could it possibly be that God would become a baby in first-century Palestine? Our mode of interceding during Christmastide can echo this theme by shifting where the prayer leader stands. The intercessions might be prayed in unexpected parts of the worship space (keeping in mind that a movable microphone may be necessary so worshipers can hear voices from the new location). Could the intercessions be prayed from the midst of the assembly? Or from the font? Or from the rear of the worship space? Or from a choir loft?

An unexpected location for the prayer leader may at first be jarring. But it may also offer a reminder that our prayers for the world are born not only in multiple locations of the worship space but also in multiple locations of our lives. We can intercede in our beds and at our desks, in the midst of new adventures and during mundane tasks, in the waiting room and behind the wheel, on a run and in a hospital room. Prayer can be incarnate everywhere, no matter our activity or our emotional state today.

Assembly Song

What does incarnation look like? It is the embodiment of something we have not quite grasped, but once it is seen, it can be known, understood, comprehended. It gives us what we need—something incarnate is the truest essence of itself, but in a form we can touch, taste, sing, and emulate.

A great challenge for planning assembly song in the Christmas season is personal nostalgia, with hymns that have been sung for many generations. Of all seasons, this one has the most recognized and beloved tunes and texts—hymns that take us to a deep place in faith or family. While these hymns should be sung, how do we balance them with newer ones? It can be difficult to try new music at any time, but at Christmas, worshipers often subtly (or not) want their favorites. And everyone has a different favorite! How can we expand the musical vocabulary of the incarnation while also honoring the memories that make the season so special for our assemblies?

One technique is to introduce a new Christmas hymn in pieces, either during Advent or during the long green season after Pentecost, looking in-depth at the text. "Peace came to earth" (ELW 285) is a wonderful text that speaks of the incarnate Christ as the fullness of God ("You show the Father none has ever seen, in flesh and blood you bore our griefs and pains," stanza 3) and is germane to other times in the church year, such as Lent and Easter. If this hymn is learned in connection with a Lenten text or on Easter 2 ("all doubts dispelled"), how much more incarnational would it be at Christmastime? The impact will be greatest at Christmas if the congregation already knows the hymn so that when they are singing it after the sermon (or perhaps interspersed within it), they aren't learning it for the first time.

In this same vein, teaching hymns like "Midnight stars make bright the skies" (ELW 280) or "'Twas in the moon of wintertime" (ELW 284) gives assemblies a chance to learn new Christmas texts through the language of other cultures. Children are adept at learning and singing other languages; they can learn the stories behind each hymn and then teach the adults! When children teach and lead, the congregation readily follows. This is a way Christ becomes incarnate in us—we see him through the eyes, music, and texts of other cultures and age groups.

Liturgically, the beloved older hymns fit right in: for the hymn of praise, "Angels we have heard on high" (all or just selected stanzas), "Hark! The herald angels sing," and "Jesus, what a wonderful child" work well. "What child is this" (especially stanza 3) could be used as an offering song in this short season.

In "Of the Father's love begotten" (ELW 295) we sing the history of our salvation through the incarnate Christ. Selected stanzas could enhance or replace sections of the thanksgiving at the table, including the Sanctus. For example, consider the intent of these words from stanza 3: "This is he whom seers in old time chanted of with one accord, whom the voices of the prophets promised in their faithful word."

The Christmas season is also the perfect time to think creatively about using instruments in worship. Many college students are home, and extended-family members visit from out of town. With careful planning, musical gifts from visitors and students can embody the true spirit of community—a community that exists as the incarnate body of Christ in the world.

Worship Space

Christmas can be complicated for worship space. The season is rich with tradition and history that can be both meaningful and complex in worshiping communities. It is often a dance to honor practices within the community while creating space for new offerings. If our Advent worship space sought to create a sacred space for something new to emerge, how can we help that come to birth in the Christmas season? The image of God incarnate as a baby thousands of years ago can be both captivating and limiting. The challenge is how to continue to see God take on flesh and dwell among us today. How does our worship space help us do that?

Here are some guiding questions for reflection:

- If we have introduced blue into our worship space, do we remove it or add the Christmas and Epiphany colors of white and gold?
- If we have some sort of tree or branch(es) from Advent, could people now slowly add to that display through the Christmas season? In our culture, where Christmas often seems to appear out of whole cloth the day after Thanksgiving and is packed away on December 26, could we instead have Christmas appear slowly from Christmas Eve through the twelve days of Christmas and perhaps even into Epiphany? Here are some thoughts about how that might unfold:
  - Could we write on yellow or gold paper where we see God incarnate or where we long to see God incarnate among us?
  - Could those papers be cut or folded into stars to hang on the branches? This slowly converts the worship space from blue to white and gold over the weeks of Christmas and the first Sundays after Epiphany.
  - Could people bring those hopes for incarnation written on paper to a "manger" of sorts throughout Christmas as prayer petitions to be incorporated into art? For example, if prayer petitions are written simply on white, gold, and yellow tissue paper, they can be painted with glue and water onto a canvas or object during the week. Painting tissue paper onto an object can be quite versatile. The paper could be molded onto a globe, a piece of furniture, or a box. These hopes could be tied to a processional practice for intercessory prayer or to another point in the service.
- Does the Advent wreath stay and have candles and lights added to it to symbolize the growing light? Or is it removed completely from the space?

Outside our worship spaces, the calendar dates surrounding these liturgical seasons are filled with a fast-paced, consumer-focused time that carries us from Thanksgiving turkeys to Black Friday sales through Christmas shopping frenzies and activities. Our faith tradition turns that pattern upside down. We celebrate the birth of a vulnerable newborn to a marginalized mother, a baby who will grow up to lead us on a new path to world peace and just living. How does our worship space create the opportunity to appreciate this radical turning of the tables and juxtaposition with our broader, cultural norms? When we pause to think about this countercultural task, we realize anew how critical the shaping of our worship space really is. Without some space apart that calls us to new thinking, we are unlikely to be able to wrap our hearts and minds around this story.

Seasonal Checklist

- Publicize Christmas services in outdoor signage, local newspapers, on your church website, through social media, and perhaps in a special local mailing. Updating your website is especially important: Visitors are coming!
- Prepare materials for Christmas flower sponsorship.
- Repair or replace seasonal environment materials and decorations as needed.
- If handheld candles are used on Christmas Eve, ensure an adequate supply is available and that fire detection and suppression systems are in working order.
- Order worship folder covers if needed for Christmas Eve, Christmas Day, and Epiphany.
- Design worship folders that are easy for guests to follow, including specific instructions for communion distribution. For tips on preparing excellent worship folders, consult *Leading Worship Matters: A Sourcebook for Preparing Worship Leaders* (Augsburg Fortress, 2013, pp. 268–272).
- If you project your service onto a screen or wall, proofread the text carefully and test it on the screen/wall beforehand to check visibility. Work with musicians to ensure that projected texts match what will be sung.
- Determine the communion distribution procedure for larger liturgies and ensure that adequate amounts of elements are available. Provide clear instructions to ushers, communion ministers, and the altar guild.
- Make arrangements for adequate seating, along with additional worship books if needed for larger assemblies on Christmas Eve.
- Schedule time after January 6 to make any changes or additions to the visual environment to prepare the worship space for the time after Epiphany.

Worship Texts for Christmas

Confession and Forgiveness

All may make the sign of the cross, the sign that is marked at baptism, as the presiding minister begins.

Blessed be the holy Trinity, ✝ one God,
Love from the beginning,
Word made flesh,
Breath of heaven.
Amen.

Let us confess our sinfulness before God and one another, trusting in God's endless mercy and love.

Silence is kept for reflection.

Merciful God,
we confess that we are not perfect.
We have said and done things we regret.
We have tried to earn your redeeming grace,
while denying it to others.
We have resisted your call
to be your voice in the world.
Forgive us, loving God.
Give us your righteousness,
the strength to put aside our failures,
and the courage to try again. Amen.

Dear people of God, hear the good news:
Christ the Savior is born!
You are loved and forgiven
in the name of ✝ Jesus, who has come among us.
You are freed from proving that you deserve to be loved,
because God's love is given to you
as the most precious gift of all.
Rejoice in this love and share it with the world.
Amen.

Offering Prayer

Generous God,
you have given us life, this community,
and these gifts of the earth
that become the meal of your grace.
Move in our hearts,
that we might use your gifts
to bring hope and blessing wherever we go,
through Christ our Lord.
Amen.

Invitation to Communion

Love has come: God's love for all people.
Come and eat, for Christ invites you.

Prayer after Communion

Emmanuel, God with us,
you grace us with life and breath
and give us bread for the journey.
Send us out in service to this world that you love,
telling the amazing news of your coming
to be Savior and Lord of all.
Amen.

Blessing

Grace from God's own heart,
peace from the ✝ Child in the manger,
and strength from the Spirit of life
be blessings for you today and forever.
Amen.

Dismissal

Christ is born!
Go tell it on the mountain and everywhere.
Thanks be to God.

Seasonal Rites for Christmas

Light Dawns on a Weary World
A Service of Lessons and Carols for Epiphany

This service of lessons and carols can be used on Epiphany of Our Lord, on a Sunday during the time after Epiphany, for a weekday service, or for any large or small gathering. It could also provide the outline for a one-week Bible study.

The readings throughout the service all relate to the theme of light. The hymn "Light dawns on a weary world" (ELW 726) is included as a suggestion for a gathering song or a sending song. Some might want to sing selected verses in both places as a way of bracketing the service.

Several suggestions for assembly song as well as keyboard settings follow each song suggestion. These settings could be used as introductions, as organ/piano stanzas of the hymn, or as additional preludes or postludes. Feel free to adapt, replace, or augment as best fits your context. Some may wish to include a brief spoken meditation after each reading or a longer homily following the final reading. In the case of the latter, feel free to add a hymn of the day from the selections offered throughout the service.

Dialogue

(based on Ps. 18:28; 27:1; 97:11; 119:105; 36:9; and Isa. 2:5)

It is you who light my lamp; you, my God,
who lights up the darkness.
The Lord is my light and my salvation;
whom then shall I fear?
The Lord is the stronghold of my life;
of whom shall I be afraid?

Light dawns for the righteous, and joy for the honest of heart.
Your word is a lamp to my feet and a light to my path.

For with you is the fountain of life; in your light we see light.
O house of Jacob, come, let us walk in the light
of the Lord!

Gathering Song

Light dawns on a weary world   ELW 726
O Morning Star, how fair and bright!   ELW 308, LBW 76
O day of rest and gladness   ELW 521, LBW 251
Soul, adorn yourself with gladness   ELW 488/489, LBW 224

Keyboard Settings

Burkhardt, Michael. "Light Dawns on a Weary World." SATB, org. AFP 9781506414058. Includes an introduction and optional descant on stanza 3.
Miller, Aaron David. "Light Dawns on a Weary World" from *Chorale Preludes for Piano in Traditional Styles*. Pno. AFP 9780800679033.
Manz, Paul. "O Morning Star, How Fair and Bright!" from *A New Liturgical Year*, vol. 1.Org. AFP 9780800656713.

Opening Prayer

Everlasting God, the radiance of all faithful people, you brought the nations to the brightness of your rising. Fill the world with your glory, and show yourself to all the world through him who is the true light and the bright morning star, your Son, Jesus Christ, our Savior and Lord, who lives and reigns with you and the Holy Spirit, one God, now and forever.
Amen.

Lessons and Carols

Lesson: Genesis 1:1-5
Carol
When long before time   ELW 861, WOV 799
Light shone in darkness   ELW 307
God created heaven and earth   ELW 738
Keyboard Settings
Wahl, Carol. "Earth and All Stars!" from *Flight of the Dove: Piano Reflections*. Pno. AFP 9781506426419.
Sedio, Mark. "Creating God, Your Fingers Trace" from *Come and Praise*, vol 3. Org. AFP 9781506426327.

Lesson: Exodus 13:17-22
Carol
When Israel was in Egypt's land   WOV 670, TFF 87
Bless now, O God, the journey   ELW 326
God the sculptor of the mountains   ELW 736
Keyboard Settings
Floeter, Valerie. "Jesus, Still Lead On" from *Jesus, Still Lead On: Piano Settings for Today*. Pno. AFP 9781506426440.
Ashdown, Franklin D. "If You But Trust in God to Guide You" from *Adagios of Hope and Peace: Ten Settings for Organ*. Org. AFP 9781506413587.

Lesson: Isaiah 9:2-7

Carol

O day of peace ELW 711, WOV 762

Each winter as the year grows older ELW 252, WOV 628

Dona nobis pacem, Domine SP 9

Keyboard Settings

Organ, Anne Krentz. "Shalom" from *Global Piano Reflections.*
Pno, opt solo inst. AFP 9780800658014.

Ringham, William. "Comfort, Comfort Now My People" from
People, Look East: Advent and Christmas Settings. Org.
AFP 9781506426365.

Lesson: Isaiah 60:1-6

Carol

Arise, your light has come! ELW 314, WOV 652

We are marching in the light ELW 866, WOV 650

Arise, shine SC 3

Keyboard Settings

Coman, Ellen. "We Are Marching in the Light" from *Dance to
the Lord: Piano Settings.* Pno. AFP 9781506426426.

Nelson, Ronald A. "Rise Up, O Saints of God!/Arise, Your Light
Has Come!" from *Easy Hymn Settings for Organ*, vol. 2.
Org. AFP 9781451420838.

Lesson: Matthew 5:14-16

Carol

This little light of mine ELW 677

We Are Called ELW 720

Drawn to the Light ELW 593

Keyboard Settings

Hampton, Keith. "This Little Light of Mine" from *Let It Rip! at
the Piano.* Pno. AFP 9780800659066.

Childs, Edwin T. "This Little Light of Mine" from *Spirituals for
Organ: For Manuals Only.* Org. AFP 9781451401141.

Lesson: Ephesians 5:8-14

Carol

I want to walk as a child of the light ELW 815, WOV 649

Awake, my soul, and with the sun ELW 557, LBW 269

Christ is our guiding light SC 7

Keyboard Settings

Floeter, Valerie. "I Want to Walk as a Child of the Light" from
Jesus, Still Lead On: Piano Settings for Today. Pno. AFP
9781506426440.

Wold, Wayne. "Houston" from *Augsburg Organ Library:
Epiphany.* AFP 9780800659349.

Lesson: 1 John 1:5-9

Carol

Christ, Be Our Light ELW 715

Through the night of doubt and sorrow ELW 327, LBW 355

Light and darkness SP 24

Keyboard Settings

Mossing, Sally Drennan. "Christ, Be Our Light" from *Christ
Be Our Light: Music for the Church Pianist.* Pno. AFP
9780800663858.

DeJong, Kenneth L. "Christ, Be Our Light" from *Star of
Promise: Ten Preludes on Advent Hymns.* Org. AFP
9781451499087.

Lesson: John 1:1-14

Carol

Love divine, all loves excelling ELW 631, LBW 315

Word of God, come down on earth ELW 510, WOV 716

Peace came to earth ELW 285, WOV 641

Keyboard Settings

Thomas, David Evan. "Of the Father's Love Begotten"
from *Wassail! Christmas Carols for Piano.* Pno. AFP
9781506413747.

MacMillan, Alan. "Of the Father's Love Begotten" from *Sing
the Year Round: Hymn Settings for Organ.* Org. AFP
9781506426389.

The service may continue with the meal.

Sending Song

Rise, shine, you people! ELW 665, LBW 393
Songs of thankfulness and praise ELW 310, LBW 90
Light dawns on a weary world ELW 726

Keyboard Settings

Hansen, Sherri. "Light Dawns on a Weary World" from *Piano Weavings*, vol. 2. Pno. AFP 9781506413723.

Osterland, Karl. "O Morning Star, How Fair and Bright!" from *A Wittenberg Collection: Lutheran Chorales for Organ*. Org. AFP 9781506413570.

December 24, 2019
Nativity of Our Lord
Christmas Eve

In winter's deepest night, we welcome the light of the Christ child. Isaiah declares that the light of the long-promised king will illumine the world and bring endless peace and justice. Paul reminds us that the grace of God through Jesus Christ brings salvation to all people. The angels declare that Jesus' birth is good and joyful news for everyone, including lowly shepherds. Filled with the light that shines in our lives, we go forth to share the light of Christ with the whole world.

I
Particularly appropriate for Christmas Eve

Prayer of the Day

Almighty God, you made this holy night shine with the brightness of the true Light. Grant that here on earth we may walk in the light of Jesus' presence and in the last day wake to the brightness of his glory; through your Son, Jesus Christ our Lord, who lives and reigns with you and the Holy Spirit, one God, now and forever.

Gospel Acclamation

Alleluia. I am bringing you good news of great joy for all the people: to you is born this day in the city of David a Savior, who is the Messiah, the Lord. *Alleluia.* (Luke 2:10-11)

Readings and Psalm

Isaiah 9:2-7

This poem promises deliverance from Assyrian oppression, a hope based on the birth of a royal child with a name full of promise. While Judah's king will practice justice and righteousness, the real basis for faith lies in God's passion for the people: The zeal of the LORD of hosts will do this!

Psalm 96

Let the heavens rejoice and the earth be glad. (Ps. 96:11)

Titus 2:11-14

The appearance of God's grace in Jesus Christ brings salvation for all humanity. Consequently, in the present we live wisely and justly while also anticipating the hope of our Savior's final appearance.

Luke 2:1-14 [15-20]

God's greatest gift comes as a baby in a manger. Angels announce the "good news of great joy" and proclaim God's blessing of peace.

Preface   Christmas

Color   White

Prayers of Intercession

The prayers are prepared locally for each occasion. The following examples may be adapted or used as appropriate.

Gathered with all who seek the Christ child, let us pray for the church, the world, and all who are in need.
A brief silence.

Wonderful counselor, on this holy night your church throughout the world celebrates the Word of God being born among us. Endow your church with a zeal for sharing your love and grace with all. Hear us, O God.
Your mercy is great.

Lord of hosts, the heavens are glad, the earth rejoices, and the trees sing for joy at your coming. Grant us wisdom to care for your creation in ways that benefit all of your creatures. Hear us, O God.
Your mercy is great.

Prince of peace, your grace has appeared and brings salvation to all. Bring healing to people and nations divided by violence (*especially*). Direct the leaders of the nations, so that in self-controlled, upright, and godly living, they may work toward peace. Hear us, O God.
Your mercy is great.

Mighty God of mercy, you come among us as a vulnerable infant. Protect all in need: those without homes or caregivers, those who grieve, all who are hungry, and all who are ill (*especially*). Hear us, O God.
Your mercy is great.

Gracious God, we praise you for gathering us tonight to worship in holy splendor. Direct our worship, fellowship, and service, so that our lives and Christian witness may be pleasing to you. Hear us, O God.
Your mercy is great.

Here other intercessions may be offered.

Everlasting God, your steadfast love never ends. Thank you for revealing your faithfulness and love to us through the saints of every time and place (*especially*). Hear us, O God.
Your mercy is great.
Into your gracious hands we commend all for whom we pray, trusting in your steadfast mercy; through Jesus Christ, our Savior and Lord.
Amen.

Ideas for the Day

- Isaiah evokes a light shining in "a land of deep darkness" (9:2), and Luke carries us to a night sky illumined with angels. Many Christmas Eve services include a moment when overhead lights are turned off and the space is slowly filled with the glow of candles. In a culture where we tend to fear darkness and banish it with our artificial light, avoid rushing through such a time. Rather, invite your people to the grace of this darkness, to observe one another's faces in the candlelight, and to delight in the collective experience of being gathered in the dark. For a deeper exploration of God's goodness discovered in darkness, check out Barbara Brown Taylor's *Learning to Walk in the Dark* (San Francisco: HarperOne, 2014) or read through Brian Wren's hymn "Joyful is the dark" at hymnary.org.

- This coming year, the United States will conduct another national census to reapportion congressional representation. For the Romans, censuses were a part of imperial occupation, an accounting that would lead to crippling taxation of Palestine. To the empire of Rome, Mary, Joseph, and Jesus each counted not as human beings with dignity but as greater funds to raise armies and expand the boundaries of the empire. Reducing people to such numbers evokes the dehumanizing experiences of prisons or detention centers. Our culture continues to reduce people to numbers like bank account balances or academic GPAs. Yet, the Christmas story shows us a different picture of who counts: poor shepherds and forgotten peasants, each precious in God's sight. In a service that often brings many guests, how will they be shown they "count" in God's story and your ministry?

- Under the pull of familiar traditions on Christmas Eve, it can be easy to lose the natural continuity that flows from Advent into Christmas. Many worship planners work hard to cultivate Advent's expectancy by creatively and prophetically calling out places in our world where we long for God's deliverance. In whatever way your assembly has explored Advent's themes of longing, Christmas Eve completes that journey at the manger, where God's response is received. How might you extend your Advent themes into the core of this service too? Isaiah may lend some resources here with his words about justice triumphing over oppression. On Christmas Eve, continue to name the forces of subjection in our world and proclaim the Savior who has come to bring their end.

Connections with Creation

Peace is a key word on this holy night. Isaiah declares that the child born this night will institute a reign of "endless peace" (9:7). In the lullaby to the infant Jesus, we sing "Sleep in heavenly peace." Our holiday cards are adorned with fancy scripts reading "Peace on Earth." What would it mean for peace to be not just *on* earth, as if the earth were just a stage for the human drama, but actually *within* earth? Can we imagine the heavens being glad because air pollution has ceased? Can we imagine the seas roaring with life because the plastics and garbage have been removed? Can we see fields exulting because they are protected from "development" in the form of shopping malls and big-box stores? What would it look like for the trees of the forest to sing for joy, knowing that they are being preserved? This holy night we can rejoice that Christ's birth is bringing righteousness to all the world.

Let the Children Come

This night shines "with the brightness of the true Light" (prayer of the day). We often assume that if children are to participate on Christmas Eve, it has to be at an earlier, simpler service. We also assume they have somehow absorbed the familiar carols. Consider teaching children a few carols to sing at a 20- to 30-minute gathering rite such as a "prelude of carols" or "procession of choirs" at the main eucharist or candlelight service. Present this well in advance to parents, who may resist the idea of keeping their kids up late—until they see how much they enjoy being part of the late service on this special night. Naps during the day are a must, and there will be yawns and wiggles, but after their carols the children may process out to join their parents in the pews for the rest of the service (where dozing is permitted).

Assembly Song
Gathering

Angels we have heard on high   ELW 289, LS 16, LBW 71
I am so glad each Christmas Eve   ELW 271, LS 22, LBW 69
O come, all ye faithful   ELW 283, LLC 309, LS 27, LBW 45

Psalmody and Acclamations

Jenkins, Stephen. "A Christmas Psalm." SATB, assembly, opt U or cant, org. MSM 80-102.
O'Brien, Francis Patrick. "Today Is Born Our Savior (Psalm 96)." SAB, assembly, kybd, fl, tr. GIA G-5920.
Wetzler, Robert. "Psalm 96" from PWA.
(GA) Haas, David. "Advent/Christmas Gospel Acclamation." Cant, 2 pt, kybd, opt gtr, 2 C inst. OCP 97089.

Hymn of the Day

From heaven above ELW 268, LBW 51 *VOM HIMMEL HOCH*

Peace came to earth ELW 285, WOV 641 *SCHNEIDER*

'Twas in the moon of wintertime ELW 284, LBW 72 *UNE JEUNE PUCELLE*

Offering

In the bleak midwinter ELW 294

What child is this ELW 296, sts. 1, 3; LBW 40, sts. 1, 3

Communion

Away in a manger ELW 277/278, WOV 644, LS 17/18, LBW 67

On Christmas night ELW 274

Silent night, holy night! ELW 281, LLC 301, LS 26, LBW 65

Sending

Go tell it on the mountain ELW 290, TFF 52, LS 23, LBW 70

Hark! The herald angels sing ELW 270, LS 25, LBW 60

Additional Assembly Songs

Gloria en las alturas/Glory in the highest LLC 297

The virgin Mary had a baby boy TFF 53

Unto us a boy is born H82 98

⊕ Creación Colectiva (Collective Creation). "Gloria en lo alto a Dios" from *Singing Peace*. U, chord symbols. WCC Publications. Out of print. Hannelore.Schmid@wcc-coe.org.

⊕ Uqueio, Zacharias M. "Wonani kupswalwa ka Jesu/How Wondrous the Birth of Jesus" from *Global Praise 3*. SATB. GBGMusik 9781890569877.

☼ Daigle, Lauren/Paul Duncan/Paul Mabury. "Light of the World" from CCLI.

☼ Morgan, Reuben. "Glory to God" from CCLI.

☼ Pettipoole, Megan/Luke Pettipoole. "Joining in the Joy" from *Swallowed Up Death*. cdomaha.bandcamp.com.

☼ Rundman, Jonathan. "Glory in the Highest (Gloria)" from *A Heartland Liturgy*. jonathanrundman.bandcamp.com.

☼ Tomlin, Chris/Ed Cash. "Hymn of Joy" from CCLI.

☼ Wardell, Isaac. "Joy! Joy!" from *Salvation Is Created*. bifrostartsmusic.bandcamp.com.

Music for the Day
Choral

Carter, Andrew. "Two Spanish Carols" SSATB, a cap. OXF 9780193432024.

Goodall, Howard. "Romance of the Angels." SATB, org. MSM 56-0037.

P ♫ Luther, Martin/arr. Daniel E. Schwandt. "From Heaven Above" from *Augsburg Chorale Book*. 2 pt mxd, org, 2 tpts. AFP 9781506426303.

P Schalk, Carl. "How Shall We Approach This Wonder?" SATB, org, fl, ob, opt str. AFP 9781506456737.

Children's Choir

Kinyon, Barbara Balzer. "A Christmas Lullaby." U/2 pt, kybd, opt fl, hb. AFP 9780800676667.

P Rameau, J. Philippe. "Wake, O Shepherds" from *ChildrenSing the Classics*. U, kybd, vln, opt vc or bsn. AFP 9781506447629.

Rutter, John. "Shepherd's Pipe Carol." U, kybd, opt desc. OXF 9780193420335.

Keyboard / Instrumental

P ♫ Bottomley, Greg. "'Twas in the Moon of Wintertime" from *This Christmas Night: Piano Settings*. Pno. AFP 9781451486117.

Larkin, Michael. "Silent Night, Holy Night" from *Rejoice! Ten Hymns for Christmas and Easter*. Pno. MSM 15-835.

P ♫ Pelz, Walter. "Vom Himmel hoch" from *A Walter Pelz Organ Anthology*. Org. AFP 9781506448039.

P Sims, David. "Infant Holy, Infant Lowly" from *Wondrous Birth: Seven Hymn Settings for Organ*. Org. AFP 9781506413662.

Handbell

♫ Delancy, Lauran. "From Heaven Above to Earth I Come." 3-5 oct, L3. CPH 977721.

♫ Eithun, Sandra. "German Carol Medley." 3-5 oct hb or hc, opt SATB, L2. CG CGB899. SATB score, CGB1428. Opt full score, CGB898.

♫ Krug, Jason. "'Twas in the Moon of Wintertime." 2-3 oct, L1. SF 286500.

⊕ = global song   ♫ = relates to hymn of the day
☼ = praise song   P = available in Prelude Music Planner

December 25, 2019
Nativity of Our Lord
Christmas Day

As on the first day of creation, on this Christmas Day the Word illumines the world, shining forth to bring all things into being. Today we celebrate the incarnate Word, God becoming flesh to live among us in the person of Jesus Christ then and now. Emboldened by the good news of Christ's birth, along with the shepherds, Mary and Joseph, and all witnesses to the light of Christ, we declare to the world that we have indeed seen and been transformed by the arrival of "the salvation of our God." O come, let us adore!

II
Particularly appropriate for Christmas Day

Prayer of the Day

All-powerful and unseen God, the coming of your light into our world has brightened weary hearts with peace. Call us out of darkness, and empower us to proclaim the birth of your Son, Jesus Christ, our Savior and Lord, who lives and reigns with you and the Holy Spirit, one God, now and forever.

Gospel Acclamation

Alleluia. A holy day has dawned upon us. Come, you nations, and adore the Lord. For today a great light has come upon the earth. *Alleluia.*

Readings and Psalm
Isaiah 62:6-12

The prophet invites the people to give God no rest until God reestablishes Jerusalem. In turn, they will receive names full of promise: The Holy People, The Redeemed of the Lord, A City Not Forsaken.

Psalm 97

Light dawns for the righteous, and joy for the honest of heart. (Ps. 97:11)

Titus 3:4-7

God saves us not because of what we do. Rather, God is a God of mercy and salvation who graciously cleanses us in baptism and renews our lives through the Holy Spirit.

Luke 2:[1-7] 8-20

The world's deep night is shattered by the light of God's new day. The glory of God is revealed to poor shepherds, who share the good news with others.

III
Particularly appropriate for Christmas Day

Prayer of the Day

Almighty God, you gave us your only Son to take on our human nature and to illumine the world with your light. By your grace adopt us as your children and enlighten us with your Spirit, through Jesus Christ, our Redeemer and Lord, who lives and reigns with you and the Holy Spirit, one God, now and forever.

Gospel Acclamation

Alleluia. I am bringing you good news of great joy for all the people: to you is born this day in the city of David a Savior, who is the Messiah, the Lord. *Alleluia.* (Luke 2:10-11)
or
Alleluia. A holy day has dawned upon us. Come, you nations, and adore the Lord. For today a great light has come upon the earth. *Alleluia.*

Readings and Psalm
Isaiah 52:7-10

Isaiah proclaims news of great joy: "Your God reigns!" Just as God saved the people from oppression in Egypt, God delivers Israel from exile. All the earth will witness the saving acts of God.

Psalm 98

All the ends of the earth have seen the victory of our God. (Ps. 98:3)

Hebrews 1:1-4 [5-12]

This letter opens with a lofty declaration of Jesus' preeminent status as the Son through whom God created the world and through whom our sins are cleansed. God speaks to us now through the Son, who is exalted even above the angels.

John 1:1-14

The prologue to the Gospel of John describes Jesus as the Word of God made flesh, the one who reveals God to be "full of grace and truth."

Preface   Christmas

Color   White

Prayers of Intercession

The prayers are prepared locally for each occasion. The following examples may be adapted or used as appropriate.

Gathered with all who seek the Christ child, let us pray for the church, the world, and all who are in need.

A brief silence.

Loving God, you come among us in Christ Jesus. Grant to your whole church the humility to recognize our sinfulness, and direct us to work toward unity. Hear us, O God.

Your mercy is great.

Lord of all the earth, all of creation rejoices in you. Endow us with wisdom to care for all that you have made as we give thanks for the beautiful intricacy of your creative work. Hear us, O God.

Your mercy is great.

O Lord, you love mercy and justice. Grant to the leaders of all nations good judgment that leads them to work for justice, peace, and equality for all. Hear us, O God.

Your mercy is great.

Merciful God, you promise to be with us always. Make your comforting presence known to new parents, families, those who live alone, those who are sick, those who are hungry, and all who grieve (*especially*). Hear us, O God.

Your mercy is great.

Merciful God, with the shepherds you call us to not be afraid. Free us from our fears so that we share the great joy of your love with everyone. Bless our ministries to the wider community (*especially*). Hear us, O God.

Your mercy is great.

Here other intercessions may be offered.

Gracious God, you guard the lives of the faithful and you have revealed your love to us through the lives of your saints (*especially*). Inspired by their witness, embolden us to share your love in word and deed. Hear us, O God.

Your mercy is great.

Into your gracious hands we commend all for whom we pray, trusting in your steadfast mercy; through Jesus Christ, our Savior and Lord.

Amen.

Ideas for the Day

- The scriptures for Christmas Day invite our meditation not just on the birth of Jesus but on the entire mystery of the incarnation—the totality of Jesus' life, death, resurrection, and ascension through which God revealed Godself to us. In Hebrews, we are told: "Long ago God spoke to our ancestors in many and various ways by the prophets, but in these last days he has spoken to us by a Son" (1:1-2). All of Christ's life speaks to us and enhances the power of the Christmas joy we experience. Preach a sermon, read a handful of key stories from Jesus' life, or use visual representations in your worship or gathering space to evoke connections across Christ's life as his presence among us is celebrated this day.

- In the powerful, poetic imagery of the opening chapter of John, we hear of the Word that becomes flesh. The Greek word *logos* that is translated as "Word" can also mean "plan." Jesus is God's plan for creation, for human life, and for our salvation taking on flesh and reality. It is powerful to watch plans and dreams become realities. In the film *Field of Dreams*, the main character dreams of a baseball field in the middle of a cornfield and the people it could gather together, and quips the famous line "If you build it, they will come." Over the course of your assembly's history, when have they seen their plans and dreams for ministry become a reality? Consider how these experiences might add depth to God's cosmic plan for our salvation taking on flesh in the person of Jesus Christ.

- On Christmas Day, both readings from Isaiah exhort enthusiastic sharing of good news. We hear of signs plastered to walls, banners carried by teeming crowds, and songs of joy. In worship, through songs like "Go tell it on the mountain" (ELW 290), our assemblies will be encouraged to participate in the proclamation of the incarnation as they are sent forth from this service. While many in your assembly may feel a strong desire in their hearts to share this joy, they may also find themselves unsure about how exactly to act on such a call. What might it look like in your context to invite people to share or practice the words and actions they might use in the coming week to pass on this story of good news?

Connections with Creation

Folks may be familiar with the old hymn "This World Is Not My Home" with these lyrics: "This world is not my home, I'm just a-passin' through . . . And I can't feel at home in this world anymore." Certainly we can appreciate the sentiment of someone drawing near to the end of a difficult life and desiring to be with the Lord. But the idea that this world—which we know God created out of God's divine love—is not our home, and that we're just passing through, is problematic. If this world is not my home, then I really don't have a reason to care about it. But

John's gospel tells us that Jesus was a person who lived on *this* earth, drank *this* water, breathed *this* air, walked on *this* soil. Jesus was born among us and made this world his home. If God cared enough about God's son to have him live on this earth, then we must care for this earth as well.

Let the Children Come

When it comes to dumbing down to the assembly, perhaps the greatest and most insidious trend is the temptation to dumb down to children. Resist the temptation! Take care not to put stumbling blocks in the path of these little ones. Some people believe that John 1 is too hard for children, with its veiled reference to Jesus as the "Word." Might not the short, powerful phrases ("In the beginning was the Word . . . the Word was with God . . . the Word was God") actually be quite memorable for them in the long run? Ask yourself whether children truly need to immediately understand everything they hear, see, and do in our liturgies, and try not to segregate them or give them a diet of lightweight programming. Plant the seed and let them grow into the rituals and words of worship. The very Word-made-flesh may thus take root and grow in them.

Assembly Song
Gathering

Angels, from the realms of glory   ELW 275, LBW 50
Jesus, what a wonderful child   ELW 297, TFF 51
Joy to the world   ELW 267, LS 24, LBW 39

Psalmody and Acclamations

Feeley, Ephrem. "Sing a New Song to the Lord." SATB, cant, assembly, kybd, gtr. GIA G-9641.
Gelineau, Joseph. "Psalm 98" from ACYG.
Christopherson, Dorothy. "Psalm 98" from *ChildrenSing Psalms*. U, kybd, fc, tamb.
Marshall, Jane. "Psalm 98." U, kybd, assembly. CG CGA427.
(GA) Haas, David. "Advent/Christmas Gospel Acclamation." Cant, 2 pt, kybd, opt gtr, 2 C inst. OCP 97089.

Hymn of the Day

All my heart again rejoices   ELW 273   *WARUM SOLLT ICH*
Let our gladness have no end   ELW 291, LBW 57   *NARODIL SE KRISTUS PAN*
Of the Father's love begotten   ELW 295, LBW 42   *DIVINUM MYSTERIUM*

Offering

Love has come   ELW 292
What child is this   ELW 296, sts. 1, 3; LBW 40, sts. 1, 3

Communion

Away in a manger   ELW 277/278, WOV 644, LS 17/18, LBW 67
Lo, how a rose e'er blooming   ELW 272, LBW 58
Midnight stars make bright the skies   ELW 280

Sending

Good Christian friends, rejoice   ELW 288, LLC 289, LBW 55
It came upon the midnight clear   ELW 282, LBW 54

Additional Assembly Songs

Christians, awake, salute the happy morn   H82 106
Emmanuel   W&P 36, TFF 45
God here among us   MSB2 S552
⊕ He came down   ELW 253
⊕ Hreib, Manal/Daphna Rosenberg. "Between Darkness and Light" from *Sing the Circle Wide: Songs of Faith from Around the World*. Kanata Centre for Worship and Global Song 9780973059359.
☼ Brown, Brenton/Henry Thomas Smart/James Montgomery/ Michael Rossback/Paul Baloche. "Angels from the Realms of Glory (Emmanuel)" from CCLI.
☼ Glover, Ben/Reuben Morgan. "We Have a Saviour" from CCLI.
☼ Gungor, David/John Arndt. "Christ the Lord Is Born" from *Advent*, vol. 2. thebrilliancemusic.com.
☼ Olson, Larry/Hans Peterson. "Glory to the Love" from *Love Can Break Through*. dakotaroadmusic.com.
☼ Redman, Matt. "Light of the World" from CCLI.
☼ Stevens, Chris/Matt Maher/Rachel Taylor Popadic. "Glory (Let There Be Peace)" from CCLI.

Music for the Day
Choral

P Burkhardt, Michael. "Gaudete." U or trbl, SATB, tamb, perc. MSM 50-1126.
P ♫ Lasky, David, "All My Heart Again Rejoices." SATB, kybd. AFP 9781451423921.
Machemer, Matthew. "Of the Father's Love Begotten." 2 pt, kybd, fl, opt hb. CPH 984312.
P Smith, Alan. "The Virgin Mary Had a Baby Boy." SAB, pno. AFP 9781506456904.

Children's Choir

Bedford, Michael. "Hodie Christus natus est." U/2 pt, kybd. CG CGA421.
Burkhardt, Michael. "Awake, Awake" from *Canons for the Church Year*, set 1. 4 vcs, hb, opt alto/bass xyl. MSM 50-9803.
Jennings, Carolyn. "Sing Merrily a Song." U, 2 pt or 3 pt. CG CGA341.

⊕ = global song   ♫ = relates to hymn of the day
☼ = praise song   P = available in Prelude Music Planner

Keyboard / Instrumental

P   Carter, John. "Go Tell It on the Mountain" from *Christmas Jazz: Suite for Piano*. Pno. AFP 9780806698007.

   Langlois, Kristina. "Joy to the World" from *Five for the Christmas Season*. Org. MSM 10-146.

♫   Phillips, Craig. "Divinum mysterium" from *Joy to the World: Three Preludes for Christmas*. Org. SEL 160-815.

P ♫   Raabe, Nancy. "Let Our Gladness Have No End" from *Grace & Peace, Volume 6: Songs of Heaven*. Pno. AFP 9781451479621.

Handbell

   Childers, Brian. "I Wonder as I Wander." 3-5 oct hb, opt 3-5 oct hc, fl, str qnt, perc. GIA G-9450. Full score, G-9450. Inst, kybd, G-9450K.

♫   Mallory, Ron. "Of the Father's Love Begotten." 2 oct, L2+. HOP 2188.

   Page, Anna Laura. "Gloria" from *Glory in the Highest*. 12-16 hb, opt pno, L2 and L2+. CG CGB1082.

Thursday, December 26
Stephen, Deacon and Martyr

Stephen was a deacon and the first martyr of the church. He was one of those seven upon whom the apostles laid hands after they had been chosen to serve widows and others in need. Later, Stephen's preaching angered the temple authorities, and they ordered him to be put to death by stoning, with Saul (later Paul) as one of the observers. As he died, he witnessed to his faith and spoke of a vision of heaven.

Friday, December 27
John, Apostle and Evangelist

John, the son of Zebedee, was a fisherman and one of the Twelve. John, his brother James, and Peter were the three who witnessed the light of the transfiguration. John and James once made known their desire to hold positions of power in the kingdom of God. Jesus' response showed them that service to others was the sign of God's reign in the world. Tradition has attributed authorship of the gospel and the three epistles bearing his name to the apostle John. John is a saint for Christmas through his proclamation that the Word became flesh and lived among us, that the light of God shines in the darkness, and that we are called to love one another as Christ has loved us.

Saturday, December 28
The Holy Innocents, Martyrs

The infant martyrs commemorated on this day were the children of Bethlehem, two years old and younger, who were killed by Herod, who worried that his reign was threatened by the birth of a new king. Augustine called these innocents "buds, killed by the frost of persecution the moment they showed themselves." Those linked to Jesus through their youth and innocence encounter the same hostility Jesus encounters later in his ministry.

December 29, 2019
First Sunday of Christmas

As we celebrate the Twelve Days of Christmas, our gospel today confronts us with the death of innocent children at the hands of Herod. The birth of Christ does not remove the power of evil from our world, but its light gives us hope as we walk with all the "holy innocents" of past generations and today who have suffered unjustly. In our gathering around word and meal, God continues to redeem us, lift us up, and carry us as in days of old.

Prayer of the Day

O Lord God, you know that we cannot place our trust in our own powers. As you protected the infant Jesus, so defend us and all the needy from harm and adversity, through Jesus Christ, our Savior and Lord, who lives and reigns with you and the Holy Spirit, one God, now and forever.

Gospel Acclamation

Alleluia. Let the peace of Christ rule in your hearts, and let the word of Christ dwell in you richly. *Alleluia.* (Col. 3:15, 16)

Readings and Psalm

Isaiah 63:7-9

God does not delegate divine intervention to a messenger or an angel. God's own presence brings salvation. The prophet and all who read these words join in celebrating God's gracious deeds. God trusts that God's people will not act falsely.

Psalm 148

The splendor of the LORD is over earth and heaven. (Ps. 148:13)

Hebrews 2:10-18

Through Jesus' suffering and death, the trail to eternal salvation has been blazed for us. We do not fear death, because he has conquered the power of death. Thus Christ, our merciful and faithful high priest, has the final say over the destiny of our lives.

Matthew 2:13-23

In a dream, Joseph is warned to flee to Egypt to protect the infant Jesus from the jealousy of Herod.

Preface   Christmas

Color   White

Prayers of Intercession

The prayers are prepared locally for each occasion. The following examples may be adapted or used as appropriate.

Gathered with all who seek the Christ child, let us pray for the church, the world, and all who are in need.

A brief silence.

Praise is on our lips and in our hearts, Holy One, for the gracious deeds and acts that you have bestowed upon your church. Give to your whole church open hearts that we might work together to share your good news in Christ Jesus. Hear us, O God.

Your mercy is great.

Praise to you, Creator of all, for you have created a rich diversity of nature and creatures: sun, moon, stars, mountains and all hills, oceans and rivers (*local bodies of waters may be named*). Sustain all that you made and keep us faithful in our care for creation. Hear us, O God.

Your mercy is great.

We bless you, Ruler of all, for the communities and nations of which we are a part. Gather into your arms the many peoples of the world and grant humility to all leaders, so that all may find blessing and peace. Hear us, O God.

Your mercy is great.

O Holy One, you overcame death and freed us from all fear. Give courage to all who are afraid and comfort to all who suffer in any way (*especially*). Give patience and compassion to those who provide care. Hear us, O God.

Your mercy is great.

Nurturing God, you care for your children in any danger. Grant courage to our congregation, that we are present with children who need our love and protection, with parents who grieve the loss of children, and with those who seek safety from hurtful situations. Hear us, O God.

Your mercy is great.

Here other intercessions may be offered.

Light of life, you claim us as your children forever. We praise you for those who have gone before us in the faith, serving as witnesses to your presence (*especially*). Hear us, O God.

Your mercy is great.

Into your gracious hands we commend all for whom we pray, trusting in your steadfast mercy; through Jesus Christ, our Savior and Lord.

Amen.

Ideas for the Day

- The holy family flees certain death by crossing borders and resettling in Egypt until it is safe to return. Allow this difficult and sometimes forgotten or ignored text to breathe through the stories shared by a speaker from Lutheran Immigration and Refugee Service (request one through lirs.org). Or consider this Sunday an opportune time for a justice moment during worship, in which postcards are filled out concerning current immigration and refugee issues and are blessed in worship before being mailed to government leaders.
- Grief and lament present both a challenge and an opportunity for worship. An essay by Steve and Joan Huyser-Honig, entitled "Bringing Our Pain to God: Michael Card and Calvin Seerveld on Biblical Lament in Worship" (June 20, 2008), discusses approaches to incorporating lament into worship. The authors also suggest additional resources for worship planners preparing for this and other lament-saturated Sundays. Find the essay in the Calvin Institute of Christian Worship's resource library: worship.calvin.edu/resources/resource-library (check resource type "feature story" or search by tag "lament").
- The death of children at the hands of those with little or no regard for human life has become part of our tragic national narrative and stirs, at least for a time, passionate debate, particularly over gun ownership. The ELCA has not been silent about this issue, as the March 6, 2018, letter from the Conference of Bishops attests (elca.org/News-and-Events/7915). Affirming the 1994 ELCA social message on "Community Violence," it quotes from that document: "We are empowered to take up the challenge to prevent violence and to attack the complex causes that make violence so pervasive" (elca.org/socialmessages). See "Gun Violence and Christian Witness" for a thorough discussion of the history of this issue and the challenges it brings (Katie Day, *Journal of Lutheran Ethics*, vol. 14, no. 5 [May 2014]; elca.org/JLE/Articles/65). On a Sunday when the gospel story unflinchingly recounts the slaughter of children at the hands of power, proclaim God's unrelenting promise to be present with us in the midst of our confusion, disagreement, and lament.

Connections with Creation

The contrasts in today's readings are stark. In Psalm 148, heaven and earth praise God. But in Matthew, mothers cry unconsolably when their children are murdered. Ecological devastation and climate disruption contribute to and exacerbate the human calamities of war and violence that result in the deaths of thousands of children today. Families caught in areas wracked by drought and battles over natural resources cry out with "wailing and loud lamentation" (Matt. 2:18) when their children suffer and die. The church is called to attend to these cries and address the conditions that make for the instability and armed conflict that cause such suffering. Advocating for climate solutions, establishing clean water sources, and mediating tensions are ways in which the church can help. All the while, we lift up the vision of a healthy and sustainable earth thriving with abundance and equity, as Psalm 148 describes, where even the fruit trees, together with the rulers and citizens, praise our creator God.

Let the Children Come

All is not "calm and bright" in the continuing Christmas story. Already in the early months after Jesus' birth, he encounters danger and tragedy. Avoid the urge to shelter your congregation's children from the story of the slaughter of the Bethlehem children. Even if they do not live in fear of genocide, children have heard much in recent years about the suffering of innocents, including the separation of children from their parents. We can assure them that God's tender affection for all children (young and old) is so great that God gave Jesus to take on our humanity—including childhood—and kept Jesus safe in Egypt, guided him back to Nazareth, and led him to his prophetic path and purpose. God, who knows what it is like to be a small child, holds them in loving care, and nothing can separate them from that embrace.

Assembly Song
Gathering

Angels, from the realms of glory ELW 275, LBW 50
Let all together praise our God ELW 287, LBW 47
Once in royal David's city ELW 269, WOV 643

Psalmody and Acclamations

Praise the Lord! O heavens ELW 823
Krentz, Michael. "Psalm 148" from PWA.
Leckebusch, Martin. "Let All Creation's Wonders" (THAXTED) from *Lift Up Your Hearts*. Faith Alive Christian Resources.
(GA) Haas, David. "Advent/Christmas Gospel Acclamation." Cant, 2 pt, kybd, opt gtr, 2 C inst. OCP 97089.

Hymn of the Day

Midnight stars make bright the skies ELW 280 HUAN-SHA-XI
O little town of Bethlehem ELW 279, LBW 41 ST. LOUIS
That boy-child of Mary ELW 293, TFF 54 BLANTYRE

Offering

Love has come ELW 292
What child is this ELW 296, sts. 1, 3; LBW 40, sts. 1, 3

Communion

All my heart again rejoices   ELW 273, LBW 46
Away in a manger   ELW 277/278, WOV 644, LS 17/18, LBW 67
Your little ones, dear Lord   ELW 286, LBW 52

Sending

Cold December flies away   ELW 299, LLC 292, LBW 53
Go tell it on the mountain   ELW 290, TFF 52, LS 23, LBW 70

Additional Assembly Songs

Lully, lullay, thou little tiny child   H82 247
Love came down at Christmas   H82 84, NCH 165
Oh, sleep now, holy baby   WOV 639

⊕ Bell, John L. "Look Up and Wonder" from *Innkeepers and Light Sleepers*. GIA G-3835.

⊕ Nhlane, Ben. "Muchindikani Yesu Mtuwa/Sing Welcome to Our Savior" from *Global Praise 1*. GBGMusik 9781890569013.

☼ Gungor, David/John Arndt. "May You Find a Light" from *Advent*, vol. 1. thebrilliancemusic.com.

☼ Rand, Lenora/Hannah Rand/Gary Rand. "Longest Nights" from *Advent & Christmas*. themany1.bandcamp.com.

☼ Sczebel, Joel. "Our Song from Age to Age" from CCLI.

☼ Strumpel, Aaron/Robin Pasley/Timothy Thornton. "Trouble Won't Go" from CCLI.

☼ Tan, Ben/Benjamin Hastings/Chris Davenport. "Seasons" from CCLI.

☼ Van Patter, Michael. "Our Song in the Night (Psalm 77)" from *Songs in the Night*. michaelvanpatter.bandcamp.com.

Music for the Day
Choral

P Hopson, Hal H. "The Christ Child." SATB, pno, opt fl. AFP 9781506456874.

P Schultz, Donna Gartman. "Cold December Winds Were Stilled" from *Augsburg Choirbook for Women*. 2 pt trbl, pno. AFP 9780800620370.

P♫ Sedio, Mark. "Midnight Stars Make Bright the Sky." SATB, hp or kybd, vln. AFP 9781506426020.

Todd, Will. "My Lord Has Come." SATB, a cap. OXF 9780193382237.

Children's Choir

P Fedak, Alfred. "A Prayer to the Child Jesus." 2 pt, alto solo, opt fl, hb. SEL 405-277.

P Schultz, Donna Gartman. "Cold December's Winds Were Stilled" from *Augsburg Choirbook for Women*. 2 pt, pno. AFP 9780800620370.

P Sedio, Mark. "The Coventry Carol." 2 pt, org. SEL 405-234.

Keyboard / Instrumental

P Burroughs, Bob. "In the Bleak Midwinter" from *Good Christian Friends, Rejoice: Carols for Piano*. Pno. AFP 9781451462630.

P♫ David, Anne Marie. "O Little Town of Bethlehem" from *Snow on Snow: Piano Settings*. Pno. AFP 9781451486100.

P♫ Kerr, J. Wayne. "Midnight Stars Make Bright the Skies" from *Amen, We Praise Your Name: World Hymns for Organ*. Org. AFP 9781451486018.

Whitsett, Eleanor. "In dulci jubilo" from *In dulci jubilo: Four Faces of a Folksong*. Org. MSM 10-154.

Handbell

♫ Dobrinski, Cynthia. "O Little Town of Bethlehem." 3-5 oct, L3. HOP 2270.

♫ Morris, Hart. "Midnight Stars Make Bright the Sky." 3-5 oct hb, opt 3 oct hc, fl, wch, L3. CG CGB359.

Rogers, Sharon Elery. "Infant Holy in a Manger." 2-3 oct, L2. AFP 0800674871.

Wednesday, January 1
Name of Jesus

The observance of the octave (eighth day) of Christmas has roots in the sixth century. Until the recent past, Lutheran calendars called this day "The Circumcision and Name of Jesus." The emphasis on circumcision is the older emphasis. Every Jewish boy was circumcised and formally named on the eighth day of his life. Already in his youth, Jesus bears the mark of a covenant that he makes new through the shedding of his blood on the cross. That covenant, like Jesus' name, is a gift that marks the children of God. Baptized into Christ, the church begins a new year in Jesus' name.

Thursday, January 2
Johann Konrad Wilhelm Loehe, renewer of the church, died 1872

Loehe (approximate pronunciation: LAY-uh) was a pastor in nineteenth-century Germany. From the small town of Neuendettelsau, he sent pastors to North America, Australia, New Guinea, Brazil, and the Ukraine. His work for a clear confessional basis within the Bavarian church sometimes led to conflict with the ecclesiastical bureaucracy. Loehe's chief concern was that a congregation find its life in the holy communion, and from that source evangelism and social ministries would flow. Many Lutheran congregations in Michigan, Ohio, and Iowa were either founded or influenced by missionaries sent by Loehe.

⊕ = global song   ♫ = relates to hymn of the day
☼ = praise song   P = available in Prelude Music Planner

January 5, 2020
Second Sunday of Christmas

Within the gospel reading's profound words lies the simple message that God is revealed in a human person. Though we may try to understand how the Word existed with God from the beginning of time, the wonder we celebrate at Christmas is that the Word continues to dwell among us. Christ comes among us in the gathered assembly, the scriptures, the waters of new birth, and the bread and the wine. Through these ordinary gifts we receive the fullness of God's grace and truth.

Prayer of the Day

Almighty God, you have filled all the earth with the light of your incarnate Word. By your grace empower us to reflect your light in all that we do, through Jesus Christ, our Savior and Lord, who lives and reigns with you and the Holy Spirit, one God, now and forever.

or

O God our redeemer, you created light that we might live, and you illumine our world with your beloved Son. By your Spirit comfort us in all darkness, and turn us toward the light of Jesus Christ our Savior, who lives and reigns with you and the Holy Spirit, one God, now and forever.

Gospel Acclamation

Alleluia. All the ends of the earth have seen the victory of our God. *Alleluia.* (Ps. 98:3)

Readings and Psalm

Jeremiah 31:7-14

God promises to bring Israel back to its land from the most remote parts of exile. In Zion Israel will rejoice over God's gift of food and livestock. Young women will express their joy in dancing; God will give gladness instead of sorrow.

or Sirach 24:1-12

The figure of Wisdom played a major role in early discussions of Christology. Wisdom is the divine word, coming from the mouth of God, and ruling over all of creation. Wisdom, created at the beginning of time, made her dwelling place in Jerusalem among God's people.

Psalm 147:12-20

Worship the LORD, O Jerusalem; praise your God, O Zion. (Ps. 147:12)

or Wisdom 10:15-21

We sing, O Lord, to your holy name. (Wis. 10:20)

Ephesians 1:3-14

In Jesus, all of God's plans and purposes have been made known as heaven and earth are united in Christ. Through Jesus, we have been chosen as God's children and have been promised eternal salvation.

John 1:[1-9] 10-18

John begins his gospel with this prologue: a hymn to the Word through whom all things were created. This Word became flesh and brought grace and truth to the world.

Preface   Christmas

Color   White

Prayers of Intercession

The prayers are prepared locally for each occasion. The following examples may be adapted or used as appropriate.

Gathered with all who seek the Christ child, let us pray for the church, the world, and all who are in need.

A brief silence.

Holy God, you make your presence known to the church in every land. Give to us a desire and will to support the diverse work of the church throughout the world (*ministries of the church around the world may be named*). Hear us, O God.

Your mercy is great.

Generous Creator, in you all things came into being and without you not one thing exists. We praise you for the snow and rain that water the earth. Move us to care for the well-being of the work of your hands. Hear us, O God.

Your mercy is great.

Savior of the nations, you gather in your care people of every age and ability, from lands near and far. Inspire the leaders of the nations to work for peace within their countries and in all the world. Hear us, O God.

Your mercy is great.

Saving God, provide for your people who begin this new year in need. Grant shelter to those who are homeless, comfort to all who are lonely, and a strong sense of your presence to those who are sick (*especially*). Hear us, O God.

Your mercy is great.

Word of truth, your good news of salvation is proclaimed among us. Bless all who proclaim your word in this community, especially teachers, pastors, deacons, musicians, and lectors. Hear us, O God.

Here other intercessions may be offered.

Your mercy is great.

Gracious One, your light shines in the darkness and it is not overcome. We thank you for the witnesses who have testified to your light (*especially*). May their lives continue to inspire us. Hear us, O God.

Your mercy is great.

Into your gracious hands we commend all for whom we pray, trusting in your steadfast mercy; through Jesus Christ, our Savior and Lord.

Amen.

Ideas for the Day

- As the season of Christmas draws to a close, the joy of Christmas has perhaps begun to fade in our homes as trees are denuded of their tinsel and lights, crèches are put away, and life returns to normal. The birth of Jesus heralds Christ's reign of joy not for just a day or a season, but as part of the ongoing power of incarnation itself. Let the words that Jeremiah declares to Israel resonate, for we too have been redeemed and gathered from the farthest parts of the earth. How will you more intentionally express that joy in worship today and on upcoming Sundays? Some creatives are opening up their faith communities to deeper and more consistent expressions of joy in interesting and surprising ways. For example, Heather Roth Johnson writes at her blog about churches living out the gospel in unexpected ways: storyboardingchurch.wordpress.com. Karen Ware Jackson, pastor at Faith Presbyterian in Greensboro, North Carolina, blogs about intergenerational worship and learning at karenwarejackson.com.
- "To all who received him, who believed in his name, he gave power to become children of God" (John 1:12). Many groups of people, including some with mental illness, struggle to be a part of any faith community. Pathways to Promise, in its Mental Health Ministry toolkit for faith communities, reminds us that "our calling as faith communities is to open the doorways of inclusion, to become centers of healing and growth." Consider living more deeply into the fullness of being an inclusive and welcoming faith community for those with mental illness. Use the toolkit found at pathways2promise.org and commit on this first Sunday of the calendar year to a strategy for welcoming these brothers and sisters in Christ.
- The first chapter of the Gospel of John represents for Christians some of the most familiar and beautiful poetry in all of scripture, full of pondering the mystery of Christ present at the beginning as the prime actor in creation, and present now as the incarnate Word made flesh. Prepare in advance to incorporate poetry that reflects upon the incarnation in worship today. This blog post by Christian Holleck describes how one congregation celebrated Holy Trinity Sunday with poetry: collegevilleinstitute.org/bearings/poetry-in-worship.

Connections with Creation

As the new year has begun, this is a good time to take stock of the ways in which your congregation is "like a watered garden," to use Jeremiah's imagery (31:12). The prophet describes a sacramental vision in which the people are "radiant" as they behold God's goodness. God sets before them grain, wine, and oil, the very elements of our worship rituals of holy communion and anointing. How is your congregation using these gifts and blessings to live out Jeremiah's description of God's transformation? During the past year, in what ways has your church turned "mourning into joy" (31:13), comforted those in need, and traded gladness for sorrow? And what is planned for the year ahead that will cause rejoicing because of God's goodness working through your congregation?

Let the Children Come

Even while much of North American culture has finished its midwinter festival of consumerism and consumption, the church is still celebrating the incarnation. The profound incarnation text of John 1, which is also proclaimed on Christmas Day, returns on this Sunday. Especially if your congregation does not offer a Christmas Day service, proclaim also the optional verses of today's gospel. Let the Word dwell in the children richly. Find Rosephanye Powell's choral anthem "The Word Was God" on YouTube and use the rhythm of the anthem to teach a spoken chant of the first verse of today's gospel reading: "In the beginning was the Word, and the Word was with God, and the Word was God" (John 1:1). There's a good chance the children will have the mantra running through their heads for a long time to come.

Assembly Song
Gathering

At the name of Jesus   ELW 416, W&P 12, LBW 179

Son of God, eternal Savior   ELW 655, LBW 364

Word of God, come down on earth   ELW 510, WOV 716

Psalmody and Acclamations

"O Praise the Lord, Jerusalem." *Psallite* A-203. Cant, assembly, alto desc.

Folkening, John. "Six Psalm Settings with Antiphons." SATB, U or cant, assembly, opt kybd. MSM 80-700.

Gelineau, Joseph. "Psalm 147" from ACYG.

(GA) Haas, David. "Advent/Christmas Gospel Acclamation." Cant, 2 pt, kybd, opt gtr, 2 C inst. OCP 97089.

Hymn of the Day

Let our gladness have no end   ELW 291, LBW 57   *NARODIL SE KRISTUS PAN*

Of the Father's love begotten   ELW 295, LBW 42   *DIVINUM MYSTERIUM*

Thy strong word   ELW 511, LBW 233   *EBENEZER*

Offering

Love has come   ELW 292

What child is this   ELW 296, sts. 1, 3; LBW 40, sts. 1, 3

Communion

Away in a manger   ELW 277/278, WOV 644, LS 17/18, LBW 67

Infant holy, infant lowly   ELW 276, LBW 44

Your little ones, dear Lord   ELW 286, LBW 52

Sending

Good Christian friends, rejoice   ELW 288, LLC 289, LBW 55

Let all together praise our God   ELW 287, LBW 47

Additional Assembly Songs

Listen! You nations   LBW 14

Many will come   MSB2 S544

Thy Word is a lamp   TFF 132, W&P 144

🌐 Heaven is singing for joy/El cielo canta alegría   ELW 664

🌐 Murray, Shirley Erena/Lim Swee Hong. "Away and in Danger" from *Faith, Hope, and Love: Songs for the Church*. HOP 8846.

☼ Daigle, Lauren/Paul Duncan/Paul Mabury. "Light of the World" from CCLI.

☼ Fielding, Ben/Reuben Morgan. "Who You Say I Am" from CCLI.

☼ Horst, Nathan. "Into the Light" from *Into the Light*. sisterbrotherband.com.

☼ Johnson, Brian/Jeremy Riddle. "You Are Good" from CCLI.

☼ McCracken, Sandra. "Grace upon Grace" from *The Builder and the Architect*. sandramccracken.com.

☼ Riddle, Jeremy/Josh Farro/Phil Wickham. "This Is Amazing Grace" from CCLI.

Music for the Day
Choral

P Behnke, John A. "Word of God, Come Down to Earth." 2 pt mxd, kybd or org. MSM 50-7506.

P Roberts, Paul, "The Word Became Flesh" from *The Augsburg Choirbook*. SATB, fl. AFP 9780800656782.

♫ Sedio, Mark. "Let Our Gladness Have No End." SATB div, kybd or hp, vln. MSM 50-1209.

♫ Willcocks, David. "Of the Father's Heart Begotten." SATB, org. OXF 9780193510852.

Children's Choir

P Behnke, John A. "Word of God, Come Down on Earth." 2 pt, kybd/org. MSM 50-7506.

Raabe, Nancy. "Peace Came to Earth." U, ob, kybd, opt assembly. MSM 60-1007.

Zimmermann, Heinz Werner. "And the Word Became Flesh" from *Five Hymns*. U, kybd. CPH 975131. Out of print.

Keyboard / Instrumental

P ♫ Kim, Marianne. "Thy Strong Word" from *My Soul Proclaims: Piano Meditations for Worship*. Pno. AFP 9781451499131.

Phillips, Craig. "Dix" from *Oxford Hymn Settings for Organists: Epiphany*. Org. OXF 9780193393455.

♫ Sedio, Mark. "Let Our Gladness Have No End" from *Six Slovak Hymn Improvisations*. Org. MSM 10-833.

P ♫ Thomas, David Evan. "Of the Father's Love Begotten" from *Wassail! Christmas Carols for Piano*. Pno. AFP 9781506413747.

Handbell

♫ Hurlbutt, Patricia. "Let Our Gladness Have No End." 3-5 oct, L2+. CG CGB967.

♫ McChesney, Kevin. "Of the Father's Love Begotten." 3-5 oct, L3+. BP HB206.

♫ Waldrop, Tammy. "Fantasia on Ebenezer." 3 or 5 oct, L2+. LOR 20/1654L.

🌐 = global song   ♫ = relates to hymn of the day
☼ = praise song   P = available in Prelude Music Planner

January 6, 2020
Epiphany of Our Lord

The feast of Epiphany ("manifestation") concludes the Christmas season with a celebration of God's glory revealed in the person of Jesus Christ. In Isaiah and Ephesians, that glory is proclaimed for all nations and people. Like the light of the star that guided the magi to Jesus, the light of Christ reveals who we are: children of God who are claimed and washed in the waters of baptism. We are sent out to be beacons of the light of Christ, sharing the good news of God's love to all people.

Prayer of the Day

O God, on this day you revealed your Son to the nations by the leading of a star. Lead us now by faith to know your presence in our lives, and bring us at last to the full vision of your glory, through your Son, Jesus Christ our Lord, who lives and reigns with you and the Holy Spirit, one God, now and forever.

or

Almighty and ever-living God, you revealed the incarnation of your Son by the brilliant shining of a star. Shine the light of your justice always in our hearts and over all lands, and accept our lives as the treasure we offer in your praise and for your service, through Jesus Christ, our Savior and Lord, who lives and reigns with you and the Holy Spirit, one God, now and forever.

or

Everlasting God, the radiance of all faithful people, you brought the nations to the brightness of your rising. Fill the world with your glory, and show yourself to all the world through him who is the true light and the bright morning star, your Son, Jesus Christ, our Savior and Lord, who lives and reigns with you and the Holy Spirit, one God, now and forever.

Gospel Acclamation

Alleluia. We have observed his star at its rising, and have come to worship him. *Alleluia.* (Matt. 2:2)

Readings and Psalm

Isaiah 60:1-6

Jerusalem is assured that nations will make a pilgrimage to her because the light of God's presence is in her midst. The bountiful food of the sea and the profits of international trade will come streaming to Jerusalem and thereby declare God's praise.

Psalm 72:1-7, 10-14

All kings shall bow down before him. (Ps. 72:11)

Ephesians 3:1-12

What had been hidden from previous generations is now made known through the gospel ministry of Paul and others. In Christ both Jews and Gentiles participate in the richness of God's promised salvation.

Matthew 2:1-12

God's promise shines bright in the night as magi follow a star to honor a new king. Strangers from a faraway land, they welcome the long-awaited messiah of Israel.

Preface   Epiphany of Our Lord

Color   White

Prayers of Intercession

The prayers are prepared locally for each occasion. The following examples may be adapted or used as appropriate.

Gathered with all who seek the Christ child, let us pray for the church, the world, and all who are in need.

A brief silence.

Faithful God, continue to provide dedicated leaders and passionate people for your church, so that wisdom and compassion in all its rich variety may be made known throughout the world. Hear us, O God.

Your mercy is great.

Creating God, your glory shines around us in every star, creature, and person. Liberate us from the ways we destroy your creation. Free us to care for the earth so that all experience your bountiful goodness. Hear us, O God.

Your mercy is great.

Give your justice to the leaders of the world, O God. Endow them with humble courage to defend the cause of the poor and give deliverance to those in need, so that peace abounds in all countries (*especially*). Hear us, O God.

Your mercy is great.

By the guidance of a star, you led the magi to pay homage to the Christ child. Protect new families, those who live alone, travelers, those who suffer loss, and all others in need (*especially*). Hear us, O God.

Your mercy is great.

Ever-present One, in Christ Jesus we boldly come before you in worship. Nurture and encourage all who gather for worship, those who serve in worship leadership roles, and all who participate in the work of this faith community. Hear us, O God.

Your mercy is great.

Here other intercessions may be offered.

Generous God, throughout time you have given us people who have shown us the gift of your grace (*especially*). Inspire us by their faithfulness to serve you and all your people. Hear us, O God.
Your mercy is great.
Into your gracious hands we commend all for whom we pray, trusting in your steadfast mercy; through Jesus Christ, our Savior and Lord.
Amen.

Ideas for the Day

- Epiphany is a day with many symbols, including stars, light, crowns, magi, and gifts. While you could decorate with all of these symbols, it is probably better to pick one theme. One option would be to add extra lights and stars to your Christmas decorations. For example, stars could be cut from shiny gold and silver wrapping paper. Ask people to write their prayers on the stars. Today and/or throughout the time after Epiphany, collect the stars and hang them from a ceiling or display them on a wall in the worship or gathering space. Instead of stars, you could use crown or gift shapes.

- Host an Epiphany gift-giving party to support a local ministry while also learning about the day. People can bring personal care items for a local women's shelter, household goods for immigration and refugee services, or food for a food pantry. During the party have intergenerational Epiphany crafts available; make and wear paper crowns, fold origami stars, and send everyone home with a piece of chalk and a copy of an Epiphany home blessing so that they can mark their doors with "20+C+M+B+20."

- During the gospel reading, pause between verses 10 and 11 and have the magi brought into the worship space in a procession: smaller figures from a nativity scene could be carried in on decorative pillows; larger figures could be pulled in a cart or wagon. Process the figures around the worship space while the choir or assembly sings an acclamation or hymn, then place them at the manger. When the gospel concludes, the magi figures can be processed out or remain at the nativity scene.

- Glow sticks could be used today to represent either the star the magi followed or the light of Christ. They could be incorporated into the confession and forgiveness, gathering rite, sermon, or prayers of intercession. Worshipers could be invited to hold them up during the readings from Isaiah ("Arise, shine; for your light has come," 60:1; "Nations shall come to your light, and kings to the brightness of your dawn," 60:3) and Matthew ("there, ahead of them, went the star that they had seen at its rising," 2:9).

Connections with Creation

"Star light, star bright, first star I see tonight . . ." There's something about stars that has captured the imagination of human beings from the time they gathered around ancient fires watching the sparks fly up into the darkened sky. The magi were practiced in the art of observing celestial phenomena, so when a special star appeared, they took notice and followed it to find Jesus. But if they were to observe our night sky today, they would likely be disappointed to see so few stars. Light pollution from street lights, cars, buildings, and other sources has obscured the observation of stars and planets and disrupted the natural cycles of animals and birds. How can your church help mitigate light pollution? Strategic outside lighting using motion sensors and timers can help. Also, raise awareness through preaching and newsletter articles about the benefits and blessings of the dark night sky.

Let the Children Come

Many congregations miss out on the opportunity to celebrate this important feast, which closes out the festive Christmas season when it doesn't fall on a Sunday. Consider doing a "back-to-school" and "back-to-church" Epiphany service and party on this Monday Epiphany evening. Gertrud Mueller Nelson's book *To Dance with God* (Paulist Press) contains numerous ideas and traditions for family, church, school, or community Epiphany celebrations, including the blessing of homes, a bean or king cake, a pageant of the magi, a follow-the-star game, and gift-giving. If the children already presented a pageant in Advent or during the twelve days of Christmas, tonight is the night for the final act: the arrival of the magi. If you have used a manger scene and kept the approaching magi at a distance, place them front and center with the holy family.

Assembly Song
Gathering

All my heart again rejoices ELW 273, LBW 46
Brightest and best of the stars ELW 303, LBW 84
Hail to the Lord's anointed ELW 311, LBW 87

Psalmody and Acclamations

Haas, David. "In the Time of God (Psalm 72)." Choir, cant, assembly, kybd, gt, opt hb, 2 C inst. GIA G-5657.
Mayernik, Luke. "Epiphany of the Lord" from 5GP.
Mummert, Mark. "Psalm 72," Refrain 1, from PSCY.
(GA) Haas, David. "Advent/Christmas Gospel Acclamation." Cant, 2 pt, kybd, opt gtr, 2 C inst. OCP 97089.

Hymn of the Day

Bright and glorious is the sky   ELW 301, LBW 75   *DEJLIG ER DEN HIMMEL BLÅ*

O Morning Star, how fair and bright!   ELW 308, LLC 320, LBW 76   *WIE SCHÖN LEUCHTET*

The First Noel   ELW 300, LBW 56   *THE FIRST NOWELL*

Offering

In the bleak midwinter   ELW 294, sts. 1, 3

O Morning Star, how fair and bright!   ELW 308, st. 3; LLC 320, st. 3; LBW 76, st. 3

Communion

Come, beloved of the Maker   ELW 306, CBM 67

I want to walk as a child of the light   ELW 815, WOV 649, LS 37

Light shone in darkness   ELW 307

Sending

As with gladness men of old   ELW 302, LBW 82

This little light of mine   ELW 677, LS 33, TFF 65

Additional Assembly Songs

Arise, shine   SC 3

Los magos que llegaron a Belén/The magi who to Bethlehem did go   LLC 317, NCH 155

We three kings   WOV 646, LLC 321

⊕ Give us light/Jyothi dho Prabhu   GTG 467

⊕ Matsikenyiri, Patrick. "Rujeko/The Light of God Comes" from *Njalo (Always)*. ABI 9780687498079.

☼ Brown, Lacey. "Follow the Star" from *Like the Tide*. poorclare.bandcamp.com.

☼ Grace, Ben. "Rejoice (The Light Has Come)" from *Epiphany*. thecalendaryears.bandcamp.com.

☼ Hughes, Tim. "Here I Am to Worship" from CCLI.

☼ Redman, Matt. "Light of the World" from CCLI.

☼ Strumpel, Aaron. "Bright Star" from CCLI.

☼ Ward, Tara/ Nathanael Washam. "Revealed" from *Songs for a Mystical Supper*. churchofthebeloved.bandcamp.com.

Music for the Day
Choral

P Highben, Zebulon M. "Hymn to Christ the Light." SATB, a cap. AFP 9781506447315.

P Neswick, Bruce. "Epiphany Carol (Sing of God Made Manifest)" from *The Augsburg Choirbook*. U, org. AFP 9780800656782.

P Perkins, Scott. "You, God, Are My Light." SATB, org. AFP 9781506456966.

Weaver, John. "Epiphany Alleluias." SATB, org. B&H 9790051456833.

Children's Choir

Burkhart, Michael. "Arise! Shine!" from *Canons for the Church Year*, set 1. 3 vcs, SATB or kybd. MSM 50-9803.

P Paradowski, John. "Arise and Shine!" U/2 pt, kybd, opt hb. CG CGA1039.

Revicki, Robert. "Dominus illuminatis mea" from *Songs of Praise*. 2 pt, tri, cym. B&H M051455973.

Keyboard / Instrumental

P ♫ Hovland, Egil. "Wie schön leuchet" from *A New Liturgical Year, Volume 2: Anthology for Organ*. Org. AFP 9781451499070.

P ♫ Organ, Anne Krentz. "Wie schön leuchet" from *Be Thou My Vision: Piano Reflections*. Pno. AFP 9780800678524.

P Sims, David. "There's a Star in the East" from *Wondrous Birth: Seven Hymn Settings for Organ*. Org. AFP 9781506413662.

P ♫ Turner, John. "The First Noel" from *Jazz Carols for Piano*. Pno. AFP 9781451499117.

Handbell

♫ Callahan, Frances. "O Morning Star, How Fair and Bright!" 2-3 oct, L3. MSM 30-201.

♫ McFadden, Jane. "Bright and Glorious Is the Sky." 3-5 hb, opt 3 or 4 oct hc, fl, L3. BP HB402.

♫ Moklebust, Cathy. "The First Noel." 3-7 oct, L3+. JEF 9480.

⊕ = global song   ♫ = relates to hymn of the day
☼ = praise song   P = available in Prelude Music Planner

Time after Epiphany

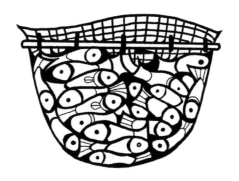

Preparing for the Time after Epiphany

Preaching

The time after Epiphany begins and ends with a festival from the life of Christ: the Baptism of Our Lord on January 12, and the Transfiguration of Our Lord on February 23. This year provides the rare opportunity to observe another festival in the middle of the season: the Presentation of Our Lord on February 2. The Presentation rarely falls on a Sunday, and both *Evangelical Lutheran Worship* rubrics and ecumenical practice suggest that, as a significant lesser festival, it replace the ordinary Sunday readings. Interspersed between these festivals are green Sundays that focus on the calling of the disciples and early sections of the Sermon on the Mount.

With Easter falling late in 2020, the time after Epiphany is quite long; when considering it as a whole, there are several things for a preacher to note. Year A is filled with more light images than other years: "I will give you as a light to the nations" (Isa. 49:6 on January 19); "The people who walked in darkness have seen a great light" (Isa. 9:2, Matt. 4:16, and Psalm 27 on January 26); "A light to reveal you to the nations" (Luke 2:32 and other images of light in the liturgy for the Presentation of Our Lord on February 2); "You are the light of the world" and "Let your light shine" (Matt. 5:14-16 on February 9). Through assembly song, preaching, and intercessory responses, this particular Epiphany can be filled with light. In fact, preachers who are looking for a sermon series might find creative options in the time after Epiphany.

However, preachers should also name the dangers in always equating light with good and darkness with evil, particularly as heard in relation to the color of one's skin. Consider other ways to speak of light such as *brightness*, *radiance*, and *luminosity*. At the same time, the entire incarnation cycle is a time to name a healthy spirituality of darkness: new life arises from the earth and places of gestation.

The Presentation of Our Lord is sometimes called Candlemas because of the reference to "a light for revelation to the Gentiles" (Luke 2:32) and the blessing of candles that is often part of the rite for this day. Believe it or not, the origins of the feast align with Groundhog Day, and there are many ways to connect shadows, light, the fortieth day of Christmas, and this hinge between Christmas and Easter. February 2 is the midpoint between the winter solstice and the spring equinox. In some traditions, Christmas decorations are left up until the Presentation, and the assembly song, environment, and preaching can enjoy a reprise of some elements from the Christmas liturgy.

Preachers will find many creative options for the Presentation, whether starting with connections to Groundhog Day or naming the longing of Anna and Simeon to see the fulfillment of God's promises. Throughout the incarnation cycle, the preacher leads the community to see with our eyes the salvation of God even as we hold in our hands the bread of life and the cup of salvation, signs of God with us.

Intercessory Prayer

The time after Epiphany gives us six full Sundays before the feast of the Transfiguration this calendar year. The time begins with the calling, marking, and sending of Jesus through baptism, and continues with stories of the disciples' calling. We then listen for a number of weeks to well-known passages from Matthew's Sermon on the Mount. These Sundays offer an opportunity in our prayers of intercession to consider *who and what we pray for,* attending to people, places, and situations that we often forget and leave out of our prayers.

First, consider for whom and what your assembly usually prays. Give some thought to how your assembly tends to pray. Do you pray generally for the earth's oceans, mountains, and forests? Or do you pray for your local lake, the designated wilderness areas nearby, and the city park where the congregation's children play? Some congregations pray regularly for local places and persons, especially those well known to the congregation, but fail to pray for those beyond their neighborhood. Other congregations pray with general language for the world, the nation, and the church but forget to add specifics (the name of your companion synod, the newly elected mayor, the teachers in your local school) that would be meaningful to the assembly.

Then, schedule a brainstorming session. At some point before the season begins, schedule a meeting with intercessory prayer leaders and/or assisting ministers. Make a list of all for whom your assembly normally prays. This list may include, among others, our president/prime minister, our bishop, our sick and homebound members. Take note of whether your congregation follows any prayer cycles: for example, your synod's, the Global Mission prayers for companion churches and mission personnel, the ELCA's Prayer Ventures (elca.org/en/Resources/Prayer-Ventures), or the World Council of Churches' prayers for the nations of the world (oikoumene.org/en/resources/prayer-cycle).

After you have brainstormed, make another list. Whom and what has your assembly not prayed for in a while? The prayer cycles noted above may be helpful, along with other templates for intercessory prayer, like those offered in the *Evangelical Lutheran Worship* rubrics (pp. 127–128) or the *Book of Common Prayer* forms for the prayers of the people (pp. 383–393). Are there specifics, or general categories, your assembly might lift up during the time after Epiphany?

Make a plan. From these lists, assign names, places, or categories to the seven weeks of this season. Add them also to any emailed or printed prayer lists. (Of course, in a given week, world or local events may suggest an additional prayer petition by Saturday night.)

If your congregation always uses an unedited version of the weekly *Sundays and Seasons* intercession templates, these additional persons and places—thought up ahead of time, or in the week prior to Sunday—could be prayed for during the space for additional petitions. On the other hand, making these lists beforehand may cause prayer preparers to significantly edit the templates you normally use (which practice is strongly encouraged both by *Sundays and Seasons* and by the ELCA's *Principles for Worship*).

In any case, at the end of these seven weeks, perhaps your assembly will have succeeded in praying for more and different people, places, occasions, events, and needs than you usually do. If in the privacy of our homes and hearts we pray primarily for the few people and situations we care about the most, then on Sunday, the prayers of intercession serve to help us pray more deeply and widely than we might on our own.

Assembly Song

The Sundays following Epiphany are weekly opportunities to hear readings and sing songs that reflect Christ's incarnational identity and, by extension, our identity as members of that body. The lectionary directs us that, just as Christ is the light to the nations (a consistent theme through the season), we are to extend that light to all, through the work of the Spirit.

This long stretch of Sundays after Epiphany is the perfect opportunity to introduce a new setting of the liturgy, though perhaps not all parts at once. This is probably best done as a slow, deliberate process, and it is an excellent opportunity to utilize both adult and children's choirs and instrumentalists. The hymn of praise is a good place to start as most in *Evangelical Lutheran Worship* (both "Glory to God" and "This is the feast") have refrains, or music that is otherwise repetitive

in nature. The choir or a soloist can sing the verses, and the assembly can join on the refrain for the first few weeks, then slowly be incorporated into the whole song. When teaching a new setting, for the unlearned sections you can also use familiar hymns that echo seasonal themes. One example is "We have seen the Lord" (ELW 869). This joyful, repetitive song can be sung as a response to the gospel or the sermon, as an offering song, as a sending song, or as a common refrain as communion is coming to a close. The tune is enough of an earworm that people may find themselves singing it during the week, bringing worship outside the church walls. The hymn can be accompanied by African drums or sung a cappella and can be sung easily in English or Swahili, with an older youth as the caller/leader.

Another liturgical piece to learn is a setting of the Nunc dimittis, "Now, Lord, you let your servant go in peace." This is the song Simeon sings when Christ is revealed to him, very appropriate on Sunday, February 2, the feast of the Presentation of Our Lord. If you don't use this song after communion on a regular basis, you could use it as a sending song, perhaps singing the same setting on the four Sundays preceding Ash Wednesday. *Evangelical Lutheran Worship* contains several settings of this song in its Holy Communion and Night Prayer liturgies (pp. 113, 135, 324) and in its hymn section (#200–203, 313, 440).

Every now and then, as an addition to spoken intercessions, it can be nice to sing prayers. If you have an evening service, a perfect prayer song is "Now it is evening" (ELW 572), a hymn that centers the assembly on how the incarnate Christ binds us together in community. For a morning or noontime service, "O God in heaven" (ELW 748) works well. Each hymn can be sung starting with the first stanza, with spoken intercessions interspersed thematically with the hymn text. During the spoken intercessions the assembly can sing a drone in the key to support entry into the next stanza. These songs can be accompanied or sung a cappella if already familiar to the congregation.

For preachers, the hymn of the day can be an extra help when shaping a sermon. The hymns suggested in *Sundays and Seasons* are carefully chosen and might give guidance to a preacher looking for a particular phrase or direction. A common refrain could be sung at specific times during the sermon to reinforce the message. Hymns such as "Christ, Be Our Light" (ELW 715, specifically the refrain) or "Goodness is stronger than evil" (ELW 721) are easily learned, and the repetitive nature of each lends itself to memory, even for those whose memories are beginning to fade.

Worship Space

Despite being the longest segment of these three seasons of incarnation, the time after Epiphany is often the most over-looked in terms of worship space and seasonal preparations as worship committees exhale from the Advent and Christmas bustle. How can we use our worship space to prevent post-Christmas or "postpartum" depression after this eventful new birth among us? Where might we find the incarnation appearing in surprising places in our lives and in our world? How can our worship space shape and express that? It can be easy to let the poinsettias and other festive decorations slowly wilt or wither in the days and weeks after Christmas. But with intentionality, we can use the space during this time to focus on incarnation among us and not simply pack up the Christmas nativity scene.

- Are there ways to position the assembly to face one another to see the embodied community in a new way?
- Could we continue a prayer or processional practice during this time that in an artistic way brings in more of the gold, yellow, or white introduced at Christmas?
- Continue writing prayers on squares or stars of tissue paper and painting them onto heavy paper, fabric canvas, or an object such as a box or a piece of furniture. Heavier butcher paper (110 lb.) can be bought in a roll at art supply stores and works well for this type of project. You can also use a pre-stretched piece of art canvas purchased directly from the store.
- During worship or educational time, write visions for incarnation onto satin or floral ribbon that could be hung or woven in different ways in the worship space or incor-porated into a banner. Floral ribbon is quite strong, afford-able, available, and versatile. It will hold up outdoors for quite some time if you wanted to extend your visions out-side the worship space to draw people in or expand the scope of incarnational imagery.
- What springs forth from this incarnation among us? Are there ways that the birch branches or bare evergreen tree can house some unfolding symbols of incarnation in the congregation, community, or world?
- Picking up on themes of streams of living water and a flow-ering wilderness could be a beautiful way to call forth incarnate care for creation.

Attending thoughtfully as a worshiping community to these three seasons of incarnation can breathe fresh life into a wor-ship space as we launch a new liturgical year. It is a new birth and life waiting to happen!

Seasonal Checklist

- If Baptism of Our Lord (January 12) will be observed as a baptismal festival, publicize the festival and arrange for baptismal preparation with parents, sponsors, and candidates.
- Order a sufficient annual quantity of *Welcome, Child of God* (a board book for infants and toddlers) and *Liv-ing the Promises of Baptism: 101 Ideas for Parents* (both Augsburg Fortress) and present them as baptismal gifts from the congregation to children and parents. Enroll-ing families with babies and toddlers in the monthly Frolic Enewsletter is one way congregations may choose to pro-vide ongoing support to families of the newly baptized (wearesparkhouse.org/kids/frolic).
- If a form of baptismal remembrance is used, evergreen branches for sprinkling may be desired.
- On the festivals of the Baptism of Our Lord and Transfigu-ration, consider using thanksgiving for baptism instead of confession and forgiveness during the gathering rite.
- Increasingly, Martin Luther King Jr. Day is observed as a day of service in many locales. Plan to participate as a church in local observances or organize your own.
- If you are hosting a catechumenal process and have a group of inquirers, use Welcome to Baptism (*ELW*, pp. 232–33) prior to the beginning of Lent.
- If the congregation is celebrating the lesser festival of Pre-sentation of Our Lord (February 2), collect supplies for refreshing or creating candles for the worship space.
- If the alleluia will be symbolically buried or bid farewell on the festival of the Transfiguration, make appropri-ate arrangements. See the seasonal rites section (p. 75) for more ideas.

Worship Texts for the Time after Epiphany

Confession and Forgiveness

All may make the sign of the cross, the sign that is marked at baptism, as the presiding minister begins.

Blessed be the holy Trinity, ✛ one God,
the eternal voice from heaven,
the anointed and beloved one,
the Spirit moving over the waters.
Amen.

As we approach the mystery of God, let us come in confession, trusting the love of Christ crucified and risen.

Silence is kept for reflection.

God who searches us and knows us,
you have shown us what is good,
but we have looked to other lights to find our way.
We have not been just in our dealings with others.
We have chosen revenge over mercy.
We have promoted ourselves
instead of walking humbly with you.
With what shall we come before you?
Forgive us our sin,
and show us your salvation
in the face of Jesus Christ our Savior. Amen.

Beloved of God,
you have not received the spirit of the world,
but the Spirit that is from God,
poured out for you in the faithfulness of Jesus Christ.
Receive the promise of baptism:
You are God's child; ✛ your sins are forgiven.
Rejoice and be glad, for yours is the reign of heaven.
Amen.

Offering Prayer

God of wonder,
you formed us in our mother's womb,
and from mother earth you bring forth this bread and wine.
We place them on your table,
together with our lives and all that you have made.
Open the heavens to us and pour out your Spirit.
We wait for your mercy;
we long for your peace;
we hunger and thirst for Jesus Christ,
our banquet of life.
Amen.

Invitation to Communion

Here is the Lamb of God who takes away the sin of the world!
Come to the table of mercy and joy.

Prayer after Communion

Faithful God,
you have kept your promise to us in this meal,
nourishing us with the gift of salvation.
Now send your servants forth in peace,
that we may testify to your goodness
and share the hope that is ours
in Jesus Christ, our Savior and Lord.
Amen.

Blessing

May Christ, the wisdom and power of God,
and the source of our life together,
keep you united in mind and purpose.
And the blessing of almighty God,
the Father, the ✛ Son, and the Holy Spirit,
be with you always.
Amen.

Dismissal

Go in peace. Let your light shine.
Thanks be to God.

Seasonal Rites for the Time after Epiphany

Week of Prayer for Christian Unity

At least once a year, Christians are reminded of Jesus' prayer for his disciples that "they may be one . . . so that the world may believe" (see John 17:21). Hearts are touched and Christians come together to pray for their unity. Congregations and parishes all over the world exchange preachers or arrange special ecumenical celebrations and prayer services. The event that touches off this special experience is the Week of Prayer for Christian Unity.

Traditionally, the week of prayer is celebrated between January 18 and 25, between the feasts of St. Peter and St. Paul. In the southern hemisphere, where January is a vacation time, churches often find other days to celebrate it, for example around Pentecost, which is also a symbolic date for unity.

In order to prepare for the annual celebration, ecumenical partners in a particular region are invited to produce a basic liturgical text on a biblical theme. Then an international editorial team of World Council of Churches (WCC) and Roman Catholic representatives refines this text to ensure that it can be prayed throughout the world, and to link it with the search for the visible unity of the church.

The text is jointly published by the Pontifical Council for Promoting Christian Unity and the WCC, through the WCC's Commission on Faith and Order, which also accompanies the entire production process of the text. The final material is sent to WCC member churches and Roman Catholic episcopal conferences, and they are invited to translate the text and contextualize or adapt it for their own use.

Liturgical resources and materials for use in congregations are available at oikoumene.org/en/resources/week-of-prayer.

Reprinted from oikoumene.org/en/resources/week-of-prayer; accessed November 2018.

Farewell to Alleluia

Congregations that keep the ancient practice of fasting from singing or speaking "alleluia" through the forty days of Lent may consider the practice of "burying" the alleluia at the end of the liturgy on the last Sunday before Ash Wednesday. This might mean simply singing an appropriate song at the end of the service. Or it might include the actual lowering of a visual alleluia (a banner created by children, perhaps) while singing. The alleluia may literally be buried in a box in the church yard or hidden away somewhere in the church (where only the children know where it is!). The alleluia should return with great joy at the first alleluias of the Easter season, perhaps at the Vigil of Easter liturgy.

For even more ideas and helps around burying the alleluia, see this post with its link to an FAQ on the ELCA's Worship blog: blogs.elca.org/worship/430.

Hymns and songs

Alleluia, song of gladness   ELW 318, WOV 654

Halle, halle, hallelujah   ELW 172

Gospel Acclamation / Celtic Alleluia   ELW 174

Schwandt, Daniel. "Farewell to Alleluia." *Music Sourcebook for All Saints through Transfiguration* S571.

January 12, 2020
Baptism of Our Lord
First Sunday after Epiphany — Lectionary 1

In the waters of the Jordan, Jesus is revealed as the beloved Son of God. Through this great epiphany, Jesus fulfills all righteousness and becomes the servant of God who will bring forth justice and be a light to the nations. In the waters of baptism we too are washed by the Word, anointed by the Spirit, and named God's beloved children. Our baptismal mission is to proclaim good news to all who are oppressed or in need of God's healing.

Prayer of the Day

O God our Father, at the baptism of Jesus you proclaimed him your beloved Son and anointed him with the Holy Spirit. Make all who are baptized into Christ faithful to their calling to be your daughters and sons, and empower us all with your Spirit, through Jesus Christ, our Savior and Lord, who lives and reigns with you and the Holy Spirit, one God, now and forever.

Gospel Acclamation

Alleluia. A voice from heaven said, "This is my Son, the Beloved, with whom I am well pleased." *Alleluia.* (Matt. 3:17)

Readings and Psalm

Isaiah 42:1-9

God's servant is endowed with God's spirit in order to bring justice to the nations. The servant will not exercise authority boisterously or with violence, nor will weariness ever prevent the fulfilling of the servant's task. God's old promises have been fulfilled; the servant's new assignment is to bring light to the nations.

Psalm 29

The voice of the LORD is upon the waters. (Ps. 29:3)

Acts 10:34-43

Peter crosses the sharp religious boundary separating Jews from Gentiles and proclaims the good news of God's inclusive forgiveness in Jesus' name to Cornelius, a Roman centurion. As a result of Peter's preaching, Cornelius and his family become the first Gentiles to be baptized in the name of Jesus Christ.

Matthew 3:13-17

Before Jesus begins his ministry, he is baptized by John, touched by the Spirit, and identified publicly as God's child.

Preface   Baptism of Our Lord

Color   White

Prayers of Intercession

The prayers are prepared locally for each occasion. The following examples may be adapted or used as appropriate.

Called together through water and the Word, we boldly pray for the church, the world, and all who long to hear God's voice.
A brief silence.

Renewing God, thank you for the gift of baptism (*especially for name/s baptized among us today*). Give your church boldness to proclaim your promises. Tear down obstacles of injustice so that your word of hope reaches the ends of the earth. Lord, in your mercy,
hear our prayer.

Almighty God, we rejoice in the glory of your creation: the beauty of rivers and streams, glaciers and oceans, lakes and ponds. Bring restoration to your earth, and free us from overuse and abuse of water, air, and land. Lord, in your mercy,
hear our prayer.

God of peace, we give thanks for order in the midst of chaos, though we long for greater justice in our world. Raise up wise and compassionate servant leaders so that all experience your reign of peace. Lord, in your mercy,
hear our prayer.

Holy God, thank you for the powerful healing we witness through doctors and nurses, medication, therapy, and holistic means. Break through clouds of pain and anguish with your voice of comfort. Proclaim hope to all who grieve, and send healing to all who are sick (*especially*). Lord, in your mercy,
hear our prayer.

God of courage, we rejoice in this community of hope. Strengthen all who are preparing for baptism and renew the faith of sponsors, mentors, parents, grandparents, friends, and all who guide the newly baptized in this life of joy. Lord, in your mercy,
hear our prayer.

Here other intercessions may be offered.

God of hope, unleash your Spirit to increase our trust in you. We give thanks for the lives of the saints who inspire us with lives of baptismal witness (*especially*). Lord, in your mercy,
hear our prayer.

We place our prayers before you, God, united in your Spirit; through your beloved Son, Jesus Christ our Lord. **Amen.**

Ideas for the Day

- Baptism of Our Lord is a great day to celebrate a baptism. If there are no baptisms planned, be sure to include a thanksgiving for baptism in the service. If your worship attendance is small, invite people to come to the font for a time of personal remembrance of baptism. Services with more worshipers could include smaller bowls dipped into the baptismal font and brought to various stations where people can come for a remembrance of baptism.

- Those living with chronic illness or disability may spend a lot of time focused on what's "wrong" with them. Baptism offers a different vision and hope for people with disabilities, and for the Christian community formed by baptism. God claims us and bestows the gifts of the Spirit without regard to abilities or disabilities. Jesus welcomes those who are weakest and makes them a living sign of the kingdom of God in our midst. Read the order for Holy Baptism in *Evangelical Lutheran Worship* (pp. 227–231) to find a blessing to remind worshipers of this hope.

- The promises in the baptism liturgy (*ELW*, p. 228) have become a theological cornerstone to summarize our baptismal calling. Have members of the congregation share how they see themselves living into these promises through their vocations, whether paid or volunteer work. Or have a Mission and Ministry Party where the various ministries within and supported by your congregation share their work and recruit new supporters in the congregation.

- Emphasize your congregation's place of baptism today with added visual elements. For example, create a simple mobile from sturdy cardstock cut into the shape of water drops or doves to hang from the ceiling above your font. Or use various shades and widths of green, blue, and white fabric or ribbon to create a simple hanging above the font. If the ceiling over your font is too high to do this safely or practically, a banner stand could be repurposed into a structure from which to hang things. With enough lead time, the names of those baptized in the congregation this day or over the past year could be written onto the water drops, doves, or strips of fabric and ribbon before they are hung.

Connections with Creation

Baptism of Our Lord is an ideal time to talk with the congregation about the necessity of protecting the sanctity of water. Ask if they know the name of their local watershed, the closest body of water to the church, and the biggest source of water pollution in their area. If Jesus were to go to one of these sites, would he want to be baptized in those waters today, or are they polluted? What is the role of the church in protecting the waters of creation in which we baptize? Perhaps your church can take part in a water cleanup at a nearby stream or river. As the psalmist says, "The voice of the LORD is upon the waters" (Ps. 29:3). God's voice is calling us to keep those waters clean!

Let the Children Come

The day we celebrate Jesus' baptism and anointing for his journey to the cross is a wonderful occasion to invite children to explore baptism as a sacrament. The rite of Holy Baptism in *Evangelical Lutheran Worship* provides for the use of oil when the sign of the cross is made on the forehead of the newly baptized. If your congregation uses oil for baptisms or for anointing during a healing service, invite children to gather at the font and show them the oil jar or stock (often a small gold container). They may be especially fascinated with the oil stock on a ring which some pastors use. Make the sign of the cross with oil on each forehead and remind them that in baptism they are "sealed by the Holy Spirit and marked with the cross of Christ forever" (*ELW*, p. 231).

Assembly Song
Gathering

Crashing waters at creation ELW 455

Oh, love, how deep ELW 322, LBW 88

This is the Spirit's entry now ELW 448, LBW 195

Psalmody and Acclamations

Sing glory to the name of God/Psalm 29 GTG 10

Mummert, Mark. "Psalm 29," Refrain 1, from PSCY.

Wetzler, Robert. "Psalm 29" from PWA.

(GA) Monteiro, Simei (Brazil). "Alleluia" from GS3. Use ELW psalm tone 1 with proper verse for Baptism of Our Lord.

Hymn of the Day

Christ, when for us you were baptized ELW 304 *LOBT GOTT, IHR CHRISTEN*

I bind unto myself today ELW 450, LBW 188 *ST. PATRICK'S BREASTPLATE*

When Jesus came to Jordan ELW 305, WOV 647 *KING'S LYNN*

Offering

O Morning Star, how fair and bright! ELW 308, st. 3; LLC 320, st. 3; LBW 76, st. 3

We know that Christ is raised ELW 449, LBW 189

Communion

Spirit of Gentleness ELW 396, WOV 684, LS 68

Spirit of God, descend upon my heart ELW 800, LBW 486

The only Son from heaven ELW 309, LBW 86

Sending

Songs of thankfulness and praise ELW 310, LBW 90

Wade in the water ELW 459, TFF 114

Additional Assembly Songs

Come to the water MSB2 S562

Jesus, the Light of the World/Rise Up! Shine! TFF 59, MSB2 S555

Song over the Waters W&P 127

⊕ Russian Orthodox trad. "When You, O Lord, Were Baptized" from *Hallelujah! Resources for Prayer and Praise,* 10th Assembly. SATB. WCC Publications. Out of print. Hannelore.Schmid@wcc-coe.org.

⊕ Shona trad., Zimbabwe. "Rakanaka Vhangeri/Come and Hear Now the Gospel" from *Agape: Songs of Hope and Reconciliation.* OXF 9780191000133. Out of print.

☼ Benedict, Bruce/Isaac Wardell. "He Will Not Cry Out" from *He Will Not Cry Out.* bifrostartsmusic.bandcamp.com.

☼ Fielding, Ben/Brooke Ligertwood. "What a Beautiful Name" from CCLI.

☼ Houge, Nate. "Treasure" from *Storm Home: A Collection of Music from Humble Walk Artists-in-Residence.* humblewalk.bandcamp.com.

☼ McCracken, Sandra. "Trinity Song." from CCLI.

☼ Rozier, Andi/James McDonald/Jason Ingram/Meredith Andrews/Stuart Garrard. "Open Up the Heavens" from CCLI.

☼ Sampson, Marty/Matt Crocker. "Open Heaven (River Wild)" from CCLI.

Music for the Day
Choral

P Folkemer, Stephen P. "Once Led to Your Font." SAB, org, fl. AFP 9781506456843.

P Keesecker, Tom. "Hail to the Lord's Anointed" from *The New Gloria Deo,* vol. 2. 2 pt mxd, pno, gtr. AFP 9781451424133.

Mclein, Lena J. "Don't You Let Nobody Turn You 'Round" from *The Oxford Book of Spirituals.* SATB, pno. OXF 9780193863040.

P Ward, Tony. "We Arise This Day." SATB, pno, opt vln, solo inst, assembly. AFP 9781506452524.

Children's Choir

Callahan, Charles. "The Baptism of Our Lord." U, opt desc, org. MSM 50-2003.

P Highben, Zebulon. "I'm Going on a Journey." U, pno, bass gtr, tenor sax, opt assembly. AFP 9780800664022.

Mauersburger, Erhard. "We Saw His Glory" from *A Second Morning Star Choir Book.* U, kybd. CPH 974702.

Keyboard / Instrumental

♫ Callahan, Charles. "King's Lynn" from *O God beyond All Praising: Seven Pieces for Organ on English Hymntunes.* Org. MSM 10-799.

P Childs, Edwin T. "Wade in the Water" from *Spirituals for Organ: For Manuals Only.* Org. AFP 9781451401141.

Locklair, Dan. "... the heavens were opened ..." from *Windows of Comfort (Two Organ Books), Organbook 1.* Org. HAL 50483050.

P♫ Wilson, Terry D. "Let All Together Praise Our God" from *Creative Spirit: Piano Settings.* Pno. AFP 9781451479607.

Handbell

♫ Hurlbutt, Patricia. "Let All Together Praise Our God (Lobt Gott, ihr Christen)." 3-5 oct, L2. CPH 977803.

Tucker, Margaret. "Shall We Gather at the River" from *Ring Around the Year.* 3-5 oct, L2, L2+. CG CGB759.

Wissinger, Kath. "Call of the Water." 3-7 oct hb, opt 3-7 oct hc, C inst, wch. Ring True Music RE8005.

Wednesday, January 15
Martin Luther King Jr., renewer of society, martyr, died 1968

Martin Luther King Jr. is remembered as an American prophet of justice among races and nations, a Christian whose faith undergirded his advocacy of vigorous yet nonviolent action for racial equality. A pastor of churches in Montgomery, Alabama, and Atlanta, Georgia, his witness was taken to the streets in such other places as Birmingham, Alabama, where he was arrested and jailed while protesting against segregation. He preached nonviolence and demanded that love be returned for hate. Awarded the Nobel Peace Prize in 1964, he was killed by an assassin on April 4, 1968. Though most commemorations are held on the date of the person's death, many churches hold commemorations near Dr. King's birth date of January 15, in conjunction with the American civil holiday honoring him. An alternate date for the commemoration is his death date, April 4.

Friday, January 17
Antony of Egypt, renewer of the church, died around 356

Antony was born in Qemen-al-Arous, Upper Egypt, and was one of the earliest Egyptian desert fathers. Born to Christian parents from whom he inherited a large estate, he took personally Jesus' message to sell all that you have, give to the poor, and follow Christ. After making arrangements to provide for the care of his sister, he gave away his inheritance and became a hermit. Later, he became the head of a group of monks that

⊕ = global song   ♫ = relates to hymn of the day

☼ = praise song   P = available in Prelude Music Planner

lived in a cluster of huts and devoted themselves to communal prayer, worship, and manual labor under Antony's direction. The money they earned from their work was distributed as alms. Antony and his monks also preached and counseled those who sought them out. Antony and the desert fathers serve as a reminder that certain times and circumstances call Christians to stand apart from the surrounding culture and renounce the world in service to Christ.

Friday, January 17
Pachomius, renewer of the church, died 346

Another of the desert fathers, Pachomius (puh-KOME-ee-us) was born in Egypt about 290. He became a Christian during his service as a soldier. In 320 he went to live as a hermit in Upper Egypt, where other hermits lived nearby. Pachomius organized them into a religious community in which the members prayed together and held their goods in common. His rule for monasteries influenced both Eastern and Western monasticism through the Rule of Basil and the Rule of Benedict, respectively.

Saturday, January 18
Confession of Peter
Week of Prayer for Christian Unity begins

The Week of Prayer for Christian Unity is framed by two commemorations, the Confession of Peter (a relatively recent addition to the calendar) and the older Conversion of Paul. Both apostles are remembered together on June 29, but these two days give us an opportunity to focus on key events in each of their lives. Today we remember that Peter was led by God's grace to acknowledge Jesus as "the Messiah, the Son of the living God" (Matt. 16:16). This confession is the common confession that unites us with Peter and with all Christians of every time and place.

January 19, 2020
Second Sunday after Epiphany
Lectionary 2

Today's gospel opens with further reflection on Jesus' baptism. He is the Lamb of God who takes away the sin of the world and the one anointed by the Spirit. In the liturgy we come and see Christ revealed among us in word and meal. We go forth to invite others to come and worship the Holy One and to receive the gifts of grace and peace made known among us.

Prayer of the Day

Holy God, our strength and our redeemer, by your Spirit hold us forever, that through your grace we may worship you and faithfully serve you, follow you and joyfully find you, through Jesus Christ, our Savior and Lord.

Gospel Acclamation

Alleluia. In the Word was life, and the life was the light of all people. *Alleluia.* (John 1:4)

Readings and Psalm
Isaiah 49:1-7

Here the servant, identified as Israel, speaks for herself and describes her honored mission. Called before her birth like Jeremiah and John the Baptist, the servant is not only to restore Israel. The servant's ultimate assignment is to bring news of God's victory to the ends of the earth. God in faithfulness has chosen Israel for this task.

Psalm 40:1-11

I love to do your will, O my God. (Ps. 40:8)

1 Corinthians 1:1-9

Though God's church in Corinth is a fractious congregation beset with many conflicts, Paul opens this letter by spotlighting the multiple ways God has enriched and sustained its life as part of the divine call into the fellowship of our Lord Jesus Christ.

John 1:29-42

John the Baptist's witness to Jesus initiates a chain of testimony as his disciples begin to share with others what they have found.

Preface   Sundays

Color   Green

Prayers of Intercession

The prayers are prepared locally for each occasion. The following examples may be adapted or used as appropriate.

Called together through water and the Word, we boldly pray for the church, the world, and all who long to hear God's voice.

A brief silence.

Faithful God, thank you for the testimony of disciples throughout the generations and for opportunities to proclaim your mercy. Reveal your truth and glory to all who ponder your word of life. Lord, in your mercy,

hear our prayer.

Creating God, we marvel at the abundance of the world you have made. Give us confidence in our calling to be stewards of the earth so that our lives are in fellowship with all creation. Lord, in your mercy,

hear our prayer.

Almighty God, we are thankful for all who have marched for justice and advocated for peace. Entrust our elected leaders (*especially*) with strength, wisdom, and a discerning spirit, so that both our words and our actions serve you. Lord, in your mercy,

hear our prayer.

God of hope, thank you for your constant presence as you walk with your children through challenges of joblessness, homelessness, grief, and sickness. Gather your community around all who need your healing power, that they find strength in you (*especially*). Lord, in your mercy,

hear our prayer.

God of persistence, we glory in the gifts of our church leaders. Bless and strengthen our council members, staff, pastors, worship leaders, and all those who offer their gifts to this community, that our work together would serve your mission. Lord, in your mercy,

hear our prayer.

Here other intercessions may be offered.

Living God, we give thanks for the whole communion of saints, each called in their own time to serve you (*especially Henry, Bishop of Uppsala*). Inspire our lives with their testimony. Lord, in your mercy,

hear our prayer.

We place our prayers before you, God, united in your Spirit; through your beloved Son, Jesus Christ our Lord.

Amen.

Ideas for the Day

- Though a pastor claiming to be a servant of God from the time in the womb (Isa. 49:1, 5) might raise eyebrows, there is a comfort and power to such boldness. Those called to the ministry of word and sacrament often feel they "have labored in vain," having "spent [their] strength for nothing and vanity" (49:4), but they continue because "[their] cause is with the LORD" (49:4). Such bold self-comfort and self-acknowledgment are life-saving for all leaders called to be "a light to the nations" (49:6) in troubling times, especially when support and affirmation are thin.

- The general mood of today's appointed psalm and the reading from 1 Corinthians is one of simple thanks and praise, but with contrasting foci. The psalmist sings of how God saved them from "the desolate pit" (Ps. 40:2), not even requiring a traditional burnt offering or sin offering (40:6). And so, the recently redeemed shares this glad news of deliverance in the great assembly (40:9), completing the circle of gratitude for what God has done for them. Paul, however, gives thanks specifically for the power of God's presence in other people—for how "the grace of God . . . has been given you in Christ Jesus" (1 Cor. 1:4) and how they were "not lacking in any spiritual gift" (1:7)—making them ideal friends and collaborators in Paul's mission throughout Asia Minor. It makes an especially Lutheran contrast with the psalm as well, as Luther regularly taught that our God works through means—through aspects of quotidian life—and not just in miracles and deeds of power.

- In the synoptic gospels, John the Baptist's power and authority nearly rival those of Jesus. But in John's gospel, the desert prophet gives regular descriptions of Jesus' authority exceeding his own. Not only does John affirm that Jesus is "the Son of God" (John 1:34) and "the Lamb of God" (1:36), but he even makes the cryptic pronouncement about Jesus' eternal nature, saying that Jesus "ranks ahead of me because he was before me" (1:30). John's dedication to God and humanity meant that when someone came along who could do a better job than he could, had more insight, and was greater than he was, he had to defer. By extension, then, it's a good practice for pastors to do the same—pointing to lay leaders, community members, anyone who is fulfilling a role better or more effectively than they can.

Connections with Creation

"Listen to me, O coastlands," the servant calls out in today's reading from Isaiah (49:1-7). What does the prophet's mission mean for *actual* coastlands? As sea levels rise from melting glaciers due to global warming, and coastal erosion renders some beaches nonexistent due to destructive storms, God's creation is in need of a prophetic voice. Advocating for environmental protection sometimes requires a "mouth like a sharp sword" and a will like "a polished arrow" to cut through the apathy and moneyed interests of those in power. And like Isaiah's servant, we may often feel like we have "labored in vain" when so little progress is made. Yet we know our "cause is with the LORD" who means for our work to be "a light to the nations." God's salvation indeed extends "to the end of the earth."

Let the Children Come

Over the next several weeks, make a big deal of "alleluia" in your music and visuals. Create a huge black-and-white outline of the word on a sturdy no-show-thru or poster-bond paper roll (available at art supply stores or online) and invite children to color it and add sequins and other decorations as they arrive each Sunday between now and Transfiguration (Feb. 23). While they work, teach hymn-based alleluia refrains or have them make up their own melodies for this special word. Encourage others in the congregation to join in the fun.

Alternatively, consider commissioning an artist or inviting a local art teacher to help children in your community design and create a bright and festive permanent fabric or wood alleluia for use every year. Remind children that they will be helping to remove and "bury" the banner for Lent at the close of the service on Transfiguration Sunday.

Assembly Song
Gathering

I want to walk as a child of the light ELW 815, WOV 649, LS 37
O God of light ELW 507, LBW 237
Thy strong word ELW 511, LBW 233

Psalmody and Acclamations

I waited patiently for God/Psalm 40 GTG 651
"Here I Am." *Psallite* A-96. Cant or SATB, assembly, kybd.
Alonso, Tony. "Here I Am." SATB, cant, assembly, kybd. GIA G-6735.
(GA) Monteiro, Simei (Brazil). "Alleluia" from GS3. Use ELW psalm tone 1 with proper verse for Epiphany 2.

Hymn of the Day

A lamb goes uncomplaining forth ELW 340, LBW 105
AN WASSERFLÜSSEN BABYLON
Here I Am, Lord ELW 574, WOV 752, TFF 230, LS 138
HERE I AM, LORD
Lamb of God/Your Only Son ELW 336 *YOUR ONLY SON*

Offering

Come to the table ELW 481, W&P 33
Take, oh, take me as I am ELW 814, SP 40

Communion

Blessing, Honor, and Glory ELW 433, W&P 21
Lamb of God, pure and sinless ELW 357, LBW 111
Now behold the Lamb ELW 341, TFF 128

Sending

Drawn to the Light ELW 593
We are marching in the light/Siyahamba ELW 866, WOV 650, TFF 63, W&P 148

Additional Assembly Songs

Arise, shine SC 3
Yo soy la luz del mundo/I am the light of nations LLC 319
You are my strength when I am weak GTG 519
⊕ Anon., Palestine. "Uhibbuka Rabbi Yasu'/I Give My Heart to You, O Christ" from *Hosanna! Ecumenical Songs for Justice and Peace*. WCC Publications 9782825416679.
⊕ Wu, Jen-se. "Lamb of God" from *Sound the Bamboo*. GIA G-6830.
☼ Bozarth, Whitney. "Come and See" from *Anchor for My Soul*. whitneybozarth.bandcamp.com.
☼ Crowder, David. "Come and Listen" from CCLI.
☼ Pakan, Joel. "Behold, the Lamb" from *Storm Home: A Collection of Music from Humble Walk Artists-in-Residence*. humblewalk.bandcamp.com.
☼ Reagan, Will. "I Can Tell" from WT.
☼ Rundman, Jonathan. "Lamb of God (Agnus Dei)" from *A Heartland Liturgy*. jonathanrundman.bandcamp.com.
☼ Tomlin, Chris/Jason Ingram/Matt Maher/Matt Redman. "Come and See" from CCLI.

Music for the Day
Choral

P Farlee, Robert Buckley. "The Only Son from Heaven" from *The Augsburg Choirbook*. SATB, a cap. AFP 9780800656782.
P Hassler, Hans Leo. "Agnus Dei" from *Chantry Choirbook: Sacred Music for All Seasons*. SATB, a cap. AFP 9780800657772.
♫ Schutte, Dan/arr. Jack Schrader. "Here I Am, Lord." 2 pt mxd, pno, opt gtr, bass gtr, drm, perc. HOP 5879.
Wesby, Barbara. "Agnus Dei." SA, pno. wesbyworksmusic.com.

Children's Choir

Miller, Aaron David. "Lamb of God." U, pno. AFP 9780800638375.
P Pooler, Marie. "Lamb of God" from *Unison and Two-part Anthems*. U/2 pt, kybd. AFP 9780800648916.
P Makeever, Ray. "Come and See" from *Dancing at the Harvest*. U/2 pt, pno/gtr. AFP 9780800655938.

Keyboard / Instrumental

P Cherwien, David. "Wojtkiewiecz" from *Augsburg Organ Library: Epiphany*. Org. AFP 9780800659349.
Ore, Charles W. "O Day Full of Grace" from *Eleven Compositions for Organ*, set VII. Org. CPH 976988.
P Raabe, Nancy M. "Christ, Be Our Light" from *Foot-Friendly Preludes*. Org. AFP 9781451479539.
P ♫ Unke, Zach. "Here I Am, Lord" from *At the Name of Jesus: Piano Settings*. Pno. AFP 9781506448046.

⊕ = global song   ♫ = relates to hymn of the day
☼ = praise song   P = available in Prelude Music Planner

Handbell

♫ Helman, Michael. "Here I Am, Lord." 3-6 oct hb, opt 3-5 oct hc, L2+. LOR 20/1847L.

♫ Ryan, Michael. "Lamb of God." 2-3 oct, L2. LOR 20/1457L. Tucker, Sondra. "I Want to Walk as a Child of the Light." 3-5 oct, L3. AFP 11-11024.

Sunday, January 19

Henry, Bishop of Uppsala, martyr, died 1156

Henry, an Englishman, became bishop of Uppsala, Sweden, in 1152 and is regarded as the patron of Finland. He traveled to Finland with the king of Sweden on a mission trip and remained there to organize the church. He was murdered in Finland by a man he had rebuked and who was disciplined by the church. Henry's burial place became a center of pilgrimage. His popularity as a saint is strong in both Sweden and Finland.

Tuesday, January 21

Agnes, martyr, died around 304

Agnes was a girl of about thirteen living in Rome who had chosen a life of service to Christ as a virgin, despite the Roman emperor Diocletian's ruling that outlawed all Christian activity. The details of her martyrdom are not clear, but she gave witness to her faith and was put to death as a result, most likely by the sword. Since her death, the church has honored her as one of the chief martyrs of her time.

Saturday, January 25

Conversion of Paul
Week of Prayer for Christian Unity ends

Today the Week of Prayer for Christian Unity comes to an end. The church remembers how a man of Tarsus named Saul, a former persecutor of the early Christian church, was turned around by God's grace to become one of its chief preachers. The risen Christ appeared to Paul on the road to Damascus and called him to proclaim the gospel. The narratives describing Paul's conversion in the Acts of the Apostles, Galatians, and 1 Corinthians inspire this commemoration, which was first celebrated among the Christians of Gaul.

♫ = relates to hymn of the day
P = available in Prelude Music Planner

January 26, 2020
Third Sunday after Epiphany
Lectionary 3

Jesus begins his public ministry by calling fishers to leave their nets and follow him. In Jesus the kingdom of God has come near. We who have walked in darkness have seen a great light. We see this light most profoundly in the cross—as God suffers with us and all who are oppressed by sickness, sin, or evil. Light dawns for us as we gather around the word, the font, and the holy table. We are then sent to share the good news that others may be "caught" in the net of God's grace and mercy.

Prayer of the Day

Lord God, your lovingkindness always goes before us and follows after us. Summon us into your light, and direct our steps in the ways of goodness that come through the cross of your Son, Jesus Christ, our Savior and Lord.

Gospel Acclamation

Alleluia. Jesus preached the good news of the kingdom and cured every sickness among the people. *Alleluia.* (Matt. 4:23)

Readings and Psalm

Isaiah 9:1-4

The northern tribes of Zebulun and Naphtali experienced the gloom of defeat by Assyrian military forces, but they are assured that their condition will be reversed when God makes a light-filled appearance. The joy they will experience will resemble celebrations of great harvests, because God will deliver them from everything that diminishes or oppresses them.

Psalm 27:1, 4-9

The Lord is my light and my salvation. (Ps. 27:1)

1 Corinthians 1:10-18

Paul calls on the Corinthians to end their dissensions and share the unified outlook of the gospel. Discord arises when we forget that we belong not to human leaders or institutions but to Christ. Indeed, the unifying word of the cross of Christ is the center of the gospel and the power of God's salvation.

Matthew 4:12-23

Jesus begins his public ministry shortly after John the Baptist is imprisoned by Herod. He proclaims the nearness of God's reign and calls four fishermen to be his first disciples.

Preface   Sundays

Color   Green

Prayers of Intercession

The prayers are prepared locally for each occasion. The following examples may be adapted or used as appropriate.

Called together through water and the Word, we boldly pray for the church, the world, and all who long to hear God's voice.
A brief silence.

Holy One, your voice calls us to follow. Thank you for raising up missionaries in every generation (*especially Timothy, Titus, and Silas*) and for all who create communities of grace today. Open our hearts to serve you near and far. Lord, in your mercy,
hear our prayer.

Maker of all, we rejoice in the beauty and abundance of the earth. Unite us in our shared calling to be stewards of creation, to reduce waste, and to simplify our lives for your sake. Lord, in your mercy,
hear our prayer.

Ruler of all, thank you for those who run for local and national office, and all who serve as elected leaders. Gather wise and courageous voices together, that your mercy and justice would dawn upon all people and nations. Lord, in your mercy,
hear our prayer.

Healer of all, thank you for sanctuary and safety. Uplift all who live where fear governs and evil divides. Give refugees and all who seek safety a path toward hope and new life. Grant healing and wholeness to all who are sick, lonely, or grieving (*especially*). Lord, in your mercy,
hear our prayer.

God of courage, thank you for faithful teachers and evangelists in this and every place. Inspire our faith formation efforts with all generations as you call us to follow you. Bless our children, youth, and adults who engage in learning. Lord, in your mercy,
hear our prayer.

Here other intercessions may be offered.

Risen Lord, we marvel at the meaning of your resurrection. Give us faith to place all hope in you as we give thanks for the faithful departed (*especially*). May their witness help us follow your call. Lord, in your mercy,
hear our prayer.

We place our prayers before you, God, united in your Spirit;
through your beloved Son, Jesus Christ our Lord.
Amen.

Ideas for the Day

- Whereas scripture does not reveal much information about what life in Galilee was like, modern archeology does. Excavations in the 1970s and '80s revealed Galilee to have long been an arid backwater only sparsely settled by landless cast-offs from Judea in the decades before Jesus' birth. It doubtless would have been a shock for Isaiah's audience to hear that "a great light" and a source of "joy" would come from such "a land of deep darkness" (9:2-3) and privation. But the Bible reliably demonstrates that God often lifts up great leaders precisely from obscurity and hardship—shepherds, discontented farmers, cave-dwelling prophets—because such penury likely produces not only an undiluted dependence upon God, but also the tenacity and adaptability necessary to initiate change in even the most troubling times.

- Silencing critical voices through calls to be "united in the same mind and the same purpose" is an eternal and some-times insipid practice (1 Cor. 1:10). Divisions and quarrels are often signs of honesty and vitality, not always strife and toxicity. Silencing or ignoring critical voices can often run the risk of stifling the Spirit's voice in a community. Luckily though, Paul's plea is for true unity, not confor-mity. Paul grounds his concerns in the mutual reminder that despite the fractious potential of "eloquent wisdom" (1:17) and charismatic personality, we can navigate diffi-culty when we ultimately seek direction and togetherness in Christ alone, and that in the cross we find our deepest reservoir of power.

- Jonathan Reed and John Dominic Crossan's book *Exca-vating Jesus: Beneath the Stones, Behind the Texts* (New York: HarperCollins, 2002) makes deep connections between the Isaiah reading and this week's gospel. Reed and Crossan share findings from a first-century fishing boat found by the Sea of Galilee in 1986, which, though largely built from low-quality materials and held together with wooden plugs and resin, is a moving testimony to ingenuity born of perpetual hardship. Though slow to understand some of Jesus' theology and rhetoric, the first apostles were likely practical, adaptive, and resourceful—just the kind of people Jesus needed to build something from almost nothing (Matt. 4:17-22). And though Isaiah, Matthew, and archeology illustrate the intractability of Galilee's social conditions, from this forsaken land would come the vanguard of a movement that would change human history.

Connections with Creation

The people of Puerto Rico know what it means to "[live] in a land of deep darkness" (Isa. 9:2). After the 2017 hurricanes that destroyed their homes, businesses, and dilapidated electricity grid, some families went without power for months, even up to a year. More than four thousand people died. Ironically, the carbon footprint of these islanders is very low because they use little electricity. Yet the "yoke of their burden" (9:4) has been laid across their shoulders by the developed world supercharg-ing global warming, which exacerbates hurricanes. They long for God to "make glorious the way of the sea" (9:1) that has sustained their people for countless generations. Lutheran Disaster Response helped by providing food, water, formula, and diapers during the days and weeks immediately following the hurricane. They are also engaged in a multi-year volunteer rebuild/repair program. How can your church help God's light to shine in these places?

Let the Children Come

Paul has no patience for the divisions among the Corinthi-ans. Though the word *reconciliation* may not be familiar to children, the action and the meaning are a part of their lives. Children fuss and fight with one another. They know the pain of separation and anger with their friends and their family. And they also know what it means to "make up." A simple word such as "sorry" along with a gesture, perhaps a hug, carries the meaning of two people once divided who are now reconciled. In your congregation, what are the ways in which children know and experience the reconciliation and peace of Jesus Christ?

Assembly Song
Gathering

All my hope on God is founded   ELW 757, WOV 782
How clear is our vocation, Lord   ELW 580
The Son of God, our Christ   ELW 584, LBW 434

Psalmody and Acclamations

The Lord is my light   TFF 61
Behnke, John A. "The Lord Is My Light and My Salvation."
    SAB, assembly, kybd, opt 2-3 oct hb. CG CGA981.
Organ, Anne Krentz. "Psalm 27:1, 4-9" from PSCY.
(GA) Monteiro, Simei (Brazil). "Alleluia" from GS3. Use ELW
    psalm tone 1 with proper verse for Epiphany 3.

Hymn of the Day

Come, follow me, the Savior spake   ELW 799, LBW 455   MACHS
    MIT MIR, GOTT
Will you come and follow me   ELW 798, W&P 137   KELVINGROVE
You have come down to the lakeshore   ELW 817, WOV 784,
    TFF 154, LLC 560   PESCADOR DE HOMBRES

Offering

God extends an invitation/Nuestro Padre nos invita   ELW 486, WOV 709, LLC 397, TFF 125

Jesus, come! for we invite you   ELW 312, WOV 648

Communion

Come, beloved of the Maker   ELW 306, CBM 67

Here I Am, Lord   ELW 574, WOV 752, TFF 230, LS 138

Take, oh, take me as I am   ELW 814, SP 40

Sending

Jesus call us; o'er the tumult   ELW 696, LBW 494

Rise, O church, like Christ arisen   ELW 548, OBS 76

Additional Assembly Songs

Called as partners in Christ's service   NCH 495

They cast their nets   LBW 449

You walk along our shoreline   NCH 504, GTG 170

🌐 Collective Creation, Matanzas, Mexico. "Las mesas partidas/ These Tables Divided" from *Hosanna! Ecumenical Songs for Justice and Peace*. SATB. WCC Publications 9782825416679.

🌐 South African trad., Zulu. "Jikelele/Everywhere" from *For Everyone Born: Global Songs for an Emerging Church*. SATB. GBGMusik 9781933663265.

☼ Culver, Caleb/Cory Asbury/Ran Jackson. "Reckless Love" from CCLI.

☼ Houston, Joel/Matt Crocker/Salomon Ligthelm. "Oceans (Where Feet May Fail)" from CCLI.

☼ Johnson, Brian/John Mohr. "Where You Go I Go" from CCLI.

☼ Rend Collective. "My Lighthouse" from CCLI.

☼ Tomlin, Chris/Jason Ingram/Reuben Morgan. "I Will Follow" from CCLI.

☼ Younker, Brett/Karl Martin/Kirby Kaple/Matt Redman/Pat Barrett. "Build My Life" from CCLI.

Music for the Day
Choral

Brusick, William. "I Want to Walk as a Child of the Light." 2 pt mxd, pno. CPH 984252.

P Hopp, Roy. "Would I Have Answered When You Called." SATB, org. AFP 9780800679262.

Stroope, Z. Randall. "The Call." SSA, org. MSM 50-6525.

P Young, Phillip M. "Jesus Calls Us." SATB, org. AFP 9781541479386.

Children's Choir

Kosche, Kenneth T. "The Lord Is My Light." 2 pt, kybd. CPH 984053.

P Simpson, F. Thomas. "Nets of Love." U/2 pt, kybd. CG CGA1301.

Southwick Cool, Jayne. "Lumen Christi." U, kybd. CG CGA1098.

🌐 = global song   🎵 = relates to hymn of the day
☼ = praise song   P = available in Prelude Music Planner

Keyboard / Instrumental

Page, Anna Laura. "I Love to Tell the Story" from *Tell the Story: Ten Gospel Hymn Arrangements for Piano*. Pno. MSM 15-850.

P🎵 Powell, Robert J. "Come, Follow Me, the Savior Spake" from *Mixtures: Hymn Preludes for Organ*. Org. AFP 9781451479553.

P🎵 Rowland-Raybold, Roberta. "You Have Come Down to the Lakeshore" from *All Praise for Music: Hymn Settings for Piano*. Pno. AFP 9781451486087.

P🎵 Wold, Wayne L. "Will You Come and Follow Me" from *Awake My Heart: Organ Suites and Settings*. Org. AFP 9781506447964.

Handbell

🎵 Eithun, Sandra. "Will You Come and Follow Me" from *Our God Reigns*. 12 bells, opt kybd, L1, L2. CG CGB1056.

🎵 Honore, Jeffrey. "Pescador de hombres." 3-5 oct, L3. WLP 3431.

Rogers, Sharon. "Followers of the Lamb." 3-5 hb, drm or tamb, L3. AGEHR AG35202.

Sunday, January 26
Timothy, Titus, and Silas, missionaries

On the two days following the usual date for the Conversion of Paul, his companions are remembered. Timothy, Titus, and Silas were missionary coworkers with Paul. Timothy accompanied Paul on his second missionary journey and was commissioned by Paul to go to Ephesus, where he served as bishop and overseer of the church. Titus was a traveling companion of Paul, accompanied him on the trip to the council of Jerusalem, and became the first bishop of Crete. Silas traveled with Paul through Asia Minor and Greece and was imprisoned with him at Philippi, where they were delivered by an earthquake.

Monday, January 27
Lydia, Dorcas, and Phoebe, witnesses to the faith

On this day the church remembers three women who were companions in Paul's ministry. Lydia was Paul's first convert at Philippi in Macedonia. She was a merchant of purple-dyed goods, and because purple dye was extremely expensive, it is likely that Lydia was a woman of some wealth. Lydia and her household were baptized by Paul, and for a time her home was a base for Paul's missionary work. Dorcas is remembered for her charitable works, particularly making clothing for needy widows. Phoebe was a *diakonos*, a deacon in the church at Cenchreae, near Corinth. Paul praises her as one who, through her service, looked after many people.

Tuesday, January 28
Thomas Aquinas, teacher, died 1274

Thomas Aquinas (uh-KWY-nus) was a brilliant and creative theologian of the thirteenth century. He was first and foremost a student of the Bible and profoundly concerned with the theological formation of the church's ordained ministers. As a member of the Order of Preachers (Dominicans), he worked to correlate scripture with the philosophy of Aristotle, which was having a renaissance in Aquinas's day. Some students of Aristotle's philosophy found in it an alternative to Christianity. But Aquinas immersed himself in the thought of Aristotle and worked to explain Christian beliefs in the philosophical culture of the day.

February 2, 2020
Presentation of Our Lord

The Presentation of Our Lord is referred to in some corners of the church as Candlemas because of an ancient tradition of blessing all the candles to be used in the church in the coming year at the mass celebrated on that day. It was a way of underscoring the truth of Simeon's confession that this baby Jesus was "a light for revelation to the Gentiles" and a light for glory to Israel. Let the light of every candle in church be a little epiphany of the love of God for all people in the person of God's Son, Jesus, the light of the world.

Prayer of the Day

Almighty and ever-living God, your only-begotten Son was presented this day in the temple. May we be presented to you with clean and pure hearts by the same Jesus Christ, our great high priest, who lives and reigns with you and the Holy Spirit, one God, now and forever.

Gospel Acclamation

Alleluia. My eyes have seen your salvation, which you have prepared in the presence of all peoples. *Alleluia.* (Luke 2:30-31)

Readings and Psalm
Malachi 3:1-4

This reading concludes a larger section (2:17—3:5) in which the prophet speaks of the coming of the God of justice. Malachi looks for that day when the wondrous power of God will purify the priestly descendants of Levi who minister in the temple at Jerusalem.

Psalm 84

How dear to me is your dwelling, O LORD. (Ps. 84:1)

or Psalm 24:7-10

Lift up your heads, O gates, that the King of glory may come in. (Ps 24:7)

Hebrews 2:14-18

Jesus shared human nature fully so that his death might be for all humans a liberation from death's power. Here the writer uses the image of priestly service in the temple as a way of describing the life and saving death of the Lord Jesus. He is the high priest who offers his life on behalf of his brothers and sisters.

Luke 2:22-40

This story is a study in contrasts: the infant Jesus with the aged prophets; the joy of birth with the ominous words of Simeon to Mary; the faithful fulfilling of the law with the presentation of the one who will release its hold over us. Through it all, we see the light of God's salvation revealed to the world.

Preface   Christmas

Color   White

Prayers of Intercession

The prayers are prepared locally for each occasion. The following examples may be adapted or used as appropriate.

Called together through water and the Word, we boldly pray for the church, the world, and all who long to hear God's voice.
A brief silence.

Almighty God, you grant wisdom to our elders in every land and generation. Give senior citizens boldness to share the faith and a spirit of curiosity and joy to continue learning as your disciples. Lord, in your mercy,
hear our prayer.

Everlasting God, you provide beauty and warmth in sun, moon, stars, and fire, and you give us abundant gifts of water, land, and air. Break our patterns of overusing resources across the world so that all experience your beautiful creation. Lord, in your mercy,
hear our prayer.

Creating God, thank you for your daily presence in our community and throughout the world. Inspire leaders with your strength and wisdom, that all communities may be safe places for children, adults, seniors, infants, and youth. Lord, in your mercy,

hear our prayer.

Incarnate God, thank you for being born among us and experiencing human pain and sorrow. Bring wholeness to all who live with chronic illness, and rest your Spirit on those who are near death. Strengthen the sick (*especially*). Bless those who care for them. Lord, in your mercy,

hear our prayer.

Merciful God, you encourage us through strong communities of faith. Open our hearts and minds to new people and ideas. Bless our vibrant traditions that bring life and hope. Lord, in your mercy,

hear our prayer.

Here other intercessions may be offered.

God of hope, thank you for the saints who have gone before us (*especially*). Keep us faithful in service to you until we are one with all the faithful departed. Lord, in your mercy,

hear our prayer.

We place our prayers before you, God, united in your Spirit; through your beloved Son, Jesus Christ our Lord.

Amen.

Ideas for the Day

- Luke offers us characters from several generations in his account of Jesus' presentation in the temple. Most prominent are Simeon and Anna, both "of a great age" (Luke 2:36). Most congregations have people "of a great age," but many have pastors who are not. It may be helpful to consider the current experiences of the older people in our congregations. In his essay "Out the Window," the first in his book *Essays after Eighty*, Donald Hall says of old age, "However alert we are, however much we think we know what will happen, antiquity remains an unknown, unanticipated galaxy. It is alien, and old people are a separate form of life" (New York: Houghton Mifflin Harcourt, 2014, p. 7). If the aging people in our settings feel alien to those who are younger, it may benefit us to read such a collection of essays and to ask some of our elderly members to share their experiences with us.

- To Simeon it is revealed that he will live to see the Messiah, and he is guided by the Spirit to the temple on the day of Jesus' presentation. Anna is open to God's word as she spends all her time in the temple. Both Simeon and Anna are aged prophets who hear and speak the truth about who God is and what God is doing, and they point to the baby who will grow and become strong, filled with wisdom and God's favor. Wisdom and truth are not limited to people of a certain age or experience. What might God be revealing to people in your setting who are teenagers, young parents, or empty-nesters? Invite some people to bear witness to what God is showing them. Alternately, interview people of various ages, and include their testimonies in your sermon or in the worship folder.

- In today's second reading we are reminded that there is no struggle we can experience through which Christ has not lived. It is, in part, why we can trust our Lord; he has been tested, betrayed, misunderstood, slandered, misjudged, beaten, abandoned, and killed. Invite people to write on a slip of paper a word or phrase to describe a current or past struggle; collect them and pray a prayer of trust and gratitude to God ". . . for abiding with us through divorce, unemployment, eating disorders, broken trust, failing health . . ."—whatever has been shared on the slips of paper.

Connections with Creation

The temple of the Lord is a prominent theme in today's readings. Jesus is brought to Jerusalem's temple as a baby to be dedicated to God. Psalm 84 speaks of "the courts of the LORD" (v. 2) as a place of joy and refreshment. Yet the psalm takes an unusual turn at verse three, describing the sparrow and swallow making a nest at the altars of the Lord. Could it be that the psalmist sees God's dwelling place not just in a human-made temple but in the earth itself? The psalm describes a place of springs and pools, and God as both a sun and a shield. What if we were to adopt this expansive understanding of God's temple to include the natural world? More than just a metaphor, the world as God's temple has ramifications for how we treat wild places, urban trees, rivers, and even our own church grounds.

Let the Children Come

Haven't put the crèche away yet? Perfect! "Re-purpose" two shepherds, angels, or magi to be Simeon and Anna, or search a dollar shore or thrift shop for miniature dolls or figurines that match the size of your holy family. Color their hair gray. Redecorate the stable (perhaps already reconfigured to look like a house in Bethlehem for the arrival of the magi) to look like the temple in Jerusalem, and tell the children the tender story of these two elderly, faithful people meeting and worshiping the Messiah. On this day of Candlemas, surround the scene with a multitude of blazing candles to show that the little Christ child is the true light that shines on all of God's people.

Assembly Song
Gathering

Christ, whose glory fills the skies ELW 553, LBW 265
I want to walk as a child of the light ELW 815, WOV 649, LS 36
Of the Father's love begotten ELW 295, LBW 42

Psalmody and Acclamations

How lovely, Lord/Psalm 84 GTG 402, PAS 84C
Feeley, Ephrem. "How Lovely Are Your Dwelling Places (Psalm 84)." SATB, cant, assembly, kybd, vc. GIA G-8164.
Gelineau, Joseph. "Psalm 84" from ACYG.
(GA) Monteiro, Simei (Brazil). "Alleluia" from GS3. Use ELW psalm tone 1 with proper verse for Presentation of Our Lord.

Hymn of the Day

In his temple now behold him ELW 417 *REGENT SQUARE*
   LBW 184 *LINDSBORG*
In peace and joy I now depart ELW 440 *MIT FRIED UND FREUD*
You, dear Lord/Tú, Señor, que brillas ELW 702, LLC 429
   TÚ SEÑOR

Offering

O Morning Star, how fair and bright! ELW 308, st. 3; LLC 320, st. 3; LBW 76, st. 3
Take, oh, take me as I am ELW 814, SP 40

Communion

At last, Lord/Ahora, Señor ELW 203
Draw us in the Spirit's tether ELW 470, WOV 703
What child is this ELW 296, LBW 40

Sending

O Lord, now let your servant ELW 313, LBW 339
Savior, again to your dear name ELW 534, LBW 262

Additional Assembly Songs

The Lord is my light TFF 61, SP 41
There's a light in the world ASG 41
⊕ Armarnad, Anto/Colin A. Gibson. "Following Jesus/Yesu ke piche jayenge ham sab" from *Sound the Bamboo*. GIA G-6830.
⊕ Ryu Hyung Sun. "Jukkeso wangwiye/The God of Glory Goes Up to the Throne" from *Hosanna! Ecumenical Songs for Justice and Peace*. U. WCC Publications 9782825416679.
☼ Colligan, Richard-Bruxvoort. "Holy One, Now Let Your Servants Go in Peace (A Nunc Dimittis)" from *Worldmaking*. worldmaking.net.
☼ Davis, Geron. "Holy Ground" from CCLI.
☼ Hoagland, Eddie/Jacob Sooter/Jonathan Smith/Matt Maher. "I See the Lord" from CCLI.

☼ Redman, Matt. "Better Is One Day" from CCLI.
☼ Rundman, Jonathan. "Canticle for Departure (Nunc Dimittis)" from *A Heartland Liturgy*. jonathanrundman.bandcamp.com.
☼ Tomlin, Chris/Jesse Reeves. "Famous One" from CCLI.

Music for the Day
Choral

Burkhardt, Michael. "How Lovely and How Pleasant." 2 pt mxd, org. MSM 50-5250.
P Buxtehude, Dietrich. "In Peace and Joy I Now Depart" from *Augsburg Chorale Book*. SATB, kybd or str trio, vln, vc. AFP 9781506426303.
Ellingboe, Bradley. "Simeon's Song." SATB, pno. KJO 8988.
P Wonacott, Glenn. "God Is Here." SATB, a cap. AFP 9781451485806.

Children's Choir

Kemp, Helen. "Nunc Dimittis" from *Magnificat and Nunc Dimittis*. U, pno, C inst, hc, hb. CG CGA954.
Lovelace, Austin. "Song of Simeon." U, org. SEL 410-852.
Mendelssohn, Felix. "How Lovely Is Your Dwelling." U/2 pt, pno. CG CGA1017.

Keyboard / Instrumental

♫ Hobby, Robert A. "Regent Square" from *Three Christmas Preludes*, set 2. Org. MSM 10-150.
♫ Manz, Paul. "In Peace and Joy I Now Depart" from *Three Lenten Hymns for Oboe and Organ*. Org, ob. MSM 20-361.
Raney, Joel. "What Child Is This?" from *Images of Christmas*. Pno. HOP 8095.
P Wilson, Terry D. "O Gladsome Light" from *Near the Cross: Piano Settings*. Pno. AFP 9781506448053.

Handbell

Afdahl, Lee. "How Lovely Is Thy Dwelling Place." 3-7 oct, L4. AGEHR AG37003.
Behnke, John. "I Want to Walk as a Child of the Light." 3 or 5 oct, L2. CPH 976611.
♫ Ingram, Bill. "Regent Square" from *Five Hymns for Twelve Bells*. 12 bells, L2. CG CGB770.

⊕ = global song   ♫ = relates to hymn of the day
☼ = praise song   P = available in Prelude Music Planner

February 2, 2020
Fourth Sunday after Epiphany
Lectionary 4

Who are the blessed ones of God? For Micah, they are those who do justice, love kindness, and walk humbly with God. For Paul, they are the ones who find wisdom in the weakness of the cross. For Jesus, they are the poor, the meek, the merciful, the pure in heart, the peacemakers, those who mourn, and those who hunger for righteousness. In baptism we find our blessed identity and calling in this countercultural way of living and serving.

Prayer of the Day

Holy God, you confound the world's wisdom in giving your kingdom to the lowly and the pure in heart. Give us such a hunger and thirst for justice, and perseverance in striving for peace, that in our words and deeds the world may see the life of your Son, Jesus Christ, our Savior and Lord.

Gospel Acclamation

Alleluia. Rejoice and be glad, for your reward is great in heaven. *Alleluia.* (Matt. 5:12)

Readings and Psalm

Micah 6:1-8

With the mountains and the foundations of the earth as the jury, God brings a lawsuit against Israel. God has "wearied" Israel with a long history of saving acts. God does not want or expect lavish sacrifices to attempt to earn divine favor. Rather God empowers the people to do justice, to love loyalty to God, and to walk shrewdly in God's service.

Psalm 15

LORD, who may abide upon your holy hill? (Ps. 15:1)

1 Corinthians 1:18-31

According to the world's standards of power and might, the message of the cross seems stupid and offensive. Yet this word reveals the paradoxical way God has chosen to work power and salvation through weakness, rejection, and suffering. Hence the message of the cross becomes true wisdom and power for believers.

Matthew 5:1-12

Jesus opens the Sermon on the Mount by naming those who are blessed in the reign of God.

Preface   Sundays

Color   Green

Prayers of Intercession

The prayers are prepared locally for each occasion. The following examples may be adapted or used as appropriate.

Trusting that God hears us, let us pray for the church, the world, and all those in need.

A brief silence.

God of liberation, you set your people free to serve others. Embolden your church, that we seek justice for the oppressed, share generously your lovingkindness, and live humbly together. Unite us as one people under the foolishness of the cross. Hear us, O God.

Your mercy is great.

God of the universe, your care is evident everywhere—from the foundations of the earth to the summit of the tallest mountains. Reconcile all of creation to itself and repair the environmental destruction caused by human carelessness and greed. Hear us, O God.

Your mercy is great.

God of the nations, you desire peace and justice among all people. Deliver us from systems of fear that seek to divide us. Guide our local and national leaders (*especially*). May their decisions empower and serve the needs of the poor and the disenfranchised. Hear us, O God.

Your mercy is great.

God of the oppressed, you raise up the lowly and comfort those in despair. We lift up to you all who are victims of exploitation, discrimination, and greed. We pray for those who are suffering in any way this day (*especially*). Hear us, O God.

Your mercy is great.

God of love, you sent your Son, Jesus Christ, to earth in the form of a baby, whose presentation in the temple we celebrate today. Fill our own house of worship with your presence, that all who enter may encounter Christ. Hear us, O God.

Your mercy is great.

Here other intercessions may be offered.

God of life, we give you thanks for all those who have died in the faith (*especially*). Thank you for the examples of our ancestors and the saints who have gone before us. Hear us, O God.

Your mercy is great.

Confident that you are able to accomplish more than we even dare to ask, we bring these prayers before you, believing in your saving grace revealed in Jesus Christ our Lord.
Amen.

Ideas for the Day

- For a modern take on the ancient language of the Beatitudes, see Pastor Nadia Bolz-Weber's two-minute video called "Blessed Are the Unemployed, Unimpressive, and Underrepresented." It was produced as a part of a film project called *Makers*. Simply search YouTube for "Nadia Bolz-Weber Beatitudes" to find it.
- How and when does your congregation use the word *blessed* in your life together? Do the people who gather to knit prayer shawls or make quilts bless these items before giving them away? When a new table is crafted to hold the communion elements, is that table blessed in worship upon its first use? Do you call the consecration of the elements "blessing" the elements? Do you bless backpacks, bicycles, or surfboards in your setting? How do these blessed things connect with the blessed people of whom Jesus speaks? Do they connect at all? If so, how? If not, is this confusing for worshipers?
- Micah 6:3 is a question that echoes throughout the solemn reproaches we pray on Good Friday: "O my people, O my church, what have I done to you? How have I offended you? Answer me." In the darkened worship space during Holy Week, these words weigh a lot. Do they feel different on this Sunday morning during the time after Epiphany? Consider including a few of the solemn reproaches from the Good Friday liturgy just prior to the creed or the prayers of intercession today (*Evangelical Lutheran Worship Leaders Edition*, pp. 639–641).

Connections with Creation

The mountains bear witness in the trial against humanity, according to Micah 6. Verse 2 tells us that "the Lord has a controversy with his people" because they have worshiped other gods. What might the mountains testify against humanity today? People raising the alarm about mountaintop removal for coal extraction have used biblical framing for their billboards denouncing this harmful practice: "Stop destroying my mountains. –God." We might also wonder what it would be like for Jesus to deliver his Sermon on the Mount at a site where one of these mountains has been cut away, leaving nothing but rock and rubble where trees and animals once made their homes. Imagine Jesus' words proclaimed from these desolate places: "Blessed are the poor in spirit . . . those who mourn . . . the meek . . ." (Matt. 5:3-5). How might our preaching and ministry follow Jesus up the mountain?

Let the Children Come

Why do we stand for the gospel reading? Because each time the gospel words are read, it is as if Jesus comes among us to speak the word of life. Just as in today's gospel reading the great multitude of people gathered to hear Jesus, we rise to greet the one who speaks God's blessing to us. Encourage children to stand—perhaps even on the pew or chair, with safe support—and to turn their bodies and eyes toward the gospel reader. Help children learn the assembly's response to the announcement of the gospel ("Glory to you, O Lord") and its conclusion ("Praise to you, O Christ") by heart. We are all paying close attention to the words of Jesus.

Assembly Song
Gathering

Light shone in darkness ELW 307
Rejoice in God's saints ELW 418, WOV 689
We Are Called ELW 720, W&P 147, LS 37

Psalmody and Acclamations

Jennings, Carolyn. "Psalm 15" from PSCY.
Nelson, Ronald A. "Psalm 15" from PWA.
Traditional, arr. Wendell Whalum. "Psalm 15" from PAS 15C.
(GA) Monteiro, Simei (Brazil). "Alleluia" from GS3. Use ELW psalm tone 1 with proper verse for Epiphany 4.

Hymn of the Day

Blest are they ELW 728, WOV 764, LS 143 BLEST ARE THEY
When the poor ones/Cuando el pobre ELW 725, LLC 508 EL CAMINO
Where cross the crowded ways of life ELW 719, LBW 429 WALTON

Offering

Let us go now to the banquet/Vamos todos al banquete ELW 523, LLC 410
We come to the hungry feast ELW 479, WOV 766, DATH 84

Communion

Bread of life from heaven ELW 474
Holy, holy, holy, holy/Santo, santo, santo, santo ELW 762, LLC 273, TFF 203, W&P 61
Take, oh, take me as I am ELW 814, SP 40

Sending

Let justice flow like streams ELW 717, WOV 763, TFF 717
To be your presence ELW 546

Additional Assembly Songs

Blessed are the poor in spirit NCH 180
Que se alegren los pobres/May the poor people be joyful LLC 459

There is a longing in our hearts GTG 470

⊕ Russian Orthodox trad. "Remember Your Servants (Blessed Are the Poor in Spirit)" from *Hallelujah! Resources for Prayer and Praise*, 10th Assembly. SATB. WCC Publications. Out of print. Hannelore.Schmid@wcc-coe.org.

⊕ Taizé Community. "The Kingdom of God." SATB. GIA G-7496.

☼ Brown, Lacey. "I Stand with You" from *I Stand with You*. poorclare.bandcamp.com.

☼ Hall, Charlie. "Micah 6:8" from CCLI.

☼ Maher, Matt. "Unwavering" from CCLI.

☼ Maher, Matt/Paul Moak/Trevor Morgan. "All the People Said Amen" from CCLI.

☼ Skinner, Anthony/Stuart Garrard. "Oh Blessed" from CCLI.

☼ Wood, Naaman/Bruce Benedict. "You Are Blessed" from *The Beatitudes EP (Fall '15)*. hopecollegeworship.bandcamp .com.

Music for the Day
Choral

℗ Bankson, Jeremy J. "Holy God, Holy and Glorious." SATB, org, opt br qrt, timp, hb, assembly. AFP 9781506456713.

℗ Haugen, Kyle. "Be Thou My Vision" from *St. Olaf Choirbook for Women*. SSA, pno. AFP 9781506426310.

Nelson, Eric. "What Does the Lord Require?" SATB, pno. MSM 50-2012.

℗ Pasch, William Allen. "You Got to Get Low." SATB, a cap. AFP 9781451479522.

Children's Choir

Beck, John Ness/Craig Courtney. "Offertory." 3 pt, kybd. BP BP1983.

Bedford, Michael. "Blessed Are They (The Beatitudes)." U/2 pt, org, fl. CG CGA1025.

Carter, Andrew. "Blest Are They" from *Blest Are They: Three Treble Anthems from Magnificat*. U, kybd, opt hb. MSM 50-9422.

Keyboard / Instrumental

Burkhardt, Michael. "Rise Up, O Saints of God" from *Hymns for the Saints*. Org. MSM 10-742.

℗♫ Organ, Anne Krentz. "Blest Are They" from *In Heaven Above: Piano Music for Funerals and Memorials*. Pno. AFP 9781451401912.

℗♫ Powell, Robert J. "Where Cross the Crowded Ways of Life" from *Prayerful Preludes*, set 9. Org. MSM 10-787.

℗♫ Roberts, Al. "Cuando el pobre" from *We Belong to God: Piano Settings of Folk Tunes*. Pno. AFP 9781451451801.

Handbell

♫ Helman, Michael. "Blest Are They." 3-5 oct hb, opt 3-5 oct hc, fl. L3-. GIA G-7043.

⊕ = global song   ♫ = relates to hymn of the day
☼ = praise song   ℗ = available in Prelude Music Planner

Lamb, Linda. "Just As I Am." 2-3 oct, L2. ALF 29950.

Stephenson, Valerie. "For the Beauty of the Earth." 3-5 oct, L2. CG CGB851.

Sunday, February 2
Presentation of Our Lord

Forty days after the birth of Christ we mark the day Mary and Joseph presented him in the temple in accordance with Jewish law. There a prophet named Anna began to speak of the redemption of Israel when she saw the young child. Simeon also greeted Mary and Joseph. He responded to the presence of the consolation of Israel in this child with the words of the Nunc dimittis. His song described Jesus as a "light for the nations."

Because of the link between Jesus as the light for the nations, and because an old reading for this festival contains a line from the prophet Zephaniah, "I will search Jerusalem with candles," the day is also known as Candlemas, a day when candles are blessed for the coming year.

Monday, February 3
Ansgar, Bishop of Hamburg, missionary to Denmark and Sweden, died 865

Ansgar was a monk who led a mission to Denmark and later to Sweden, where he built the first church. His work ran into difficulties with the rulers of the day, and he was forced to withdraw into Germany, where he served as a bishop in Hamburg. Despite his difficulties in Sweden, he persisted in his mission work and later helped consecrate Gothbert as the first bishop of Sweden. Ansgar had a deep love for the poor. He would wash their feet and serve them food provided by the parish.

Wednesday, February 5
The Martyrs of Japan, died 1597

In the sixteenth century, Jesuit missionaries, followed by Franciscans, introduced the Christian faith in Japan. But a promising beginning to those missions—perhaps as many as 300,000 Christians by the end of the sixteenth century—met complications from competition between the missionary groups, political difficulty between Spain and Portugal, and factions within the government of Japan. Christianity was suppressed. By 1630, Christianity was driven underground.

Today we commemorate the first martyrs of Japan, twenty-six missionaries and converts who were killed by crucifixion. Two hundred and fifty years later, when Christian missionaries returned to Japan, they found a community of Japanese Christians that had survived underground.

February 9, 2020
Fifth Sunday after Epiphany
Lectionary 5

Light shines in the darkness for the upright, the psalmist sings. Isaiah declares that when we loose the bonds of injustice and share our bread with the hungry, the light breaks forth like the dawn. In another passage from the Sermon on the Mount, Jesus, the light of the world, calls his followers to let the light of their good works shine before others. Through baptism we are sent into the world to shine with the light of Christ.

Prayer of the Day

Lord God, with endless mercy you receive the prayers of all who call upon you. By your Spirit show us the things we ought to do, and give us the grace and power to do them, through Jesus Christ, our Savior and Lord.

Gospel Acclamation

Alleluia. Jesus says, I am the light of the world; whoever follows me will have the light of life. *Alleluia.* (John 8:12)

Readings and Psalm

Isaiah 58:1-9a [9b-12]

Shortly after the return of Israel from exile in Babylon, the people were troubled by the ineffectiveness of their fasts. God reminds them that outward observance is no substitute for genuine fasting that results in acts of justice, such as feeding the hungry, sheltering the homeless, and clothing the naked.

Psalm 112:1-9 [10]

Light shines in the darkness for the upright. (Ps. 112:4)

1 Corinthians 2:1-12 [13-16]

Though people such as the Corinthians are enamored with human philosophy and wisdom, Paul continuously presents God's hidden wisdom which is Jesus Christ crucified. True spiritual maturity involves judging ourselves and others in light of God's revelation in the cross.

Matthew 5:13-20

In the Sermon on the Mount, Jesus encourages his followers to be the salt of the earth and the light of the world, doing good works and keeping God's commandments.

Preface   Sundays

Color   Green

Prayers of Intercession

The prayers are prepared locally for each occasion. The following examples may be adapted or used as appropriate.

Trusting that God hears us, let us pray for the church, the world, and all those in need.

A brief silence.

Holy God, it is your desire that all people might come to know you intimately. Lead our communities into deeper relationship with you. May your church radiate your righteousness to all whom we encounter. Hear us, O God.

Your mercy is great.

God of creation, you quench the dry ground, bringing water that sustains life. Satisfy the needs of all the earth, so that all living things bear witness to your verdant grace and continue to shout your praise. Hear us, O God.

Your mercy is great.

God of glory, during your time here on earth you were crucified by powerful rulers who did not understand you. Grant leaders in our day wisdom and discernment, that they may recognize you in the lives of the people they serve. Hear us, O God.

Your mercy is great.

God of justice, you free us from the oppression that binds us and exhort us to serve one another. Liberate us from all fear, bigotry, and greed, and set our hearts and minds on love, equality, and justice. Hear us, O God.

Your mercy is great.

God of life, you reveal your saving love to us through the power of your Spirit. Bless those among us who are preparing to encounter your invigorating will in a new way, especially those preparing for or affirming baptism (*name/s*). Hear us, O God.

Your mercy is great.

Here other intercessions may be offered.

God of all eternity, we give you thanks for the lives of the saints who have pointed us towards faithfulness in you (*especially*). May we trust in your endless mercy and grace. Hear us, O God.

Your mercy is great.

Confident that you are able to accomplish more than we even dare to ask, we bring these prayers before you, believing in your saving grace revealed in Jesus Christ our Lord.

Amen.

Ideas for the Day

- Those who live in cold climates with snow and ice are probably used to the idea of trampling salt underfoot! All winter, various types of snow-melt products are placed on sidewalks, driveways, and parking lots. If this is the case for your community, salt that has lost its saltiness would still seem to have value. How might you rephrase this parable to work in your context? Perhaps salt functions more like the light in Matthew 5:14-16—salt is never kept in the garage after an ice storm but is spread all over the ground to prevent falls and keep people safe!

- "The law [and] the prophets" as used in Matthew 5:17 is shorthand for the entirety of the Hebrew Bible. Do folks in your community know this? Do they know what the main messages are of the law (worship God, love neighbor) and the prophets (righteous living is worth more to God than worship)? Consider ways you might increase awareness about the Hebrew Bible. There could be a blurb in the worship folder or newsletter, a display in the gathering space, or an adult education session. Understanding "the law and the prophets" will help worshipers appreciate what it means that Jesus fulfills them.

- Isaiah 58 tells us that worship is meaningless without acts of humility and justice. This week might be a good one to dedicate a portion of your congregation's Sunday morning schedule to a service event. Consider beginning the service project with prayer and this reading from Isaiah.

- How is God's Spirit at work in the lives of your community members? In celebration of having received God's Spirit, as described in the reading from 1 Corinthians, perhaps you could incorporate an interactive element of worship. The prayers of intercession could include a time to name some of the ways the Spirit's work has been seen. Worshipers could write down one way that the Spirit has been moving in their lives. The papers could then be brought forward during the offering or added to a bulletin board after worship.

Connections with Creation

Most people think of the season of Lent as the time for fasting. Yet the reading in Isaiah today speaks of fasting from those things that lead to injustice and oppression. Given that Ash Wednesday is on the horizon, this may be a good time to help folks think about what kind of fasting they will engage in during those forty days. Consider fasting from activities that lead to environmental stress. Fast from using plastic bags or from making unnecessary consumer purchases. Consider a "carbon fast" to use less fossil fuel. Now is the time to plan for what will be needed to engage in this eco-spiritual practice of fasting. You may even suggest forming a small group to meet weekly during Lent to discuss and take actions for caring for God's creation. Let your congregation's light "rise in the darkness" (Isa. 58:10)!

Let the Children Come

The short verses of the gospel acclamation which are specific to each Sunday in the church year could be sung or even spoken by an individual or small group between the singing of the alleluias by the whole assembly. The verse is usually concise, pithy, and easy for children to learn. Today, these words of the gospel acclamation have such power: "Jesus says, I am the light of the world; whoever follows me will have the light of life" (John 8:12). Have a group of children sing or shout these sentences during the acclamation. Perhaps the theme of the gospel acclamation could also be incorporated into the day's dismissal, spoken by the assisting minister or the children: "You are the light of the world. Shine with the light of Christ!" To which the assembly responds, "Thanks be to God."

Assembly Song
Gathering

Dearest Jesus, at your word ELW 520, LBW 248

Gather Us In ELW 532, WOV 718

Let streams of living justice ELW 710

Psalmody and Acclamations

"Take Your Place at the Table." *Psallite* C-176. Cant or SATB, assembly, kybd.

Alonso, Tony. "The Just Man Is a Light in the Darkness" from TLP:A.

Mayernik, Luke. "Fifth Sunday in Ordinary Time A" from 5GP.

(GA) Monteiro, Simei (Brazil). "Alleluia" from GS3. Use ELW psalm tone 1 with proper verse for Epiphany 5.

Hymn of the Day

Break now the bread of life ELW 515, LBW 235 *BREAD OF LIFE*

Christ, Be Our Light ELW 715 *CHRIST, BE OUR LIGHT*

This little light of mine ELW 677, LS 33, TFF 65 *THIS JOY*

Offering

God extends an invitation/Nuestro Padre nos invita ELW 486, WOV 709, LLC 397, TFF 125

We come to the hungry feast ELW 479, WOV 766, DATH 84

Communion

Light shone in darkness ELW 307

Lord, whose love in humble service ELW 712, LBW 423

You satisfy the hungry heart ELW 484, WOV 711

Sending

Go, make disciples ELW 540, W&P 47

Rise, shine, you people! ELW 665, LBW 393

Additional Assembly Songs

Bring Forth the Kingdom W&P 22, LS 35, NCH 181

Come, let us return MSB1 S435

Jesus, the Light of the World/Rise Up! Shine! TFF 59, MSB2 S555

⊕ When the poor ones/Cuando el pobre ELW 725

⊕ Anon. South African. "Siph'amandla/O God, Give Us Power" from *Freedom Is Coming: Songs of Protest and Praise from South Africa*. SATB. GIA WB528 (book), WB528CD (book and CD).

☼ Avery, Brad/David Carr/Mac Powell/Mark D. Lee/Tai Anderson. "City on a Hill" from CCLI.

☼ Butler, Chuck/Ed Cash/Hillary McBride/James Tealy. "We Are" from CCLI.

☼ Cantelon, Ben/Elias Dummer/Nick Herbert. "A City on a Hill" from CCLI.

☼ Daigle, Lauren Ashley/Leslie Jordan/Paul Mabury. "Salt and Light" from CCLI.

☼ L'Ecuyer, Jan/John L'Ecuyer. "Salt and Light" from CCLI.

☼ Pino, Catherine. "Light of the World" from CCLI.

Music for the Day
Choral

♫ Farrell, Bernadette/arr. Joel Raney. "Christ, Be Our Light!" SATB, pno, hb. HOP C5851.

P Kornelis, Benjamin. "Light of the World." SATB, solo, opt perc. AFP 9781506456799.

Routley, Eric. "Salt and Light." SATB, kybd. GIA G-2300.

P Wold, Wayne L. "For the Least." 2 pt mxd, kybd. AFP 9781451462326.

Children's Choir

Powell, Robert J. "Happy Are Those Who Fear the Lord (Psalm 112)" in *Songs from the Psalms*. U, kybd. CPH 977035.

Sensmeier, Randall K. "You Are Salt, Which, Shaken Out" from *Teach Our Hearts to Sing Your Praise*. U, kybd. GIA G-5632.

P Taylor, Terry D. "Shine Your Light" from *Shine Your Light*. U, pno. CG CGA1361.

Keyboard / Instrumental

P♫ Biery, Marilyn. "Break Now the Bread of Life" from *An American Perspective: Settings of Old and New Tunes for Organ*. Org. AFP 9781451401820.

Groom te Velde, Rebecca. "Houston" from *Oxford Hymn Settings for Organists: Epiphany*. Org. OXF 9780193393455.

P♫ Miller, Aaron David. "This Little Light of Mine" from *Eight Chorale Preludes for Manuals Only*, vol. 2. Org. AFP 9780800678470.

P♫ Van der Pol, Jerry. "Christ, Be Our Light" from *Endless Song: Accessible Piano Settings*. Pno. AFP 9781506426433.

Handbell

♫ Moats, William. "This Little Light of Mine." 2-3 oct, L2+. CG CGB678.

♫ Page, Anna Laura. "Walk in the Light." 3-5 oct hb, opt 2 oct hc, L3. CG CGB1070.

♫ Thompson, Karen. "Break Now the Bread of Life." 3-5 oct hb, opt 3-5 oct hc, L2+. LOR 20/1978L.

Friday, February 14
Cyril, monk, died 869; Methodius, bishop, died 885; missionaries to the Slavs

These two brothers from a noble family in Thessalonika in northeastern Greece were priests and missionaries. After some early initial missionary work by Cyril among the Arabs, the brothers retired to a monastery. They were later sent to work among the Slavs, the missionary work for which they are most known. Since Slavonic had no written form at the time, the brothers established a written language with the Greek alphabet as its basis. They translated the scriptures and the liturgy using this Cyrillic alphabet. The Czechs, Serbs, Croats, Slovaks, and Bulgars regard the brothers as the founders of Slavic literature. The brothers' work in preaching and worshiping in the language of the people are honored by Christians in both East and West.

February 16, 2020
Sixth Sunday after Epiphany
Lectionary 6

In today's reading from Deuteronomy we are called to choose life by loving and obeying God. Much of today's gospel reading echoes portions of the Ten Commandments. Jesus' instructions to the crowd reveal a pattern of behavior that honors both God and the neighbor, resulting in life and health for the whole community. We too are invited to embrace these commandments, not out of fear of retribution, but because God has promised that to do so means life for us.

Prayer of the Day

O God, the strength of all who hope in you, because we are weak mortals we accomplish nothing good without you. Help us to see and understand the things we ought to do, and give us grace and power to do them, through Jesus Christ, our Savior and Lord.

Gospel Acclamation

Alleluia. You are the light of the world. A city set upon a hill cannot be hid. *Alleluia.* (Matt. 5:14)

Readings and Psalm

Deuteronomy 30:15-20

The LORD sets before the people of God a clear choice. Life and prosperity will come to the faithful; loss of the land will be the consequence of disobedience. Choosing life entails loving and holding fast to the LORD. Life in God's presence presupposes the promise made to the ancestors.

or Sirach 15:15-20

Wisdom literature has a high estimation of human possibilities. We are God's trusted creatures. Wisdom invites people to choose to keep God's commandments. God does not command people to be wicked or give them permission to sin.

Psalm 119:1-8

Happy are they who follow the teaching of the LORD. (Ps. 119:1)

1 Corinthians 3:1-9

Human leaders in the church are not the ones who control ministry. Rather they are coworkers who belong to God, the one who truly controls and continuously empowers the ministry of the church.

Matthew 5:21-37

In the Sermon on the Mount, Jesus exhorts his followers to embrace standards of righteousness that exceed legal requirements and traditional expectations.

Preface   Sundays

Color   Green

Prayers of Intercession

The prayers are prepared locally for each occasion. The following examples may be adapted or used as appropriate.

Trusting that God hears us, let us pray for the church, the world, and all those in need.

A brief silence.

Shepherding God, you protect and guide us with your word. Lead your church into ever closer relationship with you, that we might better know your commands, hold fast to your decrees, and live in your law. Hear us, O God.

Your mercy is great.

God of the cosmos, heaven and earth bear witness to the splendor of all you have created. Bless the ground, trees, waterways, and skies with abundant life. Restore synergy between humankind and the natural world, that we may live in harmony with the world you have made. Hear us, O God.

Your mercy is great.

God of peace, you show solidarity with all who suffer. Bring an end to violence, war, discrimination, and all other forms of deadly hate, that we may experience your love through the power of justice. Hear us, O God.

Your mercy is great.

God of hope, you provide bountifully for all people. Use our lives to alleviate global injustice and eliminate poverty, that all benefit from the abundant gifts you pour out for your people. Hear us, O God.

Your mercy is great.

God of growth, you nurture this community. Cultivate in us a spirit of service to one another, and bless us in the ministry we share (*ministries of the congregation may be named*). Hear us, O God.

Your mercy is great.

Here other intercessions may be offered.

God of our ancestors, Abraham and Sarah, Isaac and Rebecca, Jacob and Leah and Rachel, we give you thanks for our

forebears in the faith who now rest in your eternal grace and love (*especially*). Hear us, O God.
Your mercy is great.
Confident that you are able to accomplish more than we even dare to ask, we bring these prayers before you, believing in your saving grace revealed in Jesus Christ our Lord.
Amen.

Ideas for the Day

- Moses urges God's followers to "choose life" (Deut. 30:19). In American political discourse, this phrase has been used persistently in the abortion debate. But that's not what the author of Deuteronomy had in mind. Choosing life means following God faithfully. How might your congregation choose life? Perhaps you could support the lives of poor children in your community by developing a program that provides food on weekends or in the summer, when subsidized school meals aren't available. You could create a re-entry program for veterans returning from combat, to connect them with possible employment and housing opportunities and to help them work through possible PTSD. Or you could support a similar program for folks returning to society after being incarcerated. The phrase "choose life" encourages us to create a more just and life-giving society for all people.

- The church in Corinth was plagued by "jealousy and quarreling" (1 Cor. 3:3), as are many churches today. If your community has recently experienced conflict, perhaps this week's worship could contain an intentional ritual of reconciliation. If a fuller order for confession and forgiveness is desired, using selected portions of Corporate Confession and Forgiveness from *Evangelical Lutheran Worship* would be appropriate (pp. 238–242). An interactive experience might also be helpful in some circumstances. For example, worshipers could write down on long, narrow strips of paper ways in which they feel they have been wronged by or have done wrong to others in the community. These confessions could then be woven together to create a work of reconciliation art representing the interconnectedness of the community even in times of struggle.

- Matthew 5:27-30 is revolutionary! Jesus states that when a man looks lustfully at a woman, the fault is entirely his. It has nothing to do with the woman's reputation, what she is wearing, whether she is out alone, or anything else. Men have a responsibility to treat women with respect as children of God. If they cannot do so, they are to tear out their eye or cut off their hand—to remove whatever has caused them to sin. For Jesus' peers, such a profound recognition of the personhood and value of women would have been unheard of. For our congregations today, it may still be a difficult concept for many to understand.

Connections with Creation

Life, growth, and death: both Moses and Paul speak to these themes in today's readings. People living within the agrarian society of Paul's time would have been intimately familiar with the processes of planting, watering, and observing the mystery of a seed growing into a plant. Little wonder that he used this as a metaphor for the life of faith that comes from God. In the Deuteronomy reading, Moses was preparing his people to move from a hunter-gatherer existence wandering in the wilderness to an agrarian lifestyle in a new land. He warned that turning away from God's commands would lead to curses instead of blessings and long life. Today, how might we honor the integrity of soil, water, seeds, and the cycles of life? In what ways can we turn back the curses of our destructive habits that harm ecosystems and lead to public health problems? Moses' words are as valid today as they were thousands of years ago: "Choose life!" (30:19).

Let the Children Come

In the anticipation of Advent, in the incarnation of Christmas, in the revelation of Epiphany, and in the anointing at the Baptism of Our Lord, we saw God close-to-us, God-with-us, God-in-us, God-for-us. Then throughout the Sundays after Epiphany, in Jesus' own teaching, God's divine design for life in the household of faith has been laid out. It is a way of life that loves God's ways, God's voice, and God's commands. Remind children and youth that in God's world, we "put our whole self in" and choose life: full, responsible living. All the readings and the psalm today speak of living in God's ways. To love God's laws means keeping our promises, telling the truth, being reconciled with each other, honoring our commitments, respecting the relationships of others, and treating all with honor and respect as our full co-disciples in God's realm.

Assembly Song
Gathering

> In all our grief ELW 615, WOV 739
> O God of every nation ELW 713, LBW 416
> What is this place ELW 524

Psalmody and Acclamations

> "Love the Lord Your God." *Psallite* A-112. Cant or SATB, assembly, kybd.
> Mummert, Mark. "Psalm 119:1-8," Refrain 1, from PSCY.
> Nelson, Ronald A. "Psalm 119:1-8" from PWA.
> (GA) Monteiro, Simei (Brazil). "Alleluia" from GS3. Use ELW psalm tone 1 with proper verse for Epiphany 6.

Hymn of the Day

O God of love, O King of peace ELW 749 *ERHALT UNS, HERR*
LBW 414 *ACK, BLIV HOS OSS*

O God of mercy, God of light ELW 714, LBW 425 *JUST AS I AM*

The people walk/Un pueblo que camina ELW 706, LLC 520
UN PUEBLO QUE CAMINA

Offering

Come, let us eat ELW 491, sts. 1-3; LS 103, sts. 1-3; LBW 214,
sts. 1-3

God extends an invitation/Nuestro Padre nos invita ELW 486,
WOV 709, LLC 397, TFF 125

Communion

Blessed assurance ELW 638, WOV 699, TFF 118

There is a balm in Gilead ELW 614, WOV 737, TFF 185

Will you let me be your servant ELW 659

Sending

O God of light ELW 507, LBW 237

Spread, oh, spread, almighty Word ELW 663, LBW 379

Additional Assembly Songs

Christ our peace SP 5

En medio de la Vida/Mingled in all our living LLC 512

I shall not be moved TFF 147

🌐 Behold, how pleasant/Miren qué bueno ELW 649, LLC 468

🌐 Kabemba, Joseph. "As Long As We Follow/Na nzela na lola
(Malembe)" from *Global Praise 3*. SATB. GBGMusik
9781890569877.

☼ Assad, Audrey/Chris Tomlin/Matt Maher. "No Greater Love"
from CCLI.

☼ Batstone, Bill/Steve Wiggins. "Choose Life" from CCLI.

☼ Gungor, David/Ian Cron/John Arndt. "Brother" from CCLI.

☼ McClarney, Chris/Nate Moore/Tony Brown. "Yes and Amen"
from CCLI.

☼ McCracken, Sandra. "Flourishing (Psalm 119)" from *Psalms*.
sandramccracken.bandcamp.com.

☼ Powell, Aaron/Elias Dummer/Eric Fusilier/Josh Vanderlaan.
"Confession (Agnus Dei)" from CCLI.

Music for the Day
Choral

Hamilton, Gregory. "O Master, Let Me Walk with Thee." SATB,
kybd, opt fl or vln. MSM 50-6042.

Hildebrand, Kevin. "O God, My Faithful God." SATB, org. MSM
50-7073.

P Raabe, Nancy M. "Forgive Our Sins as We Forgive." SAB, mxd,
pno. AFP 9781506408644.

P Wehrspann, Deanna. "May Your Voice Be at Peace." SATB, a
cap. AFP 9781451462388.

Children's Choir

How, Martin. "Day by Day." U/2 pt/3 pt, org. GIA G-4178.

P Simon, Julia. "God Be in My Head." U, opt div, pno. AFP
9780800664039.

White, L. J. "Prayer of St. Richard of Chichester." 2 pt, kybd.
OXF 9780193510357.

Keyboard / Instrumental

P Organ, Anne Krentz. "In All Our Grief" from *Piano Reflections
on Hymns of Healing*. Pno. AFP 9781506448060.

P Pelz, Walter L. "O Christ, Our Hope" from *A Walter Pelz Organ
Anthology*. Org. AFP 9781506448039.

P Raabe, Nancy. "Detroit" from *Day of Arising: A Tapestry of
Musical Traditions*. Pno. AFP 9780800637460.

P ♫ Weber, Jacob B. "Erhalt uns, Herr" from *Organ Impressions
for the Church Year*. Org. AFP 9781506447995.

Handbell

P Compton, Matthew. "Through the Walk of Life." 3-7 oct, L4+.
CG CGB813.

♫ Eithun, Sandra. "O God of Love, O King of Peace." 3-5 oct hb,
opt 3 oct hc, SATB choir/solo, L2. CG CGB677. Full score,
CGB676.

Tucker, Margaret. "Processional and Joyful Dance" from *Joyfully Ring*. 2-3 oct hb, L1+. CG CGB1061. 3-5 oct compat-
ible. CGB1062.

Tuesday, February 18
Martin Luther, renewer of the church, died 1546

On this day in 1546, Martin Luther died at the age of sixty-two.
For a time, he was an Augustinian monk, but it is his work as
a biblical scholar, translator of the Bible, public confessor of
the faith, reformer of the liturgy, theologian, educator, and
father of German vernacular literature that holds him in our
remembrance. In Luther's own judgment, the greatest of all of
his works was his catechism, written to instruct people in the
basics of faith. And it was his baptism that sustained him in his
trials as a reformer.

🌐 = global song   ♫ = relates to hymn of the day
☼ = praise song   P = available in Prelude Music Planner

February 23, 2020
Transfiguration of Our Lord
Last Sunday after Epiphany

Today's festival is a bridge between the Advent-Christmas-Epiphany cycle that comes to a close today and the Lent-Easter cycle that begins in several days. On a high mountain Jesus is revealed as God's beloved Son, echoing the words at his baptism. This vision of glory sustains us as Jesus faces his impending death in Jerusalem. We turn this week to Ash Wednesday and our yearly baptismal journey from Lent to Easter. Some churches put aside the alleluia at the conclusion of today's liturgy. This word of joy will be omitted during the penitential season of Lent and will be sung again at Easter.

Prayer of the Day

O God, in the transfiguration of your Son you confirmed the mysteries of the faith by the witness of Moses and Elijah, and in the voice from the bright cloud declaring Jesus your beloved Son, you foreshadowed our adoption as your children. Make us heirs with Christ of your glory, and bring us to enjoy its fullness, through Jesus Christ, our Savior and Lord, who lives and reigns with you and the Holy Spirit, one God, now and forever.

Gospel Acclamation

Alleluia. This is my Son, my Chosen, listen to him! *Alleluia.* (Luke 9:35)

Readings and Psalm

Exodus 24:12-18

At Mount Sinai, Moses experienced the presence of God for forty days and forty nights. The "glory of the LORD" settled on the mountain, and on the seventh day God called out to Moses. On the mountain God gave Moses the stone tablets inscribed with the Ten Commandments.

Psalm 2

You are my son; this day have I begotten you. (Ps. 2:7)

or Psalm 99

Proclaim the greatness of the LORD; worship upon God's holy hill. (Ps. 99:9)

2 Peter 1:16-21

At the transfiguration, God's voice was heard declaring Jesus to be the beloved Son. By the activity of Holy Spirit, God's voice continues to be heard through the word of scripture.

Matthew 17:1-9

Shortly before he enters Jerusalem, where he will be crucified, Jesus is revealed to Peter, James, and John in a mountaintop experience of divine glory called the transfiguration.

Preface   Transfiguration

Color   White

Prayers of Intercession

The prayers are prepared locally for each occasion. The following examples may be adapted or used as appropriate.

Trusting that God hears us, let us pray for the church, the world, and all those in need.

A brief silence.

Holy God, your loving power is at work among us. Rouse and embolden your church, that we too might be transfigured, set alight in the world for the sake of the gospel. Hear us, O God.

Your mercy is great.

Awesome God, you speak and the earth trembles. You display your majesty in the mountains and your mystery in the clouds. Grant that we discover your magnificence in all of your created world. Hear us, O God.

Your mercy is great.

Ruler of nations, your reign extends across all human borders. Guide world leaders (*especially*) in justice and righteousness, that they may work for equity for all people and protect the world that you have made. Hear us, O God.

Your mercy is great.

Gracious God, you are a refuge for all who are neglected and abused. Bring freedom to those who are oppressed and give comfort to those experiencing pain of any kind (*especially*). Hear us, O God.

Your mercy is great.

God of Moses and Elijah, you made your dwelling place at the top of a mountain with Jesus and his disciples. Dwell also in this congregation, that all who enter this community might be transformed by your dazzling brilliance. Hear us, O God.

Your mercy is great.

Here other intercessions may be offered.

Everlasting God, you offer eternal life to all your children. Thank you for the witness of those who lived and died in the faith (*especially Polycarp, Bishop of Smyrna, whose martyrdom in the early church we remember this day*). Hear us, O God. **Your mercy is great.**
Confident that you are able to accomplish more than we even dare to ask, we bring these prayers before you, believing in your saving grace revealed in Jesus Christ our Lord.
Amen.

Ideas for the Day

- Transfiguration Sunday is a hinge point in the liturgical year. It marks the end of a journey of light that travels through the Advent wreath, Christmas Eve candlelight, and the Epiphany star. We then move to Lent, a season not typically marked by images of light. Transfiguration bears stories of experiencing God's light right up close. From these lofty spiritual spaces Moses and Jesus' disciples descend back to the everyday, carrying the experience of light with them. Consider using Transfiguration Sunday to launch a Lenten journey of carrying the experience of light. Provide a candle for each worshiper or ask worshipers in advance to bring their own this Sunday. Light the candles during the gospel reading, then send them home with people to light throughout the season as part of their Lenten prayer and reflection.
- Moses waits six days before God calls to him from the cloud, and then spends forty days and nights in the cloud. Jesus tells Peter, James, and John not to tell anyone about the transfiguration until he has been raised from the dead. In both experiences there is a time of waiting before stories are shared, a time of processing and listening before witness can happen. We move into a cloud in a different way. Screens light up our faces. With social media we can post live video, respond to events in real time, and comment on thoughts instantaneously. Our cloud does not promote or foster slow and thoughtful processing. Perhaps an interaction with the divine is too much to take in all at one time. In a culture that is always on, these encounters can be an invitation into slow reflection on the work of God in our lives.
- Exploration is the focus of the characters in the various series of the *Star Trek* franchise. As ships travel through space, they frequently stop to investigate sources of life, light, and energy. In the first moments it is not always clear to the crews what they are encountering, but the resolution is usually life-giving. Reflecting on the transfiguration, 2 Peter 1:19 encourages us to be attentive to the gospel as to a light in a dark place. Just as Moses, Peter, James, and John all experience light, life, and energy in a new way, we are called by God and sent into the world as explorers of grace.

Connections with Creation

The story of Jesus' transfiguration offers a geography of spiritual encounter. Jesus and the disciples walk up a mountain and hear the voice of God while subsumed in a cloud. The setting is not incidental and ought not to be spiritualized too quickly. The majestic and harrowing heights of mountains and the sublime and sometimes fearsome power of clouds and storms are places of divine encounter throughout the Bible. How might the transfiguration help us think about the geography of our own encounters with God under the wide horizon of creation? Further, how do the wheat and wine of communion and the water of baptism locate our sacramental encounter with God within watersheds and bioregions from which they are drawn and grown? How might our ecological neighborhood be transfigured in our own eyes into a place of encounter with God?

Let the Children Come

Jesus glows! The disciples understand that this glow is awesome. They want to capture it and keep it in a permanent fixture on top of the holy mountain. Instead, Jesus shares this glow from God with others, not through words but through his love given to all people. Today, marvel at how a child's face lights up upon receiving a smile: their entire body shifts, their face and muscle tone relaxing. During worship, share God's glow with each other by inviting children and adults to smile at one another during the sharing of the peace. Shine "like the sun" (Matt. 17:2)! Encourage families to take their shared smiles home with them and to spread the glow into their family's life. Wonder together if any dwelling can hold in the glow of God's beloveds, or if sparkles, smiles, and twinkling eyes naturally overflow into God's world.

But life involves ups and downs; just as Jesus led the disciples back down the mountain, the worship mood takes a bit of a downward turn at whatever point you and the children "bury" the alleluia in anticipation of Lent.

Assembly Song
Gathering

Arise, your light has come! ELW 314, WOV 652
Immortal, invisible, God only wise ELW 834, LBW 526
Oh, wondrous image, vision fair ELW 316, LLC 322, LBW 80

Psalmody and Acclamations

Bow down before the holy mountain of God/Psalm 99 TFF 11
Jennings, Carolyn. "Psalm 2" from PSCY.
Goreham, Norman J. "Why This Dark Conspiracy" (CHRIST IST ERSTANDEN) from *Lift Up Your Hearts*. Faith Alive Christian Resources.

Mathis, William H. Refrain for "Psalm 99" from *After the Prelude: Year A*. U/cant, hb. CG CGB658 (digital version), CGB659 (print version). Use with ELW psalm tone 6 or 10 (in C).

(GA) Monteiro, Simei (Brazil). "Alleluia" from GS3. Use ELW psalm tone 1 with proper verse for Transfiguration of Our Lord.

Hymn of the Day

How good, Lord, to be here!   ELW 315, LBW 89   POTSDAM
In a lowly manger born   ELW 718, LBW 417   MABUNE
Jesus on the mountain peak   ELW 317   BETHOLD
   WOV 653   ST. ALBINUS

Offering

Come, let us eat   ELW 491, sts. 1-3; LS 103, sts. 1-3; LBW 214, sts. 1-3
The trumpets sound, the angels sing   ELW 531, W&P 139

Communion

Beautiful Savior   ELW 838, LS 174, LBW 518
Taste and see   ELW 493, TFF 126
Yours, Lord, is the glory/Tuya es la gloria   ELW 849, LLC 605

Sending

Alleluia, song of gladness   ELW 318, WOV 654
In thee is gladness   ELW 867, LBW 552

Additional Assembly Songs

I am the light of the world   NCH 584
Lumière de Dieu   SP 26, MSB2 S568
We have come at Christ's own bidding   NCH 182
⊕ Here on Jesus Christ I will stand/Kwake Yesu nasimama GTG 832
⊕ "Tua palavra na vida/Your Word in Our Lives" from *Global Praise 1*. GBGMusik 9781890569013.
☼ Hughes, Tim. "Beautiful One" from CCLI.
☼ King, Aodhan/Brooke Ligertwood/Scott Ligertwood/Taya Smith. "Transfiguration" from CCLI.
☼ Stevens, Sufjan. "The Transfiguration" from *Seven Swans*. music.sufjan.com.
☼ Torwalt, Bryan/Katie Torwalt/Phil Wickham. "Mountain" from CCLI.
☼ Ward, Tara. "Do Not Be Afraid" from *Hope for a Tree Cut Down*. belovedschurch.org.
☼ Younker, Brett/Jimi Cravity/Melodie Malone/Mia Fieldes. "Holy Ground" from CCLI.

Music for the Day
Choral

ᴾ Bach, J. S./arr. Mark Bighley. "The Only Son from Heaven" from *The Augsburg Choirbook for Advent, Christmas, and Epiphany*. SATB, org. AFP 9780800678586.

Farlee, Robert Buckley. "Farewell to Alleluia." U, kybd. AFP 9780800649487.

ᴾ Rasbach, David. "Lord, I Was Blind." SATB, pno, opt vc. CG CGA1343.

Wesby, Roger. "Siyahamba." SATB div, a cap. wesbyworksmusic.com.

Children's Choir

ᴾ Crunk, Kris/Randy Cox. "God Alone." U/2 pt, pno. CG CGA1297.

ᴾ Neswick, Bruce. "Epiphany Carol" from *The Augsburg Choirbook*. U, org. AFP 9780800656782.

ᴾ Taylor, Terry D. "I Am the Light" from *Shine Your Light*. U, pno. CG CGA1361.

Keyboard / Instrumental

ᴾ♫ Biery, Marilyn. "Jesus on the Mountain Peak" from *An American Perspective: Settings of Old and New Tunes for Organ*. Org. AFP 9781451401820.

Callahan, Charles. "Fanfare on Agincourt Hymn" from *O God beyond All Praising: Seven Pieces for Organ on English Hymntunes*. Org. MSM 10-799.

ᴾ David, Anne Marie. "Beautiful Savior" from *Snow on Snow: Piano Settings*. Pno. AFP 9781451486100.

ᴾ♫ Sims, David. "In a Lowly Manger Born" from *Wondrous Birth: Seven Hymn Settings for Organ*. Org. AFP 9781506413662.

Handbell

Keller, Michael. "Transfiguration." 5-7 oct, L6. AGEHR AG57002.

ᴾ McChesney, Kevin. "Transformation." 3-7 oct, L2+. CG CGB794.

Moklebust, Cathy. "Meditation on Beautiful Savior." 3-5 oct, L3. CG CGB175. 2 oct, L2. CGB763.

Sunday, February 23
Polycarp, Bishop of Smyrna, martyr, died 156

Polycarp was Bishop of Smyrna (in present-day western Turkey) and a link between the apostolic age and the church at the end of the second century. He is said to have been known by John, the author of Revelation. In turn he was known by

Irenaeus, bishop of Lyon in France, and Ignatius of Antioch. At the age of eighty-six he was martyred for his faith. When urged to save his life and renounce his faith, Polycarp replied, "Eighty-six years I have served him, and he never did me any wrong. How can I blaspheme my king who saved me?" The magistrate who made the offer was reluctant to kill a gentle old man, but he had no choice. Polycarp was burned at the stake, his death a testimony to the cost of renouncing temptation.

Tuesday, February 25
Elizabeth Fedde, deaconess, died 1921

Fedde was born in Norway and trained as a deaconess. In 1882, at the age of 32, she was asked to come to New York to minister to the poor and to Norwegian seamen. Her influence was wide-ranging, and she established the Deaconess House in Brooklyn and the Deaconess House and Hospital of the Lutheran Free Church in Minneapolis. She returned home to Norway in 1895 and died there.

Lent

Preparing for Lent

Preaching

"Let the same mind be in you that was in Christ Jesus," (Phil. 2:5). It is to this Passion Sunday text, a vision of disciples remade in the mind of Christ, that all of Lent builds in year A of the Revised Common Lectionary. The season of baptismal preparation provides a rich palette of biblical texts in which the people of God both strive and fail to live faithfully into the mind of Christ. The grace of God provides a never-ending spring of encouragement. From the contrasting prayers of the hypocrites and those who pray in secret, through the amazing but flawed faithfulness of Abraham and Sarah, to the over-enthusiastic woman at the well and the reticent parents of the one given sight, we see Sunday by Sunday just how complicated and difficult it is to cultivate and live into the sacrificial, servant mind of Christ. Like a steady drumbeat, Romans provides a solid theological commentary on abundant human sin and abundant God-given grace throughout the season.

At the same time, one need not scratch too deeply beneath the surface of these texts of baptismal preparation to find the living waters. In these forty days of dry bones and lack of vision, God points us toward the paschal mystery on the horizon and the saving waters that await our renewal. Gracious encouragement abounds. Through the God who so loved that world that the self-emptying Son was given, our hope is encouraged in the living waters of a Samaritan well, in the water flowing from the rock, in the horn of oil and the mighty outpouring of the Spirit, in mud and washing.

Through a sublime and tightly woven symphony of stories across this season we see God's ancient people mirroring our own lives—the equivocation of Adam and Eve, laid against the faithfully following Abraham. Nicodemus comes with bold questions to Jesus but only under the cover and safety of darkness. The Bethany sisters both accuse and confess. In all their complexity, these characters despair and hope, work and wonder, live and die as we ourselves do. And our only real hope is every bit as complex and mysterious—the waters of baptism toward which the church of the self-emptying Christ moves. They are waters of death, then life. Of dying, then rising. Of sin swallowed up, then life given and renewed.

At Lent 5's crest, Martha confronts our Fountain of Grace: "Lord, if you had been here . . ." (John 11:21). But isn't that just the point? Christ was here, is here, all along, and we are too pre-occupied, too dried up and deserted in our own self-centeredness to notice. Yet baptismal grace calls us out of the valley, out of the tomb, out of that final resting place of desperation where our own ill-conceived agendas have landed us. Sunday after Sunday, the Jesus revealed in these texts stands before the tomb of the assembly and calls us back to life. Day after day, the wise preacher will remind us, the Risen One stands at the tomb of our defeated lives calling, "Come out!" (John 11:43). Today is a new day in which to "let the same mind be in you that was in Christ Jesus."

Intercessory Prayer

One of the first things heard by the people of God entering the Lenten season is a word of warning about how we practice our piety. Named specifically in that warning is how we pray, or rather, how we should not pray. Lent is perhaps the season for us to work on streamlining our petitions before God, not for the sake of brevity alone, but so that we might find renewed focus in our praying. Such focus might be encouraged by how we pray, not just what we pray. Shorter petitions may leave time for the assembly to silently reflect on their own need for repentance and forgiveness, or to name for themselves the people and situations that are in need of God's holy restoration. These needs might be written down and hung on some bare branches or a rudimentary cross in the chancel or near the baptismal font. Such action may allow us to pray with and for one another throughout the week.

Early in the season, the texts shed light on how far diverted our quest for righteousness can become when we rely on our own works. Scripture begs us to look for God's righteousness, no matter how difficult it may be for us to perceive, and to leave behind our own empty gestures and intentions. There is opportunity in Lent to let our prayers be confessional in that we can name before God the ways in which we have turned to our own will and desires. However, our intercessions remain the means by which we call out to God for holy work to be done in the world and not just in ourselves. Therefore, we might not only confess our shortcomings but also ask God to turn us again into the flow of righteousness and to make our words and actions reflect God's redeeming work.

The season of Lent culminates in the liturgy of the Passion. In the Passion readings we hear the things that God has desired for us all along: the faithful obedience of the suffering servant, an honest naming of the pain and distress that the psalmist has endured, a poetic description of Christ's self-emptying on the cross, and an ultimate discovery of our life, not by our own fulfilling of God's commandments, but in the death of God's Anointed One. Such immersion in our life in Christ may give shape to our prayers throughout the entire season of Lent. How might we beg God to stir up faithful obedience in us as God did in Abraham? How can we encourage such honest dialogue about the pain of the world as Jesus had with the woman at the well, and as there was between Moses and the refugees of the exodus? How might we ask God to turn us again into the flow of righteousness, from trusting in our own works to trusting in God's work that allows us to empty ourselves for the sake of our human siblings and all of creation? How could we focus on looking for God's life in the world in the most unexpected of people and places, finding it even where death's shadow looms largest, like the graves of Lazarus and Jesus? For it is at the grave where we are unmistakably bound to God in Christ, who is prepared to lead us into the new life for which we pray.

Assembly Song

As a season of baptismal preparation, Lent invites us to stock our assemblies' voices, minds, and hearts with images that will be brought into relief around the font at the Vigil of Easter. Though we begin this journey to life-giving waters with stark reminders of our mortality on Ash Wednesday, the Lenten season is not just about sackcloth and ashes, nor is it enough to sing only of these things. Rather, as we are reminded in the preceding paragraphs, this year's Lenten texts overflow with contrasts and dichotomies that mark the baptismal life.

As for any season, important questions must inform choices for each assembly—its people, space, gifts, location, and surrounding community. What texts, styles, and leadership choices emphasize Lenten disciplines of prayer, fasting, and almsgiving in our respective contexts? What suggests that the season is a pilgrimage, a forty-day journey through the Lenten wilderness toward the font? What images, nouns, and active verbs are suggested by seasonal texts such as the prayer after communion (*ELW*, p. 65) or the prayers of the day? Likewise, what songs draw attention to lectionary images such as the dust of earth mixed with oil on Ash Wednesday as a sign of mortality, or the dust of earth mixed with spit that heals the blind man (Lent 4)? What shall we sing while the culture around us sells Easter candy and flowers even as we hear of dry bones and stinking bodies (Lent 5)? Are there familiar hymns or songs that would be useful to repeat weekly in order to maintain or deepen the season's focus? For example, the stanzas of "Tree of Life and awesome mystery" (ELW 334) are especially appropriate for the Lenten Sundays of year A. In addition, the desert and water imagery in the hymn "O God, with hope I enter in" from

Susan Palo Cherwien's collection *Come, Beloved of the Maker* is worthy of repetition throughout the season.

Assembly song should not only direct attention to these words and images but also steer attention toward the justice, mercy, and peace that sprout from baptismal calling. Look beyond the "Lent" section of the hymnal (ELW 319–343) to other seasonal emphases such as "Holy Baptism" (ELW 442–459), "Grace, Faith" (ELW 587–598), "Justice, Peace" (ELW 705–729), "Prayer" (ELW 741–754), or "Trust, Guidance" (ELW 755–795) and consider the wealth of images related to exile, wandering, longing, promise, and trust in spirituals from the African American tradition.

Like the texts of hymns and songs, leadership and musical style can also reflect themes of the season. Would unaccompanied singing or simpler accompaniments such as a drone or a single melody instrument amplify seasonal ideas of focus or restraint? What styles or accompaniment choices might communicate (sonically) the dryness of the desert through which the Lenten pilgrimage takes place? Might postludes, organ Zimbelsterns, or other festive accoutrements remain buried with our alleluias until the Vigil of Easter? Perhaps the season's psalms can be chanted without refrains, chanted on a single pitch instead of using a psalm tone, or chanted without accompaniment with a single bell tone between verses. Or, in place of the Kyrie, chant the Great Litany (ELW 238) at the beginning of each service.

Finally, it may be helpful to review the guidance and suggestions in sources such as *Keeping Time* (pp. 83–93), *Worship Guidebook for Lent and the Three Days* (pp. 4–91), and *Evangelical Lutheran Worship* (pp. 247–257).

Worship Space

The church's environment can help set the tone for the liturgies during the season of Lent. Furniture, fabric, plants, natural elements, art, windows, banners, and light can be used to display themes from the scriptures. In Lent we experience barrenness like a desert, the dry bones in the valley, the darkness of questioning faith, and the despair of temptation in the wilderness. Gone are the exquisite fabrics, the fresh flowers, and the opulence of decor.

The nave's space in Lent should be sparse, with most decor stored away for this season. This unadorned setting can be accomplished by a thorough decluttering, a spring cleaning of the space. Walk through your church's front doors, through your narthex, and into the nave of your church with the eyes of a visitor. Ask what furniture, framed items, decorations, bulletin boards, or other items are necessary and welcoming for this time of year. Rid out what doesn't belong; find places in storage for things you will use in different seasons. Do all precious or historical items need to be in view all year long? A decision may be made to store away some display items to then be brought out of storage on a seasonal cycle. An environment team may choose to leave the entryway or narthex as is and focus on the nave for the decluttering. In all things, show hospitality. If the narthex is full of items, consider arranging themed areas, such as spaces for announcements, worship schedules, and visitor information, in an organized and hospitable way. Leave what is necessary and beautiful.

Every church space or nave is different, so it is important to discover what will work best in your context. The permanent physical space and floor plan will inform the placement of temporary, seasonal decorations. Some spaces have permanent features that teams need to work with creatively.

If the space has a piece of art, an architectural feature, or a stained-glass window depicting one of the scripture stories in Lent, this feature can be highlighted for worshipers. Visually specify one cross in the space as a focal point and add a purple fabric drape if desired. Perhaps a large stone vase with bare branches could grace the area near the cross. If there are many crosses, be encouraged to store some away. You may decide to veil items that cannot be removed. Any fabrics you use are best if natural, even coarse, not satiny or glossy. *Austerity* is a key word for Lent.

Artists and children can contribute to the Lenten environment. Children could make pictures from the scripture stories about Lazarus, the man born blind, or the Samaritan woman. This artwork could be featured as bulletin covers or a grouping of framed art in the entryway. If image projection is an option in the worship space, obtain traditional and modern fine art, to be illuminated during the scripture readings.

A fabric drape could enhance a doorway. On some weeks, add branches from native trees. A series of thin, wispy fabric banners in dark colors could suggest a desert or wilderness. Communion ware of local pottery could be used seasonally. Don't try to recreate Jerusalem in the first century; that is to say, don't pretend we are back in Jesus' time through decor. In the worship environment, let God's word be living—past, present, and future. Choose the best, most beautiful, most natural elements available.

Seasonal Checklist

So much happens during Lent and Holy Week that planning in advance is essential. Consider this checklist along with the checklist for the Three Days (p. 139). One helpful strategy for managing time and energy is to think about where you are going to focus your creative attention this year and what practices or traditions you will carry over from previous years.

- Review the liturgies for Ash Wednesday and the Sunday of the Passion in *Evangelical Lutheran Worship*. Plan rehearsals for these days and arrange for worship leaders, readers, musicians, liturgical artists, and technicians to be there.
- Gather or order worship participation leaflets for Ash Wednesday, the Sunday of the Passion, and the liturgies of Holy Week. Leaflets can be ordered from Augsburg Fortress.
- Gather or order ritual elements: ashes, palms, anointing oil. Consider making the switch to eco-palms (lwr.org/get-involved/buy-coffee-ecopalms/eco-palms) or use locally available branches (already on the ground).
- If you have a procession with palms on the Sunday of the Passion, consider how those with physical disabilities may participate in the procession or be seated ahead of time.
- If you are making a change in the musical setting for the liturgy in Lent, alert the musicians and those responsible for preparing printed or projected worship aids early so they can adequately prepare for that transition. Extra proofreading for the first worship folder or projected materials may be needed, as well as extra time for musicians and worship leaders to learn and practice new parts.
- Arrange for musicians, vocal groups, and soloists to support the assembly's singing throughout Lent, the Three Days, and Easter.
- If your congregation has a catechumenal ministry, review the various Lenten rites and determine how they will be introduced and conducted during Sunday worship.
- Confirm any plans for Easter baptisms.

Worship Texts for Lent

Confession and Forgiveness

All may make the sign of the cross, the sign that is marked at baptism, as the presiding minister begins.

Blessed be the holy Trinity, ☩ one God,
who is present, who gives life,
who calls into existence the things that do not exist.
Amen.

If you were to keep watch over sins, O Lord, who could stand?
Yet with you is forgiveness, and so we confess.

Silence is kept for reflection.

Gracious God,
have mercy on us.
We confess that we have turned away from you,
knowingly and unknowingly.
We have wandered from your resurrection life.
We have strayed from your love for all people.
Turn us back to you, O God.
Give us new hearts and right spirits,
that we may find what is pleasing to you
and dwell in your house forever. Amen.

Receive good news: God turns to you in love.
"I will put my spirit in you, and you shall live," says our God.
All your sin is forgiven in the name of ☩ Jesus Christ,
who is the free and abounding gift of God's grace for you.
Amen.

Offering Prayer

Holy and generous host,
you set a table where we feast as friends.
Prepare us to witness to your goodness
with every gift you have given us to share,
that all people may know your peace
through Jesus Christ, now and forever.
Amen.

Invitation to Communion

God's love is poured out in Christ for you.
Open yourselves to receive it.

Prayer after Communion

We thank you, living God,
for the body and blood of your Son,
which sustains us in the wilderness and the garden alike.
As Christ has loved us in this feast,
so send us to love Christ in our neighbors.
In Jesus' name we pray.
Amen.

Blessing

Now is the acceptable time.
Now is the day of salvation.
Holy God,
speaking, spoken, and inspiring,
☩ bless you, unbind you,
and send you in love and in peace.
Amen.

Dismissal

Go in peace. Share the good news.
Thanks be to God.

Seasonal Rites for Lent

At the Name of Jesus
A Lenten Midweek Series

Overview

This Lenten midweek service based on the second reading for Passion Sunday, Philippians 2:5-11, points the assembly toward its annual celebration of the Sunday of the Passion and has the potential to clarify and reinforce the importance of reading the passion as the central proclamation for Passion Sunday. While many congregations remain confused about Passion/Palm Sunday, the preacher in these midweek reflections can point the worshiping community toward a deeper and richer celebration of the passion of Christ on the first day of Holy Week and exploit the rich contrast between that Sunday's entrance rite shouts of "Hosanna!" over and against the passion reading's cries of "Crucify!" Both ends of the theological and emotional spectrum are significant touchstones for the coming celebration of the Three Days, and few passages give such clear voice to those contrasting touchstones as the Christ hymn in Philippians 2.

The readings and psalms offered below, selected to complement Philippians 2:5-11, are easily set within the context of Evening Prayer using settings from *Evangelical Lutheran Worship* (pp. 309–319) or other resources. They might also be adapted to a freer form of liturgy that includes only readings, hymns, and reflections and could easily be used for a noontime service or even the conclusion to a weekly Lenten Bible study on this text.

Weekly Themes from Philippians 2:5-11

Week 1 - Christ emptied and humbled himself
Week 2 - Christ became obedient
Week 3 - At the name of Jesus all knees shall bow
Week 4 - Every tongue confesses Jesus
Week 5 - Let the same mind be in you

First Reading

Week 1 - Isaiah 53:4-9
Week 2 - Genesis 12:1-9
Week 3 - 1 Kings 18:30-40
Week 4 - Genesis 28:10-15
Week 5 - Jeremiah 31:31-34

Psalm

Week 1 - Psalm 145:14-21
Week 2 - Psalm 37:1-9
Week 3 - Psalm 22:25-31
Week 4 - Psalm 148
Week 5 - Psalm 25:1-10

Second Reading

Philippians 2:5-11 is read each week. Consider different ways of presenting the text at each of the five midweek liturgies. Suggestions include but are not limited to the following:

- Five different readers.
- Five different translations.
- Readers' Theater, using the resources of five small groups within the congregation presenting an imaginative rendering of the text.
- A reading of the text that repeats the weekly theme three times. For example, during Week 1, following verse 6, the first three words of verses 7 and 8 are repeated:

  . . . did not regard equality with God as something to be exploited,
  but emptied himself,
  but emptied himself,
  but emptied himself,
  taking the form of a slave, being born in human likeness.
  And being found in human form,
  he humbled himself
  he humbled himself
  he humbled himself
  and became obedient to the point of death—even death on a cross.

- Partnering with a Sunday school or confirmation class to prepare a weekly reading of the text for midweek worship that might include movement, sound effects, or other dramatic elements.

Hymn Suggestions

Week 1 - Precious Lord, take my hand   ELW 773, TFF 193
Week 2 - O Jesus, I have promised   ELW 810, LBW 503
Week 3 - At the name of Jesus   ELW 416, LBW 179
Week 4 - All my hope on God is founded   ELW 757, WOV 782
Week 5 - When I survey the wondrous cross   ELW 803, LBW 482

February 26, 2020
Ash Wednesday

On Ash Wednesday we begin our forty-day journey toward Easter with a day of fasting and repentance. Marking our foreheads with dust, we acknowledge that we die and return to the earth. At the same time, the dust traces the life-giving cross indelibly marked on our foreheads at baptism. While we journey through Lent to return to God, we have already been reconciled to God through Christ. We humbly pray for God to make our hearts clean while we rejoice that "now is the day of salvation." Returning to our baptismal call, we more intentionally bear the fruits of mercy and justice in the world.

Prayer of the Day

Almighty and ever-living God, you hate nothing you have made, and you forgive the sins of all who are penitent. Create in us new and honest hearts, so that, truly repenting of our sins, we may receive from you, the God of all mercy, full pardon and forgiveness through your Son, Jesus Christ, our Savior and Lord, who lives and reigns with you and the Holy Spirit, one God, now and forever.

or

Gracious God, out of your love and mercy you breathed into dust the breath of life, creating us to serve you and our neighbors. Call forth our prayers and acts of kindness, and strengthen us to face our mortality with confidence in the mercy of your Son, Jesus Christ, our Savior and Lord, who lives and reigns with you and the Holy Spirit, one God, now and forever.

Gospel Acclamation

Return to the LORD, your God, who is gracious and merciful, slow to anger, and abounding in steadfast love. (Joel 2:13)

Readings and Psalm

Joel 2:1-2, 12-17

Because of the coming day of the LORD, the prophet Joel calls the people to a community lament. The repentant community declares that God is gracious and asks God to spare the people lest the nations doubt God's power to save.

or Isaiah 58:1-12

Shortly after the return of Israel from exile in Babylon, the people were troubled by the ineffectiveness of their fasts. God reminds them that outward observance is no substitute for genuine fasting that results in acts of justice, such as feeding the hungry, sheltering the homeless, and clothing the naked. Sincere repentance will lead to a dramatic improvement of their condition.

Psalm 51:1-17

Have mercy on me, O God, according to your steadfast love. (Ps. 51:1)

2 Corinthians 5:20b—6:10

The ministry of the gospel endures many challenges and hardships. Through this ministry, God's reconciling activity in the death of Christ reaches into the depths of our lives to bring us into a right relationship with God. In this way, God accepts us into the reality of divine salvation.

Matthew 6:1-6, 16-21

In the Sermon on the Mount, Jesus commends almsgiving, prayer, and fasting, but emphasizes that spiritual devotion must not be done for show.

Preface   Lent

Color   Purple

Prayers of Intercession

The prayers are prepared locally for each occasion. The following examples may be adapted or used as appropriate.

Turning our hearts to God who is gracious and merciful, we pray for the church, the world, and all who are in need.

A brief silence.

Merciful God, refresh the hearts of your faithful people across all lands and generations. Rescue your church from affliction, hardship, or persecution. Remove all obstacles standing in the way of our witness to your grace, mercy, and everlasting love. Hear us, O God.

Your mercy is great.

Renewing God, bless all wilderness places and all inhabitants of the land. Protect untouched ecosystems, satisfy parched places, and strengthen roots and seeds beneath the soil that await their time to flourish. Hear us, O God.

Your mercy is great.

Restoring God, rebuild and repair nations ravaged by war or famine (*especially*). Humble the hearts of governments and authorities, that they loose the bonds of injustice and liberate the oppressed. Hear us, O God.

Your mercy is great.

Generous God, provide bread for the hungry, shelter for the homeless, and protection for the vulnerable. Listen to the cries of all who are abused, imprisoned, and who suffer due to pain, anxiety, or illness (*especially*). Hear us, O God.
Your mercy is great.
Faithful God, renew our practices of devotion and discipleship. Make us generous in giving, steadfast in prayer, and attentive to your grace amid many distractions. Be with those who prepare for baptism and affirmation of baptism (*especially*). Hear us, O God.
Your mercy is great.
Here other intercessions may be offered.
Redeeming God, you raise us from the dust of death and mark us with the cross of salvation. Strengthen us by the faithfulness of the saints. Restore our joy and lead us by your bountiful grace. Hear us, O God.
Your mercy is great.
According to your steadfast love, O God, hear these and all our prayers as we commend them to you; through Christ our Lord.
Amen.

Ideas for the Day

- Today's reading from Matthew cautions against sounding a trumpet ahead of oneself when giving alms, yet in the readings from Joel and Isaiah we hear the prophets call for trumpet sounds. These sounds are not meant to announce the good works of the people, but to summon the people to repentance, fasting, and acts of justice. The Ash Wednesday liturgy begins with gathering in silence and then singing Psalm 51 or another penitential psalm (*ELW*, p. 251). The sounding of a trumpet or ringing of a chime could precede the psalm as a way of calling the gathered into the disciplines of Lent.

- We play multiple roles every day. Some of those roles even come with an identification badge. We may be in parent mode to get kids off to school and then take on the role of an accountant or carpenter. A retiree may be a patient at the doctor's office in the morning and then help shuttle grandkids in the afternoon. Kids may be moving from homework to sports practice to music lessons. Make peel-and-stick nametags and markers available as the assembly gathers for worship. Invite worshipers to fill in the nametag with as many roles as they played today: daughter, brother, parent, employee, neighbor, and so on. The sermon can touch on the way these roles shift and change and the gift of spiritual practices amid these movements. As people come forward later to receive ashes, they can be reminded of the temporary nature of these roles and the permanence of the cross of Christ.

- Ash Wednesday marks the beginning of the season of Lent, which will end with the celebration of Easter on April 12 this year. Our Muslim neighbors will begin the season of Ramadan at sunset on Thursday, April 23. If you have a relationship with members of a neighborhood Islamic center, consider inviting them for a meal on Ash Wednesday to share understandings about the practices and meanings of these seasons in our journeys of faith. An invitation to worship could be extended as well.

Connections with Creation

The dust of Ash Wednesday connects us not only to the soil but to the cosmos. Scientists estimate that forty thousand tons of cosmic dust fall to the earth each year. This dust is composed of the elemental building blocks of the material world. In 1990, Voyager 1 entered the fringes of our solar system and trained its lens back at Earth from a distance of four billion miles. Earth appears as a tiny point of light. Carl Sagan wrote, "Look again at that dot. . . . That's us. On it everyone you love, everyone you know, everyone you ever heard of, every human being who ever was, lived out their lives. The aggregate of our joy and suffering . . . every king and peasant, every young couple in love, every mother and father, hopeful child, . . . every saint and sinner in the history of our species lived there—on a mote of dust suspended in a sunbeam" (*Pale Blue Dot: A Vision of the Human Future in Space*, New York: Ballantine Books, 1997).

Let the Children Come

Children talk about death to somehow grasp the notion of it. They engage in play that imitates death (think of burying things in the sandbox). A key to helping children negotiate the world and the mystery of death is adults who are honest and truthful about it. Avoid euphemisms. Everything dies. At a certain level, children know that. Ash Wednesday is one way to help children speak about death with honesty. Do not be afraid to mark the foreheads of children, even babies, with ashes. Our finitude may frighten us, but it is a fact. Children are not unaware of death or loss, nor are their parents blind to the vulnerability of their little ones. Let us not pretend, but let us speak the truth that is more enduring than death: the love of God in Christ crucified and risen.

Assembly Song and Music for the Day

Because of the nature of this day, choral and instrumental music suggestions are listed by place in the service. Ch=Choral; CC=Children's Choir; KI=Keyboard/Instrumental; HB=Handbell. Many suggestions require assembly participation.

Gathering

Psalm 51 (see Psalmody and Acclamations)
Kyrie ELW 151–158 or from communion settings
Eternal Lord of love, behold your church ELW 321
⊕ "Señor, ten piedad LLC 185–186.
☼ Cron, Ian Morgan/Matt Maher/Stuart Garrard. "Oh Mercy" from CCLI.

⊕ = global song
☼ = praise song

Mozart, Wolfgang A. "Kyrie in D minor (Münchner Kyrie)." SATB, kybd or orch. Carus-Verlag 40.037. [Ch]

P ♫ Raabe, Nancy M. "Out of the Depths I Cry to You" from *Grace & Peace, Volume 8: Songs of Lament and Longing*. Pno. AFP 9781506413679. [KI]

Psalmody and Acclamations

Cherwien, David. "Psalm 51" from PSCY.

Marshall, Jane. "Create in Me, O God." U, desc or C inst, assembly, kybd. CG CGA750.

Raabe, Nancy. "Have Mercy on Me, O God (Psalm 51:1-17)." MSB1 S402.

Schalk, Carl. "Antiphon 1 for Psalm 51" from PATP. Use with ELW tone 9 in Dmin.

☼ Foreman, Jon. "White as Snow" from CCLI.

☼ Maher, Matt/Audrey Assad. "Clean Heart" from *Echoes*. mattmahermusic.com.

(GA) Farlee, Robert Buckley. "Let Your Steadfast Love." MSB1 S421 with proper verse for Ash Wednesday.

Hymn of the Day

Jesus, priceless treasure ELW 775, LBW 457 *JESU, MEINE FREUDE* LBW 458 *GUD SKAL ALTING MAGE*

Out of the depths I cry to you ELW 600, LBW 295 *AUS TIEFER NOT*

Restore in us, O God ELW 328 *BAYLOR* WOV 662 *CATECHUMEN*

Confession of Sin

Music Sourcebook for Lent and the Three Days (MSB1) includes four musical settings of texts for corporate confession of sin, one using the text in the Ash Wednesday service (S408), and others using the text from Corporate Confession and Forgiveness, Evangelical Lutheran Worship Leaders Edition, p. 603 (S409-S411).

Imposition of Ashes

Once we sang and danced ELW 701

Savior, when in dust to you ELW 601, LBW 91

Now quit your care H82 145

Ah, what shame I have to bear NCH 203

☼ Rundman, Jonathan. "Ashes" from *Reservoir*. jonathanrundman.bandcamp.com.

P Cool, Jayne Southwick. "O Lord, I Call to You." SAB, pno, assembly. AFP 9781451479423. [Ch]

Burkhardt, Michael. "Out of the Depths" from *Canons for the Church Year*, set 1. U/4 vcs (canon). MSM 50-9803. [CC]

♫ Bach, J. S. "Aus tiefer Not" from *Clavier-Übung III*. Various editions. [KI]

♫ Lamb, Linda. "Jesus, Priceless Treasure." 3-5 oct hb, opt 3 oct hc, fl, L3. CPH 977467. [HB]

Setting the Table

⊕ Anon., Zimbabwe/arr. and trans. Patrick Matsikenyiri and Daniel Charles Damon. "Njalo/Always" from *Njalo (Always)*. ABI 9780687498079.

Chilcott, Bob. "Be Thou My Vision" from *The New Oxford Easy Anthem Book*. OXF 9780193533189. [Ch]

P Schram, Ruth Elaine. "Brighter Than Snow (Psalm 51)." U/2 pt, pno. AFP 9780800676346. [CC]

♫ Manz, Paul. "Jesus, Priceless Treasure" from *Improvisations on Classic Chorales*. Org. MSM 10-843. [KI]

♫ Mallory, Ron. "Jesus, Priceless Treasure." 2-3 oct, L2. SF 202039. [HB]

Communion

Change my heart, O God ELW 801, W&P 28

Softly and tenderly Jesus is calling ELW 608, WOV 734, TFF 155

Thy holy wings ELW 613, WOV 741

☼ Quilala, Chris/Joshua Silverberg/Ran Jackson/Ricky Jackson. "Make Us One" from CCLI.

P Douroux, Margaret/arr. John Helgen. "Give Me a Clean Heart" SAB, pno. AFP 9780800677152. [Ch]

P Van der Pol, Jerry. "Savior, When in Dust to You" from *Endless Song: Accessible Piano Settings*. Pno. AFP 9781506426433. [KI]

Edwards, Dan. "Lord Jesus, Think on Me" from *Three for Communion*. 2-3 oct, L2. CPH 977636. [HB]

Sending

Chief of sinners though I be ELW 609, LBW 306

Lord Jesus, think on me ELW 599, LBW 309

☼ Scott, Jeremy/Sharon Damazio. "Create in Me" from CCLI.

⊕ = global song ♫ = relates to hymn of the day
☼ = praise song P = available in Prelude Music Planner

March 1, 2020
First Sunday in Lent

Today's gospel tells of Jesus' temptation in the desert. His forty-day fast becomes the basis of our Lenten pilgrimage. In the early church Lent was a time of intense preparation for those to be baptized at the Easter Vigil. This catechetical focus on the meaning of faith is at the heart of our Lenten journey to the baptismal waters of Easter. Hungry for God's mercy, we receive the bread of life to nourish us for the days ahead.

Prayer of the Day

Lord God, our strength, the struggle between good and evil rages within and around us, and the devil and all the forces that defy you tempt us with empty promises. Keep us steadfast in your word, and when we fall, raise us again and restore us through your Son, Jesus Christ, our Savior and Lord, who lives and reigns with you and the Holy Spirit, one God, now and forever.

Gospel Acclamation

One does not live by bread alone, but by every word that comes from the mouth of God. (Matt. 4:4)

Readings and Psalm

Genesis 2:15-17; 3:1-7

Human beings were formed with great care, to be in relationship with the creator, creation, and one another. The serpent's promise to the first couple that their eyes would be opened led, ironically, to the discovery only that they were naked.

Psalm 32

Mercy embraces those who trust in the LORD. (Ps. 32:10)

Romans 5:12-19

Through Adam's disobedience, humanity came under bondage to sin and death, from which we cannot free ourselves. In Christ's obedient death, God graciously showers on us the free gift of liberation and life.

Matthew 4:1-11

Jesus experiences anew the temptations that Israel faced in the wilderness. As the Son of God, he endures the testing of the evil one.

Preface   Lent

Color   Purple

Prayers of Intercession

The prayers are prepared locally for each occasion. The following examples may be adapted or used as appropriate.

Turning our hearts to God who is gracious and merciful, we pray for the church, the world, and all who are in need.
A brief silence.

God of the wilderness, we pray for the church. Lead us in showing grace and hospitality to all who struggle with doubt or shame. Make your church holy ground where all people can be seen and loved for who you have created them to be. Hear us, O God.

Your mercy is great.

We pray for creation. Show your glory in deserts and on mountaintops. Nourish gardens and orchards and bless those who tend them. Forgive us for our desire to dominate creation instead of serving as faithful stewards and caretakers. Hear us, O God.

Your mercy is great.

We pray for the nations. Liberate leaders and governments from the temptation to exercise unjust dominion over those whom they are called to lead and serve. Hear us, O God.

Your mercy is great.

We pray for those in need. Sustain those who are hungry and alone, those who are anxious, those facing difficult decisions, and those facing a recent diagnosis or new grief. (*We pray especially for . . .*) Hear us, O God.

Your mercy is great.

We thank you for putting new songs on our lips and in our hearts. Hear our voices as we join in songs of lament and praise. We give thanks for musicians, composers, and poets (*especially George Herbert; other musicians or music ministries of the local congregation may be named*). Hear us, O God.

Your mercy is great.

Here other intercessions may be offered.

We praise you for bringing us through the desert into the promised land of your kingdom. We give thanks for saints who have guided us in times of trial and joy (*especially*). Hear us, O God.

Your mercy is great.

According to your steadfast love, O God, hear these and all our prayers as we commend them to you; through Christ our Lord.

Amen.

Ideas for the Day

- The forty days of Lent echo Jesus' time in the wilderness as well as other sacred periods measured by forty. The season is also an echo of the forty weeks of human pregnancy. People who have recently been pregnant have probably experienced a version of the traditional Lenten discipline of fasting (from caffeine, alcohol, smoking) in the interest of providing safe gestational space for new life. How do we hold space for the new things that God is creating? What new life is growing quietly in the darkness while hidden from view? What is waiting to be (re)born in us and in our congregation or community?

- Although the Genesis reading may seem to suggest otherwise, curiosity is not the same as temptation. When Eve relays God's instructions to the serpent, she adds that they are not even supposed to touch the tree. The story snowballs in its interpretation, until we are not supposed to look at or even think about the tree. It is not a sin to open our eyes, pay attention, and ask questions. Unfortunately, many have formed an impression of Christianity that requires them to keep their mouth shut and pretend to agree as a form of piety and resisting temptation. In Jesus' temptation, he engages and argues against the tempter. How does our church community encourage active, engaged resistance rather than hiding from or denying temptation and evil?

- In a 2016 Seattle Children's Theater production of Maurice Sendak's classic *Where the Wild Things Are* (New York: HarperCollins, 1963), audience members were invited to participate in acting out the story: gnashing their terrible teeth as wild things, then stepping into young Max's role to command the chaos to "Be still!" Max's "wild things" as an embodiment of inner demons may resonate more powerfully for people today than cartoonish images of the devil. Just as Jesus renounced the devil three times in his temptation, in the rite of Holy Baptism we are invited three times to renounce the forces of evil (*ELW*, p. 229). If anyone in your congregation is preparing for baptism, what parallels can you lift up between Jesus' temptation in the wilderness and the rejection of sin in the baptismal rite and their own daily lives?

Connections with Creation

The Greek word translated "desert" or "wilderness" names places beyond the scope of human habitation or agricultural life. These are forbidding places where human life is vulnerable, physically and spiritually. To sojourn in such places is to be brought to the limits of endurance. Though they may be forbidding for us, it is important to bear in mind that they are biomes with their own God-given ecological integrity, independent of human beings. Preachers might resist the temptation to spiritualize or psychologize the idea of desert/wilderness in this text or to see it as simply the backdrop to the story of Jesus' temptation. Instead, one might explore the ways we commonly dismiss the value of ecological communities that we do not see as hospitable or having utility for us. The human tendency to reduce creation's value to its utility is itself a temptation to sin against the intrinsic value of God's good creation.

Let the Children Come

The three classic Lenten disciplines are fasting, prayer, and works of love. To encourage children to participate in the offering and to understand how our gifts become signs of God's gracious love for others, place a large basket in the chancel and invite children to bring nonperishable food items to worship each week during Lent. While the offering plates are passed, let the children come and place their gifts in the basket. Keep a stash of canned goods for visiting children so they can participate as well.

At the end of the season, older children can sort, box, and help deliver these gifts to a local food bank. A Sunday school class could spend a Saturday afternoon volunteering there. In small ways like these, children learn what it means to be signs of God's presence, feeding the world with God's love.

Assembly Song
Gathering

O Lord, throughout these forty days   ELW 319, LBW 99

Through the night of doubt and sorrow   ELW 327, LBW 355

Your Heart, O God, Is Grieved   ELW 602, LBW 96

Psalmody and Acclamations

Helgen, John. "Psalm 32" from *ChildrenSing Psalms*. U, assembly, kybd.

Schalk, Carl. "Antiphon for Psalm 32" from PATP. Use with ELW tone 9 in Dmin.

Schwarz, May. "Psalm 32" from PWA.

(GA) Farlee, Robert Buckley. "Let Your Steadfast Love." MSB1 S421 with proper verse for Lent 1.

Hymn of the Day

I want Jesus to walk with me   ELW 325, WOV 660, TFF 66, LS 41   *SOJOURNER*

Let us ever walk with Jesus   ELW 802, LBW 487   *LASSET UNS MIT JESU ZIEHEN*

Lord Jesus, you shall be my song/Jésus, je voudrais te chanter   ELW 808   *LES PETITES SOEURS*

Offering

Come, ye disconsolate   ELW 607, TFF 186

Tree of Life and awesome mystery   ELW 334 (sts. 1-3, Lent 1)

Communion

As the sun with longer journey   ELW 329, WOV 655
Now We Remain   ELW 500, W&P 106
Strengthen for service, Lord   ELW 497, LBW 218

Sending

Bless now, O God, the journey   ELW 326
Guide me ever, great Redeemer   ELW 618, LBW 343

Additional Assembly Songs

Crea en mí, oh Dios/Create in me a clean heart   LLC 442
Forty days and forty nights   H82 150, NCH 205, GTG 167
Satan, we're going to tear your kingdom down   TFF 207

⊕ Cassina, Miguel/trans. Andrew Donaldson. "Tu fidelidad/I Depend Upon Your Faithfulness" from *With Many Voices*. U, pno. Binary Editions 9790900140104.

⊕ South African trad. "Senzeni na?/What Have We Done?" from *More Voices*. SATB, cant. Wood Lake Publishing 9781551341484.

☼ Byrd, Anna/Kyle Lee/Michael Farren. "Wilderness" from CCLI.

☼ Foreman, Jon. "Your Love Is Strong" from CCLI.

☼ Hooper, Matthew/Richie Fike/Travis Ryan. "We Believe" from CCLI.

☼ Ingram, Jason/Kristian Stanfill. "This We Know" from CCLI.

☼ Moen, Don. "God Will Make a Way" from CCLI.

☼ Parker, Abbie/Adam Palmer/Matt Maher/Matthew Hein. "What a Friend" from CCLI.

Music for the Day
Choral

℘ Hurlbutt, Patricia. "At the Cross." 2 pt mxd, a cap. AFP 9781451479317.

℘ Sedio, Mark. "Take Us As We Are, O God." SATB, org. AFP 9781506426204.

℘ Shute, Linda Cable. "Lord, Who throughout These Forty Days." SATB, pno. AFP 9781506452500.

℘ Trinkley, Bruce. "I Want Jesus to Walk with Me" from *Augsburg Choirbook for Men*. TB, pno. AFP 9780800676834.

Children's Choir

Behnke, John A. "In Adam We Have All Been One/The King Shall Come When Morning Dawns." 2 pt, org. CPH 983886pdf.

Bender, Jan. "Begone, Satan" from *A Third Morning Star Choir Book*. 2 pt, org. CPH 974972.

Krentz Organ, Anne. "Follow Jesus." 2 pt, pno. AFP 9780800677428.

Keyboard / Instrumental

♫ Costello, Michael D. "Let Us Ever Walk with Jesus" from *God Will Guide You: Five Hymn Arrangements for Organ*. Org. MSM 10-620.

⊕ = global song   ♫ = relates to hymn of the day
☼ = praise song   ℘ = available in Prelude Music Planner

℘ ♫ Sedio, Mark. "Lord Jesus, You Shall Be My Song" from *Come and Praise*, vol. 3. Org. AFP 9781506426327.

℘ Wahl, Carol. "Tree of Life and Awesome Mystery" from *Cry of the Dove: Piano Settings*. Pno. AFP 9781451479614.

℘ ♫ Wilson, Terry D. "I Want Jesus to Walk with Me" from *Near the Cross: Piano Settings*. Pno. AFP 9781506448053.

Handbell

♫ Behnke, John. "Let Us Ever Walk with Jesus." 3 oct, L2. CPH 977106.

♫ Edwards, Dan. "I Want Jesus to Walk with Me." 3 or 5 oct, L2+. CG CGB383.

♫ Sherman, Arnold. "The Journey." 3-6 oct, L3+. HOP 1897.

Sunday, March 1
George Herbert, hymnwriter, died 1633

As a student at Trinity College, Cambridge, England, George Herbert excelled in languages and music. He went to college with the intention of becoming a priest, but his scholarship attracted the attention of King James I. Herbert served in parliament for two years. After the death of King James and at the urging of a friend, Herbert's interest in ordained ministry was renewed. He was ordained a priest in 1630 and served the little parish of St. Andrew Bremerton until his death. He was noted for unfailing care for his parishioners, bringing the sacraments to them when they were ill, and providing food and clothing for those in need. Herbert is best remembered, however, as a writer of poems and hymns such as "Come, my way, my truth, my life" (ELW 816).

Monday, March 2
John Wesley, died 1791; Charles Wesley, died 1788; renewers of the church

The Wesleys were leaders of a revival in the Church of England. Their spiritual discipline (or method) of frequent communion, fasting, and advocacy for the poor earned them the name "Methodists." The Wesleys were missionaries in the American colony of Georgia for a time, but returned to England discouraged. Following a conversion experience while reading Luther's *Preface to the Epistle to the Romans*, John was perhaps the greatest force in eighteenth-century revival. The brothers' desire was that the Methodist Societies would be a movement for renewal in the Church of England, but after their deaths the societies developed a separate status.

Charles wrote more than six hundred hymns, including "Hark! The herald angels sing" (ELW 270), "Christ, whose glory fills the skies" (ELW 553), and "Love divine, all loves excelling" (ELW 631).

Saturday, March 7
Perpetua and Felicity and companions, martyrs at Carthage, died 202

In the year 202 the emperor Septimius Severus forbade conversions to Christianity. Perpetua, a noblewoman, Felicity, a slave, and other companions were all catechumens at Carthage in North Africa. They were imprisoned and sentenced to death. Perpetua's father, who was not a Christian, visited her in prison and begged her to lay aside her Christian convictions in order to spare her life and spare the family from scorn. Perpetua responded and told her father, "We know that we are not placed in our own power but in that of God."

March 8, 2020
Second Sunday in Lent

During Lent we journey with all those around the world who will be baptized at the Easter Vigil. In today's gospel Jesus tells Nicodemus that he must be born of water and Spirit. At the font we are a given a new birth as children of God. As God made a covenant with Abraham, in baptism God promises to raise us up with Christ to new life. From worship we are sent forth to proclaim God's love for all the world.

Prayer of the Day

O God, our leader and guide, in the waters of baptism you bring us to new birth to live as your children. Strengthen our faith in your promises, that by your Spirit we may lift up your life to all the world through your Son, Jesus Christ, our Savior and Lord, who lives and reigns with you and the Holy Spirit, one God, now and forever.

Gospel Acclamation

The Son of Man must be lifted up, that whoever believes in him may have eternal life. (John 3:14-15)

Readings and Psalm

Genesis 12:1-4a

God's call of Abram and Sarai has a clear purpose—that through them all the families of the earth would gain a blessing. As they set out on their journey, they are accompanied by promises of land, nation, and a great reputation.

Psalm 121

I lift up my eyes to the hills; my help comes from the LORD. (Ps. 121:1, 2)

Romans 4:1-5, 13-17

In the person and example of Abraham we discover that a right relationship with God does not involve earning a reward from God but entails trusting God's promises. Abraham is the forebear and model for both Jews and Gentiles, because we too trust that ours is a God who gives life to the dead.

John 3:1-17

A curious Pharisee visits Jesus by night to learn from the teacher his friends reject. Jesus speaks to him about life in the Spirit and the kingdom of God.

Preface   Lent

Color   Purple

Prayers of Intercession

The prayers are prepared locally for each occasion. The following examples may be adapted or used as appropriate.

Turning our hearts to God who is gracious and merciful, we pray for the church, the world, and all who are in need.
A brief silence.

God of rebirth, empower your church throughout the world to be a voice of hope for those who fear judgment or condemnation. Assure us of your faithfulness and give us confidence to proclaim your salvation for all. Hear us, O God.
Your mercy is great.

God of rebirth, your Spirit hovered over the waters and you called creation into being. Nurture and bless all signs of rebirth around us: budding trees and new shoots, thawing lakes and warm breezes, and animals awaking from hibernation. Hear us, O God.
Your mercy is great.

God of rebirth, lead the nations in your way of righteousness. Protect those who advocate for the needs of children, migrants, and victims of violence. Give courage to lawmakers, lawyers, judges, and law enforcement officers, guiding them to do justice and to love mercy. Hear us, O God.
Your mercy is great.

God of rebirth, give us a new vision of your healing power among us. Restore hope to those who remain in the depths of depression or despair. Bring mercy and relief to those who are injured, sick, or suffering (*especially*). Hear us, O God.
Your mercy is great.

God of rebirth, we thank you for the children of this community and for the people and ministries that care for them (*individuals and ministries in the congregation may be named*). Bless new and expectant parents. Console those who have lost children and those whose desire for children remains unfulfilled. Hear us, O God.
Your mercy is great.

Here other intercessions may be offered.

God of rebirth, by wind and spirit you call us into life renewed. We give you thanks for all your saints who have inherited your promises (*especially*). Bring us, with them, into your everlasting kingdom. Hear us, O God.
Your mercy is great.

According to your steadfast love, O God, hear these and all our prayers as we commend them to you; through Christ our Lord.
Amen.

Ideas for the Day

- Nicodemus's confusion over being born from above offers an obvious time to explore the imagery of God as Mother and what it means to be formed in the womb of God. The hymn "Mothering God, you gave me birth" (ELW 735) draws on imagery from the fourteenth-century mystic Julian of Norwich: Jesus is like a mother to us, feeding us from his own body as a mother nurses her child. The medieval church drew many parallels between nursing mothers and Jesus feeding the church from his body (see Caroline Walker Bynum, *Holy Feast and Holy Fast* [Berkeley and Los Angeles, CA: University of California Press, 1987]). If there are any current (or former) nursing mothers in the congregation, how might their experience offer insights that reawaken the mystery of Holy Communion?

- There are many possible translations and meanings of Jesus' image of being born from above or born again—and many are weighed down with the connotations of modern evangelical usage. The same concept may also be translated (literally) as rebirth or renaissance, stirring up very different connotations that may be worth exploring. In Lawrence Ferlinghetti's poem "I Am Waiting" (*A Coney Island of the Mind* [New York: New Directions, 1958], p. 49), he returns again and again to the phrase "rebirth of wonder." The season of Lent invites worshipers to consider where in their lives and in the world they are waiting for rebirth—or resurrection.

- North Americans are frequently in states of transition, moving to new housing, new employment, or new phases of life (such as parenthood, retirement, assisted living).

When God called Abram to make a new start in a new land, it was for the sake of becoming a blessing for all the families of the earth. When our worshipers are discerning God's calling in their own times of transition, whose needs—and whose blessings—are considered? If God also calls us to be a blessing to all families—not just our own—we must ask how our choices impact others: for example, Will this housing opportunity contribute to gentrification or wasteful energy usage? Are people whose services we depend on paid a fair wage? How does this company impact the world for good or for ill? What are our children learning about injustice in the world and advocating for others?

Connections with Creation

Nicodemus comes to Jesus with questions and struggles to understand what Jesus has to say about being born of water and Spirit. Nicodemus's inquiry is an opportunity to ask our own probing questions about the watery sacrament of baptism. The water in which we baptize is drawn from our local watersheds, nurturing farms and fields and feeding municipal water systems that supply water for our drinking, cooking, and washing. Lutheran Christians dare to call the water of the font holy because it is the common, precious stuff from which our holy God nurtures all life. In and through it, we are "sealed by the Holy Spirit and marked with the cross of Christ forever" (*ELW*, p. 231). In all our rites related to baptism (don't forget confession and forgiveness, which Luther called a daily crawling back to baptism), we are sacramental members in our local watersheds. Worship leaders can dive deeply into these ecological and sacramental connections.

Let the Children Come

The serpent raised up in the wilderness and described by Jesus in the gospel finds a counterpart in the church's use of the processional cross. A stationary or permanent cross can get lost in the worship space and not be noticed. A cross carried in procession can regularly bring to mind the gift of God in the cross. For children, a processional cross can be a visual cue to understanding that Jesus' cross leads the way to our salvation and leads us into service in the world. Let an older child lift high the cross in a procession as the people gather to hear the word and share the meal, and then let the child carry the cross out of the worship space—and out the front door of the church and into the world—when worship ends. Let the children lead the others in following the cross and Jesus into the places they are sent to serve and live.

Assembly Song
Gathering

Lord, take my hand and lead me   ELW 767, LBW 333
Lift high the cross   ELW 660, LLC 489, LS 88, LBW 377
Seed that in earth is dying   ELW 330

Psalmody and Acclamations

I to the hills will lift my eyes/Psalm 121 GTG 45

Gelineau, Joseph. "Psalm 121" from ACYG.

O'Brien, Frances Patrick. "Our Help Is from the Lord." SAB, cant, assembly, kybd, opt gtr, fl, vc. GIA G-5449.

(GA) Farlee, Robert Buckley. "Let Your Steadfast Love." MSB1 S421 with proper verse for Lent 2.

Hymn of the Day

God loved the world ELW 323 ROCKINGHAM OLD LBW 292
DIE HELLE SONN LEUCHT

Lord Christ, when first you came to earth ELW 727, LBW 421
MIT FREUDEN ZART

There's a wideness in God's mercy ELW 587 ST. HELENA
ELW 588, LBW 290 LORD, REVIVE US

Offering

As the grains of wheat ELW 465, WOV 705, W&P 10

Tree of Life and awesome mystery ELW 334 (sts. 1-3, Lent 2)

Communion

Mothering God, you gave me birth ELW 735, WOV 769

Now We Remain ELW 500, W&P 106

That priceless grace ELW 591, TFF 68

Sending

For by grace you have been saved ELW 598

In the cross of Christ I glory ELW 324, LBW 104

Additional Assembly Songs

By grace we have been saved W&P 25, ASG 4

By the waters of Babylon TFF 67

For God so loved the world ASG 10, LS 45

⊕ Taizé Community. "By Night/De noche iremos" from *Songs and Prayers from Taizé*. SATB. GIA G-3719.

⊕ Lee, Song-chon/Song-suk Im. "To the High and Kindly Hills" from *Sound the Bamboo*. U, fl, zither, drm. GIA G-6830.

☼ Bridges, Michael/George Baum. "Psalm 121" from *Something*. speedwood.com.

☼ Brown, Lacey. "To the Hills" from *Closer than My Breathing*. poorclare.bandcamp.com.

☼ Bruxvoort-Colligan, Richard. "God Is Holding Your Life" from *Sharing the Road*. psalmimmersion.com.

☼ Crowder, David/Mark Waldrop/Matt Maher. "Oh, Great Love of God" from CCLI.

☼ Johnson, Brian/Joel Case/Jonathan David Helser. "No Longer Slaves" from CCLI.

☼ Sampson, Marty/Matt Crocker. "God So Loved" from CCLI.

Music for the Day
Choral

P Farlee, Robert Buckley. "To Christ Belong." SATB, org, fl, opt assembly. AFP 9781451420791.

P Franck, Melchior/ed. William Braun. "For God So Loved the World." SATB, a cap. AFP 9781506452456.

P Schütz, Heinrich. "The Blood of Jesus Christ/Das Blut Jesu Christi" from *Chantry Choirbook: Sacred Music for All Seasons*. SAB, cont. AFP 9780800657772.

Weber, Paul. "All Who Believe and Are Baptized." SATB, org, fl. CPH 984033.

Children's Choir

Haas, David and Jane Holstein. "Baptized in Water." 2 pt, pno, opt fl. HOP C5574.

Hildebrand, Kevin. "God So Loved the World." 2 pt, kybd. CPH 984275.

Kemp, Helen. "A Mountain Psalm: A Meditation on Psalm 121." 2 pt, pno, opt assembly. CG CGA1061.

Keyboard / Instrumental

Cherwien, David M. "Prelude on Lift High the Cross" from *Lift High the Cross: Prelude and Postlude*. Org. MSM 10-726.

P ♫ Christiansen, Clay. "Lord Christ, When First You Came to Earth" from *All Things Bright and Beautiful: Eight Hymn Settings for Organ*. Org. MSM 10-664.

P Hansen, Sherri. "Mothering God, You Gave Me Birth" from *Piano Weavings*, vol. 2. Pno. AFP 9781506413723.

P ♫ Miller, Aaron David. "God Loved the World" from *Eight Chorale Preludes for Manuals Only*, vol. 2. Org. AFP 9780800678470.

Handbell

♫ Glasgow, Michael. "Contemplation on the Cross." 3-6 oct hb, opt 3-6 oct hc, L4-. LOR 20/1700L.

Rogers, Sharon Elery. "Two Songs of Hope and Rest." 2-3 oct, L1. FLA HP5465.

♫ Tucker, Sondra. "There's a Wideness in God's Mercy." 3-5 oct, L3. AFP 0800674901.

Tuesday, March 10
Harriet Tubman, died 1913; Sojourner Truth, died 1883; renewers of society

Harriet Tubman was born into slavery in Maryland and remained a slave until about age thirty when, fearing she would be sold and moved farther south, she escaped with the help of the Underground Railroad. After that, she helped about three hundred others to escape until slavery was abolished. After the Civil War, her home in Auburn, New York, became a center for women's rights and served the aged and poor.

⊕ = global song   ♫ = relates to hymn of the day
☼ = praise song   P = available in Prelude Music Planner

Sojourner Truth, too, was born a slave, in New York state. Her birth name was Isabella. After slavery was abolished in New York in 1827, she was freed and, while working as a house-keeper, became deeply involved in Christianity. A number of years later, she discerned a call to become a preacher. Taking the name Sojourner Truth, she set out on an evangelistic jour-ney, where people found her testimony to be deeply moving. In later life, she also became a popular speaker against slavery and for women's rights.

Thursday, March 12
Gregory the Great, Bishop of Rome, died 604

Gregory was born into a politically influential family. At one time he held political office and at another time he lived as a monk, all before he was elected to the papacy. Gregory's work was extensive. He influenced public worship through the establishment of a lectionary and prayers to correlate with the readings. He established a school to train church musicians. Gregorian chant is named in his honor. He wrote a treatise underscoring what is required of a parish pastor serving a con-gregation. He sent missionaries to preach to the Anglo-Saxons who had invaded England. And at one time he organized distri-bution of grain during a shortage of food in Rome.

March 15, 2020
Third Sunday in Lent

In today's gospel the Samaritan woman asks Jesus for water, an image of our thirst for God. Jesus offers living water, a sign of God's grace flowing from the waters of baptism. The early church used this gospel and those of the next two Sundays to deepen baptismal reflection during the final days of preparation before baptism at Easter. As we journey to the resurrec-tion feast, Christ comes among us in word, bath, and meal—offering us the life-giving water of God's mercy and forgiveness.

Prayer of the Day

Merciful God, the fountain of living water, you quench our thirst and wash away our sin. Give us this water always. Bring us to drink from the well that flows with the beauty of your truth through Jesus Christ, our Savior and Lord, who lives and reigns with you and the Holy Spirit, one God, now and forever.

Gospel Acclamation

Lord, you are truly the Savior of the world; give me this living water that I may never thirst again. (John 4:42, 15)

Readings and Psalm
Exodus 17:1-7

Because the thirsty Israelites quarreled with Moses and put God to the test, Moses cried out in desperation to God. God commanded Moses to strike the rock to provide water for the people. The doubt-filled question—"Is the Lord among us or not?"—received a very positive answer.

Psalm 95

Let us shout for joy to the rock of our salvation. (Ps. 95:1)

Romans 5:1-11

Though we often hear that God helps those who help them-selves, here Paul tells us that through Jesus' death God helps utterly helpless sinners. Since we who had been enemies are reconciled to God in the cross, we now live in hope for our final salvation.

John 4:5-42

Jesus defies convention to engage a Samaritan woman in con-versation. Her testimony, in turn, leads many others to faith.

Preface Lent

Color Purple

Prayers of Intercession

The prayers are prepared locally for each occasion. The following examples may be adapted or used as appropriate.

Turning our hearts to God who is gracious and merciful, we pray for the church, the world, and all who are in need.
A brief silence.

God of living water, send your church beyond boundaries to proclaim your grace. May its witness be a source of refresh-ment for thirsty souls. Strengthen our voices, that all people can know and believe that Jesus is truly the savior of the world. Hear us, O God.

Your mercy is great.

God of living water, protect from pollution or misuse all rivers, lakes, oceans, and streams (*local water sources may be named*). Bless the work of those who dig wells and those who advocate for access to clean water, that all people and animals have enough to drink. Hear us, O God.

Your mercy is great.

God of living water, open the hearts of leaders and authorities, that they hear the cries of the suffering and act with compassion toward them. Bring peace to disputed lands and bring reconciliation to people divided by race, culture, or nationality. Hear us, O God.

Your mercy is great.

God of living water, mend the hearts of those who grieve broken relationships, whether by conflict, abuse, divorce, or death. Draw near to all who are ill (*especially*). Assure those questioning your presence in the midst of doubt or suffering. Hear us, O God.

Your mercy is great.

God of living water, renew us in the promises of baptism. Join us together in worship, fellowship, and sharing your good news. Embolden us to serve others and to work for justice and peace. Hear us, O God.

Your mercy is great.

Here other intercessions may be offered.

God of living water, we thank you for those who endured suffering and who now boast in the glory of God (*especially*). Pour your Holy Spirit into our hearts and give us peace as we live in the hope of our salvation. Hear us, O God.

Your mercy is great.

According to your steadfast love, O God, hear these and all our prayers as we commend them to you; through Christ our Lord. **Amen.**

Ideas for the Day

- On this Sunday in the middle of Lent, consider incorporating a healing service with prayer and laying on of hands into your worship experience. You might choose to use scented anointing oil to trace a cross on the foreheads of those prayed for. See the Service of Healing in *Evangelical Lutheran Worship Occasional Services for the Assembly*, pages 271–283 (also available on sundaysandseasons.com).

- Everything in this gospel reading is wrong, and that makes it right. Jews like Jesus do not talk to Samaritans. Women do not come to the well alone in the middle of the day. Men do not talk to women they are not related to. Jesus breaks through all of these barriers to share the promise of living water. What barriers exist in your community preventing people from sharing living water? What might you do to break through those barriers?

- Many Samaritans said to the woman, "It is no longer because of what you said that we believe, for we have heard for ourselves, and we know that this is truly the Savior of the world" (John 4:42). Faith might begin when the people hear the woman's word, but the good-news transformation takes place when they encounter Jesus for themselves. Is there a time in your life when hearing led you to fully experiencing, and that experience changed everything? Hearing about the wonders of walking in the woods is one thing. Putting on a backpack with everything you need to eat and live for a week and heading into the woods is an experience that changes you.

- Much has been made of the Samaritan woman's five husbands. Could it be she is a woman bearing the weight of grief from the loss of so many people in her life? Could it be she lives dreading the vicious combination of cruel gossip and cold shoulders she receives from others? Piercing through her experience of alienation, Jesus looks at her brokenness with mercy and compassion.

Connections with Creation

Living water is a biblical phrase for water that participates in the great hydrological cycles: falling as rain, bubbling from springs, and flowing through streams and lakes. Living water is an essential ingredient to life on Earth. It is this living water that God's Spirit "moves over" and that flows through Eden in Genesis 1 and 2, that gushes from the rock to sustain the weary Hebrew people in the desert in Exodus 17, and that Jesus promises to give the Samaritan woman. Preachers are encouraged to resist the temptation to jump too quickly to living-water-as-metaphor, thus losing the dense ecological and sacramental meanings at play here. How might modern ecological understandings enrich the biblical sense of living water? How does the living water of baptism nourish both our ecological and theological habitat?

Let the Children Come

Let's face a basic truth: we all whine and quarrel, especially when our basic needs for food, water, sleep, and shelter are not met. In the Exodus text, we hear how the Israelites feel distressed not knowing when and how they will eat and drink. Learning to trust that God will care for them is a hard lesson, even after witnessing the miracle of water from a rock. Today encourage everyone, especially children, to dip their hands into the waters of the baptismal font as they go to or return from communion. Invite worshipers to feel the coolness and notice the texture of the water as it clings to their skin. Ask them to breathe in as they dip their hands into the water, and to breathe out as they watch the water cascade off and thread back into the font. Let breath and water today teach trust in God.

Assembly Song
Gathering

Give Me Jesus ELW 770, TFF 165, WOV 777

Jesus, we are gathered/Jesu, tawa pano ELW 529, TFF 140

Oh, that the Lord would guide my ways ELW 772, LBW 480

Psalmody and Acclamations

"Listen! Listen! Open your Hearts!" *Psallite* A-36. Cant or
SATB, assembly, kybd.

Haugen, Marty. "If Today You Hear His Voice" from TLP:A.

Oh, come, let us worship DATH 5

(GA) Farlee, Robert Buckley. "Let Your Steadfast Love." MSB1
S421 with proper verse for Lent 3.

Hymn of the Day

As the deer runs to the river ELW 331 *JULION*

Come to me, all pilgrims thirsty ELW 777 *BEACH SPRING*

I heard the voice of Jesus say ELW 332, LBW 497 *THIRD MODE
MELODY* ELW 611 *KINGSFOLD* TFF 62 *SHINE ON ME*

Offering

Come to the table ELW 481, W&P 33

Tree of Life and awesome mystery ELW 334 (sts. 1-3, Lent 3)

Communion

Come with us, O blessed Jesus ELW 501, LBW 219

O Jesus, blessed Lord ELW 541, LBW 220

One bread, one body ELW 496, WOV 710, TFF 122, W&P 111

Sending

Glorious things of you are spoken ELW 647, LBW 358

Praise the One who breaks the darkness ELW 843, ASG 34

Additional Assembly Songs

My soul thirsts for God SP 28

Aqui del pan Partido tomaré LLC 384

Surely it is God who saves me WOV 635, H82 678/679

⊕ Lee, Geonyong. "O Lord, as a Deer Longs for Cool Water/Chuyo
sasumi shinaenmul ch'attut" from *Sound the Bamboo*.
U with echoes. GIA G-6830.

⊕ Matsikenyiri, Patrick. "Iropa/By the Blood" from *Africa Praise
Songbook*. SATB, cant. GBGMusik 1890569070.

☼ Bannister, Ben/Ellie Holcomb. "Living Water" from CCLI.

☼ Houston, Joel/Jonas Myrin. "Broken Vessels (Amazing Grace)"
from CCLI.

☼ McMillan, John Mark/Sarah McMillan. "King of My Heart"
from CCLI.

☼ Neese, Simeon/Zach Neese. "Living Water" from CCLI.

☼ Peterson, Hans. "There Is a Mountain" from *Harvest of a
Heart*. dakotaroadmusic.com.

☼ Stanfill, Kristian. "Spring of Life" from WT.

⊕ = global song   ♫ = relates to hymn of the day
☼ = praise song   P = available in Prelude Music Planner

Music for the Day
Choral

Busarow, Donald. "I Heard the Voice of Jesus Say/O God,
Whose Will Is Life and Peace." SATB, org, fl. CPH
982619POD.

P ♫ Highben, Zebulon M. "Come to Me, All Pilgrims Thirsty."
SATB, assembly, org, C or B-flat inst. AFP 9780800621414.

P Pilkington, Steve. "Wondrous Love." 2 pt mxd, pno, hb. SEL
405-463.

Scheidt, Samuel. "O Jesu süss, wer dein gedenkt (O Jesus, Joy of
Loving Hearts)." TBB, cont. Alliance Music Publications
AMP 0864.

Children's Choir

How, Martin. "O Come, Let Us Sing unto the Lord." 2 pt, org.
MSM 50-7301.

P Schoenfeld, William M. "Oh, Come, Let Us Sing!" from *Augsburg Easy Choirbook*, vol. 3. 2 pt trbl or mxd, kybd. AFP
9781506414041.

P ♫ Witherup, William. "I Heard the Voice of Jesus Say." 2 pt, fl,
ob, org. SEL 420-451.

Keyboard / Instrumental

♫ Biery, James. "The Woman at the Well" from *Three Gospel
Scenes Quoting Familiar Hymns*. Org. MSM 10-317.

P ♫ Langlois, Kristina. "As the Deer Runs to the River" from
Ride On in Majesty: Organ Inspirations. Org. AFP
9781451451771.

♫ Near, Gerald. *Solemn Prelude on a Theme of Thomas Tallis*.
Org. MSM 10-168.

P ♫ Shaw, Timothy. "Beach Spring" from *Hymn Settings for the
Year: 55 Piano Gems*. Pno. AFP 9781506413693.

Handbell

♫ Ingram, Bill. "Come to Me, All Pilgrims Thirsty" from *Five
Hymns for Twelve Bells*. 3 oct (12 bells), L2. CG CGB770.

Thompson, Karen. "As the Deer." 3-5 oct hb, opt 3-5 oct hc, L2+.
GIA G-8364.

♫ Tucker, Sondra. "Canticle on Kingsfold." 3-5 oct hb, opt 3 oct
hc, L4-. BP HB408.

Tuesday, March 17
Patrick, bishop, missionary to Ireland, died 461

At sixteen, Patrick was kidnapped by Irish pirates and sold into slavery in Ireland. He himself admitted that up to this point he cared little for God. He escaped after six years, returned to his family in southwest Britain, and began to prepare for ordained ministry. He later returned to Ireland, this time to serve as a bishop and missionary. He made his base in the north of Ireland

and from there made many missionary journeys with much success. In his autobiography he denounced the slave trade, perhaps from his own experience as a slave. Patrick's famous baptismal hymn to the Trinity, "I bind unto myself today" (ELW 450), can be used as a meditation on Lent's call to return to our baptism.

Thursday, March 19
Joseph, Guardian of Jesus

The gospels are silent about much of Joseph's life. We know that he was a carpenter or builder by trade. The Gospel of Luke shows him acting in accordance with both civil and religious law by returning to Bethlehem for the census and by presenting the child Jesus in the temple on the fortieth day after his birth. The Gospel of Matthew tells of Joseph's trust in God, who led him through visionary dreams. Because Joseph is not mentioned after the story of a young Jesus teaching in the temple, it is assumed that he died before Jesus reached adulthood.

Saturday, March 21
Thomas Cranmer, Bishop of Canterbury, martyr, died 1556

Cranmer was serving as bishop of Taunton in England when he was chosen by King Henry VIII to become archbishop of Canterbury, largely because Cranmer would agree to the king's divorce from Catherine of Aragon. Cranmer's lasting achievement is contributing to and overseeing the creation of the Book of Common Prayer, which in revised form remains the worship book of the Anglican Communion. He was burned at the stake under Queen Mary for his support of the Protestant Reformation.

March 22, 2020
Fourth Sunday in Lent

Baptism is sometimes called enlightenment. The gospel for this Sunday is the story of the man born blind healed by Christ. "I was blind, now I see," declares the man. In baptism God opens our eyes to see the truth of who we are: God's beloved children. As David was anointed king of Israel, in baptism God anoints our head with oil, and calls us to bear witness to the light of Christ in our daily lives.

Prayer of the Day

Bend your ear to our prayers, Lord Christ, and come among us. By your gracious life and death for us, bring light into the darkness of our hearts, and anoint us with your Spirit, for you live and reign with the Father and the Holy Spirit, one God, now and forever.

Gospel Acclamation

Jesus says, I am the light of the world; whoever follows me will have the light of life. (John 8:12)

Readings and Psalm
1 Samuel 16:1-13

Samuel anointed David even though he was the eighth-oldest son of Jesse and did not match his brothers in height or other physical characteristics. With the anointing came endowment with the spirit of the Lord, designating David as the Lord's chosen successor to Saul.

Psalm 23

You anoint my head with oil. (Ps. 23:5)

Ephesians 5:8-14

Because we now live in the divine light which is Jesus Christ, we conduct our lives in ways that reflect the light of Christ, so that our activity is truly pleasing to God.

John 9:1-41

Jesus heals a man born blind, provoking a hostile reaction that he regards as spiritual blindness to the things of God.

Preface Lent

Color Purple

Prayers of Intercession

The prayers are prepared locally for each occasion. The following examples may be adapted or used as appropriate.

Turning our hearts to God who is gracious and merciful, we pray for the church, the world, and all who are in need.

A brief silence.

God of insight, open the hearts of the church and the world to all who testify to your deeds of power (*like Jonathan Edwards, whom we commemorate today*). Raise up voices in your church that are often silenced or overlooked due to age, gender expression, race, or economic status. Hear us, O God.

Your mercy is great.

God of insight, empower us to care for the land and all living things that dwell in it and beneath it. Provide rich soil for crops to grow. Bring rain to lands suffering drought. Protect hills and shorelines from damage caused by erosion. Hear us, O God.

Your mercy is great.

God of insight, bring peace to all people and nations. Anoint leaders who seek goodness, righteousness, and truth on behalf of all. Frustrate the efforts of those who would seek to cause violence or terror. Hear us, O God.

Your mercy is great.

God of insight, you care for our needs even before we ask. Come quickly to all who seek prayer this day (*especially*). Accomplish healing through the work of doctors, nurses, physical therapists, nutritionists, and all who tend to human bodies. Hear us, O God.

Your mercy is great.

God of insight, help this assembly lift up the unique gifts of each person who enters, no matter their physical capacity, cognitive ability, or sensory need. Help us to be creative and brave in making our facilities and our ministries accessible to all. Hear us, O God.

Your mercy is great.

Here other intercessions may be offered.

God of insight, you call out to those who are asleep and awaken them to new life with you. We give thanks for your saints (*especially*). Join us together with them as your children in this world and the next. Hear us, O God.

Your mercy is great.

According to your steadfast love, O God, hear these and all our prayers as we commend them to you; through Christ our Lord.

Amen.

Ideas for the Day

- A woman died of lung cancer. Her family was always quick to point out that, unlike most lung cancer victims, she never smoked cigarettes. They did not want people to blame her for her illness. It is comforting to find some reason when people are afflicted with a disease. But not all those who smoke get lung cancer, and not everyone with lung cancer smoked.

- Parents and others who bring for baptism children who are not able to answer for themselves are entrusted with responsibilities, including nurturing these children so that they "may learn to trust God, . . . care for others and the world God made, and work for justice and peace" (*ELW*, p. 228). This means the baptized are trained to spot indifference to others and God's creation. They are trained to recognize injustice and abuse. It means once we are baptized, we cannot turn our backs on the injustice we see. As God's people, we are called to respond, sometimes by political action and other times through acts of generosity and mercy.

- David was the least likely candidate to be anointed by Samuel, but he was the one God chose. Who in your congregation might be among the "least likely"? Everyone has a faith story. Could you discover the story of the quiet older woman who always sits alone? What about the teen who attended confirmation camp or participated in a mission trip for the first time last summer? Who are the "least likely" who have powerful stories to share?

- In the second reading Paul encourages his listeners to "try to find out what is pleasing to the Lord" (Eph. 5:10), but he doesn't really tell them *how* to do that. It all sounds so vague. And aren't the things that please God obvious, anyway? Why would followers of Jesus need to be told that? Paul knows we are human beings with limited vision. Perhaps there is an invitation in his words to explore and experiment. Can you think of an example or two of something that pleases God that is not immediately obvious? Ask worshipers to reflect on this question for a few minutes after the reading from Ephesians or during the sermon.

Connections with Creation

In the service of Holy Baptism, oil is often used for anointing the head of the newly baptized, as the minister prays, "Child of God, you have been sealed by the Holy Spirit and marked with the cross of Christ forever" (*ELW*, p. 231). Why oil? Biblically speaking, anointing with oil is a ritual action of great significance. David is anointed with oil to signify his being chosen by God to be a king. In Psalm 23, the anointing of the head with oil is a pledge of God's abiding presence. Baptismal anointing harks back to David's royal anointing; the baptized are a "royal priesthood, a holy nation" (1 Peter 2:9). Biologically speaking, oil forms the membranes of every living cell, making life as we know it possible. Chemically speaking, it captures and stores the energy of the sun in remarkable ways. While the burning of fossil fuel–oil contributes to the degradation of creation, the olive oil of baptismal anointing is renewable, both ecologically and spiritually.

Let the Children Come

In our gospel story today, a man blind from birth sees for the first time. He once "saw" only through his hands, fingertips, ears, and nose by touch, sound, and smell. Sometimes we close our eyes during a prayer, sermon, song, or hymn that speaks to us. When we open our eyes, we see everything around us differently: brightness, colors, shapes, sizes, and truths. Today's gospel may be particularly powerful for children if it's listened to with eyes shut tight. Invite everyone to close their eyes; encourage listeners to feel the mud on their eyes and the cool water of the pool washing the mud away. In the reading, help the assembly truly hear the neighbors' gossip and the Pharisees' questioning and derision, and to feel in their hearts the man's happiness and elation.

Assembly Song
Gathering

Christ, Be Our Light ELW 715
God, whose almighty word ELW 673, LBW 400
If you but trust in God to guide you ELW 769, LBW 453

Psalmody and Acclamations

Comer, Marilyn. "Psalm 23" from *ChildrenSing Psalms*. U, assembly, kybd.
Daigle, Gary. "The Lord Is My Shepherd." 2 pt, assembly, kybd, gtr, fl, vc. GIA G-8283.
Haugen, Marty. "The Lord Is My Shepherd." from TLP:A.
(GA) Farlee, Robert Buckley. "Let Your Steadfast Love." MSB1 S421 with proper verse for Lent 4.

Hymn of the Day

Come, follow me, the Savior spake ELW 799, LBW 455 *MACHS MIT MIR, GOTT*
Lead me, guide me ELW 768, TFF 70, W&P 84 *LEAD ME, GUIDE ME*
You, dear Lord/Tú, Señor, que brillas ELW 702, LLC 429 *TÚ SEÑOR*

Offering

Seed that in earth is dying ELW 330
Tree of Life and awesome mystery ELW 334 (sts. 1-3, Lent 4)

Communion

Amazing grace, how sweet the sound ELW 779, LLC 437, LBW 448
O living Bread from heaven ELW 542, LBW 197
You Are Mine ELW 581, W&P 158

Sending

Awake, O sleeper, rise from death ELW 452
What God ordains is good indeed ELW 776, LBW 446

⊕ = global song   ♬ = relates to hymn of the day
☼ = praise song   P = available in Prelude Music Planner

Additional Assembly Songs

My good shepherd is the Lord ASG 23
Open our eyes, Lord TFF 98, LS 31, W&P 113
⊕ Goodness is stronger than evil ELW 721, GTG 750
⊕ Chelliah, Calvin/Thamilz melody, Malaysia. "Your Word Will Be a Lamp to Guide Our Feet" from *Sound the Bamboo*. GIA G-6830.
☼ Guglielmucci, Mike. "Healer" from CCLI.
☼ Hastings, Benjamin/Joel Houston/Michael Fatkin. "So Will I (100 Billion X)" from CCLI.
☼ Houston, Joel/Matt Crocker. "Wonder" from CCLI.
☼ Rand, Lenora/Gary Rand. "Lovely Needy People–Kyrie" from *All Belong Here*. themany1.bandcamp.com.
☼ Riddle, Jeremy/Josh Farro/Phil Wickham. "This Is Amazing Grace" from CCLI.
☼ Tomlin, Chris/John Newton/Louie Giglio. "Amazing Grace (My Chains Are Gone)" from CCLI.

Music for the Day
Choral

♬ Akers, Doris/arr. John Carter. "Lead Me, Guide Me." SATB, pno. HOP C5225.
P Carter, John. "Amazing Grace." SATB, pno. AFP 9780800621377.
Goodall, Howard. "The Lord Is My Shepherd (Psalm 23)." SATB, org or pno or str qrt. MSM 12-0571520480.
P Organ, Anne Krentz. "Come, My Light" from *Augsburg Easy Choirbook*, vol. 2. 2 pt mxd, pno. AFP 9780800675813.

Children's Choir

P Anderson, Shari. "I Want to Walk as a Child of the Light" from *ChildrenSing in Worship*, vol. 2. U/2 pt, fl, pno. AFP 9781451424126.
P Taylor, Terry D. "Walk as Children of Light" from *Shine Your Light*. U, pno. CG CGA1361.
Wienhorst, Richard. "Amazing Grace." 2 pt, 2 fl/vln. ECS 4698.

Keyboard / Instrumental

P Organ, Anne Krentz. "You Are Mine" from *Piano Reflections on Hymns of Healing*. Pno. AFP 9781506448060.
Phillips, Craig. "Prelude on Slane" from *O Love, How Deep: Three Hymn Settings for Organ*. Org. MSM 10-240.
P ♬ Powell, Robert J. "Come, Follow Me, the Savior Spake" from *Mixtures: Hymn Preludes for Organ*. Org. AFP 9781451479553.
Schrader, Jack. "Amazing Grace" from *Amazing Grace: Blues Gospel Piano*. Pno. HOP 8138.

Handbell

Gross, William. "For God So Loved the World." 3 or 5 oct, L3. FTT 20455.

♫ Thompson, Karen. "The Summons." 3-5 oct, L3-. GIA G-8717.

P Waldrop, Tammy. "The GatheRing" from *Spring Ring!* 3-5 oct hb or hc, L1, L1+, L2-. CG CGB830. 2-3 oct. CGB829.

Sunday, March 22
Jonathan Edwards, teacher, missionary to American Indians, died 1758

Edwards was a minister in Connecticut and described as the greatest of the New England Puritan preachers. One of Edwards's most notable sermons found its way into contemporary anthologies of literature. In this sermon, "Sinners in the Hands of an Angry God," he spoke at length about hell. However, throughout the rest of his works and his preaching he had more to say about God's love than God's wrath. His personal experience of conversion came when he felt overwhelmed with a sense of God's majesty and grandeur, rather than a fear of hell. Edwards served a Puritan congregation, where he believed that only those who had been fully converted ought to receive communion; his congregation thought otherwise. Edwards left that congregation and carried out mission work among the Housatonic Indians of Massachusetts. He became president of the College of New Jersey, later to be known as Princeton University.

Tuesday, March 24
Oscar Arnulfo Romero, Bishop of El Salvador, martyr, died 1980

Romero is remembered for his advocacy on behalf of the poor in El Salvador, though it was not a characteristic of his early priesthood. After being appointed as archbishop of San Salvador, he preached against the political repression in his country. He and other priests and church workers were considered traitors for their bold stand for justice, especially defending the rights of the poor. After several years of threats to his life, Romero was assassinated while presiding at the eucharist. During the 1980s thousands died in El Salvador during political unrest.

Wednesday, March 25
Annunciation of Our Lord

Nine months before Christmas the church celebrates the annunciation. In Luke the angel Gabriel announces to Mary that she will give birth to the Son of God, and she responds, "Here am I, the servant of the Lord." Ancient scholars believed that March 25 was also the day on which creation began and was the date of Jesus' death on the cross. Thus, from the sixth to eighth centuries, March 25 was observed as New Year's Day in much of Christian Europe.

March 29, 2020
Fifth Sunday in Lent

In today's gospel Jesus reveals his power over death by raising Lazarus from the dead. The prophet Ezekiel prophesies God breathing new life into dry bones. To those in exile or living in the shadows of death, these stories proclaim God's promise of resurrection. In baptism we die with Christ that we might also be raised with him to new life. At the Easter Vigil we will welcome the newly baptized as we remember God's unfailing promise in our baptism.

Prayer of the Day

Almighty God, your Son came into the world to free us all from sin and death. Breathe upon us the power of your Spirit, that we may be raised to new life in Christ and serve you in righteousness all our days, through Jesus Christ, our Savior and Lord, who lives and reigns with you and the Holy Spirit, one God, now and forever.

Gospel Acclamation

I am the resurrection and the life; whoever believes in me will never die. (John 11:25, 26)

Readings and Psalm

Ezekiel 37:1-14

Ezekiel's vision of the valley of dry bones is a promise that Israel as a nation, though dead in exile, will live again in their land through God's life-giving spirit. Three times Israel is assured that through this vision they will know that "I am the LORD."

Psalm 130

I wait for you, O LORD; in your word is my hope. (Ps. 130:5)

Romans 8:6-11

For Paul, Christian spirituality entails living in the reality of the Holy Spirit. The driving force behind our actions and values is not our sinful desire for self-satisfaction but the very Spirit by which God raised Jesus from the dead and will also raise us from the dead.

John 11:1-45

Jesus is moved to sorrow when his friend Lazarus falls ill and dies. Then, in a dramatic scene, he calls his friend out of the tomb and restores him to life.

Preface   Lent

Color   Purple

Prayers of Intercession

The prayers are prepared locally for each occasion. The following examples may be adapted or used as appropriate.

Turning our hearts to God who is gracious and merciful, we pray for the church, the world, and all who are in need.
A brief silence.

God of life, bind your faithful people into one body. Enliven the church with your Spirit and bless the work of those who work for its renewal (*like Hans Nielsen Hauge, whom we commemorate today*). Accomplish your work of salvation in us and through us, for the sake of the world. Hear us, O God.
Your mercy is great.

God of life, you love the world you have made and you grieve when creation suffers. Restore polluted lands and waterways. Heal areas of the world ravaged by storms, floods, wildfires, droughts, or other natural disasters (*especially*). Bring all things to new life. Hear us, O God.
Your mercy is great.

God of life, show redemption to all who watch and wait with eager expectation: those longing for wars to cease, those waiting for immigration paperwork to finalize, those seeking election, and those in dire need of humanitarian relief. Come quickly with your hope. Hear us, O God.
Your mercy is great.

God of life, you weep with those who grieve. Unbind all who are held captive by anxiety, despair, or pain (*especially*). Fill us with compassion and empathy for those who struggle, and keep us faithful in prayer. Hear us, O God.
Your mercy is great.

God of life, we give thanks for opportunities for this congregation to collaborate with our community in caring for the needs of our neighbors. (*Particular ministry partnerships may be named.*) Strengthen our ties with other local congregations, agencies, and services. Hear us, O God.
Your mercy is great.

Here other intercessions may be offered.

God of life, you are our resurrection. We remember all those who have died and trust that, in you, they will live again (*especially*). Breathe new life into our dry bones, that we, too, might live with you forever. Hear us, O God.
Your mercy is great.

According to your steadfast love, O God, hear these and all our prayers as we commend them to you; through Christ our Lord. **Amen.**

Ideas for the Day

- Notice how little of this gospel text is about Jesus dealing with Lazarus. He addresses Lazarus in only one verse, John 11:43. In the rest of the text, Jesus is dealing with Lazarus's sisters or the community around him. So often it is said that funerals are for the living, not for the dead. At a funeral, the person who died is already in God's care. It is those who are living who need the reminder that God cares for them too. Amid questions and doubts—such as "Lord, if you had been here, my brother would not have died" (11:21, 32)—we need Jesus to interact with us, and he does. Jesus not only brings new life to Lazarus; he also brings new life to the sisters and the community—and to us. Jesus is Lord of the dead and the living.
- From 2014 to 2015, ABC aired a drama called *Resurrection*. The premise was that people's deceased loved ones had come back from the dead. Despite its title, the show misunderstood the biblical notion of resurrection. The resurrection that we receive through Christ is new life now and later. It is not people from the past appearing in the present, like in the TV show. Although many people wish that their loved ones would return like Lazarus from the grave or like the people in the TV show, we know that doesn't happen. However, we also know that death does not have the last word. Through the one who is the resurrection and the life, we have the promise of new life—even though we don't know what that life will look like. The raising of Lazarus can give us comfort because Jesus is stronger than death.
- Lauren Daigle's song "Come Alive (Dry Bones)" (from the album *How Can It Be*, Centricity, 2015) is based on today's first reading from Ezekiel. She puts this text into a modern-day prayer, calling for God's breath to breathe upon us. It is also a song about having the courage to proclaim the good news in the face of lies and a world that has turned away from God. Just as God commanded Ezekiel to "prophesy to these bones" (Ezek. 37:4), so God calls us to do the same in our world.

Connections with Creation

A clear-eyed look at the reality of desolation and death is essential for both our lectionary passages and our own ecological moment. The prophet Ezekiel contemplates the seemingly hopeless scene of a valley littered with the bones of his people. The story of Lazarus is the story of Mary and Martha's inability, despite their every attempt, to keep their brother from dying. Scientists warn that we are currently experiencing the sixth mass extinction event, an extinction of plant and animal life not seen for sixty-five million years. Our current geological age is being called the Anthropocene, because the effects of human culture have become the defining feature of Earth's future. Can the bones of a desecrated creation live? Can the bones of a human culture implicated in creation's desecration yet find a way forward? We celebrate the baptismal festival of Easter because we believe God is able to make it so.

Let the Children Come

Lent can feel like a time of waiting, especially for children. But Lent offers no visual cues, like Advent candles, to mark the passage of time week by week. The "buried" alleluia lies quietly hidden, perhaps forgotten in young minds or its absence too abstract to understand. Psalm 130 laments the endless waiting of God's people in exile: "My soul waits for the Lord more than those who keep watch for the morning" (Ps. 130:6). We feel Lent's exile from Easter joy, and we wonder when the return of Easter will find us once again. Take time today during worship to count the Sundays of Lent already lived through as a community. Count one, two, three, four, five! Lift up today as the last number of Lenten Sundays. Next week will be something else, Passion/Palm Sunday. Our wait is almost over.

Assembly Song
Gathering

Christ, the life of all the living ELW 339, LBW 97

Jesus lives, my sure defense ELW 621, LBW 340

Veni Sancte Spiritus ELW 406, WOV 686

Psalmody and Acclamations

Gelineau, Joseph. "Psalm 130" from ACYG.

Grotenhuis, Dale. "Out of the Depths I Cry to You." SATB, opt assembly, org. MSM 50-3015.

Pelz, Walter L. "Psalm 130." U, assembly, org. CG CGA980.

(GA) Farlee, Robert Buckley. "Let Your Steadfast Love." MSB1 S421 with proper verse for Lent 5.

Hymn of the Day

Jesus is a rock in a weary land ELW 333 *WEARY LAND*

Lord, thee I love with all my heart ELW 750, LBW 325 *HERZLICH LIEB*

The Word of God is source and seed ELW 506, WOV 658 *GAUDEAMUS DOMINO*

Offering

O blessed spring ELW 447, WOV 695, OBS 71

Tree of Life and awesome mystery ELW 334 (sts. 1-3, Lent 5)

Communion

I am the Bread of life ELW 485, WOV 702

Thee we adore, O Savior ELW 476, LBW 199

We who once were dead ELW 495, LBW 207

Sending

Restore in us, O God ELW 328, WOV 662
What wondrous love is this ELW 666, LBW 385

Additional Assembly Songs

In the bulb there is a flower LS 56
Let this season be ASG 19
Rich in promise OBS 75
⊕ Bell, John L. "O Christ, You Wept" from *When Grief Is Raw*. SATB. GIA G-4829.
⊕ Haitian trad./adapt. Andrew Donaldson. "Haitian Kyrie." SATB. andrewdonaldson.ca. Also from *Sing the Circle Wide: Songs of Faith from Around the World*. Kanata Centre for Worship and Global Song 9780973059359.
☼ Cash, Ed/Jonathan David Helser/Melissa Helser. "You Came (Lazarus)" from CCLI.
☼ Daigle, Lauren/Michael Farren. "Come Alive (Dry Bones)" from CCLI.
☼ Gungor, Michael. "When Death Dies." praisecharts.com.
☼ McMillan, John Mark. "Death in Reverse" from *Mercury & Lightning*. johnmarkmcmillan.com.
☼ Seay, Robbie. "Psalm 130 (I Wait)" from CCLI.
☼ Tibbs, John. "Swallowing Death, Breathing Life" from *Swallowing Death, Breathing Life*. johntibbsmusic .bandcamp.com.

Music for the Day
Choral

P Carter, John. "When I Survey the Wondrous Cross." SAB, pno. AFP 9781506452531.
P Cool, Jayne Southwick. "O Lord, I Call to You." SAB, pno, opt assembly. AFP 9781451479423.
P Fleming, Larry L. "Give Me Jesus" from *The Augsburg Choirbook*. SATB, a cap. AFP 9780800656782.
♬ Johnson, Kyle. "Jesus Is a Rock in a Weary Land." SATB, pno. MSM 50-6106.

Children's Choir

P Burrows, Mark. "Love Can Never End" from *Again, I Say Rejoice!* U/2 pt, pno/gtr. CG CGC56.
Pelz, Walter. "Psalm 130." U, org, opt assembly. CG CGA980.
P Scott, K. Lee. "Out of the Depths I Cry to Thee." 2 pt, kybd. AFP 9780800647322. Also in *Augsburg Easy Choirbook*, vol. 1. AFP 9780800676025.

Keyboard / Instrumental

P♬ Carter, John. "Jesus Is a Rock in a Weary Land" from *Spirituals for Piano*. Pno. AFP 9780800621698.
♬ Costello, Michael D. "Lord, Thee I Love with All My Heart" from *God Will Guide You: Five Hymn Arrangements for Organ*. Org. MSM 10-620.

P♬ Hansen, Sherri. "The Word of God Is Source and Seed" from *Piano Weavings*. Pno. AFP 9781451494129.
P Powell, Robert J. "Eternal Lord of Love, Behold Your Church" from *Our Cheerful Songs: Hymn Preludes for Organ*. Org. AFP 9781451486070.

Handbell

♬ Eithun, Sandra. "Lord, Thee I Love with All My Heart." 3-6 oct hb, opt 3-6 oct hc, tpt. L2+. CPH 977677.
Moats, William. "In the Shadow of the Cross." 3-5 oct hb, opt 3-5 oct hc, L2+. CG CGB821.
Morris, Hart. "Dry Bones" from 10 Essential Classics, vol. 1. 3-5 oct, L2. HOP 2831.

Sunday, March 29
Hans Nielsen Hauge, renewer of the church, died 1824

Hans Nielsen Hauge was a layperson who began preaching about "the living faith" in Norway and Denmark after a mystical experience that he believed called him to share the assurance of salvation with others. At the time, itinerant preaching and religious gatherings held without the supervision of a pastor were illegal, and Hauge was arrested several times. He also faced great personal suffering: his first wife died, and three of his four children died in infancy.

Tuesday, March 31
John Donne, poet, died 1631

This priest of the Church of England is commemorated for his poetry and spiritual writing. Most of his poetry was written before his ordination and is sacred and secular, intellectual and sensuous. He saw in his wife, Anne, glimpses of the glory of God and a human revelation of divine love. In 1615 he was ordained and seven years later he was named dean of St. Paul's Cathedral in London. By that time his reputation as a preacher was firmly in place. In his poem "Good Friday, 1613. Riding westward," he speaks of Jesus' death on the cross: "Who sees God's face, that is self life, must die; What a death were it then to see God die?"

Saturday, April 4
Benedict the African, confessor, died 1589

Born a slave on the island of Sicily, Benedict first lived as a hermit and labored as a plowman after he was freed. When the bishop of Rome ordered all hermits to attach themselves to a religious community, Benedict joined the Franciscans, where he served as a cook. Although he was illiterate, his fame as a

⊕ = global song   ♬ = relates to hymn of the day
☼ = praise song   P = available in Prelude Music Planner

confessor brought many visitors to the humble and holy cook, and he was eventually named superior of the community. A patron saint of African Americans, Benedict is remembered for his patience and understanding when confronted with racial prejudice and taunts.

April 5, 2020
Sunday of the Passion
Palm Sunday

Today, we encounter the paradox that defines our faith: Jesus Christ is glorified king and humiliated servant. We too are full of paradox: like Peter, we fervently desire to follow Christ, but find ourselves afraid, denying God. We wave palms in celebration today as Christ comes into our midst, and we follow with trepidation as his path leads to death on the cross. Amid it all we are invited into this paradoxical promise of life through Christ's broken body and outpoured love in a meal of bread and wine. We begin this week that stands at the center of the church year, anticipating the completion of God's astounding work.

Prayer of the Day

Everlasting God, in your endless love for the human race you sent our Lord Jesus Christ to take on our nature and to suffer death on the cross. In your mercy enable us to share in his obedience to your will and in the glorious victory of his resurrection, who lives and reigns with you and the Holy Spirit, one God, now and forever.

or

Sovereign God, you have established your rule in the human heart through the servanthood of Jesus Christ. By your Spirit, keep us in the joyful procession of those who with their tongues confess Jesus as Lord and with their lives praise him as Savior, who lives and reigns with you and the Holy Spirit, one God, now and forever.

or

O God of mercy and might, in the mystery of the passion of your Son you offer your infinite life to the world. Gather us around the cross of Christ, and preserve us until the resurrection, through Jesus Christ, our Savior and Lord, who lives and reigns with you and the Holy Spirit, one God, now and forever.

Gospel Acclamation

Christ humbled himself and became obedient to the point of death—even death on a cross. Therefore God also highly exalted him and gave him the name that is above every name. (Phil. 2:8-9)

Readings and Psalm

Procession with Palms: **Matthew 21:1-11**
Isaiah 50:4-9a

The servant of the Lord expresses absolute confidence in his final vindication, despite the fact that he has been struck and spit upon. This characteristic of the servant played an important role in the early church's understanding of the suffering, death, and resurrection of Jesus.

Psalm 31:9-16

Into your hands, O LORD, I commend my spirit. (Ps. 31:5)

Philippians 2:5-11

Paul uses an early Christian hymn to help us comprehend Jesus' obedient selflessness on the cross and how God has made Christ lord over all reality. The perspective of the cross becomes the way we rightly understand God, Christ, our own lives, and fellowship within the community of Christ.

Matthew 26:14—27:66 *or* **Matthew 27:11-54**

In fulfillment of scripture and obedience to God's will, Jesus goes to the cross so that a new covenant in his blood may bring forgiveness of sins. Even the soldiers who crucify him recognize him to be the Son of God.

Preface   Sunday of the Passion

Color   Scarlet *or* Purple

Prayers of Intercession

The prayers are prepared locally for each occasion. The following examples may be adapted or used as appropriate.

Turning our hearts to God who is gracious and merciful, we pray for the church, the world, and all who are in need.

A brief silence.

God of mercy, awaken your church to new proclamations of your faithfulness. By your Spirit, give us bold and joyful words to speak, that we sustain the weary with the message of your redemption. Hear us, O God.

Your mercy is great.

God of mercy, quiet the earth where it trembles and shakes. Protect vulnerable ecosystems, threatened habitats, and endangered species. Prosper the work of scientists, engineers, and researchers who find ways to restore creation to health and wholeness. Hear us, O God.

Your mercy is great.

God of mercy, drive away fear and anger that cause us to turn against one another. Give courage to leaders who seek liberation for the oppressed. Bring peace and hope to those who are in prison and those who face execution. Hear us, O God.

Your mercy is great.

God of mercy, send your saving help to all who suffer abuse, insult, discrimination, or contempt. Heal the wounded. Comfort the dying. Bring peace to those suffering chronic or terminal illness. Tend to all who cry out for relief (*especially*). Hear us, O God.

Your mercy is great.

God of mercy, we pray for all who will prepare and lead worship in this Holy Week. In all things, show us the ways that you call us to die to self, to live for you, and to give of ourselves for the sake of others. Hear us, O God.

Your mercy is great.

Here other intercessions may be offered.

God of mercy, when we breathe our last, you raise us to eternal life. With all your witnesses in heaven and on earth (*especially*), let us boldly confess the name of Jesus Christ, our resurrection and our hope. Hear us, O God.

Your mercy is great.

According to your steadfast love, O God, hear these and all our prayers as we commend them to you; through Christ our Lord.

Amen.

Ideas for the Day

- The duality of Palm Sunday and Passion Sunday can be emphasized by thinking of inside vs. outside. Many assemblies will start their Palm Sunday procession outside the worship space and perhaps even outside the building. This is a public display. However, once the assembly enters the worship space, it will hear the story of Jesus' passion. How often do we try to display the celebrations and joy in life while hiding the pain and suffering? For example, consider what people decide to post and not post on social media. How would our life of faith be different if we were more public about our suffering—and, more importantly, more public about the one who meets us in our suffering?

- In Leonardo da Vinci's famous painting of the Last Supper, the scene he captures is not the moment when Jesus says, "Take, eat; this is my body." Instead, he captures the moment when Jesus says, "Truly I tell you, one of you will betray me." Find this image online and look closely at it. All of the disciples are reacting to this accusation in their body language and facial expressions ("Surely not I, Lord?" [Matt. 26:22]). The disciples do not automatically think, "I wonder who he's talking about." Instead, they all realize that they are capable of betraying their teacher. (Notice in the painting that Judas is leaning away from Jesus but does not seem shocked like the other disciples. He knows Jesus is talking about him.) As today's texts move from "Hosanna!" ("Save us") to "Crucify him!" we see that we too are capable of turning on Jesus.

- The refrain of Mark Schultz's song "Love Has Come" connects to today's famous Christ hymn from Philippians 2: "Every knee shall bow, every tongue confess / That God is love and love has come for us all" (from the album *Come Alive*, Word Records, 2009). In our world, where love is about happy feelings and pleasant experiences, Paul's hymn shows us that real love is sacrificial. In his death on the cross, Jesus showed how that kind of love has come to us all.

Connections with Creation

The use of palms in procession on this Sunday links our worshiping communities to the geography of the palm-growing Holy Land. Alternatively, worship planners might consider cutting local leaves and branches from a sustainable source as a way of celebrating Jesus' incarnational entry into their local ecological realm. One congregation playfully calls their celebration "Pine Sunday," waving branches in procession cut from the surrounding conifer forest. As Jesus and his disciples celebrated Passover, we are reminded of the ways in which our liturgical celebrations locate us within Earth's cycles and seasons. Passover/Holy Week/Easter celebrations are springtime festivals (in the Northern Hemisphere), as the natural world bursts with new life. Christians in the southern parts of the world will lift up the ecological context of their celebrations in different (but no less rich) ways.

Let the Children Come

Children love a parade, and this day the whole assembly participates. The procession with palms, whether done outside the building, throughout the building, or inside the worship space, allows worshipers to walk and sing and wave their branches. Choose a hymn or song with an easily memorized refrain (ELW 344, MSB1 S423–S424), or, if outside, an ostinato hosanna that can be sung accompanied by hand-carried instruments (DATH 59, GS2 13, GS3 34). Then people do not need to look at printed words or music, and even those who do not read can join in the singing.

The reading of the passion narrative, using a variety of voices with readers stationed around the worship space, will engage the attention of children. Let them look around as the story unfolds. Sitting still is not the highest good. Consider breaking up the narrative with a simple sung refrain the children could easily learn.

Assembly Song
Gathering
All glory, laud, and honor ELW 344, LS 48, LBW 108
Jesus, I will ponder now ELW 345, LBW 115
Ride on, ride on in majesty! ELW 346, LBW 121

Psalmody and Acclamations
Gelineau, Joseph. "Psalm 31" from ACYG.
Schalk, Carl. "Antiphon for Psalm 31" from PATP. Use with ELW tone 9 in Dmin.
Sedio, Mark. "Psalm 31," Refrain 1, from PSCY.
(GA) Farlee, Robert Buckley. "Let Your Steadfast Love." MSB1 S421 with proper verse for Sunday of the Passion.

Hymn of the Day
A lamb goes uncomplaining forth ELW 340, LBW 105
AN WASSERFLÜSSEN BABYLON
Calvary ELW 354, TFF 85 *CALVARY*
O sacred head, now wounded ELW 351/352, LLC 342, LBW 116/117 *HERZLICH TUT MICH VERLANGEN*

Offering
Come to the table ELW 481, W&P 33
We place upon your table, Lord ELW 467, LBW 217

Communion
Beneath the cross of Jesus ELW 338, LBW 107
Jesus, remember me ELW 616, WOV 740, LLC 457
Were you there ELW 353, TFF 81, LLC 344, LBW 92

Sending
Go to dark Gethsemane ELW 347, LBW 109
Praise and thanks and adoration ELW 783, LBW 470

Additional Assembly Songs
Jerusalén, ciudad de Dios/Jerusalem, the city of God LLC 335, MSB1 S428
Mantos y palmas/Filled with excitement LLC 333, MSB1 S422,
⊕ Ho Lung, Richard. "Enter into Jerusalem" from *Lead Me, Guide Me* (2nd ed.). GIA G-7000.

⊕ = global song ♫ = relates to hymn of the day
☼ = praise song P = available in Prelude Music Planner

⊕ Tanzanian trad./arr. Patrick Matsikenyiri. "Sanna, sannanina" from *Africa Praise Songbook*. SATB. GBGMusik 1890569070.
☼ Brown, Brenton/Paul Baloche. "Hosanna (Praise Is Rising)" from CCLI.
☼ Kocian, James/Judi Tyler. "This Changes Everything" from *Love Will*. jameskocian.com.
☼ Lubben, Dave. "Save Us" from CCLI.
☼ Retherford, Will. "At Your Cross" from *Walk*. willretherford .com.

Music for the Day
Choral
P Engelsdorfer, Amy Lynne. "When I Survey the Wondrous Cross." SAB, pno. AFP 9781506422206.
Halls, David. "Hosanna to the Son of David" from *The New Oxford Easy Anthem Book*. SATB, org or kybd. OXF 9780193533189.
Pooler, Marie. "Hosanna" from *Unison and Two-part Anthems*. 2 pt, kybd. AFP 9780800648916.
Schütz, Heinrich. "Ehre sei Dir, Christe (Christ to You Be Honor)" from *Passion According to St. Matthew*. SATB, a cap. HAL 08596787.

Children's Choir
Anderson, Norma S. "The Walk to Calvary." U/2 pt, kybd. CG CGA739.
Burkhardt, Michael. "Hosanna." 2 pt, hb, bass inst (bsn/vc/ bass xyl). MSM 50-3754.
Gerike, Henry V. "Guide Me, Savior, through Your Passion." U, org, opt canon. GIA G-2767.

Keyboard / Instrumental
P ♫ Cherwien, David. "A Lamb Goes Uncomplaining Forth" from *Good Friday Reflections: Organ Meditations on Stations of the Cross*. Org. MSM 10-365.
P ♫ Raabe, Nancy M. "O Sacred Head, Now Wounded" from *Grace & Peace, Volume 2: Hymn Portraits for Piano*. Pno. AFP 9780800679019.
P ♫ Wilson, Terry D. "Calvary with They Crucified My Lord" from *Near the Cross: Piano Settings*. Pno. AFP 9781506448053.

Handbell
♫ Glasgow, Michael. "Dies irae." 3-7 oct hb, ob or C inst, opt 2 oct hc, L3-. CG CGB682.
♫ Ingram, Bill. "Passion Suite." 3 oct, L2. GIA G-6399.
♫ Tucker, Sondra. "Contemplation on Passion Chorale." 3-5 oct hb, opt 3 oct hc, L3. CG CGB1042.

April 6, 2020
Monday in Holy Week

During Holy Week some communities gather each day to meditate on Jesus' final days before his death on the cross. Today's gospel commemorates the anointing of Jesus by Mary, a foreshadowing of his death and burial. Isaiah speaks of the suffering servant who is a light for the nations and who faithfully brings forth justice. For Christians, Jesus' suffering is the path to resurrection and new life. We eagerly await the celebration of the great Three Days later this week.

Prayer of the Day

O God, your Son chose the path that led to pain before joy and to the cross before glory. Plant his cross in our hearts, so that in its power and love we may come at last to joy and glory, through Jesus Christ, our Savior and Lord, who lives and reigns with you and the Holy Spirit, one God, now and forever.

Gospel Acclamation

May I never boast of anything except the cross of our Lord Jesus Christ. (Gal. 6:14)

Readings and Psalm

Isaiah 42:1-9

God's servant is endowed with God's spirit in order to bring justice to the nations. The servant will not exercise authority boisterously or with violence, nor will weariness ever prevent the fulfilling of the servant's task. God's old promises have been fulfilled; the servant's new assignment is to bring light to the nations.

Psalm 36:5-11

All people take refuge under the shadow of your wings. (Ps. 36:7)

Hebrews 9:11-15

Prior to Christ, forgiveness was mediated through animal sacrifice. Christ came as the great high priest to establish a new covenant. Through his blood we are liberated from our sins and promised eternal life.

John 12:1-11

A few days after raising Lazarus from the dead, Jesus visits the man's home. Lazarus's sister Mary anoints the feet of Jesus with costly perfume.

Preface   Sunday of the Passion

Color   Scarlet *or* Purple

Monday, April 6
Albrecht Dürer, died 1528; Matthias Grünewald, died 1529; Lucas Cranach, died 1553; artists

These great German artists revealed through their work the mystery of salvation and the wonder of creation. Dürer's work reflected the apocalyptic spirit of his time. Though he remained a Roman Catholic, he was sympathetic to Martin Luther's reforming work. Grünewald's paintings are known for their dramatic forms, vivid colors, and depiction of light. Cranach's work includes many fine religious examples and several portraits of Martin Luther. Cranach was also widely known for his woodcuts.

April 7, 2020
Tuesday in Holy Week

As the great Three Days draw near, some communities gather each day of Holy Week for worship. Paul proclaims Christ crucified as the wisdom and power of God. Jesus speaks of the grain of wheat that falls into the earth and dies in order that it may bear fruit. We die with Christ in baptism that we may be raised with him to new life. We will celebrate this great mystery of death and resurrection at the Easter Vigil later this week.

Prayer of the Day

Lord Jesus, you have called us to follow you. Grant that our love may not grow cold in your service, and that we may not fail or deny you in the time of trial, for you live and reign with the Father and the Holy Spirit, one God, now and forever.

Gospel Acclamation

May I never boast of anything except the cross of our Lord Jesus Christ. (Gal. 6:14)

Readings and Psalm
Isaiah 49:1-7

Here the servant, identified as Israel, speaks for herself and describes her honored mission. Called before her birth like Jeremiah and John the Baptist, the servant is not only to restore Israel. The servant's ultimate assignment is to bring news of God's victory to the ends of the earth. God in faithfulness has chosen Israel for this task.

Psalm 71:1-14

From my mother's womb you have been my strength. (Ps. 71:6)

1 Corinthians 1:18-31

To the world, the word of the cross is silly, because it claims God's power is most fully revealed in complete, utter weakness. For those who are being saved, however, the word of the cross unveils God's true wisdom, power, and source of true life.

John 12:20-36

Knowing that his hour has come, Jesus announces that his death will be an exaltation. When he is lifted up in death, drawing people to new life, God's name will be glorified.

Preface   Sunday of the Passion

Color   Scarlet *or* Purple

April 8, 2020
Wednesday in Holy Week

This day was formerly called "Spy Wednesday," an allusion to the gospel reading, in which Judas is identified as the betrayer of Jesus. As Jesus endured the suffering of the cross, we are called to run the race of life with perseverance, confident of the joy to come. In the Three Days, which begin tomorrow evening, we will journey with Christ from darkness to light, from captivity to freedom, from death to life.

Prayer of the Day

Almighty God, your Son our Savior suffered at human hands and endured the shame of the cross. Grant that we may walk in the way of his cross and find it the way of life and peace, through Jesus Christ, our Savior and Lord, who lives and reigns with you and the Holy Spirit, one God, now and forever.

Gospel Acclamation

May I never boast of anything except the cross of our Lord Jesus Christ. (Gal. 6:14)

Readings and Psalm
Isaiah 50:4-9a

The servant of the Lord expresses absolute confidence in his final vindication, despite the fact that he has been struck and spit upon. This characteristic of the servant played an important role in the early church's understanding of the suffering, death, and resurrection of Jesus.

Psalm 70

Be pleased, O God, to deliver me. (Ps. 70:1)

Hebrews 12:1-3

In the way of the cross, Jesus has blazed the trail for our salvation. With faithful perseverance, we follow in his footsteps.

John 13:21-32

At the last supper, Jesus identifies Judas Iscariot as the one who will betray him, and sends him on his way.

Preface   Sunday of the Passion

Color   Scarlet *or* Purple

The Three Days

Preparing for the Three Days

Preaching

These are the days to proclaim, not explain. There are no words that will explain the complex series of texts, actions, and rites that bridge the church's baptismal preparation of Lent and the mystery of Easter's dying and rising. The Three Days are not meant as a passion play, but rather as the assembly's annual encounter with the deepest mysteries of faith, laid out before them, celebrated. Rather than reenacting these desperate, dying moments of Christ and his Passover from death to life, the preacher's amazing privilege and responsibility is to point and proclaim: To point to the Savior bent to wash his friends' feet and proclaim servanthood. To point to the Savior breaking loaf and lifting cup and proclaim remembrance poured out. To point to the altar's stripping and proclaim surrender. To point to the cross and proclaim a love that knows no limits, not even death.

The *mandatum* for which this holiest of Thursdays gets its name is perhaps the centering point for the preacher's proclamation of the Three Days. To "love one another [just] as I have loved you" (John 13:34) is both the law and the gospel of it all, the dying and the rising. It can never be done in human life apart from Christ, but that still remains the mandate. Because it cannot be done, we enter deeply into the remembrance, through this sacred Holy Week journey, that Christ has done it for us, making these liturgies and their pointed proclamation the most compelling story that we can tell as preachers of the gospel.

Good Friday is not a funeral for Jesus but rather, as the Passion from the Gospel of John would lead us, a triumph of the cross. In John's version, Jesus' own words from the cross are a two-edged, law-and-gospel sword. "It is finished" (John 19:30) is Christ's last, triumphant cry, to be sure. But echoing the completion of creation in Genesis 2:2, Christ's cry is also a birth announcement of the new creation. "It is finished," Christ proclaims, and so should we. All things are made new.

The Easter Vigil's compelling recap of God at work in the epic of God's people allows the congregation to tell, to hear, and to remember the sweeping story of its very own salvation. God comes now in the Spirit's breath across the waters, in the saving ark, in the revival of dry bones, and in men and women tried by fire for their stands of justice. These come to fruition on the promised land side of baptism with Paul's summary of the baptismal mystery from Romans 6 and the first telling of the resurrection.

Intercessory Prayer

If we think of Lent as a time of fasting and preparation for the salvation that God in Christ is accomplishing for the whole world, then we enter into the great Three Days ready to behold such holy, mysterious work. The people of the exodus awaited their promised deliverance from slavery by eating a meal, already dressed for travel, as though they were certain that their salvation would come that night. We too gather to listen, eat, and pray with trust that our deliverance from sin, death, and all that separates us from God is also near. Like our ancestors, we call on the name of the Lord, we lift up the cup of salvation, and we eat of Christ, the Lamb of God who takes away the sin of the world. In his life giving and his death enduring, we witness the faithful service and love that save us and shape us into the body of people who reflect Christ's life into the world.

Through our liturgy of the Three Days, our praying speaks urgency: the urgency of the world seeking God's deliverance and the urgency of Christ's saving act. We know that Christ understands the pain of the world when he cries out on the cross to a God who seemingly forsakes him. Who are the people on whose behalf we might cry out? Who are the people who feel that God has forsaken them in time of death or desperate need? God is revealed as the caretaker, the midwife, the wet nurse of those who are forsaken, and God is made known right in the depths of suffering, not apart from it.

Present in our Good Friday liturgy are already some prayers that shed light on the urgency and wide expanse that our praying encompasses during this primary observance of the church. The Bidding Prayer (*ELW Leaders Edition*, pp. 636–638) encourages us to imagine all different kinds of people who may be seeking salvation and to ask for God's revealing among them, including people of other faiths or no faith at all. Although we might be cautious in speaking to such neighbors about our own religious beliefs and life, we are still encouraged to ask God's salvation for them, trusting that there is no barrier, not even death, that can contain the abundant life and salvation Christ gives.

The Solemn Reproaches (*ELW Leaders Edition*, pp. 639–641) also offer ancient words that gather all the voices of the faithful in the Trisagion: "Holy God, holy and mighty, holy and immortal, have mercy on us." This spoken or sung response (see ELW 159–161) can be something that people learn by heart through repeated praying during the Three Days. It can also become a verse they incorporate into their personal prayer life at home. As the urgency for God's salvation builds into the Easter Vigil, the prayers with Trisagion could be used in the section of the Vigil leading up to the announcement of Christ's resurrection. Such petitions may be used as responses to the readings, employing the imagery of Hebrew scripture.

After the announcement of the resurrection during the Easter Vigil, and on Easter morning and Easter evening, we remember that our life in Christ has been revealed. Our praying moves out from Jerusalem, into Galilee, and beyond to all nations. The great need of the world continues to be lifted up, but now it is mixed with a feeling of great joy at what God in Christ has accomplished.

Assembly Song

Like the preacher's imperative described above, the task of assembly song during the Three Days is to point and to proclaim. This is the center of our common worship life, the source from which Christian identity flows and expands outward like the widening scope of Good Friday prayers. These days brim with ritual actions that fully engage all of the body's senses. How can we sing the importance of these days for the rest of the church year, and for everything else in our lives? What texts and melodies can hold all that we bring and pour into them across these days? What treasures from the past help us remember the depth and breadth of the salvation stories we hear at the Vigil of Easter? What new songs crackle like the new fire? What melodies and harmonies help write the command to love deep in our hearts?

The ritual actions of the Three Days—footwashing, stripping of the altar, the procession of the cross, movements around fire and font—present a number of logistical considerations for assembly singing. It may be useful to consider shorter, repetitive songs or refrains (ELW 350, 354) or call-and-response songs that can be taught by rote, that are easily committed to memory, or that are already familiar in the assembly. Be especially mindful of choices that assume whether or not the assembly will carry bulletins, hymnals, or nothing at all from place to place during these services. What texts, melodies, and rubrics in the assembly's bulletin will support their singing?

For Maundy Thursday, consult the "love" and "Maundy Thursday" portions of the topical index of hymns for options best suited to the assembly's movements, space, and other leadership considerations. On Good Friday, seek choices that proclaim the triumph of the cross with appropriate solemnity, remembering that the day's visual starkness—with paraments, flowers, and other adornments removed from the worship space—will be served well by a complementary aural starkness: less is more. Seek texts that embrace and give strong voice to the paradoxes and mysteries of these days and their central symbols, such as "Sing, my tongue" (ELW 355/356), "There

in God's garden" (ELW 342), or Sylvia Dunstan's "You, Lord, are both Lamb and Shepherd" (GTG 274), which is sometimes referred to by its Latin subtitle, "Christus paradox." For some, it may be meaningful to intersperse chorale or other hymn and song stanzas throughout the Passion gospel as was customary in musical settings from the time of Bach.

At the Vigil of Easter, consider shorter call-and-response songs for the sung responses to the readings that may be more conducive to singing with reduced lighting as is practiced in many places. In addition to the hymnal, consult the *Music Sourcebook for Lent and the Three Days*, which, in addition to providing several options to accompany the rituals of the Three Days, presents musical responses for all twelve readings of the Vigil of Easter. It may also be helpful to review the guidance and suggestions in sources such as *Keeping Time* (pp. 93–122), *Worship Guidebook for Lent and the Three Days* (pp. 93–182), and *Evangelical Lutheran Worship* (pp. 258–270). Together, these resources remind musicians and assembly song leaders that the overarching pattern of the Three Days is inherently dramatic, that we can trust the wisdom of the rituals we have inherited to help us point to, proclaim, and sing of the Christ who loves, serves, gathers all to himself, and passes from death to life.

Worship Space

The placement of furniture and decor during the Three Days can greatly enhance the assembly's liturgies. The scriptural texts will take the environment through Christ's crucifixion, burial, and resurrection, making this the central time of year for the church's practices and beliefs. There will be furniture moving, additions to decor, and changing of liturgical colors in an already very busy time at church. It is important to recruit help and have a plan so the changes can be made smoothly.

Some of the images during the Three Days are from Old Testament stories about creation, the flood, the deliverance at the Red Sea, the deliverance of Jonah, and the valley of dry bones. Featuring the stories through art is a way to set the climate for worship. Children can participate in such demonstrations through a Lenten art project, listening to each biblical story and then illustrating it with paint on newsprint. The students home in on an image from the scriptural account. Then the paintings become fine-tuned, ultimately reproduced on high-quality paper. An experienced artist incorporates the students' paintings into large murals, each representing one story. The murals then are hung in the worship space. During the Vigil of Easter, each can be spotlighted in the darkened room for dramatic effect during the corresponding reading. The murals can be displayed through the Easter season in a prominent place.

One must plan for furniture placement for footwashing, the eucharist meal, stripping of the altar, baptisms, and more, keeping in mind how darkness and light can be incorporated into each service. The focus in the space can be the barren table, the cross, or the baptismal font. If the nave's cross has a drape of fabric or a vase filled with bare branches, plan how these will be changed through the Three Days and into Easter.

Consider a worship binder for the Three Days, perhaps covered in exquisite fabric, to be used by the presider. Decide on vesture for the catechumenates who will be baptized during the Easter Vigil. Present the paschal candle at the font in a place of honor. One may decide to use more candles to represent the catechumenates and which can remain near the font until Pentecost.

Art images proclaiming the mystery of dying and rising can be displayed near the entrance to the worship space. If projected images are used in the space, consider showing both traditional and modern works of fine art during the liturgies, such as to accompany the readings. Public domain digital fine art is obtainable for projected images and service booklets. Consider using decor authentic to the community. Expand the use of visuals to include the global community of faith, always mindful to use such material in ways that are authentic and respectful.

While purple is the color used in Lent, scarlet can be added on Passion Sunday. Palm branches can also be used effectively in the surroundings on Passion Sunday. As the community enters the nave at Easter, the colors will be gold and white, and Easter's opulence will be readily observed.

Throughout the Three Days, provide a thoughtful and beautiful environment for worshipers. Make best decisions for the space, taking into consideration the scale of the room and the amount of time the environment team has to make changes.

Seasonal Checklist

- Review the liturgies for Maundy Thursday, Good Friday, and the Vigil of Easter in *Evangelical Lutheran Worship* (Assembly Edition, pp. 258–270; Leaders Edition, including the Notes on the Services, pp. 628–653 and 36–42).
- Prepare a detailed leaders book for worship leaders for all the Three Days liturgies, including all texts and music. Place them in three-ring binders (ceremonial binders are available from Augsburg Fortress). Highlight speaking parts and instructions for each worship leader in individual copies.
- Create worship folders for these services, or a single booklet-style worship folder for Maundy Thursday, Good Friday and the Easter Vigil. One booklet will illustrate that these services are one. Order preprinted covers as needed. For tips on preparing excellent worship folders, consult *Leading Worship Matters: A Sourcebook for Preparing Worship Leaders* (Augsburg Fortress, 2013, pp. 268–272).

- Arrange rehearsals for all the liturgies of the Three Days. These unique services must be remembered and practiced each year, even by seasoned worship leaders.
- Equip and inform (and thank!) altar guild members for their work in these busy days.
- Publicize Holy Week and Easter services in local newspapers, your church's website, and through social media.
- Determine how many footwashing stations your assembly will need on Maundy Thursday.
- If you are going to strip the altar on Maundy Thursday, do theater-style blocking and plan and practice all the movements and actions ahead of time. Practice at least once with the lights as dim as you plan on them being at the time. This is especially important for musicians who may be singing or playing as the altar is stripped.
- Arrange for a thorough cleaning of the worship space between Maundy Thursday and the Easter Vigil.
- Purchase a new paschal candle and new congregational handheld candles.
- If there will be baptisms of children and/or adults at the Easter Vigil (or on Easter Sunday), see the many suggestions in *Washed and Welcome: A Baptismal Sourcebook* and *Go Make Disciples: An Invitation to Baptismal Living* (Augsburg Fortress 2010, 2012).
- Determine the communion distribution procedure for larger liturgies and ensure that adequate amounts of elements are available. Provide clear instructions to ushers, communion ministers, and the altar guild.
- Make arrangements for adequate seating, along with additional worship books if needed for larger assemblies on Easter Sunday.
- Make arrangements for the church office to be closed and all staff to have a paid day off on Easter Monday.

Worship Texts for the Three Days

MAUNDY THURSDAY

Confession and Forgiveness

Friends in Christ, in this Lenten season we have heard our Lord's call to struggle against sin, death, and the devil—all that keeps us from loving God and each other. This is the struggle to which we were called at baptism. [We have shared this discipline of Lent with new brothers and sisters in Christ who will be baptized at the Easter Vigil.]

Within the community of the church, God never wearies of forgiving sin and giving the peace of reconciliation. On this night let us confess our sin against God and our neighbor, and enter the celebration of the great Three Days reconciled with God and with one another.

Silence is kept for reflection and self-examination.

Most merciful God,
we confess that we are captive to sin
and cannot free ourselves.
We have sinned against you in thought, word, and deed,
by what we have done and by what we have left undone.
We have not loved you with our whole heart;
we have not loved our neighbors as ourselves.
For the sake of your Son, Jesus Christ,
have mercy on us.
Forgive us, renew us, and lead us,
so that we may delight in your will
and walk in your ways,
to the glory of your holy name. Amen.

God, who is rich in mercy, loved us
even when we were dead in sin,
and made us alive together with Christ.
By grace you have been saved.
In the name of + Jesus Christ, your sins are forgiven.
Almighty God strengthen you with power
through the Holy Spirit,
that Christ may live in your hearts through faith.
Amen.

Offering Prayer

God of glory,
receive these gifts and the offering of our lives.
As Jesus was lifted up from the earth,
draw us to your heart in the midst of this world,
that all creation may be brought from bondage to freedom,
from darkness to light, and from death to life;
through Jesus Christ, our Savior and Lord.
Amen.

Invitation to Communion

Come to Jesus, our host and our meal.

Prayer after Communion

Lord Jesus, in a wonderful sacrament
you strengthen us with the saving power
of your suffering, death, and resurrection.
May this sacrament of your body and blood
so work in us that the fruits of your redemption
will show forth in the way we live,
for you live and reign with the Father and the Holy Spirit,
one God, now and forever.
Amen.

VIGIL OF EASTER

Greeting

The grace of our Lord Jesus Christ, the love of God,
and the communion of the Holy Spirit be with you all.
And also with you.

Sisters and brothers in Christ, on this most holy night when our
Savior Jesus Christ passed from death to life, we gather with
the church throughout the world in vigil and prayer. This is the
passover of Jesus Christ. Through light and the word, through
water and oil, bread and wine, we proclaim Christ's death and
resurrection, share Christ's triumph over sin and death, and
await Christ's coming again in glory.

Offering Prayer

God of glory,
receive these gifts and the offering of our lives.
As Jesus was lifted up from the earth,
draw us to your heart in the midst of this world,
that all creation may be brought from bondage to freedom,
from darkness to light, and from death to life;
through Jesus Christ, our Savior and Lord.
Amen.

Invitation to Communion

Come to the banquet. Behold the risen Christ.

Prayer after Communion

Life-giving God,
in the mystery of Christ's resurrection
you send light to conquer darkness,
water to give new life,
and the bread of heaven to nourish your people.
Send us forth as witnesses to Jesus' resurrection,
that we may show your glory to all the world;
through the same Jesus Christ, our risen Lord.
Amen.

Blessing

May God who has brought us from death to life
fill you with great joy.
Almighty God, Father, ✛ Son, and Holy Spirit,
bless you now and forever.
Amen.

Dismissal

Alleluia! Christ is risen.
Christ is risen indeed. Alleluia!
Go in peace. Share the good news. Alleluia!
Thanks be to God. Alleluia!

Worship texts for Easter Day and Easter Evening begin on page 168.

Seasonal Rites for the Three Days

"The Jews" in John's Passion

On Good Friday, the many churches around the world that are restoring the great Three Days proclaim the Passion from John 18–19, and contemporary Christians are rightly concerned about how the fourth gospel describes "the Jews." Pastors, church musicians, and parish educators may find these comments and this emendation of the New Revised Standard Version of John's Passion helpful.[1]

About the evangelist: The author of the Gospel according to John was a Jewish Christian. By the year 100, about when the gospel was composed, those who accepted Jesus as the Messiah and Son of God and those who did not were separating into two distinct religious communities that became Christianity and post-biblical Judaism. In the Johannine community, which was probably located in present-day Turkey, the relationship between these two groups was antagonistic.[2] So, although honoring the Jewish tradition, the evangelist is critical of those local Jews—mostly Pharisees—who did not in the 90s accept Jesus as the embodiment of the Torah and the replacement of the destroyed temple. The evangelist has backdated these diaspora Jews to those in Jerusalem in the 30s and designates this group with the Greek noun *Ioudaioi*.

About *Ioudaioi*: The word *Ioudaioi* is literally "the Judeans," that is, people currently or originally residents of Judea who shared a common history and religion. Some biblical scholars urge that "Judeans" is the best English rendering of the Johannine designation.[3] During medieval times, Middle English dropped the "d" in "Judean," producing our word "Jew."[4] Thus, the English language suggests two different entities, Judeans and Jews, and this linguistic situation much complicates our reception of John 18–19.

About the historicity of John 18–19: The evangelist engaged in some generalizations and exaggerations. Thus, while blaming the Pharisees for Jesus' capture, the evangelist describes the Pharisee Nicodemus as a follower of Jesus.

Furthermore, despite a popular misperception that the gospels are historically accurate narratives, John's gospel includes many details that reflect and describe the year 100 rather than the year 30, and much historical data—for example, the precise political role of the Sanhedrin in the 30s—is unknown to us.[5] Thus, when the evangelist writes of "the Jews," a careful reader will ask, Which Jews, when? Biblical scholars agree that only a small number of Judeans in the 30s, probably mostly Sadducees, would have been somehow involved in Jesus' execution.

About contemporary English Bible translations: In the New Revised Standard Version of the Bible, which attempted a relatively close translation of the Greek into English, chapters 18–19 cite "the Jews" twenty-one times. The word refers variously to an assembled crowd (for example, 19:7), the adherents of a religion (19:31), the temple authorities (18:12), and the residents of the province of Judea (19:20).[6] Sometimes the referent is unclear (for example, 18:31). Several Bible translations sometimes replace "the Jews" with wording that more explicitly designates which Jews the narrative is referring to. In 19:7, Today's English Version and the Contemporary English Version write "the crowd." In 19:31, the TEV writes "the Jewish authorities," and in 19:38, the CEV writes "the Jewish leaders."

About contemporary English: To further complicate our translation task, our noun "Jews" has many referents: adherents of the religion of Judaism; members of a historic ethnicity; participants, by birth or choice, in a cultural community; subjects of an ancient religious and ethnic nation-state; even citizens of the State of Israel. An ethnic Jew may be a practicing Christian; an observant participant of Judaism may be of any ethnicity. Some usage replaces the noun "Jew" with the adjective "Jewish." The word has been used as an anti-Semitic slur.

So: Given the various referents of "the Jews" in the Gospel of John and its many meanings in our speech, the proclamation of John's Passion on Good Friday may prove a stumbling block. The hope is that, as always, catechesis and preaching will assist believers in receiving the good news of Jesus Christ for their lives in, with, and under the words of the Bible, which always proclaims God's word in ancient cultural speech. To minimize misunderstandings on Good Friday and to counteract possible anti-Semitism, the following emendation of the NRSV John

---

1 For background to the following considerations, see Andrew Chester, "The Jews of Judaea and Galilee," pp. 9–26, John Barclay, "The Jews in the Diaspora," pp. 27–40, and D. Moody Smith, "John," pp. 96–111, in *Early Christian Thought in Its Jewish Context*, ed. John Barclay and John Sweet (Cambridge: Cambridge University Press, 1996).

2 Philip F. Esler, *The First Christians in Their Social Worlds* (New York: Routledge, 1994), 84–86.

3 Philip A. Harland, *Dynamics of Identity in the World of the Early Christians* (New York: T & T Clark, 2009), 14. See, for example, David Bentley Hart, *The New Testament: A Translation* (New Haven: Yale University Press, 2017), 210–14.

4 See the entry "Jew" in the *Oxford English Dictionary* (New York: Oxford University Press, 1971).

5 Raymond E. Brown, *The Gospel According to John*, vol. 2 (Garden City, NY: Doubleday & Company, 1970), 787–803, and 814–962, passim.

6 A somewhat different listing is in "The Jews," *Worship Guidebook for Lent and the Three Days* (Minneapolis: Augsburg Fortress, 2009), 127.

18–19 attempts to clarify who in each episode of the narrative is meant by "the Jews." Substitutions are denoted in italics. This proposal comes with awareness that any such rendering of the Greek *Ioudaioi* necessarily involves interpretation of the narrative, yet with no presumption of historical accuracy.

Finally, about liturgical proclamation: It is never pastorally wise to distribute a printed biblical text to the assembly and then to proclaim a different translation; the result can be worshipers speculating about the disparity, rather than receiving the word of God. Thus, please ensure that, if a printed text is provided, it corresponds precisely to the proclaimed text.

Gail Ramshaw
Liturgical Scholar

The Passion according to John, emended: John 18:1—19:42

[1][Jesus] went out with his disciples across the Kidron valley to a place where there was a garden, which he and his disciples entered. [2]Now Judas, who betrayed him, also knew the place, because Jesus often met there with his disciples. [3]So Judas brought a detachment of soldiers together with police from the chief priests and the Pharisees, and they came there with lanterns and torches and weapons. [4]Then Jesus, knowing all that was to happen to him, came forward and asked them, "Whom are you looking for?" [5]They answered, "Jesus of Nazareth." Jesus replied, "I am he." Judas, who betrayed him, was standing with them. [6]When Jesus said to them, "I am he," they stepped back and fell to the ground. [7]Again he asked them, "Whom are you looking for?" And they said, "Jesus of Nazareth." [8]Jesus answered, "I told you that I am he. So if you are looking for me, let these men go." [9]This was to fulfill the word that he had spoken, "I did not lose a single one of those whom you gave me." [10]Then Simon Peter, who had a sword, drew it, struck the high priest's slave, and cut off his right ear. The slave's name was Malchus. [11]Jesus said to Peter, "Put your sword back into its sheath. Am I not to drink the cup that the Father has given me?"

[12]So the soldiers, their officer, and the *temple* police arrested Jesus and bound him. [13]First they took him to Annas, who was the father-in-law of Caiaphas, the high priest that year. [14]Caiaphas was the one who had advised the Jews that it was better to have one person die for the people.

[15]Simon Peter and another disciple followed Jesus. Since that disciple was known to the high priest, he went with Jesus into the courtyard of the high priest, [16]but Peter was standing outside at the gate. So the other disciple, who was known to the high priest, went out, spoke to the woman who guarded the gate, and brought Peter in. [17]The woman said to Peter, "You are not also one of this man's disciples, are you?" He said, "I am not." [18]Now the slaves and the police had made a charcoal fire because it was cold, and they were standing around it and warming themselves. Peter also was standing with them and warming himself.

[19]Then the high priest questioned Jesus about his disciples and about his teaching. [20]Jesus answered, "I have spoken openly to the world; I have always taught in synagogues and in the temple, where all the *Jewish people* come together. I have said nothing in secret. [21]Why do you ask me? Ask those who heard what I said to them; they know what I said." [22]When he had said this, one of the police standing nearby struck Jesus on the face, saying, "Is that how you answer the high priest?" [23]Jesus answered, "If I have spoken wrongly, testify to the wrong. But if I have spoken rightly, why do you strike me?" [24]Then Annas sent him bound to Caiaphas the high priest.

[25]Now Simon Peter was standing and warming himself. They asked him, "You are not also one of his disciples, are you?" He denied it and said, "I am not." [26]One of the slaves of the high priest, a relative of the man whose ear Peter had cut off, asked, "Did I not see you in the garden with him?" [27]Again Peter denied it, and at that moment the cock crowed.

[28]Then they took Jesus from Caiaphas to Pilate's headquarters. It was early in the morning. They themselves did not enter the headquarters, so as to avoid ritual defilement and to be able to eat the Passover. [29]So Pilate went out to them and said, "What accusation do you bring against this man?" [30]They answered, "If this man were not a criminal, we would not have handed him over to you." [31]Pilate said to them, "Take him yourselves and judge him according to your law." The *Jewish authorities* replied, "We are not permitted to put anyone to death." [32](This was to fulfill what Jesus had said when he indicated the kind of death he was to die.)

[33]Then Pilate entered the headquarters again, summoned Jesus, and asked him, "Are you the King of the Jews?" [34]Jesus answered, "Do you ask this on your own, or did others tell you about me?" [35]Pilate replied, "I am not a Jew, am I? Your own nation and the chief priests have handed you over to me. What

have you done?" [36]Jesus answered, "My kingdom is not from this world. If my kingdom were from this world, my followers would be fighting to keep me from being handed over to the *Jewish authorities*. But as it is, my kingdom is not from here." [37]Pilate asked him, "So you are a king?" Jesus answered, "You say that I am a king. For this I was born, and for this I came into the world, to testify to the truth. Everyone who belongs to the truth listens to my voice." [38]Pilate asked him, "What is truth?"

After he had said this, he went out to the *crowd* again and told them, "I find no case against him. [39]But you have a custom that I release someone for you at the Passover. Do you want me to release for you the King of the Jews?" [40]They shouted in reply, "Not this man, but Barabbas!" Now Barabbas was a bandit.

[19:1]Then Pilate took Jesus and had him flogged. [2]And the soldiers wove a crown of thorns and put it on his head, and they dressed him in a purple robe. [3]They kept coming up to him, saying, "Hail, King of the Jews!" and striking him on the face. [4]Pilate went out again and said to them, "Look, I am bringing him out to you to let you know that I find no case against him." [5]So Jesus came out, wearing the crown of thorns and the purple robe. Pilate said to them, "Here is the man!" [6]When the chief priests and the *temple* police saw him, they shouted, "Crucify him! Crucify him!" Pilate said to them, "Take him yourselves and crucify him; I find no case against him." [7]The *crowd* answered him, "We have a law, and according to that law he ought to die because he has claimed to be the Son of God."

[8]Now when Pilate heard this, he was more afraid than ever. [9]He entered his headquarters again and asked Jesus, "Where are you from?" But Jesus gave him no answer. [10]Pilate therefore said to him, "Do you refuse to speak to me? Do you not know that I have power to release you, and power to crucify you?" [11]Jesus answered him, "You would have no power over me unless it had been given you from above; therefore the one who handed me over to you is guilty of a greater sin." [12]From then on Pilate tried to release him, but the *crowd* cried out, "If you release this man, you are no friend of the emperor. Everyone who claims to be a king sets himself against the emperor."

[13]When Pilate heard these words, he brought Jesus outside and sat on the judge's bench at a place called The Stone Pavement, or in Hebrew Gabbatha. [14]Now it was the day of Preparation for the Passover; and it was about noon. He said to the *crowd*, "Here is your King!" [15]They cried out, "Away with him! Away with him! Crucify him!" Pilate asked them, "Shall I crucify your King?" The chief priests answered, "We have no king but the emperor." [16]Then he handed him over to them to be crucified.

So they took Jesus; [17]and carrying the cross by himself, he went out to what is called The Place of the Skull, which in Hebrew is called Golgotha. [18]There they crucified him, and with him two others, one on either side, with Jesus between them. [19]Pilate also had an inscription written and put on the cross. It read, "Jesus of Nazareth, the King of the Jews." [20]Many of the *Judeans* read this inscription, because the place where Jesus was crucified was near the city; and it was written in Hebrew, in Latin, and in Greek. [21]Then the chief priests of the *temple* said to Pilate, "Do not write, 'The King of the Jews,' but, 'This man said, I am King of the Jews.'" [22]Pilate answered, "What I have written I have written." [23]When the soldiers had crucified Jesus, they took his clothes and divided them into four parts, one for each soldier. They also took his tunic; now the tunic was seamless, woven in one piece from the top. [24]So they said to one another, "Let us not tear it, but cast lots for it to see who will get it." This was to fulfill what the scripture says,

"They divided my clothes among themselves,
and for my clothing they cast lots."

[25]And that is what the soldiers did.

Meanwhile, standing near the cross of Jesus were his mother, and his mother's sister, Mary the wife of Clopas, and Mary Magdalene. [26]When Jesus saw his mother and the disciple whom he loved standing beside her, he said to his mother, "Woman, here is your son." [27]Then he said to the disciple, "Here is your mother." And from that hour the disciple took her into his own home.

[28]After this, when Jesus knew that all was now finished, he said (in order to fulfill the scripture), "I am thirsty." [29]A jar full of sour wine was standing there. So they put a sponge full of the wine on a branch of hyssop and held it to his mouth. [30]When Jesus had received the wine, he said, "It is finished." Then he bowed his head and gave up his spirit.

[31]Since it was the day of Preparation, the *Jewish authorities* did not want the bodies left on the cross during the sabbath, especially because that sabbath was a day of great solemnity. So they asked Pilate to have the legs of the crucified men broken and the bodies removed. [32]Then the soldiers came and broke the legs of the first and of the other who had been crucified

with him. [33]But when they came to Jesus and saw that he was already dead, they did not break his legs. [34]Instead, one of the soldiers pierced his side with a spear, and at once blood and water came out. [35](He who saw this has testified so that you also may believe. His testimony is true, and he knows that he tells the truth.) [36]These things occurred so that the scripture might be fulfilled, "None of his bones shall be broken." [37]And again another passage of scripture says, "They will look on the one whom they have pierced."

[38]After these things, Joseph of Arimathea, who was a disciple of Jesus, though a secret one because of his fear of the *temple authorities*, asked Pilate to let him take away the body of Jesus. Pilate gave him permission; so he came and removed his body. [39]Nicodemus, who had at first come to Jesus by night, also came, bringing a mixture of myrrh and aloes, weighing about a hundred pounds. [40]They took the body of Jesus and wrapped it with the spices in linen cloths, according to the burial custom of the Jews. [41]Now there was a garden in the place where he was crucified, and in the garden there was a new tomb in which no one had ever been laid. [42]And so, because it was the Jewish day of Preparation, and the tomb was nearby, they laid Jesus there.

Vigil of Easter: Creation
Genesis 1:1—2:4a

Preparation

The three readers are equal voices and should stand together. Inspiration for this reading can be found in the Rubilev icon of the Holy Trinity, also called the Visitation to Abraham. While the readers sometimes are the voice of God, all three are messengers of the word of God at creation. Emphasis is placed on certain words and phrases by all three speaking in unison.

Script

1: A reading from Genesis.

1: In the beginning when God created the heavens and the earth, the earth was a formless void and darkness covered the face of the deep, while a

All: wind

1: from God swept over the face of the waters. Then God said,

2: Let there be light;

3: and there was light. And God saw that the light was

All: good;

3: and God separated the light from the darkness.

2: God called the light Day, and the darkness God called Night.

1: And there was evening

2: and there was morning,

3: the first day.

1: And God said,

2: Let there be a dome in the midst of the waters, and let it separate the waters from the waters.

3: So God made the dome and separated the waters that were under the dome from the waters that were above the dome.

2: And it was so.

1: God called the dome

All: Sky.

1: And there was evening

2: and there was morning,

3: the second day.

1: And God said,

2: Let the waters under the sky be gathered together into one place, and let the dry land appear.

3: And it was so.

1: God called the dry land

All: Earth,

2: and the waters that were gathered together God called

All: Seas.

3: And God saw that it was

All: good.

1: Then God said,

2: Let the earth brought forth vegetation: plants yielding seed, and fruit trees of every kind on earth that bear fruit with the seed in it.

3: And it was so.

1: The earth brought forth vegetation: plants yielding seed of every kind, and trees of every kind bearing fruit with the seed in it. And God saw that it was

All: good.

1: And there was evening

2: and there was morning,

3: the third day.

1: And God said,

2: Let there be lights in the dome of the sky to separate the day from the night; and let them be for signs and for seasons and for days and years, and let them be lights in the dome of the sky to give light upon the earth.

3: And it was so.

1: God made the two great lights—the greater light to rule the day and the lesser light to rule the night—and the

All: stars.

2: God set them in the dome of the sky to give light upon the earth, to rule over the day and over the night, and to separate the light from the darkness. And God saw that it was

All: good.

1: And there was evening

2: and there was morning,

3: the fourth day.

1: And God said,

2: Let the waters bring forth swarms of living creatures, and let birds fly above the earth across the dome of the sky.

3: So God created the great sea monsters and every living creature that moves, of every kind, with which the waters swarm, and every winged bird of every kind. And God saw that it was

All: good.

1: God blessed them, saying,

2: Be fruitful and multiply and fill the waters in the seas, and let birds multiply on the earth.

1: And there was evening

2: and there was morning,

3: the fifth day.

1: And God said,

2: Let the earth bring forth living creatures of every kind: cattle and creeping things and wild animals of the earth of every kind.

3: And it was so.

1: God made the wild animals of the earth of every kind, and the cattle of every kind, and everything that creeps upon the ground of every kind. And God saw that it was

All: good.

2: Then God said,

3: Let us make humankind in our image, according to our likeness; and let them have dominion over the fish of the sea, and over the birds of the air, and over the cattle, and over all the wild animals of the earth, and over every creeping thing that creeps upon the earth.

1: So God created humankind in God's image, in the image of God, God created them; male and female God created them. God blessed them, and God said to them,

2: Be fruitful and multiply, and fill the earth and subdue it; and have dominion over the fish of the sea and over the birds of the air and over every living thing that moves upon the earth.

3: See, I have given you every plant yielding seed that is upon the face of all the earth, and every tree with seed in its fruit; you shall have them for food.

1: And to every beast of the earth, and to every bird of the air, and to everything that creeps on the earth, everything that has the breath of life, I have given every green plant for food.

2: And it was so.

3: God saw everything that God had made, and indeed, it was

All: very good.

1: And there was evening

2: and there was morning,

3: the sixth day.

1: Thus the heavens and the earth were finished, and all their multitude.

2: And on the seventh day God finished the work that God had done, and God rested on the seventh day from all the work that God had done.

3: So God blessed the seventh day and hallowed it, because on it God rested from all the work that God had done in creation.

1: These are the generations of the heavens and the earth when they were created.

All: The word of the Lord.

April 9, 2020
Maundy Thursday

This evening our Lenten observance comes to an end, and we gather with Christians around the world to celebrate the Three Days of Jesus' death and resurrection. Tonight we remember Christ's last meal with his disciples, but the central focus is his commandment that we live out the promise embodied in this meal. As Jesus washed his disciples' feet, so we are called to give and receive love in humble service to one another. Formed into a new body in Christ through this holy meal, we are transformed by the mercy we have received and carry it into the world. Departing worship in solemn silence, we anticipate the coming days.

Prayer of the Day

Holy God, source of all love, on the night of his betrayal, Jesus gave us a new commandment, to love one another as he loves us. Write this commandment in our hearts, and give us the will to serve others as he was the servant of all, your Son, Jesus Christ, our Savior and Lord, who lives and reigns with you and the Holy Spirit, one God, now and forever.

or

Eternal God, in the sharing of a meal your Son established a new covenant for all people, and in the washing of feet he showed us the dignity of service. Grant that by the power of your Holy Spirit these signs of our life in faith may speak again to our hearts, feed our spirits, and refresh our bodies, through Jesus Christ, our Savior and Lord, who lives and reigns with you and the Holy Spirit, one God, now and forever.

Gospel Acclamation

I give you a new commandment, that you love one another just as I have loved you. (John 13:34)

Readings and Psalm
Exodus 12:1-4 [5-10] 11-14

Israel remembered its deliverance from slavery in Egypt by celebrating the festival of Passover. This festival featured the Passover lamb, whose blood was used as a sign to protect God's people from the threat of death. The early church described the Lord's supper using imagery from the Passover, especially in portraying Jesus as the lamb who delivers God's people from sin and death.

Psalm 116:1-2, 12-19

I will lift the cup of salvation and call on the name of the LORD. (Ps. 116:13)

1 Corinthians 11:23-26

In the bread and cup of the Lord's supper, we experience intimate fellowship with Christ and with one another because it involves his body given for us and the new covenant in his blood. Faithful participation in this meal is a living proclamation of Christ's death until he comes in the future.

John 13:1-17, 31b-35

The story of the last supper in John's gospel recalls a remarkable event not mentioned elsewhere: Jesus performs the duty of a slave, washing the feet of his disciples and urging them to do the same for one other.

Preface   Maundy Thursday

Color   Scarlet *or* White

Prayers of Intercession

The prayers are prepared locally for each occasion. The following examples may be adapted or used as appropriate.

Turning our hearts to God who is gracious and merciful, we pray for the church, the world, and all who are in need.

A brief silence.

God of love, unite your church in its commitment to humble service. Make us your faithful disciples. Speak words of truth and grace through us. Encourage us in self-giving acts of kindness. Let us love one another as you have loved us. Hear us, O God.

Your mercy is great.

God of love, tend to flocks, fields, and vineyards. Bring favorable weather for crops to grow. Guide the hands of those who cultivate, farm, and garden. Let the earth flourish so that all may eat and be satisfied. Hear us, O God.

Your mercy is great.

God of love, you give us a new commandment, to have love for one another. We give thanks for organizations that respond to disasters and for agencies that offer relief and humanitarian aid to populations in need (*particular organizations may be named*). Hear us, O God.

Your mercy is great.

God of love, give ear to all who call upon you for any need of body or spirit (*especially*). Provide for those who do not have enough to eat, those who are unemployed or underemployed, and those who rely on the generosity of others. Hear us, O God.

Your mercy is great.

God of love, you invite us to your table of mercy. Heal all divisions between members of this assembly. Extend the hospitality of this table beyond these walls, that your love and welcome be made known to all. Hear us, O God.

Your mercy is great.

Here other intercessions may be offered.

God of love, glorify your servants who walked by faith in this life and who now feast with you. Inspire us by the sacrifice of those who were imprisoned, persecuted, or martyred for their faith (*especially Dietrich Bonhoeffer*). Hear us, O God.

Your mercy is great.

According to your steadfast love, O God, hear these and all our prayers as we commend them to you; through Christ our Lord.

Amen.

Ideas for the Day

- As with any words we hear or say repeatedly, it is easy to forget the significance of the words "In the night in which he was betrayed . . ." In fact, they highlight the amazing grace and good news that, even as humanity did its worst, Jesus gave them his very best. Walter Wangerin Jr. offers a powerful reflection on these words in his book *Reliving the Passion: Meditations on the Suffering, Death, and Resurrection of Jesus as Recorded in Mark*: "Can we comprehend the joining of two such extremes, the good and the evil together? In the night of gravest human treachery he gave the gift of himself. And the giving has never ceased. . . . This is grace" ([Grand Rapids, MI: Zondervan, 1992], p. 55).

- In recent years on Maundy Thursday, Pope Francis has publicly washed the feet of marginalized people, such as inmates in detention centers. Keeping that practice in mind, as well as a recent movement to provide "ashes to go" on Ash Wednesday, how could you "take church to the streets" on Maundy Thursday (using the phrase from ashestogo.org)? In what alternative location could you hold your Maundy Thursday service or offer footwashing—a care facility, a jail, a university? With what partner community could you hold a joint service so that members could wash one another's feet? The many logistical, social, and philosophical challenges would be good opportunities to ponder the meaning and symbolism of Jesus' simple action. The goal is simple too: that "everyone will know that you are [Jesus'] disciples, if you have love for one another" (John 13:35).

- When Peter understandably resists having his feet washed, Jesus says, "Unless I wash you, you have no share with me" (John 13:8). Having his feet washed gives Peter a part in Jesus' ongoing life. These words are intriguing in light of what has been called an "epidemic of loneliness" in the United States, in which many people do not feel a "share" in the life of others. (An internet search on that phrase yields many statistics and reflections.) Through Jesus and especially his meal, individuals are reconnected into his body. How can your community share more widely this powerful antidote to loneliness and disconnection?

Connections with Creation

We begin the great Three Days with Jesus stooping to wash the feet of his disciples. This radical act of humility and service is given as the model for Jesus' disciples to follow. It also encapsulates the loving service that will lead him to the cross. Breaking with the tradition of ritually washing only the feet of fellow priests, Pope Francis has made the radical gesture of visiting prisons on Maundy Thursday to wash the feet of inmates, including women and Muslims. How might Francis's example challenge us to think in fresh ways about renewing and reorienting our relationship to creation? What would it mean to "wash creation's feet"? How would such humility reorient our relationship to God, creation, and one another? Given the human suffering brought by environmental degradation, how might this give new meaning to Jesus' call to "love one another" (John 13:34)?

Let the Children Come

Does your congregation practice a kind of "representational" footwashing where only a few people actively participate in this liturgical action? Make an invitation to the whole worshiping assembly to share in the footwashing. Establish stations, not unlike communion stations, to which people may process and take a seat. A minister would wash the feet of the first person in line. That person would, in turn, wash the feet of the next person in line, and so on, until all have shared in the footwashing. This way parents can wash the feet of children. Siblings, who might usually be rivals, can minister to one another. Have a footwashing minister remain at each station (this could be an older child or youth) to distribute clean towels, provide fresh ewers of water, wipe water from the floor, and offer other assistance as needed.

Assembly Song and Music for the Day

Because of the nature of this day, choral and instrumental music suggestions are listed by place in the service. Ch=Choral; CC=Children's Choir; KI=Keyboard/Instrumental; HB=Handbell. Many suggestions require assembly participation.

Laying On of Hands

Our Father, we have wandered ELW 606, WOV 733

Softly and tenderly Jesus is calling ELW 608, WOV 734, TFF 155

Forgive your people/Perdona a tu pueblo, Señor LLC 337, MSB1 S437

☼ Nockels, Christy. "By Our Love" from CCLI.

Leighton, Kenneth. "Solus ad victimam." SATB, org. OXF 9780193851696. [Ch]

⊕ = global song   ♫ = relates to hymn of the day
☼ = praise song   P = available in Prelude Music Planner

Schalk, Carl. "Where Charity and Love Prevail." 2 pt, ob, org. CPH 982701POD. [CC]

P ♫ Floeter, Valerie A. "Where Charity and Love Prevail" from *Jesus, Still Lead On: Piano Settings for Today*. Pno. AFP 9781506426440. [KI]

McMichael, Catherine. "Contemplation on Ubi caritas." 3-6 oct, L3+. AGEHR 36036. [HB]

Psalmody and Acclamations

What shall I render to the Lord/Psalm 116 GTG 655

McRae, Shirley W. "Psalm 116" from *ChildrenSing Psalms*. U, assembly, kybd, 5 hb.

Schalk, Carl. "Antiphon 2 for Psalm 116" from PATP. Use with ELW tone 8 in Emin.

(GA) Farlee, Robert Buckley. "Let Your Steadfast Love." MSB1 S421 with proper verse for Maundy Thursday.

Hymn of the Day

Great God, your love has called us ELW 358, WOV 666 RYBURN

Jesu, Jesu, fill us with your love ELW 708, WOV 765, TFF 83, LS 146 CHEREPONI

Where charity and love prevail ELW 359, LBW 126 TWENTY-FOURTH

☼ Assad, Audrey/Isaac Wardell/Madison Cunningham. "Little Things with Great Love" from *Work Songs*. theporters gate.bandcamp.com.

Footwashing

Love consecrates the humblest act ELW 360, LBW 122

Ubi caritas et amor/Where true charity and love abide ELW 642, WOV 665

Where true charity and love abide/Ubi caritas et amor ELW 653

Where charity and love are shown/Donde hay caridad LLC 337, MSB1 S442

☼ Brown, Brenton. "Humble King" from CCLI.

P Barton, David. "A New Commandment." SATB, kybd. AFP 9781506408491. [Ch]

P Farlee, Robert Buckley. "When Twilight Comes" from *Augsburg Easy Choirbook*, vol. 1. 2 pt mxd, pno. AFP 9780800675578. [Ch]

P ♫ Kerr, J. Wayne. "Jesu, Jesu, Fill Us with Your Love" from *Amen, We Praise Your Name: World Hymns for Organ*. Org. AFP 9781451486018. [KI]

Setting the Table

O Lord, we praise you ELW 499, LBW 215

We place upon your table, Lord ELW 467, LBW 217

☼ Brown, Lacey. "Love" from *Like the Tide*. poorclare.band camp.com.

Proulx, Richard. "A New Commandment: Communion Proces-sional." SATB, solo, ob, org. GIA G-4853. [Ch]

Althouse, Jay. "Come to the Table of the Lord." 2 pt, pno. HOP C6034. [CC]

P ♫ Raabe, Nancy M. "Great God, Your Love Has Called Us" from *Grace & Peace, Volume 8: Songs of Lament and Longing*. Pno. AFP 9781506413679. [KI]

♫ McChesney, Kevin. "Jesu, Jesu, Fill Us with Your Love." 2-3 oct, L2. AFP 11-10985. [HB]

Communion

Around you, O Lord Jesus ELW 468, LBW 496

Stay with me ELW 348, WOV 743

When twilight comes ELW 566, WOV 663, GS2 42

Sharing Paschal bread and wine GTG 207

⊕ O Lamb of God/Oi, Jumalan Karitsa ELW 197

⊕ Maher, Matt/Matt Redman. "Remembrance (The Communion Song)" from CCLI.

Nelson, Ronald A. "If You Love One Another. U/2 pt, kybd. SEL 422-841. [CC]

Haan, Raymond H. "What Wondrous Love Is This" from *Ah, Dearest Jesus: Three Lenten Pieces for Cello or Viola*. Org, vc or vla. MSM 20-363. [KI]

Sherman, Arnold. "Ah, Holy Jesus." 3-5 oct hb, opt 3 oct hc. L3. HOP 1612. [HB]

Stripping the Altar

P Highben, Zebulon. "Lord, I Cry to You (Psalm 88)." MSB1 S446.

St. Gregory of Nyssa Episcopal Church. "My God, My God (Psalm 22)." MSB1 S447.

Schalk, Carl. "Antiphon for Psalm 22" from PATP. Use with ELW tone 8 in Emin.

Bell, John L. "O Lord My God." SATB, a cap, assembly. GIA G-5163.

Sending

None

Thursday, April 9
Dietrich Bonhoeffer, theologian, died 1945

Bonhoeffer (BON-heh-fer) was a German theologian who, at the age of twenty-five, became a lecturer in systematic theol-ogy at the University of Berlin. In 1933, and with Hitler's rise to power, Bonhoeffer became a leading spokesman for the Confessing Church, a resistance movement against the Nazis. He was arrested in 1943. He was linked to a failed attempt on Hitler's life and sent to Buchenwald, then to Schönberg prison. After leading a worship service on April 8, 1945, at Schönberg prison, he was taken away to be hanged the next day. His last words as he left were, "This is the end, but for me the beginning of life." *Evangelical Lutheran Worship* includes a hymn (626) by Bonhoeffer, "By gracious powers."

April 10, 2020
Good Friday

Life and death stand side by side as we enter into Good Friday. In John's passion account, Jesus reveals the power and glory of God, even as he is put on trial and sentenced to death. Standing with the disciples at the foot of the cross, we pray for the whole world in the ancient bidding prayer, as Christ's death offers life to all. We gather in solemn devotion, but always with the promise that the tree around which we assemble is indeed a tree of life. We depart silently, and we anticipate the culmination of the Three Days in the Easter Vigil.

Prayer of the Day

Almighty God, look with loving mercy on your family, for whom our Lord Jesus Christ was willing to be betrayed, to be given over to the hands of sinners, and to suffer death on the cross; who now lives and reigns with you and the Holy Spirit, one God, forever and ever.

or

Merciful God, your Son was lifted up on the cross to draw all people to himself. Grant that we who have been born out of his wounded side may at all times find mercy in him, Jesus Christ, our Savior and Lord, who lives and reigns with you and the Holy Spirit, one God, now and forever.

Gospel Acclamation

Look to Jesus, who for the sake of the joy that was set before him endured the cross, disregarding its shame, and has taken his seat at the right hand of the throne of God. (Heb. 12:2)

Readings and Psalm

Isaiah 52:13—53:12

The fourth servant poem promises ultimate vindication for the servant, who made his life an offering for sin. The servant pours himself out to death and is numbered with the transgressors, images that the early church saw as important keys for understanding the death of Jesus.

Psalm 22

My God, my God, why have you forsaken me? (Ps. 22:1)

Hebrews 10:16-25

In the death of Jesus, forgiveness of sins is accomplished and access to God is established. Hence, when we gather together for worship and when we love others, we experience anew the benefits of Jesus' death.

or Hebrews 4:14-16; 5:7-9

In his death Jesus functions as great high priest who experiences temptation and suffering in order that we would receive mercy and find grace, because he is the source of true salvation.

John 18:1—19:42

On Good Friday, the story of Jesus' passion—from his arrest to his burial—is read in its entirety from the Gospel of John.

Holy communion is normally not celebrated on Good Friday; accordingly, no preface is provided. The worship space having been stripped on the preceding evening, no paraments are used today.

Prayers of Intercession

On Good Friday, the church's ancient Bidding Prayer is said or sung. See Evangelical Lutheran Worship Leaders Edition, *pp. 636-638.*

Ideas for the Day

- When Jesus says he has "spoken openly to the world" (John 18:20), he uses the Greek word *cosmos*, an important word in John's gospel. His death and resurrection change the whole cosmos. Help people envision the cross in its cosmic significance as a tree of life by sharing the 1894 mosaic by Edward Burne-Jones, found in the American Episcopal Church in Rome. Christ crucified is pictured on a tree of life, with Adam and Eve on either side. You can download an image of the watercolor sketch at collections.vam.ac.uk (search for "Tree of Life American Episcopal Church"). Consider pairing this image with Marty Haugen's Lenten hymn, "Tree of Life and awesome mystery" (ELW 334).
- Through its Good Friday worship, the church communicates to the broader community that it is a safe place to hold everything in life that is painful, tragic, confusing, and unbearable. On this day especially, the church practices being this place not only for its members but also for the world. How has your congregation offered that "safe place" to the broader community, or what inspiration could you find from other congregations who have done so? You can find some recent examples with an online search of "church hosts vigil."
- As John's gospel tells the story of Christ's passion and death, the story is set in five different locations. You could read each of those five portions from a different vantage point in your worship space, or you could intersperse

them with reflections, prayers, or meditative music. As each location also highlights different characters in the story, you could have each reflection come from a different character: Simon Peter, Jesus' mother, or Nicodemus, for example.

- How can we remember to "approach the throne of grace with boldness" (Heb. 4:16) not only on this day but every day? During worship, you could give people a small cross to wear or display. Then interpret that action: What is the *good* news of *Good* Friday that we might "wear" or carry with us? How is that different from or similar to other reasons people wear a cross as jewelry, either as a reminder to the wearer or as a message to others? A 2011 BBC article, "The Cross" (bbc.co.uk/religion/religions/christianity /symbols/cross_1.shtml) offers some reflections about this practice from a secular point of view.

Connections with Creation

Who is speaking in Psalm 22? Traditionally, Christians have read it as the voice of Jesus. Indeed, it is on the lips of Jesus as he dies. Yet the first-person voice of the psalm invites readers to find themselves in the words. That is part of the story of the cross: Jesus' sufferings are ours. Might we in turn hear in the words of Psalm 22 the voice of the suffering creation, feeling mocked and forsaken? Might the story of the crucifixion encompass the story of environmental degradation in our own day? How might the solemnity of Good Friday awaken the worshipers to a new awareness of their ecological context? How might God's promise of new life through the cross awaken hopeful, Spirit-filled action amid ecosystems that seem to have more in common with Good Friday than with Easter?

Let the Children Come

Is the Good Friday liturgy a service in which children are welcome? Think about how your congregation marks Good Friday. Does your worship perpetuate the trauma of the story? The service as presented in *Evangelical Lutheran Worship* is quiet, prayerful, and reflective. There is more silence than usual. The bidding prayer takes time. Put together, does this mean that there are fewer children present? If a special family service is offered in your congregation, assess to what extent it is in character with the solemn nature of this day. Good Friday needs to be the way it is. Make sure worship planners and leaders attend to the details of this day that may interest children: darkness and light, the texture of a rough-hewn cross, reverencing the cross with a bow or touch. Parents and caregivers with small children should be assured that they can leave or step out and back in at any time without apology.

Assembly Song and Music for the Day

Because of the nature of the Good Friday liturgy, music suggestions are listed by place in the service. Many suggestions require assembly participation.

Gathering

None

Psalmody and Acclamations

My God, my God/Psalm 22 TFF 2

Schalk, Carl. "Antiphon for Psalm 22" from PATP. Use with ELW tone 8 in Emin.

Witte, Marilyn. "My God, My God (Psalm 22)." MSB1 S448.

(GA) Farlee, Robert Buckley. "Let Your Steadfast Love." MSB1 S421 with proper verse for Good Friday.

Hymn of the Day

Holy God, holy and glorious ELW 637 NELSON

My song is love unknown ELW 343, WOV 661 LOVE UNKNOWN LBW 94 RHOSYMEDRE

When I survey the wondrous cross ELW 803, TFF 79 HAMBURG LBW 482 ROCKINGHAM OLD

Procession of the Cross: Dialogue

Alonso, Tony. "Behold the Wood of the Cross" from *Music for the Adoration of the Holy Cross*. SAB, cant, assembly, gtr, kybd. WLP 005292.

McGoff, Kevin G. "This Is the Wood of the Cross." SATB, assembly. Use with refrain or verses only. GIA G-7794.

P Organ, Anne Krentz. "Behold, the Life-Giving Cross" and "We Adore You, O Christ." MSB1 S459.

Procession of the Cross: Solemn Reproaches

de Victoria, Tomás, arr. Geoffrey Cox. "The Reproaches." SATB, cant, a cap. OCP 4525.

Farlee, Robert Buckley. "Solemn Reproaches of the Cross." Solo, SATB, pno. AFP 9780800674724.

P Witte, Marilyn. "Solemn Reproaches." MSB1 S461.

Procession of the Cross: We Glory in Your Cross

Alonso, Tony. "Faithful Cross" from *Music for the Adoration of the Holy Cross*. SAB, cant, assembly, kybd. WLP 005292.

Haugen, Marty. "Adoramus te Christe." MSB1 S469.

Pearson, Donald. "We Glory in Your Cross, O Lord." SAB, a cap. OCP 4537.

Proulx, Richard. "We Adore You, O Christ." SATB, a cap. PAR 9836.

P = available in Prelude Music Planner

Procession of the Cross: Other Choral Music

P   Anerio, Giovanni F. "Christ Humbled Himself (Christus factus est)" from *Augsburg Motet Book*. SATB, a cap or cont. AFP 9781451423709.

Bouman, Paul. "Behold the Lamb of God." U/2 pt, org. CPH 981088POD.

Brahms, Johannes. "O Sacred Head, Now Wounded." U, kybd, opt vc. MSM 50-2655.

P   Jennings, Carolyn. "Ah, Holy Jesus" from *Augsburg Choirbook for Women*. SA, vc. AFP 9780800620370.

P   Mummert, Mark. "This Cross" from *O Lord of Light: Nine Two-Part Mixed Anthems for the Church Year*. 2 pt mxd, org. MSM 55-9930.

Hymn of Triumph

Jesus, keep me near the cross   ELW 335, TFF 73

Sing, my tongue   ELW 355/356, LBW 118

There in God's garden   ELW 342, WOV 668

P   Scott, K. Lee. "The Tree of Life (There in God's Garden)." SATB, assembly, org, opt br qt, opt hb. MSM 50-3000.

Additional Music Suggestions

The suggestions listed below may also be appropriate, especially for services other than the liturgy of Good Friday.

Assembly Songs

Lamb of God most holy/Santo cordero   LLC 340, MSB1 S453

On a barren hilltop   GTG 217

You, Lord, are both Lamb and Shepherd   GTG 274

⊕   Feliciano, Francisco F. "How Deep Your Love, O Master" from *Sound the Bamboo*. SATB. GIA G-6830.

⊕   Pagura, Federico J. "Tenemos esperanza/We Have Hope" from *Tenemos Esperanza/We Have Hope*. U, pno. GBGMusik 1890569453.

☼   Figueroa, Andres/Hank Bentley/Mariah McManus/Mia Fieldes. "Tremble" from CCLI.

☼   Getty, Keith/Stuart Townend. "In Christ Alone" from CCLI.

☼   Gungor, David/John Arndt. "Does Your Heart Break?" from *Lent*. thebrilliancemusic.com.

☼   Tomlin, Chris/Ed Cash/Jonas Myrin/Matt Armstrong/Matt Redman. "At the Cross (Love Ran Red)" from CCLI.

☼   Van Patter, Michael. "Our Song in the Night (Psalm 77)" from *Songs in the Night*. michaelvanpatter.bandcamp.com.

☼   Watts, Keith/Isaac Wardell/Madison Cunningham. "Wood and Nails" from *Work Songs*. theportersgate.bandcamp.com.

Choral

Sherman, Kim D. "Graveside" from *Service for the Dead in Bosnia-Herzegovina*. SSAATB, a cap. kdsherman.com.

Children's Choir

Rorem, Ned. "The Mild Mother." U, pno. ECS 2584.

Keyboard / Instrumental

P ♫   Biery, James. "Holy God, Holy and Glorious" from *The Paschal Lamb: Easter Settings for Organ*. Org. AFP 9781451494099.

P   Langlais, Jean. "Herzlich tut mich verlangen" from *A New Liturgical Year, Volume 2: Anthology for Organ*. Org. AFP 9781451499070.

P ♫   Lind, Robert. "When I Survey the Wondrous Cross" from *Cross of Jesus: Piano Settings*. Pno. AFP 9781451494105.

Oines, Sylvia Berg. "Were You There? and My Lord, What a Morning" from *Bread of Life: Hymn Settings for Piano*. Pno. MSM 15-834.

Handbell

♫   Ingram, Bill. "When I Survey the Wondrous Cross" from *Five Hymns for Twelve Bells*. 3 oct (12 bells), L2. CG CGB770.

♫   McChesney, Kevin. "When I Survey the Wondrous Cross." 3-5 oct hb, opt 2 oct hc, L2-. LOR 20/1070L.

♫   Stults, Tyleen. "My Song Is Love Unknown." 3 oct, L2. CPH 977679.

Friday, April 10
Mikael Agricola, Bishop of Turku, died 1557

Agricola was consecrated as the bishop of Turku in 1554 without papal approval. As a result, he began a reform of the Finnish church along Lutheran lines. He translated the New Testament, the prayerbook, hymns, and the mass into Finnish, and through this work set the rules of orthography that are the basis of modern Finnish spelling. His thoroughgoing work is particularly remarkable in that he accomplished it in only three years. He died suddenly on a return trip from negotiating a peace treaty with the Russians.

⊕ = global song   ♫ = relates to hymn of the day
☼ = praise song   P = available in Prelude Music Planner

April 11, 2020
Resurrection of Our Lord
Vigil of Easter

This is the night of salvation! At the Vigil of Easter, we gather around fire, word, water, bread, and wine, proclaiming through story and song that ours is a God who continuously brings life out of death. On this night we experience again the heart of God's baptismal promise and the center of our faith: we are claimed and cleansed, renewed in the death and resurrection of Christ. We gather with all the saints of every time and place to celebrate the good news: Christ is risen indeed! Alleluia!

Prayer of the Day

Eternal giver of life and light, this holy night shines with the radiance of the risen Christ. Renew your church with the Spirit given us in baptism, that we may worship you in sincerity and truth and may shine as a light in the world, through your Son, Jesus Christ our Lord, who lives and reigns with you and the Holy Spirit, one God, now and forever.

or

O God, you are the creator of the world, the liberator of your people, and the wisdom of the earth. By the resurrection of your Son free us from our fears, restore us in your image, and ignite us with your light, through Jesus Christ, our Savior and Lord, who lives and reigns with you and the Holy Spirit, one God, now and forever.

Gospel Acclamation

Alleluia. Let us sing to the LORD, who has triumphed gloriously; our strength and our might, who has become our salvation. *Alleluia.* (Exod. 15:1-2)

Readings and Responses

Readings marked with an asterisk are not omitted.

*1 Genesis 1:1—2:4a

Creation

Response: Psalm 136:1-9, 23-26

God's mercy endures forever. (Ps. 136:1)

2 Genesis 7:1-5, 11-18; 8:6-18; 9:8-13

Flood

Response: Psalm 46

The LORD of hosts is with us; the God of Jacob is our stronghold. (Ps. 46:7)

3 Genesis 22:1-18

Testing of Abraham

Response: Psalm 16

You will show me the path of life. (Ps. 16:11)

*4 Exodus 14:10-31; 15:20-21

Deliverance at the Red Sea

Response: Exodus 15:1b-13, 17-18

I will sing to the LORD, who has triumphed gloriously. (Exod. 15:1)

*5 Isaiah 55:1-11

Salvation freely offered to all

Response: Isaiah 12:2-6

With joy you will draw water from the wells of salvation. (Isa. 12:3)

6 Proverbs 8:1-8, 19-21; 9:4b-6
or **Baruch 3:9-15, 32—4:4**

The wisdom of God

Response: Psalm 19

The statutes of the LORD are just and rejoice the heart. (Ps. 19:8)

7 Ezekiel 36:24-28

A new heart and a new spirit

Response: Psalms 42 and 43

I thirst for God, for the living God. (Ps. 42:2)

8 Ezekiel 37:1-14

Valley of the dry bones

Response: Psalm 143

Revive me, O LORD, for your name's sake. (Ps. 143:11)

9 Zephaniah 3:14-20

The gathering of God's people

Response: Psalm 98

Lift up your voice, rejoice, and sing. (Ps. 98:4)

10 Jonah 1:1—2:1

The deliverance of Jonah

Response: Jonah 2:2-3 [4-6] 7-9

Deliverance belongs to the LORD. (Jonah 2:9)

11 Isaiah 61:1-4, 9-11

Clothed in the garments of salvation

Response: Deuteronomy 32:1-4, 7, 36a, 43a

Great is our God, the Rock, whose ways are just. (Deut. 32:3-4)

*12 Daniel 3:1-29

Deliverance from the fiery furnace

Response: Song of the Three 35-65

Praise and magnify the Lord forever. (Song of the Three 35)

New Testament Reading and Gospel

Romans 6:3-11

We were incorporated into the death of Jesus Christ in baptism and so were liberated from the dominion of sin. We also anticipate that we will be incorporated into the resurrection of Christ and so will be liberated from the hold death has over our mortal bodies.

John 20:1-18

John's gospel describes the confusion and excitement of the first Easter: the stone is moved, disciples race back and forth, and angels speak to a weeping woman. Then, Jesus himself appears.

Preface   Easter

Color   White *or* Gold

Prayers of Intercession

The prayers are prepared locally for each occasion. The following examples may be adapted or used as appropriate.

Turning our hearts to God who is gracious and merciful, we pray for the church, the world, and all who are in need.

A brief silence.

God of resurrection, this is the night when your holy church gathers around fire and water, bread and wine, story and celebration. Make us eager to go into all the world with the news that Christ is alive and death is conquered. Hear us, O God.

Your mercy is great.

God of resurrection, in the beginning you created all things and declared them good. Where floods and fires threaten to overwhelm and destroy, speak peace against the chaos. Set rainbows in the skies as signs of your faithfulness. Shine your glory through each twinkling star. Hear us, O God.

Your mercy is great.

God of resurrection, you are deliverance for people enslaved by conflict, corruption, and inequality. Grant wisdom to governments and world leaders. Lead them in the way of righteousness and along paths of justice. Hear us, O God.

Your mercy is great.

God of resurrection, hold vigil with all who watch and wait this night: those sitting beside dying loved ones, those working the night shift at hospitals and care centers, emergency first responders, those awaiting test results or diagnoses, those who are in labor, and those who long for healing (*especially*). Hear us, O God.

Your mercy is great.

God of resurrection, stir up the waters of salvation and bring renewed life to all who receive or affirm the gift of baptism this night. (*Those receiving or affirming baptism may be named.*) Claim us as your beloved children, clothe us in the garments of salvation, and raise us from death to life. Hear us, O God.

Your mercy is great.

Here other intercessions may be offered.

God of resurrection, bless the memory of all the faithful witnesses who boldly proclaimed, "We have seen the Lord!" Give us confidence that because Christ has been raised, we too will be raised to new life. Hear us, O God.

Your mercy is great.

According to your steadfast love, O God, hear these and all our prayers as we commend them to you; through Christ our Lord. **Amen.**

Ideas for the Day

- The number and length of readings for this evening may appear excessive to those not acquainted with the Easter Vigil, so creative ways of presenting them may be called for. In *To Dance with God*, Gertrud Mueller Nelson describes how readers in her congregation were "typecast" for the readings: "The reader of the creation story was an old man with a fine, large beard. He looked like a patriarch. A father, his only son standing at his side, read the story of Abraham and his only son Isaac. A woman told, rather than read, the story of the march through the sea. She used simple words and powerful gestures" (New York: Paulist, 1986, p. 177). Such coordinating of readers may be part of the prayer life of the worship planner: who in your community most identifies with these stories?

- Some worshipers may need something in their hands during these readings. Provide copies of a finger labyrinth (labyrinthsociety.org/download-a-labyrinth). The labyrinth can be a tool to illustrate the journey of God's people in the scriptural narrative as it mirrors the twists and turns of the salvation story. Listeners may discover both the distance and nearness of God for themselves as they follow the winding path leading them at times toward, and at others away from, the center (God).

- The readings for the Easter Vigil are ideal instruction for young people in the stories of the deliverance of God's people from situations of despair. Provide a short list of some of these Bible stories to households with children with the encouragement to read these stories from children's Bibles and storybooks at home (creation, Noah's ark, the exodus, the dry bones, Jonah, and the three men in the fiery furnace would be plenty). Have books and Bibles ready for borrowing from the church too. Children will be more prepared to hear these stories told at the Vigil with their church family.

- In his essay "On Fairy-Stories," J. R. R. Tolkien coined the term *eucatastrophe*, which he describes in a letter to his son as "the sudden happy turn in a story which pierces you with a joy that brings tears" (*The Letters of J. R. R. Tolkien*, New York: Houghton Mifflin Harcourt, 2000, p. 100). Easter is the "eucatastrophe of the incarnation," but throughout all of tonight's readings the eucatastrophic turn of events is present. What eucatastrophes has your community experienced in the past year to name and celebrate during a short, spoken reflection at the Vigil?

Connections with Creation

The Easter Vigil invites engagement with the wide horizon of creation. Traditionally beginning outdoors around the new fire, the lectionary readings inspire us to read scripture sacramentally. The lectionary readings contain stories of waters that feed the river of our baptismal theology, like a "baptismal watershed" flowing through the scriptures: from the primordial waters of Genesis 1–2; to the flood and God's covenant with all creation; to the Red Sea crossing; to God's word nourishing the earth like rain in Isaiah 55; to the cleansing waters of Ezekiel 36, and the new life to dry bones in Ezekiel 37; to the seas, rivers, and springs blessing the Lord in the Song of the Three; to Paul's reflection on dying and rising with Christ in baptism. We might even imagine this watershed flowing on to John 20, where we find Jesus, the firstborn of the new creation, risen in a garden in springtime.

Let the Children Come

This long-anticipated night is one of opposites. Genesis begins tonight's vigil with the oppositions of creation: formlessness and form, absence of light and light, waters and sky, evening and morning. Watch and listen tonight for more opposites: captivity and freedom, old and new, dry bones and living beings. Even the cross becomes a sign of opposites. What was once a symbol of shame and death now becomes a sign of God's radical love and life. During the Easter Vigil, we hold all these opposites close to our hearts. We cannot have one without the other. There is no light without lightlessness. There is no land without sky. There is no life without death.

Invite the children to help resurrect the Alleluia banner tonight, perhaps as an alleluia verse, an extended alleluia, or a hymn with alleluias is sung as the gospel acclamation. The solemnity of Lent gives way to unbridled joy!

Assembly Song and Music for the Day

Because of the nature of this day, choral and instrumental music suggestions are listed both by place in the service and categorized by type of leadership (in brackets): Ch=Choral; CC=Children's Choir; KI=Keyboard/Instrumental; HB=Handbell. Many suggestions require assembly participation.

Fire and Procession

Alonso, Tony. "This Is the Night: Procession of the Paschal Candle and Exsultet." SATB, cant, assembly, kybd, opt gtr, fl, ob, vc. WLP 005314.

P Haugen, Marty. "Light of Christ, Rising in Glory (Easter Vigil Procession)." MSB1 S472.

P Highben, Zebulon. "Processional Refrains (Stanza 1)." MSB1 S471.

Easter Proclamation

Alonso, Tony. "This Is the Night: Procession of the Paschal Candle and Exsultet." SATB, cant, assembly, kybd, opt gtr, fl, ob, vc. WLP 005314.

Hillebrand, Paul. "Exsultet." Cant, SATB, assembly, kybd, gtr. OCP 30113062.

Repulski, John. "Exsultet." Cant, SATB, hb. OCP 30103338.

Readings and Responses

Responses to each reading are included in Music Sourcebook for Lent and the Three Days *and* Psalter for Worship Year C. *Related hymns are listed in* Indexes to Evangelical Lutheran Worship. *The responses listed below are from other resources.*

1 Creation

Cooney, Rory. "Genesis Reading for the Great Vigil." SATB, cant, assembly, kybd, gtr, fl. GIA G-5018.

Haugen, Marty. "Your Love Endures." SATB, cant, assembly, kybd, gtr, 2 ww in C. GIA G-4842.

P de Lassus, Rudolph. "Stars in the Sky Proclaim" from *Augsburg Motet Book*. SAB, a cap. AFP 9781451423709. [Ch]

P Hansen, Sherri. "God Created Heaven and Earth" from *Piano Weavings*, vol. 2. Pno. AFP 9781506413723. [KI]

2 Flood

"A River Flows." *Psallitè* A-238. Cant or SATB, assembly, kybd.

Bedford, Michael. "Be Still and Know (Psalm 46:10-11)" from *Two Psalms for Young Singers*. U, kybd, opt hb. CG CGA1140. [CC]

P Horman, John. "God Told Noah" from *Sing the Stories of God's People*. U, kybd. AFP 9780806698397. [CC]

Moore, James E., Jr. "Be Still." SATB, assembly, kybd, gtr. GIA G-5731.

P = available in Prelude Music Planner

3 Testing of Abraham

Gelineau, Joseph. "Psalm 16" from ACYG. [Ch]

Lawton, Liam. "Evermore I'll Sing Your Praise." Cant, assembly, kybd, gtr. GIA G-5294.

P Miller, Aaron David. "I Want Jesus to Walk with Me." U, pno, opt desc. AFP 9781451421606. [CC]

Stachowski, Zack. "Keep Me Safe." U or 2 pt choir, assembly, kybd, gtr, opt oboe, str qrt. GIA G-8324. [Ch]

4 Deliverance at the Red Sea

O Mary, don't you weep   TFF 88

When Israel was in Egypt's land   TFF 87

Bell, John. "When Israel Came Out of Egypt's Land." SATB. GIA G-4674. [Ch]

Cooney, Rory. "Exodus Reading for the Great Vigil." SATB, cant, assembly, kybd, gtr, opt fl. GIA G-4117.

Keesecker, Thomas. "Go Down, Moses." U/2 pt, pno. CG CGA1368. [CC]

5 Salvation freely offered to all

"Joyfully You Will Draw Water." *Psallite* A-57.

Haas, David. "The Easter Vigil in the Holy Night: After the Fifth Reading" from *Cry Out with Joy* (festivals). GIA G-8480.

Haugen, Marty. "You Will Draw Water Joyfully" from TLP:S.

6 The wisdom of God

Alonso, Tony. "Lord, You Have the Words of Everlasting Life" from TLP:S.

Birks, Thomas R. "The Heavens Declare Your Glory" (FAITH-FUL; alternate tunes AURELIA, ELLACOMBE) from *Lift Up Your Hearts*. Faith Alive Christian Resources.

P de Lassus, Rudolf. "Stars in the Sky Proclaim" from *Augsburg Motet Book*. SAB. AFP 9781451423709. [Ch]

7 A new heart and a new spirit

⊕ Mulrain, George. "The Thirsty Deer Longs for the Stream" from *Global Praise 1*. U, pno. GBGMusik 1890569011.

Kean, Daniel. "Psalm 42." SATB, cant, assembly, pno, ob. GIA G-4895.

P Leavitt, John. "As Pants the Hart." SATB, pno. AFP 9781506445540. [Ch]

8 Valley of the dry bones

Daw, Carl P. Jr. "Hear My Prayer, O God" (HYMN CHANT) from PAS 143A.

Gelineau, Joseph. "Psalm 143" from ACYG. [Ch]

Show Me the Way/Psalm 143   DATH 45

9 The gathering of God's people

Behnke, John. "Psalm 98: Sing to the Lord a New Song." SATB, cant, assembly, kybd, 2 tpt, hb. CPH 983666WEB.

P Christopherson, Dorothy. "Psalm 98" from *ChildrenSing Psalms*. U, assembly, kybd, fc, tamb.

Trapp, Lynn. "All the Ends of the Earth." SATB, assembly, kybd, tr, 2 C inst. GIA G-5623.

10 The deliverance of Jonah

Guimont, Michel. "Easter Vigil X" from *Psalms for the Revised Common Lectionary*. SATB, assembly, kybd, gtr. GIA G-5616.

P Horman, John D. "Jonah" from *Sing the Stories of God's People*. U, kybd. AFP 9780806698397. [CC]

Pavlechko, Thomas. "Jonah 2:2-3 [4-6] 7-9" from PSCY.

11 Clothed in the garments of salvation

Guimont, Michel. "Easter Vigil XI" from *Psalms for the Revised Common Lectionary*. SATB, assembly, kybd, gtr. GIA G-5616.

Mummert, Mark. "Deuteronomy 32:1-4, 7, 36a, 43a" from PSCY.

12 Deliverance from the fiery furnace

Consiglio, Cyprian. "Song of the Three Young Men." Cant, assembly, perc. OCP 10199.

P Jennings, Kenneth. "All You Works of the Lord, Bless the Lord." SATB, org. AFP 9780800645311. [Ch]

Joncas, Jan Michael. "Canticle of the Three Young Men." SATB, assembly, 2 cant, org. GIA G-8441.

MacKenzie, Valerie. "Cool Under Fire." U, pno. LOR CIM1051. [CC]

Gospel Acclamation

Haugen, Marty. "Easter Alleluia." SATB, cant, kybd, gtr, 2 ww in C. GIA G-3594.

Procession to the Font

I'm going on a journey   ELW 446, TFF 115

We know that Christ is raised   ELW 449, LBW 189

Handel, George Frederic/arr. Walter Ehret. "All Who Are Thirsty, Come to the Spring." 2 pt or 2 pt mxd, kybd. GIA G-5838. [Ch or CC]

Haugen, Marty. "Come to the Feast." SATB or U, pno, gtr, ww in C, opt br qrt, hb. GIA G-3543.

☀ Hastings, Benjamin/Dean Ussher/Marty Sampson. "O Praise the Name (Anástasis)" from CCLI.

Setting the Table

At the Lamb's high feast we sing   ELW 362, sts. 2, 4; LBW 210, sts. 2, 4

The trumpets sound, the angels sing   ELW 531, W&P 139

¡Cristo vive!/Christ is living   NCH 235

☀ Chapman, John Wilbur/Mark Hall/Michael Bleecker. "Glorious Day (Living He Loved Me)" from CCLI.

⊕ = global song
☀ = praise song   P = available in Prelude Music Planner

☼ Gungor, David/John Arndt/Matt Maher. "Gravity of Love" from CCLI.

P Ferguson, John. "This Joyful Eastertide." 2 pt mxd, org. AFP 9781506413990. [Ch]

P Hobby, Robert A. "I've Just Come from the Fountain." SATB, a cap. AFP 9780800659196. [Ch]

Carter, John. "Let Us Talents and Tongues Employ" from *You Satisfy the Hungry Heart: Piano Settings for Communion*. Pno. HOP 8008. [KI]

Communion

Blessing, Honor, and Glory ELW 433, W&P 21

United at the table/Unidos en las fiesta ELW 498, LLC 408

We who once were dead ELW 495, LBW 207

⊕ South African trad. "We Walk His Way/Ewe thina" from *We Walk His Way*. SATB, cant. GIA G-7403.

☼ Maher, Matt. "Your Grace Is Enough" from CCLI.

☼ Moore, Joshua/Sandra McCracken. "We Will Feast in the House of Zion" from CCLI.

☼ Phillips, Latifah/David Wilton. "Roll Away the Stone" from *Good Friday to Easter*. pagecxvi.com.

Sending

Christ is risen! Alleluia! ELW 382, LBW 131

Come, you faithful, raise the strain ELW 363, LBW 132

With high delight let us unite ELW 368, LBW 140

Hildebrand, Kevin. "Awake, O Sleeper, Rise and See." SATB, org, br qrt, opt assembly. CPH 983935. [Ch]

P Farlee, Robert Buckley. "Gaudeamus pariter" from *Augsburg Organ Library: Easter*. Org. AFP 9780800659363. [KI]

Ferguson, John "Easter Hymn" from *In Quiet Joy: Easter Triptych*. Org. MSM 10-422. [KI]

April 12, 2020
Resurrection of Our Lord
Easter Day

This is the day the Lord has made! Christ is risen, and through him all creation is made new! Indeed, "God shows no partiality" (Acts 10:34): Christ's resurrection truly brings life to everyone. We sing hymns of praise, gather around sacred words, and proclaim God's faithfulness, power, and love in the feast of holy communion. With the women at the tomb, we are astonished, elated, and grateful. We depart with joy to proclaim the good news of God's endless love.

Prayer of the Day

O God, you gave your only Son to suffer death on the cross for our redemption, and by his glorious resurrection you delivered us from the power of death. Make us die every day to sin, that we may live with him forever in the joy of the resurrection, through your Son, Jesus Christ our Lord, who lives and reigns with you and the Holy Spirit, one God, now and forever.

or

God of mercy, we no longer look for Jesus among the dead, for he is alive and has become the Lord of life. Increase in our minds and hearts the risen life we share with Christ, and help us to grow as your people toward the fullness of eternal life with you, through Jesus Christ, our Savior and Lord, who lives and reigns with you and the Holy Spirit, one God, now and forever.

Gospel Acclamation

Alleluia. Christ, our paschal lamb, has been sacrificed. Therefore, let us keep the feast. *Alleluia*. (1 Cor. 5:7, 8)

Readings and Psalm
Acts 10:34-43

Peter's sermon, delivered at the home of Cornelius, a Roman army officer, is a summary of the essential message of Christianity: Everyone who believes in Jesus, whose life, death, and resurrection fulfilled the words of the prophets, "receives forgiveness of sins through his name."

or Jeremiah 31:1-6

God's final word is always "Yes." Because God's love is everlasting, God always remains faithful. Ancient Israel is assured that it will be rebuilt and have plentiful crops. The people of God too will ultimately be reunited.

Psalm 118:1-2, 14-24

This is the day that the LORD has made; let us rejoice and be glad in it. (Ps. 118:24)

Colossians 3:1-4

Easter means new life for us as it first meant new life for Christ. His resurrection reshapes the entire focus and motivation for our lives since we are now hidden with the risen Christ in God.

or **Acts 10:34-43**

See above.

Matthew 28:1-10

Sorrow gives way to "fear and great joy" when two women are sent by an angel to proclaim the good news: Jesus is risen!

or **John 20:1-18**

John's gospel describes the confusion and excitement of the first Easter: the stone is moved, disciples race back and forth, and angels speak to a weeping woman. Then, Jesus himself appears.

Preface   Easter

Color   White *or* Gold

Prayers of Intercession

The prayers are prepared locally for each occasion. The following examples may be adapted or used as appropriate.

Uplifted by the promised hope of healing and resurrection, we join the people of God in all times and places in praying for the church, the world, and all who are in need.

A brief silence.

God of resurrection, from the very beginning you give the church the gift of women as your witnesses: as preachers, teachers, and leaders (*especially*). Open our ears to their proclamation this day and always. Lord, in your mercy,
hear our prayer.

All your creation praises you—the earth hums, the seas pulse, the stars shine, and the galaxies whirl in glorious harmonies to honor you. Let us hear and blend our voices in the song. Lord, in your mercy,
hear our prayer.

The countries of the world experience disunity and conflict; we set our minds on fear and greed rather than on your rule of justice and steadfast love. Build up all countries on your cornerstone of peace. Lord, in your mercy,
hear our prayer.

We still weep with those who weep, and mourn with those who mourn. Cradle the fearful, the suffering, and the dying, assuring them of your loving presence (*especially*). Lord, in your mercy,
hear our prayer.

Bless the creative and helpful service of worship leaders this day: musicians, ushers, greeters, worship assistants, preachers, readers, and all others who provide welcome and hospitality in our midst. Lord, in your mercy,
hear our prayer.

Here other intercessions may be offered.

Risen Lord, you went ahead of us into the grave and defeated the powers of evil. We remember those who have died

(*especially*). Inspire us to live our lives in this resurrection hope and draw us to you in our final days. Lord, in your mercy,
hear our prayer.

With bold confidence in your love, almighty God, we place all for whom we pray into your eternal care; through Christ our Lord.
Amen.

Ideas for the Day

- In *Meal from Below* (Tacoma: Street Psalms Press, 2012, p. 119), Scott Dewey recounts that before the 2010 earthquake in Haiti a seminary in Port-au-Prince would seldom interact with neighboring slums. In the aftermath of the devastation, both physical and social barriers were torn down. A seminary professor showed Dewey his tent where he was living with other refugees, and described vital new ministries created in response to need. "Here in Haiti," Dewey says, "in one corner at least, the devastating earthquake has served to break down social divides few had been willing to cross." How does the groundbreaking news of the resurrection (Matt. 28:2) tear down barriers we continue to create?

- The "Easter earthquake" of the gospel upsets the familiar terrain of despair with the unexpected uprising of life. In the wake of the 1906 San Francisco earthquake, the decision was quickly made to rebuild the city. Within three years the renovation was well underway, with running cable cars, a redesigned Chinatown with landmark pagodas, and twenty thousand new buildings. Similarly, we now inhabit the new topography of resurrection as we live into Christ's victory over sin and death. What frontiers in this altered landscape of new life is your community called to explore?

- The traditional orthodox *anastasis* icon symbolically depicts the resurrected Christ hovering over an open chasm as Adam and Eve, representing the whole human race, rise to greet him. The icon reminds us that Easter is not just for those first witnesses in today's gospel, nor is it only for the ones who accept their proclamation. Easter is for everyone: it is global and cosmic, and all creation benefits from Christ's victory! View a variety of icons of the resurrection at orthodoxwiki.org/Resurrection.

- Both the guards and the women were terrified at the angel's proclamation (Matt. 28:4-5) as they witnessed phenomena unparalleled in their experience. Neil deGrasse Tyson reminds us in his show *Cosmos* that laws of nature are so called because they are always and everywhere true. In the law of conservation of energy, both sides of the equation must balance out: "The energy accounting books are always strictly balanced" (Season 1, Episode 6; 34:15—35:47). But today a lifeless body becomes energized seemingly on its own. Resurrection steals in to our hermetically sealed understanding of the cosmos; it upsets our accounting books, and that is unsettling, to say the least!

Connections with Creation

Matthew's account of the resurrection comes with natural signs and metaphors, inviting reflection on how the natural world is not simply the backdrop of the gospel message but participates in its proclamation. As the women arrive at the tomb, Matthew includes the narrative detail that the sun is dawning. The symbolic meaning is clear: Jesus' resurrection is the dawning of a new day, what the early church would call the "eighth day" of creation. The earth quakes and an angel alights, whose appearance is as lightning, and whose clothing is white as snow. While these details are easily passed over on the way to what is considered the essence of the Easter story, these natural phenomena and metaphors—at once awe-inspiring, overwhelming, beautiful, terrifying, destructive, and always beyond human control—communicate an aspect of Easter in their own way. How does attentiveness to creation prepare us to receive the Easter message?

Let the Children Come

Today many worshipers speak to each other and to God in an age-old call and response. The call goes out: "Alleluia! Christ is risen!" The response returns: "Christ is risen indeed! Alleluia!" This joyous exchange weaves throughout worship, ensuring that this most important of holy days remains a celebration of God's true power rather than a performance trap. Build on today's call-and-response pattern using the familiar words of Psalm 118, appointed for Easter Day each year. Ask the children to make the call: "This is the day that the Lord has made!" Encourage the assembly to respond: "Let us rejoice and be glad in it!" Like the Israelites led in song by Miriam, celebrate with tambourines and hand drums, all played by children. Let these words carry the assembled body of Christ into praise, thanksgiving, and prayer, repeating the call to rejoice, over and over again.

Assembly Song
Gathering

That Easter day with joy was bright ELW 384, LBW 154
The day of resurrection! ELW 361, LBW 141
The strife is o'er, the battle done ELW 366, LBW 135

Psalmody and Acclamations

Chepponis, James. "Eastertime Psalm: Psalms for Easter, Ascension, and Pentecost." SATB, cant, org, assembly, opt 4 tpts, hb. GIA G-3907.
Organ, Anne Krentz. "This Is the Day." SATB, org, assembly. AFP 9781506445755.
Shields, Valerie. "Psalm for Easter." SATB, cant, assembly, org, opt tpt, hb, perc. MSM 80-405.

(GA) Browning, Carol/arr. Tom Andion. "Deo Gloria Alleluia (Easter Gospel Acclamation)" with proper verse for Easter. SATB, cant, assembly, kybd, gtr, opt fl, 2 tpt, perc. GIA G-6402.

Hymn of the Day

Christ has arisen, alleluia/Mfurahini, haleluya ELW 364, WOV 678, TFF 96, LLC 349 *MFURAHINI, HALELUYA*
Christ is risen! Shout Hosanna! ELW 383 *TURNBULL* WOV 672 *JACKSON NEW*
Christ Jesus lay in death's strong bands ELW 370, LBW 134 *CHRIST LAG IN TODESBANDEN*

Offering

At the Lamb's high feast we sing ELW 362, sts. 2, 4; LBW 210, sts. 2, 4
The trumpets sound, the angels sing ELW 531, W&P 139

Communion

Christ the Lord is risen today! ELW 373, LS 64, LBW 130
Now the feast and celebration ELW 167, WOV 789
United at the table/Unidos en las fiesta ELW 498, LLC 408

Sending

Hallelujah! Jesus lives! ELW 380, LBW 147
This joyful Eastertide ELW 391, WOV 676, LBW 149

Additional Assembly Songs

Christ has risen while earth slumbers GTG 231
Lift your voice rejoicing, Mary H82 190
Low in the grace he lay TFF 94
⊕ You are holy/Du är helig ELW 525
⊕ Monteiro, Simei. "Aleluia" from *Global Praise 1*. U. GBGMusik 1890569011.
☼ Brown, Chris/Mack Brock/Matthew Ntlele/Steven Furtick/Wade Joye. "Resurrecting" from CCLI.
☼ Critz, Jordan/Matt Boswell. "Christ Is Risen Indeed" from CCLI.
☼ Ingram, Jason/Jonathan Smith/Kristian Stanfill/Sean Curran. "Glorious Day" from CCLI.
☼ Johnson, Brian/Phil Wickham. "Living Hope" from CCLI.
☼ Maher, Matt/Mia Feldes. "Christ Is Risen" from CCLI.
☼ Tomlin, Chris/Daniel Carson/Ed Cash/Gloria Gaither/Jason Ingram/Matt Maher/William J. Gaither. "Because He Lives (Amen)" from CCLI.

Music for the Day
Choral

P Bankson, Jeremy J. "Good Christian Friends, Rejoice and Sing!" SATB, org, opt br qrt, timp, sus cym, assembly. AFP 9781506452463.

⊕ = global song
☼ = praise song   P = available in Prelude Music Planner

Praetorius, Michael/arr. Michael Burkhardt. "Heut triumphieret Gottes Sohn (Today in Triumph Christ Arose)" from *O Come, Ye Servants of the Lord: Renaissance and Baroque Anthems for the Church Year*. SATB, a cap or cont. CPH 984136.

Organ, Anne Krentz. "Awake, My Heart, with Gladness." SATB, org, opt str, ww. AFP 9781451451542.

P Whitehill, Erik. "Now the Green Blade Rises" from *Wade in the Water: Easy Choral Music for All Ages*. 2 pt mxd, pno. AFP 9780800678616.

Children's Choir

Running, Joseph. "An Easter Carol." U/solo, kybd. MSM 50-4751.

Sedio, Mark. "In the Fair Morning." U, desc or C inst, kybd. LOR AM709.

Sleeth, Natalie. "This Is the Day." U/2 pt, kybd. HIN HMC229.

Keyboard / Instrumental

P ♫ Biery, James. "Christ Has Arisen, Alleluia" from *The Paschal Lamb: Easter Settings for Organ*. Org. AFP 9781451494099.

P Bottomley, Greg. "Jesus Christ Is Risen Today" from *Piano Sunday Morning*. Pno. AFP 9780800663841.

P ♫ Burkhardt, Michael. "Christ lag in Todesbanden" from *Living Voice of the Gospel: The Hymns of Martin Luther*. Org. MSM 10-683.

Handel, George Frideric/arr. Mark Thewes. "Hallelujah Chorus." Pno and org (4 players). MSM 20-867.

Handbell

♫ Lohr, Alan. "Christ lag in Todesbanden." 5 oct, L4. SF 118349.

♫ Moats, William. "Haleluya." 3 oct, L2. Genesis Press GP2040.

Moklebust, Cathy. "African Alleluia." 2, 3, or 4 oct, opt African perc, L4. CG CGB229.

April 12, 2020
Resurrection of Our Lord
Easter Evening

Isaiah proclaims the great feast to come, when God will swallow up death forever. Paul invites us to celebrate the paschal feast with the unleavened bread of sincerity and truth. The Easter evening gospel tells of the risen Christ being made known to the disciples in the breaking of the bread. Our hearts burn within us as the hope of the resurrection is proclaimed in our midst and as Jesus appears to us at the holy table.

Prayer of the Day

O God, whose blessed Son made himself known to his disciples in the breaking of bread, open the eyes of our faith, that we may behold him in all his redeeming work, Jesus Christ, our Savior and Lord, who lives and reigns with you and the Holy Spirit, one God, now and forever.

Gospel Acclamation

Alleluia. Our hearts burn within us while you open to us the scriptures. *Alleluia.* (Luke 24:32)

Readings and Psalm
Isaiah 25:6-9

The prophet portrays a wonderful victory banquet at which death, which in ancient Canaan was depicted as a monster swallowing everyone up, will be swallowed up forever. The prophet urges celebration of this victory, which is salvation.

Psalm 114

Tremble, O earth, at the presence of the LORD. (Ps. 114:7)

1 Corinthians 5:6b-8

In preparation to celebrate Passover, God's people cleaned out all the old leaven from their homes. Paul draws on this practice to portray Christ as our Passover lamb whose sacrifice means that we now clean out the old leaven of malice and wickedness from our lives and replace it with sincerity and truth.

Luke 24:13-49

On the day of his resurrection, Jesus joins two disciples on the road to Emmaus and makes himself known to them in the breaking of bread.

Preface   Easter

Color   White *or* Gold

♫ = relates to hymn of the day
P = available in Prelude Music Planner
162

Easter

Preparing for Easter

Preaching

"But we had hoped . . ." On the third Sunday of Easter the Lukan text reports that the two disciples on the Emmaus road say to Jesus, "But we had hoped . . ." (Luke 24:21).

Easter is the season to proclaim with joy and boldness that all in which we had previously falsely hoped has been put to death. Now is the time, "the queen of seasons, bright" ("Come, you faithful, raise the strain," ELW 363), to raise our voice to proclaim the one true hope—an inheritance that is imperishable, undefiled, and unfading—the hope of Jesus Christ risen from the dead.

"But we had hoped . . ." We had hoped for a better diagnosis, and we were disappointed. We had hoped for a better return on our investment, and the market failed us. We had hoped that homelessness and hunger would somehow have miraculously disappeared in our nation, rather than becoming worse, and the stark truth stands before us that without our own participation and sacrifice in its eradication, there is no hope. In other words, this is the season, a week of weeks, in which to unabashedly proclaim that the false projects and easy answers on which we repeatedly pin our hopes have been pinned instead to the cross and destroyed in the empty tomb. For the first time there is new hope. Real hope. Hope that even death cannot destroy.

It is with this conviction and faithful resolve that the preacher is called in this season to navigate a path from Matthew's fearful ones present around the tomb on Easter morning, through the doubt-filled upper room, on the Emmaus road, and all the way to where the disciples find themselves on Pentecost, "all together in one place" (Acts 2:1). Through all the doubts and fears, in spite of all the "what ifs," amid the places and situations that the gospel spreads before the Easter season assembly, the witness of the early church—almost exclusively from 1 Peter—is of a hope that is unrelenting. Those to whom the author of 1 Peter writes are not the privileged, so this hermeneutic of hope will have to be unpacked for most congregations who are still as burdened by their fears as those first witnesses of the resurrection.

It is a splendid season in which to include in the proclamation the witness and testimony of the newly baptized, or the parents of infants or children baptized at the Vigil. They will have their own stories to tell of hope born or reborn, of a passage from old to new that is the source of this season's name: *paschal*.

One might do well to choose a central theme or image from the overall arc of these readings to anchor the preaching for the season. Hope, of course, could be such an anchor. But so also could a phrase from so many of the lectionary texts: "a new birth into a living hope" (1 Peter 1:3), "I came that they may have life" (John 10:10), or "because I live, you also will live" (John 14:19). Each of these is sturdy enough to stretch the span of the season and to connect the message of the failure of our human plans and hopes over and against the death-defeating hope that Christ freely offers all.

Intercessory Prayer

The women who seek Jesus at the tomb are ushered into the new age of Christ's resurrection with fear and great joy. It is possible that both of these emotions arise from an uncertainty about what is going on. Undoubtedly, fear drives many of the prayers that are spoken in our homes and also in our faith communities. What might our devotion to prayer look like when shaped instead by the great joy that arises from uncertainty? It is not difficult to imagine the excitement with which the women run from the tomb or the enthusiasm with which Thomas confesses, "My Lord and my God!" (John 20:28).

Often in our congregations the time of praying for the church, those in need, and all of creation bears a somber tone. Easter may be a season in which we pray with excitement, great joy, and even a little bit of fear of the unknown, as we look for what our resurrecting God is doing in the world. How do we express our great joy in the resurrection, especially when interceding for the sake of the world? Our prayers of praise and thanksgiving might lead us to lift our hands up. Praise and thanksgiving are often set to music that causes us to sway and move with the Spirit. Even our intercessions can speak of the joy and excitement we have in anticipation of the great things God will bring to fruition. In the Easter season we pray with joyful anticipation because we are rooted in the sure sign of all God's promises fulfilled: the death and resurrection of Jesus Christ. Maybe this is the season to teach all people in the congregation joyful prayer gestures, such as the ancient *orans* position or other gestures that express uplifting within our being. Musically inclined faith communities might intersperse a sung refrain from *Evangelical Lutheran Worship* with the petitions (consider ELW 741, 744, or 752).

The texts of the Easter season call us to see our identity renewed in Christ. We were once not a people, and now we are God's people (1 Peter 2:10). In year A some of the texts from Lent are repeated soon after in the season of Easter. Do we receive these words in a new way in light of the resurrection? Now we lift up the cup of salvation, call on the name of the Lord, and pay our vows in the glory of Christ's new life. In Easter we become the witnesses of the resurrection and are, therefore, called to mindfulness before God of the people most in need of this salvation: those who suffer oppression, those who are persecuted for their faith, and especially those whose lives are endangered when they practice their faith.

Having witnessed how Christ's death and resurrection are God's age-old prophecy and promise fulfilled, the disciples devote themselves to prayer while they wait for a new promise, the Advocate whom Jesus will send. As the Easter season draws to a close, we cling to the presence of the Holy Spirit, who keeps us in the way of Christ, and we are called into a heightened awareness of the work that God is doing now, among us and throughout the world. It is that same Holy Spirit who guides our praying, and even utters prayers on our behalf when we do not know what to pray (Romans 8:26). This Holy Spirit flows from the fearful and joyful hearts of believers out into a needy world.

Assembly Song

Like the readings for the Easter season, assembly song should invite ever-widening reflection on what it means to be Easter people fully living into our baptismal calling as witnesses of the resurrection. The Christ into whose death we are born journeys with us on the way (Easter 3) and becomes the way (Easter 5). Though Jesus was hidden by a cloud at his ascension, we find his presence among us in our assemblies, communities, and friends; in strangers; and each week around word and meal, a foretaste of the great and promised feast.

Unlike secular observances of Christmas and Easter, the church's celebrations of these festivals do not end the following morning; we do well to annually remind our assemblies of this throughout the twelve days of Christmas and the fifty days of Easter. Consider beginning each Sunday of Easter—a week of weeks—with one of the many rousing hymns with exclamatory titles and bold tunes, such as "Alleluia! Jesus is risen!" (ELW 377), "Christ is risen! Alleluia!" (ELW 382), "Christ is risen! Shout Hosanna!" (ELW 383), "Christ is alive! Let Christians sing" (ELW 389), and "We know that Christ is raised" (ELW 449), all of which encourage us to keep festival, and to keep hope. Or, given the abundance of wonderful Easter hymns, consider using select stanzas or refrains as gospel acclamations throughout the season: consider the third stanza of "Christ is arisen" (ELW 372) or alleluias excerpted from "The strife is o'er, the battle done" (ELW 366), "Good Christian friends, rejoice and sing!" (ELW 385), and "O sons and daughters, let us sing" (ELW 386). Instrumental descants, bells, Zimbelsterns, choral stanzas, and other celebratory adornments are appropriate for the entire season, not just Easter Sunday.

Perhaps this season would be an appropriate time to replace instrumental preludes with a gathering song (or songs) as a means of keeping festival, or of teaching the assembly one or more new Easter or baptism hymns or songs that nurture and strengthen their collective voice. For example, consider songs such as "Alleluia," "Come to the table," "God who has saved," "Haleluya! Pujilah Tuhanmu," and the Palestinian "Hallelujah" in the collection *Singing in Community: Paperless Music for Worship* (Augsburg Fortress, 2017).

As noted in the 2017 edition of *Sundays and Seasons Preaching, Year A* (p. 148), the gospel readings for the second through seventh Sundays of Easter can be paired with sections of the catechism, a correlation that can readily be explored through assembly song. After all, these are the days in which the newly baptized now gather as members of the assembly! The following list may be useful for thinking intentionally about hymns and songs that trace the long arc of Lent's baptismal preparation through Easter's baptismal living: the Apostles' Creed (Easter 2), Holy Communion (Easter 3), Holy Baptism (Easter 4), the Lord's Prayer (Easter 5), the Ten Commandments (Easter 6), and Confession and Forgiveness (Easter 7).

Finally, as has been suggested in previous seasonal essays, it may be helpful to review the guidance and suggestions in sources such as *Keeping Time* (pp. 122–130), the "Scripture Index—Service Music and Hymns" section of *ELW Leaders Edition* (pp. 906–920), and the "Music" section of *Principles for Worship*.

Worship Space

The art and environment in your church can reflect the glorious and wondrous resurrection of Christ. The fasting is over; the time of feasting is at hand. It is a season when the worship space can point to the risen Christ in our midst.

Easter is the church's greatest festival; the worship space can have even more adornment than it does in the Christmas season. Strive to be authentic in any decor that is chosen, and consider displaying art or furniture from the local community of believers. Always use the very best elements for decor at church. Plastic, silk, and artificial flowers don't have a role of honor in the worship space. Keep the ambo, table, and font unobstructed. Add flowers or other decor to the room, but add nothing that gets in the way of the movement of the people during the liturgies.

Fabric can be used to enhance the space during Easter. Simple swaths of sheer fabric placed high above the heads of the congregation can be effective. Banners can also be used. It is not necessary to have banners with words or slogans; sometimes less is more. Rainbows and doves are often symbols used in Easter decor. Suggest rainbow motifs in sheer fabrics instead of hanging the stereotypical rainbow arch of intense colors. Let some shimmering white banners suggest the dove instead of the overused image of a dove. Add a depiction of the olive branch in a creative way, appropriate to the scale of your space. Images of the empty cross and the risen Christ may be displayed to show visual revelation. Change the nave's cross drape to white and use a vase that held bare branches in Lent to now hold lush, green, living plants, depicting the change of the church season from barrenness to abundance, fasting to feasting.

Art depicting scripture stories that was created during Lent can stay in place for the season of Easter. Set up a large floor easel to display a work of art that is stationary through the season. Choose some fine art for service booklets or for projection in the nave. An excellent resource for fine art is the National Gallery in Washington, DC. It provides open access to thousands of digital images in public domain, free of charge (images.nga.gov).

Wreaths and garlands are often underused in Easter. Wreaths are appropriate for the season as they signify triumph and eternity. The paschal candle can be placed near the table to illuminate the incarnation of Christ's body in the meal. Or the candle may be placed near the font to reflect new birth in baptism. If placing the paschal candle near the font, consider adding large new candles near the paschal candle representing the newly baptized. The candles could burn every Sunday in the season and be taken home after Pentecost.

The last day of Easter is the day of Pentecost. The focus of the seating arrangement, if movable, could be the font. Drape the nave's cross in red. Flames are a strong image of the Holy Spirit, as are wind, breath, and the image of a dove. Experiment with red ribbons flowing abundantly down from a large hoop to hang gracefully in the nave. Create an aura of flames by using seven sheer fabric banners in hues of red and orange. Add white doves to cascading red ribbons. Consider an alcohol type candle to float on the baptismal waters during a reading of the Pentecost story. Alternately, if your space would allow, place forty-nine smaller glass votive candles in addition to the paschal candle on Pentecost Sunday to visually represent the fifty days of Easter.

Seasonal Checklist

- If your assembly keeps the tradition of burying the alleluia in Lent, celebrate its return with lavish alleluias during the Easter season.
- Light the paschal candle on each of the Sundays of Easter, including the Day of Pentecost.
- It is particularly appropriate during the Easter season to use thanksgiving for baptism as an alternative to confession and forgiveness. A new form is available in the seasonal worship texts section (p. 168).
- If your congregation doesn't already use a full thanksgiving at the table, do so in Easter. Forms VII and X (*ELW*, pp. 67, 69) use fresh, poetic language that pulls together many of the images in the Easter readings. Form IV (pp. 111, 133) can be used from Ash Wednesday through the Day of Pentecost, creating an intentional unity through the whole Easter cycle. Form IX (p. 68) calls to mind the cosmic reach of the resurrection.
- Schedule an ecumenical Ascension Day service with other local congregations or, if geographically possible, with other Lutheran congregations in your conference/cluster. Rotate the host congregation each year.
- Consider observing the Day of Pentecost as the next baptismal festival after the Vigil of Easter.
- If you will use a diversity of languages for the Day of Pentecost, make preparations in advance with musicians and readers.

Worship Texts for Easter

Thanksgiving for Baptism

All may make the sign of the cross, the sign that is marked at baptism, as the presiding minister begins.

Alleluia! Christ is risen.
Christ is risen indeed. Alleluia!

Joined to Christ in the waters of baptism,
we are raised with him to new life.
Let us give thanks for the gift of baptism.

Water may be poured into the font as the presiding minister gives thanks.

We give you thanks, O God,
for in the beginning you created us in your image
and planted us in a well-watered garden.
In the desert you promised pools of water for the parched,
and you gave us water from the rock.
When we did not know the way,
you sent the Good Shepherd to lead us to still waters.
At the cross, you watered us from Jesus' wounded side,
and on this day, you shower us again with the water of life.

We praise you for your salvation through water,
for the water in this font,
and for all water everywhere.
Bathe us in your forgiveness, grace, and love.
Satisfy the thirsty, and give us the life only you can give.

To you be given honor and praise
through Jesus Christ our Lord
in the unity of the Holy Spirit, now and forever.
Amen.

Offering Prayer

Merciful God,
our ordinary gifts seem small for such a celebration,
but you make of them an abundance,
just as you do with our lives.
Feed us again at this table
for service in your name,
in the strength of the risen Christ.
Amen.

Invitation to Communion

Come to the banquet. Behold the risen Christ.

Prayer after Communion

Life-giving God,
you have fed us with your word,
and our hearts burn within us.
Through this meal you have opened us to your presence.
Now send us forth to share the gifts of Easter with all in need;
through Jesus Christ our Lord.
Amen.

Blessing

May the One who brought forth Jesus from the dead
raise you to new life, fill you with hope,
and turn your mourning into dancing.
Almighty God, Father, ☩ Son, and Holy Spirit,
bless you now and forever.
Amen.

Dismissal

Christ is risen, just as he said.
Go in peace. Share the good news. Alleluia!
Thanks be to God. Alleluia!

Seasonal Rites for Easter

Blessing of a Community Garden

This brief service of blessing and prayer may be used when a congregation gathers at a garden on church grounds or in the community.

Blessing

God of creation, we thank you that in this time and place you have granted us a community garden where your children may gather and grow together. Bless our footsteps as we walk upon this holy ground. Bless our hands as we plant new seeds and relationships. Keep us ever vigilant to see the growth you bring, that all who partake of this harvest might find in it a foretaste of the heavenly banquet prepared for us in your kingdom. **Amen.**

One or more of the following readings and hymns may be used.

Readings

Isaiah 55:6-13
Psalm 148:1-6
Mark 13:31-32
1 Corinthians 3:5-9

Hymns

All creatures, worship God most high! ELW 835
As saints of old ELW 695
Taste and see ELW 493, TFF 126
All things bright and beautiful WOV 767
God, whose farm is all creation ELW 734

Prayer

God of abundance, who breathes life into humanity and speaks creation into being, you have graciously entrusted us with the care of all your creatures and called us to encounter you in the breaking of bread and the sharing of a common cup. Pour out your Spirit upon this garden, that it might be a place of devotion and care; of reconciliation with our wounded planet and with one another; of growth and flourishing within this soil and within our bodies. May the fruits of our labor be acceptable in your sight, to the well-being of all your beloved creation and your eternal glory. **Amen.**

April 19, 2020
Second Sunday of Easter

In today's gospel the risen Christ appears to the disciples and offers them the gift of peace. Even amid doubts and questions, we experience the resurrection in our Sunday gathering around word and meal, and in our everyday lives. Throughout the coming Sundays of Easter the first two readings will be from the Acts of the Apostles and the first letter of Peter. Even as the early Christians proclaimed the resurrection, we rejoice in the new birth and living hope we receive in baptism.

Prayer of the Day

Almighty and eternal God, the strength of those who believe and the hope of those who doubt, may we, who have not seen, have faith in you and receive the fullness of Christ's blessing, who lives and reigns with you and the Holy Spirit, one God, now and forever.

Gospel Acclamation

Alleluia. Blessed are those who have not seen and yet have come to believe. *Alleluia.* (John 20:29)

Readings and Psalm

Acts 2:14a, 22-32

After the Holy Spirit comes to the apostles on Pentecost, Peter preaches the gospel to the gathered crowd. He tells them that Jesus, who obediently went to his death according to God's plan, was raised from the dead by God. Finally, he appeals to scripture, quoting Psalm 16:8-11, to show that Jesus is the Messiah: though crucified, the risen Jesus is now enthroned.

Psalm 16

In your presence there is fullness of joy. (Ps. 16:11)

1 Peter 1:3-9

This epistle was written to encourage Christians experiencing hardships and suffering because of their faith in Christ. The letter opens by blessing God for the living hope we have through Christ's resurrection even amid difficult circumstances and surroundings.

John 20:19-31

The risen Jesus appears to his disciples, offering them a benediction, a commission, and the gift of the Holy Spirit. But one of their number is missing, and his unbelief prompts another visit from the Lord.

Preface   Easter

Color   White

Prayers of Intercession

The prayers are prepared locally for each occasion. The following examples may be adapted or used as appropriate.

Uplifted by the promised hope of healing and resurrection, we join the people of God in all times and places in praying for the church, the world, and all who are in need.

A brief silence.

Open the doors we close, O God, when we fear those who worship you in different ways. Guide us to unity and harmony so that we may come to respect and cherish our commonalities. Lord, in your mercy,

hear our prayer.

Open the paths we ignore, O God, when we prioritize financial gain and convenience over listening to the groaning of the earth. Inspire all to care for the world you have made so that living things might thrive. Lord, in your mercy,

hear our prayer.

Open the rooms we lock, O God, to those who live without a homeland or place of safety. We pray that generous nations offer refuge and peace for all. Lord, in your mercy,

hear our prayer.

Open the hearts we close, O God, to the cries of those in pain. We pray for those isolated physically or emotionally through incarceration, addiction, mental illness, chronic suffering, grief, and all in need (*especially*). Lord, in your mercy,

hear our prayer.

Open the ways of love, O God, in the pursuit of peace throughout the world, and bless the efforts of missionaries, healthcare professionals, activists for women and children, and relief workers, especially those who find themselves in harm's way. (*Here other worldwide ministries may be named.*) Lord, in your mercy,

hear our prayer.

Here other intercessions may be offered.

Open the way to eternal life, O God, as we remember those who have died in faith (*especially Olavus Petri and Laurentius Petri, renewers of the church*). Free us from the fear of death, that we embrace the peace you have promised. Lord, in your mercy,

hear our prayer.

With bold confidence in your love, almighty God, we place all for whom we pray into your eternal care; through Christ our Lord.
Amen.

Ideas for the Day

- "The Room Where It Happens" from the Broadway musical *Hamilton* is sung by Aaron Burr, who enviously recounts how a major political compromise was reached during a mysterious dinner table bargain. Burr laments his absence from that meeting and ends with the refrain, "I wanna (I've got to) be in the room where it happens" (Lin-Manuel Miranda, Atlantic Records, 2015). Likewise, Thomas is missing from the room when it happens: the resurrected Jesus mysteriously appears and bestows the gift of the Holy Spirit upon the disciples. Thomas wants to share that experience. Jesus ends this exclusion by coming to Thomas so that he is once again included in the community of disciples. We might wonder who is being left out by our worship, church leadership, ministry programs, and outreach projects. Who are we excluding? Do we expect those on the outside to come to us, or do we join Jesus and go to them?
- On his resurrected body, Jesus still bears the wounds and scars of his crucifixion. We often seek to hide our imperfections and flaws through makeup, Instagram filters, or surgery. Oliver Cromwell allegedly instructed his portrait's artist: "Paint me as I am, warts and all." The risen Christ is made known in our brokenness and imperfections, and we share the good news of resurrection when we too can courageously show our scars to others. On the podcast *On Being*, host Krista Tippett interviews palliative care physician Dr. BJ Miller about reframing his relationship to his body after losing multiple limbs. He discusses the moment he stopped covering up his scars and the transformative effect it has had on his patients ("Reframing Our Relationship to That We Don't Control," January 28, 2016; onbeing.org). Consider reading the ELCA social message on "People Living with Disabilities" from 2010 (elca.org).
- Jesus invites Thomas to experience the resurrection by touching his hands and side. Brain researcher Helena Backlund Wasling discusses the science behind the importance of touch in our everyday life in her TEDx presentation, "Fight Off Loneliness with Touch" (*TedxGöteborg*, December 30, 2014; tedxgoteborg.com). She lifts up the healing power of touch and its role in forming connection, offering comfort, and creating emotional bonds. Provide space during worship for experiences that focus on the sense of touch: blessing of hands, laying on of hands, or the sign of the cross rite found in the Welcome to Baptism section of *Evangelical Lutheran Worship Leaders Edition* (pp. 593–594).

Connections with Creation

Jesus breathes the Holy Spirit onto the disciples huddled in fear, opening to them a new future borne along by resurrection promise. In making connections to creation during the Easter season, it is vital to link resurrection hope and our belief in God as creator. It is precisely the God who creates and delights in the world who can bring new life and hope out of death. Our gospel text makes this point in its powerful allusion to the Genesis creation: as Jesus breathes the Spirit into his disciples, he mirrors God breathing the Spirit into Adam's lungs. The Holy Spirit creates and sustains all creatures, and the breath in our lungs, which we share with every dog and hamster, every sparrow and sea lion, is our participation together in God's holy and sustaining presence. As Psalm 104:30 puts it, "You send forth your Spirit, and they are created; and so you renew the face of the earth."

Let the Children Come

The old adage "seeing is believing" holds true for children and youth. Children are concrete learners. They need to see and feel to learn. Youth tend to be black-or-white, either/or thinkers. In that way, children and youth are like Thomas in today's gospel. So what do children and youth see, feel, and hear during worship today that helps them believe Jesus is risen? Greeting one another with a sign of Christ's peace as the risen Christ greets the disciples in the gospel story today? The worship space still dressed in its festive Easter garb? Adults, who normally do not shout during worship, raising their voices in loud alleluias? The table set with bread and wine for all to be fed? Easter songs and hymns sung with gusto? How will your congregation show the children in your midst your assembly's belief in the risen Christ?

Assembly Song
Gathering

Come, you faithful, raise the strain   ELW 363, LBW 132
Good Christian friends, rejoice and sing!   ELW 385, LBW 144
The risen Christ   ELW 390

Psalmody and Acclamations

Alonso, Tony. "Lord, You Will Show Us the Path of Life" from TLP:A.
Miller, Aaron David. "Psalm 16," Refrain 3, from PSCY.
Sedio, Mark. "Psalm 16" from PWA.
(GA) Browning, Carol/arr. Tom Andion. "Deo Gloria Alleluia (Easter Gospel Acclamation)" with proper verse for Easter 2. SATB, cant, assembly, kybd, gtr, opt fl, 2 tpt, perc. GIA G-6402.

Hymn of the Day

Alleluia! Christ is arisen/¡Aleluya! Cristo resucitó ELW 375, LLC 361 *SANTO DOMINGO*

O sons and daughters, let us sing ELW 386/387, LBW 139 *O FILII ET FILIAE*

We walk by faith ELW 635 *SHANTI* WOV 675 *DUNLAP'S CREEK*

Offering

Day of arising ELW 374, sts. 3-4; OBS 54, sts. 3-4

The peace of the Lord/La paz del Señor ELW 646, LLC 471

Communion

Be not afraid ELW 388

Now the feast and celebration ELW 167, WOV 789

We who once were dead ELW 495, LBW 207

Sending

Peace, to soothe our bitter woes ELW 381, LBW 338

Thine is the glory ELW 376, LBW 145

Additional Assembly Songs

Day of delight and beauty unbounded GTG 242

May you look beyond seeing ASG 22

Up from the earth in dawn array CBM 106

⊕ Capri, Valerio/Jocelyn Belamide. "Pace a sia, pace a voi" from *Hosanna! Ecumenical Songs for Justice and Peace*. U. WCC Publications 9782825416679.

⊕ Matsikenyiri, Patrick. "Mambo Jesu achiwoneka" from *Njalo (Always)*. ABI 9780687498079.

☼ Baird, Jonathan/Meghan Baird/Ryan Baird/Stephen Altrogge. "Behold Our God" from CCLI.

☼ Cash, Ed/Kari Jobe. "Breathe on Us" from CCLI.

☼ Dwane, Ted/Ben Lovett/Winston Marshall/Marcus Mumford. "Believe" from *Wilder Mind*. mumfordandsons.com.

☼ Gungor, David/Michael Gungor/Lisa Gungor. "Breathe" from *The Brilliance*. thebrilliancemusic.com.

☼ King, Aodhan/Joel Davies. "To My Knees" from CCLI.

☼ Skinner, Anthony/Bobby Strand/Josh Baldwin. "Peace" from CCLI.

Music for the Day
Choral

♫ Bojos, Luis/arr. Nathan Zullinger. "¡Aleluya! Christo resucitó/Alleluia, Christ Is Arisen." SATB, a cap, perc. MSM 50-4665.

P Ellingboe, Bradley. "The Chief Cornerstone" from *Augsburg Easy Choirbook*, vol. 1. 2 pt mxd, kybd, opt tpt. AFP 9780800676391.

P Heald, Jason. "Alleluia! Alleluia! Hearts to Heaven." SAB, pno, tpt. AFP 9781506452432.

P Wold, Wayne L. "Be in My Seeing." SATB, kybd. SEL 410-672.

Children's Choir

P Bach, J. S. "Lord Jesus Christ, God's Only Son" from *Bach for All Seasons*. U, kybd. AFP 9780800658540.

Klinge, Barbara. "I Know That My Redeemer Lives." 2 pt, pno. CPH 984311.

P ♫ Organ, Anne Krentz. "We Walk by Faith." 2 pt, pno. AFP 9781451492637.

Keyboard / Instrumental

P ♫ Biery, James. "Alleluia! Christ Is Arisen/¡Aleluya! Cristo resucitó" from *The Paschal Lamb: Easter Settings for Organ*. Org. AFP 9781451494099.

♫ Callahan, Charles. An Easter Suite. Org. MSM 10-401.

P ♫ Floeter, Valerie A. "We Walk by Faith" from *Jesus, Still Lead On: Piano Settings for Today*. Pno. AFP 9781506426440.

P Raabe, Nancy M. "Now the Green Blade Rises" from *Foot-Friendly Preludes*. Org. AFP 9781451479539.

Handbell

♫ Frizzel, J. D. "Easter Triumph." 3-6 oct, L2+. LOR 20/1562L.

♫ Hurlbutt, Patricia. "O Sons and Daughters, Let Us Sing." 3-5 oct, L3. LOR 20/2025L.

♫ Stephenson, Valerie. "O Sons and Daughters, Let Us Sing." 3-5 oct hb, opt 3 oct hc, L3. GIA G-6150.

Sunday, April 19
Olavus Petri, priest, died 1552; Laurentius Petri, Bishop of Uppsala, died 1573; renewers of the church

These two brothers are commemorated for their introduction of the Lutheran movement to the Church of Sweden after studying at the University of Wittenberg. They returned home and, through the support of King Gustavus Vasa, began their work. Olavus published a catechism, hymnal, and a Swedish version of the mass. He resisted attempts by the king to gain royal control of the church. Laurentius was a professor at the university in Uppsala. When the king wanted to abolish the ministry of bishops, Laurentius persuaded him otherwise. The historic episcopate continues in Sweden to this day. Together the brothers published a complete Bible in Swedish and a revised liturgy in 1541.

Tuesday, April 21
Anselm, Bishop of Canterbury, died 1109

This eleventh- and twelfth-century Benedictine monk stands out as one of the greatest theologians between Augustine and Thomas Aquinas. He is counted among the medieval mystics who emphasized the maternal aspects of God. Of Jesus Anselm

⊕ = global song   ♫ = relates to hymn of the day

☼ = praise song   P = available in Prelude Music Planner

says, "In sickness you nurse us and with pure milk you feed us." Anselm is perhaps best known for his "satisfaction" theory of atonement. He argued that human rebellion against God demands a payment, but because humanity is fallen it is incapable of making that satisfaction. But God takes on human nature in Jesus Christ to make the perfect payment for sin.

Thursday, April 23
Toyohiko Kagawa, renewer of society, died 1960

Toyohiko Kagawa (toy-oh-hee-koh ka-ga-wa) was born in 1888 in Kobe, Japan. Orphaned early, he was disowned by his remaining extended family when he became a Christian. Kagawa wrote, spoke, and worked at length on ways to employ Christian principles in the ordering of society. His vocation to help the poor led him to live among them. He established schools, hospitals, and churches. He also worked for peace and established the Anti-War League. He was arrested for his efforts to reconcile Japan and China after the Japanese attack of 1940.

Saturday, April 25
Mark, Evangelist

Though Mark himself was not an apostle, it is likely that he was a member of one of the early Christian communities. It is possible that he is the John Mark of Acts 12 whose mother owned the house where the apostles gathered. The gospel attributed to him is brief and direct. It is considered by many to be the earliest gospel. Tradition has it that Mark went to preach in Alexandria, Egypt, became the first bishop there, and was martyred.

April 26, 2020
Third Sunday of Easter

Today's gospel begins with two disciples walking to Emmaus, overcome with sadness, loss, and disappointment. They had hoped Jesus, who was crucified, would be the one to redeem Israel! Yet the risen Christ walks with them and then opens their eyes in the breaking of the bread. Each Sunday our hearts burn within us as the scriptures are proclaimed and Christ appears to us as bread is broken and wine is poured. The story of Emmaus becomes the pattern of our worship each Lord's day.

Prayer of the Day

O God, your Son makes himself known to all his disciples in the breaking of bread. Open the eyes of our faith, that we may see him in his redeeming work, who lives and reigns with you and the Holy Spirit, one God, now and forever.

Gospel Acclamation

Alleluia. Our hearts burn within us while you open to us the scriptures. *Alleluia.* (Luke 24:32)

Readings and Psalm
Acts 2:14a, 36-41

Today's reading is the conclusion of Peter's sermon preached following the giving of the Holy Spirit to the apostles on the day of Pentecost. The center of his preaching is the bold declaration that God has made the crucified Jesus both Lord and Christ.

Psalm 116:1-4, 12-19

I will call on the name of the LORD. (Ps. 116:13)

1 Peter 1:17-23

The imagery of exile is used to help the readers of this letter understand that they are strangers in a strange land. Christians no longer belong to this age. Through the death of Christ we belong to God, so that our focus, faith, and hope are no longer on such things as silver or gold.

Luke 24:13-35

The colorful story of Jesus' appearance to two disciples on the road to Emmaus answers the question of how Jesus is to be recognized among us. Here, he is revealed through the scriptures and in the breaking of bread.

Preface   Easter

Color   White

Prayers of Intercession

The prayers are prepared locally for each occasion. The following examples may be adapted or used as appropriate.

Uplifted by the promised hope of healing and resurrection, we join the people of God in all times and places in praying for the church, the world, and all who are in need.

A brief silence.

For those whose hearts are fervent with love for your gospel, that they are empowered to tell the story of your love in their lives and to show hospitality in response to this love. Lord, in your mercy,

hear our prayer.

For the diverse natural world: for jungles, prairies, forests, valleys, mountains, and for all the wild and endangered animals who call these spaces home, that they are nurtured and protected. Lord, in your mercy,

hear our prayer.

For broken systems we have inherited and that we continue to perpetuate, forgive us. Restrain the nations from fighting over limited resources. Redeem us from the cycles of scarcity and violence. Lord, in your mercy,

hear our prayer.

For all who call upon your healing name, give rest. Stay with us, and walk with all those who are hungry, friendless, despairing, and desiring healing in body and spirit (*especially*). Lord, in your mercy,

hear our prayer.

For the faith forming ministries of this church. For those preparing for baptism, first communion, confirmation, and membership (*especially*). For those who participate in Sunday school and adult education; guide and inspire learners of every age and ability. Lord, in your mercy,

hear our prayer.

Here other intercessions may be offered.

Create in our hearts a yearning to rest in your promise of eternal and resurrected life. Give us thankful hearts for those who have died, even as we look forward to the hope of new life with you. Lord, in your mercy,

hear our prayer.

With bold confidence in your love, almighty God, we place all for whom we pray into your eternal care; through Christ our Lord.

Amen.

Ideas for the Day

- Whether we associate roads with traffic, long commutes, or wasted time, traveling on the road rarely leads to meaningful encounters anymore. Yet the road can be a place of transition and a chance to encounter the sacred. In *The Book of Joy*, Archbishop Desmond Tutu shares his practice of blessing other drivers on the road (New York: Penguin Random House, 2016, pp. 198–199). Instead of getting frustrated by the person who cuts him off in traffic, he wonders if the driver has a spouse with pancreatic cancer or is rushing to the hospital because his wife is giving birth. What are other ways we might practice recognizing Christ in the strangers we encounter on the road? Have the assembly make care bags to keep in the car to share with people in need whom they meet on the road. Create a road or labyrinth in your worship space with stations to reflect on the roads, roadblocks, intersections, and road signs in our life of faith.

- For people of color, the road may elicit feelings of danger and fear. Think about the interactions on the road between police and people of color (for example, Michael Brown, Sam Dubose, Philando Castile, Walter Scott). When we encounter someone unfamiliar on the road, is our first reaction to call the police in fear? Who has the power in these situations? The disciples offer a different model for how to encounter the stranger. They welcome him, accompany him on the road, learn from him, and show him hospitality. Ultimately, they realize this unfamiliar person is Jesus. Resurrection is the new narrative we live through embracing the unknown and striving for racial justice on the road.

- Since the meal is the centerpiece to this gospel story, consider elevating the focus on the eucharist this week by celebrating it in a new way. Stand in a circle and have each person offer the bread to the person next to them, or if you normally use wafers, try serving a full loaf of bread instead. Emphasize the presence of the risen Christ with us in the meal.

- Jesus comes upon the disciples in the midst of their grief, disappointment, and disbelief. Even though Jesus knows exactly what they are going through, he asks them about it anyway. Without trying to minimize or fix their feelings, Jesus listens. Empathic listening is transformative and leads us to resurrection and new life. Provide guidelines on how to listen well, and practice one-to-one conversations in the congregation.

Connections with Creation

Our gospel reading turns on a gesture of hospitality. The two grief-stricken disciples don't recognize the Jesus-stranger walking with them until they invite him to join them in the house and he breaks bread. We might think about how in our worship spaces we can extend hospitality to the natural world. While a special worship service outdoors may accomplish some of these goals, hospitality to the natural world extends beyond seeing it as merely the setting for worship. One congregation invited parishioners to bring stones from the nearby creek to worship and place them around and in the baptismal font before confession and forgiveness. The stones were a way of symbolically welcoming the creek and its ecology into worship and connecting the font to the local watershed. Might we even be able to see the creatures of our local ecology as fellow "members" of the worshiping congregation, in the spirit of all creation singing praise to God, such as in Psalm 148?

Let the Children Come

On the road to Emmaus, a stranger walks with stunned and grieving disciples. Walking side by side, they may not even look at each other except for a sideways glance now and then. As scripture states, "their eyes were kept from recognizing [Jesus]" (Luke 24:16). However, once at the table together, now able to look each other fully in the face, "their eyes were opened" (Luke 24:31). Children are very tuned in to faces in a way many adults have forgotten. Show children today the holiness of really looking at each other during the sharing of the peace and the sharing of communion. Do this by slowing down the assembly line of peace sharing and meal serving. Encourage everyone to take a deep breath before moving on to the next person. Embrace the grace that occurs when we truly see each other face to face. Help the assembly embody the grace of God today.

Assembly Song
Gathering

Awake, my heart, with gladness   ELW 378, LBW 129
That Easter day with joy was bright   ELW 384, LBW 154
With high delight let us unite   ELW 368, LBW 140

Psalmody and Acclamations

McRae, Shirley W. "Psalm 116" from *ChildrenSing Psalms*. U, assembly, kybd, 5 hb.
Mummert, Mark. "Psalm 116," Refrain 1, from PSCY.
Schalk, Carl. "Antiphon 2 for Psalm 116" from PATP. Use with ELW tone 8 in Emin.
(GA) Browning, Carol/arr. Tom Andion. "Deo Gloria Alleluia (Easter Gospel Acclamation)" with proper verse for Easter 3. SATB, cant, assembly, kybd, gtr, opt fl, 2 tpt, perc. GIA G-6402.

Hymn of the Day

Day of arising   ELW 374 *RAABE*   OBS 54 *BUNESSAN*
Christ is alive! Let Christians sing   ELW 389, LBW 363 *TRURO*
This joyful Eastertide   ELW 391, WOV 676, LBW 149 *VRUECHTEN*

Offering

At the Lamb's high feast we sing   ELW 362, sts. 2, 4; LBW 210, sts. 2, 4
We know that Christ is raised   ELW 449, LBW 189

Communion

Bread of life, our host and meal   ELW 464
I am the Bread of life   ELW 485, WOV 702
You satisfy the hungry heart   ELW 484, WOV 711

Sending

Christ the Lord is risen today; Alleluia!   ELW 369, LBW 128
We are baptized in Christ Jesus   ELW 451, WOV 698

Additional Assembly Songs

Open our eyes, Lord   TFF 98, LS 31, W&P 113
¿Qué venías conversando?   LLC 362
⊕ To God our thanks we give/Reamo leboga   ELW 682
⊕ Come, walk with us/Hamba nathi   GS2 6
☼ Baloche, Paul. "Open the Eyes of My Heart" from CCLI.
☼ Critz, Jordan/Matt Boswell. "Christ Is Risen Indeed" from CCLI.
☼ Gungor, David/John Arndt/Michael Rossback. "Christ Is Risen" from *The Brilliance*. thebrilliancemusic.com.
☼ Houston, Joel/Matt Crocker. "Street Called Mercy" from CCLI.
☼ Maher, Matt/Matt Redman. "Remembrance (The Communion Song)" from CCLI.
☼ McMillan, John Mark. "Heart Bleeds" from CCLI.

Music for the Day
Choral

Biery, James. "O sacrum convivium." SATB, a cap. MSM 50-8311.
P Carter, John. "I Sing the Love That Dreamed Creation." SAB, pno. AFP 9781506456768.
P ♫ Highben, Zebulon M. "Christ Is Alive! Let Christians Sing." SATB, org, br qrt, opt assembly. AFP 9781451451580.
P ♫ Schalk, Carl. "Day of Arising." SATB, org. AFP 9780800658670.

Children's Choir

P Haugen, Marty. "Now in This Banquet." 2 pt, pno, opt gtr, 2 C inst, assembly. GIA G-2918.
P Highben, Zebulon. "In the Breaking of the Bread." 2 pt, org. MSM 50-9937.
Petrich, Robert. "Alleluia! Risen Indeed." 2 pt, kybd. MSM 80-401.

Keyboard / Instrumental

P ♫ Bingham, Seth. "Truro" from *A New Liturgical Year, Volume 2: Anthology for Organ*. Org. AFP 9781451499070.
♫ Davenport, Rudy. "Morning Has Broken" from *Morning Has Broken: A Suite of Hymns for Piano*. Pno. MSM 15-833.
P ♫ Diemer, Emma Lou. "This Joyful Eastertide" from *Glory, Laud, and Honor: Organ Settings*. Org. AFP 9781451494068.

⊕ = global song   ♫ = relates to hymn of the day
☼ = praise song   P = available in Prelude Music Planner

P ♫ Raabe, Nancy M. "Day of Arising" from *Day of Arising: A Tapestry of Musical Traditions*. Pno. AFP 9780800637460.

Handbell

♫ Krug, Jason. "This Joyful Eastertide." 3-7 oct hb, opt 3-5 hc, tpt, L3. BP HB517.

♫ McFadden, Jane. "This Joyful Eastertide." 3-5 oct hb, opt 3-4 oct hc. L2+. HOP2276.

♫ Moklebust, Cathy. "Christ Is Alive! Let Christians Sing." 3-5 oct, opt C, B-flat, F or C bass inst, L2. CG CGB877. 2-3 oct, CGB876.

Wednesday, April 29
Catherine of Siena, theologian, died 1380

Catherine of Siena was a member of the Order of Preachers (Dominicans), and among Roman Catholics she was the first woman to receive the title Doctor of the Church. She was a contemplative and is known for her mystical visions of Jesus. This gift of mysticism apparently extended back into her childhood, much to the dismay of her parents, who wanted her to be like other children. Catherine was a humanitarian who worked to alleviate the suffering of the poor and imprisoned. She was also a renewer of church and society and advised both popes and any persons who told her their problems. Catherine's contemplative life was linked to her concern for the poor and suffering. She is a reminder that prayer and activism belong together.

Friday, May 1
Philip and James, Apostles

Philip was one of the first disciples of Jesus, who after following Jesus invited Nathanael to "come and see." According to tradition, Philip preached in Asia Minor and died as a martyr in Phrygia. James, the son of Alphaeus, is called "the Less" (meaning "short" or "younger") to distinguish him from another apostle named James, commemorated July 25. Philip and James are commemorated together because the remains of these two saints were placed in the Church of the Apostles in Rome on this day in 561.

Saturday, May 2
Athanasius, Bishop of Alexandria, died 373

Athanasius (ath-an-AY-shus) attended the Council of Nicea in 325 as a deacon and secretary to the bishop of Alexandria. At the council, and when he himself served as bishop of Alexandria, he defended the full divinity of Christ against the Arian position held by emperors, magistrates, and theologians. Because of his defense of the divinity of Christ, he was considered a troublemaker and was banished from Alexandria on five occasions. As bishop, one of his paschal letters to surrounding bishops gives a list for books that should be considered canonical scripture. He lists the twenty-seven New Testament books that are recognized today.

♫ = relates to hymn of the day
P = available in Prelude Music Planner
176

May 3, 2020
Fourth Sunday of Easter

Today is sometimes called "Good Shepherd Sunday." Jesus is called the "gate" of the sheep in today's gospel. The risen Christ opens the way to abundant life. He anoints our heads with oil and guides us beside the still waters of our baptism. Each Sunday he spreads a feast before us amid the world's violence and war. We go forth to be signs of the resurrection and extend God's tender care to all creation.

Prayer of the Day

O God our shepherd, you know your sheep by name and lead us to safety through the valleys of death. Guide us by your voice, that we may walk in certainty and security to the joyous feast prepared in your house, through Jesus Christ, our Savior and Lord, who lives and reigns with you and the Holy Spirit, one God, now and forever.

Gospel Acclamation

Alleluia. Jesus says, I am the good shepherd. I know my own and my own know me. *Alleluia.* (John 10:14)

Readings and Psalm

Acts 2:42-47

Today's reading is a description of life in the community following Peter's sermon on the day of Pentecost, when the Spirit was poured out on God's people. The new community is sustained in worship and fellowship, shares what they have, and ensures that everyone has enough.

Psalm 23

The LORD is my shepherd; I shall not be in want. (Ps. 23:1)

1 Peter 2:19-25

Doing the right things does not guarantee that one will not experience difficulties, hardships, rejection, or even suffering. Here Christ is presented as the model for our path of endurance and loyalty to God, particularly amid adversity.

John 10:1-10

Jesus uses an image familiar to the people of his day to make a point about spiritual leadership. Those who listen to Jesus are led to abundant life.

Preface   Easter

Color   White

Prayers of Intercession

The prayers are prepared locally for each occasion. The following examples may be adapted or used as appropriate.

Uplifted by the promised hope of healing and resurrection, we join the people of God in all times and places in praying for the church, the world, and all who are in need.

A brief silence.

Shepherding God, we thank you for the educational ministries of your church. Enrich the work of teachers, professors, mentors, advisors, and faculty at colleges, seminaries, and learning sites (*local colleges and seminaries may be named*). Lord, in your mercy,

hear our prayer.

Creating God, we praise you for those who maintain and operate farm equipment, for those who plant and harvest crops, for local farmers' markets, and for those involved in agriculture of any kind. Strengthen their hands as they feed the world. Lord, in your mercy,

hear our prayer.

Guiding God, no one should be in want. Bid the nations to return to your paths of righteousness and inspire our leaders to walk in your ways, so that all may have the opportunity to live abundantly and sustainably. Lord, in your mercy,

hear our prayer.

Comforting God, you carry us tenderly. We pray for those who walk through dark valleys overshadowed by anxiety and overwhelmed with suffering (*especially*). Lord, in your mercy,

hear our prayer.

Nurturing God, you desire justice for the hungry. Bless advocacy work, food pantries, and feeding ministries in our congregations (*local ministries may be named*). May none of our neighbors lack for basic needs. Lord, in your mercy,

hear our prayer.

Here other intercessions may be offered.

Everlasting God, your beloved have heard your voice; you have called them by name and guided them to your side in death. We thank you for their lives of faithful witness. Lord, in your mercy,

hear our prayer.

With bold confidence in your love, almighty God, we place all for whom we pray into your eternal care; through Christ our Lord.
Amen.

Ideas for the Day

- John's gospel says that Jesus came to share life abundantly. Give your congregation a heads-up that you want them to join you in finding evidence of abundant life in the world; have them post it to their social media accounts with #abundantlife or some other hashtag and tag your congregation in the post. Throughout the week, share some of their posts on your church's social media account and encourage further participation through newsletters, emails, and blog posts. You might also consider having people submit photos of abundant life a couple weeks before today to use as bulletin art, as projected art in the worship space, as a slideshow in a gathering or coffee area, or printed and displayed in an art gallery fashion.

- If the idea of sheep and shepherd is foreign to you or your ministry context, think of parallels. Who are the "sheep" and who are the "shepherds" in your community? Are certain people natural leaders who can get groups of people to follow them and their plans? Do other people prefer to have someone guide them in projects that the community takes on? It is possible that people take on the roles of both sheep and shepherd at various times, sometimes guiding others toward the gate and sometimes needing guidance themselves. Think about how your community positions itself in the surrounding area. Does your congregation act as shepherd, sheep, gate, or something else in its public proclamation of the gospel?

- This week's second reading seems like a great setup for next Sunday's account of the stoning of Stephen. Both have themes of holy people experiencing unnecessary suffering and finding redemption through it. But be careful to not glorify undeserved suffering. Some in our midst have suffered endlessly and needlessly and will not hear this passage as good news. Might it be possible that Peter has found himself complicit in the dominant narrative of oppressor rather than as the oppressed? Throughout history, oppressors have exploited the idea of redemptive suffering—that suffering now leads to heavenly rewards later. This tactic is used to control people and ensure that they believe their suffering serves a purpose (to prevent uprising against the oppressor). Has Peter accidentally fallen into this trap and taken on the oppressive message as one of liberation? What would those who find themselves on the underside of life—those who have constantly been oppressed and forced to suffer—have to say about this passage?

Connections with Creation

Psalm 23 offers rich images of God's provision and care. Green pastures are full of flourishing grasses and shrubs, providing ample sustenance for sheep and countless other creatures. The still water evoked here gives the psalm a contemplative quality, inviting reflection on the ways water not only sustains biological life but also renews our spirits, as many who have spent time at the ocean or next to a calm lake at sunset can attest. Baptism is never far from our thoughts during the Easter season, and Psalm 23 provides a kaleidoscope of images to enrich our baptismal reflection and practice. To name one: the baptismal font can be surrounded by an abundance (and *abundance* is key here) of flowers and green plants during this season (if possible, those that grow locally), making a connection between the ordinary, yet holy, water of the font and the ordinary, yet holy, water through which God creates and sustains all living things.

Let the Children Come

No matter where we assemble to worship God, we enter through a door or opening. In the gospel reading today, Jesus calls this entry point a "gate." Jesus goes on to call himself "the gate" (John 10:9). On the other side of the gate is a pasture, allowing all to live abundantly and well. How do our worship services feel like pasture to children? Is being quiet stressful for them? Is the music too loud for young, sensitive ears? Is there no place to move within the worship space while remaining a part of the flock? View your worship space from the vantage point of children. Crouch down to see what they see from their height. They might see a Bible in the pew or chair in front of them. But do they see a story Bible? Is there a space with a child-size table for coloring and comfy cushions for resting in this pasture?

Assembly Song
Gathering

> Blessing, Honor, and Glory   ELW 433, W&P 21
> My Shepherd, you supply my need   ELW 782
> The Lord's my shepherd   ELW 778, LLC 549, LBW 451

Psalmody and Acclamations

> Comer, Marilyn. "Psalm 23" from *ChildrenSing Psalms*. U, assembly, kybd.
> Gelineau, Joseph. "Psalm 23" from ACYG.
> Mayernik, Luke. "Fourth Sunday of Easter A" from 5GP.
> (GA) Browning, Carol/arr. Tom Andion. "Deo Gloria Alleluia (Easter Gospel Acclamation)" with proper verse for Easter 4. SATB, cant, assembly, kybd, gtr, opt fl, 2 tpt, perc. GIA G-6402.

Hymn of the Day

Have no fear, little flock ELW 764, LS 171, LBW 476 *LITTLE FLOCK*

Savior, like a shepherd lead us ELW 789, TFF 254 *BRADBURY* LBW 481 *HER TIL VIES*

The King of love my shepherd is ELW 502, LBW 456 *ST. COLUMBA*

Offering

At the Lamb's high feast we sing ELW 362, sts. 2, 4; LBW 210, sts. 2, 4

Now the feast and celebration ELW 167, WOV 789

Communion

Now behold the Lamb ELW 341, TFF 128

Shepherd me, O God ELW 780

You satisfy the hungry heart ELW 484, WOV 711

Sending

All people that on earth do dwell ELW 883, LBW 245

Praise the Lord, rise up rejoicing ELW 544, LBW 196

Additional Assembly Songs

Come away to the skies H82 213

I will supply your need SC 32

The Lamb TFF 89

⊕ Barros, Ernesto. "Momento novo/A New Moment" from *Tenemos Esperanza/We Have Hope*. U. GBGMusik 1890569011.

⊕ Kuyu, Daniel Lasuba/trans. Andrew Donaldson. "Yesu ini uhibuka/Yesu, I Bring My Love to You" from *Hosanna! Ecumenical Songs for Justice and Peace*. U. WCC Publications 9782825416679.

☼ Assad, Audrey/Bryan Brown. "I Shall Not Want" from CCLI.

☼ Palmer, Adam/Jonathan Smith/Matthew Hein/Stephanie Kulla/Stuart Garrard. "King of Love" from CCLI.

☼ Redman, Beth/Matt Redman. "You Never Let Go" from CCLI.

☼ Rend Collective. "Never Walk Alone" from CCLI.

☼ Rinehart, Bear/Bo Rinehart/Chris Tomlin/Ed Cash. "Goodness Love and Mercy" from CCLI.

☼ Ruis, David. "Good Shepherd (Lead On)" from CCLI.

Music for the Day
Choral

Schubert, Franz. "Psalm 23." SSAA, pno. Carus-Verlag 40.149/00.

P Taylor, Jim. "The 23rd Psalm." U/2 pt, pno. CG CGA1296.

♫ Thomson, Virgil. "My Shepherd Will Supply My Need." SATB, a cap. ALF 00-GCMR02046.

P♫ Zimmermann, Heinz Werner. "Psalm 23 (The Lord Is My Shepherd)" from *The Augsburg Choirbook*. SATB, org, DB. AFP 9780800656782.

⊕ = global song ♫ = relates to hymn of the day
☼ = praise song P = available in Prelude Music Planner

Children's Choir

Hurd, Bob. "Christ the Good Shepherd." U/SAB, pno/gtr, assembly. OCP 30133949.

Kemp, Helen. "The Good Shepherd." 2 pt, pno. CG CGA1079.

P White, David Ashley. "No More a Stranger or a Guest (Psalm 23)." 2 pt, C inst, hb/pno. SEL 410-833.

Keyboard / Instrumental

P♫ Callahan, Charles. "St. Columba" from *We Are Gathered: 12 Hymn Meditations for Piano*. Pno. MSM 15-760.

P♫ Kolodziej, Benjamin. "Savior, like a Shepherd Lead Us" from *Jesus Loves Me: Organ Settings of William Bradbury Tunes*. Org. AFP 9781506447971.

P♫ Miller, Aaron David. "Little Flock" from *Hymns in Jazz Style*. Pno. AFP 9780800678531.

Miller, Aaron David. "Maccabaeus, Festival March" from *Oxford Hymn Settings for Organists: Easter and Ascension*. Org. OXF 9780193393462.

Handbell

Childers, Brian. "The Shepherd." 3-4 oct hb solo, pno, L easy. FTT 1047.

♫ McFadden, Jane. "Have No Fear, Little Flock." 3-5 oct hb, opt 3 oct hc, L2. CPH 976922.

♫ Moklebust, Cathy. "The King of Love My Shepherd Is." 3, 4, or 5 oct hb, opt 3, 4, or 5 oct hc, L3+. CG CGB825.

Monday, May 4
Monica, mother of Augustine, died 387

Monica was married to a pagan husband who was ill-tempered and unfaithful. She rejoiced greatly when both her husband and his mother became Christian. But it is because she is the mother of Augustine that she is best known. Monica had been a disciple of Ambrose, and eventually Augustine came under his influence. Almost everything we know about Monica comes from Augustine's *Confessions*, his autobiography. She died far from her home, but said to her son, "Do not fret because I am buried far from our home in Africa. Nothing is far from God, and I have no fear that God will not know where to find me, when Christ comes to raise me to life at the end of the world." Her dying wish was that her son remember her at the altar of the Lord, wherever he was.

Friday, May 8
Julian of Norwich, renewer of the church, died around 1416

Julian (or Juliana) was most likely a Benedictine nun living in an isolated cell attached to the Carrow Priory in Norwich (nor-rich), England. Definite facts about her life are sparse. However, when she was about thirty years old, she reported visions that she later compiled into a book, *Sixteen Revelations of Divine Love*, a classic of medieval mysticism. The visions declared that love was the meaning of religious experience, provided by Christ who is love, for the purpose of love. A prayer and hymn attributed to Julian are included in *Evangelical Lutheran Worship* (p. 87, #735).

Saturday, May 9
Nicolaus Ludwig von Zinzendorf, renewer of the church, hymnwriter, died 1760

Count Zinzendorf was born into an aristocratic family and after the death of his father was raised by his Pietistic grandmother. This influence was a lasting one, and he moved away from what he felt was an overly intellectual Lutheranism. When he was twenty-two, a group of Moravians asked permission to live on his lands. He agreed, and they established a settlement they called Herrnhut, or "the Lord's watch." Eventually worldwide Moravian missions emanated from this community. Zinzendorf participated in these missions and is also remembered for writing hymns characteristic of his Pietistic faith, including "Jesus, still lead on" (ELW 624).

May 10, 2020
Fifth Sunday of Easter

As we continue to celebrate the fifty days of Easter, today's gospel includes Jesus' promise that he goes to prepare a place for his followers in his Father's house. Our baptism commissions us to share Jesus' mission in the world. As 1 Peter reminds us, we are a holy people, called to proclaim the one who called us out of darkness into light. In words and deeds we bear witness to the risen Christ—our way, our truth, our life.

Prayer of the Day

Almighty God, your Son Jesus Christ is the way, the truth, and the life. Give us grace to love one another, to follow in the way of his commandments, and to share his risen life with all the world, for he lives and reigns with you and the Holy Spirit, one God, now and forever.

Gospel Acclamation

Alleluia. I am the way, the truth, and the life. No one comes to the Father except through me. *Alleluia.* (John 14:6)

Readings and Psalm
Acts 7:55-60

Stephen was one of the seven men chosen by the apostles to serve tables so that the apostles could be free to serve the word (Acts 6:1-6). Stephen does more than distribute food, however. For his preaching of God's word, he becomes the first martyr of the faith.

Psalm 31:1-5, 15-16

Into your hands, O Lord, I commend my spirit. (Ps. 31:5)

1 Peter 2:2-10

Christ is the cornerstone of God's saving work and the foundation of our lives. We are God's chosen, holy people who continuously celebrate and declare the mercy of God we experience through Jesus Christ.

John 14:1-14

On the night that he is to be arrested, Jesus shares final words with his disciples. As the one through whom God is known, he promises to go before them and act on their behalf.

Preface   Easter

Color   White

Prayers of Intercession

The prayers are prepared locally for each occasion. The following examples may be adapted or used as appropriate.

Uplifted by the promised hope of healing and resurrection, we join the people of God in all times and places in praying for the church, the world, and all who are in need.
A brief silence.

Build us up, mothering God, as living stones united in your spiritual house. Continually strengthen your church as it is sent forth to proclaim your love. We pray especially for new congregations and those in redevelopment. Lord, in your mercy, **hear our prayer.**

Humble us, creator God, as part of your creation. Fill us with respect and awe for the world you have made, including volcanoes, ocean currents, tropical rainstorms, glaciers, and other forces that both destroy and create. Lord, in your mercy, **hear our prayer.**

Align our ways to your love, O God. We pray for countries, leaders, and other organizations as they prepare places for those seeking refuge and safety (*aid organizations may be named*). Lord, in your mercy, **hear our prayer.**

God of healing and rest, help those whose hearts are heavy and weighed down by many troubles. Comfort their suffering, ease their distress, and carry their burdens (*especially*). Lord, in your mercy, **hear our prayer.**

Nurturing God, we pray for those who tend and teach young children, for the safe pregnancies of expectant parents, and for families who struggle with infertility and miscarriage. We give thanks for all who have shown mothering care, and we remember all for whom this day is difficult. Lord, in your mercy, **hear our prayer.**

Here other intercessions may be offered.

Generous God, you call into your brilliant light all who have died. Give us faith to take hold of the promise of your eternal life. Lord, in your mercy, **hear our prayer.**

With bold confidence in your love, almighty God, we place all for whom we pray into your eternal care; through Christ our Lord.
Amen.

Ideas for the Day

- Scores of people are unjustly murdered each day, and any of them could be modern examples of Stephen for your community. *Considering Matthew Shepard* is a performance of the life and death of Matthew Shepard by Craig Hella Johnson and his choir, Conspirare. It is written as a combined poem, requiem, and memorial. The piece has deep connections to spirituality and the church in the form of the requiem mass but also translates that spirituality into a secular context. One of the more powerful moments in the piece is sung from the perspective of the fence to which Matthew was tied. The singer/fence sings, "He was heavy as a broken heart . . . I held him all night long" in a haunting melody. What do the stones that were used to kill Stephen have to say? What do the bullets used to kill schoolchildren have to say? More information about

Considering Matthew Shepard can be found at https://conspirare.org/project/considering-matthew-shepard/.

- For an interactive time of confession, have people write their sins onto stones with marker. This would be a good week to direct people to reflect on their participation in violence and have them use that as a springboard for what they write on their stones. Ensure that there are enough stones for each person to have a few, and then invite people to place their stones at the base of the font. As a community, affirm that we are complicit in the violence of the world and that we are truly sorry and humbly repent. As each person places their stones, encourage them to make the sign of the cross on themselves with water from the font as a reminder of baptism and forgiveness.

- Have a time and place during or after worship for people to write letters to elected local, state, and national officials advocating on behalf of the most vulnerable in our communities. The ELCA is committed to advocacy on behalf of God's children, and this is a good Sunday to participate in that as a community. If your synod or region has a local advocacy office, contact them for specifics about what they are advocating for in your area, or use your own knowledge of legislative actions to direct your congregational participation in advocacy.

Connections with Creation

"I am the way, and the truth, and the life" (John 14:6). Jesus' words are an invitation into a relationship with God and all creation. As we follow Jesus' way, God's sacramental immanence in creation nurtures faith and loving community, bringing healing and hope. Jesus' way leads us ever more deeply into an embrace of God's world. Jesus as the truth brings a liberating sense of freedom, as every pursuit of truth in the world can be said to be encompassed by and bring us closer to the fullness of Christ. In an age when faith and science are often seen as being in conflict, preachers can offer the pastoral message that science is neither faith's rival nor its enemy, but an ally in understanding creation and the Creator more truly. In saying that he is the life, Jesus names himself as the animating, creative Spirit of God coursing through all living things.

Let the Children Come

Children love building with their hands. Often when children are little, adults work with them building large and tall block structures. Together, children and adults build more intricate structures than children can alone. By working together, the adult constructs a learning scaffold around the children so that one day very soon children build a similar structure all by themselves. In our gospel today, the disciples struggle with how to build God's kingdom without Jesus there in human form. The scaffold Jesus provided seems to have been torn away. Yet Jesus knows his followers possess within all he has taught them. It's now time for them to take a few baby steps into leading others in building God's kingdom. In today's second reading, the apostle Peter reminds fellow believers to come to Jesus to be built into God's people. Peter became a scaffold for God's grace for others. We can too!

Assembly Song
Gathering

Alleluia! Jesus is risen! ELW 377, WOV 674, TFF 91, LS 62

Here, O Lord, your servants gather/Sekai no tomo to te o tsunagi ELW 530

Lord God, we praise you ELW 558

Psalmody and Acclamations

Bruxvoort-Colligan, Richard. "Into Your Hands (Psalm 31:5, 15)" from *Sharing the Road*. AFP 9780800678630.

Haugen, Marty. "I Put My Life in Your Hands" from *Psalms for the Church Year*, vol. l. SATB, cant, assembly, kybd, gtr. GIA G-2664.

Sedio, Mark. "Psalm 31," Refrain 1, from PSCY.

(GA) Browning, Carol/arr. Tom Andion. "Deo Gloria Alleluia (Easter Gospel Acclamation)" with proper verse for Easter 5. SATB, cant, assembly, kybd, gtr, opt fl, 2 tpt, perc. GIA G-6402.

Hymn of the Day

Come, my way, my truth, my life ELW 816, LBW 513 THE CALL

Hallelujah! Jesus lives! ELW 380, LBW 147 FRED TIL BOD

You are the way ELW 758, LBW 464 DUNDEE

Offering

Father, we thank you ELW 478, WOV 704

Let us talents and tongues employ ELW 674, WOV 754, TFF 232

Communion

Evening and morning ELW 761, LBW 465

I am the Bread of life ELW 485, WOV 702

I received the living God ELW 477, WOV 700, LS 105

Sending

I know that my Redeemer lives! ELW 619, LBW 352

Now the green blade rises ELW 379, LLC 357, LS 55, LBW 148

Additional Assembly Songs

Alleluia, alleluia, give thanks WOV 671, H82 178, GTG 240

Go in peace and serve the Lord W&P 46

I will trust in the Lord TFF 256

⊕ Irish trad. "Let Your Restless Hearts Be Still" from *Enemy of Apathy*. U, pno, or SATB. GIA G-3647.

⊕ Kenyan trad., as taught by Jonathan Gichaara. "Twende sote/Come and Go with Me" from *African Songs of Worship*. WCC Publications. Out of print. Hannelore.Schmid@wcc-coe.org.

☼ Cantelon, Ben/Nick Herbert/Tim Hughes. "The Way" from CCLI.

☼ Davis, Austin/Ben Davis/Dustin Sauder/Grant Pittman/Kari Jobe/Marty Sampson/Mia Fieldes. "I Am Not Alone" from CCLI.

☼ Mote, Edward/Eric Liljero/Jonas Myrin/Reuben Morgan/William Batchelder Bradbury. "Cornerstone" from CCLI.

☼ Mullins, Rich. "That Where I Am" from CCLI.

☼ Rand, Hannah/Lenora Rand. "Room for All of Us" from *Advent & Christmas*. themany1.bandcamp.com.

☼ Smith, Ben/Daniel Bashta/Pat Barrett. "The Way" from CCLI.

Music for the Day
Choral

P ♫ Larkin, Michael. "Come, My Way, My Truth, My Life." SATB, org. AFP 9781451492446.

P ♫ Mendelssohn, Felix. "Jesus Christ, My Sure Defense–Alleluia/Jesus, meine Zuversicht–Hallelujah" from *Chantry Choirbook: Sacred Music for All Seasons*. SATB. AFP 9780800657772.

♫ Schultz, Ralph C. "Hallelujah! Jesus Lives." SATB, trbl vcs, opt 4 oct hb. CPH 983880.

Wesley, Samuel. "Lead Me, Lord" from *The New Oxford Easy Anthem Book*. SATB, org. OXF 9780193533189.

Children's Choir

P Ellingboe, Bradley. "The Chief Cornerstone" in *Augsburg Easy Choirbook*, vol. 1. 2 pt, kybd. AFP 9780800676025.

P Leaf, Robert. "Come with Rejoicing." U, kybd. AFP 9780800645755.

Vaughan Williams, Ralph. "This Is the Truth." 2 pt, kybd. OXF 9780193857193.

Keyboard / Instrumental

P ♫ Childs, Edwin T. "Come, My Way, My Truth, My Life" from *Wedding Settings for Organ*. Org. AFP 9781506413655.

P ♫ Gabrielsen, Stephen. "Dundee" from *Augsburg Organ Library: Autumn*. Org. AFP 9780800675790.

Larkin, Michael. "All Creatures of Our God and King" from *All Creatures of Our God and King: Piano Music for Worship*. Pno. MSM 15-765.

P Organ, Anne Krentz. "I Know That My Redeemer Lives!" from *Piano Reflections on Hymns of the Faith*. Pno. AFP 9780806698069.

⊕ = global song ♫ = relates to hymn of the day
☼ = praise song P = available in Prelude Music Planner

Handbell

Buckwalter, Karen Lakey. "Processional" from *Ring and Sing the Seasons*. 3 oct, L1+. CG CGB969.

♫ McChesney, Kevin. "Come, My Way, My Truth, My Life." 2-3 oct, L2. LOR 20/1554L.

♫ McFadden, Jane. "Blessing and Honor/Hallelujah Jesus Lives." 3-5 oct, L easy. AFP 1110573.

Thursday, May 14
Matthias, Apostle

After Christ's ascension, the apostles met in Jerusalem to choose a replacement for Judas. Matthias was chosen over Joseph Justus by the casting of lots. Little is known about Matthias, and little is reported about him in the account of his election in Acts 1:15-26. Matthias traveled among the disciples from the beginning of Jesus' ministry until his ascension. His task, after he was enrolled among the eleven remaining disciples, was to bear witness to the resurrection.

May 17, 2020
Sixth Sunday of Easter

Jesus does not abandon his followers. Through the Holy Spirit, Jesus comes to abide with his disciples of every generation. As Pentecost draws near, we are reminded that the risen Christ dwells in us as the Spirit of truth. We receive this Spirit in baptism and pray that in our gathering around the Lord's table the Spirit will transform us to be the body of the risen Christ in the world.

Prayer of the Day

Almighty and ever-living God, you hold together all things in heaven and on earth. In your great mercy receive the prayers of all your children, and give to all the world the Spirit of your truth and peace, through Jesus Christ, our Savior and Lord, who lives and reigns with you and the Holy Spirit, one God, now and forever.

Gospel Acclamation

Alleluia. Those who love me will keep my word, and my Father will love them, and we will come to them and make our home with them. *Alleluia.* (John 14:23)

Readings and Psalm
Acts 17:22-31

In Athens, Paul faces the challenge of proclaiming the gospel to Greeks who know nothing of either Jewish or Christian tradition. He proclaims that the "unknown god" whom they worship is the true Lord of heaven and earth who will judge the world with justice through Jesus, whom God has raised from the dead.

Psalm 66:8-20

Bless our God, you peoples; let the sound of praise be heard. (Ps. 66:8)

1 Peter 3:13-22

The author of 1 Peter encourages Christians to remain faithful even in the face of defamation and persecution. In baptism we are made clean to act in accordance with what is right.

John 14:15-21

In final words to his disciples on the night of his arrest, Jesus encourages obedience to his commandments and speaks of the Spirit, who will be with them forever.

Preface   Easter

Color   White

Prayers of Intercession

The prayers are prepared locally for each occasion. The following examples may be adapted or used as appropriate.

Uplifted by the promised hope of healing and resurrection, we join the people of God in all times and places in praying for the church, the world, and all who are in need.

A brief silence.

Abiding God, you have revealed yourself to us in the form of your Son, Jesus Christ. Embolden your church, as your followers, to reveal your love to everyone in our speaking and in our living. Lord, in your mercy,

hear our prayer.

You are the creator of heaven and earth. Revitalize the health of oceans, rivers, lakes, springs, glaciers, and other bodies of water that give life to your creatures (*local bodies of water may be named*). Lord, in your mercy,

hear our prayer.

You call all people of the world your children. Judge the nations justly, show mercy to the oppressed, and speak truth to power through your prophets. Lord, in your mercy,

hear our prayer.

You come near to us when we are lost, and you hear our distress. We pray for those who suffer in any way (*especially*). Lord, in your mercy,

hear our prayer.

Your commands are good and merciful. Give us courage to take hold of our baptismal promises to work for justice, advocate for the voiceless, and free the oppressed and imprisoned in body, mind, or spirit. Lord, in your mercy,

hear our prayer.

Here other intercessions may be offered.

You remain with us always, O God, and your kingdom has no end. We remember the saints who have gone before us (*especially*). Unite us forever in your final victory over death. Lord, in your mercy,

hear our prayer.

With bold confidence in your love, almighty God, we place all for whom we pray into your eternal care; through Christ our Lord.

Amen.

Ideas for the Day

- Paul's address to the Athenians has all the components of a good commencement address. It was given in the equivalent of a modern-day university town to a similar crowd as gathers for graduations. We can imagine those who heard it then having these things in common with those who gather in such places at this time of year today: they like to read, write, and think, research, develop, and debate. This is a good Sunday to bless all the graduates in your community, perhaps following the service with a celebration that includes a display of their work: pieces of art, a finished dissertation, or a poster from a prized science project. It is important to also recognize at this time those who might be completing GEDs, certificate programs, certifications, or gap year projects. The point is to acknowledge the achievements of all and to encourage those who are making plans for their next steps, bless those preparing to send beloved children off to begin their adult lives, and deepen the bonds of community.
- In John 14:16 we hear the word *Advocate*. Those who do the work of advocacy in our culture are not always acknowledged. If they are acknowledged, they aren't always recognized with favor. Think about how you might acknowledge those who serve as advocates. Lift up the work of people who accompany immigrant minors, who offer legal defense to those who cannot pay, and who work to free persons who are unjustly imprisoned. Stories, statistics, and the names of individuals engaged in the work of advocacy and justice can be found through LIRS (lirs.org/) and the Southern Poverty Law Center (splcenter.org). At the 2018 ELCA Youth Gathering in Houston, Bryan Stevenson, founder of the Equal Justice Initiative in Montgomery, Alabama,

said, "I don't believe the opposite of poverty is wealth. I am persuaded that the opposite of poverty is justice." Stevenson's book *Just Mercy* (New York: Random House, 2014) is another source to consult in your planning.

Connections with Creation

Paul's speech in the Areopagus notes that God is the one "who made the world and everything in it, he who is Lord of heaven and earth" (Acts 17:24). This has profound implications for how humans are to regard the created world because it affirms humanity's position *within* the cosmos, not *above* it. If God has set boundaries within creation, humans are obligated to respect them. Paul also notes that God "commands all people everywhere to repent" (17:30), which raises the question, What would repentance from ecological sin look like? To answer this, we can turn to Jesus' teaching about the Spirit as Advocate in John 14:16. Led by the Holy Spirit, we can advocate for communities that have borne the brunt of ecological sin, calling for policies and regulations that prevent pollution and climate disruption. When we keep God's commandments to protect Earth and vulnerable people, we demonstrate our love for God.

Let the Children Come

The psalm for this day and its appointed refrain invites worshipers to "Bless our God, you peoples; let the sound of praise be heard" (Ps. 66:8). Despite knowing that God put the "wiggle" in our children, we often still hope they will be quiet in church. This may be a good Sunday to consider giving everyone eight months to eighty years old an invitation to praise God quite loudly. What would a group of excited worshipers look like? How might you invite young children to help you at the thanksgiving for baptism? Could they help sprinkle the congregation with water-filled blessings? Would their loudness at shouting "Remember your baptism!" remind us that we can rejoice as those transformed to be the body of the risen Christ in the world—all of us, all peoples, all ages?

Assembly Song
Gathering

Christ is alive! Let Christians sing ELW 389, LBW 363
Come down, O Love divine ELW 804, LBW 508
What wondrous love is this ELW 666, LBW 385

Psalmody and Acclamations

Farlee, Robert Buckley. "Psalm 66," Refrain 3, from PSCY.
Organ, Anne Krentz. "Psalm 66:8-20" from PWA.
Tate, Paul. "Sixth Sunday of Easter (A)" from *Cry Out with Joy, Year A*. GIA G-8481.
(GA) Browning, Carol/arr. Tom Andion. "Deo Gloria Alleluia (Easter Gospel Acclamation)" with proper verse for Easter 6. SATB, cant, assembly, kybd, gtr, opt fl, 2 tpt, perc. GIA G-6402.

Hymn of the Day

Dear Christians, one and all, rejoice   ELW 594, LBW 299
NUN FREUT EUCH

Love consecrates the humblest act   ELW 360, LBW 122
TWENTY-FOURTH

Love divine, all loves excelling   ELW 631, LBW 315   *HYFRYDOL*

Offering

Christ is risen! Shout Hosanna!   ELW 383, WOV 672

Come to us, creative Spirit   ELW 687, WOV 758

Communion

Jesu, Jesu, fill us with your love   ELW 708, WOV 765, TFF 83, LS 146

Jesus loves me!   ELW 595, LLC 614, TFF 249, LS 160

Ubi caritas et amor/Where true charity and love abide   ELW 642, WOV 665

Sending

Come, we that love the Lord   ELW 625, WOV 742, TFF 135, LS 164

Goodness is stronger than evil   ELW 721

Additional Assembly Songs

God sent his Son/Because He Lives   TFF 93

Seigneur, rassemble-nous/Unite us, God, in peace   SP 35

You are God's own people   MSB2 S566

⊕ Bell, John L. "God the Spirit Comes to Stay" from *Enemy of Apathy*. SATB. GIA G-3647.

⊕ Boström, Tomas, "Öppna din dörr/It Can Be a Girl" from *Sing the Circle Wide: Songs of Faith from Around the World*. Kanata Centre for Worship and Global Song 9780973059359.

☼ Corbett, Amy/Chris Brown/Steven Furtick. "Here Again" from CCLI.

☼ Crowder, David/Ed Cash. "I Am" from CCLI.

☼ Human, Brock. "Abide" from WT.

☼ McCracken, Sandra/Isaac Wardell/Liz Vice/Paul Zach. "We Abide in You" from *Work Songs*. theportersgate.bandcamp.com.

☼ Riddle, Jeremy/Josh Farro/Phil Wickham. "This Is Amazing Grace" from CCLI.

☼ Rundman, Jonathan. "This Is My Commandment" from *This Is My Commandment*. jonathanrundman.bandcamp.com.

Music for the Day
Choral

P Ellingboe, Bradley. "Glory, Glory, Hallelujah." SATB, a cap. AFP 9780800659561.

♫ Engel, James. "Dear Christians, One and All." SAB, org, tpt, assembly. CPH 982816.

P Rosewall, Michael. "Now Thank We All Our God." 2 pt mxd, kybd. AFP 9780800623852.

♫ Willcocks, David. "Love Divine, All Loves Excelling" from *The New Oxford Easy Anthem Book*. SATB, org. OXF 9780193533189.

Children's Choir

Caldara, Antonio. "Bless the Lord, All Nations." U/2 pt, 2 C inst, kybd. MSM 50-9506.

Hopson, Hal. "Children of the God Who Made Us." U/2 pt, pno, opt fl/C inst. CG CGA1506.

Marshall, Jane. "Psalm 66" from *Psalms Together*, vol. 1. U, kybd, opt assembly. CG CGC18.

Keyboard / Instrumental

♫ Larkin, Michael. "Hyfrydol" from *All Creatures of Our God and King: Piano Music for Worship*. Pno. MSM 15-765.

P ♫ Organ, Anne Krentz. "O Lamb of God, You Bear the Sin" from *Lamb of God: Reflections for Piano on Agnus Dei Settings*. Pno. AFP 9781451424232.

P ♫ Pelz, Walter L. "Dear Christians, One and All, Rejoice" from *A Walter Pelz Organ Anthology*. Org. AFP 9781506448039.

♫ Phillips, Craig. *Toccata on Hyfrydol*. Org. SEL 160-675.

Handbell

Morris, Hart. "Come Down, O Love Divine." 3-5 oct hb, opt 3-4 oct hc, org, solo, SATB, assembly, L2+. LOR 20/1711L.

Stephenson, Valerie. "I've Got the Joy (Down in My Heart)." 3-5 oct, opt bng, cym, L2. CG CGB579.

♫ Tucker, Sondra. "Meditation on Hyfrydol." 3 oct, L2. CG CGB182.

Monday, May 18
Erik, King of Sweden, martyr, died 1160

Erik, long considered the patron saint of Sweden, ruled from 1150 to 1160. He is honored for efforts to bring peace to the nearby pagan kingdoms and for his crusades to spread the Christian faith in Scandinavia. He established a protected Christian mission in Finland that was led by Henry of Uppsala. As king, Erik was noted for his desire to establish fair laws and courts and for his concern for the poor and sick. Erik was killed by a Danish army that approached him at worship on the day after the Ascension. He is reported to have said, "Let us at least finish the sacrifice. The rest of the feast I shall keep elsewhere." As he left worship he was killed.

⊕ = global song   ♫ = relates to hymn of the day
☼ = praise song   P = available in Prelude Music Planner

May 21, 2020
Ascension of Our Lord

In today's readings the risen Christ ascends into heaven and his followers are assured that the Spirit will empower them to be witnesses throughout the earth. The disciples were told to not gaze up into heaven to look for Jesus (Acts 1:11); we find his presence among us as we proclaim the word and share the Easter feast. We too long for the Spirit to enliven our faith and invigorate our mission.

Prayer of the Day

Almighty God, your only Son was taken into the heavens and in your presence intercedes for us. Receive us and our prayers for all the world, and in the end bring everything into your glory, through Jesus Christ, our Sovereign and Lord, who lives and reigns with you and the Holy Spirit, one God, now and forever.
or
Almighty God, your blessed Son, our Savior Jesus Christ, ascended far above all heavens that he might fill all things. Mercifully give us faith to trust that, as he promised, he abides with us on earth to the end of time, who lives and reigns with you and the Holy Spirit, one God, now and forever.

Gospel Acclamation

Alleluia. Go and make disciples of all nations, says the Lord; I am with you always, to the end of the age. *Alleluia.* (Matt. 28:19, 20)

Readings and Psalm

Acts 1:1-11

Before he is lifted into heaven, Jesus promises that the missionary work of the disciples will spread out from Jerusalem to all the world, and that the disciples will be accompanied and empowered by the Holy Spirit. His words provide an outline of the book of Acts.

Psalm 47

God has gone up with a shout. (Ps. 47:5)

or Psalm 93

Ever since the world began, your throne has been established. (Ps. 93:2)

Ephesians 1:15-23

The risen and exalted Christ reigns over the entire universe. The author of Ephesians prays that we are given the wisdom to know the power of the risen Christ and the empowering hope that the knowledge of this inheritance provides.

Luke 24:44-53

On the day of his ascension, Jesus leaves his disciples with a commission, a blessing, and a promise of the Holy Spirit.

Preface   Ascension

Color   White

Prayers of Intercession

The prayers are prepared locally for each occasion. The following examples may be adapted or used as appropriate.

Uplifted by the promised hope of healing and resurrection, we join the people of God in all times and places in praying for the church, the world, and all who are in need.
A brief silence.

Living God, you chose us to be your witnesses in the world. We pray for the church in every place and the congregations in our community (*especially*). Focus our hearts and minds on the ministry we share in your name. Lord, in your mercy,
hear our prayer.

Loving God, all creation sings praise to you. You delight in the oceans, and the mountains are your throne. Teach us humility and respect for our home. Lord, in your mercy,
hear our prayer.

Sovereign God, you rule the heavens, the earth, and time itself. Make this a time of justice, peace, and solidarity among all nations and peoples, so that oppression and violence rule no more. Lord, in your mercy,
hear our prayer.

Tender God, we wait with hope for your presence to heal us, bless us, restore us, and give us peace. You know all the names of those suffering for whom we pray this day (*especially*). Lord, in your mercy,
hear our prayer.

Gentle God, you guide us as we seek wisdom. We pray for teachers, professors, theologians, day care workers, and all those charged with teaching the young and old. Give them endurance and persistence in their valuable work. Lord, in your mercy,
hear our prayer.

Here other intercessions may be offered.

Infinite God, your inheritance given to all your saints is your presence in our life and in our death. We remember with thanksgiving the faithful departed (*especially Helena, mother of Constantine*). Lord, in your mercy,
hear our prayer.

With bold confidence in your love, almighty God, we place all for whom we pray into your eternal care; through Christ our Lord.
Amen.

Ideas for the Day

- Create ways for people to reflect on what it means to be witnesses and how Jesus equipped the disciples for this work. Have stations at the entrances to the worship space containing an ink pad or two. Invite every person who enters the worship space to ink one of their fingers and then place their fingerprint on the hand of someone else— a friend, an usher, a visitor—as a visual mark of the witness we share with one another. The sermon could include references to the variety of "prints" we carry that make us witnesses to events, both heinous and holy: tattoos on survivors of Auschwitz; scars that both donors and recipients of organ transplants bear; fingerprints that help solve crimes, freeing victims from the fear they experience until the perpetrator is found. Use words from Acts 1:8, "you will be my witnesses," in the benediction.
- The Ephesians reading begins with words of thanks and ends with a reference to the body of Christ. Christian writer and scholar Diana Butler Bass, author of *Grateful* (San Francisco: HarperOne, 2018), says, "We have privatized gratitude, so that it's become something only for us . . . gratitude is inherently social—gratitude always connects us. Yet somehow American individualism has managed to sever the ties that gratitude naturally brings to us" (sojo .net/articles/maybe-weve-gotten-gratitude-all-wrong). To emphasize thankfulness to others in the body of Christ, prepare pre-addressed thank-you notes and make them available after worship. The recipients of these notes will be people who are participating in a particular ministry in which your congregation is also participating. For example, an online search about the Flint Water Crisis provides stories of churches helping to sustain the people of Flint: providing bottled water and cash donations; negotiating for Flint residents to have safe showers at local hotels for a nominal fee. If your church has been sending water or financial resources to Flint, invite worshipers to sign these pre-addressed notes that extend thanks to people and places beyond your doors doing ministry similar to yours. The thank-you notes themselves might borrow phrases from Paul's letter to the Ephesians.

Connections with Creation

Just before his ascension, Jesus tells the disciples that they will be his witnesses "to the ends of the earth" (Acts 1:8). At that time two thousand years ago, there were still many places on this planet that had not yet seen human footprints. Today the only places that remain unexplored by humans are a few deserts, mountain peaks, arctic regions, and deep ocean trenches. Yet the entire planet has been affected by human activity. Those arctic regions are losing glaciers, desertification is spreading, and mountains are losing snow cover, all due to human-induced global warming. Even the Mariana Trench— the deepest part of the ocean—was found to have a plastic bag floating in it. What would it mean, then, to witness to Jesus in these farthest places? One way is to answer the call to clean up pollution and mitigate climate disruption so that the ends of the earth can be protected and survive.

Let the Children Come

Ascension Day is kept on the fortieth day of Easter. While numbers don't hold the same spiritual significance for many mainline Protestants as they did in the ancient world, it can be fascinating to children that forty seems to mean something in the Bible, to the church, and even in the secular world. There are forty days and forty nights aboard the ark; there are forty years for Israel in the wilderness; there are forty days in Lent; and people say that at age forty someone is "over the hill." Imagine forty stones lined up in a row, forty baptism candles, forty teddy bears, forty health kits, forty rings of a bell, forty hugs. How do you count to forty?

Assembly Song
Gathering

Crown him with many crowns ELW 855, LBW 170
Hail thee, festival day! ELW 394, LBW 142
Lord, I lift your name on high ELW 857, W&P 90

Psalmody and Acclamations

God, you rule with royal bearing/Psalm 93 GTG 272
Chepponis, James. "Eastertime Psalm: Psalms for Easter, Ascension, and Pentecost." SATB, cant, org, assembly, opt 4 tpts, hb. GIA G-3907.
Mayernik, Luke. "Ascension of the Lord" from 5GP.
Schalk, Carl. "Psalm 93" from PWA.
(GA) Browning, Carol/arr. Tom Andion. "Deo Gloria Alleluia (Easter Gospel Acclamation)" with proper verse for Ascension. SATB, cant, assembly, kybd, gtr, opt fl, 2 tpt, perc. GIA G-6402.

Hymn of the Day

A hymn of glory let us sing! ELW 393, LBW 157 *LASST UNS ERFREUEN*
Alleluia! Sing to Jesus ELW 392, LBW 158 *HYFRYDOL*
Lord, you give the great commission ELW 579, WOV 756 *ABBOT'S LEIGH*

Offering

Come to us, creative Spirit ELW 687, WOV 758
Now the silence ELW 460, LBW 205

Communion

Beautiful Savior ELW 838, LS 174, LBW 518

Blessing, Honor, and Glory ELW 433, W&P 21

Lord, enthroned in heavenly splendor ELW 475, LBW 172

Sending

O Christ, our hope ELW 604, LBW 300

Rejoice, for Christ is king! ELW 430, LBW 171

Additional Assembly Songs

Canten, canten himnos a Dios/Clap your hands, all you people LLC 363

Up through endless ranks of angels LBW 159

⊕ Arabic trad. "Yaa Quddsa RuuhilLaah/Come Near, O Spirit, Come" from *Hosanna! Ecumenical Songs for Justice and Peace*. SATB. WCC Publications 9782825416679.

⊕ Creación Colectiva, Matanzas, Cuba. "Envío/To the Streets" from *Hosanna! Ecumenical Songs for Justice and Peace*. SATB. WCC Publications 9782825416679.

☼ Brown, Lacey. "Love" from *Like the Tide*. poorclare.bandcamp .com.

☼ Gungor, David/Eric Marshall/John Arndt. "Night Has Passed" from CCLI.

☼ Hall, Charlie/Kendall Combes/Quint Anderson. "Rising (A Song of Ascent)" from CCLI.

☼ Ingram, Jason/Jonathan Smith/Kristian Stanfill/Sean Curran. "Glorious Day" from CCLI.

☼ Jeancake, Paxson. "Right Hand of the Father" from *Wide Awake*. paxsonandallison.com.

☼ Tomlin, Chris/Daniel Carson/Ed Cash/Jesse Reeves. "Jesus Messiah" from CCLI.

Music for the Day
Choral

Bullard, Alan, "Hail the Day that Sees Him Rise" from *Epiphany to All Saints for Choirs*. SATB, org or pno. OXF 9780193530263.

P Cherwien, David. "Up through Endless Ranks of Angels." SAB, org, opt tpt. AFP 9780800658816.

♫ Hobby, Robert A. "Alleluia! Sing to Jesus." SATB, org or br or orch. MSM 60-8842.

P Proulx, Richard. "Christ Now Sends the Spirit" from *The Augsburg Choirbook*. SAB, org, fl, opt assembly. AFP 9780800656782.

Children's Choir

Chapman, Stephen. "O Clap Your Hands." Solo/soli, 3 pt trbl, pno. GAL 7.0577.

Hunnicutt, Judy. "Clap Your Hands, All Ye Children." U, kybd. AFP 111632. Out of print.

Witherup, William C. "Look, Ye Saints/Lord, Enthroned in Heavenly Splendor." 2 pt, org. SEL 415-819.

Keyboard / Instrumental

P Diemer, Emma Lou. "Come Away to the Skies" from *Glory, Laud, and Honor: Organ Settings*. Org. AFP 9781451494068.

P♫ Langlois, Kristina. "Lasst uns erfreuen" from *Postludes for Organ on Festive Tunes*. Org. AFP 9781506413631.

P♫ Miller, Aaron David. "God Is Here!" from *Hymns in Jazz Style*. Pno. AFP 9780800678531.

♫ Raney, Joel. "Hyfrydol" from *Meditations for Quiet Worship*. Pno. HOP 8320.

Handbell

Hakes, Derek. "All Hail the Risen King." 2-3 oct, L2. LOR 20/1341L.

♫ Moklebust, Cathy. "Alleluia! Sing to Jesus!" 3-6 oct, opt org, br qrt or qnt, timp, SATB, assembly, L3. CG CGB413. Various editions.

♫ Moklebust, Cathy. "Now All the Vault of Heaven Resounds (Lasst uns erfreuen)." 3-6 oct hb, 3-5 oct hc, L3. CPH 977488.

Thursday, May 21
Helena, mother of Constantine, died around 330

Wife of the coregent of the West, Helena (or Helen) was mother of Constantine, who later became Roman emperor. After he was converted to Christianity, he influenced her also to become Christian. From that point she lived an exemplary life of faith, particularly through acts of generosity toward the poor. She is also remembered for traveling through Palestine and building churches on the sites she believed to be where Jesus was born, where he was buried, and from which he ascended.

⊕ = global song   ♫ = relates to hymn of the day
☼ = praise song   P = available in Prelude Music Planner

May 24, 2020
Seventh Sunday of Easter

In these days between Ascension and Pentecost, we gather with the disciples in the upper room, waiting for the Spirit to transform the church around the world. In today's gospel Jesus prays for his followers and for their mission in his name. Amid religious, social, and economic divisions, we seek the unity that Jesus had with his Father. Made one in baptism, we go forth to live our faith in the world, eager for the unity that God intends for the whole human family.

Prayer of the Day

O God of glory, your Son Jesus Christ suffered for us and ascended to your right hand. Unite us with Christ and each other in suffering and in joy, that all the world may be drawn into your bountiful presence, through Jesus Christ, our Savior and Lord, who lives and reigns with you and the Holy Spirit, one God, now and forever.

Gospel Acclamation

Alleluia. I will not leave you orphaned, says the Lord. I am coming to you. *Alleluia.* (John 14:18)

Readings and Psalm

Acts 1:6-14

Today's reading is part of the introduction to the narrative of the outpouring of the Spirit on Pentecost. These verses tell of the risen Lord's conversation with his disciples on the eve of his ascension, in which he promises that they will receive the power of the Holy Spirit.

Psalm 68:1-10, 32-35

Sing to God, who rides upon the clouds. (Ps. 68:4)

1 Peter 4:12-14; 5:6-11

Our faith in Christ does not make us immune from the scorn of others. Nevertheless, we are to resist the designs of evil when we experience disparagement from others because we trust God's grace will strengthen and guide us.

John 17:1-11

On the night before his crucifixion, Jesus prays to his heavenly Father, asking that those who continue his work in this world will live in unity.

Preface   Ascension

Color   White

Prayers of Intercession

The prayers are prepared locally for each occasion. The following examples may be adapted or used as appropriate.

Uplifted by the promised hope of healing and resurrection, we join the people of God in all times and places in praying for the church, the world, and all who are in need.
A brief silence.

O God, call your people to be one, as you are one. Unite your church in the truth of your gospel, the love of our neighbor, and the call to proclaim your reign to all people. Lord, in your mercy,
hear our prayer.

Breathe life into your creation. Guide your people as we explore the mysteries of the universe. We pray for the work of scientists and mathematicians whose skill enriches our understanding (*like Nicholas Copernicus and Leonard Euler, whom the church commemorates today*). Lord, in your mercy,
hear our prayer.

Make your justice known among the nations of the earth. Protect the vulnerable (*especially in nations currently in crisis*). Redirect those who use violence and greed as weapons. Lord, in your mercy,
hear our prayer.

Come to the aid of your children. We pray for those engulfed in grief, those without supportive families, and for all who are isolated, powerless, or afraid, that all may rest their anxieties in your care. Lord, in your mercy,
hear our prayer.

Give courage to all who embark on new ventures. We especially remember this day those who risked their lives to serve in our armed forces. Grant safety to those serving at home or abroad, and assure them of your never-failing strength. Lord, in your mercy,
hear our prayer.

Here other intercessions may be offered.

Raise all your saints to eternal life. Until that day, we give you thanks for the faithful examples of those who have listened to your voice and now rest in you. Lord, in your mercy,
hear our prayer.

With bold confidence in your love, almighty God, we place all for whom we pray into your eternal care; through Christ our Lord.
Amen.

Ideas for the Day

- Jesus prays for our unity. To create a visual representation of your assembly's unity, construct a quilt together. In the weeks prior to Easter 7, have each person decorate a quilt square with symbols or words that represent their life. This could happen in Sunday school, during adult education time, or at a station in the gathering space. You can simply use fabric markers, or you could enlist creatives in the congregation to suggest other ways to decorate the squares. Have a quilter stitch them together into a banner by Easter 7, and hang it in the worship space as a symbol of unity on this day when we hear our Lord pray that we would all be one.
- Jesus' prayer for unity is as true and bold as it gets. He prays that all may be one. One of the ways we can work toward unity is by reaching into a world we don't understand, asking others to teach us something true about a part of life about which we might stand in judgment. The podcast *Ear Hustle* (earhustlesq.com) brings the listener into San Quentin prison. If you spend half an hour listening to the episode called "Looking Out" (Season 1, Episode 3), you will learn to know, and likely love, an inmate named Rauch, and in a small and holy way, your life will be stitched to his. You will be one.
- The idea and image of Jesus' ascension can be a difficult one to help people process. Jan Richardson's poem "Stay: A Blessing for Ascension Day" would work nicely in worship today. After all the readings, preaching, peace, and meal, the words of this blessing encourage the hearers to "still yourself and turn toward one another" when the inclination might be to scurry around trying to fulfill Jesus' mandate to witness to the ends of the earth. Visit the website painted prayerbook.com and search for the title of the blessing.

Connections with Creation

Sister Dorothy Mae Stang was a nun murdered in 2005 for her work to protect impoverished Brazilian communities in the Amazon. She had dedicated her life to defending the Brazilian rain forest from depletion due to agriculture and had advocated for the rural poor since the early 1970s. Sister Dorothy received death threats for years but never faltered in her mission. The words of 1 Peter encourage the faithful during "the fiery ordeal" (4:12), and Sister Dorothy exemplifies this kind of courage. She is a model of the sacrificial love of God, who steadfastly proclaims that the most vulnerable—including Earth itself—are worth dying for. Her faithfulness humbles us and teaches us what is worth living for.

Let the Children Come

Lions are powerful creatures. They are the king of beasts for a reason! In 1 Peter, evil ("your adversary the devil," 5:8) is compared to a lion, and it might be that this image frightens children (and adults) in your congregation. It's noteworthy, then, that our text instructs resistance. It seems also that courage for this resistance comes not from being strong ourselves but in knowing that we have a community of faith that is with us. If your congregation is paying special attention to baptism this Easter season, why not practice some hearty renouncing using the threefold renunciations from the baptismal rite before reciting the creed: "Do you renounce the devil and all the forces that defy God? . . . I renounce them" (*ELW*, p. 229). Gather around the font. If you can't shout away a lion on your own, maybe you need a community to help you be loud enough.

Assembly Song
Gathering

Behold, how pleasant/Miren qué bueno ELW 649, LLC 468, GS2 21

In Christ there is no east or west ELW 650, TFF 214, LBW 359

Rise, O Sun of righteousness ELW 657

Psalmody and Acclamations

Cooney, Rory. "You Have Made a Home for the Poor" from *Psalms for the Church Year*, vol. 4. SATB, cant, assembly, kybd, gtr, opt fl or vln. GIA G-3612.

Messner, Sally. "Psalm 68:1-10, 32-35" from PWA.

Pavlechko, Thomas. "Psalm 68:1-10, 32-35" from PSCY.

(GA) Browning, Carol/arr. Tom Andion. "Deo Gloria Alleluia (Easter Gospel Acclamation)" with proper verse for Easter 7. SATB, cant, assembly, kybd, gtr, opt fl, 2 tpt, perc. GIA G-6402.

Hymn of the Day

Come now, O Prince of peace ELW 247, LS 13 OSOSŎ

Son of God, eternal Savior ELW 655, LBW 364 IN BABILONE

You Are Mine ELW 581, W&P 158 YOU ARE MINE

Offering

Come to us, creative Spirit ELW 687, WOV 758

I come with joy ELW 482

Communion

Father, we thank you ELW 478, WOV 704

Lord, Be Glorified ELW 744, TFF 248, W&P 89

Lord, who the night you were betrayed ELW 463, LBW 206

Sending

Blest be the tie that binds ELW 656, LBW 656

We are all one in Christ/Somos uno en Cristo ELW 643, TFF 221, LLC 470, LS 130

Additional Assembly Songs

Grains of wheat/Una espiga WOV 708, LLC 392

Mirad cuán bueno/Behold, how good and delightful LLC 475

You are the seed WOV 753, TFF 226, LLC 486, LS 139

🌐 Carpintero, Mireya and Raoul. "Hola! Como estás?" from *Hosanna! Ecumenical Songs for Justice and Peace.* WCC Publications 9782825416679.

🌐 Murray, Shirley Erena/Brian Mann. "For Everyone Born" from *For Everyone Born: Global Songs for an Emerging Church.* U. GBGMusik 9781933663265.

☼ Brewster, Lincoln/Paul Baloche. "Today Is the Day" from CCLI.

☼ Gungor, David/John Arndt. "Now and At the Hour" from *Lent.* thebrilliancemusic.com.

☼ Keyes, Aaron/Bryan Brown/Evan Wickham/Michael Gungor. "Make Us One" from WT.

☼ Nockels, Christy/Ellie Holcomb. "Everything Is Mine in You" from CCLI.

☼ Pasley, Ben/Don Chaffer/Robin Pasley. "You Are So Good to Me" from CCLI.

☼ Quilala, Chris/Joshua Silverberg/Ran Jackson/Ricky Jackson. "Make Us One" from CCLI.

Music for the Day
Choral

♫ Ellingboe, Bradley. "Oh, Love, How Deep." SATB, kybd, tamb, perc. KJO 8831.

P Ferguson, John. "This Is My Song." SATB, org, tbn, opt assembly. AFP 9781506456928.

P Highben, Zebulon, M. "I Come with Joy." SAB, pno. AFP 9781506422060.

P Wold, Wayne L. "Enviado (The Lord Now Sends Us Forth)." 2 pt, kybd, opt perc. AFP 9781506422022.

Children's Choir

Marshall, Jane. "Psalm 68" from *Psalms Together*, vol. 2. U, kybd, assembly. CG CGC21.

Willan, Healy. "I Will Not Leave You Comfortless" from *We Praise Thee, II*. 2 pt, org. CPH 977610pdf.

P Wold, Wayne. "Sisters and Brothers, Family of God" from *ChildrenSing in Worship*. U/2 pt, kybd. AFP 9781451401806.

Keyboard / Instrumental

P ♫ Culli, Benjamin. "In Babilone" from *Praise the One: Ten Organ Impressions for Worship*, vol. 2. Org. AFP 9780806696935.

Groom te Velde, Rebecca. "Llanfair Toccata" from *Oxford Hymn Settings for Organists: Easter and Ascension*. Org. OXF 9780193393462.

Oliver, Curt. "I Come with Joy" from *Four Communion Hymn Settings for Piano*, set 2. Pno. MSM 15-825.

P ♫ Wahl, Carol. "You Are Mine" from *Cry of the Dove: Piano Settings*. Pno. AFP 9781451479614.

Handbell

♫ Griffin, Jackie. "Festive Celebration (In Babilone)." 5 oct, L3. FTT 201885.

♫ Larson, Lloyd. "You Are Mine." 3-5 oct, L2+. HOP 2696.

Phillips, Judy. "Dove of Peace." 3-6 oct, L3+. GIA G-7292.

Sunday, May 24
Nicolaus Copernicus, died 1543; Leonhard Euler, died 1783; scientists

Remembering scientists such as Copernicus and Euler offers an opportunity to ponder the mysteries of the universe and the grandeur of God's creation. Copernicus is an example of a renaissance person. He formally studied astronomy, mathematics, Greek, Plato, law, medicine, and canon law. He also had interests in theology, poetry, and the natural and social sciences. Copernicus is chiefly remembered for his work as an astronomer and his idea that the sun, not the earth, is the center of the solar system.

Euler (OY-ler) is regarded as one of the founders of the science of pure mathematics and made important contributions to mechanics, hydrodynamics, astronomy, optics, and acoustics.

Wednesday, May 27
John Calvin, renewer of the church, died 1564

John Calvin began his studies in theology at the University of Paris when he was fourteen. In his mid-twenties he experienced a conversion that led him to embrace the views of the Reformation. His theological ideas are systematically laid out in his *Institutes of the Christian Religion*. He is also well known for his commentaries on scripture. He was a preacher in Geneva, was banished once, and then later returned to reform the city under a theocratic constitution.

Friday, May 29
Jiří Tranovský, hymnwriter, died 1637

Jiří Tranovský (YEAR-zhee truh-NOF-skee) is considered the "Luther of the Slavs" and the father of Slovak hymnody. Trained at the University of Wittenberg in the early seventeenth century, Tranovský was ordained in 1616 and spent his life preaching and teaching in Prague, Silesia, and finally Slovakia. He produced a translation of the Augsburg Confession and published his hymn collection *Cithara Sanctorum* (Lyre of the Saints), the foundation of Slovak Lutheran hymnody.

🌐 = global song   ♫ = relates to hymn of the day
☼ = praise song   P = available in Prelude Music Planner

May 30, 2020
Vigil of Pentecost

At this liturgy we gather in vigilant prayer as the disciples did in the days preceding Pentecost. Our world waits for an end to war and violence. The whole creation waits for an end to suffering. With undying hope we pray for the crowning gift of Easter—the Spirit of the risen Christ among us.

Prayer of the Day

Almighty and ever-living God, you fulfilled the promise of Easter by sending the gift of your Holy Spirit. Look upon your people gathered in prayer, open to receive the Spirit's flame. May it come to rest in our hearts and heal the divisions of word and tongue, that with one voice and one song we may praise your name in joy and thanksgiving; through Jesus Christ, our Savior and Lord, who lives and reigns with you and the Holy Spirit, one God, now and forever.

Gospel Acclamation

Alleluia. Come, Holy Spirit, fill the hearts of your faithful, and kindle in us the fire of your love. *Alleluia.*

Readings and Psalm

Exodus 19:1-9

At Sinai God assured Israel that they were God's prized possession and commissioned them to serve as mediating priests for the nations. God's word spoken to Moses is the basis of the people's trust.

or Acts 2:1-11

As Jesus promised his disciples, the Holy Spirit is sent to them. The disciples are empowered to witness to God's powerful deeds to people of all nations.

Psalm 33:12-22

The LORD is our helper and our shield. (Ps. 33:20)

or Psalm 130

There is forgiveness with you. (Ps. 130:4)

Romans 8:14-17, 22-27

The Holy Spirit has made us God's children who eagerly await the glorious future God has prepared for all of creation. While we cannot fully see what God has in store for us and creation, we eagerly anticipate it in hope. Even when we are unable to pray, the same Spirit prays for us.

John 7:37-39

Jesus describes the Holy Spirit as living water, quenching the thirst of all who come to him and filling the hearts of believers until they overflow.

Preface   Vigil and Day of Pentecost

Color   Red

May 31, 2020
Day of Pentecost

Pentecost derives its name from the Jewish festival celebrating the harvest and the giving of the law on Mount Sinai fifty days after Passover. Fifty days after Easter, we celebrate the Holy Spirit as God's presence within and among us. In Acts the Spirit arrives in rushing wind and flame, bringing God's presence to all people. Paul reminds us that though we each have different capacities, we are unified in the Spirit that equips us with these gifts. Jesus breathes the Holy Spirit on his disciples, empowering them to forgive sin. We celebrate that we too are given the breath of the Holy Spirit and sent out to proclaim God's redeeming love to all the world.

Prayer of the Day

O God, on this day you open the hearts of your faithful people by sending into us your Holy Spirit. Direct us by the light of that Spirit, that we may have a right judgment in all things and rejoice at all times in your peace, through Jesus Christ, your Son and our Lord, who lives and reigns with you and the Holy Spirit, one God, now and forever.

Gospel Acclamation

Alleluia. Come, Holy Spirit, fill the hearts of your faithful, and kindle in us the fire of your love. *Alleluia.*

Readings and Psalm

Acts 2:1-21

Pentecost was a Jewish harvest festival that marked the fiftieth day after Passover. Luke portrays the Holy Spirit being poured out upon the disciples before the gathered and astonished people assembled in Jerusalem for the festival. Filled with the Spirit, the disciples were able to witness to the power of Christ's resurrection.

or Numbers 11:24-30

The spirit of God rested upon seventy elders in Israel who had been chosen to share the burden of leadership with Moses. When some became jealous that two others also had the spirit and could prophesy, Moses said that he hoped that all of God's people would be prophets.

Psalm 104:24-34, 35b

Send forth your Spirit and renew the face of the earth. (Ps. 104:30)

1 Corinthians 12:3b-13

Paul is helping the Corinthians understand the relationship between our God-given unity and Spirit-created diversity. The Spirit creates the unity of faith and gives all Christians diverse gifts for the common benefit of all. We need one another's diverse spiritual gifts because the same Spirit has given them to each person for the common good.

or Acts 2:1-21

See above.

John 20:19-23

The risen Jesus appears to his disciples, offering them a benediction, a commission, and the gift of the Holy Spirit.

or John 7:37-39

Jesus describes the Holy Spirit as living water, quenching the thirst of all who come to him and filling the hearts of believers until they overflow.

Preface   Vigil and Day of Pentecost

Color   Red

Prayers of Intercession

The prayers are prepared locally for each occasion. The following examples may be adapted or used as appropriate.

Uplifted by the promised hope of healing and resurrection, we join the people of God in all times and places in praying for the church, the world, and all who are in need.

A brief silence.

We call on your spirit of unity, giving thanks for our different vocations. Activate and utilize the diverse gifts present in your church, that they reveal your love for all. Lord, in your mercy,
hear our prayer.

We call on your spirit of life, present in air, wind, humidity, storms, and oxygen in our atmosphere, breathing energy into all things. Heal with your breath the whole creation, especially those who struggle to breathe due to air pollution. Lord, in your mercy,
hear our prayer.

We call on your spirit of righteousness. Wherever we as a people are divided, unite us. Wherever we are prideful, humble us. Give each one of us a heart for justice and empathy. Lord, in your mercy,
hear our prayer.

We call on your spirit of healing. Bless nurses, doctors, midwives, chaplains, counselors, and hospice workers as they care for those in need. We pray for all who long for comfort (*especially*). Lord, in your mercy,
hear our prayer.

We call on your spirit of friendship. As Elizabeth welcomed Mary to her home, give us a spirit of welcome to those whom we meet in this congregation and outside these doors. Surprise us daily with unexpected grace, that we rejoice in every blessing you send. Lord, in your mercy,
hear our prayer.

Here other intercessions may be offered.

We call on your spirit of hope. As you have led your saints in all times and places, stir in us the desire to follow their example, leading us from death to new life in you. Lord, in your mercy,
hear our prayer.

With bold confidence in your love, almighty God, we place all for whom we pray into your eternal care; through Christ our Lord.
Amen.

Ideas for the Day

- See the excellent suggestions for Pentecost worship space in the "Preparing for Easter" introduction (pp. 165–167).
- The folks at The Bible Project have created a four-minute video tracing the Holy Spirit from the beginning hovering over the water, all the way through the scriptural narrative, and into our lives today (thebibleproject.com/explore /holy-spirit). They describe the Holy Spirit as "God's personal presence" and show the Spirit moving through the prophets, Jesus' baptism, the resurrection, and the Day of Pentecost.
- The bestowal of multiple languages in the reading from Acts and the varieties of gifts described in the reading from 1 Corinthians reveal that God is glorified in diversity. Knowing your own context, write a sending blessing that includes the gifts you know are present in your assembly. Perhaps include a line about being drawn from the worship experience out into the world and empowered by the Holy Spirit as nurses, teachers, Uber drivers, food servers, medical transcriptionists—whatever is particular to your community—to heal, teach, transport, feed, manage details, and so forth, in the lives of our neighbors in the name of Jesus.
- On this day we celebrate our being clothed with the power from on high. Now comes the promised Holy Spirit poured out on all, and it is not exclusively, or even primarily, about speaking in tongues. The speech required of us is quite simple: our response to the Spirit's anointing is to proclaim God's love through Jesus Christ. And this is duty and joy not just for the pastor or church professionals but for every believer.

- Those watching the newborn church that first Pentecost wondered what was going on. Some thought they were a little tipsy. Others probably didn't know what to think. What do people think as they observe our Spirit-filled worship services today? Do they sense God's Spirit moving among us, or does it just seem odd to them? Do people feel like they can follow what we're doing, or does it seem like something from another country or century? We need to worship as the Spirit leads us, but we need also to pay attention to the visitor who for the first time is catching a glimpse of God's Spirit. We may be doing things that seem perfectly normal to us but that are quite strange to newcomers; let us seek friendly and hospitable ways to help them understand.

Connections with Creation

"Your sons and your daughters shall prophesy" (Acts 2:17), and your young men and women shall see visions. What faith-inspired visions do our young people have today? What are they prophesying? In 2018, twenty-one teens and young adults filed a lawsuit against the U.S. government to push for a plan to reduce greenhouse gas emissions and drastically curb climate disruption. These young people are holding up a vision in which the climate system can sustain human life for their generation and beyond. We might say that the Holy Spirit has anointed them with "tongues of fire" to speak truth to power and call for their elders to protect this planet. The courage and foresight of this group of young people in the organization called Our Children's Trust is empowering others with what Christians would call an outpouring of the Holy Spirit.

Let the Children Come

Pentecost is not just a day for celebrating together with other Christians; it is also a day about being fed by the Holy Spirit in order to go out and share the good news. Surround your baptismal font with red votive candles or tealights (real or battery-operated) in mason jars. For a fun touch, wrap the jar rim with red yarn to draw the eyes to it. This great festival calls for a procession of fire and wind. Every child who wants to could be involved with very little rehearsal. Older children can carry the mason jars with the candles to the front. Tie silver, white, and red streamers or ribbons to the wrists of smaller children. Let them "blow where they will" as they enter dancing or skipping and twirling their arms. Make sure you also have a recessional to bring that fire and wind of the Holy Spirit out into the world.

Assembly Song
Gathering

Come, Holy Ghost, God and Lord ELW 395, LBW 163
Gracious Spirit, heed our pleading ELW 401, WOV 687,
    TFF 103, LS 66
O Holy Spirit, enter in ELW 786, LBW 459

Psalmody and Acclamations

Alonso, Tony. "Lord, Send Out Your Spirit/Señor, envía tu Espíritu." SAB, cant, assembly, pno, gtr. GIA G-7241.

Lawton, Liam. "Send Forth Your Spirit." SATB, assembly, kybd, gtr, fl. GIA G-5295.

Mayernik, Luke. "Pentecost Vigil and Pentecost Day" from 5GP.

(GA) Browning, Carol/arr. Tom Andion. "Deo Gloria Alleluia (Easter Gospel Acclamation)" with proper verse for Pentecost. SATB, cant, assembly, kybd, gtr, opt fl, 2 tpt, perc. GIA G-6402.

Hymn of the Day

Creator Spirit, heavenly dove ELW 577, LBW 472 VENI CREATOR SPIRITUS ELW 578, LBW 284 KOMM, GOTT SCHÖPFER

Like the murmur of the dove's song ELW 403, WOV 685 BRIDEGROOM

O living Breath of God/Soplo de Dios viviente ELW 407, LLC 368 VÅRVINDAR FRISKA

Offering

Come to us, creative Spirit ELW 687, WOV 758

O Holy Spirit, root of life ELW 399, WOV 688

Communion

Eternal Spirit of the living Christ ELW 402, LBW 441

O Spirit of life ELW 405, WOV 680

Spirit of Gentleness ELW 396, WOV 684, LS 68

Sending

God of tempest, God of whirlwind ELW 400

O day full of grace ELW 627, LS 71, LBW 161

Rise, O church, like Christ arisen ELW 548, OBS 76

Additional Assembly Songs

As the wind song GTG 292

Santo Espíritu, plenitud pascual/Holy Spirit, our font of love LLC 370

There's a sweet, sweet Spirit in this place TFF 102

🌐 Sosa, Pablo. "Que esta iglesia sea un árbol/May This Church Be like a Tree" from *Hosanna! Ecumenical Songs for Justice and Peace*. SATB. WCC Publications 9782825416679.

🌐 Wang, Wei-fang. "Holy Spirit, You're like the Wind/Sheng ling ru feng" from *Global Praise 3*. SATB. GBGMusik 9781890569877.

☼ Assad, Audrey. "Spirit of the Living God" from CCLI.

☼ Brown, Chris/Matthew Ntlele/Steven Furtick. "Fullness" from CCLI.

☼ Gungor, David/John Arndt/Lisa Gungor/Michael Gungor. "Breathe" from CCLI.

☼ Smith, Caroline Cobb. "Breath of God" from CCLI.

☼ Van Patter, Michael. "Breathe on Me, Breath of God" from *Pentecost Songs*. cardiphonia.bandcamp.com.

☼ Wilton, David. "Wash Me Clean" from *Hymns IV*. pagecxvi.com.

Music for the Day
Choral

Hassell, Michael. "Spirit, Spirit of Gentleness." SATB, pno, sax or cl. AFP 9780800657116.

P Miller, Aaron David. "Holy Ghost, with Light Divine." 2 pt, pno. AFP 9780800677947.

Mozart, Wolfgang A. "Veni Sancte Spiritus (KV 47)" from *Shorter Sacred Works*. SATB, org. BAR 9790006527977.

Muczynski, Robert. "Alleluia" from *Five Centuries of Choral Music*. SATB, a cap. HAL 50330320.

Children's Choir

Bach, J. S. "Come, Let Us All This Day." U, kybd. CPDL.

Bedford, Michael. "Sing and Dance, Children of God." 2 pt, kybd. HIN HMC379.

Owen, Harold. "Breathe on Me, Breath of God." U, kybd. GIA G-5113.

Keyboard / Instrumental

Burkhardt, Michael. "Intrada and Trio on Komm, Heiliger Geist, Herre Gott" from *Living Voice of the Gospel: The Hymns of Martin Luther*. Org. MSM 10-683.

P ♫ Culli, Benjamin. "Like the Murmur of the Dove's Song" from *New Songs of Celebration: Ten Settings for Organ*. Org. AFP 9781451494082.

P ♫ Organ, Anne Krentz. "Creator Spirit, Heavenly Dove" from *Piano Reflections on Pentecost Tunes*. Pno. AFP 9781451499148.

P ♫ Roberts, Al. "Soplo de Dios viviente" from *We Belong to God: Piano Settings of Folk Tunes*. Pno. AFP 9781451451801.

Handbell

♫ McFadden, Jane. "Like the Murmur of a Dove's Song." 3-5 oct hb, opt 3-5 hc, C inst, L3. BP HB310.

♫ Tucker, Sondra. "Come, Holy Spirit (Invocation)." 3, 4, or 5 oct, L3. CG CGB630.

♫ Wagner, Doug. "Come, Creator Spirit." 3-5 oct hb or hc, L2. LOR 20/1559L.

Sunday, May 31
Visit of Mary to Elizabeth

Sometime after the Annunciation, Mary visited her cousin Elizabeth. This occasion is sometimes referred to simply as "The Visitation." Elizabeth greeted Mary with the words "Blessed are you among women," and Mary responded with her famous song, the Magnificat. Luke's gospel tells that even John the Baptist rejoiced and leapt in his mother's womb when

🌐 = global song   ♫ = relates to hymn of the day
☼ = praise song   P = available in Prelude Music Planner

Elizabeth heard Mary's greeting. On this festival two women are seen: one, seemingly too old to have a child, bears the last prophet of the old covenant, and the other, quite young, bears the incarnate Word and the new covenant.

Monday, June 1
Justin, martyr at Rome, died around 165

Justin was born of pagan parents. At Ephesus he was moved by stories of early Christian martyrs and came under the influence of an elderly Christian man he met there. Justin described his conversion by saying, "Straightway a flame was kindled in my soul and a love of the prophets and those who are friends of Christ possessed me." Justin was a teacher of philosophy and engaged in debates about the truth of Christian faith. He was arrested and jailed for practicing an unauthorized religion. He refused to renounce his faith, and he and six of his students, one a woman, were beheaded.

Justin's description of early Christian worship around the year 150 is the foundation of the church's pattern of worship, East and West.

Wednesday, June 3
The Martyrs of Uganda, died 1886

Christianity had been introduced to Uganda after 1877, but was made available primarily to those in the court of King Mutesa. His successor, King Mwanga, was angered by these Christian members of the court whose first allegiance was not to him but to Christ. On June 3, 1886, thirty-two young men were burned to death for refusing to renounce Christianity. Other martyrs followed. But many were impressed by the confident manner in which these Christians went to their deaths, and the persecution led to a much stronger Christian presence in the country.

Wednesday, June 3
John XXIII, Bishop of Rome, died 1963

In his ministry as a bishop of Venice, John (then Archbishop Roncalli) was loved by his people. He visited parishes and established new ones. He had warm affection for the working class—he himself was the child of Italian peasants—and he worked at developing social-action ministries. At age seventy-seven he was elected bishop of Rome. Despite the expectation that he would be a transitional pope, he had great energy and spirit. He convened the Second Vatican Council to open the windows of the church and "let in the fresh air of the modern world." The council brought about great changes in Roman Catholic worship, changes that have influenced Lutherans and many other Protestant churches as well.

Friday, June 5
Boniface, Bishop of Mainz, missionary to Germany, martyr, died 754

Boniface (his name means "good deeds") was born Wynfrith in Devonshire, England. He was a Benedictine monk who at the age of thirty was called to missionary work among the Vandal tribes in Germany. His first missionary attempt was unsuccessful, but he returned two years later and was able to plant the gospel in an area filled with superstitious and violent practices. He led large numbers of Benedictine monks and nuns in establishing churches, schools, and seminaries. Boniface was also a reformer. He persuaded two rulers to call synods to put an end to the practice of selling church offices to the highest bidder. Boniface was preparing a group for confirmation on the eve of Pentecost when he and they were killed by a band of pagans.

Summer

Preparing for Summer

Preaching

Summer preaching is a great time to reframe how God continues to make a claim on the beloved community of the church against all odds. God's persistence in the life of the church is truly a treasure! Accounts of Jesus forming his followers through storytelling and with mighty acts inspire us to persevere and even flourish.

Jeremiah the prophet was compelled to speak even though he had no assurance that his words would have any effect (Lectionary 12/13, June 21/28). The great fertility of God's word produces fruit like rain promotes crop growth (Lectionary 15, July 12). In Jesus' parable of the wheat and weeds, we are to shine like the sun even when weeds are planted because God is the gardener and God will reap what is sown (Lectionary 16, July 19).

Maybe your congregation has a community garden whose produce is given to hungry people. Perhaps there is one person in your congregation with an amazing gift for hospitality who knows how to welcome newcomers. Maybe your youth take time for a mission trip. These are all examples of the beloved community following in the ways of Jesus. Talk about them in preaching.

Jesus promotes a singular focus on what he calls the "kingdom of heaven." Parable after parable speaks about glorious things coming from a small seed, a little yeast, or a treasure hidden in a field (Lectionary 17, July 26). Jesus brings the abundance of God to a hungry crowd with just a little bread and a couple of fish (Lectionary 18, August 2). God works in small, hidden things here and now. What are the gifts that we have received that look small but really are not small? What treasures are hidden in our communities that spark the imagination to see the kingdom of heaven right in front of us?

Preaching close to the summer texts can reveal a sense of awe in Jesus' command of wind and wave, his healing power, and his own identity as the one who saves. Notice the disciples' fear of the storm at sea and their mistaking Jesus for a ghost. Notice Peter, the "Rock," sinking into the water before being pulled out by the hand of Jesus. And then see how those in the boat worshiped Jesus (Lectionary 19, August 9). Weaving this narrative into our own patterns of fear and doubt, how might we be reassured by Jesus' attention to the fearful, terrified ones in the rocking boat? How do we experience Jesus attending to our doubts? How can we receive his power and presence in the tumult of our lives, and how does such receiving lead us to worship?

The beloved community we call the church is continually being shaped by its attention to the word of God. Each day, and particularly on Sunday, our baptismal callings are formed in Christ for life. Despite our setbacks, misunderstandings, or distractions, God continues to come close. The prophet Isaiah declares that "the Lord will comfort Zion; he will comfort all her waste places, and will make her wilderness like Eden, her desert like the garden of the Lord" (Isa. 51:3; Lectionary 21, August 23). We are given a precious gift through Christ's life, death, and resurrection. We might find renewal in this gift in the summertime. And we might receive the keys to the kingdom of heaven.

Intercessory Prayer

Summer is often a time of fewer people in church, a more informal atmosphere, and less programming around worship. So it's a great time to try out different ways of praying or simply work toward more lay leadership in the form you already use.

If you currently use the weekly petitions provided in *Sundays and Seasons* with little adaptation, you could stick with that while also developing a pattern of lay prayer leadership. People might be more willing to do this for the first time if it's explicitly cast as summer experimentation. You could give individuals and teams the weekly *Sundays and Seasons* petitions and ask them to add each week (1) something current from the news and (2) something local. The "something local" could be either an ongoing issue and the people addressing it (refugee resettlement, opioid addiction) or references to the seasons, weather, and environment.

Alternatively, you could give prayer writers guidelines for crafting the intercessions, such as Gail Ramshaw's *Praying for the Whole World: A Handbook for Intercessors* (Augsburg Fortress, 2016). Or give them a topical outline with the six foci of our prayer: the church in all its forms worldwide, the earth/environment, the nations/society, this congregation, those in particular need, and our communion with those who have died. You might also encourage them to use one or more cycles of prayer (see some examples on pages 71–72 of this volume), praying in turn for various missionaries or for social service or other nonprofit organizations supported by the congregation or its members.

Depending on the makeup of the congregation, you might assign a month or a week of prayers to individuals, families/ households, small groups within the congregation (Bible study group, women's group, VBS participants), or teams formed for prayer writing. Teams could well include children, teenagers, and the elderly homebound. If you have laypersons who bring communion to folks who are homebound or in care facilities, the communion visitor and the visitee could be a team to draft one or more petitions for the next week's prayers. Not all visitors/visitees will be up for this, but when the homebound person is thoughtful and "with it," they might enjoy the challenge. Ideally, some of the people who have experimented with prayer writing during the summer will be willing to continue this ministry into the program year.

Here are a few other summer prayer experiments you might try:

- *Sung prayer refrains.* The choir may now be sitting scattered through the assembly and can help support its singing!
- *Bidding prayer.* This form of prayer leaves silent space for the assembly to pray for what has been named. The leader may say, "I ask your prayers for justice and peace in the world." After a period of silence, the leader says the lead-in to the assembly's response. Since many of us are so uneasy in silence, it might help to have some sort of music accompany the space for prayer: a singing bowl, a gentle gong or chime, or an instrument repeating a short melody.
- *Visual symbols.* Adults or kids could choose or create a symbol for each of the six prayer categories (a clear bowl of water for church, a potted plant for the earth, a globe for the nations), and someone could hold up each symbol in turn to help focus prayer. (Invite the assembly to keep eyes open in this case so the symbols don't go unseen.)
- *Encourage the assembly's own prayers.* Invite the assembly to voice the names of those who are sick. Then start including other categories to name aloud: their own godchildren, nations where there is conflict, places dealing with natural disaster, communities still recovering from tragedies long out of the news, children in unsafe situations, and so on.

Assembly Song

"Summertime, and the livin' is easy," say the lyrics of a familiar song. But summertime is not always easy for musicians, choirs, and leaders of song as we take breaks, travel, rest, and enjoy the long days of this season. Your usual leadership may not be available, and each week could bring a change in available resources. But take comfort! This really is an age-old challenge; even J. S. Bach composed some cantatas for one singer or a handful of instruments when resources were scarce. So, use what you

have and rejoice in one, many, or, well, just you! Pull out a few beloved and known pieces of music for preludes and postludes. Take a break and enjoy those favorites again. Or if summer brings extra time to practice, what a great opportunity to work on something special and have it under your fingers for the upcoming year.

Summer is a wonderful chance to include all those who are available, from singers to instrumentalists to anyone who wants to join you in leading the church's song. Often during this season, we experience both droughts and floods when it comes to musicians. Explore *Evangelical Lutheran Worship's* Holy Communion Setting Eight with the help of Paul Friesen-Carper's ensemble setting (Augsburg Fortress, 2015). These arrangements allow you to include every singer and almost every instrument available. Invite those in your assembly who can read music to attend a rehearsal and coaching session at the start of summer (or several during). Give them music in advance. Then, have them join you when they are able and create a summer band, choir, and/or orchestra. Some weeks you will have more participants, some weeks fewer. Just make sure you are well rehearsed in your own vocal part and/or leadership at the keyboard. Make sure you practice leading the song before you teach others to lead with you! Even the most experienced musicians sometimes forget that.

Intergenerational choirs and song leaders are another wonderful summer tool. Children who have attended camp or Vacation Bible School could sing songs from that experience and then teach them to the assembly. You could also add impromptu percussion or even dance to a simple gospel acclamation. Consider using "Halle, halle, hallelujah" (ELW 172), which can be led by organ, band, piano, or even a cappella voices. Children could use simple egg shakers or hand drums, and adults could shake their keys along with the music. Be creative. A simple box can make a drum. Fill a container with dried beans and you have a simple shaker instrument that anyone can play.

Summer is also a great time to explore singing a response during the prayers of intercession. Conclude each petition with ". . . we sing and pray" or "Lord, hear our song." Both *Evangelical Lutheran Worship's* Service Music section (#178–180) and the *Hear Our Prayer* collection (Augsburg Fortress, 2007) contain excellent sung prayer responses and, in the latter resource, guidance on how to lead them successfully. You might also use a simple hymn refrain that fits the day's lectionary texts or your assembly's resources.

Worship Space

Renewing worship space for the summer months might start with the practical. Does worship attendance increase or decrease? Does seating need to be added or removed? If seating is fixed, and attendance decreases, rope off sections and encourage the assembly to sit closer together for more robust congregational song and voice and the strengthening of fellowship. Are music ministries on break over the summer? If possible, refresh their space. For example, don't leave bell tables up all summer that won't be used for months. Find a new seasonal use for the space—for children or a configuration for special summer musicians. As you shift or reconfigure space, take the opportunity to declutter both worship space and common areas. We can become immune to noticing our own clutter, but visitors will not be immune, and a clean, well-tended space communicates both welcome and care for God's house.

Many Sunday school and faith formation programs take a break over the summer, allowing for a time of planning and renewal. Yet this sometimes sends the message that there isn't anything for children on Sunday mornings. Find ways to communicate that children are welcome, wanted, expected, and needed in worship over the summer. Refresh or create areas for children in worship. Set up an eye-level display of children's Bibles inviting kids to pick one and take it with them into worship. If possible, buy new children's Bibles (the *Spark Story Bible*, *Whirl Story Bible*, *Frolic First Bible*, and *Frolic Preschool Bible*, all available from Augsburg Fortress, are excellent choices). If you offer children's activity bags, refresh and restock their contents. Try out a "pray-ground" in an area that is unused in the summer. A pray-ground is a designated space for children that encourages them to be in worship while also engaging them in child-friendly ways (toys, small chairs, large children's rug, books). Plan liturgical elements that engage children. Set out a bowl of egg shakers and other child-friendly percussion instruments. Greeters or ushers can invite children to take an instrument and play for a designated hymn.

In the summer green season, celebrate growth, fruitfulness, and the beauty of God's creation. Instead of purchasing flowers from a florist, in summer months have gardeners in the congregation bring in arrangements of flowers or colorful plants.

Find a large glass or plastic bowl and set it where people will see it as they come in to worship. Add to it each week items that relate to the gospel such as coins, a water cup, plastic pearls, seeds, grains of wheat, a rock. This makes for an easy intro into a children's time: "What was (new) in the bowl today?" Or each week, before or after worship, invite children to draw one of these items with chalk on a sidewalk near your building. Draw worshipers' attention to these images as they enter or leave.

An easy way to include the assembly in creating art for worship is with large illustrated coloring posters (see illus tratedchildrensministry. com). Tape the poster to a table and invite people to color on it before or after worship, at a special summer event, during youth events, or at any church gathering,

and then display it in your worship space for the summer season. Even if your group doesn't fully finish the coloring project, hang it up and use it as a reminder that we are all works in progress and that God is continually shaping and growing us.

Seasonal Checklist

- If summer worship and education schedules change, update websites, social media, newspaper listings, answering machine messages, outdoor signs, and internal publications such as a newsletter.
- Schedule and plan commissioning services for any special ministries organized by the congregation (vacation Bible school, mission trips, church camps). Use Blessing and Sending for Mission (*Occasional Services for the Assembly*, pp. 159–60) on the Sunday prior to departure. Consider inviting participants to assist with worship leadership upon completion of their program.
- Use Farewell and Godspeed (*ELW*, p. 75) when people leave the congregation to move to a new community or to bid farewell to graduates leaving for college, other study, or other opportunities.
- Encourage people to worship with a local congregation while traveling. Publicize the "Find a Congregation" tool at elca.org so that travelers can research churches in the places they are visiting.
- If you are planning to use a different worship space or to rearrange your existing space, find volunteers to help with moving furniture and preparing the visual environment. Consult with musicians, ushers, and altar guild members about the practical needs of a worship space.
- Recruit volunteers for any special ministries you may be starting this summer or fall—freshly baked communion bread, community garden, food drive, etc.
- Find musicians to serve as cantors or to play instruments if your regular music leaders will be taking a break over the summer.
- If you intend to offer a back-to-school blessing or blessing of workers on Labor/Labour Day weekend, begin planning and advertising now.
- Make plans for "God's work. Our hands" Sunday if your congregation plans to participate. This annual day of service is generally scheduled for a Sunday in early September (check elca.org for the 2020 date and planning resources). Begin organizing service projects and advertise the schedule for the day.

Worship Texts for Summer

Confession and Forgiveness

All may make the sign of the cross, the sign that is marked at baptism, as the presiding minister begins.

Blessed be the holy Trinity, ☩ one God,
whose steadfast love is everlasting,
whose faithfulness endures from generation to generation.
Amen.

Trusting in the mercy of God, let us confess our sin.

Silence is kept for reflection.

Reconciling God,
we confess that we do not trust your abundance,
and we deny your presence in our lives.
We place our hope in ourselves
and rely on our own efforts.
We fail to believe that you provide enough for all.
We abuse your good creation for our own benefit.
We fear difference and do not welcome others
as you have welcomed us.
We sin in thought, word, and deed.
By your grace, forgive us;
through your love, renew us;
and in your Spirit, lead us;
so that we may live and serve you in newness of life.
Amen.

Beloved of God,
by the radical abundance of divine mercy
we have peace with God through ☩ Christ Jesus,
through whom we have obtained grace upon grace.
Our sins are forgiven.
Let us live now in hope.
For hope does not disappoint,
because God's love has been poured into our hearts
through the Holy Spirit.
Amen.

Offering Prayer

God of goodness and growth,
all creation is yours,
and your faithfulness is as firm as the heavens.
Water and word, wine and bread:
these are signs of your abundant grace.
Nourish us through these gifts,
that we might proclaim your steadfast love
in our communities and in the world,
through Jesus Christ, our strength and our song.
Amen.

Invitation to Communion

Friends of Jesus, come to the table.
Receive nourishment for your journey.

Prayer after Communion

God of the welcome table,
in this meal we have feasted on your goodness
and have been united by your presence among us.
Empower us to go forth sustained by these gifts
so that we may share your neighborly love with all,
through Jesus Christ, the giver of abundant life.
Amen.

Blessing

Neither death, nor life, nor angels, nor rulers,
nor things present, nor things to come,
nor powers, nor height, nor depth,
nor anything else in all creation,
will be able to separate us from the love of God in Christ Jesus.

God, the creator, ☩ Jesus, the Christ,
and the Holy Spirit, the comforter,
bless you and keep you in eternal love.
Amen.

Dismissal

Go in peace. Christ is with you.
Thanks be to God.

Seasonal Rites for Summer

Blessings and Prayers

The following blessings and prayers can be included in the worship of the whole assembly. Those being prayed for can gather with the presiding and assisting ministers at the font or in another location in the worship space. These prayers could also be adapted for use in other settings such as a home or workplace.

Beginning a New Job

The following reading from Jeremiah may precede the prayer and blessing.

For surely I know the plans I have for you, says the Lord, plans for your welfare and not for harm, to give you a future with hope. (Jeremiah 29:11)

The presiding minister continues with the prayer and blessing.
Let us pray.
O God of our labor, we give you thanks for the gifts of your Spirit poured out on your people. We pray, as *name/s begin* this new work, that it may help to fulfill *their* calling and purpose in this life, for the sake of the world you love.
Amen.

May God who loves you and calls you into meaningful work, walk with you as you move forward into a future filled with hope.
Amen.

Retirement

The following reading from Philippians may precede the sharing, prayer, and blessing.

The Apostle Paul writes: I thank my God every time I remember you, constantly praying with joy in every one of my prayers for all of you, because of your sharing in the gospel from the first day until now. I am confident of this, that the one who began a good work among you will bring it to completion by the day of Jesus Christ. (Philippians 1:3-5)

The presiding minister may invite worshipers to share how the retiree has been a blessing to them and the community.

The presiding minister continues with the prayer and blessing.
Let us pray.
For the life and ministry of *name*, we give you thanks, O God. For the gifts you have given *her/him* that *she/he* might serve your people, for opportunities to grow and learn, for relationships built through years of connection, we give you thanks, O God. As *name* now transitions to a new phase of rest and play, direct *her/him* in new ways of serving you and one another.
Amen.

or
Gracious God, we thank you for the work and witness of your servant *name*, who has enriched this community and brought gladness to friends and family. Now bless and preserve *her/him* at this time of transition. Day by day, guide *her/him* and give *her/him* what is needed, friends to cheer *her/his* way, and a clear vision of that to which you are now calling *her/him*. By your Holy Spirit be present in *her/his* pilgrimage, that *she/he* may travel with the one who is the way, the truth, and the life, Jesus Christ our Lord.
Amen.

The presiding minister continues:
You have been a blessing to the world. We now bless you as you enter a new phase of life.

The presiding minister may invite the assembly to raise a hand in a gesture of blessing.
Go with love. Go with joy. Go with peace.
The Spirit of God goes with you. Amen.

Transition from School to Summer

The following reading from Proverbs may precede the sharing, prayer, and blessing.

Trust in the Lord with all your heart, and do not rely on your own insight. In all your ways acknowledge God, and God will make straight your paths. (Proverbs 3:5-6)

The presiding minister may invite students and teachers to share one piece of insight they gained during the school year.

The presiding minister continues with the prayer and blessing.

Let us pray.

We give you thanks, O God, for the ways you speak to us and through us. Increase in us a desire for wisdom and insight that we may use what we have learned for the sake of the common good. We pray in the name of the one who taught disciples and told stories, Jesus our Savior.

Amen.

The presiding minister continues:

You have learned and taught.

Thanks be to God!

You have grown and matured.

Thanks be to God!

You have explored and created.

Thanks be to God!

You have loved and been loved.

Thanks be to God!

Now, enter into rest and play, the re-creation of summer.

And all God's people said:

Amen!

June 7, 2020
The Holy Trinity
First Sunday after Pentecost

Though the word *trinity* is not found in the scriptures, today's second reading includes the apostolic greeting that begins the liturgy: The grace of our Lord Jesus Christ, the love of God, and the communion of the Holy Spirit be with you all. In the gospel Jesus sends his disciples forth to baptize in the name of the Father, and the Son, and the Holy Spirit. More than a doctrine, the Trinity expresses the heart of our faith: we have experienced the God of creation made known in Jesus Christ and with us always through the Holy Spirit. We celebrate the mystery of the Holy Trinity in word and sacrament, as we profess the creed, and as we are sent into the world to bear witness to our faith.

Prayer of the Day

Almighty Creator and ever-living God: we worship your glory, eternal Three-in-One, and we praise your power, majestic One-in-Three. Keep us steadfast in this faith, defend us in all adversity, and bring us at last into your presence, where you live in endless joy and love, Father, Son, and Holy Spirit, one God, now and forever.

or

God of heaven and earth, before the foundation of the universe and the beginning of time you are the triune God: Author of creation, eternal Word of salvation, life-giving Spirit of wisdom. Guide us to all truth by your Spirit, that we may proclaim all that Christ has revealed and rejoice in the glory he shares with us. Glory and praise to you, Father, Son, and Holy Spirit, now and forever.

Gospel Acclamation

Alleluia. Holy, holy, holy is the LORD of hosts; God's glory fills the whole earth. *Alleluia*. (Isa. 6:3)

Readings and Psalm

Genesis 1:1—2:4a

At the beginning of time, God the Creator, God the powerful Word, and God the life-giving Spirit form the earth and all its inhabitants. God sees that all this created work is good and then rests on the seventh day.

Psalm 8

How majestic is your name in all the earth! (Ps. 8:1)

2 Corinthians 13:11-13

Paul closes a challenging letter to the Corinthians with an appeal to Christian fellowship grounded in the triune harmony of Christ's grace, God's love, and the Spirit's partnership.

Matthew 28:16-20

After his resurrection, Jesus summons his remaining disciples and commissions them to baptize and teach all nations in the name of the Father, Son, and Holy Spirit.

Preface   Holy Trinity

Color   White

Prayers of Intercession

The prayers are prepared locally for each occasion. The following examples may be adapted or used as appropriate.

Called into unity with one another and the whole creation, let us pray for our shared world.

A brief silence.

God of community, you form us as your church. Guide our bishops, pastors, deacons, and all the baptized in sharing your life-giving good news with all the world. Strengthen us to be bold in our proclamation. Hear us, O God.

Your mercy is great.

God of creation, you called everything into being. Sustain this world with your renewing care. Inspire us to see waterways, plant life, birds, fish, insects, and mammals and call them good. Hear us, O God.

Your mercy is great.

God of counsel, all authority belongs to you. Encourage the leaders of this and every land to seek peace, equality, and unity. Instill wisdom in advocates who work toward justice in often ignored communities (*like Chief Seattle, whom we commemorate today*). Hear us, O God.

Your mercy is great.

God of care, you created us in your image. Help us see your likeness in one another. Open our eyes to see and attend to all who face oppression and suffering. Console, heal, and nourish all in need (*especially*). Hear us, O God.

Your mercy is great.

God of companionship, you accompany this body of faith. As the rhythms of summer begin, protect all who travel, renew all who will enjoy a time of sabbath, and shelter all who will not be protected from the sun's heat. Hear us, O God.
Your mercy is great.
Here other intercessions may be offered.
God of compassion, you comfort us in our grief with the promise of the resurrection. We give you thanks for the saints of all time and in our lives (*especially*). Hear us, O God.
Your mercy is great.
Receive these prayers, O God, and those too deep for words; through Jesus Christ our Lord.
Amen.

Ideas for the Day

- Fans of Madeleine L'Engle's young adult science fiction novel *A Wrinkle in Time* may well have read the other books in the series, including the third, *A Swiftly Tilting Planet* (a winner of the National Book Award for Young People's Literature). If so, they may recognize the Trinity-focused text of "I bind unto myself today" (ELW 450), based on a prayer by St. Patrick commonly called "St. Patrick's Breastplate." The protagonist of this book, Charles Wallace, invokes St. Patrick's Breastplate throughout the story as he is engaged in a profound struggle between good and evil. This could be a delightful point of connection for young people—and others—who may be surprised to see how a favorite science fiction author draws from the ancient traditions and liturgies of the church.
- While somewhat acerbic in tone, the video "St. Patrick's Bad Analogies" on the YouTube channel LutheranSatire offers an amusing explanation of why all our attempts to describe the Trinity are inadequate and end up falling into heresy. The point is not that St. Patrick was wrong for using a shamrock to illustrate the Trinity, but that we should not spend our energy trying to find the best way to define a mystery that can be neither fully comprehended nor explained by mortals. *Explaining* the Trinity isn't the point; *trusting* the presence and power of the triune God is.
- A fresco in St. Jakobus Church in Urschalling, Germany, depicts Abraham worshiping, with a nearby inscription reading, "Abraham tres vidit unum adoravit" ("Abraham sees three, he worships one"). Facing Abraham is a notably unusual depiction of the Trinity: the figure in the center, representing the Holy Spirit, is female. The fresco dates from the twelfth to fourteenth centuries. Several photographs of this Trinity are available on Wikimedia Commons; search "Holy Trinity Urschalling."

Connections with Creation

Elizabeth Johnson's classic book *She Who Is* presents a way of seeing the Trinity from a feminist perspective in which Sophia-Spirit, Sophia-Jesus, and Sophia-God engage in an eternal exchange of holy wisdom. That wisdom births the world and "calls forth human responsibility for the good of the world." Wherever people, communities, or Earth itself is threatened, damaged, or destroyed, the power of the triune God is at work to bring about new life and new hope. One way to celebrate this day is to invite the congregation to list all the ways in which they notice the Holy Trinity active in creation. If, as Johnson says, Sophia "is an expression of the most intense divine presence in the world," helping people make the connection between creation and the Sophia-Creator can both enhance faith and infuse the world with the sacredness intended by the creative Trinity.

Let the Children Come

This week we are given the rare gift of listening to some ancient poetry in Genesis 1. Our creative God inspired this work of artistry. Help children (and adults) notice that the poem isn't complete until the holy day of rest. Like the people of Israel, we are invited to rest in God. Rest can be difficult in our fast-paced world where success is measured by how busy we are. Perhaps this is an opportunity to invite your congregation to pause. Invite the children to help you hold silences. Can they ring a bell when a time for silence is over after the sermon? It's often when we're still that we find we have time to be truly creative. We're made in the image of a creative God. How might God inspire you to create this week in celebration of God's good earth?

Assembly Song
Gathering

Come, all you people/Uyaimose ELW 819, WOV 717, TFF 138
Holy, holy, holy, Lord God Almighty! ELW 413, LLC 371, LBW 165
I bind unto myself today ELW 450, LBW 188

Psalmody and Acclamations

O Lord, our God, how excellent/Psalm 8 GTG 25
Burkhardt, Michael. "Psalm 8" from *Psalms for the Church Year*. 3 pt equal vcs, a cap or with org and/or hb. MSM 80-708.
Valentine, Timothy, SJ. "How Majestic Your Name." SAB, cant, assembly, gtr, kybd, opt inst. GIA G-4833.
(GA) ELW 175 with proper verse for Holy Trinity. (Tone in ELW Accompaniment Edition: Service Music and Hymns.)

Hymn of the Day

Come, join the dance of Trinity ELW 412 *KINGSFOLD*
Mothering God, you gave me birth ELW 735, WOV 769 *NORWICH*
We all believe in one true God ELW 411, LBW 374 *WIR GLAUBEN ALL*

Offering

My Lord of light   ELW 832, WOV 796
Praise and thanksgiving be to God   ELW 458, LBW 191

Communion

Isaiah in a vision did of old   ELW 868, LBW 528
Holy, holy, holy/Santo, santo, santo   ELW 473, W&P 62
You are holy/Du är helig   ELW 525

Sending

Go, make disciples   ELW 540, W&P 47
Holy God, we praise your name   ELW 414, LBW 535

Additional Assembly Songs

In the name of the Father   TFF 142
May the Sending One   NCH 79
Womb of life and source of being   NCH 274, GTG 3
⊕ Joseph, Ravela, as taught by Vinita Manchala. "Margam, Satyam, Jivam, Nive/Living, Moving, End and Beginning" from *Hosanna! Ecumenical Songs for Justice and Peace*. SATB. WCC Publications 9782825416679.
⊕ Kang, Unsu/Edward Poltras/rev. Andrew Donaldson. "God Who Created" from songs submitted to the World Council of Churches' 10th Assembly. Out of print. Hannelore .Schmid@wcc-coe.org.
☼ Assad, Audrey. "Receive" from CCLI.
☼ Clark, Derek Samuel/Fred Hammond/Shelton Summons. "Father Spirit Jesus" from CCLI.
☼ Fielding, Ben/Matt Crocker. "This I Believe (The Creed)" from CCLI.
☼ Gungor, Lisa. "God Our Mother" from CCLI.
☼ McCracken, Sandra. "Trinity Song" from CCLI.
☼ Roth, Spencer/Bobby Smith/Jordan Watts. "Trinity Song" from *Always Only Jesus*. jfworship.com.

Music for the Day
Choral

P Burrows, Mark. "Santo." SATB, pno, perc. CG CGA1349.
P♫ Highben, Zebulon. "Mothering God, You Gave Me Birth." SAB, gtr, fl. AFP 9781451424249.
Mathias, William. "As Truly as God Is Our Father" from *Epiphany to All Saints for Choirs*. SATB, org. OXF 9780193530263.
P Ward, Tony. "We Arise This Day." SATB, pno, opt vln, solo inst, assembly. AFP 9781506452524.

Children's Choir

P Helgen, John. "Psalm 8" from *ChildrenSing Psalms*. U/2 pt, kybd, hb, fc. AFP 9780800663872.
Hopson, Hal H. "I Sing a Song of Thanks and Joy." U, pno, opt hb. MSM 50-7504.

P Sleeth, Natalie. "Go into the World" from *LifeSongs*. U, kybd, opt. descant. AFP 9780806642703.

Keyboard / Instrumental

P♫ Callahan, Charles. "Variations on Kingsfold" from *English Hymn Tune Suite*. Org. MSM 10-989.
P♫ Hansen, Sherri. "Mothering God, You Gave Me Birth" from *Piano Weavings*, vol. 2. Pno. AFP 9781506413723.
P Shaw, Timothy. "Holy, Holy, Holy, Lord God Almighty!" from *My Redeemer Lives: Hymns of Comfort and Praise*. Pno. AFP 9781451451795.
Wold, Wayne L. "Holy God, We Praise Your Name" from *Credo for Organ and Trumpet: Settings for Festive Occasions*. Org, tpt. AFP 9781506413754.

Handbell

♫ Eithun, Sandra. "I Heard the Voice of Jesus Say." 3-6 oct hb, opt 3-5 hc, L2+. SF 202037.
♫ Lamb, Linda. "Bell Peal on Holy, Holy, Holy." 2 oct, L1. ALF 25341.
♫ Tucker, Sondra. "Canticle on Kingsfold." 3-5 oct hb, opt 3 oct hc, L4-. BP HB408.

Sunday, June 7
Seattle, chief of the Duwamish Confederacy, died 1866

Noah Seattle was chief of the Suquamish tribe and later became chief of the Duwamish Confederacy, a tribal alliance. When the tribes were faced with an increasing number of white settlers, Seattle chose to live and work peacefully with them rather than engage in wars. After Seattle became a Roman Catholic, he began the practice of morning and evening prayer in the tribe, a practice that continued after his death. On the centennial of his birth, the city of Seattle—named for him against his wishes—erected a monument over his grave.

Tuesday, June 9
Columba, died 597; Aidan, died 651; Bede, died 735; renewers of the church

These three monks from the British Isles were pillars among those who kept alive the light of learning and devotion during the Middle Ages. Columba founded three monasteries, including one on the island of Iona, off the coast of Scotland. That monastery was left in ruins after the Reformation but today is home to an ecumenical religious community. Aidan, who helped bring Christianity to the Northumbria area of England, was known for his pastoral style and ability to stir people to

⊕ = global song   ♫ = relates to hymn of the day
☼ = praise song   P = available in Prelude Music Planner

charity and good works. Bede was a Bible translator and scripture scholar. He wrote a history of the English church and was the first historian to date events anno Domini (A.D.), "year of our Lord." Bede is also known for his hymns, including "A hymn of glory let us sing!" (ELW 393).

Thursday, June 11
Barnabas, Apostle

The Eastern church commemorates Barnabas as one of the Seventy commissioned by Jesus. Though he was not among the Twelve mentioned in the gospels, the book of Acts gives him the title of apostle. His name means "son of encouragement." When Paul came to Jerusalem after his conversion, Barnabas took him in over the fears of the other apostles, who doubted Paul's discipleship. Later, Paul and Barnabas traveled together on missions. At the Council of Jerusalem, Barnabas defended the claims of Gentile Christians in relation to the Mosaic law.

June 14, 2020
Time after Pentecost — Lectionary 11

Moses tells the Israelites that they are called to be a priestly kingdom and a holy people. Jesus sends out the disciples as laborers into the harvest. In baptism we too are anointed for ministry, sharing God's compassion with our needy world. From the Lord's table we go forth to proclaim the good news, to heal the sick, and to share our bread with the hungry.

Prayer of the Day

God of compassion, you have opened the way for us and brought us to yourself. Pour your love into our hearts, that, overflowing with joy, we may freely share the blessings of your realm and faithfully proclaim the good news of your Son, Jesus Christ, our Savior and Lord.

Gospel Acclamation

Alleluia. The kingdom of God has come near; repent, and believe in the good news. *Alleluia.* (Mark 1:15)

Readings and Psalm
Exodus 19:2-8a

At Sinai God assured Israel, "You shall be my treasured possession," and commissioned them to serve as mediating priests for the nations. The people commit themselves completely to God's will.

Psalm 100

We are God's people and the sheep of God's pasture. (Ps. 100:3)

Romans 5:1-8

We are no longer God's enemies but have peace with God because we were brought into a right relationship with God through Christ's death.

Matthew 9:35—10:8 [9-23]

The mission of Jesus' followers is to continue the mission of Jesus himself. Here, he instructs his first disciples as to how they might proclaim the gospel through their words and deeds.

Semicontinuous Reading and Psalm
Genesis 18:1-15 [21:1-7]

God, in the form of three messengers, announces to Sarah and Abraham that they will have a child. Sarah, because of her advanced age, laughs at this seeming impossibility. But nothing is impossible for God, and in due course Isaac is born (Gen. 21:1-7). Now, Sarah confesses, everyone will share in her joyous laughter.

Psalm 116:1-2, 12-19

I will call on the name of the LORD. (Ps. 116:13)

Preface   Sundays

Color   Green

Prayers of Intercession

The prayers are prepared locally for each occasion. The following examples may be adapted or used as appropriate.

Called into unity with one another and the whole creation, let us pray for our shared world.

A brief silence.

Holy One, you bring us together and call us your own. Bless theologians, teachers, and preachers who help us grow in faith (*following the examples of Basil the Great, Gregory of Nyssa, Gregory of Nazianzus, and the teacher Macrina, whom we commemorate today*). Guide your church, that we might be a holy people. Hear us, O God.

Your mercy is great.

Holy One, the whole earth is yours. Where there is fire, bring cool air and new growth. Where there is flooding, bring abatement. Where there is drought, bring rain. Inspire us to care for what you have provided. Hear us, O God.

Your mercy is great.

Holy One, we have created divisions you will not own. In places of conflict (*especially*), raise up leaders who work to develop lasting peace and reconciliation. Encourage organizations and individuals who care for all forced to leave their homes. Hear us, O God.

Your mercy is great.

Holy One, you care for those who are harassed and helpless. Protect and defend those who are abused. Heal those who are sick. Feed all who hunger. Empower all whose voices go unheard, and help us respond to the pressing needs of our neighbors. Hear us, O God.

Your mercy is great.

Holy One, you provide a plentiful harvest of gifts and resources. Prepare us to labor and gather the fruits of this congregation, that we might discover new ways of living. Minister to us in our work, that we do not lose heart. Hear us, O God.

Your mercy is great.

Here other intercessions may be offered.

Holy One, you bring all people to yourself. We give thanks for the holy people who have gone before us (*especially*). Sustain us in your mission until the day you bear us up to join the saints in light. Hear us, O God.

Your mercy is great.

Receive these prayers, O God, and those too deep for words; through Jesus Christ our Lord.

Amen.

Ideas for the Day

- In the short video "The Devil = Your Inner Critic," part of the *Have a Little Faith* series at Makers (www.makers .com/playlists), ELCA pastor and author Nadia Bolz-Weber speaks about our fears of never overcoming the distance between our actual selves and our ideal selves. The sense of this distance is what holds many Christians back from believing that they are worthy of truly having a calling, that they have any authority as a believer in Jesus, or that they have any ability to fulfill their calling. In the video, Pastor Bolz-Weber reminds us that the person God knows, loves, and calls is not an idealized version of ourselves; God chose to love and call us as we actually already are.

- A liturgy including an anointing of hands for service can be a powerful reminder that we are all called and equipped to serve. You might set up several stations for anointing and prayer around the altar, designated for various types of service: healing, teaching, nurturing/caring, building/ creating, worshiping/praying, and so on. You could invite worshipers to go to the station they most identify with or would most like prayer for. It would be important to include a category like worshiping/praying that will apply to everyone in the room; no one should be left out of this rite.

- A 2016 *Living Lutheran* article, "The Future Is Here" (livinglutheran.org/2016/09/the-future-is-here), outlines the scope of a significant clergy shortage facing the ELCA. Even with the decline in the number of full-time calls available, within a few years the church will still not have enough pastors and deacons to fill the need. In addition to lifting up the priesthood of all the baptized, today would be an appropriate day to pray for seminaries, encourage members to provide financial support for students, and ask people to actively pray for and lift up young children who may have a calling to rostered ministry in the years to come. See a blessing for seminarians in the seasonal rites section on page 255.

Connections with Creation

Psalm 100 appears to personify Earth by poetically describing creation's ability to worship God "with gladness" and to come into God's presence "with singing" (v. 2). But in her poem "Such Singing in the Wild Branches," Mary Oliver describes a holy encounter with a wood thrush that elevates her soul with its song. Perhaps the psalmist had it right—those gates of God through which we are to enter with thanksgiving may be the very trees themselves. Maybe those courts are the tall grasses that bow in reverence as the Spirit-wind passes by. As summer begins in the Western Hemisphere, this is an ideal time to remind those in worship that God's temple is Earth itself. And if our own souls need comforting, we can heed Oliver's urging: "Quick, then—open the door and fly on your heavy feet; the song may already be drifting away."

Let the Children Come

Our gospel this week is the sending out of the twelve disciples to care for people in very practical ways. Sometimes in the church we get caught up in what we should and shouldn't do, and we make the gift of being able to serve in love into a law of duty. It's rather lonely for church members when they get caught up keeping tabs on who last washed dishes from coffee hour, who brought cookies last week, who remembered to show up to acolyte and who forgot. This is an opportunity to help inspire and model joyful service and genuine love of one another. Children are watching. It seems significant that Jesus didn't send out the disciples on their own. What service project can you do this Sunday as a whole congregation? Make sure the children are in the thick of it—they are servants too.

Assembly Song
Gathering

Gather Us In   ELW 532, WOV 718

In Christ called to baptize   ELW 575

We all are one in mission   ELW 576, WOV 755

Psalmody and Acclamations

Come with joy/Psalm 100   DATH 41

Pelz, Walter L. "Psalm 100" from PWA.

Roberts, William Bradley. "Psalm 100" from PSCY.

(GA) ELW 175 with proper verse for Lectionary 11.

Hymn of the Day

The Son of God, our Christ   ELW 584, LBW 434   SURSUM CORDA

There's a wideness in God's mercy   ELW 587   ST. HELENA

ELW 588, LBW 290   LORD, REVIVE US

Will you come and follow me   ELW 798, W&P 137   KELVINGROVE

Offering

We Are an Offering   ELW 692, W&P 146

We give thee but thine own   ELW 686, LBW 410

Communion

For by grace you have been saved   ELW 598

Send me, Jesus   ELW 549, TFF 245

You satisfy the hungry heart   ELW 484, WOV 711

Sending

Holy Spirit, ever dwelling   ELW 582, LBW 523

Rise up, O saints of God!   ELW 669, LBW 383

Additional Assembly Songs

Bring Forth the Kingdom   W&P 22, LS 35, NCH 181

For the healing of the nations   SP 12a

⊕ You are the seed   WOV 753, TFF 226, LLC 486, LS 139

⊕ Enviado soy de Dios/The Lord now sends us forth   ELW 538, LLC 415

⊕ Pakistani trad. "Be Joyful in the Lord, All Lands/Ae sab Zami-inde loko" from *Sound the Bamboo*. U. GIA G-6830.

☼ Aronson, Elena/David M. Bailey/Deleyse Rowe/Ryan Martin. "The Earth Shall Know" from *Urban Doxology*. urban doxology.bandcamp.com.

☼ Assad, Audrey. "Teresa" from CCLI.

☼ Brown, Chris/Mack Brock/Steven Furtick. "There Is a Cloud" from CCLI.

☼ Hammond, Fred/Kim Rutherford/Noel Hall. "Lord of the Harvest" from CCLI.

☼ McDowell, William. "Send Me" from CCLI.

☼ Reagan, Wen/Naaman Wood. "Help Us to Follow" from *Among the Thorns*. cardiphonia.bandcamp.com.

Music for the Day
Choral

♫ Bell, John/arr. Gary Daigle. "The Summons." 2 pt, kybd, opt fl, gtr. GIA G-5410.

Haydn, Johann Michael/arr. Patrick M. Liebergen "Come Follow Me Forever." 2 pt, kybd. GIA G-5387.

P Le Jeune, Claude. "All You That Dwell upon Earth" from *Augsburg Motet Book*. SAB, a cap. AFP 9781451423709.

P ♫ Moore, Bob. "There's a Wideness in God's Mercy." SAB, pno. AFP 9781506422152.

Children's Choir

Dietterich, Philip R. "Come One, Come All, Come Follow." U, kybd. CG CGA553.

P Shaw, Timothy. "A Psalm of Thanksgiving." U/2 pt, kybd, opt C inst. CG CGA1321.

Shields, Valerie. "Psalm 100." U/2 pt, kybd, opt 1 or 2 C inst. ECS 5782.

Keyboard / Instrumental

♫ Callahan, Charles. "Kelvingrove" from *Four Celtic Preludes: Guitar and Organ or Piano*. Gtr, org or pno. MSM 20-735.

P ♫ Childs, Edwin T. "Lord, Revive Us" from *American Folk Hymns for Organ*. Org. AFP 9781451494051.

P ♫ Raabe, Nancy M. "There's a Wideness in God's Mercy" from *Grace & Peace, Volume 6: Songs of Heaven*. Pno. AFP 9781451479621.

Raney, Joel. "This Is My Father's World" from *This Is My Story, This Is My Song*. Pno. HOP 8193.

Handbell

Eithun, Sandra. "Raise Your Joys and Triumphs High." 3-6 oct. L2+. LOR 20/1468L.

♫ Nelson, Susan T. "Will You Come and Follow Me." 3-5 oct hb, opt C inst, L3. AGEHR 35289.

♫ Tucker, Sondra. "There's a Wideness in God's Mercy." 3-5 oct, L3. AFP 0800674901.

⊕ = global song   ♫ = relates to hymn of the day   + = semicontinuous psalm

☼ = praise song   P = available in Prelude Music Planner

Sunday, June 14

Basil the Great, Bishop of Caesarea, died 379; Gregory, Bishop of Nyssa, died around 385; Gregory of Nazianzus, Bishop of Constantinople, died around 389; Macrina, teacher, died around 379

The three men in this group are known as the Cappadocian fathers; all three explored the mystery of the Holy Trinity. Basil was influenced by his sister Macrina to live a monastic life, and he settled near the family estate in Caesarea. Basil's Longer Rule and Shorter Rule for monastic life are the basis for Eastern monasticism to this day and express a preference for communal monastic life over that of hermits. Gregory of Nazianzus (nah-zee-AN-zus) was sent to preach on behalf of the Orthodox faith against the Arians in Constantinople, though the Orthodox did not have a church there at the time. He defended Orthodox trinitarian and christological doctrine, and his preaching won over the city. Gregory of Nyssa (NISS-uh) was the younger brother of Basil the Great. He is remembered as a writer on spiritual life and the contemplation of God in worship and sacraments.

Macrina (muh-CREE-nuh) was the older sister of Basil and Gregory of Nyssa. She received an excellent education centered on the Bible, and when her fiancé died, she devoted herself to the pursuit of Christian perfection. She was a leader of a community, based at the family estate, dedicated to asceticism, meditation, and prayer. Macrina's teaching was influential within the early church.

June 21, 2020
Time after Pentecost — Lectionary 12

God does not promise that the path of the disciple will be easy. Jeremiah feels the pain of rejection from those who do not want to hear what he has to say. Jesus declares that his words may bring stark division. Even so, we need not be afraid for God accounts for each hair on our heads. Though we may experience rejection, frustration, division, and death, God's grace and love make us a new creation each day. Marked with the cross and filled with holy food, we are sent from worship to witness to Christ in the world.

Prayer of the Day

Teach us, good Lord God, to serve you as you deserve, to give and not to count the cost, to fight and not to heed the wounds, to toil and not to seek for rest, to labor and not to ask for reward, except that of knowing that we do your will, through Jesus Christ, our Savior and Lord.

Gospel Acclamation

Alleluia. Jesus says, The Spirit of the Lord will testify on my behalf, and you also are to testify. *Alleluia.* (John 15:26, 27)

Readings and Psalm
Jeremiah 20:7-13

Jeremiah accuses God of forcing him into a ministry that only brings him contempt and persecution. Yet Jeremiah is confident that God will be a strong protector against his enemies and commits his life into God's hands.

Psalm 69:7-10 [11-15] 16-18

Answer me, O LORD, for your love is kind. (Ps. 69:16)

Romans 6:1b-11

In baptism we were incorporated into the reality of Christ's death and resurrection. We have been made new in Christ through his death and resurrection to live freed from sin.

Matthew 10:24-39

Jesus warns his disciples that their ministry in his name will meet with opposition. However, he assures them that they need not fear for the truth will come to light. Life is found in Christ.

Semicontinuous Reading and Psalm
Genesis 21:8-21

Sarah demands that Abraham send Hagar and her son, Ishmael, away. Abraham is distressed because he is Ishmael's father. Sarah wants to ensure that her son, Isaac, will be the one to inherit God's blessing. God, however, hears Hagar's cry and promises to also make of Ishmael a great nation.

Psalm 86:1-10, 16-17

Have mercy on me; give your strength to your servant. (Ps. 86:16)

Preface   Sundays

Color   Green

Prayers of Intercession

The prayers are prepared locally for each occasion. The following examples may be adapted or used as appropriate.

Called into unity with one another and the whole creation, let us pray for our shared world.

A brief silence.

Expansive God, you bring diverse voices together to form your church. Open our hearts and unstop our ears to learn from one another, that differences might not overshadow our baptismal unity. Hear us, O God.

Your mercy is great.

Providing God, your creation shows us that life comes from death. Renew the places where our land, air, and waterways have been ill for too long (*local environmental concerns may be prayed for*). Direct the work of all who care for birds and their habitats. Hear us, O God.

Your mercy is great.

Protecting God, sustain and keep safe all who work to defend others across the world (*especially*). Revive and strengthen organizations dedicated to caring for refugees and migrants while their homelands struggle for peace. Hear us, O God.

Your mercy is great.

Loving God, you promise to be with all who are persecuted for your sake. Guide all who speak your word of justice and console any who are tormented or targeted for being who they are. Hear us, O God.

Your mercy is great.

Compassionate God, you are with us and we are never alone. Bless all fathers and father figures who strive to love and nurture as you do. Comfort all who long to be fathers and all for whom this day is difficult. Hear us, O God.

Your mercy is great.

Here other intercessions may be offered.

Reigning God, you bless us with guides and caretakers in the faith. As we give thanks for those who have died (*especially Onesimos Nesib, translator and evangelist*), increase our care for one another until we walk with them in newness of life. Hear us, O God.

Your mercy is great.

Receive these prayers, O God, and those too deep for words; through Jesus Christ our Lord.

Amen.

Ideas for the Day

- Theologian James H. Cone was fond of saying, "You can't preach the gospel without being opposed." Today's Jeremiah text agrees. People ridicule his words and work (20:7), others threaten his livelihood, and even friends try to undermine everything he works for (20:10). Yet to contain the "burning fire shut up in [Jeremiah's] bones"— the call to prophetic words and work—is too great a burden, and so he bursts forth (20:9)—not unlike Cone—to share the words, decisions, and deeds that God has put on his heart. Are there consequences? Sure. But when God blesses followers with such fire, to resist being consumed by it is both a refusal of God's call and a missed opportunity to see what God has in store for our lives.

- Overzealous Christians who claim to be "cured" of their sinful nature often merit suspicion. Lutheran theology teaches that nothing we do can ever free us from sin's power. Hypocritical televangelists in these and olden days serve as a reminder, exhorting followers to tithe generously from their own lavish mansions, and counseling marital fidelity while concealing their own affairs. Skeptics rightly point out that if Christian life didn't purge the sinful nature of these loud-and-proud followers of Jesus, is such a claim even believable, let alone possible? Paul's distinction is helpful here: being "dead to sin" is inseparable from being "alive to God in Christ Jesus" (6:11). Since our own sinful nature kills us daily, it's only in Christ that we may be "dead to sin and alive to God." Righteousness is never "ours" by anything except God's work through Christ—and ironically, the more righteous we proclaim ourselves to be, the more likely we're not.

- This wonderful cluster of pithy proclamations in Matthew makes for delightful reflection as Jesus touches on everything from power dynamics (10:24-25) to prophetic honesty (10:34-36) and even pastoral care (10:29-31). As quotable as these statements are, they don't much connect to each other, suggesting that Jesus may have had Jeremiah's "fire in the bones" inspiring him (Jer. 20:9), each pronouncement tumbling impatiently out as Jesus gave inspiration free rein. If you must find a uniting thread, one might say eschatology joins these phrases, but you may just as easily say the passage simply shows the value of speaking boldly as the Holy Spirit prompts—whether while reading a prepared text or during a moment of passion.

Connections with Creation

When Jesus says in Matthew 10:31 that humans are worth more than many sparrows, his words could be read as putting humans above the birds. This, in turn, could be used to justify the destruction of wildlife and its habitation in favor of extracting wood from trees, methane from shale, and coal from mountains for human use. But such a reading ignores the prior verses where Jesus acknowledges that God is aware of every fallen bird and counts every hair on a human head. What if humans were to care enough about the birds to mourn when the last of a species like the kakapo or California condor falls to the ground? What if Christians partnered with scientists to count and track endangered species? Perhaps this could be seen as a "ministry of the sparrows."

Let the Children Come

This week is the week of the summer solstice. In the Northern Hemisphere the hours of daylight will now begin to grow shorter until just around Christmas, when we see very clearly Emmanuel, God-with-us. The gospel reminds us that existing in Christian community is not always easy, and Jesus knows this. The gift in the text is the assurance that we are deeply valued by God (Matt. 10:29-31). What might it look like for the children to practice noticing how God has given them the gift of existence and to remember that they can be sure God values them deeply? Maybe you make a paper chain out of paper where each person writes or draws one thing they are thankful for each week until the winter solstice. What color paper would you choose? Where would you hang it?

Assembly Song
Gathering

Lift high the cross ELW 660, LLC 489, LS 88, LBW 377
O God, my faithful God ELW 806, LBW 504
We know that Christ is raised ELW 449, LBW 189

Psalmody and Acclamations

Mayernik, Luke. "Twelfth Sunday in Ordinary Time A" from 5GP.
Haugen, Marty. "Lord, in Your Great Love, Answer Me" from TLP:A.
+ Keesecker, Thomas. "Psalm 86:1-10, 16-17" from PWA. (GA) ELW 175 with proper verse for Lectionary 12.)

Hymn of the Day

Let us ever walk with Jesus ELW 802, LBW 487 *LASSET UNS MIT JESU ZIEHEN*
Oh, praise the gracious power ELW 651, WOV 750 *CHRISTPRAISE RAY*
Take up your cross, the Savior said ELW 667 *BOURBON* LBW 398 *NUN LASST UNS DEN LEIB BEGRABEN*

Offering

Take my life, that I may be ELW 583/685, LLC 570, LBW 406
We Are an Offering ELW 692, W&P 146

Communion

Borning Cry ELW 732
Let us break bread together ELW 471, TFF 123, LBW 212
Strengthen for service, Lord ELW 497, LBW 218

Sending

I love to tell the story ELW 661, TFF 228, LS 154, LBW 390
O Christ, your heart, compassionate ELW 722

Additional Assembly Songs

By grace God calls us into life BCM 64
Keep in mind that Jesus Christ LBW 13
Weary of all trumpeting WOV 785
⊕ Bell, John L. "Don't Be Afraid" from *Come All You People*. SATB. GIA G-4391.
⊕ Neto, Rodolfo Gaede Neto. "Pelas dores deste mundo/For the Troubles and the Sufferings" from *Global Praise 3*. U. GBGMusik 9781890569877.
☼ Assad, Audrey/Kyle Lee. "Sparrow" from CCLI.
☼ Ligertwood, Brooke/Scott Ligertwood. "Beneath the Waters (I Will Rise)" from CCLI.
☼ Keyes, Aaron/Andy Lehman. "Take Up My Cross" from *Through It All*. aaronkeyes.com.
☼ Kidd, Matthew/Robbie Seay. "Baptize Me in the River" from CCLI.
☼ Williams, Ryan. "All for the One Who Saved Me" from CCLI.
☼ Younker, Brett/Daniel Carson/Jason Ingram/Judson Wheeler Van DeVenter/Kristian Stanfill/Winfield Scott Weeden. "My Heart Is Yours" from CCLI.

Music for the Day
Choral

Forrest, Dan. "Children of the Heavenly Father." 2 pt trbl or mxd, pno. BP BP1920.
P Giamanco, Anthony. "Take Up Your Cross." 2 pt mxd, pno. AFP 9780800678968.
♫ Manz, Paul. "Let Us Ever Walk with Jesus." 2 pt mxd. MSM 50-9405.
P Mendelssohn, Felix. "For the Lord Will Lead" from *To God Will I Sing: Vocal Solos for the Church Year*. Solo, pno. AFP 9780800674335.

Children's Choir

P Highben, Zebulon M. "I'm Going on a Journey." U, pno, bass gtr, tenor sax, opt assembly. AFP 9780800664022.
Hopson, Hal H. "Children of the God Who Made Us." U/2 pt, pno, opt fl. CG CGA1506.
♫ Manz, Paul. "Let Us Ever Walk with Jesus." U, org. MSM 50-9405.

Keyboard / Instrumental

P♫ Langlois, Kristina. "Oh, Praise the Gracious Power" from *Postludes for Organ on Festive Tunes*. Org. AFP 9781506413631.
P♫ Manz, Paul. "Lasset uns mit Jesu ziehen" from *Augsburg Organ Library: Marriage*. Org. AFP 9781451486025.

⊕ = global song   ♫ = relates to hymn of the day   + = semicontinuous psalm
☼ = praise song   P = available in Prelude Music Planner

Page, Anna Laura. "Children of the Heavenly Father" from *Blest Be the Tie: Ten Hymn Arrangements for Piano.* Pno. MSM 15-838.

P Unke, Zach. "How Firm a Foundation" from *Wondrous Love: Piano Settings.* Pno. AFP 9781506426457.

Handbell

♫ Behnke, John. "Let Us Ever Walk with Jesus." 3 oct, L2. CPH 977106.

P Lamb, Linda. "Glorify Thy Name." 3-5 oct hb, opt 3 oct hc, L3-. HOP 2661.

Waugh, Tim. "Fancye." 3-5 oct, L4+. JEF JHS9336.

Sunday, June 21
Onesimos Nesib, translator, evangelist, died 1931

Onesimos Nesib (oh-NESS-ee-mus neh-SEEB) was born into the Oromo people of Ethiopia. He was captured by slave traders and taken from his homeland to Eritrea, where he was bought, freed, and educated by Swedish missionaries. He translated the Bible into Oromo and returned to his homeland to preach the gospel. His tombstone includes a verse from Jeremiah 22:29, "O land, land, land, hear the word of the Lord!"

Wednesday, June 24
John the Baptist

The birth and life of John the Baptist is celebrated exactly six months before Christmas Eve. For Christians in the Northern Hemisphere, these two dates are deeply symbolic. John said that he must decrease as Jesus increased. According to tradition, John was born as the days are longest and then steadily decrease, while Jesus was born as the days are shortest and then steadily increase. In many countries this day is celebrated with customs associated with the summer solstice.

Thursday, June 25
Presentation of the Augsburg Confession, 1530

On this day in 1530 the German and Latin editions of the Augsburg Confession were presented to Emperor Charles of the Holy Roman Empire. The Augsburg Confession was written by Philipp Melanchthon and endorsed by Martin Luther and consists of a brief summary of points in which the reformers saw their teaching as either agreeing with or differing from that of the Roman Catholic Church of the time. In 1580 when the *Book of Concord* was drawn up, the unaltered Augsburg Confession was included as the principal Lutheran Confession.

Thursday, June 25
Philipp Melanchthon, renewer of the church, died 1560

Though he died on April 19, Philipp Melanchthon (meh-LAHNK-ton) is commemorated today because of his connection with the Augsburg Confession. Colleague and co-reformer with Martin Luther, Melanchthon was a brilliant scholar, known as "the teacher of Germany." The University of Wittenberg hired him as its first professor of Greek, and there he became a friend of Luther. Melanchthon was a popular professor—even his classes at six in the morning had as many as six hundred students. As a reformer he was known for his conciliatory spirit and for finding areas of agreement with fellow Christians. He was never ordained.

Saturday, June 27
Cyril, Bishop of Alexandria, died 444

Remembered as an outstanding theologian as well as a contentious personality, Cyril defended the orthodox teachings about the person of Christ against Nestorius, bishop of Constantinople. Nestorius taught that the divine and human natures of Christ were entirely distinct, and therefore Mary could not be referred to as the *theotokos*, or bearer of God. This conflict, which also had roots in a rivalry for preeminence between Alexandria and Constantinople, involved all of the major Christian leaders of the time, including the patriarchs of Rome, Antioch, and Jerusalem, and finally also the emperor. In the end it was decided that Cyril's interpretation, that Christ's person included both divine and human natures, was correct.

♫ = relates to hymn of the day
P = available in Prelude Music Planner

June 28, 2020
Time after Pentecost — Lectionary 13

The welcome of baptism is for all God's children. This baptismal gift sets us free from the power of sin and death. In today's gospel, Christ promises that the disciple who gives a cup of cold water to the little ones serves Christ himself. From worship we are sent on our baptismal mission: to serve the little ones of this world and to be a sign of God's merciful welcome.

Prayer of the Day

O God, you direct our lives by your grace, and your words of justice and mercy reshape the world. Mold us into a people who welcome your word and serve one another, through Jesus Christ, our Savior and Lord.

Gospel Acclamation

Alleluia. You are a chosen race, a royal priesthood, a holy nation, in order that you may proclaim the mighty acts of the one who called you out of darkness into his marvelous light. *Alleluia.* (1 Peter 2:9)

Readings and Psalm

Jeremiah 28:5-9

Through a symbolic action Jeremiah insisted that Judah and all the surrounding nations should submit to the king of Babylon (Jer. 27). Hananiah contradicted the word of Jeremiah, who in reply insisted that Hananiah's rosy prediction should not be believed until it came true. God confirmed the word of Jeremiah and sentenced the false prophet Hananiah to death (vv. 16-17).

Psalm 89:1-4, 15-18

Your love, O Lord, forever will I sing. (Ps. 89:1)

Romans 6:12-23

Sin is an enslaving power which motivates us to live self-serving, disobedient lives. Sin's final payoff is death. We, however, have been set free from sin's slavery to live obediently under God's grace, whose end is the free gift of eternal life.

Matthew 10:40-42

When Jesus sends his disciples out as missionaries, he warns them of persecution and hardships they will face. He also promises to reward any who aid his followers and support their ministry.

Semicontinuous Reading and Psalm

Genesis 22:1-14

Abraham was prepared to obey God's command amid extreme contradiction: the child to be sacrificed is the very child through whom Abraham is to receive descendants. God acknowledged Abraham's obedient faith, and Abraham offered a ram in the place of his son Isaac.

Psalm 13

I trust in your unfailing love, O Lord. (Ps. 13:5)

Preface   Sundays

Color   Green

Prayers of Intercession

The prayers are prepared locally for each occasion. The following examples may be adapted or used as appropriate.

Called into unity with one another and the whole creation, let us pray for our shared world.

A brief silence.

God of companionship, encourage our relationships with our siblings in Christ. Bless our conversations. Shape our shared future and give us hearts eager to join in a festal shout of praise. Hear us, O God.

Your mercy is great.

God of abundance, you make your creation thrive and grow to provide all that we need. Inspire us to care for our environment and be attuned to where the earth is crying out. Hear us, O God.

Your mercy is great.

God of mercy, your grace is poured out for all. Inspire authorities, judges, and politicians to act with compassion. Teach us to overcome fear with hope, meet hate with love, and welcome one another as we would welcome you. Hear us, O God.

Your mercy is great.

God of care, accompany all who are in deepest need. Comfort those who are sick, lonely, or abandoned (*especially*). Strengthen those who are in prison or awaiting trial. Renew the spirits of all who call upon you. Hear us, O God.

Your mercy is great.

God of community, we give thanks for this congregation. Give us passion to embrace your mission and the vision to recognize where you are leading us. Teach us how to live more faithfully with each other. Hear us, O God.

Your mercy is great.

Here other intercessions may be offered.

God of love, you gather in your embrace all who have died (*especially Irenaeus, Bishop of Lyon*). Keep us steadfast in our faith and renew our trust in your promise. Hear us, O God.
Your mercy is great.
Receive these prayers, O God, and those too deep for words; through Jesus Christ our Lord.
Amen.

Ideas for the Day

- Killing themselves *en masse* rather than submit to Roman siege, the Jewish zealots of first-century Palestine cut a dashing figure of resistance, holed up in the towering fortress of Masada in the Negev Desert. However, contemporary Israeli historians, like Nachman Ben-Yehuda in *The Masada Myth* (Madison, WI: University of Wisconsin Press, 1995), criticize such lionization for the needless death it brings. Jeremiah is right to lovingly yet firmly rebuke Hananiah for his foolhardy prophecies (28:6-7). Preaching resilience and the acceptance of hardship over victory is sobering and bleak, but unlike the zealots at Masada, Jeremiah didn't want his people to sacrifice themselves—even if it meant indefinitely suffering under a tyrant. When God promises deliverance, it's because God wants us to live, and in God's eyes surviving and thriving is better than being a dead hero any day.
- It is good that Paul reminds us of the "natural limitations" of words like *slavery* and *obedience* in theological discourse (Rom. 6:19). They were just as shocking in Paul's day as ours and can still get you into quite the pickle if used carelessly. A man blithely preaching on obedience and slavery to God is likely to get told off by a woman or two—same thing with any white person using such rhetoric with people of color. Obedience under chattel slavery is imposed through violence and terror. What is clear from Paul, though, is that slavery and obedience to God are chosen and embraced via faith. Consequently, the decision to choose being a slave to faith, as opposed to remaining a slave to the world, is a breathtaking act of resistance and rebellion.
- In this week's gospel Jesus focuses on welcoming, but it bears noting precisely whom Jesus says to welcome. Prophets, a "righteous person," and even children deserved welcome not solely for their unique status, but rather because they were often vulnerable and subject to terrific violence. The twenty-first century is no different—where whistle-blowers and uncompromising public leaders are often harassed, and children's voices are often ignored by those charged to protect them. Jesus could likely even relate to all three, as a righteous prophet who barely escaped death as a child (Matt. 2:13-18). By speaking so clearly about welcoming, he sagely adjures his followers

to provide the care and protection he too needed but often lacked.

Connections with Creation

"Whoever welcomes a prophet . . . will receive a prophet's reward," says Jesus in Matthew 10:41. The word *prophet* literally means "one who comes before another to speak," based on the Greek word *prophetes*, from *pro*, meaning "before," and *phenai*, meaning "speak." The prophet speaks on behalf of and before God and God's people, particularly those who are most vulnerable to the systems and leaders that abuse their power. Did you know there are prophets who speak and act on behalf of God's creation? Groups such as Lutherans Restoring Creation encourage the "greening" of congregations, urge action on global warming, and take part in grassroots efforts for environmental protection in communities throughout the United States. So, what is the "prophet's reward"? Bringing faith values to intersect with creation care enhances the work of Christians and their secular partners by building bridges to protect and cherish the world God has made.

Let the Children Come

What does it look like to live as faithful followers of Jesus? Our gospel gives us a good metaphor with the "cup of cold water" (Matt. 10:42). Because some in our world truly suffer from thirst, perhaps this is a good opportunity to consider the radical and practical side of Christian hospitality. What does it look like for a child to practice welcoming Christ with a cup of water? Can you hand out water at a local 5K without any expectation of church membership? Can you invite children to collect coins all July for a water project through a Lutheran or community organization? Can they help set out water bowls for neighborhood dogs near your church this summer? Water is life.

Assembly Song
Gathering

All my hope on God is founded ELW 757, WOV 782
Baptized and Set Free ELW 453
Salvation unto us has come ELW 590, LBW 297

Psalmody and Acclamations

Martinson, Joel. "Psalm 89." Cant, opt SATB, assembly, org, ob. MSM 80-006.
Trapp, Lynn. "Four Psalm Settings." U or cant, assembly, org, opt SATB. MSM 80-701.
+ Idle, Christopher. "How Long Will You Forget Me, Lord" (MARTYRDOM) from *Lift Up Your Hearts*. Faith Alive Christian Resources.
(GA) ELW 175 with proper verse for Lectionary 13.

Hymn of the Day

All Are Welcome ELW 641 *TWO OAKS*

Amazing grace, how sweet the sound ELW 779, LLC 437, LBW 448 *NEW BRITAIN*

That priceless grace ELW 591, TFF 68 *THAT PRICELESS GRACE*

Offering

Here is bread ELW 483, W&P 58

Take my life, that I may be ELW 583/685, LLC 570, LBW 406

Communion

Dear Christians, one and all, rejoice ELW 594, LBW 299

There's a wideness in God's mercy ELW 587/588, LBW 290

This is my Father's world ELW 824, LBW 554

Sending

Give to our God immortal praise! ELW 848, LBW 520

Where cross the crowded ways of life ELW 719, LBW 429

Additional Assembly Songs

For everyone born GTG 769

Hope of the world H82 472, LBW 493, GTG 734

May the God of hope go with us/Canto de esperanza GTG 765

⊕ Gaëtan, Niriko, Madagascar, as taught by Sharon Lee Ranotahinjanahary. "Rombaho/From All that Turns Us from You." SATB. andrewdonaldson.ca.

⊕ Wyatt, Nélida. "Mari, mari" from *Put Your Arms around the World*. U. GBGMusik 9781933663166.

☼ Gungor, David/John Arndt/Matt Maher/Stuart Garrard. "Makers of the Peace" from CCLI.

☼ Hastings, Benjamin/Bryan Fowler/Rend Collective. "Rescuer" from CCLI.

☼ Jensen, Richard. "A Slave to Righteousness, and Free" from *Regenerate*. richjens.bandcamp.com.

☼ Keyes, Aaron/Chris Spring/Paul Oakley/Stuart Townend. "O God of Boundless Mercy" from CCLI.

☼ Philip, Abe/Liza Philip. "I Have Been Baptized into Christ" from *Arise My Soul*. songsfromscripture.bandcamp.com.

☼ Townend, Stuart. "Streets of the City" from CCLI.

Music for the Day
Choral

P Cherwien, David M. "I Want Jesus to Walk with Me." SAB or 2 pt mxd, pno. MSM 50-3435.

Hallock, Peter R. "Your Love, O Lord, For Ever I Will Sing." SATB, org. GIA G-2078.

♫ Haugen, Marty. "All Are Welcome." SATB, kybd, gtr, opt 2 wws or br qrt, assembly. GIA G-4166.

P♫ Helgen, John. "That Priceless Grace" from *Augsburg Easy Choirbook*, vol. 1. U, desc, pno. AFP 9780800676025.

Children's Choir

♫ Eithun, Sandra. "Amazing Grace." U, pno. CG CGA1269.

P Ferguson, John. "Jesus, My Lord and God" from *ChildrenSing in Worship*, vol. 3. U, kybd. AFP 9781451462548.

P Horman, John D. "Jesus and the Children" from *Sing the Stories of Jesus*. U, kybd. AFP 9780800679453.

Keyboard / Instrumental

Callahan, Charles. "Voluntary on Engelberg." Org. MSM 10-702.

♫ Carter, John. "Amazing Grace" from *Folk Hymns for Piano*. Pno. HOP 240.

P♫ Maxwell, David. "All Are Welcome" from *We Walk by Faith: Organ Settings*. Org. AFP 9781451479584.

P♫ Raabe, Nancy. "That Priceless Grace" from *Grace & Peace, Volume 8: Songs of Lament and Longing*. Pno. AFP 9781506413679.

Handbell

♫ McAninch, Diane. "Prelude on All Are Welcome." 3-5 oct hb, opt 3 oct hc, fl, L3. GIA G-7083.

♫ Moklebust, Cathy. "God of Amazing Grace." 3-5 oct hb, opt 3 oct hc, L3-. CG CGB878.

P♫ Waldrop, Tammy. "Amazing Grace" from *Spring Ring!* 3-5 oct hb or hc, L1, L1+, L2-. CG CGB830. 2-3 oct hb or hc, CGB829.

Sunday, June 28
Irenaeus, Bishop of Lyons, died around 202

Irenaeus (ee-ren-AY-us) believed that the way to remain steadfast to the truth was to hold fast to the faith handed down from the apostles. He believed that only Matthew, Mark, Luke, and John were trustworthy gospels. Irenaeus was an opponent of gnosticism and its emphasis on dualism. As a result of his battles with the gnostics, he was one of the first to speak of the church as "catholic." By catholic he meant that local congregations did not exist by themselves but were linked to one another in the whole church. He also maintained that this church was not contained within any national boundaries. He argued that the church's message was for all people, in contrast to the gnostics and their emphasis on "secret knowledge."

Monday, June 29
Peter and Paul, Apostles

These two are an odd couple of biblical witnesses to be brought together in one commemoration. It appears that Peter would have gladly served as the editor of Paul's letters: in a letter attributed to him, Peter says that some things in Paul's letters

---

⊕ = global song ♫ = relates to hymn of the day + = semicontinuous psalm
☼ = praise song P = available in Prelude Music Planner

are hard to understand. Paul's criticism of Peter is more blunt. In Galatians he points out ways that Peter was wrong. One of the things that unites Peter and Paul is the tradition that says they were martyred together on this date in 67 or 68. What unites them more closely is their common confession of Jesus Christ. Together Peter and Paul lay a foundation and build the framework for our lives of faith through their proclamation of Jesus Christ.

Wednesday, July 1
Catherine Winkworth, died 1878; John Mason Neale, died 1866; hymn translators

Neale was an English priest associated with the movement for church renewal at Cambridge. Winkworth lived most of her life in Manchester, where she was involved in promoting women's rights. These two hymnwriters translated many hymn texts into English. Catherine Winkworth devoted herself to the translation of German hymns, nineteen of which are included in *Evangelical Lutheran Worship*; the fourteen hymn translations of John Mason Neale in the collection represent his specialization in ancient Latin and Greek hymns.

Friday, July 3
Thomas, Apostle

Thomas is perhaps best remembered as "Doubting Thomas." But alongside this doubt, the Gospel of John shows Thomas as fiercely loyal: "Let us also go, that we may die with him" (John 11:16). And John's gospel shows Thomas moving from doubt to deep faith. Thomas makes one of the strongest confessions of faith in the New Testament, "My Lord and my God!" (John 20:28). From this confession of faith, ancient stories tell of Thomas's missionary work to India, where Christian communities were flourishing a thousand years before the arrival of sixteenth-century missionaries.

July 5, 2020
Time after Pentecost — Lectionary 14

The mystery of God's ways is sometimes hidden from the wise and intelligent. Jesus associates with those often excluded from the religious community. Like Paul, we struggle with our own selfish desires and seek God's mercy and forgiveness. We gather to be refreshed by Christ's invitation: "Come to me, all you that are weary." Gathered around word, water, and meal, we find rest for our souls.

Prayer of the Day

You are great, O God, and greatly to be praised. You have made us for yourself, and our hearts are restless until they rest in you. Grant that we may believe in you, call upon you, know you, and serve you, through your Son, Jesus Christ, our Savior and Lord.

Gospel Acclamation

Alleluia. Blessed are you, Lord of heav'n and earth; you have revealed these things to infants. *Alleluia.* (Matt. 11:25)

Readings and Psalm
Zechariah 9:9-12

The coming messianic king will inaugurate an era of disarmament and prosperity. Because of God's covenant with Israel, the people are designated as "prisoners of hope."

Psalm 145:8-14

The LORD is gracious and full of compassion. (Ps. 145:8)

Romans 7:15-25a

Life captive to sin is a catch-22 existence in which we know good but do not do it and do things we know to be wrong. Through Jesus Christ, God has set us free from such a futile existence.

Matthew 11:16-19, 25-30

Jesus chides people who find fault with both his ministry and that of John the Baptist. He thanks God that wisdom and intelligence are not needed to receive what God has to offer.

Semicontinuous Reading and Psalm
Genesis 24:34-38, 42-49, 58-67

The marriage of Isaac and Rebekah helped to fulfill God's promise that Abraham and Sarah would become the ancestors of many nations.

Psalm 45:10-17

God has anointed you with the oil of gladness. (Ps. 45:7)

or Song of Solomon 2:8-13

Arise, my love, my fair one, and come away. (Song of Sol. 2:10)

Preface Sundays

Color Green

Prayers of Intercession

The prayers are prepared locally for each occasion. The following examples may be adapted or used as appropriate.

Called into unity with one another and the whole creation, let us pray for our shared world.

A brief silence.

We pray for the church. Sustain us as we share your word. Embrace us as we struggle to find our common ground. Lift up leaders with powerful and prophetic voices. Free us from stagnant faith. Hear us, O God.

Your mercy is great.

We pray for the well-being of creation. Protect the air, water, and land from abuse and pollution. Free us from apathy in our care of creation and direct us toward sustainable living. Hear us, O God.

Your mercy is great.

We pray for the nations (*especially the United States and Canada, celebrating their nationhood*). Guide leaders in developing just policies and guide difficult conversations. Free us from patriotism that hinders relationship-building. Lead us to expansive love for our neighbor. Hear us, O God.

Your mercy is great.

We pray for all in need. For all who are tired, feeling despair, sick, or oppressed (*especially*). Take their yoke upon you and ease their burdens. Give your consolation and free us from all that keeps us bound. Hear us, O God.

Your mercy is great.

We pray for this congregation. Bless pastors, deacons, and congregational leaders. Energize children's ministry volunteers, church administrators, and those who maintain our building. Shine in this place that we might notice the ways your love transforms our lives. Hear us, O God.

Your mercy is great.

Here other intercessions may be offered.

We give thanks for those who have died in faith (*especially*). Welcome them into your eternal rest and comfort us in our grief until we are joined with them in new life. Hear us, O God.

Your mercy is great.

Receive these prayers, O God, and those too deep for words; through Jesus Christ our Lord.

Amen.

Ideas for the Day

- While yokes are not well known today, there are other modern products that do similar jobs. Scrum sleds are used frequently in football and other athletic training; a team of people pushes the sled across a field. Videos of a team using a sled can be found online and used to demonstrate a group sharing the burden. With advance planning, you could also create your own video by contacting your local high school athletic department; the church staff could be the team pushing the sled.

- Like a yoke, lifting and moving straps can make it possible for two people to easily lift furniture. In worship, you can demonstrate how carrying a heavy object is easier with two people, but even easier with a tool that efficiently disperses the weight between itself and the individuals using it. Another option to illustrate the concept of a yoke is to fill a backpack with rocks for someone to carry around. The rocks represent our heavy burdens, which can then be distributed to various people in the assembly to represent how much easier it is when we do not bear our burdens alone but share them with God and fellow members of the body of Christ who support and pray for us.

- Today's reading from Zechariah is usually associated with Palm Sunday. How does the image of a peace-bringing, triumphant king riding humbly on a donkey square with the militaristic and nationalistic themes that are present in the culture, especially so close to Independence Day in both Canada and the United States?

- For a fascinating discussion of Jesus' story about the children in the marketplace (Matt. 11:16-19), see Jerome Berryman's book *Becoming Like a Child: The Curiosity of Maturity beyond the Norm* (New York: Church Publishing, 2017). Berryman writes, "At first this looks like a simple example story. The adults of this generation are like indecisive children who can't decide whether to follow John or Jesus and wind up following neither and losing touch with the kingdom" (pp. 84–85). But Berryman suggests that if we assume that children show the way to the kingdom, as Jesus says in various places in the gospels that they do, then the children in this story were "holding out for the Easter Game, which integrates the ultimate sadness of Holy Week (the wailing and mourning) and the ultimate happiness and wonder of Easter morning (the happiness of music and dancing) to make Christian joy" (p. 87).

Connections with Creation

What does it mean to be "prisoners of hope"? The prophet Zechariah uses that term to describe the people of Israel who had suffered in exile but have now returned to Jerusalem (9:12). Will they be able to see the vision of God's intended restoration and then take action? Those working to preserve old-growth forests, restore healthy ecosystems, and replenish potable water to communities could be described as "prisoners of hope." They work against all odds to align with a vision of restoration for our planet. Jesus suggests that such a vision is invisible to "the wise and the intelligent" and seen only by "infants" (Matt. 11:25). In other words, it takes a certain kind of childlike creativity and freshness to perceive what God is doing all around us to restore the health of ecosystems. Will we notice and take action?

Let the Children Come

This week's psalm refrain is "The LORD is gracious and full of compassion" (Ps. 145:8). It is the assembly's response to the promises we hear in Zechariah—a triumphant king riding humbly on a donkey, the end of war, and freedom for the prisoners. In Jesus and the body of Christ, we see the completion of these promises and respond with song. What does it look like for us to remember that grace and compassion—not military might, war, or keeping prisoners—are the markers of a Christian life? Can the children help sing or lead the psalm refrain and help the whole congregation remember the graciousness of God?

Assembly Song
Gathering

Come, join the dance of Trinity ELW 412

Let the whole creation cry ELW 876, LBW 242

Oh, sing to God above/Cantemos al Señor ELW 555, WOV 726, LLC 600

Psalmody and Acclamations

Trapp, Lynn. "Four Psalm Settings." U or cant, assembly, org, opt SATB. MSM 80-701.

Whitney, Rae E. "O My God and King and Savior" (HOLY MANNA) from PAS 145F.

+ Pelz, Walter E. "Psalm 45:10-17" or "Song of Solomon 2:8-13" from PWA.

(GA) ELW 175 with proper verse for Lectionary 14.

Hymn of the Day

Come, follow me, the Savior spake ELW 799, LBW 455 *MACHS MIT MIR, GOTT*

How clear is our vocation, Lord ELW 580 *REPTON*

I heard the voice of Jesus say ELW 332, LBW 497 *THIRD MODE MELODY* ELW 611 *KINGSFOLD* TFF 62 *SHINE ON ME*

Offering

Here is bread ELW 483, W&P 58

We give thee but thine own ELW 686, LBW 410

Communion

Come to me, all pilgrims thirsty ELW 777

Lord of all hopefulness ELW 765, LS 169, LBW 469

What a friend we have in Jesus ELW 742, LBW 439

Sending

Come, gracious Spirit, heavenly dove ELW 404, LBW 475

Light dawns on a weary world ELW 726

Additional Assembly Songs

I will give you rest SC 30

My soul finds rest in God alone ASG 26

This is the day TFF 262

🌐 German trad. "Gifts of the Spirit" from *Heaven Shall Not Wait.* U, pno. GIA G-3646S.

🌐 Taizé Community. "Mon âme se repose/In God Alone" from *Songs and Prayers from Taizé.* SATB. GIA G-3719.

☼ Assad, Audrey/Isaac Wardell. "In the Fields of the Lord" from *Work Songs.* theportersgate.bandcamp.com.

☼ Baloche, David. "Come to Me" from CCLI.

☼ Glover, Ben/David Crowder/Matt Maher. "Come as You Are" from CCLI.

☼ Kimborough, Wendell. "Come to Me" from CCLI.

☼ McCracken, Sandra. "Come to Me" from CCLI.

☼ Ogden, Jonathan. "So Easy" from CCLI.

Music for the Day
Choral

P Larson, Lloyd. "There's Something About That Name" from *Contemporary Classics for Two Voices: Medium Voice Duets.* HOP 8570.

P Leaf, Robert. "Come with Rejoicing." U, kybd. AFP 9780800645755.

Peloquin, Alexander C. "A Prayer for Us." SATB, org, br qrt, timp, hb. GIA G-1982.

P Scott, K. Lee. "Jesus Calls Us" from *Treasures in Heaven.* 2 pt, org. AFP 9780800679477.

Children's Choir

♫ Cherwien, David. "I Heard the Voice of Jesus Say." U, org, opt C inst. CG CGA643.

P Patterson, Mark. "Come into God's Presence (Echo Song)" from *The Joy of Part Singing.* U, pno, opt Orff inst. CG CGBK67.

P Berg, Ken. "Somebody's Knockin'." U, pno. CG CGA1303.

Keyboard / Instrumental

Carter, John. "America, the Beautiful" from *Patriotic Songs for Piano.* Pno. HOP 8225.

P Cherwien, David M. "Softly and Tenderly Jesus Is Calling" from *In Heaven Above: Piano Music for Funerals and Memorials.* Pno. AFP 9781451401912.

P ♫ Powell, Robert J. "Come, Follow Me, the Savior Spake" from *Mixtures: Hymn Preludes for Organ.* Org. AFP 9781451479553.

P ♫ Weber, Jacob B. "Repton" from *Christ Is King: Organ Hymn Preludes.* Org. AFP 9781451486032.

🌐 = global song   ♫ = relates to hymn of the day   + = semicontinuous psalm
☼ = praise song   P = available in Prelude Music Planner

Handbell

♫ Afdahl, Lee. "Dear Lord, Lead On." 3, 5, or 6 oct. L3+. AFP 11-10770.

♫ Eithun, Sandra. "I Heard the Voice of Jesus Say" from *Bells and Keys, More or Less.* 1½-2 oct hb, opt kybd, L2. CG CGB880.

♫ Hakes, Derek. "Kingsfold Fantasia." 3 oct solo hb, 1 oct hc, fl, pno, opt bell tree, L3. FTT 1113.

Monday, July 6
Jan Hus, martyr, died 1415

Jan Hus was a Bohemian priest who spoke against abuses in the church of his day in many of the same ways Luther would a century later. He spoke against the withholding of the cup at the eucharist and because of this stance was excommunicated, not for heresy but for insubordination toward his archbishop. He preached against the selling of indulgences and was particularly mortified by the indulgence trade of two rival claimants to the papacy who were raising money for war against each other. He was found guilty of heresy by the Council of Constance and burned at the stake. The followers of Jan Hus became known as the Czech Brethren and eventually continued as the Moravian Church.

Saturday, July 11
Benedict of Nursia, Abbot of Monte Cassino, died around 540

Benedict is known as the father of Western monasticism. He was educated in Rome but was appalled by the decline of life around him. He went to live as a hermit, and a community of monks came to gather around him. In the prologue of his rule for monasteries, he wrote that his intent in drawing up his regulations was "to set down nothing harsh, nothing burdensome." It is that moderate spirit that characterizes his rule and the monastic communities that are formed by it. Benedict still encourages a generous spirit of hospitality in that visitors to Benedictine communities are to be welcomed as Christ himself.

July 12, 2020
Time after Pentecost — Lectionary 15

God's word is like the rain that waters the earth and brings forth vegetation. It is also like the sower who scatters seed indiscriminately. Our lives are like seeds sown in the earth. Even from what appears to be little, dormant, or dead, God promises a harvest. At the Lord's table we are fed with the bread of life, that we may bear fruit in the world.

Prayer of the Day

Almighty God, we thank you for planting in us the seed of your word. By your Holy Spirit help us to receive it with joy, live according to it, and grow in faith and hope and love, through Jesus Christ, our Savior and Lord.

Gospel Acclamation

Alleluia. The word is very near to you; it is in your mouth and in your heart. *Alleluia.* (Deut. 30:14)

Readings and Psalm

Isaiah 55:10-13

God's word to Israel's exiles is as sure and effective as never-failing precipitation. Their return to the Holy Land in a new exodus is cheered on by singing mountains and by trees that clap their hands.

Psalm 65:[1-8] 9-13

Your paths overflow with plenty. (Ps. 65:11)

Romans 8:1-11

There is no condemnation for those who live in Christ. God sent Christ to accomplish what the law was unable to do: condemn sin and free us from its death-dealing ways. The Spirit now empowers proper actions and values in our lives and gives us the promise of resurrected life.

Matthew 13:1-9, 18-23

In Matthew's gospel, both Jesus and his disciples "sow the seed" of God's word by proclaiming the good news that "the kingdom of heaven is near." Now, in a memorable parable, Jesus explains why this good news produces different results in those who hear.

Semicontinuous Reading and Psalm
Genesis 25:19-34

Although Jacob was younger than his twin, Esau, he eventually takes the birthright away from his brother. Jacob is portrayed in the Bible as deceptive, gripping his brother when he came out of the womb and driving a hard bargain by buying the birthright for a bowl of lentils.

Psalm 119:105-112

Your word is a lamp to my feet and a light upon my path. (Ps. 119:105)

Preface   Sundays

Color   Green

Prayers of Intercession

The prayers are prepared locally for each occasion. The following examples may be adapted or used as appropriate.

Called into unity with one another and the whole creation, let us pray for our shared world.

A brief silence.

Gracious God, your word has been sown in many ways and places. We pray for missionaries and newly planted congregations around the world. Inspire us by their witness to the faith we share. Hear us, O God.

Your mercy is great.

Creating God, the mountains and hills burst into song and the trees and fields clap their hands in praise. We pray for the birds and animals who make their home in the trees, and for lands stripped bare by deforestation. Empower us to sustainably use what you have given. Hear us, O God.

Your mercy is great.

Reigning God, we pray for our nation's leaders. Increase their desire for justice and equality. We pray for our enemies. Bridge the chasms that divide us and guide authorities to a deep and lasting peace. Hear us, O God.

Your mercy is great.

Abiding God, care for all who are in need (*especially*). For those who are doubting, renew faith. For those who are worrying, provide release. For those who are struggling, ease burdens. For those in fear, give hope. Hear us, O God.

Your mercy is great.

Renewing God, revive your church in this place. Nourish and nurture the seeds you have planted, that we might grow as disciples. Replace what has been depleted. Sustain our ministries (*especially*) and deepen relationships with the wider community. Hear us, O God.

Your mercy is great.

Here other intercessions may be offered.

Eternal God, we give thanks for all who have died (*especially Nathan Söderblom, Bishop of Uppsala, whom we commemorate today*). Comfort us in the sure and certain hope of the resurrection. Hear us, O God.

Your mercy is great.

Receive these prayers, O God, and those too deep for words; through Jesus Christ our Lord.

Amen.

Ideas for the Day

- Today's psalm and the readings from Isaiah and Matthew celebrate creation. Plan an outdoor worship service today, either on the church grounds or at a local park. Before or after the service worshipers could do some caring for creation by picking up trash. If you want to do more, contact your local parks department to see if there is a project your congregation can contribute to after worship. Alternatively, write to government officials to advocate for environmental protections, or consider how your congregation's practices could be more environmentally friendly.

- A visual illustration of the parable of the sower can be helpful. A week or more in advance, prepare four clear containers for planting. Place sand in the first, rocks in the second, an already-thriving weed in the third, and fresh potting soil in the fourth. Plant seeds in each of the containers, ideally something that germinates quickly like beans. Use these four containers to show how the new seeds did. If the seeds did not have time to sprout, just the four containers are helpful to demonstrate different kinds of soil. Place the four types of "soil" on a tray or activity table at the front of the worship space for everyone to experience.

- Pastor Delmer Chilton tells the story of working on a tobacco farm in eastern North Carolina when he was in college. One day when he was out harvesting the tobacco, the conveyer system on the mechanized harvester kept malfunctioning. Instead of carrying the picked leaves to a platform ten feet above, the machine kept dropping leaves on the ground. Chilton relates, "We kept stopping and starting while trying to fix the machine. There was a precocious 6-year-old boy watching us work. He observed our troubles for a while and then walked up to the farmer and said, 'Well, you can't elevate 'em all, can you, Mr. Virgil.'" Read the rest of Chilton's blog post for a reflection on the parable of the sower (livinglutheran.org/2017/07/lectionary-blog-sowing-seed).

- Give people packets of seeds to sow, such as wildflower seeds that are native to your area. Encourage the assembly to grow the seeds at their home or scatter them in a place where the flowers might bring joy to others, such as on the side of the road, edge of the woods, etc. You can also give two packets to each person or family, one for them to keep for themselves and another to give away to a friend.

Connections with Creation

When it comes to preaching that addresses environmental issues, it can seem like the scenario Jesus describes in his parable: most of the seeds fall on rocky or thorny ground, or they disappear like kernels eaten by the birds. In a sermon for the book *Earth and Word* (ed. David Rhoads, Continuum, 2007), Steven Charleston notes that "environmental ministries find few fertile grounds for growth in the life of the church." He suggests, however, that we should follow Jesus' lead by using parables and telling stories in order to do the planting. In terms of strategies, Charleston suggests creating modern parables that communicate deep truths in Earth-centered language. These need to be stories of everyday life with images easily accessible to everyday people. Craft the sermon with an illustration that invites change and a call to repentance that sounds more like a promise than a stern warning. Finally, allow space for hearers to decide what this call means to them.

Let the Children Come

Sometimes Jesus' parables seem easy to understand and sometimes they are more difficult. That's okay. We can come back to them again and again and each time find something new there. In today's gospel, Jesus tells a parable about where faith grows. How might our assembly be a place of good, nurturing soil? One place where good soil abounds is in the structure or pattern of our worship. The scripture readings and the reflection on them is followed by the feast of holy communion. Fertile ground for faith to grow is not cultivated merely through didactic instruction but also through visceral experiences of God's abundant grace. We know what the body of Christ looks like as we gather at the table. Invite and train a youth to serve as the assisting minister this week. Elementary-age and younger children will notice who is serving them.

Assembly Song
Gathering

> Many and great, O God/Wakantanka taku nitawa ELW 837, WOV 794
>
> Open now thy gates of beauty ELW 533, LBW 250
>
> What is this place ELW 524

Psalmody and Acclamations

> Alonso, Tony. "The Seed That Falls on Good Ground" from TLP:A.
>
> Makeever, Ray. "Psalm 65:[1-8] 9-13" from PWA.
>
> + Mummert, Mark. "Psalm 119:105-112" from PSCY.
>
> (GA) ELW 175 with proper verse for Lectionary 15.

+ = semicontinuous psalm

Hymn of the Day

Almighty God, your word is cast ELW 516, LBW 234
ST. FLAVIAN

Lord, let my heart be good soil ELW 512, WOV 713, TFF 131,
W&P 713, LS 83 *GOOD SOIL*

The Word of God is source and seed ELW 506, WOV 658
GAUDEAMUS DOMINO

Offering

As the grains of wheat ELW 465, WOV 705, W&P 10

The numberless gifts of God's mercy ELW 683

Communion

As rain from the clouds ELW 508

God, whose farm is all creation ELW 734

Lord, your hands have formed ELW 554, WOV 727

Sending

Build us up, Lord ELW 670

On what has now been sown ELW 550, LBW 261

Additional Assembly Songs

As sunshine to a garden ASG 1

When seed falls on good soil LBW 236

You shall go out with joy GTG 80

⊕ You are the seed/Sois la semilla WOV 753, TFF 226

⊕ Come, O Holy Spirit, come/Wa wa wa Emimimo WOV 681,
TFF 106, GTG 283

☼ Edge, Colin/Israel Houghton/Joshua Dufrene. "Take Heart"
from CCLI.

☼ Kimbrough, Wendell. "The Seeds of the Kingdom" from CCLI.

☼ Morgan, Anabeth/David Linhart/James Moscardini. "My
Foundation (Found in You)" from CCLI.

☼ Peterson, Andrew/Ben Shive. "The Sower's Song" from CCLI.

☼ Staples, Mavis. "Sow Good Seeds" from *One True Vine*.
mavisstaples.com.

☼ Zimmer, David/Ed Cash/Keith Getty/Kristyn Getty/Stuart
Townend. "May the Peoples Praise You" from CCLI.

Music for the Day
Choral

Haydn, Franz Joseph. "How Marvelous Is the Power of God."
Solo, kybd. ECS 1.1914.

P Mendelssohn, Felix/arr. K. Lee Scott. "I Will Sing of Thy
Mercies" from *Sing a Song of Joy*. Solo, kybd. AFP
9780800652821.

P Parker, Alice. "For the Fruit of All Creation." 2 pt mxd or SATB,
kybd, opt assembly. GIA G-6264.

P Scott, K. Lee. "Gracious Spirit, Dwell with Me." 2 pt, org. AFP
9780800646134.

Children's Choir

Bedford, Michael. "It Is Good to Give Thanks" from *Two
Psalms for Young Singers*. U, kybd, opt hb. CG CGA1140.

P Burrows, Mark. "Thank You, God, for Ears" from *Again, I Say
Rejoice!* U, pno or gtr. CG CGC56.

P Hobby, Robert A. "Open Your Ears, O Faithful People" from
ChildrenSing Around the World. U, opt desc, assembly, hb,
fl, fc, tamb. AFP 9781451485998.

Keyboard / Instrumental

P ♫ Biery, Marilyn. "Lord, Let My Heart Be Good Soil" from *Gathered into One: Organ Settings of Contemporary Tunes*.
Org. AFP 9781451486063.

Ferguson, John. "Rhapsody on Go, My Children, with My Blessing" from *A Wedding Triptych*. Org. MSM 10-650.

P ♫ Hansen, Sherri. "The Word of God Is Source and Seed" from
Piano Weavings. Pno. AFP 9781451494129.

Palmer, Nicholas. "Let All Things Now Living" from *For the
Care of the Earth: Hymn Reflections for Piano*. Pno. MSM
15-751.

Handbell

P Buckwalter, Karen. "As Rain from the Clouds." 3-5 oct, opt hp.
L2. CG CGB927.

Starks, Howard. "Beside Still Waters." 3 oct, L3. HOP1047. 3-5
oct, opt 3 oct hc, L3. HOP 2394.

Wissinger, Kathleen. "The Sower." 3-5 oct, L3. GIA G-6149.

Sunday, July 12
Nathan Söderblom, Bishop of Uppsala, died 1931

In 1930, this Swedish theologian, ecumenist, and social activist
received the Nobel Prize for peace. Söderblom (ZAY-der-blom)
saw the value of the ancient worship of the church catholic and
encouraged the liturgical movement. He also valued the work of
liberal Protestant scholars and believed social action was a first
step on the path toward a united Christianity. He organized the
Universal Christian Council on Life and Work, one of the organizations that in 1948 came together to form the World Council
of Churches.

Friday, July 17
Bartolomé de Las Casas, missionary to the Indies, died 1566

Bartolomé de Las Casas was a Spanish priest and a missionary
in the Western Hemisphere. He first came to the West while
serving in the military, and he was granted a large estate that
included a number of indigenous slaves. When he was ordained

⊕ = global song   ♫ = relates to hymn of the day
☼ = praise song   P = available in Prelude Music Planner

224

in 1513, he granted freedom to his servants. This act characterized much of the rest of Las Casas's ministry. Throughout the Caribbean and Central America, he worked to stop the enslavement of native people, to halt the brutal treatment of women by military forces, and to promote laws that humanized the process of colonization.

July 19, 2020
Time after Pentecost — Lectionary 16

It is an age-old question: why is there evil in the world? In the parable of the wheat and the weeds Jesus suggests that both grow together until the harvest. With Paul, we long for the day when all creation will be set free from bondage and suffering. Having both weeds and wheat within us, we humbly place our hope in the promises of God, and from the Lord's table we go forth to bear the fruit of justice and mercy.

Prayer of the Day

Faithful God, most merciful judge, you care for your children with firmness and compassion. By your Spirit nurture us who live in your kingdom, that we may be rooted in the way of your Son, Jesus Christ, our Savior and Lord.

Gospel Acclamation

Alleluia. My word shall accomplish that which I purpose, and succeed in the thing for which I sent it. *Alleluia.* (Isa. 55:11)

Readings and Psalm
Isaiah 44:6-8

There are no other gods besides God: the word of the LORD does not fail to come to pass. We can trust in God, through whom Israel—and we—are redeemed.

or Wisdom 12:13, 16-19

God's deeds of forgiveness and gift of hope indicate that God's faithful people must also show kindness. No other god cares for all people.

Psalm 86:11-17

Teach me your way, O LORD, and I will walk in your truth. (Ps. 86:11)

Romans 8:12-25

For Paul, true spirituality means that we experience the reality of the Spirit, which enables us to pray as God's children, keeps us in solidarity with creation, and gives us unseen hope that God will liberate us and creation from bondage to death and decay.

Matthew 13:24-30, 36-43

Jesus tells a parable about the coexistence of good and evil in this world. God's judgment will remove all evildoers and causes of sin, but not until the end of human history.

Semicontinuous Reading and Psalm
Genesis 28:10-19a

God's graciousness to Jacob is shown in God's revelation of the divine self to the patriarch, who is running for his life after cheating his brother Esau out of the family inheritance. Jacob promises that if God brings him back to the land, he will be loyal to God and give God a tenth of everything (vv. 20-22).

Psalm 139:1-12, 23-24

You have searched me out and known me. (Ps. 139:1)

Preface   Sundays

Color   Green

Prayers of Intercession

The prayers are prepared locally for each occasion. The following examples may be adapted or used as appropriate.

Confident of your care and helped by the Holy Spirit, we pray for the church, the world, and all who are in need.
A brief silence.

God of the harvest, you sow the good seed of the gospel of Jesus Christ into your field. Help your church throughout the world to be both diligent and patient, full of resolve and gentleness, that our witness may be faithful to your intentions. Lord, in your mercy,
hear our prayer.

God of all space and time, your whole creation groans in labor pains, awaiting the gift of new birth. Renew the earth, sky, and sea, so that all your creation experiences freedom from the bondage of decay. Lord, in your mercy,
hear our prayer.

God of the nations, teach us your ways, that we may walk in your truth. Mend the fabric of the human family, now torn apart by our fearful and warring ways (*regions and nations in*

conflict may be named). Guide us by your mercy, grace, and steadfast love. Lord, in your mercy,
hear our prayer.

God of hope, you accompany those who suffer and are near to the brokenhearted. Open our hearts to your children who are lonely and abandoned, who feel trapped by despair, and all who suffer in any way (*especially*). Lord, in your mercy,
hear our prayer.

God of the seasons, in the midst of summer, give us refreshment, renewal, and new opportunities. We pray for the safety of those who travel. We pray for those who cannot take the rest they need. Lord, in your mercy,
hear our prayer.

Here other intercessions may be offered.

God of life, those who have died in you shine like the sun in your endless kingdom. We remember with thanksgiving the saints of all times and places and saints close to us (*especially*). Gather us with them on the day of salvation. Lord, in your mercy,
hear our prayer.

In the certain hope that nothing can separate us from your love, we offer these prayers to you; through Jesus Christ our Lord.
Amen.

Ideas for the Day

- In our first reading, God, speaking though the prophet Isaiah, asks, "Is there any god besides me?" (44:8). While God answers firmly in the negative, our own struggles in this life allow the question to spark important conversation about faith and our daily need for repentance. To God's declaration here in Isaiah, "Is there any god besides me?" our answer is both a resounding "No!" and a grudging "Yes." In our gospel reading Jesus says, "The Son of Man will send his angels, and they will collect out of his kingdom all causes of sin" (Matt. 13:41). As a confessional response to the sermon, have slips of fast-dissolving paper (readily available online) and pens or markers available and invite people to write the "god" with which they struggle most. These may be placed in a water-filled baptismal font in which the slips will readily dissolve.

- The parable of the weeds (or tares, or weeds and wheat) gets a fresh and helpful look by noted preacher and author Barbara Brown Taylor, who suggests: "What if my job is not to select the seed but to prepare the soil? What if my call is to give myself to the work without getting too attached to the results?" (christiancentury.org/article/2011-10/gardener-question). When it comes time to prepare end-of-year reports for congregational annual meetings, what guidance might this gospel offer for how such reports are organized and what they emphasize?

- Focusing on the gospel, consider asking for a few volunteers to assist with part of the sermon. Divide them into two groups. Give each group a good hymn's-worth of time to prepare to tell the parable from the perspective of the wheat (group one) and the weeds (group two), giving them permission to be creative. After the hymn, have each group present their version of the story. Invite the congregation to consider the viewpoint of One Green Planet, an independent online publishing platform: "In nature, there are no 'weeds.' All plants have their roles, and if we can start to see the good in our weeds, perhaps they'll be welcome additions, or at least visitors, to our gardens" (onegreenplanet.org). Solicit from the congregation their reaction to the idea that God does not sow weeds, but we do by our own labels and then we act accordingly.

Connections with Creation

Paul says that "creation waits with eager longing for the revealing of the children of God" (Rom. 8:19). In what ways will creation benefit when those who follow God's teachings are revealed? Paul explains that creation is in "bondage to decay" and "groaning in labor pains" (8:21-22). As such, when we see oceans choked with islands of plastic trash, more than two thousand landfills in the United States alone, and the very atmosphere in bondage to greenhouse gases, we know that the redemption of our bodies is directly linked to the redemption of Earth's body. Consider an activity where non-wet trash is dumped in your worship space and ask if this is how we should treat the place where we worship. Then explain that the whole world is God's temple, and that Christians must work to clean up pollution (as others help you clean up the trash from the floor!). Visit zerowastechurch.org to learn ways for ushering your congregation into a cleaner, greener future.

Let the Children Come

Sometimes it's hard to tell the difference between weeds and wheat. They can look a lot alike. Sometimes we want to judge who is a weed and who is wheat. Sometimes we judge ourselves to be weeds, unworthy of love and compassion. But God looks at us with love and wants us to look at others the same way—even those we might want to label as weeds. In church today, how might you foster compassion for self and others? What if every time people came to church, they dipped their hands in the baptismal font, remembered their baptism, and were reminded that they are a beloved child of God? Children can be very good at helping people remember that everyone is beloved. Provide supplies today for children to create cards for homebound members.

Assembly Song
Gathering

My hope is built on nothing less   ELW 596/597, TFF 192, LBW 293/294

Oh, that I had a thousand voices   ELW 833, LBW 560

When morning gilds the skies   ELW 853, LBW 545/546

Psalmody and Acclamations

Sedio, Mark. "Psalm 86:11-17" and (+) "Psalm 139:1-12, 23-24" from PWA.

Trapp, Lynn. "Four Psalm Settings." U or cant, assembly, org, opt SATB. MSM 80-701.

+ Feeley, Ephrem. "Guard Us, Lord." SAB, cant, assembly, kybd, vla. GIA G-9624.

(GA) ELW 175 with proper verse for Lectionary 16.

Hymn of the Day

Beloved, God's chosen   ELW 648, OBS 48   *ANDREW'S SONG*

Build us up, Lord   ELW 670   *BUILD US UP*

We plow the fields and scatter   ELW 680, LLC 492   *SAN FERNANDO*   ELW 681, LS 102, LBW 362   *WIR PFLÜGEN*

Offering

As the grains of wheat   ELW 465, WOV 705, W&P 10

Praise and thanksgiving   ELW 689, LBW 409

Communion

Let us break bread together   ELW 471, TFF 123, LBW 212

Neither death nor life   ELW 622

The numberless gifts of God's mercy   ELW 683

Sending

Come, ye thankful people, come   ELW 693, LBW 407

For the fruit of all creation   ELW 679, WOV 760, LBW 563

Additional Assembly Songs

Abba's Lullaby   MSB2 S563

Stars and planets flung in orbit   NCH 567

⊕ Here on Jesus Christ I will stand/Kwake Yesu nasimama   GTG 832

⊕ Cambodian trad. "Now I Know/E lou nis" from *Sound the Bamboo*. GIA G-6830.

⊕ Matsikenyiri, Patrick. "Mweya Mutsvene Uyai Pano/ Holy Spirit, Come By Here" from *Njalo (Always)*. ABI 9780687498079.

☼ Benedict, Bruce. "Among the Thorns" from *Among the Thorns*. cardiphonia.bandcamp.com.

☼ Green Carpet Players. "All Things New" from *Morning to Evening*. redeemerknoxville.bandcamp.com.

☼ Kauflin, Bob/Jon Underhill. "Glory Awaits" from CCLI.

☼ Wardell, Isaac. "In Labor All Creation Groans" from CCLI.

☼ Wardell, Isaac/Paul Zach/Wendell Kimbrough. "Your Labor Is Not in Vain" from CCLI.

☼ Wuest, Tom. "He Shall Reign" from CCLI.

Music for the Day
Choral

Handel, George F. "Lord, You Have Searched Me." 2 pt mxd, kybd. MSM 50-5118.

Marcello, Benedetto/arr. Dale Grotenhuis. "Teach Me Now, O Lord." SA or 2 pt mxd, kybd. MSM 50-9418.

P Wold, Wayne L. "As This Bread Is Broken" from *Augsburg Easy Choirbook*, vol. 1. 2 pt mxd, org. AFP 9780800676025.

P Wonacott, Glenn. "Sing Praise to God." SAB, pno. AFP 9781451401738.

Children's Choir

P Attenberry, John. "What Then Will God Do with Me." U/2 pt, pno. CG CGA1400.

P Patterson, Mark. "Now We Give Thanks" from *Young ChildrenSing*. U, kybd. AFP 9780800676803.

Shaw, Timothy. "Teach Me Your Way." U/2 pt, opt C inst. CG CGA1081.

Keyboard / Instrumental

Fedak, Alfred V. "Puer nobis" from *Epiphanies: Three Hymn Settings for the Season of Ephipany for Oboe or Trumpet and Organ or Piano*. Org, ob. SEL 160-925.

P♫ Hansen, Sherri. "Beloved, God's Chosen" from *Piano Weavings*. Pno. AFP 9781451494129.

P♫ Kerr, J. Wayne. "We Plow the Fields and Scatter" from *Amen, We Praise Your Name: World Hymns for Organ*. Org. AFP 9781451486018.

P Linneweber, Edie. "Morning Song" from *Christ Is Near: Hymn Settings for the Church Pianist*. Pno. AFP 9781451401158.

Handbell

♫ Edwards, Dan. "Praise and Thanksgiving." 2-3 oct hb or hc, L2. LOR 20/2013L.

Mizell, Carol Lynn. "As the Wind Song." 5-6 oct hb, fl, perc, opt 5-6 oct hc, SATB choir, L3. CG CGB836. Full score, CGB835.

Page, Anna Laura. "Grace and Thanksgiving." 3-5 oct, L2. ALF 25348.

⊕ = global song   ♫ = relates to hymn of the day   + = semicontinuous psalm

☼ = praise song   P = available in Prelude Music Planner

Wednesday, July 22
Mary Magdalene, Apostle

The gospels report Mary Magdalene was one of the women of Galilee who followed Jesus. She was present at Jesus' crucifixion and his burial. When she went to the tomb on the first day of the week to anoint Jesus' body, she was the first person to whom the risen Lord appeared. She returned to the disciples with the news and has been called "the apostle to the apostles" for her proclamation of the resurrection. Because John's gospel describes Mary as weeping at the tomb, she is often portrayed in art with red eyes. Icons depict her standing by the tomb and holding a bright red egg, a symbol of the resurrection.

Thursday, July 23
Birgitta of Sweden, renewer of the church, died 1373

Birgitta (beer-GEET-uh) was married at age thirteen and had four daughters with her husband. She was a woman of some standing who, in her early thirties, served as the chief lady-in-waiting to the queen of Sweden. She was widowed at the age of thirty-eight, shortly after she and her husband had made a religious pilgrimage. Following the death of her husband, the religious dreams and visions that had begun in her youth occurred more regularly. Her devotional commitments led her to give to the poor and needy all that she owned, and she began to live a more ascetic life. She founded an order of monks and nuns, the Order of the Holy Savior (Brigittines), whose superior was a woman. Today the Society of St. Birgitta is a laypersons' society that continues her work of prayer and charity.

Saturday, July 25
James, Apostle

James is one of the sons of Zebedee and is counted as one of the twelve disciples. Together with his brother John they had the nickname "sons of thunder." One of the stories in the New Testament tells of their request for Jesus to grant them places of honor in the kingdom. They are also reported to have asked Jesus for permission to send down fire on a Samaritan village that had not welcomed them. James was the first of the Twelve to suffer martyrdom and is the only apostle whose martyrdom is recorded in scripture. He is sometimes called James the Elder to distinguish him from James the Less, commemorated with Philip on May 1, and James of Jerusalem, commemorated on October 23.

July 26, 2020
Time after Pentecost — Lectionary 17

As Solomon prays for wisdom, we seek to more deeply know the treasures of faith. In today's gospel Jesus offers everyday images that reveal to us the reign of God: a tree that becomes a sheltering home, yeast that penetrates and expands, a treasured pearl, a net that gains a great catch. Even as we seek the riches of God's reign, the great surprise is that God's grace finds us first!

Prayer of the Day

Beloved and sovereign God, through the death and resurrection of your Son you bring us into your kingdom of justice and mercy. By your Spirit, give us your wisdom, that we may treasure the life that comes from Jesus Christ, our Savior and Lord.

Gospel Acclamation

Alleluia. Many will come from east and west and will eat in the kingdom of heaven. *Alleluia.* (Matt. 8:11)

Readings and Psalm

1 Kings 3:5-12

Because Solomon did not ask for long life, riches, or the defeat of his enemies, God gave him what he asked for: wisdom to govern the people well.

Psalm 119:129-136

When your word is opened, it gives light and understanding. (Ps. 119:130)

Romans 8:26-39

These words celebrate the depth of God's actions for us. Through Christ's death for us and the activity of the Spirit praying for us, we are fused to God's love poured out in Jesus Christ. Nothing, not even death itself, is able to separate us from such incredible divine love.

Matthew 13:31-33, 44-52

Throughout Matthew's gospel, Jesus and his disciples proclaim the good news that "the kingdom of heaven is near!" Here, Jesus offers several brief parables that explore the implications of this announcement for people's lives.

Semicontinuous Reading and Psalm

Genesis 29:15-28

Laban deceives Jacob by giving his older daughter, Leah, to Jacob in marriage instead of the promised younger daughter, Rachel. Because of his love for Rachel, Jacob agrees to work for Laban for an additional seven years so that he may also be married to her.

Psalm 105:1-11, 45b

Make known the deeds of the LORD among the peoples. Hallelujah! (Ps. 105:1, 45)

or **Psalm 128**

Happy are they who follow in the ways of God. (Ps. 128:1)

Preface   Sundays

Color   Green

Prayers of Intercession

The prayers are prepared locally for each occasion. The following examples may be adapted or used as appropriate.

Confident of your care and helped by the Holy Spirit, we pray for the church, the world, and all who are in need.
A brief silence.

Merciful God, your reign is revealed to us in common things: a mustard shrub, a woman baking bread, a fishing net. Help your church witness to the surprising yet common ways you encounter us in daily life. Lord, in your mercy,
hear our prayer.

When your word is opened, it gives light and understanding. Increase our understanding and awe of your creation; guide the work of scientists and researchers. Treasuring the earth, may we live as grateful and healing caretakers of our home. Lord, in your mercy,
hear our prayer.

As the birds of the air nest in branches of trees, gather the nations of the world into the welcoming shade of your merciful reign. Direct leaders of nations to build trust with each other and walk in the way of peace. (*Here a particular world struggle may be named.*) Lord, in your mercy,
hear our prayer.

Your Spirit helps us in our weakness and intercedes for the saints according to your will. Help us when we do not know how to pray. Give comfort to the dying, refuge to the weary, justice to those who are oppressed, and healing to the sick (*especially*). Lord, in your mercy,
hear our prayer.

You show steadfast love and direct us to ask of you what we need. Help this congregation ask boldly for what is most needed. Refresh us with new dreams of being your people in this place and time. Lord, in your mercy,
hear our prayer.
Here other intercessions may be offered.
In you our lives are never lost. Strengthen us by the inspiring witness of your people in all times and places. Embolden our witness now and one day gather us with all your saints in light (*especially*). Lord, in your mercy,
hear our prayer.
In the certain hope that nothing can separate us from your love, we offer these prayers to you; through Jesus Christ our Lord.
Amen.

Ideas for the Day

- Solomon in his dream encounter with God asks for understanding and discernment to lead. During your regular weekly liturgy's time of prayer, how do you lift up your local, state, and national elected leaders? How might spending more time in crafting contextual prayer for your elected officials serve the cause of unity to which we are called? Consider the example here of Pastor Andrew Black's prayer for the opening day of the New Mexico House of Representatives: pres-outlook.org/2018/01 /a-prayer-for-government. Note how contextual prayers for local leaders need not avoid gospel imperatives and yet can affirm the vocation of political leadership.

- In the reading from Romans, the apostle Paul declares through a most comprehensive and breathless listing the stickiness of God's abounding and abiding love. In worship, communities of faith experience that love in numerous ways, from the grace-filled sacramental power of baptism and communion, to the proclaimed word of promise, to being in community, to prayer and hymnody and more. The intentional use in whole or in part of the order for healing (*ELW*, pp. 276–278) provides an additional opportunity for the experience of God's love in a multisensory and personal way. As summer worship has in many contexts been a time of trying new things, consider how you might introduce this order or increase its frequency of use.

- In this collection of Jesus' teachings about the kingdom of heaven, we can imagine the engagement of his hearers as they absorb each image, each comparison, each simile. Author Paula LaRocque, writing on the subject of simile for KERA News, states: "Good similes use just a few words to create a picture in the mind's eye—and sometimes the imagined image is more suggestive than the real image. That's how we can remember a simile long after we've forgotten where we heard it" (keranews.org/post/power-simile). Consider putting together a box full of miscellaneous objects, and at the sermon time invite people to form small groups of three people or so. Have the groups send one person up who, without looking, chooses an object from the box. Give the groups a few minutes to prepare a simile: "The kingdom of heaven is like *the object* . . ."; have them complete the simile by explaining how. Consider inviting groups to share their simile, and weave the remainder of the sermon around the similes that have been shared.

Connections with Creation

A mustard bush is not a stately tree or even a well-maintained, tightly clipped shrub. The truth is, they usually grow wild. They're ill-mannered, bushy, homely plants that no one would pick to landscape their garden. Apparently, this is not a problem for Jesus. Sturdy trunks, gorgeous flowers, and well-behaved branches matter not at all to this gardener. What seems to impress Jesus is simply the fact that the shrub grows, and grows, and grows. Tiny beginnings are where many of us find ourselves when trying to cultivate an eco-centric faith in a world that feels so inhospitable to green spirituality. For some of us, our faith is no bigger than that mustard seed. Yet as Jesus reminds us, a few small seeds are sometimes all that is needed to alter the culture, the way we think, and our values.

Let the Children Come

In this week's gospel, Jesus tells a series of short parables about what the kingdom of heaven is like: a mustard seed, yeast, treasure, a merchant, a net. Such riches! Perhaps the easiest one to have some fun with is the hidden treasure. If God's kingdom is like something so precious that when someone comes across it, they sell everything they have in order to obtain it, it must be very important. Ponder with children, "I wonder what the most important thing in our worship space is. I wonder why." Receive all answers without judgment. If you have the time and opportunity to distribute stickers and can find ones depicting a treasure chest (alternatively, print stick-on labels with the words "hidden treasure"), consider inviting the children to hand them out to each member of the assembly and to one another.

Assembly Song
Gathering

Awake, my soul, and with the sun ELW 557, LBW 269
God, who stretched the spangled heavens ELW 771, LBW 463
Neither death nor life ELW 622

Psalmody and Acclamations

Kallman, Daniel. "Psalm 119:129-136" from PWA.
Mummert, Mark. "Psalm 119:129-136" from PSCY.
+ Arnatt, Ronald. "Psalm 128." Cant, assembly, kybd. ECS 5417.
(GA) ELW 175 with proper verse for Lectionary 17.

Hymn of the Day

God, when human bonds are broken   ELW 603, WOV 735
  MERTON

Jesus, priceless treasure   ELW 775, LBW 457 *JESU, MEINE FREUDE*
  LBW 458 *GUD SKAL ALTING MAGE*

What God ordains is good indeed   ELW 776, LBW 446
  WAS GOTT TUT

Offering

Accept, O Lord, the gifts we bring   ELW 691, WOV 759

Let us go now to the banquet/Vamos todos al banquete
  ELW 523, LLC 410

Communion

Children of the heavenly Father   ELW 781, LS 167, LBW 474

My faith looks up to thee   ELW 759, LBW 479

Soul, adorn yourself with gladness/Vengo a ti, Jesús amado
  ELW 488/489, LLC 388, LBW 224

Sending

Sent forth by God's blessing   ELW 547, LBW 221

We've come this far by faith   ELW 633, TFF 197

Additional Assembly Songs

If you only had faith   GTG 176

Seek ye first   WOV 783, TFF 149, W&P 122, H82 711, GTG 175

You are the seed   WOV 753, TFF 226, LLC 486, LS 139

⊕ Korean trad. "Abba, Abba, Hear Us, We Cry" from *Sing! A New Creation*. U. Faith Alive 9781562128111.

⊕ Monteiro, Simei. "Tua Palavra/I Know Your Word" from *More Voices*. U, pno. Wood Lake Publishing 9781551341484.

☼ Baloche, David/Rita Baloche. "Nothing Can Separate" from CCLI.

☼ Greene, Travis/Victor Navejae. "Intentional" from CCLI.

☼ Hamilton, Emily/Jason Ingram/Jeff Luckey/Randy Charlson. "Common Love" from CCLI.

☼ Hodge, Charles/CJ Blount/John Larson/Justin Jackson. "You Change Everything" from CCLI.

☼ Holt, Andrew/Mia Fieldes/Natalie Grant/Seth Mosley. "Isn't He (This Jesus)" from CCLI.

☼ Howard, Alex/Jesse Reeves. "I Found a Treasure" from CCLI.

Music for the Day
Choral

Durow, Peter J. "I'm Goin' Home on a Cloud." SA, kybd, cl. Colla Voce 20-96470.

P Lund, Emily. "Dona nobis pacem." 2 pt, pno, desc, opt assembly. HOP C5821.

P Pooler, Marie. "Be Thou My Vision" from *Augsburg Easy Choirbook*, vol. 1. U, kybd, opt desc. AFP 9780800676025.

P Raabe, Nancy. "God's Plan." 2 pt mxd, pno, cl. AFP 9781451479348.

Children's Choir

Bolt, Conway A. Jr. "The Kingdom of God." 2 pt, kybd. CG CGA677.

P Horman, John D. "Solomon" from *Sing the Stories of God's People*. U, kybd. AFP 9780806698397.

P Pooler, Marie. "Be Thou My Vision" from *Augsburg Easy Choirbook*, vol. 1. U, kybd, opt desc. AFP 9780800676025.

Keyboard / Instrumental

P ♫ Benson, Robert. "Merton" from *Augsburg Organ Library: Advent, Series II*. Org. AFP 9781506448077.

P ♫ Hamilton, Gregory. "Jesus, Priceless Treasure" from *Piano Stylings on Hymn Tunes*. Pno. AFP 9781451486094.

P ♫ Markull, Friedrich W. "Was Gott tut, das ist wohlgetan" from *Twenty-Four Chorale Preludes by Friedrich Wilhem Markull: Opus 123*. Org. AFP 9781451401875.

P Organ, Anne Krentz. "Slane" from *Be Thou My Vision: Piano Reflections*. Pno. AFP 9780800678524.

Handbell

♫ Krug, Jason. "Jesus, Priceless Treasure." 3-6 oct, L3. BP HB516.

♫ Mallory, Ron. "Jesus, Priceless Treasure." 2-3 oct hb or hc, L2. SF 20/2039.

Stephenson, Valerie. "God's Grace." 3-6 oct, L1+. LOR 20/1203L.

Tuesday, July 28
Johann Sebastian Bach, died 1750; Heinrich Schütz, died 1672; George Frederick Handel, died 1759; musicians

These three composers have done much to enrich the worship life of the church. Johann Sebastian Bach drew on the Lutheran tradition of hymnody and wrote about two hundred cantatas, including at least two for each Sunday and festival day in the Lutheran calendar of his day. He has been called "the fifth evangelist" for the ways he proclaimed the gospel through his music. George Frederick Handel was not primarily a church musician, but his great work *Messiah* is a musical proclamation of the scriptures. Heinrich Schütz wrote choral settings of biblical texts and paid special attention to ways his composition would underscore the meaning of the words.

Wednesday, July 29
Mary, Martha, and Lazarus of Bethany

Mary and Martha are remembered for the hospitality and refreshment they offered Jesus in their home. Following the characterization drawn by Luke, Martha represents the active life, Mary the contemplative. Mary is identified in the fourth

⊕ = global song   ♫ = relates to hymn of the day   + = semicontinuous psalm
☼ = praise song   P = available in Prelude Music Planner

gospel as the one who anointed Jesus before his passion and who was criticized for her act of devotion. Lazarus, Mary's and Martha's brother, was raised from the dead by Jesus as a sign of the eternal life offered to all believers. It was over Lazarus's tomb that Jesus wept for love of his friend.

Wednesday, July 29
Olaf, King of Norway, martyr, died 1030

Olaf is considered the patron saint of Norway. In his early career he engaged in war and piracy in the Baltic and in Normandy. In Rouen, though, he was baptized and became a Christian. He returned to Norway, succeeded his father as king, and from then on Christianity was the dominant religion of the realm. He revised the laws of the nation and enforced them with strict impartiality, eliminating the possibility of bribes. He thereby alienated much of the aristocracy. The harshness that he sometimes resorted to in order to establish Christianity and his own law led to a rebellion. After being driven from the country and into exile, he enlisted support from Sweden to try to regain his kingdom, but he died in battle.

August 2, 2020
Time after Pentecost — Lectionary 18

In today's first reading God invites all who are hungry or thirsty to receive food and drink without cost. Jesus feeds the hungry multitude and reveals the abundance of God. At the eucharistic table we remember all who are hungry or poor in our world today. As we share the bread of life, we are sent forth to give ourselves away as bread for the hungry.

Prayer of the Day

Glorious God, your generosity waters the world with goodness, and you cover creation with abundance. Awaken in us a hunger for the food that satisfies both body and spirit, and with this food fill all the starving world; through your Son, Jesus Christ, our Savior and Lord.

Gospel Acclamation

Alleluia. One does not live by bread alone, but by every word that comes from the mouth of God. *Alleluia.* (Matt. 4:4)

Readings and Psalm
Isaiah 55:1-5

God invites Israel to a great feast at which both food and drink are free. God also promises to make an everlasting covenant with all peoples, with promises that previously had been limited to Israel. As David was a witness to the nations, these nations shall now acknowledge the ways in which God has glorified Israel.

Psalm 145:8-9, 14-21

You open wide your hand and satisfy the desire of every living thing. (Ps. 145:16)

Romans 9:1-5

This begins a new section in Paul's letter in which he will deal with the place of Israel in God's saving plan. He opens by highlighting how Israel's heritage and legacy include being God's children, having God's covenants, being given God's law, participating in worship of God, and receiving divine promises.

Matthew 14:13-21

After John the Baptist is murdered, Jesus desires a time of solitude. Still, his compassion for others will not allow him to dismiss those who need him, and he is moved to perform one of his greatest miracles.

Semicontinuous Reading and Psalm
Genesis 32:22-31

Jacob wrestled all night with God, and when God wanted to get away as dawn was breaking, Jacob would not let God go until God had blessed him. Jacob's name is changed to Israel to mark his new relationship with God as he enters the land. Jacob is astonished that he remains alive after seeing God face-to-face.

Psalm 17:1-7, 15

I shall see your face; when I awake, I shall be satisfied. (Ps. 17:15)

Preface   Sundays

Color   Green

Prayers of Intercession

The prayers are prepared locally for each occasion. The following examples may be adapted or used as appropriate.

Confident of your care and helped by the Holy Spirit, we pray for the church, the world, and all who are in need.

A brief silence.

You take resources that appear to be meager, bless them, and there is enough. May your church trust that what you bless and ask us to share with the world is abundantly sufficient. Lord, in your mercy,

hear our prayer.

Your bountiful creation offers sustenance and life for all creatures. Protect this abundance for the well-being of all. Reverse the damage we have caused your creation (*local needs may be named*). Replenish ground water supplies, provide needed rains in places of drought, and protect forests from wildfires. Lord, in your mercy,

hear our prayer.

You offer yourself to all the nations and peoples of the earth, inviting everyone to abundant life. Bring the prophetic vision to fullness, that all nations will run to you and that nations who do not know you will find their joy in you. Lord, in your mercy,

hear our prayer.

You open your hand and satisfy the desire of every living thing. Hear the anguish of tender hearts who cry to you in suffering and satisfy their deepest needs. Bring wholeness and healing to those who suffer in body, heart, soul, and mind (*especially*). Lord, in your mercy,

hear our prayer.

You offer freely the fullness of salvation. Give our congregation (*name*) such a welcoming heart, that our words and actions may extend your free and abundant hospitality to all whom we encounter. Lord, in your mercy,

hear our prayer.

Here other intercessions may be offered.

You gather your saints as one, united in the body of Jesus. Bring us with all your saints to the heavenly banquet. We remember with love and thanksgiving the saints we have known (*especially*). Lord, in your mercy,

hear our prayer.

In the certain hope that nothing can separate us from your love, we offer these prayers to you; through Jesus Christ our Lord.

Amen.

Ideas for the Day

- Jesus and the disciples find themselves in a deserted place without food. Some neighborhoods in the United States are labeled "food deserts" because their residents do not have access to affordable, nutritious food. The U.S. Department of Agriculture developed a food desert locator to identify communities in which at least a third of the people live a mile or more from a grocery store. Check it out to find the nearest food desert to your congregation. Go to usda.gov and search for the Food Access Research Atlas. How can your church work locally to partner with these communities and advocate for food justice?

- Jesus takes a meager offering of food and multiplies its impact to feed a crowd. Yet we often interpret smallness as inadequacy or failure. Whether the discouragement stems from dwindling attendance, aging members, or changing neighborhoods, churches tend to react to a decline with self-limiting behaviors, as if they have little or nothing left to offer. But the size of the congregation does not have to determine the size of its mission. For example, forty-one members of Shekinah Chapel in Riverdale, Illinois, pledged to build a church for Lutherans in Zambia, and St. Gregory Armenian Apostolic Church, a small church in Vancouver, helped to settle more than one hundred Syrian refugees (Francine Knowles, "Rewriting the narrative," *Living Lutheran*, May 9, 2018). Introduce an asset-mapping exercise to your congregation this week, and brainstorm how God can use your resources, as limited as they may be, to create abundance for all. Read *Claiming Resurrection in the Dying Church* for an imaginative retelling of this gospel passage and further ideas on creating a culture of possibility rather than inadequacy in small churches (Anna B. Olson, Louisville, KY: Westminster John Knox Press, 2016, pp. 42–43).

- How often do you echo the words of scarcity coming from the disciples: "We have nothing here but five loaves and two fish" (Matt. 14:17)? Brené Brown refers to scarcity as the "never enough" problem. We are never (good, perfect, thin, etc.) enough, nor do we have enough (time, money, etc.). Her research suggests that scarcity thrives in shame-prone environments that are deeply steeped in comparison and fractured by disengagement (*Daring Greatly*, New York: Penguin Group, 2012). The gospel moves us from a mindset of deficiency to one of sufficiency by providing a counter-narrative of worthiness, compassion, and connection. We will never experience a moment of not being enough or having enough for Jesus.

Connections with Creation

Water, wine, milk, bread, fish—today's readings are a feast! Yet hunger is experienced both in the Bible and in our world today. Hunger and environmental issues are inextricably connected. The sermon could acknowledge how climate change affects crop production, causes blight, and leads to the devastation of agriculture due to catastrophic weather events (witness Puerto Rico's decimated farming industry after Hurricane Maria in 2017). Consider taking up a special hunger collection for an area affected by drought, wildfires, or rising sea levels. At the same time, encourage congregants to advocate for policies that curb greenhouse gas emissions and mitigate climate change. Aiding those who suffer can coincide with addressing the circumstances that lead to that very suffering.

Let the Children Come

It can be helpful to let children (and adults) know that Christ feeds us from two tables: the table of the word and the table of the eucharist. From the table of the word, the assembly moves to the table of the eucharist. In today's gospel, we hear that children were present when Jesus fed the multitudes. There is bread enough for them. This week when you speak the words of invitation to the communion meal, consider adding a clause that specifically speaks to the children in the room. Remind them that they are welcome at the table. If you're able, this would be a fantastic week to have real, homemade bread at the eucharist and to think about how every meal is a reminder of the feast that is a foretaste of the heavenly one to come. Children can ably serve as gift-bearers with advance preparation.

Assembly Song
Gathering

All who hunger, gather gladly ELW 461
Lord, whose love in humble service ELW 712, LBW 423
Praise and thanksgiving ELW 689, LBW 409

Psalmody and Acclamations

Alonso, Tony. "The Hand of the Lord Feeds Us" from TLP:A.
Makeever, Ray. "Psalm 145:8-9, 14-21" from PWA.
+ Marshall, Jane. "Psalm 17." U, kybd. CG CGA891.
(GA) ELW 175 with proper verse for Lectionary 18.

Hymn of the Day

Break now the bread of life ELW 515, LBW 235 *BREAD OF LIFE*
Let us talents and tongues employ ELW 674, WOV 754,
   TFF 232 *LINSTEAD*
The church of Christ, in every age ELW 729, LBW 433
   WAREHAM

Offering

Bread of life, our host and meal ELW 464
God extends an invitation/Nuestro Padre nos invita ELW 486,
   WOV 709, LLC 397, TFF 125

Communion

Eat this bread/Jesus Christ, bread of life ELW 472, WOV 709,
   TFF 125
O bread of life from heaven ELW 480, LBW 222
We come to the hungry feast ELW 479, WOV 766, DATH 84

Sending

Amen, we praise your name/Amen siakudumisa ELW 846,
   WOV 786, TFF 279
Praise the One who breaks the darkness ELW 843, ASG 34

Additional Assembly Songs

This is my body TFF 121
We the Lord's people H82 51
⊕ Bell, John L. "We Will Take What You Offer" from *There Is One Among Us*. SAB. GIA G-5111.
⊕ Taizé Community. "Let All Who Are Thirsty, Come" from *Let All Who Are Thirsty, Come/See, I Am Near*. SATB, ww, br, vc, gtr. GIA G-8518.
☼ Burton, Henry/Luke Brawner. "Come, for the Feast Is Spread" from *Lex Orandi*. lukebrawner.bandcamp.com.
☼ Curtis, Cody. "Lamentation (9:1-5)" from *Romans*. Psallos. bandcamp.com.
☼ Dalton, David/Nate Moore/Pat Barrett/Tony Brown. "Come to the River" from CCLI.
☼ Foley, John/Matt Maher. "Come to the Water/I Will Run to You" from *Spirit and Song*. ocp.org.
☼ Morton, Luke. "Bread of Life" from *Let the Little Children Come*. glkids.bandcamp.com.
☼ Smith, Caroline Cobb. "There Is a Mountain" from CCLI.

Music for the Day
Choral

Curry, Craig. "Hungry I Come." SATB, pno. FB HAL.8747081.
P Haugen, Marty, "Now in This Banquet/God of Our Journeys/ Lord, You Can Open." 2 pt, pno, gtr, 2 ww in C, opt assembly. GIA G-2918.
Nelson, Ronald A. "You Hear the Hungry Crying." SATB, kybd, opt assembly. AFP 9781451401790.
P Proulx, Richard. "Blessing" from *To God Will I Sing: Vocal Solos for the Church Year*. Solo or duet, kybd. AFP 9780800674335.

Children's Choir

♫ James, Gary. "Break Now the Bread of Life." U, kybd. MSM 50-8306.
Mayo, Becki Slagle/Lynn Shaw Bailey. "More Than Enough." U, pno. CG CGA1545.
P Raabe, Nancy. "All Things Are Possible with God" from *ChildrenSing in Worship*, vol. 2. U/2 pt, pno. AFP 9781451424126.

Keyboard / Instrumental

P Carter, John. "Holy Manna" from *Hymn Miniatures for Piano*. Pno. AFP 9781506413686.
Larkin, Michael. "Come, Thou Fount of Every Blessing" from *Be Thou My Vision: 10 Meditative Hymns for Piano*. Pno. MSM 15-832.

⊕ = global song   ♫ = relates to hymn of the day   + = semicontinuous psalm
☼ = praise song   P = available in Prelude Music Planner

P ♫ Sedio, Mark. "Linstead" from *Augsburg Organ Library: Summer.* Org. AFP 9780800676872.

♫ Speed, Robert M. "Fanfares and Variations on Wareham" from *Marilyn Mason Music Library*, vol. 2. Org. MSM 10-991.

Handbell

♫ Afdahl, Lee. "The Church of Christ in Every Age." 3-5 oct hb, opt 3-5 oct hc, L2. AGEHR AG35306.

♫ Prins, Matthew. "Break Thou the Bread of Life." 2-3 oct, L2+. FTT 20322.

♫ Tucker, Sondra. "Let Us Talents and Tongues Employ." 3-5 oct, L3. HOP 2146.

Saturday, August 8
Dominic, founder of the Order of Preachers (Dominicans), died 1221

Dominic was a Spanish priest who preached against the Albigensians, a heretical sect that held gnostic and dualistic beliefs. Dominic believed that a stumbling block to restoring heretics to the church was the wealth of clergy, so he formed an itinerant religious order, the Order of Preachers (Dominicans), who lived in poverty, studied philosophy and theology, and preached against heresy. The method of this order was to use kindness and gentle argument, rather than harsh judgment, to bring unorthodox Christians back to the fold. Dominic was opposed to burning Christians at the stake. Three times Dominic was offered the office of bishop, which he refused so that he could continue in his work of preaching.

August 9, 2020
Time after Pentecost — Lectionary 19

Elijah finds the presence of God not in earthquake, wind, or fire, but in the sound of sheer silence. When the disciples face a great storm on the sea, they cry out with fear. Jesus says: "Take heart, it is I; do not be afraid." Amid the storms of life, we gather to seek the calm presence of Christ that soothes our fears. In comforting words of scripture and in the refreshing bread and cup of the eucharist, God grants us peace and sends us forth to be a sign of God's presence to others.

Prayer of the Day

O God our defender, storms rage around and within us and cause us to be afraid. Rescue your people from despair, deliver your sons and daughters from fear, and preserve us in the faith of your Son, Jesus Christ, our Savior and Lord.

Gospel Acclamation

Alleluia. I wait for you, O Lord; in your word is my hope. *Alleluia.* (Ps. 130:5)

Readings and Psalm
1 Kings 19:9-18

On Mount Horeb, where God had appeared to Moses with typical signs of God's presence—earthquake, wind, and fire—Elijah now experienced God in "sheer silence." God assured Elijah that he is not the only faithful believer. Seven thousand Israelites are still loyal. God instructed Elijah to anoint two men as kings and to anoint Elisha as his own successor.

Psalm 85:8-13

I will listen to what the Lord God is saying. (Ps. 85:8)

Romans 10:5-15

A right relationship with God is not something we achieve by heroic efforts. It is a gift received in the proclamation whose content is Jesus Christ. This proclaimed word creates our faith in the Lord Jesus Christ. Hence Christian proclamation is an indispensable component of God's saving actions.

Matthew 14:22-33

Matthew's gospel typically portrays Jesus' disciples as people of "little faith," who fail despite their best intentions. In this story, Matthew shows how Jesus comes to the disciples when they are in trouble and sustains them in their time of fear and doubt.

Semicontinuous Reading and Psalm
Genesis 37:1-4, 12-28

Though Joseph was Jacob's favorite son, his jealous brothers sold him into slavery. Judah, who protected Joseph's life, later gives a moving speech before Joseph in Egypt, indicating that the brothers had changed their ways (44:18-34).

Psalm 105:1-6, 16-22, 45b

Make known the deeds of the Lord among the peoples. Hallelujah! (Ps. 105:1, 45)

Preface   Sundays

Color   Green

Prayers of Intercession

The prayers are prepared locally for each occasion. The following examples may be adapted or used as appropriate.

Confident of your care and helped by the Holy Spirit, we pray for the church, the world, and all who are in need.

A brief silence.

For your whole church throughout the world. Give courage in the midst of storms, so that we see and hear Jesus calling: "Take heart, it is I: do not be afraid." May we follow Christ wherever he leads. Lord, in your mercy,

hear our prayer.

For the well-being of your creation. Protect waterways, forests, lands, and wildlife from exploitation and abuse. Help the human family endeavor to sustain and be sustained by the resources of your hand. Lord, in your mercy,

hear our prayer.

For the nations and their leaders. In you, steadfast love and faithfulness meet, and righteousness and peace kiss. May nations in conflict know the peace that is the fruit of justice, and the justice that is the path to peace. Lord, in your mercy,

hear our prayer.

For those in need. Everyone who calls upon your name will be saved. Accompany all who are lonely, hear the voices of those who cry out in anguish, and support those who are frustrated in their search for an affordable place to live. We pray for those suffering this day (*especially*). Lord, in your mercy,

hear our prayer.

For our congregation. You have gathered us here today as your people and we thank you for this gift. We pray for those who are new to this community, for students and teachers preparing for a new school year, and for those struggling with unexpected hardship. Supply us generously with your grace for our life together. Lord, in your mercy,

hear our prayer.

Here other intercessions may be offered.

We give you thanks, O God, for the saints of the whole church from all times and places, and for the saints in our lives and in our community whom you have gathered to yourself (*especially*). Lord, in your mercy,

hear our prayer.

In the certain hope that nothing can separate us from your love, we offer these prayers to you; through Jesus Christ our Lord.

Amen.

Ideas for the Day

- In walking on water and calming the storm, Jesus demonstrates his power over nature. Where do we locate God's power in the wind and waves of devastating hurricanes and floods? Where do we locate our own ecological footprint in these natural disasters? The gospel is also paired with Elijah's encounter with God, which occurs in the silence rather than the powerful acts of nature. How do we understand God's relationship to nature based on these examples? How do we interpret divine intervention in nature and its limitations? Consider reading the ELCA social statement "Caring for Creation: Vision, Hope and Justice" (elca.org) as a congregation, and ponder its implications for your assembly's life together.

- Peter exhibits boldness when he asks Jesus to help him walk on the water. Depending on your context, your members may not be as assertive about stepping up to lead. Asian Americans, women, and members who identify with other minority or oppressed groups may often wait to be invited into leadership due to socialization or internalized belief about capability. Yet Jesus empowers his followers to live confidently into God's grace. Resources like *Breaking the Bamboo Ceiling* (Jane Hyun, New York: HarperCollins, 2006) and *Lean In* (Sheryl Sandberg, New York: Alfred A. Knopf, 2013) provide helpful tools for empowering leadership among these groups. For those in positions of power and authority, how might you empower others to step into the water? Consider what barriers may exist to the priesthood of all believers being fully realized in your community and how your actions, individually and collectively, may be disempowering others. Lift up organizations that respond to the storms of poverty, injustice, and violence by empowering victims—such as the ELCA Global Mission ministries, the National Survivor Network, and the Equal Justice Initiative.

- In the midst of life's storms, our prayers are often for Jesus to immediately rescue us and restore a sense of calm. But instead, Jesus calls us out of the boat and into the storm. This is a risky and frightening invitation. When Peter's courage is shaken by a strong wind, he begins to sink, and he once again turns to Jesus for strength. Is fear and doubt a hindrance to living faithfully, or are they simply part of the process? In her TED Talk on "How to Make Stress Your Friend," Kelly McGonigal reframes the physiological indications of stress—sweat, shortness of breath, racing heart—as indications that your body is preparing you to meet the challenge ahead (TEDGlobal, June 2013, ted.com). Peter's distress reorients his trust in Jesus and prepares him for his ministry ahead. How might our fears and stressors turn us toward Christ and propel forward our ministry?

Connections with Creation

Elijah heard the voice of God while standing in silence at the entrance of a mountain cave. The disciples witnessed Jesus' miracle while on a boat at sea. Consider asking the congregation where in nature they experience the presence of God. Invite them to turn to their neighbor and share their answer. But then ask how they would feel if that sacred place was destroyed—like mountains scalped for coal, or seas inked with oil spills. The question to wrestle with is this: Are we limiting, compromising, or eliminating our opportunities to experience the divine presence by polluting and destroying the very places God has chosen to reveal Godself? What if there were no mountain for Elijah? What if the ocean were too polluted to even set out for fishing? Even as we as a civilization are sinking, however, Jesus' hand reaches for us. Now is the time for great faith.

Let the Children Come

We're hearing a water story this week, and this one takes place in a boat, making it a good Sunday to take a "field trip" to the center of your worship space, also called the nave (think "navy"). If your worship space has visible beams, it's highly likely that it was constructed to remind your congregation that they're all in the boat together. When we're very afraid and feel alone, God, the one who made the wind and the waves, is with us. We also have one another. In the coming week there are commemorations of the faithful departed who helped shape our understanding of what it means to be in this nave together with the whole church. In gratitude for their lives and witness, tell one of their stories in the center of your space: Lawrence, Clare, Florence Nightingale, Clara Maass, Maximilian Kolbe, Kaj Munk, or Mary.

Assembly Song
Gathering

Almighty God, your word is cast ELW 516, LBW 234
Listen, God is calling/Neno lake Mungu ELW 513, WOV 712,
    TFF 130, LS 79
Open your ears, O faithful people ELW 519, WOV 715, LS 84

Psalmody and Acclamations

Dancing at the Harvest/Psalm 85 DATH 40
de Silva, Chris. "Lord, Let Us See Your Kindness." SAB, assembly, kybd, gtr, 2 C inst. GIA G-8307.
+ Woehr, Roland. "Psalm 105" from PSCY.
    (GA) ELW 175 with proper verse for Lectionary 19.

Hymn of the Day

Eternal Father, strong to save ELW 756, LBW 467 *MELITA*
God of tempest, God of whirlwind ELW 400 *CWM RHONDDA*
Praise, praise! You are my rock ELW 862, ASG 33 *ZACHARY*
    WOODS ROCK

Offering

Accept, O Lord, the gifts we bring ELW 691, WOV 759
We eat the bread of teaching ELW 518

Communion

My faith looks up to thee ELW 759, LBW 479
Precious Lord, take my hand ELW 773, WOV 731, TFF 193
When peace like a river ELW 785, TFF 194, LBW 346

Sending

Jesus, Savior, pilot me ELW 755, LBW 334
My life flows on in endless song ELW 763, WOV 781

Additional Assembly Songs

For the healing of creation MSB2 S522, SP 12b
Now there is no male or female GTG 493
Will your anchor hold TFF 255
⊕ Bell, John L. "Be Still and Know" from *There Is One Among Us*. SATB. GIA G-5111. Also SP2.
⊕ de Brébeuf, Jean/Andrew Donaldson. "O Holy God, There Was a Time" from *Hosanna! Ecumenical Songs for Justice and Peace*. U. WCC Publications 9782825416679.
☼ Assad, Audrey. "Winter Snow" from CCLI.
☼ Holt, Andrew/Hope Darst/Mia Fieldes. "Peace Be Still" from CCLI.
☼ Houston, Joel/Matt Crocker/Salomon Ligthelm. "Oceans (Where Feet May Fail)" from CCLI.
☼ Ivey, Aaron/Brett Land/Dietrich Schmidt/Jimmy McNeal/Logan Garza/Logan Walter/Marcus Dawes. "All Because of Christ" from CCLI.
☼ Oliver, Lane. "Yours Alone" from CCLI.
☼ Sooter, Jacob/Meredith Andrews/Mia Fieldes. "Not for a Moment (After All)" from CCLI.

Music for the Day
Choral

Marcello, Benedetto. "Give an Ear to Me" from *Anthems for Choir 2: Twenty-four Anthems for Sopranos & Altos*. SA, kybd. OXF 9780193532403.
P ♫ Miller, Aaron David. "You Are My Rock." SAB, pno. AFP 9781451492583.
P Neswick, Bruce. "Hearken to My Voice, O Lord, When I Call" from *The Augsburg Choirbook*. SA or TB, org. AFP 9780800656782.
Vulpius, Melchior. "Abide with Us, Our Savior" from *Unison and Two-part Anthems*. AFP 9780800648916.

Children's Choir

Burkhardt, Michael. "How Can I Keep from Singing?" U/2pt, pno. CG CGA852.
P Burrows, Mark. "Do Not Be Afraid" from *Again, I Say Rejoice!* U, pno. CG CGC56.
P Cox, Randy. "Dance on the Water." U, pno. CG CGA1328.

⊕ = global song   ♫ = relates to hymn of the day   + = semicontinuous psalm
☼ = praise song   P = available in Prelude Music Planner

Keyboard / Instrumental

P ♫ Hansen, Sherri. "Praise, Praise! You Are My Rock" from *Piano Weavings*. Pno. AFP 9781451494129.

P ♫ Hobby, Robert A. "Eternal Father, Strong to Save" from *For All the Saints: Hymn Preludes for Funerals*, vol. 3. Org. AFP 9781451486056.

P ♫ Kim, Marianne. "Cwm Rhondda" from *My Soul Proclaims: Piano Meditations for Worship*. Pno. AFP 9781451499131.

P ♫ Manz, Paul. "God of Grace" from *Five Hymn Improvisations for Weddings and General Use*. Org. MSM 10-850.

Handbell

♫ Behnke, John. "Eternal Father, Strong to Save." 3-6 oct hb, opt 3-5 oct hc, L2. CPH 977434.

Krug, Jason. "All Praise to Thee" from *All Praise to Thee*, vol. 1. 12 bells, L2, L3. CG CGB920.

♫ Moklebust, Cathy. "God of Amazing Grace." 3-5 oct hb, opt 3 oct hc, L3-. CG CGB878.

Monday, August 10
Lawrence, deacon, martyr, died 258

Lawrence was one of seven deacons of the congregation at Rome and, like the deacons appointed in Acts, was responsible for financial matters in the church and for the care of the poor. Lawrence lived during a time of persecution under the emperor Valerian. The emperor demanded that Lawrence surrender the treasures of the church. Lawrence gathered lepers, orphans, the blind and lame. He brought them to the emperor and said, "Here is the treasure of the church." This act enraged the emperor, and Lawrence was sentenced to death. Lawrence's martyrdom was one of the first to be observed by the church.

Tuesday, August 11
Clare, Abbess of San Damiano, died 1253

At age eighteen, Clare of Assisi heard Francis preach a sermon in a church in town. From that time, she determined to follow in his example of Christian living. With Francis's help (and against the wishes of her father) she and a growing number of companions established a women's Franciscan community, called the Order of Poor Ladies, or Poor Clares. She became a confidante and advisor to Francis, and in standing up against the wishes of popes for the sake of maintaining complete poverty, she helped inspire other women to pursue spiritual goals.

Thursday, August 13
Florence Nightingale, died 1910; Clara Maass, died 1901; renewers of society

When Florence Nightingale decided she would be a nurse, her family was horrified. In the early 1800s nursing was done by people with no training and no other way to earn a living. Florence trained at Kaiserswerth, Germany, with a Lutheran order of deaconesses. She returned home and worked to reform hospitals in England. Nightingale led a group of thirty-eight nurses to serve in the Crimean War, where they worked in appalling conditions. She returned to London as a hero and resumed her work there for hospital reform.

Clara Maass was born in New Jersey and served as a nurse in the Spanish-American War, where she encountered the horrors of yellow fever. She later responded to a call for subjects in research on yellow fever. During the experiments, which included receiving bites from mosquitoes, she contracted the disease and died. The commemoration of these women invites the church to give thanks for all who practice the arts of healing.

Friday, August 14
Maximilian Kolbe, died 1941; Kaj Munk, died 1944; martyrs

Father Kolbe was a Franciscan priest, born Raymond Kolbe. After spending some time working in Asia, he returned in 1936 to his native Poland, where he supervised a friary that came to house thousands of Polish war refugees, mostly Jews. The Nazis were watching, however, and he was arrested. Confined in Auschwitz, Kolbe gave generously of his meager resources and finally volunteered to be starved to death in place of another man who was a husband and father. After two weeks, he was executed by a lethal injection.

Kaj (pronounced kye) Munk, a Danish Lutheran pastor and playwright, was an outspoken critic of the Nazis, who occupied Denmark during the Second World War. His plays frequently highlighted the eventual victory of the Christian faith despite the church's weak and ineffective witness. The Nazis feared Munk because his sermons and articles helped to strengthen the Danish resistance movement. He was executed by the Gestapo on January 5, 1944.

Saturday, August 15
Mary, Mother of Our Lord

The church honors Mary with the Greek title *theotokos*, meaning "God-bearer." Origen first used this title in the early church, and the councils of Ephesus and Chalcedon upheld it.

Luther upheld this same title in his writings. The honor paid to Mary as *theotokos* and mother of our Lord goes back to biblical times, when Mary herself sang, "from now on all generations will call me blessed" (Luke 1:48). Mary's life revealed the presence of God incarnate, and it revealed God's presence among the humble and poor. Mary's song, the Magnificat, speaks of reversals in the reign of God: the mighty are cast down, the lowly are lifted up, the hungry are fed, and the rich are sent away empty-handed.

August 16, 2020
Time after Pentecost — Lectionary 20

In Isaiah we hear that God's house shall be a house of prayer for all people and that God will gather the outcasts of Israel. The Canaanite woman in today's gospel is a Gentile, an outsider, who is unflinching in her request that Jesus heal her daughter. As Jesus commends her bold faith, how might our church extend its mission to those on the margins of society? In our gathering around word and meal we receive strength to be signs of comfort, healing, and justice for those in need.

Prayer of the Day

God of all peoples, your arms reach out to embrace all those who call upon you. Teach us as disciples of your Son to love the world with compassion and constancy, that your name may be known throughout the earth, through Jesus Christ, our Savior and Lord.

Gospel Acclamation

Alleluia. Jesus preached the good news of the kingdom and cured every sickness among the people. *Alleluia.* (Matt. 4:23)

Readings and Psalm

Isaiah 56:1, 6-8

The prophet calls upon Israel to do justice in view of God's imminent intervention to save. Righteousness and obedience define who belongs to the Israelite community—not race, nationality, or any other category.

Psalm 67

Let all the peoples praise you, O God. (Ps. 67:3)

Romans 11:1-2a, 29-32

God has not rejected Israel. Rather, the call and gifts of God are irrevocable so that, while all have been disobedient, God has mercy upon all.

Matthew 15:[10-20] 21-28

Jesus teaches his disciples that true purity is a matter of the heart rather than outward religious observances. Almost immediately, this teaching is tested when a woman considered to be a religious outsider approaches him for help.

Semicontinuous Reading and Psalm

Genesis 45:1-15

Moved to tears by Judah's plea on behalf of Benjamin, Joseph declares, "I am Joseph!" and asks, "Is my father still alive?" Despite the brothers' evil intent, God used Joseph to preserve many lives at a time of famine.

Psalm 133

How good and pleasant it is to live together in unity. (Ps. 133:1)

Preface Sundays

Color Green

Prayers of Intercession

The prayers are prepared locally for each occasion. The following examples may be adapted or used as appropriate.

Confident of your care and helped by the Holy Spirit, we pray for the church, the world, and all who are in need.

A brief silence.

Lord, you gather the church to be part of your mission as ambassadors of Jesus Christ. As Jesus acknowledged the great faith of a woman from outside his people, help your church discover and find blessing in the faith of people we might reject. Lord, in your mercy,

hear our prayer.

You have blessed us with the bounty of the earth. Grant your grace to all your creatures, that the earth will flourish. Relieve waters choked by garbage, renew soils stripped of nutrients, and refresh the air all creatures need to live. Lord, in your mercy,

hear our prayer.

You call the nations to be glad and sing for joy. Let your way be known among all the nations of the world, now divided by competing interests, contending alliances, and consumed by enormous worry. Bless us and make your face shine upon all. Lord, in your mercy,
hear our prayer.

You show unexpected mercy, kindness, and generosity. We pray for those who do not have enough, for outcasts in our villages, cities, and town, and for those who need your healing (*especially*). Lord, in your mercy,
hear our prayer.

In you we live and move and have our being. Grant our congregation (*name*) grace to find our life refreshed in you. Accompany us in the rhythms of late summer. Give us rest and renewal, and strengthen us for mission in your name. Lord, in your mercy,
hear our prayer.

Here other intercessions may be offered.

Your eternal promises are more than we could ever imagine. As you gather all the saints (*especially*), join us also with them on the great day of your salvation. Lord, in your mercy,
hear our prayer.

In the certain hope that nothing can separate us from your love, we offer these prayers to you; through Jesus Christ our Lord.
Amen.

Ideas for the Day

- Nelson Rivera, in an article entitled "Freedom in Reading the Scripture," describes some of Martin Luther's approaches to interpreting the Bible. In what Rivera calls a "striking example of the boldness with which Luther handled biblical texts and interpretation," he demonstrates how Luther allows seemingly disparate passages to speak to one another by pairing the story of Jacob wrestling until daybreak with a heavenly creature and the Canaanite woman who "wrestles" with Jesus in today's gospel (*LW* 6:139). Rivera concludes, "As it turns out, this Canaanite woman—a foreigner, with no known name—is Jacob in the gospel story. Moreover, faith is not passive but active and demanding. What faith demands is the promise of God, to be fulfilled in us here and now" (*Journal of Lutheran Ethics*, January 1, 2018; elca.org/JLE/Articles/1220).

- The purity codes in Jesus' time around eating and handwashing made it easy to distinguish between the righteous and the unrighteous, the good and the bad. These days it is tempting to make the same judgments according to people's clothing choices, among other things. How do somewhat arbitrary distinctions, like clothing, make it easier to exclude people? What barriers might exist making it difficult for people to conform to these norms? Are there some norms that truly matter? Who decides?

- What happens to any wine that is left after everyone has communed? What isn't sent to be shared with the absent could be consumed by the worship leaders or poured on the ground after worship in a place where people don't walk. Pouring it into a sink is discouraged, however, because sinks drain into the sewer and it is not respectful to mix the blood of Christ with what is in the sewer. Some churches have a piscina installed in or near the sacristy. This might resemble a normal sink, but the water and leftover wine drain into the earth, not the sewer. How does your worshiping community honor any bread and wine that is not consumed during communion? How is the community's faith or piety reflected in these practices?

- Paul writes in Romans: "For the gifts and the calling of God are irrevocable" (Rom. 11:29). This might sound like good news, and it might also sound daunting or scary. When is it easy to step into the gifts and calling God has given to each of us? When would we rather decline the challenges that come with the gifts and calling?

Connections with Creation

Jesus' initial treatment of the Canaanite woman appears to be in direct contradiction to the vision in Isaiah where "foreigners . . . join themselves to the LORD" (56:6). Yet Jesus relents, and the woman's daughter is healed. In this way God "gathers . . . others . . . besides those already gathered" (Isa. 56:8). This would be a good opportunity to highlight the ways in which Christians work with interfaith partners on environmental issues in order to bring healing to their communities. Look for story examples at interfaithpowerandlight.org and greenfaith .org to see how religious communities are helping people move beyond the negative cultural and religious stereotypes of the past in order to build eco-ethical bridges of cooperation into the future. If Jesus' mind and heart can be changed, ours can too.

Let the Children Come

While there are many layers to the gospel, what's striking here is how Jesus allows himself to be changed by an experience with someone whose customs and culture are so different from his own. We could say he was testing her to make a point or testing the disciples to make a point, but perhaps it would be more fruitful to wonder with the children (with adults listening in) from the perspective of the woman. "I wonder, What was most important to the Canaanite woman? . . . to Jesus? . . . to the disciples?" How might your congregation foster a conversation that expands definitions of who is in and who is out? How can the church better recognize that the circle is wide and see our kin in the one we might at first want to disparage?

Order Now for Year B 2021

Sundays and Seasons Year B 2021

Sundays and Seasons supports comprehensive week-by-week planning with content and ideas for liturgy and music, preaching and visuals, shaped by the Revised Common Lectionary, the church year, and the assembly gathered around word and sacrament.

978-1-5064-4974-6..$39.00
(2 or more $32.00 ea.)

Sundays and Seasons: Preaching Year B 2021

Encourages and provides helps for lectionary preaching, taking into account all the readings for the day, in addition to the rest of the worship service and the day itself in the church year. Features new commentary and ideas for proclamation, contributed by practicing preachers as well as scholars, together with succinct notes on each day and its readings. Also available as an add-on subscription to sundaysandseasons.com.

978-1-5064-4980-7..$29.00

Planning Guide and Preaching Combo Pack

Purchase *Sundays and Seasons* and *Sundays and Seasons: Preaching* together, and save!

978-1-5064-4986-9..$55.00
($68.00 if purchased separately)

Worship Planning Calendar Year B 2021

A two-page per week calendar helpful for worship planners, with space to record appointments and notes for each day. New compact size, 5½" x 8½". Specially designed to complement *Sundays and Seasons*. Features the daily lectionary in *Evangelical Lutheran Worship*.

978-1-5064-4976-0..$19.00

Planning Guide and Calendar Combo Pack

Sundays and Seasons and *Worship Planning Calendar* work together to save you time and provide all you need to prepare engaging worship.

978-1-5064-4985-2..$49.00
($58.00 if purchased separately)

sundaysandseasons.com

A rich and reliable resource for worship planning, Sundays and Seasons online worship planner follows the three-year lectionary cycle and provides everything you need to support your worship ministry in one convenient location, always accessible online. Learn more at sundaysandseasons.com

AUGSBURG FORTRESS

Worship Planning Resources
Year B 2021 Order Form

To order by mail, detach, fold, and seal your completed card. Please be sure to attach postage. You can also order by calling 1-800-328-4648, faxing 1-800-722-7766, or visiting our online store at augsburgfortress.org.

SHIP TO _____

Address _____

City _____

State_____ ZIP _____

Phone _____

Email _____

BILL TO _____

Address _____

City _____

State_____ ZIP _____

Phone _____

METHOD OF PAYMENT *(select one)*

AF Account #_____

Credit Card #_____

Exp. Date_____ *Card must be valid through Oct. 2020. Products ship by Sept. 2020.*

Signature_____
Signature required on all credit card orders.

Sundays and Seasons 2021
QTY: _____ 978-1-5064-4974-6..................$39.00*
QTY: _____ SUNSEASONS.....................Standing Order

Sundays and Seasons: Preaching 2021
QTY: _____ 978-1-5064-4980-7..................$29.00*
QTY: _____ SUNSEPREAC.....................Standing Order

Planning Guide and Preaching Combo Pack 2021
QTY: _____ 978-1-5064-4986-9..................$55.00*
QTY: _____ SUNSEAPPC.....................Standing Order

Worship Planning Calendar 2021
QTY: _____ 978-1-5064-4976-0..................$19.00*
QTY: _____ WRSHPPLNCL.....................Standing Order

Planning Guide and Calendar Combo Pack 2021
QTY: _____ 978-1-5064-4985-2..................$49.00*
QTY: _____ SUNSEAWPC.....................Standing Order

Calendar of Word and Season 2021
QTY: _____ 978-1-5064-4981-4..................$10.95*
QTY: _____ CALWRDSESN.....................Standing Order

Church Year Calendar 2021
QTY: _____ 978-1-5064-4977-7..................$1.95*

Church Year Calendar 2021 PDF
ONLINE 978-1-5064-4978-4..................$9.96

Bread for the Day 2021
QTY: _____ 978-1-5064-4982-1..................$8.95*

Ritual Lectionary, Year B
QTY: _____ 978-0-8066-5611-3..................$115.00*

Study Edition Lectionary, Year B
QTY: _____ 978-0-8066-5612-0..................$27.50*

More Days for Praise
QTY: _____ 978-1-4514-9621-5..................$15.00*

* Prices are for U.S. sales only and do not include shipping. Prices subject to change.

sundays and seasons

AUGSBURG FORTRESS
Attn: Mailing Center
P.O. Box 1209
Minneapolis, MN 55440-1209

Place
Stamp
Here

Detach this card, fold it in half here, and seal the edges.

Order Now
for Year B 2021

Great gifts and useful resources for living the church's year!

Bread for the Day 2021: Daily Bible Readings and Prayers

Scripture texts for individual or group prayer based on the daily lectionary in *Evangelical Lutheran Worship*.

978-1-5064-4982-1

Quantity	1–9	10–99	100–299	300–499	500–999	1,000+
Price	$8.95	$7.16	$6.71	$6.27	$5.37	$4.48

Calendar of Word and Season Year B 2021: Liturgical Wall Calendar

Full-color calendar with room for adding your events. Features beautiful artwork and identifies church festivals, national holidays, the color of the day, and Revised Common Lectionary citations. $8^{3}/_{8}$" x $10^{7}/_{8}$". Spiral-bound and punched for hanging.

978-1-5064-4981-4

Quantity	1–11	12–49	50–99	100–499	500+
Price	$10.95	$4.50	$3.50	$3.00	$2.50

Church Year Calendar Year B 2021

Provides dates, lectionary readings, hymn of the day, and the liturgical color for each Sunday and festival. Two-sided. 11" x 8½".

978-1-5064-4977-7

Quantity	1–11	12–99	100+
Price	$1.95	$0.83	$0.75

More Days for Praise: Festivals and Commemorations in Evangelical Lutheran Worship

A guide to help you include festivals and commemorations of the lives of saints in your prayer life. This volume shows that those whom the church has lifted up are both faithful and fascinating.

978-1-4514-9621-5 .... *$15.00*

Lectionary for Worship, Ritual Edition Year B
978-0-8066-5611-3 .... *$115.00*

Lectionary for Worship, Study Edition Year B
978-0-8066-5612-0 .... *$27.50*

Shipping and Handling

Prices and Product Availability are subject to change without notice.

Sales Tax: Exempt customers must provide Augsburg Fortress with a copy of their state-issued exemption certificate prior to purchase. Customers without tax-exempt status must add applicable state and local sales tax for their area.

Shipping Charges are additional on all orders. U.S. orders (except U.S. cash orders) are assessed actual shipping charges based on standard group rates. Additional shipping charges are assessed for expedited service requests and international shipments.

Return Policy: Return Policy (U.S.): With proof of purchase, non-dated, in print product in saleable condition may be returned for credit. Please contact Sales and Service at salesandservice@augsburgfortress.org or 1-800-328-4648 for assistance if you receive items that are damaged, defective, or were shipped in error. Specific return restrictions apply to some product lines. Please contact us before returning a special order item or item shipped directly from the manufacturer. Send order returns by a secure, prepaid, traceable method to the Augsburg Fortress Distribution Center, PBD Worldwide, c/o AF Distribution, 905 Carlow Dr., Unit B, Bolingbrook, IL 60490.

* For Canadian orders, please contact Parasource at custserv@parasource.com or 1-800-263-2664.

Assembly Song
Gathering

All Are Welcome ELW 641

O God, why are you silent ELW 703

Praise to the Lord, the Almighty ELW 858/859, LLC 580,
LBW 543

Psalmody and Acclamations

Let the peoples praise you, O God/Psalm 67 TFF 7

O God, show mercy to us/Psalm 67 GTG 341

+ Alonso, Tony. "How Good It Is." SATB, pno, opt assembly, str
qrt, horn in F. GIA G-7242.

(GA) ELW 175 with proper verse for Lectionary 20.

Hymn of the Day

Healer of our every ill ELW 612, WOV 738 *HEALER OF OUR
EVERY ILL*

In Christ there is no east or west ELW 650, TFF 214, LBW 359
MCKEE

When pain of the world surrounds us ELW 704 *CALLED TO
FOLLOW*

Offering

As the grains of wheat ELW 465, WOV 705, W&P 10

We eat the bread of teaching ELW 518

Communion

Creating God, your fingers trace ELW 684, WOV 757

God, my Lord, my strength ELW 795, LBW 484

Praise, praise! You are my rock ELW 862, ASG 33

Sending

Oh, for a thousand tongues to sing ELW 886, LLC 578, LS 185,
LBW 559

We've come this far by faith ELW 633, TFF 197

Additional Assembly Songs

Hands of healing SC 25

Revealed in Christ, the word of God CBM 104

Welcome Table TFF 263

⊕ P Sosa, Pablo. "Miren que bueno/Oh, Look and Wonder" from
Este es el Día. GIA G-7021. Also ELW 649, LLC 468.

⊕ Syrian Orthodox chant. "Moran ethra hama'lain (Lord, have
mercy)." WCC Publications. Out of print. Hannelore.
Schmid@wcc-coe.org.

☼ Brown, Chris/Jason Ingram/Mack Brock/Steven Furtick/
Wade Joye. "Let Us Adore" from CCLI.

☼ Horst, Nathan. "Christ in Me" from CCLI.

☼ James, Eddie. "House of Prayer" from CCLI.

☼ James, Jonathan/Matthew Hooper. "His Kingdom Is Here"
from CCLI.

☼ La Fleur, Joanna/Chris Vacher/Steve Lensink. "Great Love of
God" from *Hallelujah.* c4churchworship.com.

☼ Rand, Lenora/Gary Rand. "Lovely Needy People – Kyrie" from
All Belong Here. themany1.bandcamp.com.

Music for the Day
Choral

Courtney, Craig. "Praise Him!" 2 pt, pno, opt br qrt. BP BP1350.

♫ Haugen, Marty. "Healer of Our Every Ill." 2 pt, pno, C inst. GIA
G-3478.

P Hellerman, Fred/Fran Minkoff/arr. David Cherwien. "O Healing River" from *To God Will I Sing: Vocal Solos for the
Church Year.* Solo, kybd. AFP 9780800674335.

P Kohrs, Jonathan. "When to Our World the Savior Came." SATB,
pno. AFP 9781506452548.

P White, Clayton. "I Cried All Night Long." SATB, a cap. AFP
9781506456751.

Children's Choir

Burrows, Mark. "You Are Welcome Here." U/2 pt, pno or gtr.
CG CGA1525.

P Patterson, Mark. "Gloria Deo (Round)" from *The Joy of Part
Singing.* U/2 pt, pno. CG CGBK67.

P Wold, Wayne. "Jesus, Be Our Bread." U/2 pt, kybd. GIA G-5439.

Keyboard / Instrumental

♫ Corl, Matthew H. "McKee" from *Oxford Hymn Settings for
Organists: Autumn Festivals.* Org. OXF 9780193400689.

Fedak, Alfred V. "Variations on Beach Spring." Org. SEL
160-641.

P ♫ Organ, Anne Krentz. "Healer of Our Every Ill" from
Piano Reflections on Hymns of Healing. Pno. AFP
9781506448060.

P ♫ Wilson, Terry D. "When Pain of the World Surrounds
Us" from *Creative Spirit: Piano Settings.* Pno. AFP
9781451479607.

Handbell

Biery, James. "In Silent Pain the Eternal Son." 3-5 oct, L2. GIA
G-8943.

♫ Larson, Lloyd. "In Christ There Is No East or West." 3-5 oct,
L2+. BP HB584.

♫ McAninch, Diane. "Healer of Our Every Ill." 2-3 oct hb, opt 2
oct hc, L2. GIA G-7286.

Thursday, August 20
Bernard, Abbot of Clairvaux, died 1153

Bernard was a Cistercian monk who became an abbot of great
spiritual depth. He was a mystical writer deeply devoted to
the humanity of Christ who emphasized the inner human

⊕ = global song   ♫ = relates to hymn of the day   + = semicontinuous psalm

☼ = praise song   P = available in Prelude Music Planner

experience of prayer and contemplation. He was critical of one of the foremost theologians of the day, Peter Abelard, because he believed Abelard's approach to faith was too rational and did not provide sufficient room for mystery. Bernard's devotional writings are still read today. His sermon on the Song of Solomon treats that Old Testament book as an allegory of Christ's love for humanity. Bernard wrote several hymns that are still sung today in translation, including "Jesus, the very thought of you" (ELW 754).

August 23, 2020
Time after Pentecost — Lectionary 21

In Isaiah the people are advised to look to their spiritual ancestors as the rock from which they were hewn. Jesus declares that the church will be built on the rock of Peter's bold confession of faith. God's word of reconciliation and God's mercy are keys to the church's mission. Paul urges us to not be conformed to this world but to offer our bodies as a living sacrifice, using our individual gifts to build up the body of Christ. From the table we go forth to offer our spiritual worship through word and deed.

Prayer of the Day

O God, with all your faithful followers of every age, we praise you, the rock of our life. Be our strong foundation and form us into the body of your Son, that we may gladly minister to all the world, through Jesus Christ, our Savior and Lord.

Gospel Acclamation

Alleluia. You are the Messiah, the Son of the living God. *Alleluia.* (Matt. 16:16)

Readings and Psalm

Isaiah 51:1-6

Just as God had called Abraham and Sarah and given them many descendants, so now God offers comfort to Zion. God's deliverance will come soon and will never end.

Psalm 138

O LORD, your steadfast love endures forever. (Ps. 138:8)

Romans 12:1-8

In response to God's merciful activity, we are to worship by living holistic, God-pleasing lives. Our values and viewpoints are not molded by the time in which we live but are transformed by the Spirit's renewing work. God's grace empowers different forms of service among Christians, but all forms of ministry function to build up the body of Christ.

Matthew 16:13-20

At a climactic point in Jesus' ministry, God reveals to Peter that Jesus is "the Messiah, the Son of the living God," and Jesus responds with the promise of a church that will overcome the very gates of Hades.

Semicontinuous Reading and Psalm

Exodus 1:8—2:10

The brave Hebrew midwives defied Pharaoh to save many infants from death. When the mother of Moses placed him in a basket in the Nile, the daughter of Pharaoh found him, adopted him, and raised him. Moses' sister and mother also played crucial roles in this drama.

Psalm 124

We have escaped like a bird from the snare of the fowler. (Ps. 124:7)

Preface   Sundays

Color   Green

Prayers of Intercession

The prayers are prepared locally for each occasion. The following examples may be adapted or used as appropriate.

Confident of your care and helped by the Holy Spirit, we pray for the church, the world, and all who are in need.
A brief silence.

Lord our rock, you are our foundation in Jesus Christ, your Son, whom we confess as the living God. Prepare your church for its mission in bearing witness to Christ, both here at home and throughout the world. Lord, in your mercy,
hear our prayer.

You call forth praises from the far reaches of the universe to the smallest of creatures. Join our songs to theirs, that a spirit of praise and thanksgiving will arouse us to cherish this wondrous home you give us. Lord, in your mercy,
hear our prayer.

All the kings of the earth shall praise you, O Lord. Direct the leaders of countries, legislators and magistrates, mayors and councils, to walk in your ways. Help leaders regard those in need with mercy and fulfill your loving purposes in the governance of peoples. Lord, in your mercy,

hear our prayer.

Though we walk in the midst of trouble, you preserve us, deliver us, and fulfill your purpose for us. According to your steadfast love, grant healing and wholeness to those who are bereaved, in trouble or adversity, or sick and in need of care (*especially*). Lord, in your mercy,

hear our prayer.

You call us into this community (*name*), in which we, though many, are one in Christ. May we recognize in ourselves and in one another the unique gifts you have given us for the building up of the church for the sake of the world. Lord, in your mercy,

hear our prayer.

Here other intercessions may be offered.

You are the everlasting Rock from which we were hewn, and you restore your people to joy and gladness. In blessed memory and hope, we thank you for the lives of our beloved dead (*especially*). Bring us with them to our heavenly home. Lord, in your mercy,

hear our prayer.

In the certain hope that nothing can separate us from your love, we offer these prayers to you; through Jesus Christ our Lord.

Amen.

Ideas for the Day

- In the time of Jesus, a grotto where the god Pan was worshiped was located prominently in Caesarea Philippi. On the cliff walls adjacent to that grotto were any number of niches holding images of other gods. This was a place where many different gods were worshiped. In this context, Jesus asks the disciples, "But who do you say that I am?" (Matt. 16:15). Peter's confession of faith is even more powerful because of where Jesus and his disciples are gathered.
- Jesus tells Peter he will be given the keys of the kingdom of heaven. Keys and locks actually date back some six thousand years. They have been made of wood, iron, steel, and more. From the beginning, keys and locks were meant to provide safety and security. You can learn about both locks and keys at historyofkeys.com. How might the history of keys inform proclamation today?
- In the second reading Paul admonishes the people, "For by the grace given to me I say to everyone among you not to think of yourself more highly than you ought to think" (Rom. 12:3). While thinking too highly of oneself is an issue for some, there are plenty of people who do not think of themselves highly enough. The challenge this day is to

take Paul's words and offer a balance to them. What a joy to remind people that everyone has gifts that are valued.

- In the reading from Romans we are invited to "be transformed by the renewing of [our] minds, so that [we] may discern what is the will of God—what is good and acceptable and perfect" (Rom. 12:2). Many of the clichés that are intended to comfort people in difficult times do more harm than good, suggesting that God's will is anything but good, acceptable, or perfect: "God needed another angel" or "The Lord works in mysterious ways." How might the measuring stick of "good, acceptable, and perfect" be used when talking about the will of God? Do we even dare point to something as the will of God?

Connections with Creation

"Look to the rock from which you were hewn," Isaiah reminds the Israelites (51:1). In the gospel reading, Jesus renames Simon "Peter," meaning "rock." For many cultures, sacred rock formations are places of deep spiritual connection to the earth and the divine. Places like Garden of the Gods in Colorado and Pipestone National Monument in Minnesota have fascinating rock formations and quarries that are revered by native tribes. Yet places like Bears Ears Monument in Utah and other national lands are under threat for gas and oil development. How can we "look . . . to the quarry from which [we] were dug" (51:1) if the place is desecrated or destroyed? One way that Christians can assist native peoples is by advocating for the protection of these national parks, monuments, and sacred places.

Let the Children Come

Before Jesus' death and resurrection, we hear Peter's confession: "You are the Messiah, the Son of the living God" (Matt. 16:16). Jesus tells us that it is upon "this rock," the rock of faith, that the church will be built. Rocks provide a solid foundation. What's funny about this particular rock, the rock of faith, is that it changes as we change (1 Cor. 13:11). As we grow up, how we understand God, faith, community, and church will change. This Sunday, then, might be a good opportunity to invite older youth to give a testimony about how their faith has changed since confirmation. Work with them on it, and help them to notice what you've seen in them and to speak what they maybe have never said aloud. Invite the children up close when the testimony is being given.

Assembly Song
Gathering

Lord Jesus Christ, be present now   ELW 527, LBW 253

We all are one in mission   ELW 576, WOV 755

We are all one in Christ/Somos uno en Cristo   ELW 643,
    TFF 221, LLC 470, LS 130

Psalmody and Acclamations

Feeley, Ephrem. "In the Presence of Your Holy Angels." SAB, cant, assembly, kybd, cl. GIA G-9622.

Mayernik, Luke. "Twenty-First Sunday in Ordinary Time A" from 5GP.

+ Weber, Paul D. "Psalm 124," Refrain 1, from PSCY. (GA) ELW 175 with proper verse for Lectionary 21.

Hymn of the Day

Built on a rock ELW 652, LBW 365 KIRKEN DEN ER ET GAMMELT HUS

There's a wideness in God's mercy ELW 587 ST. HELENA ELW 588, LBW 290 LORD, REVIVE US

We sing to you, O God ELW 791 LOVE UNKNOWN

Offering

Bread of life, our host and meal ELW 464

Now the silence ELW 460, LBW 205

Communion

Faith of our fathers ELW 812/813, LBW 500

Take my life, that I may be ELW 583/685, LLC 570, LBW 406

We sing to you, O God ELW 791

Sending

Alleluia! Voices raise ELW 828

Sing praise to God, the highest good ELW 871, LBW 542

Additional Assembly Songs

Praised be the rock TFF 290

Seek ye first WOV 783, W&P 122, TFF 149, H82 711, GTG 175

⊕ Tú diste a Israel/God, with a mighty hand LLC 476

⊕ Kihaya melody. "Psalm 136" from *Halle, Halle: We Sing the World Round.* Solo, SATB. CG CGC42.

⊕ Swahili trad./arr. J. Nathan Corbitt. "Mwamba ni Yesu/The Rock Is Jesus" from *Halle, Halle: We Sing the World Round.* Solo, SATB. CG CGC42.

☼ Binion, David/Joshua Dufrene/William McDowell. "Standing" from CCLI.

☼ Lavik, Jadon. "His Name Shall Be Called" from CCLI.

☼ Lindsey, Aaron W./Tina Campbell. "I Call You Jesus" from CCLI.

☼ McDowell, William. "Spoken" from CCLI.

☼ Paris, Antonne. "Gloria a Dios solo" from CCLI.

☼ Yang, Josiah. "Take All I Am" from *Breakthroughs.* generations.sg.

Music for the Day

Choral

P ♫ Keesecker, Thomas. "We Sing to You, O God." 2 pt mxd, pno. AFP 9781506414027.

P Martinson, Joel. "By All Your Saints" from *Augsburg Easy Choirbook,* vol. 2. 2 pt mxd, org. AFP 9780800677510.

P Mendelssohn, Felix/arr. Sue Ellen Page. "For the Mountains Shall Depart" from *Elijah.* 2 pt mxd, org, ob. GIA G-8004.

P Shaw, Timothy. "How Can I Keep from Singing." U/2 pt, pno. HOP C5799.

Children's Choir

Hogan, Christopher. "God Is Here with Me." U/2 pt, pno. CG CGA1483.

Meyer, Daniel C. "With My Whole Heart." U, kybd. GIA G-5116.

P Shaw, Timothy. "How Can I Keep from Singing?" U/2 pt, opt C inst. HOP C5799.

Keyboard / Instrumental

P Callahan, Charles. "Prelude on Two Hymntunes (Aurelia and Nicaea)" from *We Are Gathered: 12 Hymn Meditations for Piano.* Pno. MSM 15-760.

P ♫ Held, Wilbur. "Kirken den er et gammelt hus" from *Augsburg Organ Library: November.* Org. AFP 9780800658960.

P ♫ Miller, Aaron David. "Built on a Rock" from *Chorale Preludes for Piano in Traditional Styles.* Pno. AFP 9780800679033.

P ♫ Wold, Wayne L. "My Song Is Love Unknown" from *Awake My Heart: Organ Suites and Settings.* Org. AFP 9781506447964.

Handbell

♫ Helman, Michael. "Built on a Rock." 3-5 oct, L3. ALF 00-19006.

Ingram, Bill. "The Solid Rock." 3-5 oct, L3-. Ring Out Press RO3340.

Page, Anna Laura. "The Solid Rock." 3-5 oct hb, opt 3 oct hc, L3. CG CGB269.

Monday, August 24
Bartholomew, Apostle

Bartholomew is mentioned as one of Jesus' disciples in Matthew, Mark, and Luke. The list in John does not include him but rather Nathanael. These two are often assumed to be the same person. Except for his name on these lists of the Twelve, little is known. Some traditions say Bartholomew preached in India or Armenia following the resurrection. In art, Bartholomew is pictured holding a flaying knife to indicate the manner in which he was killed.

⊕ = global song   ♫ = relates to hymn of the day   + = semicontinuous psalm
☼ = praise song   P = available in Prelude Music Planner

Friday, August 28
Augustine, Bishop of Hippo, died 430

Augustine was one of the greatest theologians of the Western church. Born in North Africa, he was a philosophy student in Carthage, where he later became a teacher of rhetoric. Much of his young life was a debauched one. As an adult he came under the influence of Ambrose, the bishop of Milan, and through him came to see Christianity as a religion appropriate for a philosopher. Augustine was baptized by Ambrose at the Easter Vigil in 387. He was ordained four years later and made bishop of Hippo in 396. Augustine was a defender of the Christian faith and argued, against the Donatists, that the holiness of the church did not depend on the holiness of its members, particularly the clergy, but that holiness comes from Christ, the head of the church. Augustine's autobiography, *Confessions*, tells of his slow move toward faith and includes the line "Late have I loved thee."

Friday, August 28
Moses the Black, monk, martyr, died around 400

A man of great strength and rough character, Moses the Black was converted to Christian faith toward the close of the fourth century. Prior to his conversion he had been a thief and a leader of a gang of robbers. The story of his conversion is unknown, but eventually he became a desert monk at Skete. The change in his heart and life had a profound impact on his native Ethiopia. He was murdered when Berber bandits attacked his monastery.

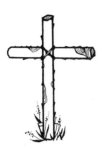

August 30, 2020
Time after Pentecost — Lectionary 22

The prophet Jeremiah speaks of the incurable wound of his suffering yet finds in God's words the delight of his heart. When Peter doesn't grasp Jesus' words about suffering, Jesus tells the disciples they will find their lives in losing them. Such sacrificial love is described by Paul when he urges us to associate with the lowly and not repay evil with evil. In worship we gather as a community that we might offer ourselves for the sake of our suffering world.

Prayer of the Day

O God, we thank you for your Son, who chose the path of suffering for the sake of the world. Humble us by his example, point us to the path of obedience, and give us strength to follow your commands, through Jesus Christ, our Savior and Lord.

Gospel Acclamation

Alleluia. May the God of our Lord Jesus Christ enlighten the eyes of our hearts, so that we may know the hope to which God has called us. *Alleluia.* (Eph. 1:17, 18)

Readings and Psalm
Jeremiah 15:15-21

Jeremiah's delight in the word of the Lord is contradicted by the heaviness of God's hand upon him and God's seeming unfaithfulness. God's tough love to Jeremiah says that if he repents, he will be allowed to continue in his strenuous ministry. Jeremiah is strengthened by the simple words, "I am with you."

Psalm 26:1-8

Your love is before my eyes; I have walked faithfully with you. (Ps. 26:3)

Romans 12:9-21

Paul presents benchmarks for faithful relationships with Christians and non-Christians. Love is the unflagging standard of our behavior. When we encounter evil, we do not resort to its tactics but seek to overcome it with good. While Christians cannot control the actions and attitudes of others, we seek to live at peace with all people.

Matthew 16:21-28

After Peter confesses that Jesus is "the Messiah, the Son of the living God" (16:16), Jesus reveals the ultimate purpose of his ministry. These words prove hard to accept, even for a disciple whom Jesus has called a "rock."

Semicontinuous Reading and Psalm
Exodus 3:1-15

Moses experienced the call of God when God appeared to him in a bush that burned but was not consumed. When Moses expressed his unworthiness, God promised to be with him. When Moses objected that people would demand to know God's name, God revealed his personal name, Yahweh (I AM WHO I AM), or the LORD. Israel discovered God's true identity when God took them out of Egypt.

Psalm 105:1-6, 23-26, 45b

Make known the deeds of the LORD among the peoples. Hallelujah! (Ps. 105:1, 45)

Preface   Sundays

Color   Green

Prayers of Intercession

The prayers are prepared locally for each occasion. The following examples may be adapted or used as appropriate.

Confident of your care and helped by the Holy Spirit, we pray for the church, the world, and all who are in need.

A brief silence.

God of faithfulness, you bid your people to follow Jesus. Set the mind of your church on divine things. Grant us trust in you, that we lose our lives for the sake of Christ and thereby discover joy in life through him. Lord, in your mercy,
hear our prayer.

God of wonder, the earth is yours and all that is in it. Heal your creation and give us eyes to see the world as you do. As the seasons change, pattern the rhythm of our lives in harmony with all creation. Lord, in your mercy,
hear our prayer.

God of all nations, you call us to live peaceably with all. Give us ears to hear one another, even those we name as enemies. Fill all leaders with mercy and understanding, that they advocate and genuinely care for those who are poor and most vulnerable in their communities. Lord, in your mercy,
hear our prayer.

God of salvation, you promise to deliver us. Give those who suffer a strong sense of your presence and love. Accompany those who are uncertain, raise the spirits of those who are despairing, and heal the sick (*especially*). Lord, in your mercy,
hear our prayer.

God of community, you call us to rejoice in hope, be patient in suffering, and persevere in prayer. Make our congregation a workshop of your love. When we quarrel, bring reconciliation. Help us overcome evil with good. Lord, in your mercy,
hear our prayer.

Here other intercessions may be offered.

God of all grace, you give us everlasting life. In love we recall your holy ones who now live in your undying light (*especially*). In our remembering, give us a foretaste of the feast to come. Lord, in your mercy,
hear our prayer.

In the certain hope that nothing can separate us from your love, we offer these prayers to you; through Jesus Christ our Lord. **Amen.**

Ideas for the Day

- Contemporary Christian artist TobyMac has a song called "Lose My Soul" (*Portable Sounds*, Forefront Records, 2007), based on Matthew 16:25-26. The music video (youtube.com/watch?v=coHKdhAZ9hU) is set in a pawn shop with various people selling different items (forfeiting their lives) in exchange for money. Watch the video for the twist at the end. Even if we don't literally sell items at a pawn shop, how often do we "sell out"? How often do we give in to what our culture expects? How often do we seek approval, acceptance, or accolades but give up ourselves in the process? This is especially a struggle for teens and young adults. The only good way of losing ourselves is for the sake of Christ. He gives us our true identity.

- The cross is the central image and symbol of our faith. Many church buildings display crosses and many Christians wear the cross as jewelry. We like the idea of the cross as something comforting, but when we see how disturbing it is—that it involves "losing" our lives—we probably echo Peter's words: "God forbid it, Lord!" (Matt. 16:22). If taking up our cross means dying to ourselves—meaning, dying to our own flawed notions of worth, connection, or work, and living into our true identity as unique children of God—then what we "sacrifice" is not necessarily something good or desirable. The least healthy things in our lives are often the hardest things to sacrifice because we feel comfortable with them or because they are self-medication for pain we don't want to face or bring to Jesus. We may not even *like* them, but we do them because the truth, the reality, and the healing of the cross seem more painful.

- When Jesus says, "Get behind me, Satan!" (Matt. 16:23), it is obviously a rebuke to Peter. However, it has a twofold meaning: 1) Get out of my way. 2) Get behind me and follow me. Sometimes we still think we know better than Jesus. We want him to follow our lead and do things the way we want. However, our proper place as disciples is in following him. Christian hip-hop artist Lecrae has a song called "Background" (*Rehab*, Reach Records, 2010; youtube.com/watch?v=LHnZRZiCYHE), in which he talks about how we are called to play the background parts for Jesus. He is the star. We are not.

Connections with Creation

Read from an individualistic, human-centered frame, it can be puzzling to know how to faithfully enact Jesus' call for his followers to lose their lives in order to find them. Few of us are going to literally give up our heart-pumping, oxygen-breathing lives for the sake of the gospel. However, read with an ecological worldview in which the workings of the natural world remind us that all of life is interconnected, Christ-followers might hear a call to die to the sins of individualism and disconnection in order to find new life in the interdependent body of Christ. The life we lose in the cross is one of loneliness and isolation; the life we find is one of mutuality and delight. Taking up a cross is a communal act that members of the body of Christ do together in order to witness to God's transforming love in a way that is more powerful than what any one of us could do on our own.

Let the Children Come

In today's gospel story, Jesus tells his disciples that he is going to die. Peter does not like it and objects. Jesus responds by saying that anyone who wants to be his follower must take up their cross and follow him. Look around the worship space. How many crosses can you find? Where do you see them? Some may be easy to spot, like a processional cross or a large cross hanging at the front of the worship space. Where else? Look at Bibles, hymnals, banners, paraments, stained-glass windows, artwork, carvings, on the baptismal font, in the worship folder, on the pastor's vestments, on the choir's robes, people's jewelry, and other places. Invite someone to carry one of the (portable) crosses you have found, and play Follow the Leader around the worship space. When is it easy to follow Jesus? When is it hard?

Assembly Song
Gathering

Come, follow me, the Savior spake ELW 799, LBW 455
Let streams of living justice ELW 710
O Jesus, I have promised ELW 810, LBW 503

Psalmody and Acclamations

Messner, Sally. "Psalm 26:1-8" from PWA.
Warner, Steven C. "Harbor of My Heart" from PAS 16B.
+ Pelz, Walter L. "Psalm 105:1-6, 23-26, 45b" from PWA.
(GA) ELW 175 with proper verse for Lectionary 22.

Hymn of the Day

Lord Jesus, you shall be my song/Jésus, je voudrais te chanter
    ELW 808 LES PETITES SOEURS
Take up your cross, the Savior said ELW 667 BOURBON
    LBW 398 NUN LASST UNS DEN LEIB BEGRABEN
You have come down to the lakeshore ELW 817, WOV 784,
    TFF 154, LLC 560 PESCADOR DE HOMBRES

Offering

All who hunger, gather gladly ELW 461
Now the silence ELW 460, LBW 205

Communion

Let us ever walk with Jesus ELW 802, LBW 487
Lord, take my hand and lead me ELW 767, LBW 333
Will you come and follow me ELW 798, W&P 137

Sending

Praise and thanks and adoration ELW 783, LBW 470
Send me, Jesus ELW 549, TFF 245

Additional Assembly Songs

By grace God calls us into life CBM 64
Step by Step W&P 132
What does the Lord require SC 56, GTG 70
🌐 Santo, santo, santo, santo ELW 762
🌐 Jacobson-Drozi, M., "Hinei ma tov/How Good and Pleasant It Is" from *Sing the Circle Wide: Songs of Faith from Around the World.* Kanata Centre for Worship and Global Song 9780973059359.
☼ DiMare, Alex. "Nothing Can Separate" from *Know the Truth.* foursquareworship.org.
☼ Harvie, Callum/Eby Corydon/Nick Herbert. "Fearless Abandon" from CCLI.
☼ Leonard, David/Don Chaffer/Leslie Jordan. "Wake Up" from CCLI.
☼ Santistevan, David. "All for Jesus" from CCLI.
☼ Williams, Ryan. "All for the One Who Saved Me" from CCLI.
☼ Zschech, Darlene/Leeland Mooring/William Casey Moore. "Beloved" from CCLI.

Music for the Day
Choral

Cherwien, David M. "Prayer for Peace." 2 pt mxd, org. MSM 50-9209.
di Lasso, Orlando. "Qui vult venire post me" from *Cantiones darum vocum.* TB, a cap. CPDL (various versions).
P Engelsdorfer, Amy Lynne. "What Wondrous Love Is This." SATB, pno. AFP 9781506445779.
P Proulx, Richard. "Weary of All Trumpeting" from *The Augsburg Choirbook.* SAB, org. AFP 9780800656782.

Children's Choir

P Burrows, Mark. "Cooperate" from *Again, I Say Rejoice!* U, pno or gtr. CG CGC56.
Dietterich, Philip R. "Come One, Come All, Come Follow." U, kybd. CG CGA553.
P Patterson, Mark. "Let All God's Children Sing" from *ChildrenSing with Instruments.* U/2 pt, pno, opt perc. AFP 9780800620349.

🌐 = global song ♫ = relates to hymn of the day + = semicontinuous psalm
☼ = praise song P = available in Prelude Music Planner

247

Keyboard / Instrumental

P Bottomley, Greg. "Blest Be the Tie That Binds" from *Piano Sunday Morning*, vol. 2. Pno. AFP 9781451462654.

P ♫ Cherwien, David. "Lord Jesus, You Shall Be My Song" from *Lord, Thee I Love: Hymn Settings for Organ*. Org. AFP 9781506426372.

Manz, Paul. "Seelenbräutigam" from *Augsburg Organ Library: Lent*. Org. AFP 9780800658977.

P ♫ Roberts, Al. "Pescador de hombres" from *We Belong to God: Piano Settings of Folk Tunes*. Pno. AFP 9781451451801.

Handbell

McAninch, Diane. "Lift High the Cross." 2-3 oct, L2-. HOP 2357.

Moklebust, Cynthia. "Jesus Shall Reign" from *Joyfully Ring*. 3-5 oct, L1+. CG CGB1062. 2-3 oct, CGB1061.

♫ Rose, William. "Lord, You Have Come to the Lakeshore." 3-5 oct hb, opt 3 oct hc, tr, perc, gtr. L3. GIA G-7036. Inst parts, G-7036INST.

Wednesday, September 2
Nikolai Frederik Severin Grundtvig, bishop, renewer of the church, died 1872

Grundtvig was one of two principal Danish theologians of the nineteenth century; the other was Søren Kierkegaard. Grundtvig's ministry as a parish pastor had a difficult start. He was officially censured after his first sermon, though he did receive approval a year later to be ordained. He served with his father for two years but was unable to receive a call for seven years after that. In 1826 he was forced to resign after he attacked the notion that Christianity was merely a philosophical idea rather than God's revelation made known to us in Christ and through word and sacrament. This belief would be a hallmark of Grundtvig's writing. He spent his last thirty-three years as a chaplain at a home for elderly women. From his university days he was convinced that poetry spoke to the human spirit better than prose. He wrote more than a thousand hymns, including "God's word is our great heritage" (ELW 509).

♫ = relates to hymn of the day
P = available in Prelude Music Planner
248

Autumn

Preparing for Autumn

Preaching

Autumn brings a return to school and the resumption of a fuller schedule of congregational activities. It's an opportune time to wonder where we stand before God. What is it that God wants from us? How can we be shaped again and again by God's word in our worshiping assemblies? What is this life with God that Jesus came to bring?

As fall rhythms return, in addition to backpack blessings or lifting up various people's occupations in prayer, *Evangelical Lutheran Worship*'s "Affirmation of Christian Vocation" could be used at a sermon's beginning or conclusion to punctuate the commitment to living a life of faith together. And preaching could be framed from this question in the rite: "Will you endeavor to pattern your life on the Lord Jesus Christ . . . all the days of your life?" (p. 84).

In the gospels, Jesus tells a series of parables to describe this life with God that in Matthew is called "the kingdom of heaven." In Jesus' parables we find that mercy meets justice head on. In one parable, a king is the model of unexpected forgiveness for a great debt (Lectionary 24, September 13). In another, a landowner hiring day laborers pays the same wage to all, no matter what time of day they began their work (Lectionary 25, September 20). And in yet another, a king extends a wedding invitation to those in the streets when others more likely to respond reject the initial invitation (Lectionary 28, October 11). Jesus' stories surprise his listeners, causing them to rethink their place.

Effective and faithful preaching captures the surprise that God's ways are not our ways. God surprises those who are on the *outside* and invites them in. In what ways have we found ourselves on the margins, or noticed others who are neglected? God also surprises those who are on the *inside*, confronting them with their privilege. In what ways have we exploited our status at the expense of others? In Philippians, Paul the apostle puzzles about his own elevated station in life as a Pharisee, but then rethinks everything that might be considered "gain" now as "loss," "because of the surpassing value of knowing Christ Jesus my Lord" (Phil. 3:7-8; Lectionary 27, October 4).

Classic Lutheran preaching of law and gospel pairs well with autumn's readings. In preaching the law, we find ourselves tangled in a web of judgment and cannot make our way out. We feel convicted. In preaching the gospel, we recognize that Christ's death and resurrection, his teaching, and his pattern of life break open the ways of God's mercy and forgiveness to those who need it (which is all of us).

Mercy might be the joyful refrain for our communal lives with God. We can laugh at Jonah, and at ourselves, as we say along with the reluctant prophet, "I knew that you are a gracious God and merciful, slow to anger, and abounding in steadfast love, and ready to relent from punishing" (Jonah 4:2; Lectionary 25, September 20). Can we imagine a church named "The Church of Second Chances" (or third, fourth, fifth, sixth, or seventh)? Are there stories you can tell or invite others to tell about starting over that might be connected to renewal of ministries in your congregation? In those stories, and in the readings that shape this season, we can come to realize that the adage "The church is a hospital for sinners, not a museum for saints" is just right for us!

Intercessory Prayer

The readings for September and October touch on mutual forgiveness, laboring in the vineyard, loving God and neighbor, service, and who is really doing the will of God. Put that together with the fact that the school year and the congregation's program year are newly begun, and it might make sense to emphasize the theme of vocation in the intercessory prayers. All of the months between Pentecost and Advent are in some sense about living out our callings, our mission in the world. The new beginnings of the early fall are especially a time when we may consider who we're called to be and what we're called to do.

If you have laypeople who craft the petitions each week, suggest to them that most petitions could be written with a two-part structure: asking God to do something about a concern, and praying for people (categories or named individuals) who are called to address that concern, either officially by job role or less officially (such as people who demonstrate or volunteer, or people who have to deal with a situation by virtue of their life circumstances). This shouldn't have to make the petitions excessively long. Instead, the focus on praying in each petition for one group of people with a relevant calling can make the petitions more specific and vivid. "Protect people who have fled their unsafe home country and are trying to make a new life here. Support the folks of Lutheran Social

Services who are helping to resettle them." "Make our schools, playgrounds, and online spaces safe for the children who gather there. Support kids and adults who speak out against bullying and value kindness more than popularity."

In the Summer section we discussed having people in the congregation speak aloud the names of persons or places in a category mentioned in the petition. In fall, some of these categories could relate directly to specific vocations. For instance, godparents could name their godchildren. Caregivers could name the persons they care for. Kids could name adults who show them how to do stuff: teachers, coaches, scout leaders. People undergoing medical treatment could name doctors and other medical professionals. Anyone could name political leaders, sheriffs or police commissioners, judges or justices.

You could choose a vocational group within the congregation each week, people who share a certain relational, occupational, or volunteer calling. That group could be asked to contribute to a petition in the prayers. The person writing the prayers could contact them the week before and ask them, "From your point of view as a [scientist, stepparent, farmer, school athlete, IT person, food service worker, activist, artist, caregiver for an elderly person], what does your calling make you aware of that we need to pray about?" Write a petition based on what they say, and identify the petition as coming from people with that calling.

Assembly Song

Autumn brings us back into what some might consider the normal rhythm of life. School has started, regular programming has begun, choirs are back in session, and the excitement of a new year is upon us. Take advantage of this energy and enthusiasm and fire up your musicians. Make a list of every musician in your congregation, and then try to use every single person this fall. If you have a beginning band or orchestra student, have them join in on a simple hymn to build confidence and trust. Tap that newly retired musician who has more time to attend rehearsals. Spend some time this autumn doing inventory and using all your resources! Start small if you haven't done this before. And if you aren't sure how best to use an instrumentalist, just ask them; chances are they can help you!

The last time we worked our way through the year A lectionary we were busily preparing for the 500th anniversary of the Reformation. Now beyond that milestone and those celebrations, we can explore other themes in this season that we might have missed or set aside three years ago. For example, the assembly's song this season might center on vocation, creation, stewardship, or love.

The energy and recharge of autumn make this the perfect time to explore some of the lesser used and known hymnody in *Evangelical Lutheran Worship*. For example, look closely at the global music in each thematic section, and consider teaching an unknown hymn to your assembly. Reach outside your comfort zone and ask for help in leading an unfamiliar musical style. Have the choir, band, or even a soloist offer it the first week as a prelude. Then build each week to include the assembly as able. It is wonderful to repeat a song over several weeks, and it builds trust and partnership between the song leaders and assembly—just try it! Autumn is also a perfect time to harness fresh energy and teach the assembly to sing in a language other than its primary one. *Evangelical Lutheran Worship* contains many hymns with one or more stanzas (provided phonetically) in a language other than English.

The stewardship theme present in many autumn lectionary texts makes this a good season to sing an offering hymn, especially if that is not your normal practice. The communion table may be set as the assembly sings a song of feasting and abundance such as "Let us go now to the banquet" (ELW 523) or "The trumpets sound, the angels sing" (ELW 531). If these are unfamiliar, what a perfect season for the assembly to learn the notes, words, and rhythms. Keep it simple and highlight the melody as you start; then add percussion, perhaps inviting all the children forward after the sharing of the peace and giving them egg shakers or simple percussion instruments (even sets of keys from other worshipers) as they surround the table and participate in the excitement and action of the feast.

Autumn is generally accompanied by a return to regular educational and faith formation programming for children, youth, and adults. Consider including in worship some beloved Sunday school songs/hymns that have been passed down for generations, as well as songs that might have been used in previous years. Let the children teach a beloved Sunday school song. If that isn't possible, or your congregation doesn't have a Sunday school, everyone loves to sing "Jesus loves me!" (ELW 595).

Worship Space

September and October bring about a shifting of gears for families with school-age children, for programmatic ministries in the church, and in the outside environment especially in northern climates. Reflect this shift; reconfigure the worship space if you downsized or upsized seating for the summer. Reset music areas to signal that choirs that have been on break are back in session.

The green season, liturgically, might be feeling long. Find ways to refresh the space. If you have more than one set of green paraments, change them out at the beginning of September. If you have a quilting group, ask them to create an altar parament using various shades of green fabric.

If you have a back-to-school Sunday or a blessing of teachers and students, plan for some visual enhancement. Ask educators to bring their lesson plan books (or another symbol of their role) and kids to bring their backpacks to worship. Have students and teachers stand with their backpacks and school materials as you pray for them. Or call up students and teachers for a prayer and final blessing at the sending, and then have them recess during the sending hymn carrying their school items, representing their heading out into the world and the new school year. Repurpose the popular Dakota Road "Kyrie" from Holy Communion Setting Eight (*ELW*, pp. 184-185) as a sending hymn for the recessional ("Kyrie eleison, on our world and on our way. Kyrie eleison, every day").

Labor/Labour Day is a wonderful opportunity to give thanks to God for the gift of work and purpose. Invite worshipers to pin a business card or a note card describing what they do for paid or unpaid work onto a bulletin board. Invite children and youth to add their vocations (student, household helper, volunteer, babysitter, caregiver of pets, school newspaper). Invite those who are retired to share the ways in which they continue to live out their vocations. Give thanks for all the work listed on the board that gives us purpose and meaning, a way to provide for our families and contribute to the welfare of our communities.

The gospel readings for the last two Sundays in September and the first Sunday in October include three different parables, all set in vineyards. Bring in a potted grapevine or other vine-growing plant as a visual for these three weeks. If you live in an area where wine is produced, use local wine on these Sundays for holy communion (if you don't already do this year-round).

The commemoration of Francis of Assisi (October 4) falls on a Sunday this year. Invite people to bring pictures of their pets to worship and provide a way to display them. Include an icon or other artwork depicting St. Francis if you have one. Prayer petitions can include thanksgiving for all of God's creatures, including our pets.

If you celebrate affirmation of baptism/confirmation on Reformation Sunday, visually center the font and table. Gather the students around the baptismal font for the affirmation of baptism, and then invite them to gather around the table during the eucharistic liturgy. Reformation Sunday can also be a wonderful day to give first Bibles to children. When you call the children up and present the Bibles, share how Martin Luther was passionate about putting the word of God into the hands of the people.

Seasonal Checklist

- If you are returning to a school-year worship and education schedule, update websites, social media, newspaper listings, answering machine messages, outdoor signs, and internal publications such as a newsletter.
- If a blessing of teachers and students will be held, see possible forms in the seasonal rites section (p. 255).
- Some congregations present Bibles to young readers at the start of Sunday school. If that is part of your tradition or one you'd like to start, make sure Bibles are ordered, delivered, and inscribed, and that parents and baptismal sponsors have been notified and invited. A blessing to accompany a presentation of the Bible is available in *Evangelical Lutheran Worship* Leaders Edition (p. 594).
- If you intend to have a pet blessing on October 4, get the word out now. This is an ideal opportunity for community outreach. See a form for blessing animals on pages 255–256.
- Begin asking for "harvest" contributions to enliven the worship space, interior gathering spaces, and exterior areas. Cornstalks, pumpkins and squash, fall flowers, and produce that has been canned can all be gathered during September for a colorful autumnal display.
- Begin planning for Advent if you have not started already.

Worship Texts for Autumn

Confession and Forgiveness

All may make the sign of the cross, the sign that is marked at baptism, as the presiding minister begins.

Blessed be the holy Trinity, ☩ one God,
who creates, redeems, and sustains us and all of creation.
Amen.

Let us confess our sin in the presence of God and of one another.

Silence is kept for reflection.

Faithful God,
have mercy on us.
We confess that we are captive to sin
and cannot free ourselves.
We turn from your loving embrace
and go our own ways.
We pass judgment on one another
before examining ourselves.
We place our own needs before those of our neighbors.
We keep your gift of salvation to ourselves.
Make us humble, cast away our transgressions,
and turn us again to life in you
through Jesus Christ, our Savior and Lord. Amen.

God hears the cries of all who call out in need,
and through his death and resurrection,
Christ has made us his own.
Hear the truth that God proclaims:
Your sins are forgiven in the name of ☩ Jesus Christ.
Led by the Holy Spirit, live in freedom and newness
to do God's work in the world.
Amen.

Offering Prayer

Blessed are you, O God, maker of all things.
You have set before us these gifts of your good creation.
Prepare us for your heavenly banquet,
nourish us with this rich food and drink,
and send us forth to set tables in the midst of a suffering world,
through the bread of life, Jesus Christ, our Savior and Lord.
Amen.

Invitation to Communion

Come to the banquet table
where Christ gives himself as food and drink.

Prayer after Communion

We give you thanks, gracious God,
that you have once again fed us with food beyond compare,
the body and blood of Christ.
Lead us from this place, nourished and forgiven,
into your beloved vineyard
to wipe away the tears of all who hunger and thirst,
guided by the example of the same Jesus Christ
and led by the Holy Spirit, now and forever.
Amen.

Blessing

Mothering God,
Father, ☩ Son, and Holy Spirit,
bless you and lead you into the way of truth and life.
Amen.

Dismissal

Go in peace. Remember the poor.
Thanks be to God.

Seasonal Rites for Autumn

Blessing and Prayer for Seminarians

Patient and loving God,
we praise you for those among us preparing for
word, sacrament, and service leadership within your church.
We give you thanks for these servants' willingness
to hear and answer your call,
make life changes,
and take up your work throughout creation.
Spread your Spirit's stirring energy over all our seminarians.
Sustain them with your living word and meal.
Give them holy breath for enduring life's struggles,
for studying your word, and for trusting in your call.
May we as congregations, seminaries, and synods
hold our seminarians in love, support, and prayer,
through your Son, Jesus Christ our Lord.
Amen.

Blessings for Teachers and Students

For the marvels of your creation,
we praise you, O God.
For the opportunity to explore and study,
we praise you, O God.
For those who guide us, teachers and mentors,
we praise you, O God.
Teach us your ways and guide us in your path,
for you are the creator of all that is seen and unseen.
Amen.
or
Let us pray for all who are beginning a new school year,
that both students and teachers
will be blessed in their academic endeavors.

Almighty God, you give wisdom and knowledge.
Grant teachers the gift of joy and insight,
and students the gift of diligence and openness,
that all may grow in what is good and honest and true.
Support all who teach and all who learn,
that together we may know and follow your ways;
through Jesus Christ our Lord.
Amen.

Blessing of Animals

Francis of Assisi composed the Canticle of the Sun (ELW 835, "All creatures, worship God most high!") shortly before his death. In it, God is praised through familial creation: brothers wind and fire, sister water, and mother earth. The hymn commands each creature to find its voice, praising God by and in their very beings. A commemoration of Francis of Assisi, renewer of the church, 1226 (October 4) could begin with or be centered on this hymn that seeks to gather a whole people ("All who for love of God forgive, all who in pain or sorrow grieve," stanza 4) alongside the manifold creatures who fill earth, sky, and sea.

Confession of our failures to tend the creation entrusted to human care and a ritual for blessing animals may appropriately be included in a commemoration of this one who is widely regarded as a patron saint of animals and ecology.

Litany of Repentance and Longing

In the beginning, the Spirit over the deep;
new life daily unfolding at God's call.
Darkness and light: Good.
Skies, lands, and seas: Good.
The earth and all that fills it—plants and rocks,
the finned, the feathered, the furry: Good.
At the last, humankind in God's image: Very good.

Yet we have failed to draw from that goodness
in care for God's creation.
**Forgive us, God, for the ways we have
exploited earth and its creatures.**

We have misunderstood our calling
to be protectors of God's creation.
**Forgive us, God, for the ways we have
exploited earth and its creatures.**

We long for new relationships with God's creation
that has been entrusted to us.
**Help us, God, to make a new community
with all that lives alongside us.**

May the merciful God who calls us
to tend earth and all its creatures,
deepen our knowledge of creation's interweaving,
so that our lives are shaped in wholeness and peace
with all living things; in Jesus' name.
Amen.

Greeting and Prayer

The grace of our Lord Jesus Christ, the love of God,
and the communion of the Holy Spirit be with you all.
And also with you.

Let us pray.
Holy God, we thank you for the gift of life. Recalling Francis
who celebrated your love for all creation, today we embrace
our connectedness to all: to wind, sea, and sky; to earthworm,
giraffe, and chicken; to fish and puppy, to cats of the jungle and
in our homes. Deepen our care for all that lives; in the name of
Jesus, our teacher, savior, and friend.
Amen.

Readings

*The reading of scripture is followed by silence for reflection. Other
forms of reflection may also follow, such as brief commentary,
teaching, or personal witness; non-biblical readings; interpretation
through music or other art forms; or guided conversation among
those present.*

Genesis 1:1, 20-28
Genesis 6:17-22
Job 38:1-11, 16-18
Psalm 8
Psalm 84:1-4
Psalm 148

Suggested non-biblical readings

First Nation storytelling, poetry, and histories
An excerpt from the Inaugural Mass of Pope Francis, who
began his ministry as Bishop of Rome by describing a vocation for the church and for humanity to be "protectors" of
creation
Poetry of Mary Oliver

Song

God of the sparrow ELW 740
God, whose farm is all creation ELW 734
All things bright and beautiful WOV 767
God, who stretched the spangled heavens ELW 771, LBW 463
Touch the earth lightly ELW 739
Let all things now living ELW 881, LBW 557
Many and great, O God ELW 837, WOV 794
Light dawns on a weary world ELW 726

Blessing of Animals

*The leader may invite all who have brought pets (or a picture or
toy, in the case of those animals who would not find it a blessing
to be present) to come forward for a prayer of blessing.*

Holy God, we thank you for the gift of *animal's name* in the
life of *person's name*. Through this animal you have brought
many blessings. Today we pause to name our gratitude, and to
pray a blessing on *animal's name*. For the companionship of
our pets we say thanks. Bless this animal's life in our care; may
she/he/it know love through all *her/his/its* days.
Amen.

*When all have returned to their places, a wider blessing may be
offered in these or similar words.*

Gracious and loving God, you place all living things into the
care of humankind. We pray that companionship with household pets will deepen our care for animals everywhere. Help
us to balance our needs with theirs, and lead us in ways of life
together that will be sustainable for all. We pray in Jesus' name.
Amen.

September 6, 2020
Time after Pentecost — Lectionary 23

Conflict is a part of relationships and life in community. Jesus' words in today's gospel are often used in situations having to do with church discipline. The prophet Ezekiel tells of warning the wicked to turn from their ways, and Paul reminds us that love is the fulfilling of the law. We gather in the name of Christ, assured that he is present among us with gifts of peace and reconciliation.

Prayer of the Day

O Lord God, enliven and preserve your church with your perpetual mercy. Without your help, we mortals will fail; remove far from us everything that is harmful, and lead us toward all that gives life and salvation, through Jesus Christ, our Savior and Lord.

Gospel Acclamation

Alleluia. In Christ God was reconciling the world to himself, entrusting the message of reconciliation to us. *Alleluia.* (2 Cor. 5:19)

Readings and Psalm

Ezekiel 33:7-11

God appointed Ezekiel as a sentinel for the house of Israel. Ezekiel must faithfully convey God's warnings to the people. Remarkably, God—who is about to attack Jerusalem—gives a warning with the hope that repentance will make the attack unnecessary.

Psalm 119:33-40

I desire the path of your commandments. (Ps. 119:35)

Romans 13:8-14

The obligation of Christians is to love one another and so fulfill the heart and goal of the law. Clothes make the person as we "put on the Lord Jesus Christ" and live today in light of the future God has in store for us.

Matthew 18:15-20

Jesus offers practical advice to his disciples on how individuals—and the church as a whole—should go about restoring relationships when one member has sinned against another.

Semicontinuous Reading and Psalm

Exodus 12:1-14

Israel remembered its deliverance from slavery in Egypt by celebrating the festival of Passover. This festival featured the Passover lamb, whose blood was used as a sign to protect God's people from the threat of death. The early church described the Lord's supper using imagery from the Passover, especially in portraying Jesus as the lamb who delivers God's people from sin and death.

Psalm 149

Sing the LORD's praise in the assembly of the faithful. (Ps. 149:1)

Preface Sundays

Color Green

Prayers of Intercession

The prayers are prepared locally for each occasion. The following examples may be adapted or used as appropriate.

Drawn together in the compassion of God, we pray for the church, the world, and all those in need.

A brief silence.

Unite your church, O God. Grant us the gifts of repentance and reconciliation. Bless the cooperative work of churches in this community (*especially*). Strengthen ecumenical partnerships; guide the work of the Lutheran World Federation and the World Council of Churches. Lord, in your mercy,
hear our prayer.

Protect your creation, O God. Teach us ways that do not harm what you have entrusted to our care. Renew and enliven places suffering from drought, flood, storms, or pollution (*especially*). Lord, in your mercy,
hear our prayer.

Turn nations and leaders from ways that lead to death. Shape new paths toward peace and cooperation, teaching us to recognize one another as neighbors. Guide legislators, civil servants, judges, and police toward laws that protect the well-being of all. Lord, in your mercy,
hear our prayer.

Tend to all in need of your compassion. Hear the cries of those awaiting justice and those yearning for forgiveness. Give community to the lonely and neighbors to the outcast. Shelter all who are vulnerable in body, mind, or spirit (*especially*). Lord, in your mercy,
hear our prayer.

Sustain us in our work, O God, and give work to those who need it. Shape societies to ensure fair treatment for all who labor. Help us to love our neighbors in and through our work. Lord, in your mercy,
hear our prayer.

Here other intercessions may be offered.

We remember with thanksgiving those who have died in faith. As you equipped them, equip us with your protection and power, until with them we see your salvation. Lord, in your mercy,

hear our prayer.

All these things and whatever else you see that we need, we entrust to your mercy; through Christ our Lord.

Amen.

Ideas for the Day

- There is something about wearing certain clothes that makes you feel like a different person. Maybe it's a power suit. Maybe it's a uniform. Maybe it's liturgical vestments. In today's passage from Romans, Paul tells us to "put on the armor of light" (Rom. 13:12). Two verses later he says to "put on the Lord Jesus Christ" (13:14). In the early church, the new converts were baptized naked and then clothed in a white robe to symbolize putting on Christ. As Christians we "wear" our baptism, which shapes our identity.

- In the reality competition shows *Big Brother* and *Survivor*, groups of strangers are put together in a certain location for a certain period of time and expected to figure out how to live together. They then vote each other off one by one until only one person remains. Sometimes the church feels like that too. We are a bunch of people put together in a certain place for a certain amount of time, and sometimes we want to vote each other out of the community. Today's reading from Matthew is often used to think about and guide church discipline. Although some behaviors are inappropriate in the life of the church because they could hurt the community, the way we are called to treat each other is with forgiveness and love—not with votes "off the island."

- Jesus said, "For where two or three are gathered in my name, I am there among them" (Matt. 18:20). Sometimes this saying is taken out of context and used to assuage disappointment when only a few people show up to worship or for a church activity. However, notice that Jesus' words come in the context of a call to forgiveness. To be "gathered in my name" is to be gathered in the spirit of forgiveness. Two or three people can get together in many locations. That doesn't necessarily make them united in Christ. Instead, we are united in Christ when we forgive each other.

Connections with Creation

Many of the biggest challenges facing the human community today relate to our entanglement in a wide array of social and ecological sins that we knowingly and unknowingly commit against one another and the earth. For example, any one of us who drives a gas-powered car is contributing to oil spills that destroy marine ecosystems, to rising carbon dioxide levels in the earth's atmosphere, and to environmental racism that forces people with darker skin tones to bear a greater proportion of the health burdens caused by pollution and climate change. We often feel that these issues are too controversial to discuss in the church, yet Jesus calls us to be a community of direct truth-telling, open-hearted listening, accountability, and restoration. An honest naming with one another of how we are being harmed by these sinful systems will make a new way forward possible for the church and the world.

Let the Children Come

Today's gospel provides an opportunity to encourage people to engage in the process of confessing sin in order to receive comfort and to strengthen faith. We lay our sins at the foot of the cross, where Christ has redeemed us, in order to receive from the crucified and risen Lord his gifts of forgiveness, healing, and restoration. Children can begin to understand the gift of reconciliation when they acknowledge behavior that has been hurtful to another. Leading a child to a genuine "I'm sorry" takes special care. Encourage a child hearing such words to respond with "I forgive you," not simply "That's okay."

We hear in the words of the absolution that our sins are forgiven. Later, the assisting minister sends us out into the world: "Go in peace. Serve the Lord." Perhaps it isn't only because this signals the "end of church" that children respond enthusiastically, "Thanks be to God!"

Assembly Song
Gathering

Built on a rock   ELW 652, LBW 365

Oh, that the Lord would guide my ways   ELW 772, LBW 480

Praise, my soul, the God of heaven   ELW 864/865, LBW 549

Psalmody and Acclamations

"Change Your Heart and Mind." *Psallite* A-171. Cant or SATB, assembly, kybd.

Becker, John W. "Psalm 119:33-40" from PWA.

+ Pelz, Walter L. "Psalm 149" from PWA.

(GA) Iona Community (Scotland). "Alleluia 1" from *Come All You People*. U/SATB. GIA G-4391. Use ELW psalm tone 1 with verse for Lectionary 23.

Hymn of the Day

Day of arising   ELW 374 *RAABE*   OBS 54 *BUNESSAN*

Draw us in the Spirit's tether   ELW 470, WOV 703 *UNION SEMINARY*

Lord of all nations, grant me grace   ELW 716, LBW 419 *BEATUS VIR*

Offering

As the grains of wheat   ELW 465, WOV 705, W&P 10
As we gather at your table   ELW 522

Communion

Blessed be the name/Heri ni jina   ELW 797
In all our grief   ELW 615, WOV 739
When we are living/Pues si vivimos   ELW 639, LLC 462

Sending

Joyful, joyful we adore thee   ELW 836, LBW 551
Send me, Lord   ELW 809, WOV 773, TFF 244

Additional Assembly Songs

Come, labor on   H82 541, NCH 532, GTG 719
Let us, with a gladsome mind   H82 389
O God, with hope I enter in   CBM 98

⊕ Doloksaribu, J.A.U. "Hidup bersama/Doors Open Wide in Welcome" from *Hosanna! Ecumenical Songs for Justice and Peace*. SATB. WCC Publications 9782825416679.

⊕ Sosa, Pablo. "Si fui motivo de dolor/If I Have Been the Source of Pain" from *Este es el Día*. U, pno, gtr. GIA G-7021. LLC 441.

☼ Brewster, Lincoln/Mia Fieldes. "There Is Power" from CCLI.

☼ Hackett, Erna/Erin O'Neill. "Teach Us to Pray" from *Urbana 15 Worship Live*. urbana.org.

☼ Heaton, Paddy. "Your Ways" from *Great and Glorious*. htcambridge.org.uk.

☼ Nockels, Christy. "By Our Love" from CCLI.

☼ Pagnam, Marcus. "Faithful God (Hear Our Prayer)" from CCLI.

☼ Wells, Tauren. "When We Pray" from CCLI.

Music for the Day
Choral

P Keesecker, Thomas. "In All Our Grief We Turn to You." 2 pt mxd, kybd. AFP 9780806697352.

♫ Moore, Bob. "Draw Us in the Spirit's Tether." SAB, desc, kybd. WLP WL.008939.

P Nelson, Ronald. "Tears Will Dry" from *Augsburg Choirbook for Women*. 2 pt trbl, kybd. AFP 9780800620370.

Scroogins, Debra. "An Instrument of Thy Peace." 2 pt trbl, pno. CG CGA1330.

Children's Choir

P Burrows, Mark. "Cooperate" from *Again, I Say Rejoice!* U, pno or gtr. CG CGC56.

Burrows, Mark. "The Light of God's Love." U/2 pt, pno, opt perc. CG CGA1496.

P Wold, Wayne L. "Build New Bridges" from *ChildrenSing in Worship*, vol. 3. U/2pt, kybd. AFP 9781451462548.

Keyboard / Instrumental

♫ Bullard, Alan. "Bunessan" from *Oxford Hymn Settings for Organists: Autumn Festivals*. Org. OXF 9780193400689.

P ♫ Childs, Edwin T. "Draw Us in the Spirit's Tether" from *Wedding Settings for Organ*. Org. AFP 9781506413655.

P Miller, Aaron David. "Day of Arising" from *Chorale Preludes for Piano in Traditional Styles*. Pno. AFP 9780800679033.

Rodriguez, Penny. "In Babilone" from *He Leadeth Me: Ten Hymn Arrangements for Piano*. Pno. MSM 15-840.

Handbell

♫ Krug, Jason. "Draw Us in the Spirit's Tether." 3-5 oct hb, opt 3-5 oct hc, L3-. BP HB553.

Moklebust, Cathy. "Morningdance." 3-5 oct, L3. CG CGB218.

♫ Tucker, Sondra. "Draw Us in the Spirit's Tether." 3-6 oct hb, opt hc. L3. ALF 46230.

Wednesday, September 9
Peter Claver, priest, missionary to Colombia, died 1654

Peter Claver was born into Spanish nobility and was persuaded to become a Jesuit missionary. He served in Cartagena (in what is now Colombia) by teaching and caring for the slaves. The slaves arrived in ships, where they had been confined in dehumanizing conditions. Claver met and supplied them with medicine, food, clothing, and brandy. He learned their dialects and taught them Christianity. He called himself "the slave of the slaves forever." Claver also ministered to the locals of Cartagena who were in prison and facing death.

⊕ = global song   ♫ = relates to hymn of the day   + = semicontinuous psalm
☼ = praise song   P = available in Prelude Music Planner

September 13, 2020
Time after Pentecost — Lectionary 24

In today's second reading Paul questions why we judge one another, since we all stand before the judgment of God. Yet we do sin against one another, and Jesus' challenge that we forgive seventy-seven times reveals God's boundless mercy. When we hear the words of forgiveness in worship and sign ourselves with the cross, we are renewed in baptism to be signs of reconciliation in the world.

Prayer of the Day

O Lord God, merciful judge, you are the inexhaustible fountain of forgiveness. Replace our hearts of stone with hearts that love and adore you, that we may delight in doing your will, through Jesus Christ, our Savior and Lord.

Gospel Acclamation

Alleluia. We have an advocate, Jesus Christ the righteous; your sins are forgiven on account of his name. *Alleluia.* (1 John 2:1, 12)

Readings and Psalm

Genesis 50:15-21

After Jacob's death the brothers of Joseph begged for forgiveness for the crime they had done against him. You intended to do me harm, Joseph said, but God used this as an opportunity to do good and save many lives.

Psalm 103:[1-7] 8-13

LORD, you are full of compassion and mercy. (Ps. 103:8)

Romans 14:1-12

This Christian community has significant struggles with diversity. Here Paul helps us understand that despite different practices in worship and personal piety, we do not judge one another. All Christians belong to the Lord Jesus Christ who died for all of us and will judge each of us.

Matthew 18:21-35

When Peter asks about the limits of forgiveness, Jesus responds with a parable that suggests human forgiveness should mirror the unlimited mercy of God.

Semicontinuous Reading and Psalm

Exodus 14:19-31

Having decided to let the Israelites go from Egypt, Pharaoh had second thoughts and sent his army after them (14:5-8). Though the passage through the Red Sea became a sign of salvation for the people of Israel, Pharaoh's forces drowned in the waters. As a result the Israelites believed in the LORD and in the LORD's servant Moses.

Psalm 114

Tremble, O earth, at the presence of the LORD. (Ps. 114:7)

or Exodus 15:1b-11, 20-21

I will sing to the LORD, who has triumphed gloriously. (Exod. 15:1)

Preface   Sundays

Color   Green

Prayers of Intercession

The prayers are prepared locally for each occasion. The following examples may be adapted or used as appropriate.

Drawn together in the compassion of God, we pray for the church, the world, and all those in need.

A brief silence.

You welcome us when we are weak in faith. Uphold your church throughout the world; make it a place of welcome. Strengthen faith through Bible studies and Sunday schools, confirmation classes and youth ministries. Nurture new ministries of education and growth (*especially*). Lord, in your mercy,

hear our prayer.

The heights of the heavens show us the vastness of your steadfast love. Have compassion on your creation. Where human selfishness has brought ruin and destruction, we look to you to heal, renew, and redeem your world. Lord, in your mercy,

hear our prayer.

Make your ways known to the nations. Speak kindness to our bitter grudges. Settle our hearts when we want to settle accounts with violence. Bless our leaders with patience and wisdom (*especially*). Lord, in your mercy,

hear our prayer.

Bring healing and justice wherever harm is dealt. Provide vindication for all who are oppressed. Free victims of human trafficking and forced labor; deliver all who are bound by debt. Feed all who hunger, and guard refugees fleeing famine, poverty, and war. Lord, in your mercy,

hear our prayer.

Teach us to forgive. Remind us that you do not always accuse us. Still our tongues when we are tempted to pass judgment and argue over opinions. Make this congregation a community of mercy for one another and for all our neighbors. Lord, in your mercy,

hear our prayer.

Here other intercessions may be offered.

Whether we live or whether we die, we are yours. We thank you for those who have showed us faithfulness, for the knees that taught us how to bow to you and the tongues that taught us to praise you (*especially John Chrysostom, Bishop of Constantinople, whom we commemorate today*). Lord, in your mercy,

hear our prayer.

All these things and whatever else you see that we need, we entrust to your mercy; through Christ our Lord.

Amen.

Ideas for the Day

- The story of Jameel McGee and Andrew Collins has gained national attention in recent years as they share their experience of forgiveness. Lilly Sullivan, a producer of *This American Life*, explores another angle of the story, namely those who cannot forgive the wrongful actions of former police officer Collins. The segment "You Have the Right to Remain Angry" (thisamericanlife.org/650/change-you-can-maybe-believe-in) challenges us to consider the obstacles to forgiveness, also highlighted in our gospel text (Matt. 18:30).

- In her book *The Limits of Forgiveness* (Fortress, 2015), Maria Mayo offers a corrective to the "idolatry of forgiveness" that can sometimes be read into these texts. She underscores the importance of repentance on the part of the offender, which is also a salient piece of this parable (Matt. 18:26). Mayo cautions against undue expectation for victims to forgive, and reminds us that while the forgiveness described in the gospel (Matt. 18:21-22) is boundless, in Luke (17:4) it is also predicated on the offender's repeated pleas for forgiveness (pp. 47–96).

- If the command to forgive seventy-seven times counters the seventy-sevenfold revenge of Lamech (Gen. 4:24), nothing captures the effects of escalating violence like Greek tragedy. Euripides's *Hecuba* portrays the murderous revenge of the defeated queen of Troy following the murder of two of her children. While she wants to keep to the *lex talionis* ("render evil for evil" [845]), the bloodshed spirals beyond limits toward a tragic ending for her and her enemies alike. Truly, they are entrapped in a system of revenge until the last penny is paid. Read the translation by Anne Carson in *Grief Lessons* (New York: NYRB, 2006, pp. 99–159).

- On Holocaust Remembrance Day in 2000, survivor Elie Wiesel requested that the German Bundestag officially ask the Jewish people for forgiveness for the atrocities committed by the Third Reich. In his address he mentioned that such a request for forgiveness will have "extraordinary repercussions in the world." Two weeks later, President Johannes Rau visited the Knesset in Israel to ask for forgiveness on behalf of the people of Germany. As a result, an exchange program was set up in which young people from Israel visit Berlin each year. View the story in the video *The Power of Forgiveness* (First Run Features, 2008; 20:32—23:56).

Connections with Creation

Through the oxygen cycle, the earth provides the oxygen we need to be alive on this planet. However, unless our bodies breathe in the air, the earth's abundant oxygen will be of no use to us. The water cycle ensures that the earth creates plentiful sources of water, but if we do not collect and drink that water, we will become dehydrated. Similarly, through the life, death, and resurrection of Jesus, God has made God's free gift of forgiveness available to the world. Jesus suggests in this gospel reading from Matthew that the act of forgiving helps us both to tap into God's abundant stores of mercy and to extend that mercy to others. Knowing that God's forgiveness is available for us should, Jesus teaches, empower us to be generous in the ways we show forgiveness to our neighbors who do us harm.

Let the Children Come

In many congregations this may be the day that begins a new term of Sunday school and faith formation programs. As children, families, and the congregation's teachers gather for this new start, worship planners may want to set aside time in worship for a blessing of children, youth, and their teachers and mentors. See the seasonal rites section for some examples of blessings (p. 255). As part of this blessing, consider the possibility of having the children and youth remain seated in the assembly but raising their hands in blessing (along with everyone else) over the teachers who are gathered near the altar. Or have the children and youth form a circle around the teachers and have students and teachers participate in mutual blessing, perhaps with a hand on one another's shoulder or head.

Assembly Song
Gathering

Heaven is singing for joy/El cielo canta alegría ELW 664, LLC 575

Immortal, invisible, God only wise ELW 834, LBW 526

In thee is gladness ELW 867, LBW 552

Psalmody and Acclamations

Alonso, Tony. "The Lord Is Kind and Merciful/El Señor es compasivo." SATB, pno, gtr, assembly. GIA G-7868.

Folkening, John. "Six Psalm Settings with Antiphons." SATB, U or cant, assembly, opt kybd. MSM 80-700.

+ Schwandt, Daniel E. "Psalm 114" from PSCY.

+ Sedio, Mark. "Exodus 15:1b-11, 20-21" from PWA.

+ = semicontinuous psalm

(GA) Iona Community (Scotland). "Alleluia 1" from *Come All You People.* U/SATB. GIA G-4391. Use ELW psalm tone 1 with verse for Lectionary 24.

Hymn of the Day

Forgive our sins as we forgive ELW 605, LBW 307 *DETROIT*

Our Father, we have wandered ELW 606, WOV 733 *HERZLICH TUT MICH VERLANGEN*

Where charity and love prevail ELW 359, LBW 126 *TWENTY-FOURTH*

Offering

I come with joy ELW 482

To God our thanks we give/Reamo leboga ELW 682, GS2 8

Communion

By your hand you feed your people ELW 469

O Jesus, blessed Lord ELW 541, LBW 220

When we are living/Pues si vivimos ELW 639, LLC 462

Sending

O Christ, our hope ELW 604, LBW 300

Rise, shine, you people! ELW 665, LBW 393

Additional Assembly Songs

If we live SP 16

Keep in mind LBW 13

King of glory, King of peace H82 382

⊕ Your will be done/Mayenziwe ELW 741, TFF 243

⊕ Egyptian trad., as taught by Michael Ghattas. "Bariki ya nafsi arrab/Praise, Oh, Praise God, O My Soul" from *Hosanna! Ecumenical Songs for Justice and Peace.* U. WCC Publications 9782825416679.

☼ Baker, Lee/Russell Allen. "Awakening (Let Your Glory Fall)" from CCLI.

☼ Davis, Eric/J. J. Hairston. "It Pushed Me" from CCLI.

☼ Holland, Hannah. "At the Name of Jesus" from CCLI.

☼ Keyes, Aaron/Matt Papa. "I Have a Peace" from CCLI.

☼ Myrin, Jonas/Aodhan King. "Heart of God" from WT.

☼ Riddle, Jeremy/Peter Mattis/Ran Jackson/Steffany Gretzinger. "All Hail King Jesus" from CCLI.

Music for the Day
Choral

P Capon, Michael. "Bless God's Holy Name: Psalm 103." SATB, kybd, opt br qnt. AFP 9781506456690.

♫ Hobby, Robert A. "Forgive Our Sins as We Forgive." SAB, org. CPH 982870.

Mozart, Wolfgang A./arr. R. Paul Crabb. "Kyrie." SA, kybd. Colla Voce 1896810.

P Schulz-Widmar, Russell. "Here, O My Lord." 2 pt, pno, opt vln or ob. AFP 9780800664220.

⊕ = global song   ♫ = relates to hymn of the day
☼ = praise song   P = available in Prelude Music Planner

Children's Choir

P Horman, John D. "Jacob's Sons" from *Sing the Stories of God's People.* U, kybd. AFP 9780806698397.

P Wold, Wayne L. "Build New Bridges" from *ChildrenSing in Worship,* vol. 3. U/2 pt, kybd. AFP 9781451462548.

Wold, Wayne L. "Kyrie eleison: Lord, Have Mercy." U, kybd. MSM 80-303.

Keyboard / Instrumental

♫ Carter, John. "O Sacred Head, Now Wounded" from *The Wondrous Cross: Piano Collection.* Pno. HOP 1747.

P Cherwien, David M. "Dove of Peace" from *Augsburg Organ Library: Summer.* Org. AFP 9780800676872.

♫ Hurd, David. "Partita on Detroit" from *African-American Organ Music Anthology,* vol. 6. Org. MSM 10-586.

P Nelson, Ronald A. "Goodness Is Stronger than Evil" from *Easy Hymn Settings for Organ,* vol. 4. Org. AFP 9781451486049.

Handbell

Eithun, Sandra. "Tranquil Chimings." 2-3 oct hb or hc, L1-. CG CGB600.

♫ Honore, Jeffrey. "Where Charity and Love Prevail." 3 or 5 oct, L3. WLP 3417.

♫ Sherman, Arnold. "O Sacred Head, Now Wounded." 3-5 oct, L3. BP HB274.

Sunday, September 13
John Chrysostom, Bishop of Constantinople, died 407

John was a priest in Antioch and an outstanding preacher. His eloquence earned him the nickname "Chrysostom" ("golden mouth"), but it also got him into trouble. As bishop of Constantinople he preached against corruption among the royal court. The empress, who had been his supporter, sent him into exile. His preaching style emphasized the literal meaning of scripture and its practical application. This interpretation stood in contrast to the common style at the time, which emphasized the allegorical meaning of the text. Chrysostom's skill in the pulpit resulted in the description of him as the patron of preachers.

Monday, September 14
Holy Cross Day

Helena, the mother of Constantine, made a pilgrimage to Israel to look for Christian holy sites. She found what she believed were the sites of the crucifixion and burial of Jesus, sites that modern archaeologists believe may be correct. Here Constantine built two churches. The celebration of Holy Cross Day originated with the dedication of the Church of the Resurrection in 335. Today the festival provides the church an opportunity to lift up the victory of the cross with a spirit of celebration that might be less suitable on Good Friday.

Wednesday, September 16

Cyprian, Bishop of Carthage, martyr, died around 258

Cyprian worked for the unity of the church and cared for his flock in North Africa during a time of great persecution. During Cyprian's time as bishop many people had denied the faith under duress. In contrast to some who held the belief that the church should not receive these people back, Cyprian believed they should be welcomed into full communion after a period of penance. He insisted on the need for compassion in order to preserve the unity of the church. His essay *On the Unity of the Catholic Church* stressed the role of bishops in guaranteeing the visible, concrete unity of the church. Cyprian was also concerned for the physical well-being of the people under his care. He organized a program of medical care for the sick during a severe epidemic in Carthage.

Thursday, September 17

Hildegard, Abbess of Bingen, died 1179

Hildegard lived virtually her entire life in convents yet was widely influential within the church. After an uneventful time as a nun, she was chosen as abbess of her community. She reformed her community as well as other convents. Around the same time, she began having visions and compiled them, as instructed, in a book she called *Scivias*. Hildegard's importance went beyond mysticism. She also advised and reproved kings and popes, wrote poems and hymns, and produced treatises in medicine, theology, and natural history. She was also a musician and an artist.

Friday, September 18

Dag Hammarskjöld, renewer of society, died 1961

Dag Hammarskjöld (HAH-mar-sheld) was a Swedish diplomat and humanitarian who served as secretary general of the United Nations. He was killed in a plane crash on this day in 1961 in what is now Zambia while he was on his way to negotiate a cease-fire between the United Nations and the Katanga forces. For years Hammarskjöld had kept a private journal, and it was not until that journal was published as *Markings* that the depth of his Christian faith was known. The book revealed that his life was a combination of diplomatic service and personal spirituality, and of contemplation on the meaning of Christ in his life and action in the world.

September 20, 2020
Time after Pentecost — Lectionary 25

Matthew narrates one of Jesus' controversial parables in which Jesus says that the reign of God is like that of a landowner who pays his workers the same wage no matter what time of day they began to work. When God changes God's mind about punishing Nineveh for their evil ways, Jonah is angry. Yet God is gracious and merciful, abounding in steadfast love. In baptism we receive the grace of God that is freely given to all. As Martin Luther wrote, in the presence of God's mercy we are all beggars.

Prayer of the Day

Almighty and eternal God, you show perpetual lovingkindness to us your servants. Because we cannot rely on our own abilities, grant us your merciful judgment, and train us to embody the generosity of your Son, Jesus Christ, our Savior and Lord.

Gospel Acclamation

Alleluia. Open our hearts, O Lord, to give heed to what is said by your Son. *Alleluia.*

Readings and Psalm
Jonah 3:10—4:11

After Jonah's short sermon in 3:4, the Ninevites all repented and God decided to spare the city. Jonah objected to this and became even more angry when God ordered a worm to destroy a plant that was providing shade. The book ends with a question that challenges any who are not ready to forgive: You, Jonah, are all worked up about a bush, but shouldn't I be concerned about a hundred and twenty thousand Ninevites?

Psalm 145:1-8

The LORD is slow to anger and abounding in steadfast love. (Ps. 145:8)

Philippians 1:21-30

Paul writes to the Philippians from prison. Though he is uncertain about the outcome of his imprisonment, he is committed to the ministry of the gospel and calls on the Philippians to live lives that reflect and enhance the gospel mission.

Matthew 20:1-16

Jesus tells a parable about God's generosity, challenging the common assumption that God rewards people according to what they have earned or deserve.

Semicontinuous Reading and Psalm
Exodus 16:2-15

Faced with hunger in the wilderness, the Israelites longed for life back in Egypt and wished they had never left. Then God miraculously and graciously gave them quails and manna to eat.

Psalm 105:1-6, 37-45

Make known the deeds of the LORD among the peoples. Hallelujah! (Ps. 105:1, 45)

Preface   Sundays

Color   Green

Prayers of Intercession

The prayers are prepared locally for each occasion. The following examples may be adapted or used as appropriate.

Drawn together in the compassion of God, we pray for the church, the world, and all those in need.
A brief silence.

Generous God, you make the last first, and the first last. Where this gospel challenges the church, equip it for its works of service. Strengthen those who suffer for Christ (*especially*). Lord, in your mercy,
hear our prayer.

Sun and wind, bushes and worms, cattle and great cities—nothing in creation is outside your concern, mighty God. In your mercy, tend to it all. Give us a spirit of generosity toward all you have made. Lord, in your mercy,
hear our prayer.

Where we find envy and create enemies, you provide enough for all. Bring peace to places of conflict and violence (*especially*). Inspire leaders with creativity and wisdom. Bless the work of negotiators, peacekeepers, and development workers. Lord, in your mercy,
hear our prayer.

Reveal yourself to all in need as you are gracious and merciful, slow to anger, abounding in steadfast love, ready to relent from punishing. Accompany judges and lawyers, victims of crime and those serving sentences. Give fruitful labor and a livelihood to those seeking work. Lord, in your mercy,
hear our prayer.

Even beyond our expectations, you choose to give generously. Grant life, health, and courage to all who are in need (*especially*). Lord, in your mercy,
hear our prayer.

Here other intercessions may be offered.

We praise you for the generations that have declared your power to us. Give us faithfulness to follow them, living for Christ, until you call us to join them in the joyful song around his throne. Lord, in your mercy,
hear our prayer.
All these things and whatever else you see that we need, we entrust to your mercy; through Christ our Lord.
Amen.

Ideas for the Day

- The "grumbling" of the first group of laborers in the gospel story for this week has parallels in the wider animal kingdom. Primatologist Frans de Waal's TED Talk on the behavior of capuchin monkeys who perceive unfair treatment illustrates how easily envy is ignited among them. The video (youtube.com/watch?v=meiU6TxysCg) provides a humorous example of what we also see in human behavior. In today's parable, however, the payment is the same for everybody. How can God and the church help us deal with envious responses to grace and forgiveness toward those we perceive as "undeserving"?

- This week's gospel reading is an occasion to highlight the issue of wage stagnation and widening income inequality between rich and poor. The Institute for Policy Studies' audit on the fiftieth anniversary of Martin Luther King Jr.'s Poor People's Campaign indicates that economic, political, and social inequalities in the United States have deepened, with economic and political power increasingly concentrated in the hands of a very few. For the full report, visit ips-dc.org/souls-of-poor-folks. The segment on income inequality begins on page 52.

- In *Short Stories by Jesus* (New York: HarperOne, 2014), Amy-Jill Levine makes the case that the householder (*oikodespotēs*) of this story represents both God and people of means who follow Jesus. As such, *oikodespotēs* who are discipled for the kingdom (Matt. 13:52) ought to seek out the unemployed and underemployed and pay a living wage. In so doing they support laborers (regardless of time on the job) and ensure that the necessary work gets done. As a result, each group gets what it needs from the other: "Maybe the concern is to work within the localized system and provide, if resources allow, funds so that everyone has enough food" (p. 216).

- The multiple attempts by the employer to find workers mimic what theologian and philosopher John Caputo calls the "insistence of God." God's continuing insistence on the well-being of creation constitutes an invitation for humans to practice hospitality and mutual concern. God's call, however, is not coercive, just as the workers in the parable are not violently compelled to enter the vineyard. View Dr. Caputo's lecture from *Homebrewed Christianity* at youtube.com/watch?v=3xBMYzPuDtQ.

Connections with Creation

Our bodies rely on nutrients from food to get the energy we need to grow, work, and thrive. Food does not just appear in the grocery store; it is cultivated and harvested by agricultural workers who put their hands into the soil and pick the fruit off the plants. The people who grow and gather our food are also the most likely to be food insecure. This means that they and their families often do not have enough food to meet their own basic nutritional needs even as they labor to provide food for others. This dynamic of injustice related to the way that societies build and maintain their food systems has been going on for thousands of years. In the parable Jesus tells about the generous vineyard owner we learn that Jesus was aware of this injustice and that living within the logic of the reign of God means that we are called to engage in acts that right our relationships with people who labor on the land.

Let the Children Come

The story of Jonah is a popular Bible story for children but only comes up in the three-year lectionary at the Vigil of Easter, on a Sunday during the time after Epiphany in year B (and then only a few verses), and this Sunday. Some children may never have heard this story in worship. Today's first reading picks up the story after Jonah has spent three days in the belly of the fish and has finally made his way to Nineveh as originally commanded by God. Consider telling the first part of the story (Jonah 1–2) from a children's Bible or picture book as a lead-in to the first reading (for example, from the *Spark Story Bible* or from the classroom or lectionary editions of the *Whirl Story Bible*). Have the children gather around the storyteller near the place where the first reading will then be proclaimed.

Assembly Song
Gathering

> Blessing and honor ELW 854, LBW 525
> Golden breaks the dawn ELW 852
> Great is thy faithfulness ELW 733, WOV 771, TFF 283

Psalmody and Acclamations

> Harmon, Kathleen. "Twenty-Fifth Sunday in Ordinary Time (A)" from *Cry Out with Joy, Year A*. GIA G-8481.
> Whitney, Rae E. "O My God and King and Savior" (HOLY MANNA) from PAS 145F.
+ Tell What God Has Done for Us/Psalm 105 DATH 97
> (GA) Iona Community (Scotland). "Alleluia 1" from *Come All You People*. U/SATB. GIA G-4391. Use ELW psalm tone 1 with verse for Lectionary 25.

+ = semicontinuous psalm

265

Hymn of the Day

Great God, your love has called us   ELW 358, WOV 666   *RYBURN*

There's a wideness in God's mercy   ELW 587   *ST. HELENA*
ELW 588, LBW 290   *LORD, REVIVE US*

Will you let me be your servant   ELW 659   *THE SERVANT SONG*

Offering

As saints of old   ELW 695, LBW 404

God, whose giving knows no ending   ELW 678, LBW 408

Communion

All who love and serve your city   ELW 724, LBW 436

Give me Jesus   ELW 770, TFF 165, WOV 777

O living Bread from heaven   ELW 542, LBW 197

Sending

How small our span of life   ELW 636

On our way rejoicing   ELW 537, LBW 260

Additional Assembly Songs

In the Lord I'll be ever thankful   SP 18

God recycles, reconciles us   ASG 13

Welcome Table   TFF 263

⊕ Anon. India. "Ever and Always Be Praise" from *Sound the Bamboo*. GIA G-6830.

⊕ Ave Virgo Virginem/John L. Bell. "Sisters and Brothers, With One Voice" from *One Is the Body*. GIA G-5790.

☼ Anna & Elizabeth. "Here in the Vineyard" from *Hop High/Here in the Vineyard*. annaandelizabeth.bandcamp.com.

☼ Boyd, Estella/Marvin Winans. "If I Labor" from CCLI.

☼ Llewellyn, Chris/Ed Cash/Gareth Gilkeson. "Christ Lives in Me" from CCLI.

☼ McDonald, Ben/Casey Brown/David Frey/Jonathan Smith. "To Live Is Christ" from CCLI.

☼ Snoke, Daniel/Michael Savinsky. "Joy and Toil" from *Among the Thorns*. cardiphonia.bandcamp.com.

☼ Tomlin, Chris/Jonas Myrin/Matt Redman. "Let It Be Jesus" from CCLI.

Music for the Day
Choral

Blersch, Jeffrey. "Voices Raised to You We Offer." SATB, br qrt, timp. CPH 984105.

P Doerksen, Brian/arr. Patrick Tierney. "Purify My Heart (Refiner's Fire)." SATB, pno. HOP C5850.

P Nelson, Ronald A. "Whoever Would Be Great among You" from *The Augsburg Choirbook*. SAB, gtr or kybd. AFP 9780800656782.

P Walter, Johann. "Salvation unto Us Has Come" from *Augsburg Chorale Book*. SATB, a cap. AFP 9781506426303.

Children's Choir

P Cox, Randy. "The Fish Caught Him." U/2 pt, pno. CG CGA1401.

P Horman, John D. "Jonah" from *Sing the Stories of God's People*. U, kybd. AFP 9780806698397.

Patterson, Mark. "How Can I Give You Thanks?" U, pno. CG CGA957.

Keyboard / Instrumental

♫ Burkhardt, Michael. "Will You Let Me Be Your Servant" from *Then Sings My Soul: Five Hymn Preludes for Organ*. Org. MSM 10-045.

Carter, John "You Satisfy the Hungry Heart" from *You Satisfy the Hungry Heart: Piano Settings for Communion*. Pno. HOP 8008.

Ferguson, John. "Laudes Domine" from *Three About Jesus: A Triptych*. Org. MSM 10-572.

P ♫ Raabe, Nancy. "Great God, Your Love Has Called Us" from *Grace & Peace, Volume 8: Songs of Lament and Longing*. Pno. AFP 9781506413679.

Handbell

♫ Moklebust, Cathy. "Gentle Shepherd, Joyful Servant." 3 or 5 oct, L3. National Music Publications HB625.

Thompson, Karen. "Jesus Calls Us." 3-6 oct hb, opt 3-5 oct hc, L2+. CG CGB868.

♫ Tucker, Sondra. "There's a Wideness in God's Mercy." 3-5 oct, L3. AFP 0800674901.

Monday, September 21
Matthew, Apostle and Evangelist

Matthew ("Levi" in the gospels of Mark and Luke) was a tax collector for the Roman government in Capernaum. Tax collectors were distrusted because they were dishonest and worked as agents for a foreign ruler, the occupying Romans. In the gospels, tax collectors are mentioned as sinful and despised outcasts, but it was these outcasts to whom Jesus showed his love. Matthew's name means "gift of the Lord." Since the second century, tradition has attributed the first gospel to him.

⊕ = global song   ♫ = relates to hymn of the day
☼ = praise song   P = available in Prelude Music Planner

September 27, 2020
Time after Pentecost — Lectionary 26

Jesus' parable about two sons who don't do what they say reveals surprises in the reign of God. In the reading from Ezekiel the people claim the ways of the Lord are unfair, while God offers repentance and new life. Paul urges us to look to Christ as a model of humility, putting the interests of others above our own. Nourished by the broken bread and shared cup, we offer our lives for the sake of our needy world.

Prayer of the Day

God of love, giver of life, you know our frailties and failings. Give us your grace to overcome them, keep us from those things that harm us, and guide us in the way of salvation, through Jesus Christ, our Savior and Lord.

Gospel Acclamation

Alleluia. My sheep hear my voice, says the Lord; I know them and they follow me. *Alleluia.* (John 10:27)

Readings and Psalm

Ezekiel 18:1-4, 25-32

Ezekiel challenges those who think they cannot change because of what their parents were and did, or who think they cannot reverse their own previous behavior. God insistently invites people to turn and live.

Psalm 25:1-9

Remember, O LORD, your compassion and love. (Ps. 25:6)

Philippians 2:1-13

As part of a call for harmony rather than self-seeking, Paul uses a very early Christian hymn that extols the selflessness of Christ in his obedient death on the cross. Christ's selfless perspective is to be the essential perspective we share as the foundation for Christian accord.

Matthew 21:23-32

After driving the moneychangers out of the temple (21:12), Jesus begins teaching there. His authority is questioned by the religious leaders, who are supposed to be in charge of the temple.

Semicontinuous Reading and Psalm

Exodus 17:1-7

Because the thirsty Israelites quarreled with Moses and put God to the test, Moses cried out in desperation to God. God commanded Moses to strike the rock to provide water for the people. The doubt-filled question—"Is the LORD among us or not?"—received a very positive answer.

Psalm 78:1-4, 12-16

We will recount to generations to come the power of the LORD. (Ps. 78:4)

Preface   Sundays

Color   Green

Prayers of Intercession

The prayers are prepared locally for each occasion. The following examples may be adapted or used as appropriate.

Drawn together in the compassion of God, we pray for the church, the world, and all those in need.

A brief silence.

In all the world, give your church unity. Inspire all the baptized with the mind of Christ. Where the church is powerful and where it struggles, shape us with humility and obedience so that your love may be at work in us. Lord, in your mercy,

hear our prayer.

Your Son took on all of bodily life in our world, even to death. Preserve and keep your creation, O God. Mend and redeem places that are polluted and damaged, so that all of creation confesses you as Lord. Lord, in your mercy,

hear our prayer.

Turn the nations toward life. Where our ways are unfair, give us new hearts and new spirits. Where sin permeates our cultures and institutions (*especially*), change our minds and teach us to trust your authority. Lord, in your mercy,

hear our prayer.

Our lives are yours, O God. Relieve the suffering of those who are ill in body, mind, or spirit. Defend the lives and welfare of children who are abused or neglected, hungry or exploited, bullied or lonely. Lord, in your mercy,

hear our prayer.

Turn this congregation away from our own interests toward the interests of others. Fill us with your compassion and sympathy. Bless ministries of care in our community (*especially*); make us into signs of your mercy and justice for our neighbors. Lord, in your mercy,

hear our prayer.

Here other intercessions may be offered.

Thank you for those who have gone into the kingdom ahead of us—tax collectors and prostitutes, likely and unlikely, obedient

and slow to learn. By their witness, teach us to confess Jesus Christ as Lord in life and in death. Lord, in your mercy,
hear our prayer.
All these things and whatever else you see that we need, we entrust to your mercy; through Christ our Lord.
Amen.

Ideas for the Day

- "You've got to give it away to keep it" is a popular expression in recovery circles, based on the final step of 12-step programs in which those in recovery are called to mentor others on the path. This type of servant leadership is embodied in the kenotic Christ of Philippians 2, who gives away even the divine form and his own human life. In his compelling book *Forgiveness and Power in the Age of Atrocity: Servant Leadership as a Way of Life* (Lanham, MD: Lexington Books, 2012), Gonzaga University professor Shann Ray Ferch offers stories of many servant leaders, illustrating the power of self-giving love to create hope and healing.

- When public officials claim biblical authority for policies that do harm to the most vulnerable among us, how do Lutheran Christians respond? Jesus was shrewd in responding to the temple leaders who questioned the authority he claimed in cleansing the temple. Asking direct questions about power (who has it, where does it come from, and how is it maintained?) is essential in a church that is always reforming, always asking who gets to claim the authority to speak for God. Episcopal priest Eric Law and his ministry, the Kaleidoscope Institute (kscopeinstitute.org), help congregations identify and address power dynamics in order to move toward more inclusive, just, and sustainable communities.

- Who did the will of his father: the son who begged off and then showed up, or the one who said he would do the work and didn't? Who does the work of God: the one who posts on social media or the one who is out in the streets working for justice? If only it were so simple, but much of today's work for the healing of the world consists in winning hearts and minds, and the internet is today's public square. Although Jesus and the chief priests agree that actions speak louder than words, our current political sphere and mediascape often give more weight to appearances than to reality. Lutheran theology of proclamation reminds us that words have transformative power.

Connections with Creation

The theme of humility runs through the lectionary readings this week. In particular, the New Testament passages point out the need for humans to adopt a posture of genuine humility in order to participate in the reign of God on Earth. Humility has often been wrongly interpreted to mean that people should restrain themselves, make themselves small, and hold back from using their talents in ways that are too powerful. However, when we spend time in the natural world, we might learn a different way of thinking about humility. Whether pondering the size of a universe that is ninety-three billion light-years in diameter or considering the fact that one billion microbes live within a teaspoon of soil, we are called to wonder at the vastness of God's creation and understand appropriately our place in this larger community of life. To be humble is to be fully and powerfully all that one is capable of being, while also seeing oneself as part of a larger web of connection.

Let the Children Come

Teach the children how and when to make the sign of the cross. If this is an unfamiliar gesture to most worshipers, then let the children teach the adults. Tell them that this sign is made upon all who are baptized into the name of the holy Trinity. Show them how to touch their foreheads with the fingers of their right hand, then to touch their chest, one shoulder, the other shoulder, and their chest again at the words, "Father, Son, and Holy Spirit." The sign of the cross may be made at the beginning of the confession and forgiveness or thanksgiving for baptism, at the announcement of the gospel, before receiving communion, and along with the presiding minister at the final blessing.

Assembly Song
Gathering

Awake, my soul, and with the sun ELW 557, LBW 269
Come, ye disconsolate ELW 607, TFF 186
Dearest Jesus, at your word ELW 520, LBW 248

Psalmody and Acclamations

Mathis, William H. Refrain for "Psalm 25" from *After the Prelude: Year A*. U/cant, hb. CG CG CGB658 (digital version), CGB659 (print version). Use with ELW psalm tone 6 or 7 (in C).
Parker, Val. "Psalm 25: To You, O Lord, I Lift My Soul." SATB, assembly, kybd, gtr. OCP 21060.
+ Nicholson, Paul. "Psalm 78," Refrain 1, from PSCY.
(GA) Iona Community (Scotland). "Alleluia 1" from *Come All You People*. U/SATB. GIA G-4391. Use ELW psalm tone 1 with verse for Lectionary 26.

Hymn of the Day

Change my heart, O God ELW 801, W&P 28 *CHANGE MY HEART*
Lord, whose love in humble service ELW 712, LBW 423 *BEACH SPRING*
O God, my faithful God ELW 806, LBW 504 *WAS FRAG ICH NACH DER WELT*

Offering

Let us talents and tongues employ   ELW 674, WOV 754, TFF 232

The trumpets sound, the angels sing   ELW 531, W&P 139

Communion

In the singing   ELW 466

O Master, let me walk with you   ELW 818, LBW 492

Strengthen for service, Lord   ELW 497, LBW 218

Sending

Hallelujah! We sing your praises   ELW 535, WOV 722, LLC 420, TFF 158

Voices raised to you   ELW 845

Additional Assembly Songs

Jesus Christ is Lord   MSB1 S429

People of the Lord   GTG 632

The church of Christ cannot be bound   GTG 766

⊕ World Council of Churches/RedCreate. "Caminando con Dios/ By Singing, and Praying, and Reading" from *Songs: Walking with the God of Life*. WCC 10th Assembly. Out of print. Hannelore.Schmid@wcc-coe.org.

⊕ Sizohamba naye/We will go with God   GS2 10, SC 55

☼ Brown, Joel. "He Reigns" from *He Reigns*. resurrectionchurch .com.

☼ Eichelberger, Brian/Charlotte Elliott/William Batchelder Bradbury. "Just As I Am" from CCLI.

☼ Hoisington, Anthony/Chris Hoisington/Chris Llewellyn/ Gareth Gilkerson. "You Shine Through" from CCLI.

☼ Reagan, Wen. "Your Will Be Done" from CCLI.

☼ Vargas, Julie Anne/Zachary Hicks. "Most Merciful God" from CCLI.

☼ Wilson, Jono/Nathan de Jong. "Revive" from CCLI.

Music for the Day
Choral

P Bankson, Jeremy J. "Lord, Keep Us Steadfast in Your Word" from *Augsburg Chorale Book*. SATB, org, tpt. AFP 9781506426303.

Burkhardt, Michael. "The Lord Now Sends Us Forth." SA or SATB, pno, perc, opt assembly. MSM 50-5412.

P Goudimel, Claude. "As the Deer, for Water Yearning" from *Chantry Choirbook: Sacred Music for All Seasons*. SATB, a cap. AFP 9780800657772.

P ♫ Keesecker, Thomas. "We Sing to You, O God." 2 pt mxd, pno. AFP 9781506414027.

Children's Choir

Bach, J. S./Michael Burkhardt. "What You, My God, Ordain Is Good." U, 2 C inst, kybd, opt bass inst. MSM 50-9455.

P Burrows, Mark. "God's Hands" from *Again, I Say Rejoice!* U, pno or gtr. CG CGC56.

P Cool, Jayne Southwick. "Psalm 25" from *ChildrenSing Psalms*. U/2 pt, kybd, assembly, opt perc. AFP 9780800663872.

Keyboard / Instrumental

♫ Burkhardt, Michael. "O God, My Faithful God" from *Praise and Thanksgiving*, set 8. Org. MSM 10-030.

P Organ, Anne Krentz. "O Blessed Spring" from *In Heaven Above: Piano Music for Funerals and Memorials*. Pno. AFP 9781451401912.

♫ Shackley, Larry. "Change My Heart, O God" from *Time to Worship*. Pno. HOP 8246.

P ♫ Young, Philip M. "Beach Spring" from *Preludes on American Tunes for Organ*. Org. AFP 9781451451764.

Handbell

♫ Compton, Matthew. "Beach Spring." 3-6 oct, L4. HOP 2743.

♫ Cota, Patricia. "Change My Heart, O God." 3-5 oct, L3. HOP 2136.

McKlveen, Paul. "Faith." 3-5 oct, L2+. JEF JHS9396.

Tuesday, September 29
Michael and All Angels

On this festival day the church ponders the richness and variety of God's created order and the limits of human knowledge of it. The scriptures speak of angels (the word means "messengers") who worship God in heaven, and in both testaments angels speak for God on earth. They are remembered most vividly as they appear to the shepherds and announce the birth of the Savior. Michael is an angel whose name appears in Daniel as the heavenly being who leads the faithful dead to God's throne on the day of resurrection. In Revelation, Michael fights in a cosmic battle against Satan.

Wednesday, September 30
Jerome, translator, teacher, died 420

Jerome is remembered as a biblical scholar and translator. Rather than choosing classical Latin as the basis of his work, he translated the scriptures into the Latin that was spoken and written by the majority of the persons in his day. His translation is known as the Vulgate, from the Latin word for *common*. While Jerome is remembered as a saint, he could be anything but saintly. He was well known for his short temper and his arrogance, although he was also quick to admit to his personal faults. Thanks to the work of Jerome, many people received the word in their own language and lived a life of faith and service to those in need.

⊕ = global song   ♫ = relates to hymn of the day   + = semicontinuous psalm
☼ = praise song   P = available in Prelude Music Planner

October 4, 2020
Time after Pentecost — Lectionary 27

In today's gospel reading, Jesus tells a vineyard parable, which serves as an image of Israel, the prophets' mission, and Christ's death. For Christians, the vineyard also speaks of God's love poured out in the blood of Christ, given to us for the forgiveness of sin. Grafted onto Christ the vine at baptism, we are nourished with wine and bread so that we may share Christ's sufferings and know the power of his resurrection.

Prayer of the Day

Beloved God, from you come all things that are good. Lead us by the inspiration of your Spirit to know those things that are right, and by your merciful guidance, help us to do them, through Jesus Christ, our Savior and Lord.

Gospel Acclamation

Alleluia. Jesus says, I chose you and appointed you to go and bear fruit that will last. *Alleluia.* (John 15:16)

Readings and Psalm

Isaiah 5:1-7

The prophet sings a sad, parable-like love song about the relationship between God and Israel. In this song Israel is compared to a promising vineyard. Despite God's loving care, the vineyard that is Israel has brought forth "wild grapes" of injustice and distress, when fine grapes of justice and righteousness were expected.

Psalm 80:7-15

Look down from heaven, O God; behold and tend this vine. (Ps. 80:14, 15)

Philippians 3:4b-14

Paul reviews some of his supposed credentials, which no longer have any bearing in comparison to the right relationship he has been given through the death of Christ. The power of Christ's resurrection motivates him to press on toward the ultimate goal, eternal life with Christ.

Matthew 21:33-46

Jesus tells a parable to the religious leaders who are plotting his death, revealing that their plans will, ironically, bring about the fulfillment of scripture.

Semicontinuous Reading and Psalm

Exodus 20:1-4, 7-9, 12-20

The God of the exodus graciously gave Israel the Ten Commandments. Primarily stated as negative imperatives, the Ten Commandments forbid gross sins such as murder, adultery, theft, and perjury. In most of life they grant Israel freedom to live righteously, with maximum love for God and neighbor.

Psalm 19

The statutes of the Lord are just and rejoice the heart. (Ps. 19:8)

Preface   Sundays

Color   Green

Prayers of Intercession

The prayers are prepared locally for each occasion. The following examples may be adapted or used as appropriate.

With confidence in God's grace and mercy, let us pray for the church, the world, and all those in need.

A brief silence.

Holy God, you call us to work for peace and justice in your vineyard. Refresh the church with your life, that we may bear fruit through work and service. Lord, in your mercy,

hear our prayer.

Thank you for the abundant harvest of the earth. Bless and care for those whose hands bring the fruits of the earth to the tables of all who hunger. May we be inspired by your servants who cared deeply for your creation (*especially Francis of Assisi, whom we commemorate today*). Lord, in your mercy,

hear our prayer.

Curb the impulses of greed and pride that lead us to take advantage of others. Grant that world leaders (*especially*) seek the fruits of the kingdom for the good and welfare of all people. Lord, in your mercy,

hear our prayer.

Sustain all who suffer with the promise of new life. Assured of your presence, heal our pain and suffering, and equip us to embrace all bodies aching for wholeness of mind, body, and soul. We call to mind those who are struggling today (*especially*). Lord, in your mercy,

hear our prayer.

We pray for all managers in our community and for all who seek employment. Give hope and a future to those who lack meaningful work, those who have been marginalized or abused in the workplace, and those who desire new opportunities. Lord, in your mercy,

hear our prayer.

Here other intercessions may be offered.

Thank you for the saints who teach us to live faithfully in your vineyard (*especially Theodor Fliedner, renewer of society*). May our chorus join theirs until our labor is complete. Lord, in your mercy,
hear our prayer.
Listen as we call on you, O God, and enfold in your loving arms all for whom we pray, in the name of Jesus Christ our Lord.
Amen.

Ideas for the Day

- Most regions now have at least some local vineyards. Where does your church's communion wine come from? Is there a potential local source? The images of the vineyard in Isaiah and Matthew invite us to remember that wine comes not from a bottle but from a real vineyard with farmers who are children of God.

- Although Jesus was speaking of and to the religious leaders of his time in the parable of the wicked tenants, we would do well to examine our own leadership: how have we become invested in being gatekeepers of the kingdom of God? We are called to be a church that is always reforming, examining where we may be falling into patterns of claiming privileged access to God. Peter Rollins's provocative book *The Idolatry of God: Breaking Our Addiction to Certainty and Satisfaction* (New York: Howard Books, 2012) challenges church insiders to notice where we have allowed beliefs about God to become idols prioritized before the divine mystery that cannot be fully grasped or contained.

- The Pew Research Center reports that the membership of the ELCA is 96 percent white, making it the most monocultural denomination in the United States (pewforum .org/religious-landscape-study). If we are the tenants of the vineyard of the church, how are we living into God's vision of a place where all are truly welcome? What are the fruits of our congregations? We may unintentionally and unknowingly perpetuate the sour wine of bias, segregation, and racial injustice. The ELCA's Racial Justice Resources (elca.org/Resources/Racial-Justice) and numerous statements from Presiding Bishop Elizabeth Eaton invite congregations to actively work toward advancing racial justice.

- Do people in your congregation mostly rent or own their homes? Who do listeners most naturally identify with: landlords or tenants? Can they imagine this story told from another point of view? In the parable, Jesus identifies God with the powerful (the landowner). In other parables and gospel narratives, Jesus identifies with the vulnerable and the unstably housed. The good news brings liberation to both the powerful and the powerless. If there are tensions in your community about tenant rights or other housing issues, this parable may invite listeners to consider others' perspectives.

Connections with Creation

To produce good wine, a landowner must have grapevines that produce fruit with the right amount of sugar and ripeness. Two factors impact the production of good grapes: weather and soil health. Weather is beyond the grower's control, but an astute landowner will invest resources in soil health. The biblical authors often use the metaphors of landowner, vineyard, vine, and fruit to speak about a community's faithfulness or disobedience; the people are evaluated based on the evidence of their fruit. Good fruit comes from good soil, and good soil contains a diverse microbial community rich in nutrients and with the ability to absorb and retain water. Science is discovering more and more about this unseen and dynamic set of processes and relationships between fungi, bacteria, viruses, and crops that lead to the production of good fruit. In the faithful life, developing the personal and communal characteristics that lead to fruits of compassion, generosity, and joy requires paying attention to the movement of God's Spirit and the nurturing of mutually beneficial relationships within the body of Christ.

Let the Children Come

This year the church's commemoration of Francis of Assisi falls on a Sunday (see a brief biographical sketch on page 272). This commemoration has been a traditional time to bless pets and animals, creatures Francis called his brothers and sisters. Invite worshipers, especially children and their families, to bring pets for a blessing today, whether during the regular Sunday assembly or at a separate time before or after the service. Invite children who do not have a pet, or whose pet would be happier staying at home, to bring a photo or a favorite stuffed animal. A new order for such a blessing is included in the seasonal rites section (pp. 255–256). Teach children the song "All God's Critters Got a Place in the Choir" by Bill Staines and have them sing it today, with the assembly joining in on the refrain.

Assembly Song
Gathering

> God the sculptor of the mountains ELW 736, TFF 222
> How clear is our vocation, Lord ELW 580
> The church's one foundation ELW 654, LLC 479, LBW 369

Psalmody and Acclamations

> Alonso, Tony. "The Vineyard of the Lord" from TLP:A.
> Becker, John W. "Psalm 80:7-15" from PWA.
> + Cool, Jayne Southwick. "Psalm 19" from *ChildrenSing Psalms*. U, kybd.
> (GA) Iona Community (Scotland). "Alleluia 1" from *Come All You People*. U/SATB. GIA G-4391. Use ELW psalm tone 1 with verse for Lectionary 27.

+ = semicontinuous psalm

Hymn of the Day

Christ is made the sure foundation ELW 645, WOV 747
WESTMINSTER ABBEY LBW 367 *EDEN CHURCH*

If you but trust in God to guide you ELW 769, LBW 453
WER NUR DEN LIEBEN GOTT

Lord Christ, when first you came to earth ELW 727, LBW 421
MIT FREUDEN ZART

Offering

Accept, O Lord, the gifts we bring ELW 691, WOV 759

Let us go now to the banquet/Vamos todos al banquete
ELW 523, LLC 410

Communion

Jesus loves me! ELW 595, LLC 614, TFF 249, LS 160

Lord our God, with praise we come ELW 730, LBW 244

My song is love unknown ELW 343, WOV 661, LBW 94

Sending

How firm a foundation ELW 796, LS 80, LBW 507

The Lord now sends us forth/Enviado soy de Dios ELW 538,
LLC 415

Additional Assembly Songs

Beloved and most loving Source CBM 61

Help us accept each other GTG 754

Make me a channel of your peace W&P 95

⊕ Pandopo, H.A./Andrew Donaldson. "Lihatlah sekelilingmu/
Lift Your Eyes and Look Around" from Yayasan Musik
Gereja, Indonesia. Out of print. Hannelore.Schmid@
wcc-coe.org.

⊕ Shona trad. "Hakuna Wakaita sa Jesu" from *Njalo (Always)*.
ABI 9780687498079.

☼ Gifford, Christa Black/Jeremy Riddle/William Matthews. "My
Great Reward" from CCLI.

☼ Houston, Joel/Matt Crocker. "Mountain" from CCLI.

☼ Myrin, Jonas/Reuben Morgan. "Christ Is Enough" from CCLI.

☼ Nockels, Christy/Nathan Nockels. "For Your Splendor" from
CCLI.

☼ Noël, Jonathan. "The Stone" from *The Stone EP*. jonathannoel
.bandcamp.com.

☼ Vice, Elizabeth/Isaac Wardell/Madison Cunningham/Orlando
Palmer/Paul Zach/Sandra McCracken. "We Abide, We
Abide in You" from CCLI.

Music for the Day
Choral

♫ Cherwien, David M. "If You But Trust in God to Guide You."
SATB, solo, org, opt fl, vc. MSM 60-9027.

P Ferguson, John. "Creating God, Your Fingers Trace." SATB,
org, opt assembly. AFP 9781506456706.

⊕ = global song   ♫ = relates to hymn of the day
☼ = praise song   P = available in Prelude Music Planner

P Grundahl, Nancy. "When I Survey the Wondrous Cross"
from *Augsburg Choirbook for Women*. SSA, pno. AFP
9780800620370.

P Schalk, Carl. "Thine the Amen, Thine the Praise" from *The
Augsburg Choirbook*. SATB, desc, org, opt assembly. AFP
9780800656782.

Children's Choir

Hobby, Robert A. "Song of Hope." U or 2 pt, kybd, perc. MSM
50-8112.

Holden-Holloway, Deborah. "Come, Let Us Sing to the Lord." U,
kybd. SEL 422-731.

P Horman, John D. "Psalm 80" from *ChildrenSing Psalms*. U,
kybd, assembly, opt tamb. AFP 9780800663872.

Keyboard / Instrumental

P Hansen, Sherri. "Thine the Amen" from *Piano Weavings*, vol.
2. Pno. AFP 9781506413723.

P ♫ Miller, Aaron David. "If You But Trust in God to Guide You"
from *Hymns in Jazz Style*. Pno. AFP 9780800678531.

P ♫ Westenkuehler, Jerry. "Trumpet Tune on Westminster
Abbey" from *Three Festive Trumpet Tunes*. Org, tpt.
MSM 10-685.

♫ Wolniakowski, Michael. "Partita on With High Delight Let Us
Unite." Org. MSM 10-416.

Handbell

♫ Gramann, Fred. "Fantasy on King's Weston." 3-6 oct, L adv.
HOP 1671.

♫ Hakes, Derek. "To God All Praise and Glory." 3-5 oct hb, opt 3-4
oct hc, L2+. LOR 20/1543L.

♫ Morris, Hart. "Celebration on Westminster Abbey." 3-5 oct hb,
opt 3 oct hc, L2+. CPH 977224.

Sunday, October 4
Francis of Assisi, renewer of the church, died 1226

Francis was the son of a wealthy cloth merchant. In a public con-
frontation with his father, he renounced his wealth and future
inheritance and devoted himself to serving the poor. Francis
described this act as being "wedded to Lady Poverty." Under
his leadership the Order of Friars Minor (Franciscans) was
formed, and they took literally Jesus' words to his disciples that
they should take nothing on their journey and receive no payment for their work. Their task in preaching was to "use words if
necessary." Francis had a spirit of gladness and gratitude for all
of God's creation. This commemoration has been a traditional
time to bless pets and animals, creatures Francis called his
brothers and sisters. A prayer and hymn attributed to St. Francis are included in *Evangelical Lutheran Worship* (p. 87, #835).

Sunday, October 4
Theodor Fliedner, renewer of society, died 1864

Fliedner's (FLEED-ner) work was instrumental in the revival of the ministry of deaconesses among Lutherans. While a pastor in Kaiserswerth, Germany, he also ministered to prisoners in Düsseldorf. Through his ministry to prisoners, he came in contact with Moravian deaconesses, and it was through this Moravian influence that he was convinced that the ministry of deaconesses had a place among Lutherans. His work and writing encouraged women to care for those who were sick, poor, or imprisoned. Fliedner's deaconess motherhouse in Kaiserswerth inspired Lutherans all over the world to commission deaconesses to serve in parishes, schools, prisons, and hospitals.

Tuesday, October 6
William Tyndale, translator, martyr, died 1536

William Tyndale was ordained in 1521, and his life's desire was to translate the scriptures into English. When his plan met opposition from Henry VIII, Tyndale fled to Germany, where he traveled from city to city, living in poverty and constant danger. He was able to produce a New Testament in 1525. Nine years later he revised it and began work on the Old Testament, which he was unable to complete. He was tried for heresy and burned at the stake. Miles Coverdale completed Tyndale's work, and the Tyndale-Coverdale version was published as the "Matthew Bible" in 1537. For nearly four centuries the style of this translation has influenced English versions of the Bible such as the King James (Authorized Version) and the New Revised Standard Version.

Wednesday, October 7
Henry Melchior Muhlenberg, pastor in North America, died 1787

Muhlenberg (MYOO-len-berg) was prominent in setting the course for Lutheranism in North America. He helped Lutheran churches make the transition from the state churches of Europe to a new identity on American soil. Among other things, he established the first Lutheran synod in America and developed an American Lutheran liturgy. His liturgical principles became the basis for the Common Service of 1888, used in many North American service books for a majority of the past century. That Muhlenberg and his work are remembered today was anticipated at his death. The inscription on his grave reads in Latin, "Who and what he was, future ages will know without a stone."

October 11, 2020
Time after Pentecost — Lectionary 28

In Isaiah we are given a vision of the great feast to come, when God will wipe away death forever. In Jesus' parable about a great banquet, those invited do not come, so the invitation is extended to others. In our liturgy God spreads a table before us. Even amid anxiety and hardship we rejoice in the peace of God which surpasses all understanding. With great joy we feast at the table of the Lord, and we go forth to share the wonderful invitation with others hungering and thirsting for the abundant life of God.

Prayer of the Day

Lord of the feast, you have prepared a table before all peoples and poured out your life with abundance. Call us again to your banquet. Strengthen us by what is honorable, just, and pure, and transform us into a people of righteousness and peace, through Jesus Christ, our Savior and Lord.

Gospel Acclamation

Alleluia. This is the LORD for whom we have waited; let us be glad and rejoice in God's salvation. *Alleluia.* (Isa. 25:9)

Readings and Psalm

Isaiah 25:1-9

After a hymn of praise acknowledging God as a shelter for the poor, the prophet portrays a wonderful victory banquet at which death—which in ancient Canaan was depicted as a monster swallowing up everyone—will be swallowed up forever. The prophet urges celebration of this victory of salvation.

Psalm 23

You prepare a table before me, and my cup is running over. (Ps. 23:5)

Philippians 4:1-9

Though writing from prison and facing an uncertain future, Paul calls on the Philippians to rejoice and give thanks to God no matter what the circumstance. God's peace is with us and binds together our hearts and minds in Jesus Christ, especially when things around us do not seem peaceful.

Matthew 22:1-14

Jesus tells a parable indicating that the blessings of God's kingdom are available to all, but the invitation is not to be taken lightly.

Semicontinuous Reading and Psalm

Exodus 32:1-14

After Israel sinned by worshiping the golden calf, Moses interceded with God to spare Israel, lest the Egyptians conclude that God had evil intents in the exodus. Moses reminds God of the promises God made to Israel's matriarchs and patriarchs.

Psalm 106:1-6, 19-23

Remember, O LORD, the favor you have for your people. (Ps. 106:4)

Preface   Sundays

Color   Green

Prayers of Intercession

The prayers are prepared locally for each occasion. The following examples may be adapted or used as appropriate.

With confidence in God's grace and mercy, let us pray for the church, the world, and all those in need.

A brief silence.

Gracious host, fill your church with a spirit of joyous hospitality. We pray for bishops, teachers, church leaders, and all children of God as they invite others to your table of boundless grace. Lord, in your mercy,

hear our prayer.

Gracious host, as creation waits with eager longing for redemption, protect your creatures that are mistreated. Restore valleys, mountains and pastures, and still and running waters. Lord, in your mercy,

hear our prayer.

Gracious host, as you set a table in the presence of enemies, so bless the efforts of diplomats, international peace workers, and world leaders who navigate conflict. May they proceed with dialogue and understanding, so that justice and peace prevails. Lord, in your mercy,

hear our prayer.

Gracious host, let your gentleness be known among those who are weary or ill (*especially*). Strengthen doctors, medical care workers, and caretakers who see to their needs. Lord, in your mercy,

hear our prayer.

Gracious host, when we are quick to judge outward appearance, remind us how you clothe all in your mercy. We pray for ministries that provide needed clothing and other personal care assistance in this community (*local ministries can be named*). Lord, in your mercy,

hear our prayer.

Here other intercessions may be offered.

Gracious host, as we remember those who have died and are gathered at the heavenly banquet, comfort us with your presence. Assure us of your peace at all times. Lord, in your mercy, **hear our prayer.**

Listen as we call on you, O God, and enfold in your loving arms all for whom we pray, in the name of Jesus Christ our Lord. **Amen.**

Ideas for the Day

- *Christian Century* published an article in 2015 entitled "Reading the Parable of the Great Banquet in Prison" by Chris Hoke. In the article, Hoke describes his time leading a Bible study in prison. One particularly enthusiastic member of the study brought guys from every cell one night because he found the story of Christianity so infectious and was eager to share the good news with as many of his fellow inmates as possible. This parable was the focus of the night's study. When an inmate read the parable aloud, there was considerable anger in the room regarding the guest's banishment to the outer darkness. The discussion that followed offered a novel perspective on this tricky parable. Read it at christiancentury.org/article/2015-01/reading-parable-prison.

- Psalm 23 is so woven into the fabric of our world as a funeral psalm that it can be hard to separate it from that context. Today we are invited to hear the psalm in light of the wedding banquet described in the gospel. The verse "You prepare a table before me in the presence of my enemies" (23:5) evokes a great banquet table spread out in front of the psalmist but also in front of the psalmist's enemies. What does it mean to have a table spread for us in front of our enemies? Does it show that the enemies are excluded from the feast—or that they are welcome to join us? Is the feast a means to seek reconciliation through a shared meal? How do we wrestle with this meal in front of (or with) our enemies today?

- Consider having the assembly commune one another today. Depending on the configuration of your worship space and the size of your assembly, everyone can gather around the table together and pass the bread and wine to one another, or everyone can form a circle around the perimeter of the worship space and pass the bread and wine around, each person communing the person next to them. Be creative in your distribution practice today, and let people experience this banquet feast in a new way.

Connections with Creation

Biblical texts about feasts and banquets communicate a dual message about abundance: God's love and care for God's people is overflowing and generous, and God's creative energy working in and through the natural world aims to provide plentiful amounts of food for all. Paradoxically, to be in the role of hosting a feast puts God in a vulnerable position of being dependent on the health and functioning of the natural world, and on humankind's successful stewardship of the food-bearing lands. When we read these passages in Psalm 23 and Matthew 22, we are reminded of our need to live in right relationship with the bountiful farms, gardens, vineyards, pasturelands, nutrient-rich soil, and laborers who tend the land, so that God's abundance might be tasted and seen in a world where many experience scarcities of opportunity, community, and the basic physical necessities of life.

Let the Children Come

Who is invited to the banquet? Jesus' parables invite us to look again at our table hospitality. Who is invited to the table? How are children welcomed to the feast? Show children how to hold their hands to receive the bread and guide them in your assembly's practice of receiving the wine. Are communion ministers prepared to offer a blessing for children who do not yet commune? For children who do commune, it may be necessary for the communion minister to kneel down to the height of the child. Have communion ministers been trained to expect and graciously manage mishaps during the serving? Wine spills, bread falls, someone gets bumped. As with meals at home, the feasting is not ended, the mess is eventually cleaned up, all is well. Anticipate a response to various mishaps so that communicants of all ages feel cared for rather than embarrassed or shamed.

Assembly Song
Gathering

Oh, that I had a thousand voices   ELW 833, LBW 560

O day of rest and gladness   ELW 521, LBW 251

We Are Called   ELW 720, W&P 147, LS 37

Psalmody and Acclamations

Mayernik, Luke. "Twenty-Eighth Sunday in Ordinary Time A" from 5GP.

Pishner, Stephen. "Twenty-Eighth Sunday in Ordinary Time (A)" from *Cry Out with Joy, Year A*. GIA G-8481.

+   Mummert, Mark. "Psalm 106:1-6, 19-23" from PSCY.

(GA) Iona Community (Scotland). "Alleluia 1" from *Come All You People*. U/SATB. GIA G-4391. Use ELW psalm tone 1 with verse for Lectionary 28.

Hymn of the Day

Now we join in celebration   ELW 462, LBW 203   *SCHMÜCKE DICH*

The peace of the Lord/La paz del Señor   ELW 646, LLC 471
   LA PAZ DEL SEÑOR

Where cross the crowded ways of life   ELW 719, LBW 429
   WALTON

+ = semicontinuous psalm

Offering

Let us go now to the banquet/Vamos todos al banquete
ELW 523, LLC 410

The trumpets sound, the angels sing ELW 531, W&P 139

Communion

Come and fill our hearts/Confitemini Domino ELW 528

Soul, adorn yourself with gladness/Vengo a ti, Jesús amado
ELW 488/489, LLC 388, LBW 224

United at the table/Unidos en las fiesta ELW 498, LLC 408

Sending

God be with us till we meet again ELW 536, TFF 157

Sent forth by God's blessing ELW 547, LBW 221

Additional Assembly Songs

Grains of wheat/Una espiga WOV 708, LLC 392

To the banquet, come LS 106

Today we all are called to be disciples GTG 757

⊕ Bell, John L. "God's Table (Since the World Was Young)" from *Heaven Shall Not Wait*. U, pno. GIA G-3646S.

⊕ La Misa Popular Nicaragüense. "Somos pueblo que camina/We Are People on a Journey" from *Sing! A New Creation*. U. Faith Alive 9781562128111. Also LLC 393.

☼ Fox, Kip. "You Set a Table" from *Unheard*, vol. 1. kipfox.com.

☼ Glover, Ben/Ben McDonald/Dave Frey. "Come to the Table" from CCLI.

☼ Lawson, Jeff. "Come to the Feast" from CCLI.

☼ McCracken, Sandra/Matthew Smith/Albert Midlane. "All Things Are Ready" from *Hiding Place*. matthewsmith.bandcamp.com.

☼ Moore, Joshua/Sandra McCracken. "We Will Feast in the House of Zion" from CCLI.

☼ Paris, Flo. "Wedding Banquet" from CCLI.

Music for the Day
Choral

P Berger, Jean. "Speak to One Another of Psalms." SATB, a cap. AFP 9780800652647.

P Culli, Benjamin. "Heart and Voice to Heaven Raise." SATB, org, br qrt, assembly. AFP 9781451479362.

P Keesecker, Thomas. "Around You, O Lord Jesus." SAB, pno, opt hb. AFP 9780800664336.

P White, David Ashley. "No More a Stranger or a Guest." 2 pt mxd, C instr, hb or kybd. SEL 410-833.

Children's Choir

Bach, J. S./Hal H. Hopson. "All the Earth Sing Forth." CG CGA889.

P Comer, Marilyn. "Psalm 23" from *ChildrenSing Psalms*. U, kybd, assembly. AFP 9780800663872.

P Patterson, Mark. "Sing, Rejoice, Clap Your Hands" from *Young ChildrenSing*. U, kybd. AFP 9780800676803.

Keyboard / Instrumental

♫ Bach, J. S. "Schmücke dich, o liebe Seele" from *Leipzig Chorales*. Various editions.

P Cherwien, David. "Rejoice, Ye Pure in Heart!" from *We Sing of God: Hymn Settings for Organ*. Org. AFP 9780806698052.

♫ Rodriguez, Penny. "Germany" from *He Leadeth Me: Ten Hymn Arrangement for Piano*. Pno. MSM 15-840.

P Schelat, David. "Around You, O Lord Jesus" from *Children of the Heavenly Father: Organ Settings of Scandinavian Tunes*. Org (no pedal). AFP 9781451451733.

Handbell

Angerman, David. "A Call to Celebration." 3-5 oct, L3. CG CGB629.

♫ Buckwalter, Karen. "Songs for the Feast." 4-5 oct, L4-. BP HB192.

Dobrinski, Cynthia. "Celebration." 3-5 oct, L1. HOP 1619.

Monday, October 12, 2020
Day of Thanksgiving (Canada)

See Day of Thanksgiving (USA), pp. 313–315.

Thursday, October 15
Teresa of Avila, teacher, renewer of the church, died 1582

Teresa of Avila (AH-vee-la) is also known as Teresa de Jesús. She chose the life of a Carmelite nun after reading the letters of Jerome. Frequently sick during her early years as a nun, she found that when she was sick her prayer life flowered, but when she was well it withered. Steadily her life of faith and prayer deepened, and she grew to have a lively sense of God's presence with her. She worked to reform her monastic community in Ávila, which she believed had strayed from its original purpose. Her reforms asked nuns to maintain life in the monastic enclosure without leaving it and to identify with those who are poor by not wearing shoes. Teresa's writings on devotional life have enjoyed a wide readership.

⊕ = global song   ♫ = relates to hymn of the day
☼ = praise song   P = available in Prelude Music Planner

Saturday, October 17
Ignatius, Bishop of Antioch, martyr, died around 115

Ignatius was the second bishop of Antioch in Syria. It was there that the name "Christian" was first used to describe the followers of Jesus. Ignatius is known to us through his letters. In them he encouraged Christians to live in unity sustained with love while standing firm on sound doctrine. Ignatius believed Christian martyrdom was a privilege. When his own martyrdom approached, he wrote in one of his letters, "I prefer death in Christ Jesus to power over the farthest limits of the earth.... Do not stand in the way of my birth to real life." Ignatius and all martyrs are a reminder that even today Christians face death because of their faith in Jesus.

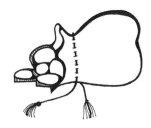

October 18, 2020
Time after Pentecost — Lectionary 29

In today's first reading God uses the Gentile ruler Cyrus to accomplish divine purposes. When the Pharisees try to trap Jesus, he tells them to give the emperor what belongs to him and to God what belongs to God. To gather for worship reminds us that our ultimate allegiance is to God rather than to any earthly authority. Created in the image of God, we offer our entire selves in the service of God and for the sake of the world.

Prayer of the Day

Sovereign God, raise your throne in our hearts. Created by you, let us live in your image; created for you, let us act for your glory; redeemed by you, let us give you what is yours, through Jesus Christ, our Savior and Lord.

Gospel Acclamation

Alleluia. Shine like stars in the world; holding fast to the word of life. *Alleluia.* (Phil. 2:15, 16)

Readings and Psalm
Isaiah 45:1-7

The prophet announces that Cyrus the Persian emperor is the one the LORD has anointed to end Israel's exile. The LORD makes this choice so that the whole world will recognize this LORD as the only God. Persia had a god of light and a god of darkness; the LORD claims sovereignty over both light and darkness.

Psalm 96:1-9 [10-13]

Ascribe to the LORD honor and power. (Ps. 96:7)

1 Thessalonians 1:1-10

Most likely this letter is the first written by Paul. Paul gives pastoral encouragement and reassurances to new Christians living in an antagonistic environment. Their commitment of faith, love, and hope makes them a model for other new Christian communities.

Matthew 22:15-22

After Jesus begins teaching in the temple, religious leaders try to trap him with questions. First they ask if God's people should pay taxes to an earthly tyrant like Caesar.

Semicontinuous Reading and Psalm
Exodus 33:12-23

Moses successfully interceded with God to accompany Israel to the promised land after their sin with the golden calf. In response to a request to display the divine glory, God recites a sentence that appears frequently in the Hebrew Scriptures: "I will be gracious to whom I will be gracious." Moses is not allowed to see God's face, but only God's back.

Psalm 99

Proclaim the greatness of the LORD our God. (Ps. 99:5)

Preface   Sundays

Color   Green

Prayers of Intercession

The prayers are prepared locally for each occasion. The following examples may be adapted or used as appropriate.
With confidence in God's grace and mercy, let us pray for the church, the world, and all those in need.
A brief silence.
Gracious God, you call us by name and invite us to share your good news. Send your Holy Spirit among preachers, missionaries, and evangelists. We give thanks for the witness of your

servant Luke, the evangelist, whom the church commemorates today. Lord, in your mercy,
hear our prayer.

God of praise, the heavens and all creation declare your salvation. From the rising of the sun to its setting, may the whole universe show forth your goodness. Raise up devoted stewards of all that you have made. Lord, in your mercy,
hear our prayer.

God of all, may your word of justice sound forth in every place. Restore divided nations and communities with reconciling truth. Lord, in your mercy,
hear our prayer.

God of light, we pray for those living with pain, illness, isolation, grief, anger, or doubt (*especially*). Join their voices in a new song, assuring them that you call them each by name. Lord, in your mercy,
hear our prayer.

God of truth, you show no partiality. May your spirit guide the work of justices, magistrates, court officials, and all vocations of the law, that your promise of restoration may be known. Lord, in your mercy,
hear our prayer.

Here other intercessions may be offered.

Living God, as you raised Jesus from the dead, so raise up those who have died in you (*especially*). We give thanks for their witness, confident of your rescuing welcome for all. Lord, in your mercy,
hear our prayer.

Listen as we call on you, O God, and enfold in your loving arms all for whom we pray, in the name of Jesus Christ, our Lord.
Amen.

Ideas for the Day

- Invite worshipers to reflect on ways in which they offer themselves to God not only through their monetary offerings but through their gifts and talents. Ask people to write down gifts on colorful sticky notes, specifically gifts that they use to glorify God. Then ask them to post the notes on a designated wall in the worship space as a reminder that our offerings are not just monetary but are manifold. This visual reminder may help people see that we give back to God what God has first given to us, and this includes our time and spiritual gifts, in addition to money.

- In your gathering space display percentages of the federal budget artistically, through jars of pennies filled according to percentages, fundraising-style thermometers drawn on paper with amounts colored in, or other creative visual aids. This display could also be part of an advocacy campaign by having a letter template for people to write to elected officials encouraging a more just distribution of tax dollars toward the most vulnerable in our society.

Various online sources provide current budget information for the United States and Canada.

- The psalmist encourages us to sing a new song to praise the Lord. The hymn "Earth and all stars!" (ELW 731) has expanded this idea of new songs to "classrooms and labs," "loud clashing cymbals," and many other illustrations. Have your congregation engage on social media with ways they see creation praising God this week. Examples can be like those of the psalmist, such as singing trees and roaring seas, or like those in the hymn, created by human beings but still used to praise God in our daily vocations. Have people share pictures or stories of where they see God being praised in unexpected places and through unexpected means.

- Paul tells the Thessalonians that he prays for them by name, and the prophet Isaiah shares that God calls people by name. Names are an important part of our identity. Have everyone who is at worship today write their name on a piece of paper and place it in a basket on their way in to worship. Then have them draw a name (not their own) on their way out. Invite the assembly to commit to pray by name throughout the week for the person whose name they drew.

Connections with Creation

What might it sound like for all the earth to sing a new song unto God, as the psalmist declares in Psalm 96? Evolutionary biology teaches us that life is always being made new through processes such as natural selection and random genetic drift. Geology reveals the ways in which the earth's physical structure has changed over billions of years. Our universe is never static; it is always transforming. With each new species of microbe, plant, and animal, the creation sings a new song unto God. As human beings, we, too, are a part of this ever-changing song of praise. As we sing alongside all these creatures, we realize that our lives are interdependent with the natural world and all its inhabitants. We learn to value the beautiful music created by this chorus of rich harmonies and varied melodies, and we give thanks to God for that which is God's: the whole universe and all within it.

Let the Children Come

How can we involve children in the time of offering? Encouraging them to put money in the offering plate is the beginning of a good discipline, but unless the children have earned the money, they may have less of a sense of what it means to give it away. As more worshipers make their financial contributions electronically and fewer bring a physical offering envelope to worship, it may appear to children that not much is being given. Some congregations provide cards in the pews that can be placed in the offering plate indicating a gift has been made electronically. Others encourage worshipers to place a hand of blessing on the plate as it passes to represent both electronic giving and the giving of resources like time and skill. Today's gospel allows us to consider how the ritual action of giving an offering becomes translated into giving "to God the things that are God's" (Matt. 22:21).

Assembly Song
Gathering

God is here! ELW 526, WOV 719

Sing praise to God, the highest good ELW 871, LBW 542

The God of Abraham praise ELW 831, LBW 544

Psalmody and Acclamations

Becker, John W. "Psalm 96:1-9 [10-13]" from PWA.

Haugen, Marty. "Give the Lord Glory and Honor" from TLP:A.

Shute, Linda Cable. "Psalm 96," Refrain 2, from PSCY.

+ Messner, Sally. "Psalm 99" from PWA.

(GA) Iona Community (Scotland). "Alleluia 1" from *Come All You People*. U/SATB. GIA G-4391. Use ELW psalm tone 1 with verse for Lectionary 29.

Hymn of the Day

Lift every voice and sing ELW 841, TFF 296, LBW 562
    LIFT EVERY VOICE AND SING

O God of every nation ELW 713 LLANGLOFFAN LBW 416
    TUOLUMNE

When our song says peace ELW 709 JENKINS

Offering

For the fruit of all creation ELW 679, WOV 760, LBW 563

We give thee but thine own ELW 686, LBW 410

Communion

Here is bread ELW 483, W&P 58

O bread of life from heaven ELW 480, LBW 222

Lord, Be Glorified ELW 744, TFF 248, W&P 89

Sending

You servants of God ELW 825, LBW 252

Your will be done/Mayenziwe ELW 741, TFF 243

Additional Assembly Songs

Give thanks TFF 292, W&P 41

God of Abraham and Sarah NCH 20

To Abraham and Sarah GTG 51

⊕ Nkuinji, Abel/trans. S. T. Kimbrough, Jr. "Tout est fait pour la gloire de Dieu/All Is Done for the Glory" from *Global Praise 3*. SATB. GBGMusik 9781890569877.

⊕ Maung, Sang. Myanmar traditional melody. "God of Region and of World" from *Sound the Bamboo*. STB. GIA G-6830.

☼ Evans, Anthony/Myron Butler. "You Deserve" from CCLI.

☼ Ivey, Aaron/Chris McClarney/Jason Ingram. "Everything and Nothing Less" from CCLI.

☼ Johnson, Aaron/Evan John/Ryan Williams/Wesley Schrock. "World Needs Jesus" from CCLI.

☼ Kull, Dave/Debora Sita/Dominik Laim. "Live Victorious" from CCLI.

☼ Ligertwood, Brooke/Joel Houston/Scott Ligertwood. "Valentine" from CCLI.

☼ Valenzuela, Aimee/Kristi Taylor/Krystle Tumlinson/Lane Oliver/Rachel Magee. "I Surrender" from CCLI.

Music for the Day
Choral

♫ Johnson, James Weldon/arr. Allen Pote. "Lift Every Voice and Sing." SAB, pno. HOP 7297.

Pärt, Arvo. "Tribute to Ceasar" SATB, a cap. Universal Edition 31137.

P Sedio, Mark. "Take My Life, That I May Be" from *Augsburg Easy Choirbook*, vol. 2. SAB, pno, fl, perc, opt gtr. AFP 9780800677510.

P Sweelinck, Jan Pieterszoon. "Sing to the Lord, New Songs Be Raising" from *Chantry Choirbook: Sacred Music for All Seasons*. SATB, a cap. AFP 9780800657772.

Children's Choir

P Benson, Robert A. "What Shall We Give to God?" from *ChildrenSing in Worship*, vol. 3. U, kybd, opt desc or C inst. AFP 9781451462548.

Pergolesi, Giovanni/Michael Burkhardt. "Sing to the Lord God." U, kybd, C inst. MSM 50-9451.

Yarrington, John. "Sing Praise and Hallelujah!" U, desc, kybd. MSM 50-7063.

Keyboard / Instrumental

♫ Burkhardt, Michael. "Festival March" from *The Balboa Park Organ Suite: A Celebration of Many Peoples*. Org. MSM 10-710.

P Hamilton, Gregory. "We Raise Our Hands to You, O Lord" from *Piano Stylings on Hymn Tunes*. Pno. AFP 9781451486094.

P Kim, Marianne. "O God beyond All Praising" from *My Soul Proclaims: Piano Meditations for Worship*. Pno. AFP 9781451499131.

P♫ Pelz, Walter L. "Bless Now, O God, the Journey" from *A Walter Pelz Organ Anthology*. Org. AFP 9781506448039.

Handbell

♫ Smith, Vicki. "Lift Every Voice and Sing." 3-5 oct, L3. CPH 976943.

♫ Page, Anna Laura. "Rejoice, Rejoice, Believers." 3-5 oct, L3. CG CGB642.

Phillips. Judy. "Dove of Peace." 3-6 oct, L3+. GIA G-7292.

⊕ = global song   ♫ = relates to hymn of the day   + = semicontinuous psalm
☼ = praise song   P = available in Prelude Music Planner

Sunday, October 18
Luke, Evangelist

St. Luke is identified by tradition as the author of both Luke and Acts. Luke is careful to place the events of Jesus' life in both their social and religious contexts. Some of the most loved parables, including the good Samaritan and the prodigal son, are found only in this gospel. Luke's gospel has also given the church some of its most beautiful songs: the Benedictus sung at morning prayer, the Magnificat sung at evening prayer, and the Nunc dimittis sung at the close of the day. These songs are powerful witnesses to the message of Jesus Christ.

Friday, October 23
James of Jerusalem, martyr, died around 62

James became an early leader of the church in Jerusalem. He is described in the New Testament as the brother of Jesus, and secular historian Josephus calls James the brother of Jesus, "the so-called Christ." Little is known about James, but Josephus reported that the Pharisees respected James for his piety and observance of the law. His enemies had him put to death.

October 25, 2020
Reformation Sunday

Rooted in the past and growing into the future, the church must always be reformed in order to live out the love of Christ in an ever-changing world. We celebrate the good news of God's grace, that Jesus Christ sets us free every day to do this life-transforming work. Trusting in the freedom given to us in baptism, we pray for the church, that Christians will unite more fully in worship and mission.

Prayer of the Day

Almighty God, gracious Lord, we thank you that your Holy Spirit renews the church in every age. Pour out your Holy Spirit on your faithful people. Keep them steadfast in your word, protect and comfort them in times of trial, defend them against all enemies of the gospel, and bestow on the church your saving peace, through Jesus Christ, our Savior and Lord, who lives and reigns with you and the Holy Spirit, one God, now and forever.
or
Gracious Father, we pray for your holy catholic church. Fill it with all truth and peace. Where it is corrupt, purify it; where it is in error, direct it; where in anything it is amiss, reform it; where it is right, strengthen it; where it is in need, provide for it; where it is divided, reunite it; for the sake of your Son, Jesus Christ, our Savior, who lives and reigns with you and the Holy Spirit, one God, now and forever.

Gospel Acclamation

Alleluia. If you continue in my word, you are truly my disciples, and you will know the truth, and the truth will make you free. *Alleluia.* (John 8:31-32)

Readings and Psalm
Jeremiah 31:31-34

The renewed covenant will not be breakable, but like the old covenant it will expect the people to live upright lives. To know the LORD means that one will defend the cause of the poor and needy (Jer. 22:16). The renewed covenant is possible only because the LORD will forgive iniquity and not remember sin. Our hope lies in a God who forgets.

Psalm 46

The LORD of hosts is with us; the God of Jacob is our stronghold. (Ps. 46:7)

Romans 3:19-28

Paul's words stand at the heart of the preaching of Martin Luther and other Reformation leaders. No human beings make themselves right with God through works of the law. We are brought into a right relationship with God through the divine activity centered in Christ's death. This act is a gift of grace that liberates us from sin and empowers our faith in Jesus Christ.

John 8:31-36

Jesus speaks of truth and freedom as spiritual realities known through his word. He reveals the truth that sets people free from sin.

Preface Sundays

Color Red

Prayers of Intercession

*The prayers are prepared locally for each occasion. The following
examples may be adapted or used as appropriate.*

With confidence in God's grace and mercy, let us pray for the
church, the world, and all those in need.

A brief silence.

Renew and inspire the church in the freedom of the gospel, O
God. Where the church is in error, reform it. Where the church
speaks your truth, strengthen it. Where the church is divided,
unify it. Ignite in us the working of the Holy Spirit. Lord, in
your mercy,

hear our prayer.

As the earth changes, as mountains shake and the waters roar,
may we care for this planet as a holy habitation for all living
things. Sustain all peoples and lands recovering from natural
disasters of any kind (*especially*). Lord, in your mercy,

hear our prayer.

Guide areas of the world divided or traumatized by conflict,
especially in our own land. Free all from slavery and human
trafficking, and protect all in harm's way. Lord, in your mercy,

hear our prayer.

Release those living in bondage to debts, chronic pain, or addiction. Grant healing touch to those who are ill (*especially*). Lord,
in your mercy,

hear our prayer.

In this family of faith we give thanks for courageous voices that
have remained firm in their commitment to the one who frees
us from sin and death. Centered in your grace, unify us in the
hope of the gospel. Lord, in your mercy,

hear our prayer.

Here other intercessions may be offered.

Even in death, you free us and give us a place in your house.
We give thanks for our ancestors who have shown us truth and
freedom, especially Martin Luther and those who work for the
renewal of the church. Lord, in your mercy,

hear our prayer.

Listen as we call on you, O God, and enfold in your loving arms
all for whom we pray, in the name of Jesus Christ, our Lord.

Amen.

Ideas for the Day

- On Reformation Sunday we celebrate the power of God's
grace to reform and reshape. The great twentieth-century
theologian Karl Barth said, "The church must always be
reformed"—a phrase often shortened to the Latin *semper
reformanda*. Rather than looking only to the past, invite
your assembly to consider the work of *continuing* reformation in the present. Explore the current call to reformation on several levels—in their personal lives and relationships, in your church and the church at large, and in your
community and society. Where might God's grace reform
us again?

- For Lutherans, Reformation Sunday carries a special
temptation toward triumphalism. Buoyed by the tale of
Martin Luther's defiant posting of the 95 Theses, our songs
and proclamations meant to praise God's grace can easily be redirected toward praising Lutheranism. One way
to move beyond this conundrum is to explore the broader
story of the renewal of the church in the sixteenth century:
by Zwingli in Switzerland, among Anabaptists, or in the
Jesuit or Carmelite orders of the Catholic Church. Keep
your celebration more honest by inviting special ecumenical guests from other denominations to join or lead your
worship this day, or ask your assembly to invite friends of
different denominations or religions to attend with them.

- In John's gospel Jesus proclaims, "You will know the truth,
and the truth will make you free" (John 8:32). Much of
what is admired about Martin Luther, among both Lutherans and others, is the image of his courage in standing up
for what he believed—a truth that was uncomfortable and
inconvenient, especially to powerful people in his own
time. We might do well to remember that Luther's arguments against indulgences were not solely theological but
had a strong component of social justice for the poor who
were the frequent victims of such sales. God's truth sets
free both souls and bodies. In our own time, businesses
offering payday loans, reverse mortgages, and subprime
housing loans often intentionally play on the hopes and
fears of those living in poverty to take advantage of them
for the benefit of the rich. On this Reformation Sunday,
how might the gospel truth invite us to set people free in
body as well as spirit?

Connections with Creation

The psalmist writes with confidence that God is our refuge
and help even in the midst of powerful and destructive natural
disasters. The earth is a bounteous planet, but it can also be
a dangerous place to live. The earth quakes and wars rage. In
a time when climate change is causing more frequent, severe
storms and warming global temperatures, we know that more
extreme weather events are on the way. Yet if we can be still and
pay close attention, we will be able to discern the presence of
God at work for the good of people and the planet. On this Sunday when we celebrate the importance of reform in our church,
we can be encouraged by the psalmist's faith in a God who calls
us to be a part of the change that God envisions for the world.

Let the Children Come

Each year we celebrate the work of Martin Luther, for whom
the Lutheran Church was named. Luther translated the Bible
into a language that the people around him could understand.
He also wrote a lot of hymns. One of Luther's hymns that we
often sing on this day is "A mighty fortress is our God" (ELW
503–505). Show children where in *Evangelical Lutheran*

Worship they can find this hymn. The words of this hymn are based on today's psalm, Psalm 46. Show them where to find Psalm 46 in *Evangelical Lutheran Worship* and then read the first verse: "God is our refuge and strength, a very present help in trouble." Saying (or singing) "A mighty fortress is our God" is like saying "God is our refuge and strength." Invite the assembly to check the source index (p. 1191) and count how many hymns by Luther are in *Evangelical Lutheran Worship*.

Assembly Song
Gathering

A mighty fortress is our God   ELW 503–505, LLC 403, LBW 228/229

Built on a rock   ELW 652, LBW 365

Christ is made the sure foundation   ELW 645, WOV 747, LBW 367

Psalmody and Acclamations

Cherwien, David. "Psalm 46: God Is Our Refuge." U, assembly, org. MSM 80-800.

The Lord of hosts is with us/Psalm 46   TFF 6

Mummert, Mark. "Psalm 46." SATB, org, assembly. AFP 9781451462449.

(GA) Iona Community (Scotland). "Alleluia 1" from *Come All You People*. U/SATB. GIA G-4391. Use ELW psalm tone 1 with verse for Reformation.

Hymn of the Day

Amazing grace, how sweet the sound   ELW 779, LLC 437, LBW 448   *NEW BRITAIN*

Lord, keep us steadfast in your word   ELW 517, LLC 399, LBW 230   *ERHALT UNS, HERR*

That priceless grace   ELW 591, TFF 68   *THAT PRICELESS GRACE*

Offering

Father, we thank you   ELW 478, WOV 704

Praise, praise! You are my rock   ELW 862, sts. 1, 4; ASG 33, sts. 1, 4

Communion

Although I speak with angel's tongue   ELW 644

O Lord, we praise you   ELW 499, LBW 215

Wash, O God, our sons and daughters   ELW 445, WOV 697, TFF 112

Sending

How firm a foundation   ELW 796, LS 80, LBW 507

Rise, O church, like Christ arisen   ELW 548, OBS 76

Additional Assembly Songs

Here on Jesus Christ I will stand/Kwake Yesu nasimama   GTG 832

Renew your church   NCH 311

Tú diste a Israel/God, with a mighty hand   LLC 476

⊕ Come now, O Prince of peace/Ososŏ, ososŏ   ELW 247, LS 13

⊕ Anon., Latin America. "Somos uno/We Are One" from *Tenemos Esperanza/We Have Hope*. U, pno. GBGMusik 1890569453.

☼ Brumley, Albert E./Crystal Yates/Drew Ley/Joshua Sherman/ Micah Tyler/The Emerging Sound. "What Mercy Did for Me" from CCLI.

☼ Fielding, Ben/Reuben Morgan. "Who You Say I Am" from CCLI.

☼ Korocz, Daniel/Jordi White. "Free Indeed" from CCLI.

☼ Marcus, Andrew/Scott Cash. "We Are Redeemed" from CCLI.

☼ Santistevan, David/Jesse Denaro. "Beautiful Mystery" from CCLI.

☼ Wilmot, Carol. "Free Indeed" from *Know the Truth*. foursquareworship.org.

Music for the Day
Choral

P Betinis, Abbie. "Blessed Be the Lord, My Rock" from *Augsburg Motet Book*. SAB, a cap. AFP 9781451423709.

♫ Hayes, Mark. "How Sweet the Sound." SATB, pno, bass, drm, perc, sax. LO 10/3434M.

P Highben, Zebulon. "God Alone Be Praised: Ad Lucem." SAB, pno, vln or ob, assembly. AFP 9781506447209.

Wesby, Roger. "Come, Holy Spirit, Come." SATB, a cap. wesbymusicworks.com.

Children's Choir

P Bedford, Michael. "Be Still and Know That I Am God" from *Two Psalms for Young Singers*. U, pno, opt hb. CG CGA1140.

Bertalot, John. "God Is Our Hope." 2 pt, kybd. CG CGA444.

P Patterson, Mark. "Psalm 46" from *ChildrenSing Psalms*. U or 2 pt, kybd. AFP 9780800663872.

Keyboard / Instrumental

P ♫ Organ, Anne Krentz. "Lord, Keep Us Steadfast in Your Word" from *Piano Reflections on Chorale Tunes*. Pno. AFP 9781506413716.

Ore, Charles. "A Mighty Fortress" from *Eleven Compositions for Organ*, set VIII. Org. CPH 977287.

♫ Proulx, Richard. "New Britian" from *Still More Intonations*, vol. VIII. Org. SEL 160-728.

P Shaw, Timothy. "The Solid Rock" from *Hymn Settings for the Year: 55 Piano Gems*. Pno. AFP 9781506413693.

⊕ = global song   ♫ = relates to hymn of the day
☼ = praise song   P = available in Prelude Music Planner

Handbell

♩ Delancy, Lauran. "Reformation Ringing." 3 or 5 oct, L2+. CPH 977683.

♩ Moklebust, Cathy. "Amazing Grace" from *Easy Favorites for the Handbell Soloist.* 3-4 oct, pno. CG CGB862.

Sherman, Arnold. "A Mighty Fortress Is Our God." 3-6 oct, L4. HOP 2112.

October 25, 2020
Time after Pentecost — Lectionary 30

Jesus' summary of the law in today's gospel echoes our first reading from Leviticus. We are called not only to love God with heart, soul, and mind, but also to love our neighbor as ourselves. It is out of such deep care that Paul shares the gospel with the Thessalonian community. In the confession of sins, we acknowledge that we have not loved God, neighbor, and self; yet we gather to hear the word of forgiveness and to be strengthened by word and meal to be signs of God's love and mercy in the world.

Prayer of the Day

O Lord God, you are the holy lawgiver, you are the salvation of your people. By your Spirit renew us in your covenant of love, and train us to care tenderly for all our neighbors, through Jesus Christ, our Savior and Lord.

Gospel Acclamation

Alleluia. Beloved, since God loved us so much, we also ought to love one another. *Alleluia.* (1 John 4:11)

Readings and Psalm

Leviticus 19:1-2, 15-18

The Holiness Code in Leviticus urges people to be holy because God is holy. Holiness is lived out as God's people exercise justice and love in their dealings with one another. We are to love our neighbors as ourselves.

Psalm 1

Their delight is in the law of the Lord. (Ps. 1:2)

1 Thessalonians 2:1-8

Paul uses intimate maternal imagery to depict the caring and nurturing relationship he shares with the Thessalonian Christians. When he first came to their city it was not to benefit himself but to share the gospel with them, which was his responsibility as an apostle of Christ.

Matthew 22:34-46

Put on the spot by the Pharisees, Jesus displays wisdom by summarizing the law of God in just two commandments and by demonstrating the Messiah must be more than the son of David.

Semicontinuous Reading and Psalm

Deuteronomy 34:1-12

Moses was not allowed to enter the promised land, but he was granted the right to see it from Mount Nebo before he died. The statement that no prophet has arisen in Israel like Moses (34:10) stands in tension with Deuteronomy 18:15 (God will "raise up for you a prophet like me") and led to the expectation that another Moses would still come. In several New Testament passages Jesus is identified as that prophet.

Psalm 90:1-6, 13-17

Show your servants your works, and your splendor to their children. (Ps. 90:16)

Preface   Sundays

Color   Green

Prayers of Intercession

The prayers are prepared locally for each occasion. The following examples may be adapted or used as appropriate.

With confidence in God's grace and mercy, let us pray for the church, the world, and all those in need.

A brief silence.

In your love, you speak to your church. Give courage and the bond of love to all who gather in your name, that this love turn toward our neighbors. Lord, in your mercy,

hear our prayer.

In your love, you create our earth filled with living things of every kind. Sustain the intricate connections among plants, insects, animals, and organisms we don't even know or recognize. Bless the work of scientists who help us extend neighbor love to the natural world. Lord, in your mercy,

hear our prayer.

In your love, you guide with justice. Inspire leaders for truthful conversations and wise policies, that decisions are made for the good of all. Lord, in your mercy,

hear our prayer.

In your love, you tenderly care for your children and nurse them to health. Bring relief to all those who need healing, hope, or restoration this day (*especially*). Lord, in your mercy,

hear our prayer.

In your love, you accompany us in life's transitions. We pray for new parents, those grieving a loss, those who are retiring, and those embarking on new ventures. Lord, in your mercy,

hear our prayer.

Here other intercessions may be offered.

In your love, we remember those who were dear to us and now rest in you. We give thanks for Martin Luther and all who seek to reform and renew your church. Give us courage to live out your gospel, revealing your love until our days on earth have ended. Lord, in your mercy,

hear our prayer.

Listen as we call on you, O God, and enfold in your loving arms all for whom we pray, in the name of Jesus Christ, our Lord.

Amen.

Ideas for the Day

- As both Leviticus and Matthew call us to love our neighbors as ourselves, it is worth pausing to think of what makes that so hard. Why do we show partiality? There are many things in our society that lull us into thinking that it is okay to make divisions among people and treat some better than others: race, socioeconomic status, professional titles, political party, sexual orientation, gender, grades, ability. Compose or modify a confession and forgiveness where we confess to God our failure to love our neighbors as ourselves. Enhance the word *neighbor* with pairings of words by which we often divide ourselves— male *and* female neighbors, Democrat *and* Republican neighbors, rich *and* poor neighbors, and so on.

- In a field of academic study known as post-colonial studies, scholars have pointed out the pervasive and harmful condescension by which European colonizers attempted to forcefully "civilize" people indigenous to the places they "discovered." These critiques have much to say to the ways our congregations continue to think about evangelism, outreach, and service to populations we perceive as different from ourselves. In 1 Thessalonians, Paul defends his own ethics of evangelism—rejecting force, flattery, and pretense. Evangelism and service should be carried out in ways that show love of our neighbors as ourselves. What

kinds of relationships does your assembly have with "others" served by its ministries? How do you challenge one another to love with the depth that Christ speaks of?

- Fundamentalism is pervasive in our contemporary situation—in Christianity, other religions, and politics. In an increasingly complex world, people yearn for clear and simple ways to understand what to believe and how to act. Fundamentalisms of all kinds falsely promise that a few basic beliefs held absolutely can remove the discomfort of ambiguity felt all around us. Yet when Jesus is asked about the fundamentals in today's gospel, he speaks only of love—toward God and others. Love does not remove complexity. It holds the ambiguity of every situation and the whole range of present needs and people involved. It is vulnerable, taking bold action, and even risking failure. This is the love that Christ showed us. It is the simple foundation that embraces the complexity of our whole lives as Christians. Among all the things you are doing as a congregation, how are you equipping your people in the challenging, yet fundamental, task of loving others?

Connections with Creation

Microbiology and ecology are teaching us the extent to which we are interdependent earth creatures. We are not merely individual humans; our bodies are communities made up of billions of tiny living organisms. Because we need food, water, and air to sustain our lives, we are dependent on the intricate and complex communities of microbes, plants, and animals that live with us on this planet. Therefore, we must see that Jesus' call for us to love our neighbors as ourselves is not merely a call to love our human neighbors. It is an ethical imperative that we also love our non-human neighbors who share Earth's ecosystems with us. The trees, bees, and bacteria are also our neighbors. In order to love these fellow earth neighbors, we might do well to give thanks for scientists, who help us appreciate the diversity of life in the natural world and who are learning to more fully identify and describe the connections, communication, and symbiotic relationships that foster life—including our own—on Earth.

Let the Children Come

Jewish tradition recognizes 613 commandments (or *mitzvot*)— including what we call the ten commandments—in the Torah (the first five books of the Bible). That is a lot of commandments! Illustrate how many with a jar containing 613 beads or dried beans or a sheet of paper with 613 dots on it. Like the ten commandments, some of the *mitzvot* focus on what to do, and some of them focus on what not to do. In today's gospel, Jesus tells us that the two most important commandments are to love God and to love our neighbor. Two things. Help the whole assembly learn these words by heart: "You shall love the Lord your God with all your heart, and with all your soul, and with all your mind.... You shall love your neighbor as yourself" (Matt. 22:37, 39). Add simple gestures as memory prompts if you wish.

Assembly Song
Gathering
Come, let us join our cheerful songs ELW 847, LBW 254
God is here! ELW 526, WOV 719
Lord Jesus Christ, be present now ELW 527, LBW 253

Psalmody and Acclamations
How happy are the saints of God/Psalm 1 GTG 457
Arnatt, Ronald. "Psalm 1." U or cant, assembly, kybd. ECS 5463.
+ True, Lori. "You Have Been Our Dwelling Place." Cant, SATB, assembly, kybd, gtr, C inst. GIA G-6067.
(GA) Iona Community (Scotland). "Alleluia 1" from *Come All You People*. U/SATB. GIA G-4391. Use ELW psalm tone 1 with verse for Lectionary 30.

Hymn of the Day
Great God, your love has called us ELW 358, WOV 666 *RYBURN*
Lord, thee I love with all my heart ELW 750, LBW 325
 HERZLICH LIEB
We Are Called ELW 720, W&P 147, LS 37 *WE ARE CALLED*

Offering
Come, ye thankful people, come ELW 693, LBW 407
We raise our hands to you, O Lord ELW 690

Communion
Spirit of God, descend upon my heart ELW 800, LBW 486
Ubi caritas et amor/Where true charity and love abide ELW 642, WOV 665
Where true charity and love abide/Ubi caritas et amor ELW 653

Sending
I love to tell the story ELW 661, TFF 228, LS 154, LBW 390
To be your presence ELW 546

Additional Assembly Songs
Today we are all called to be disciples GTG 757
By grace God calls us into life CBM 64
For the healing of the nations SP 12a
⊕ Bell, John L. "Behold, I Make All Things New" from *Come All You People*. SATB. GIA G-4391. Also SC 5
⊕ Samoan trad. "Faafetai I le Atua/Source of Life and All That's Living" from *Em Tua Graça*. SATB. WCC Publications 2825414492. Out of print. Hannelore.Schmid@wcc-coe.org.

☼ Armstrong, Matt/Micah Massey/Nate Moore/Ryan Flanigan. "Let Us Be Known by Our Love" from CCLI.
☼ Brewster, Lincoln. "Love the Lord" from CCLI.
☼ Ligertwood, Brooke/Marty Sampson. "Depths" from CCLI.
☼ Lindsey, Aaron/Israel Houghton/Tommy Sims. "Yahweh (The Lifter)" from CCLI.
☼ Mak Wai Yew, Adrian/Nathan de Jong/Samuel de Jong/Samuel Witherspoon. "All My Heart" from CCLI.
☼ Ogden, Jonathan. "You Saved My Soul" from *Take Everything*. riversandrobots.bandcamp.com.

Music for the Day
Choral
P Campbell, Jonathan D. "The Poor and the Refugee." SATB, a cap. AFP 9781506456881.
♫ Haas, David/arr. Mark Hayes. "We Are Called." SATB, pno, vln, perc. HOP C5896.
P Helman, Michael. "Love Your Neighbor." SATB, pno. AFP 9780800676247.
P Jennings, Carolyn. "Our Mission Bold and Blest." SATB, pno or org, trbl inst. AFP 9781451498950.

Children's Choir
P Burrows, Mark. "Do to Others" from *Again, I Say Rejoice!* U, pno or gtr. CG CGC56.
Butler, Donna. "Song of Peace." U/2 pt, kybd. SHW HL35028252.
P Mozart, W. A./Schram, Ruth Elaine. "To Love the Lord" from *ChildrenSing in Worship*, vol. 1. U/2 pt, kybd. AFP 9781451401806.

Keyboard / Instrumental
P ♫ Biery, Marilyn. "We Are Called" from *Gathered into One: Organ Settings of Contemporary Tunes*. Org. AFP 9781451486063.
Carter, John. "Jesu, Jesu, Fill Us with Your Love" from *Contemporary Hymns and Songs II for Piano/4 Hands*. Pno. HOP 8196.
♫ Costello, Michael. "Lord, Thee I Love with All My Heart" from *God Will Guide You: Five Hymn Arrangements for Organ*. Org. MSM 10-620.
P Shaw, Timothy. "Hyfrydol" from *Easy Hymns for the Church Pianist*, vol. 2. Pno. AFP 9781451494112.

Handbell
♫ Eithun, Sandra. "Lord, Thee I love with All My Heart." 3-6 oct hb or hc, opt tr, L2+. CPH 977677.
♫ Prins, Matthew. "We Are Called" from *We Are Called*. 2-3 oct hb or hc, L2. GIA G-8543. 3-5 oct hb or hc, G-8544.
Sherman, Arnold. "Canticle." 3-5 oct, L4. HOP 1676.

⊕ = global song ♫ = relates to hymn of the day + = semicontinuous psalm
☼ = praise song P = available in Prelude Music Planner

Monday, October 26
Philipp Nicolai, died 1608; Johann Heermann, died 1647; Paul Gerhardt, died 1676; hymnwriters

These three outstanding hymnwriters all worked in Germany during times of war and plague. When Philipp Nicolai was a pastor in Westphalia, the plague killed thirteen hundred of his parishioners. One hundred seventy people died in one week. His hymns "Wake, awake, for night is flying" (ELW 436) and "O Morning Star, how fair and bright!" (ELW 308) were included in a series of meditations he wrote to comfort his parishioners during the plague. The style of Johann Heermann's hymns moved away from the more objective style of Reformation hymnody toward expressing the emotions of faith. Among his hymns is the plaintive text "Ah, holy Jesus" (ELW 349). Paul Gerhardt lost a preaching position at St. Nicholas Church in Berlin because he refused to sign a document stating he would not make theological arguments in his sermons. The author of beloved hymns such as "O sacred head, now wounded" (ELW 351), some have called Gerhardt the greatest of Lutheran hymnwriters.

Wednesday, October 28
Simon and Jude, Apostles

Little is known about Simon and Jude. In New Testament lists of the apostles, Simon the "zealot" or Cananaean is mentioned, but he is never mentioned apart from these lists. Jude, sometimes called Thaddeus, is also mentioned in lists of the Twelve. At the last supper Jude asked Jesus why he had chosen to reveal himself to the disciples but not to the world. A traditional story about Simon and Jude says that they traveled together on a missionary journey to Persia and were both martyred there.

Saturday, October 31
Reformation Day

By the end of the seventeenth century, many Lutheran churches celebrated a festival commemorating Martin Luther's posting of the Ninety-five Theses, a summary of the abuses in the church of his time. At the heart of the reform movement was the gospel, the good news that it is by grace through faith that we are justified and set free.

November

TIME AFTER PENTECOST

SUMMER

AUTUMN

NOVEMBER

Preparing for November

Preaching

November's themes focus on the end—the end of the church year, the end times, and the end of our earthly lives. The readings include topsy-turvy language and vivid images of judgment. But for listeners from all times and places who see with the eyes of faith, they also provide solid ground for hope. The apostle Paul wrote, "We do not want you to be uninformed . . . about those who have died, so that you may not grieve as others do who have no hope" (1 Thess. 4:13; Lectionary 32, November 8). November is a time to honor grief and to preach hope.

Where Jesus is, there is hope for the faithful. On All Saints Day, November 1, which falls on a Sunday this year, in the first reading from Revelation we hear from those "who have come out of the great ordeal," who are imaged as worshiping around the throne (Rev. 7:14). We stand on the shoulders of saints and martyrs and beloved friends and family who have died, who for us have demonstrated the blessedness of those Jesus names in his Beatitudes (Matt. 5:1-12). Perhaps a carefully crafted sermon bracketed by the stanzas of "Behold the host arrayed in white" (ELW 425) might include stories about those who stood firm in faith until the end.

For the rest of the month, while facing uncertainties, distress, and failure, we might pay heed to Paul's admonition to the Thessalonians to "encourage one another and build up each other, as indeed you are doing" (1 Thess. 5:11; Lectionary 33, November 15). Exegeting the injustices in our world and communities will be as important as interpreting the truth-telling of the prophets and the challenge of Jesus to pay attention to those who squander their resources instead of sharing God's abundance. Name the actions your congregation has taken that participate in God's justice. Allow the parables Jesus tells in these November Sundays to light a fire through your proclamation, effecting change, matching what we say with how we live.

On Christ the King Sunday, the last Sunday of the church year, alongside images of the last judgment from Matthew's gospel, we might lift up examples from our communities where we have delighted to serve others and, in doing so, served the Christ in our midst. Can we count the ways we have made our faith active in love? For example, through organizations addressing hunger or suffering caused by natural disasters, through prison ministries, through food pantries and shelter programs, through letter-writing and protest, through advocating gender equality or speaking out against racism.

For communities that hold Thanksgiving services, preaching about the abundance of God is a great counterbalance to the human tendency to focus on scarcity. When sharing the eucharist, thanksgivings at the table bubble over with blessings, with *berakahs* to God. In all circumstances we give thanks to a God who creates and saves, in whom all our hope is founded. Here is one story of hope: it is a Hasidic folk tale with distinct images of hell and heaven. In hell, there is a great feast spread out. People have their arms splinted so that they are prevented from spooning the food into their mouths. In heaven, the same feast is there, and people also have their arms splinted. The difference is that in heaven, folks are feeding one another. Generosity overcomes scarcity. We do not lose hope.

Intercessory Prayer

The eschatological focus of this month could be highlighted by having the sung or spoken assembly response to the petitions be some form of "your kingdom come." In the sermon, during the time with the children within the service, or in the worship folder, it could be pointed out that "your kingdom come" is the heart of the Lord's Prayer. We are asking God to bring the kingdom Jesus imaged in his parables into being here and now. The line "your will be done, on earth as in heaven" is another way of saying the same thing. We are not saying "Whatever happens today is God's will; help us accept it." We are saying "Your will is not currently being done on earth as it is done in heaven—may your will also be done here!" We are asking God to change the world. As Desmond Tutu would put it, may God's dream come true! That dream looks like daily bread for everyone, and mutual forgiveness, and safety in the midst of threats.

In our focus on the "last things" in November, we also particularly stand with those who have died. We believe they have found their completion in God, but at the same time we believe that they wait with us for the fulfillment of God's dream. We are, all of us—on this side of death and on the other side of it—united in the communion of saints. We all pray for each other and we all pray together for God to heal this broken world: "Your kingdom come."

You might want to have a symbolic focus for the month representing our connection with those who have died. This could be some thing—a book of remembrance, a banner, wide ribbons—in or on which people could be invited throughout the month of October to write the names of those they remember. See the "Worship Space" section for suggestions on how to receive and display the names. If you have such a focus symbolizing the congregation's remembered saints, the prayers could be led by a minister standing next to that display. This could be explained as a way of reminding us that all the saints, living on earth or living with God, are praying together for God's kingdom to come.

Another symbolic way of remembering the dead in prayer during November can involve candle-lighting. People can be invited to light candles in memory of persons who have died—either tapers that they can place in a box of sand, or votive candles in glass holders that can be placed on a table. These candles can be left burning throughout the service. Again, the assisting minister can lead the prayers while standing beside the burning candles. (Note: Be sure that candles can be easily and safely lighted by worshipers and that they are situated in places free of drafts and away from ceiling fans.)

The general prayers in Thanksgiving services, especially ecumenical ones, can benefit from a sung response that helps the assembly feel unified. Even if each congregation contributes a petition/thanksgiving in its own familiar format of prayer, a common sung response will draw all the prayers together. Possible responses include the refrain of "We plow the fields and scatter" (ELW 681; also in the Episcopal hymnal); the second half of the first stanza of "Come, ye thankful people, come" (ELW 693; "God, our maker, doth provide . . ."); or the refrain from "For the beauty of the earth" as presented in *The United Methodist Hymnal* ("Lord of all, to thee we raise this our hymn of grateful praise"). "For the fruit of all creation" (ELW 679) with its widely familiar traditional Welsh tune (AR HYD Y NOS) can be woven together with spoken petitions. For example, before the first stanza, pray for the planet and the harvest; before the second stanza, pray for the nations, society, and people in need; before the third stanza, pray for the church, this congregation/community, and the communion of saints.

Assembly Song

Sundays in November can feel like each has its own focus or theme (and the colors change from white to green to white again in quick succession), and assembly song can feel equally all-over-the-map, with selections coming from almost every section of the hymnal. First, we sing of the saints (November 1), then with waiting bridesmaids (Lectionary 32, November 8), into the end times (Lectionary 33, November 15), and finally on to Christ the King and Thanksgiving. Look for a unifying piece of music or setting of the liturgy to help the assembly stay centered and focused. Holy Communion Setting Ten in *Evangelical Lutheran Worship* uses familiar hymn tunes, which might be simple and perfect for this busy, ever-changing month.

For worship on All Saints Day, consider singing a setting of the Beatitudes to accompany the remembrance of those who have died. See *Music Sourcebook for All Saints through Transfiguration* (Augsburg Fortress, 2013) for newer settings, including one with a simple refrain that the assembly could learn and sing from memory. Read the names of the beloved dead aloud in between singing a simple refrain that includes the word *Blessed*. Or consider naming both those who have died and the newly baptized during the thanksgiving at the table of the communion liturgy or during a thanksgiving for baptism. All Saints is also a perfect festival to sing a setting of the hymn of praise "This is the feast," which uses words straight from the reading from Revelation. Singing this liturgical text on All Saints as well as during Eastertide highlights the baptismal connection between these two parts of the church year. You can also sing this as the gathering or sending hymn; this canticle of praise is very flexible!

The parable of the wise and foolish bridesmaids is the gospel reading on November 8 (Lectionary 32). Sing the beloved African American spiritual "Keep your lamps trimmed and burning." Perhaps the choir leads and the assembly joins on the refrain. Consider teaching the verses to a children's choir, or to soloists if a choir is not available. You could also sing only the refrain as the sending song that day and keep the refrain going as people leave the worship space, reminding them of the cry to stay awake during the coming week, for the time of Christ is coming soon.

The church year ends with the festival of Christ the King. Sing songs about service to others as we are reminded in the gospel reading to care for the poor and for the whole kingdom of God. Consider singing the simple rhythmic setting of Psalm 95 from the Service Music section of *Evangelical Lutheran Worship* (#225) using a cantor, choir, and the whole assembly on this festival that often receives less attention as we busily prepare for Advent and Christmas. Another great option is to sing "Soon and very soon" (ELW 439) as you leave worship. This is a wonderful time to include a procession of youth or even adults playing percussion instruments as they leave worship and anticipate the coming of the King in Advent.

If your community worships on Thanksgiving or Thanksgiving Eve, consider having an intergenerational choir or instrumental group. Keep the music as simple as possible, and invite visiting family or friends to participate with a short rehearsal just before worship. It is also a wonderful chance to give thanks for the many musicians, both beginning and advanced, in your congregation who faithfully join in leading the assembly's song.

Worship Space

November can be a wonderful time to give special visual attention to the assembly's table. Many families in the United States will gather around tables in their homes for Thanksgiving. Find visual ways to emphasize how the family of God gathers around God's table every Sunday for eucharist (Thanksgiving!). Do you have a movable altar table? If so, bring it closer to the assembly for the month of November, or just on All Saints Day when you might place candles on or around it. When celebrating specific milestones such as first communion, have the children gather in a circle around or on the sides of the altar table for the eucharistic liturgy. Do the same when receiving new members, commissioning ministry leaders, or sending ministers of communion to those who are homebound, hospitalized, or in prison.

On All Saints Day there are many visual ways to remember the saints of the church. If you are inviting worshipers to write the names of their beloved dead, here are a few ways you might collect and display those names: The names could be written on a banner, on a decorated cardboard box with no ends fitted around the font, on thick ribbons attached to or wound around the font, or on a plain piece of fabric hanging on the altar table, lectern, pulpit, or font. The font is appropriate as the source of "all saints." But another placement may work better in your space. Once people have written names, the visual object can be put in place for All Saints Day and left up throughout November. Some congregations have produced more elaborate symbolic remembrances of all the congregation's saints by inviting people to bring physical photos or submit digital photos and then creating a collage, or even by giving people shoeboxes and inviting them to make a "Day of the Dead"–style *ofrenda* including symbols and pictures of loved ones.

Even though Thanksgiving is not a liturgical holiday, it has strong Christian themes of giving thanks, sharing abundance, and remembering that all we have is a gift from God. Create a cornucopia with collected items. Research the material needs of a local ministry (such as a transitional shelter, refugee and immigration services, veterans services, chemotherapy or dialysis center) and pick a theme such as harvested food, prepared casseroles, household items, canned goods, toiletries, new packages of socks and undershirts, or care bags for those in chemotherapy or dialysis. Invite worshipers to pile these items around the altar table or in another visible area during worship. Then have them carry the items out during the sending hymn and into a waiting truck or vehicle that will take them to the place they will be shared. You might accompany this procession with the same Kyrie suggested in the autumn notes on worship space (pp. 252–253).

Seasonal Checklist

- Consider using harvest decorations during November, from All Saints Day through the end of the church year.
- All Saints Day can be an occasion to celebrate baptisms in addition to remembering those who have died. If All Saints (November 1) will be observed as a baptismal festival, publicize the festival and arrange for baptismal preparation with parents, sponsors, and candidates.
- Provide a book of remembrance for All Saints Day and the month of November in which the names of loved ones may be written and remembered aloud in prayer.
- Incorporate the names of those who have died into a baptismal remembrance or into the prayers of intercession on All Saints Day.
- If you will hold events in your congregation focused on death and dying, be sure to line up speakers and resources in advance. Consider using *In Sure and Certain Hope: A Funeral Sourcebook* and *Remembering God's Promises: A Funeral Planning Handbook* (both Augsburg Fortress).
- If your congregation provides a community meal on Thanksgiving, publicize it well in advance in local newspapers, on your church website, and through social media.
- Publicize any special food collections and arrange for delivery to the appropriate agency.
- Continue planning for Advent 2020.
- Begin publicizing the schedule of Advent and Christmas worship services.

Worship Texts for November

Confession and Forgiveness

All may make the sign of the cross, the sign that is marked at baptism, as the presiding minister begins.

Blessed be the holy Trinity, ✝ one God,
in whose image we are made,
who claims us and calls us beloved.
Amen.

Silence is kept for reflection.

Holy One,
we confess that we are not awake for you.
We are not faithful in using your gifts.
We forget the least of our siblings.
We do not see your beautiful image in one another.
We are infected by sin
that divides your beloved community.
Open our hearts to your coming,
open our eyes to see you in our neighbor,
open our hands to serve your creation. Amen.

Beloved, we are God's children,
and Jesus, our Beloved, opens the door to us.
Through ✝ Jesus you are forgiven,
by Jesus you are welcome,
in Jesus you are called to rejoice!
Let us live in the promises prepared for us
from the foundation of the world.
Amen.

Offering Prayer

God of all goodness,
generations have turned to you,
gathered around your table,
and shared your abundant blessings.
Number us among them
that, as we gather these gifts from your abundance,
and give thanks for your rich blessings,
we may feast upon your very self
and care for all that you have made,
through Jesus Christ, our Sovereign and Servant.
Amen.

Invitation to Communion

There is a place for you at the banquet.
Come and feast at Jesus' table.

Prayer after Communion

Lord Jesus,
in this simple meal you have set a banquet.
Sustain us on the journey,
strengthen us to care for the least of your beloved children,
and give us glad and generous hearts
as we meet you on the way.
Amen.

Blessing

May the God of all creation,
in whose image we are made,
who claims us and calls us beloved,
who strengthens us for service,
give you reason to rejoice and be glad!

The blessing of God,
Sovereign, ✝ Savior, and Spirit,
be with you today and always.
Amen.

Dismissal

Beloved of God,
go in peace to love and serve the Lord.
Thanks be to God.

Seasonal Rites for November

Remembering the Saints

Remembering the Saints combines naming saints of the Bible, the church, and the local worshiping community with litanies and hymns for choir/cantor and assembly. It is structured to symbolize and commemorate the great "cloud of witnesses" (Hebrews 12:1-2). The sequence may be used at the beginning of the service as part of the gathering rite or following the sermon, hymn of the day, or creed as part of the prayers. It may also be used at times other than the congregation's principal weekly service, such as during an evening midweek service or a service of daily prayer.

For a visual image to accompany this rite, the names of saints could be written on paper stars and hung or posted around the worship space, creating a visual "cloud of witnesses" surrounding the assembly. The stars may remain up through the festival of Christ the King.

Resources and Preparation

Hymns
Behold the host arrayed in white ELW 425
For all the saints ELW 422

Leadership
Organist or pianist to lead the hymn stanzas and the sung
    responses in the litanies
Choir (small or large) or soloist/s to sing "Behold the host
    arrayed in white" and to help lead the assembly's responses
    in the litanies and the stanzas of "For all the saints"
Conductor to cue choir entrances
Reader/s to read the three lists of saints' names
Cantor to lead the three sung litanies

Other resources
G handbell (G4 is suggested, but other octaves will work)

Ringing of a Bell

A handbell rings three times to begin the time of remembrance.

Choral Hymn

The choir or a soloist sings the first eight measures of "Behold the host arrayed in white."

Reading 1: Saints of the Bible

The following list of names of saints of the Bible (or a selection from the list) may be read. As the names are read, a choir or soloist softly sings or hums "Behold the host," gradually becoming softer until all the names are read.

> Adam, Eve, Mary, Joseph, Abraham, Sarah, Rachel, Isaac, Rebekah, Leah, Jacob, Esau, Miriam, Moses, Rahab, Gideon, Deborah, Samson, David, Hannah, Samuel, Solomon, Isaiah, Zechariah, Elizabeth, Simeon, Peter, James, John, Joanna, Susanna, Priscilla, Mary Magdalene, Nathanael, Timothy, Zacchaeus, Philemon, Onesimus, Lydia, Paul, Simon of Cyrene, Ezekiel, Daniel, Silas, Barnabas, Ruth, Elijah, Esther, Martha, Jeremiah, Luke, Dorcas, Micah, Titus, Timothy, Phoebe, Naomi, Eunice, Lois, the Woman at the Well

A handbell rings once to conclude the reading.

Litany

The following litany may be sung or spoken by a cantor and assembly. For a sung setting, see Evangelical Lutheran Worship, *page 316, from which this litany is adapted.*

In peace, let us pray to the Lord.
Lord, have mercy.
For the peace from above, and for our salvation,
let us pray to the Lord.
Lord, have mercy.
For the peace of the whole world,
for the well-being of the church of God,
and for the unity of all, let us pray to the Lord.
Lord, have mercy.
For the faithful who have gone before us and are at rest,
let us give thanks to the Lord.
Alleluia.

Assembly Song

As the litany concludes and following a brief keyboard introduction, the assembly and choir sing stanzas 1–2 of "For all the saints." A handbell rings three times following the hymn.

Choral Hymn

The choir or a soloist sings the next eight (or repeats the first eight) measures of "Behold the host arrayed in white."

Reading 2: Saints of the Church

The following list of names of saints of the church (or a selection from the list) may be read. As the names are read, a choir or soloist softly sings or hums "Behold the host," gradually becoming softer until all the names are read.

> Francis of Assisi, Dag Hammarskjöld, Chief Seattle, Bernard of Clairvaux, John Donne, Thomas Aquinas, Hildegard of Bingen, Martin Luther, John Calvin, Elizabeth of Hungary, Dietrich Bonhoeffer, John Wesley, Johann Sebastian Bach, Teresa of Avila, Heinrich Schütz, Martin Luther King Jr., Florence Nightingale, Albrecht Dürer, Catherine Winkworth, Elizabeth Fedde, Perpetua and Felicity, Toyohiko Kagawa, Søren Kierkegaard, Birgitta of Sweden, Clara Maas, Augustine of Hippo, Isaac Watts, Julian of Norwich, Catherine of Siena

A handbell rings once to conclude the reading.

Litany

The following litany may be sung or spoken by a cantor and assembly. For a sung setting, see Evangelical Lutheran Worship, *page 316.*

For public servants, the government
and those who protect us, that they may be
upheld and strengthened in every good deed,
let us pray to the Lord.
Lord, have mercy.
For those who work to bring peace,
justice, healing, and protection
in this and every place, let us pray to the Lord.
Lord, have mercy.
For all servants of the church, for this assembly,
and for all people who await from the Lord
great and abundant mercy,
let us pray to the Lord.
Lord, have mercy.
For renewers of the church,
whose prophetic voices call us together
around the gospel of salvation,
let us give thanks to the Lord.
Alleluia.

Assembly Song

As the litany concludes and following a brief keyboard introduction, the assembly and choir sing stanzas 3–5 of "For all the saints." A handbell rings three times following the hymn.

Choral Hymn

The choir or a soloist sings the final eight (or repeats the first eight) measures of "Behold the host arrayed in white."

Reading 3: Saints of This Community

Saints from the worshiping community are named. This list will need to be gathered in advance and typically includes those from the local worshiping community who have died in the past year. As the names are read, a choir or soloist softly sings or hums "Behold the host," gradually becoming softer until all the names are read.

A handbell rings once to conclude the reading.

Litany

The following litany may be sung or spoken by a cantor and assembly. For a sung setting, see Evangelical Lutheran Worship, *page 316.*

For this assembly, for all who have shared
their lives and faith among us,
for all who have done good works in this congregation,
let us pray to the Lord.
Lord, have mercy.
For those who teach and those who learn,
for those who serve and share the gospel,
for those who are still to come,
that faithfulness and service may abound,
let us pray to the Lord.
Lord, have mercy.
For deliverance in the time of affliction,
wrath, danger, and need, let us pray to the Lord.
Lord, have mercy.
Rejoicing in the communion of all the saints,
let us commend ourselves, one another,
and our whole life to Christ our Lord.
To you, O Lord.

Prayer

Let us pray. O God, remember your church throughout the world. Make all its members grow in love for you and for one another. As you have received our sisters and brothers who have gone to their rest in the hope of the resurrection to eternal life, bring us at last with them into the light of your presence, that in union with all your saints we may give you glory forever; through your Son, Jesus Christ our Lord.
Amen.

Assembly Song

Following a brief keyboard introduction, the assembly and choir sing stanzas 6–7 of "For all the saints." A handbell rings three times following the hymn.

Final Reading and Blessing

Therefore, since we are surrounded by so great a cloud of witnesses, let us also lay aside every weight and the sin that clings so closely, and let us run with perseverance the race that is set before us, looking to Jesus the pioneer and perfecter of our faith, who for the sake of the joy that was set before him endured the cross, disregarding its shame, and has taken his seat at the right hand of the throne of God. (Hebrews 12:1-2)

Looking to Jesus
and surrounded by the cloud of witnesses,
may we live forgiven,
running the race God has set before us
both now and to eternity,
in the name of the Father, and of + the Son,
and of the Holy Spirit.
Amen.

Notes and Ideas

- For congregations with larger choirs, members of the choir may read the list of saints' names as the rest of the choir softly sings or hums "Behold the host."
- If the worship space and size of the choir is suitable, the choir may form a circle surrounding the assembly for this rite, furthering the effect of being surrounded by a great cloud of witnesses.
- Lists of the names of saints of the Bible and the church may be adapted as desired. See *Evangelical Lutheran Worship* for a list of commemorations (pp. 15–17). For other lists of those commemorated on the church's calendar, see *Libro de Liturgia y Cántico* (pp. 10–12), *This Far by Faith* (pp. 114–118), and *Lutheran Book of Worship* (pp. 10–12).
- A pronunciation guide to biblical names is available in *Getting the Word Out: A Handbook for Readers* (Augsburg Fortress, 2013; pp. 63–80).
- A choral descant may enhance the final stanza of "For all the saints."

November 1, 2020
All Saints Day

All Saints celebrates the baptized people of God, living and dead, who are the body of Christ. As November heralds the dying of the landscape in many northern regions, the readings and liturgy call us to remember all who have died in Christ and whose baptism is complete. At the Lord's table we gather with the faithful of every time and place, trusting that the promises of God will be fulfilled and that all tears will be wiped away in the new Jerusalem.

Prayer of the Day

Almighty God, you have knit your people together in one communion in the mystical body of your Son, Jesus Christ our Lord. Grant us grace to follow your blessed saints in lives of faith and commitment, and to know the inexpressible joys you have prepared for those who love you, through Jesus Christ, our Savior and Lord, who lives and reigns with you and the Holy Spirit, one God, now and forever.

Gospel Acclamation

Alleluia. They are before the throne of God, and the one who is seated on the throne will shelter them. *Alleluia.* (Rev. 7:15)

Readings and Psalm

Revelation 7:9-17

The book of Revelation is written to seven churches in western Asia Minor during a time of great oppression. Today's reading is a response to the question asked in 6:17: "Who is able to stand?" The writer gives the faithful the assurance of God's protection and a vision of victory.

Psalm 34:1-10, 22

Fear the LORD, you saints of the LORD; for those who fear the LORD lack nothing. (Ps. 34:9)

1 John 3:1-3

A saint is one who has been set apart by God for God's purposes. God, out of divine love, set us apart to be the children of God. Our holy hope is that we shall see God as God really is.

Matthew 5:1-12

In the Beatitudes, Jesus provides a unique description of those who are blessed with God's favor. His teaching is surprising and shocking to those who seek wealth, fame, and control over others.

Preface All Saints

Color White

Prayers of Intercession

The prayers are prepared locally for each occasion. The following examples may be adapted or used as appropriate.

Longing for Christ's reign to come among us, we pray for the outpouring of God's power on the church, the world, and all in need.

A brief silence.

Lord of all the saints, we praise you for evangelists and martyrs whose sacrifices witness to your gospel across time and space. Inspire us by their courage to carry our faith to new people and places around us. Hear us, O God.

Your mercy is great.

Lord of every place, the universe proclaims your greatness from generation to generation. Bless the work of naturalists, conservationists, and park rangers who train our attention to the wonders of the world you have made. Hear us, O God.

Your mercy is great.

Lord of every nation, guide this country—red states and blue states, rural voters and urban voters, young and old—as we share in another national election. Kindle hearts eager to understand our common needs and seek our common good. Hear us, O God.

Your mercy is great.

Lord of every blessing, your Son's blessing came to those living with poverty, grief, hunger, thirst, and persecution. Shape our vision of the saints to match his own. Awaken in us your call to serve all who suffer. Hear us, O God.

Your mercy is great.

Lord of every venture, anoint us with the missionary spirit of the early church. Bless all new missions of our synod (*especially*). Empower testimony from new communities of faith to shape a diverse witness to your saving power. Hear us, O God.

Your mercy is great.

Here other intercessions may be offered.

Lord of every time, countless are the multitudes you have called by name and gathered to yourself. Comfort us as we grieve those who have died in the past year (*here the names of those who have died in the previous year may be read*). In faith, may we join with them in ceaseless praise. Hear us, O God.

Your mercy is great.

Receive our prayers in the name of Jesus Christ our Savior, until that day when you gather all creation around your throne where you will reign forever and ever.
Amen.

Ideas for the Day

- See the excellent suggestions for All Saints throughout the "Preparing for November" introduction (pp. 289–291).
- On All Saints Sunday we remember those who have died for the faith and those who have died in the faith. We also recognize this day all the baptized. We are sinners. Remember that the next time you look in the mirror. We are saints, as well. Remember that too. We are sinners in our own right and saints by virtue of Christ's death and resurrection for us. In the Sermon on the Mount, Jesus speaks his blessings on all his saints. Today, as every Sunday, we saints on earth join the saints in heaven in singing God's praises. We join them at the meal as well, keeping in mind that what we receive here is but an appetizer from the heavenly banquet table.
- In the imagery of All Saints we see the tablecloth of the heavenly banquet, the baptismal robes of those in the new Jerusalem, the celestial cloud of witnesses who have gone before us. This is rich, profound imagery for a time in the church year that in many locations looks out on a darkening and bare natural world. This environment, combined with unresolved grief over death and loss, leaves many people vulnerable during this part of the year. Such vulnerability is intensified (especially in the United States) by our cultural awareness of Thanksgiving as the threshold to the holiday season. The holiday expectations of good cheer and warm relations may trigger deep feelings of abandonment and isolation. The church has an opportunity to create an environment in which people can acknowledge and explore the dimensions of loss, both individually and as part of a larger community of the living and the dead.
- Funerals with the body or ashes present are increasingly being set aside in favor of a memorial at a much later date, or a gathering that does not include elements of faith. This is particularly true when those planning the funeral do not have a connection to a faith community. Families who live far apart geographically have similar experiences of not being able to share in funeral rites that provide healing. Consider adding the funeral commendation rite (*ELW*, p. 283) to today's service at the sending. Invite worshipers to submit the names of those whose death they have not been able to publicly acknowledge and incorporate those names into the commendation. One man whose parents had both died decades prior said that he didn't know how much he yearned to acknowledge their transition into the arms of God until he heard their names in this type of context, so many years later.

Connections with Creation

Compared with the human species, most other life forms on the earth are currently in a very vulnerable position. They lack the ability to advocate for the welfare of their habitats, and many creatures are on the edge of extinction. The animals that live in threatened habitats such as rain forests, prairies, and oceans are most certainly meek. In the Sermon on the Mount, Jesus proclaims, "Blessed are the meek, for they will inherit the earth" (Matt. 5:5). An ecological interpretation of this part of Jesus' message might humbly acknowledge the almost certain truth that if humans disappeared from the planet, many other creatures would be more likely to thrive. However, if the other creatures died in great numbers, Homo sapiens would become extinct. On All Saints Day, Christians influenced by Martin Luther's theology are called to confess that we are simultaneously saint and sinner; we are capable of great harm and also are called to live in the hope that death is not the end of God's story or our own.

Let the Children Come

Children are continuing stories. Marked with the cross of Christ and sealed by the Holy Spirit, they join the community of saints, part of the ongoing narrative of God's love through the ages. On this Sunday we remember with thanksgiving those who have gone before us. Our children need this connection to the past, for it is part of who they are now and will be in the future. Show them the special ways that your community remembers those who have died today: lighting candles, speaking or singing their names as part of the prayers, ringing a bell, writing their names in a special book, displaying photos of loved ones, or other practices. Candles could be lit at home for family members who have died, with prayers offered thanking God for their lives. Families could talk about spiritual legacies left behind to strengthen and guide the present generations.

Assembly Song
Gathering

Rejoice in God's saints ELW 418, WOV 689
Give Thanks for Saints ELW 428
Ye watchers and ye holy ones ELW 424, LBW 175

Psalmody and Acclamations

Feeley, Ephrem. "Taste and See." SAB, cant, assembly, kybd. GIA G-9625.
Hobby, Robert A. "Psalm 34: I Will Bless the Lord." U, assembly, org. MSM 80-707.
Taste and see the goodness of the Lord/Psalm 34 TFF 5
(GA) ELW 170 with verse for All Saints.

Hymn of the Day

For all the saints   ELW 422, LBW 174   *SINE NOMINE*

In our day of thanksgiving   ELW 429   *ST. CATHERINE'S COURT*

Sing with all the saints in glory   ELW 426, WOV 691   *MISSISSIPPI*

Offering

Eat this bread/Jesus Christ, bread of life   ELW 472, WOV 709, TFF 125

For the bread which you have broken   ELW 494, LBW 200

Communion

Behold the host arrayed in white   ELW 425, LBW 312

Jerusalem, my happy home   ELW 628, LBW 331

Taste and see   ELW 493, TFF 126

Sending

Rejoice, ye pure in heart!   ELW 873/874, LBW 553

Shall we gather at the river   ELW 423, WOV 690, TFF 179

Additional Assembly Songs

I sing a song of the saints of God   H82 293, NCH 295

Oh, when the saints go marching in   TFF 180

⊕ Cameroon trad./trans. Andrew Donaldson. "Comment ne pas te louer/How Can We Not Praise Your Name?" from *Hosanna! Ecumenical Songs for Justice and Peace*. SAB. WCC Publications 9782825416679.

⊕ Scottish trad., Iona Community. "The Strangest of Saints" from *Heaven Shall Not Wait*. U. GIA G-3646S.

☼ Cantelon, Ben/Elias Dummer/Nick Herbert. "A City on a Hill" from CCLI.

☼ Graves, Devon/Jonathan Taylor Martin. "Poor in Spirit" from CCLI.

☼ Meyer, Jesse. "All for You, Jesus" from CCLI.

☼ Rozier, Andi/Jason Ingram/Jonathan Smith/Meredith Andrews. "All the Earth" from CCLI.

☼ Skinner, Anthony/Stuart Garrard. "Oh Blessed" from CCLI.

☼ Wood, Naaman/Bruce Benedict. "You Are Blessed" from *The Beatitudes EP*. cardiphonia.bandcamp.com.

Music for the Day
Choral

℗ Bankson, Jeremy J. "By All Your Saints." SATB, org, opt br qnt, timp. AFP 9781451485769.

℗ Beard, Stanley G. "Through the Legacy of Years." SATB, pno. AFP 9781506456935.

Betinis, Abbie. "Jerusalem luminosa." SA, a cap. KJO 6323.

Schulz-Widmar, Russell. "Jerusalem, Jerusalem." 2 pt mxd, kybd. AFP 9780800655211.

Children's Choir

℗ Christopherson, Dorothy. "Psalm 34" from *ChildrenSing Psalms*. U, assembly, kybd, opt vc. AFP 9780800663872.

Lowenberg, Kenneth. "Blessed Are the Poor in Spirit." U/2 pt, kybd. SEL 410-557.

℗ Miller, Aaron David. "I Will Bless the Lord at All Times." U, pno. AFP 8080067750. Out of print.

Keyboard / Instrumental

℗♫ Raabe, Nancy. "Sing with All the Saints in Glory" from *Grace & Peace, Volume 6: Songs of Heaven*. Pno. AFP 9781451479621.

Raney, Joel. "Shall We Gather at the River" from *Keyboard Excursions for Piano and Organ*. Pno and org. HOP 8209.

℗♫ Weber, Jacob B. "In Our Day of Thanksgiving" from *Organ Impressions for the Church Year*. Org. AFP 9781506447995.

♫ Wright, Paul Leddington. "Sine nomine" from *Oxford Hymn Settings for Organists: Autumn Festivals*. Org. OXF 9780193400689.

Handbell

♫ Glasgow, Michael. "Faith of the Saints." 3-7 oct hb, opt tr, L2+. LOR 20/1614L.

♫ Kinyon, Barbara. "For All the Saints." 4-6 oct, L2+. CG CGB357. 2-3 oct. CGB356. Opt kybd, CGB358.

♫ Waugh, Tim. "For All the Saints." 3 or 5 oct, L2. CPH 977317.

⊕ = global song   ♫ = relates to hymn of the day
☼ = praise song   ℗ = available in Prelude Music Planner

November 1, 2020
Time after Pentecost — Lectionary 31

Micah declares God's condemnation of those who abhor justice. Jesus warns against hypocrisy. Paul urges the Thessalonians to lead a life worthy of God. Called to be humble servants, we gather for worship, seeking justice and welcoming all people to share the banquet of life.

Prayer of the Day

O God, generous and supreme, your loving Son lived among us, instructing us in the ways of humility and justice. Continue to ease our burdens, and lead us to serve alongside of him, Jesus Christ, our Savior and Lord.

Gospel Acclamation

Alleluia. You have one instructor, the Messiah; the greatest among you will be your servant. *Alleluia.* (Matt. 23:10, 11)

Readings and Psalm

Micah 3:5-12

The Lord announces judgment against prophets who can be bribed to give favorable oracles. Because rulers too can be bribed to practice injustice, Micah announces the coming destruction of Jerusalem. Later, Jeremiah escaped execution because of Micah's daring precedent (Jer. 26:18-19).

Psalm 43

Send out your light and truth, that they may lead me. (Ps. 43:3)

1 Thessalonians 2:9-13

Paul uses paternal imagery to depict the guidance and encouragement he provided to the Thessalonians. They received from Paul the word of God, which energizes their faith.

Matthew 23:1-12

Jesus encourages his disciples to obey the words of Moses they hear from their teachers but to shun the hypocrisy and pretension of those who do not practice what they teach.

Semicontinuous Reading and Psalm

Joshua 3:7-17

The Lord promises to be with Joshua as the Lord was with Moses. The entry into the promised land was a liturgical procession in which the priests carried the ark of the covenant, the sign of the Lord's presence.

Psalm 107:1-7, 33-37

We give thanks to you, Lord, for your wonderful works. (Ps. 107:8)

Preface   Sundays

Color   Green

Prayers of Intercession

The prayers are prepared locally for each occasion. The following examples may be adapted or used as appropriate.

Longing for Christ's reign to come among us, we pray for the outpouring of God's power on the church, the world, and all in need.

A brief silence.

Gracious God, you invite those who feel most unworthy of love to a seat at the head of your table. Through the humility, vulnerability, and repentance of your church, bring a compassionate welcome to all in need of your grace. Hear us, O God.

Your mercy is great.

Sustaining God, guide all people of the earth through harsh extremes in the cycles of creation—drought and monsoon, blistering heat and freezing cold. Hold in your mercy all places where lives have been disrupted by natural disasters (*especially*). Hear us, O God.

Your mercy is great.

Sovereign God, gather our country around a shared table this week during our national election. Open fruitful dialogue between people of every political party, place, age, and socioeconomic status so that we may discern the common good you desire for us. Hear us, O God.

Your mercy is great.

Merciful God, protect those whose human dignity has been denied and oppressed in our nation (*especially*). Raise the voices of those who have been silenced and bring justice where power has been abused for personal gain. Hear us, O God.

Your mercy is great.

Loving God, accompany those in new and unfamiliar places who need an invitation to community. We pray especially for those who have recently moved to start their first year of college, a new job, or a missionary position in another land. Hear us, O God.

Your mercy is great.

Here other intercessions may be offered.

Eternal God, you unite all the faithful in a banquet of your abundance. This day we remember all who now feast in your eternal presence, especially all who have died in the past year

(*here the names of those who have died in the previous year may be read*). Hear us, O God.
Your mercy is great.
Receive our prayers in the name of Jesus Christ our Savior, until that day when you gather all creation around your throne where you will reign forever and ever.
Amen.

Ideas for the Day

- The prophet Micah's words sound like they could have been spoken today, directed as they are toward powerful leaders, including self-centered politicians, priests, and so-called prophets. Political, religious, and community leaders then and now need to be held accountable by those they serve. How are we, like the prophet, "filled with power, with the spirit of the Lord, and with justice and might" (3:8) to declare to powerful leaders and systems that the way things are is not the way things should be? Jesus provides an answer to this question as he schools the disciples in today's gospel: "The greatest among you will be your servant" (Matt. 23:11).

- Pray for your local political, religious, and community leaders by name today in the prayers of intercession. Ask worshipers a week or two in advance to submit the names of public servants and other leaders in their own work, school, community, or volunteer circles who could be lifted up in prayer. If the list is too long to be reasonably spoken during the intercessions, you could provide a few prayer stations in the worship space where the names of leaders in various categories or arenas of service are displayed, along with the role or place in which they serve (for example, Maria Perez, principal of Central High School; Jo Johnson, our state representative; Patricia Davenport, our synod's bishop; Hal Lee, our county sheriff). Prayers for a wide variety of leaders may be particularly meaningful so close to Election Day in the United States.

- Today's gospel text concludes, "All who exalt themselves will be humbled, and all who humble themselves will be exalted" (Matt. 23:12). Those in the final seasons of life often speak of becoming "invisible." As a person's beauty, strength, and vitality wane, society tends to look past them, assuming they can no longer contribute and forgetting the extent to which they once did contribute or still can. Consider incorporating into worship ways of lifting up the seniors in your assembly. For example, sing or speak as a prayer "When memory fades" (ELW 792). Alternatively, name those elders whose talents of artistry and carpentry have created furnishings or paraments for your worship space as a way of informing newer members of the story of these holy things and honoring the contributions of those who made them.

Connections with Creation

Throughout the Gospel of Matthew, Jesus emphasizes that if people want to participate in the reign of God on Earth, right and merciful action is more important than proper doctrine or public demonstrations of prayer and fasting. In compassionately serving others in ways that create justice and equity, God's people live into God's saving and healing mission. The eco-justice movement recognizes that environmental health and socioeconomic justice are interrelated. Unjust societies often burden the most economically insecure communities with hazardous waste, polluted air and water, and garbage dumps. These environmental factors contribute to higher rates of asthma, childhood lead poisoning, and other chronic illnesses that negatively impact quality of life. Working for justice means being aware of the connections between how we treat the natural world and how we address economic and racial disparities in our communities.

Let the Children Come

Children understand well the difference between big shots and nobodies. They know what it is to be ignored or overlooked by adults. We are reminded today that there is no place in the reign of God for big shots and nobodies. We are all students of the one teacher, Christ Jesus. Instead of towering over children when speaking to them, lean, squat, or kneel down (to the extent your physical mobility allows) so that you are at their eye level. Show them you are really listening. Suggest these actions to parents, whether orally or in the worship folder: in worship, hold smaller children up so they can see what is happening. Whisper in their ear, "Rico is reading to us from the Bible." "Pastor Martha is blessing the bread and wine." Help the children know that all of worship is for them too.

Assembly Song
Gathering

In heaven above ELW 630, LBW 330
Jesus lives, my sure defense ELW 621, LBW 340
On Jordan's stormy bank I stand ELW 437, TFF 49

Psalmody and Acclamations

Schalk, Carl. "Antiphon for Psalm 43" from PATP. Use with ELW tone 7 or tone 9 in Dmin.
Woehr, Roland. "Psalm 43," Refrain 1, from PSCY.
+ Wold, Wayne L. "Psalm 107," Refrain 2, from PSCY.
(GA) ELW 170 with verse for Lectionary 31.

Hymn of the Day

Gather Us In ELW 532, WOV 718 GATHER US IN
Praise the Almighty! ELW 877, LBW 539 LOBE DEN HERREN, O MEINE SEELE
Precious Lord, take my hand ELW 773, WOV 731, TFF 193 PRECIOUS LORD

Offering

Lord of light   ELW 688, LBW 405

We raise our hands to you, O Lord   ELW 690

Communion

Blessing, Honor, and Glory   ELW 433, W&P 21

Lord, Be Glorified   ELW 744, TFF 248, W&P 89

Lord of all hopefulness   ELW 765, LS 169, LBW 469

Sending

I'm so glad Jesus lifted me   ELW 860, WOV 673, TFF 191, LS 121

What a fellowship, what a joy divine   ELW 774, WOV 780, TFF 220

Additional Assembly Songs

Camina, pueblo de Dios   LLC 436

For the troubles and the sufferings/Pelas dores deste mundo GTG 764

Jesus, Savior, Lord, now to you I come/Saranam, saranam GTG 789

⊕ Anon. Sierra Leone/arr. Greg Scheer. "We Are Coming, Lord, to the Table" from *Global Songs for Worship*. SATB. Calvin Institute for Christian Worship and Faith Alive 9781592554423. Out of print.

⊕ Taizé Community. "Nada te turbe/Nothing Can Trouble" from *Songs and Prayers from Taizé*. SATB. GIA G-3719.

☼ Gungor, David/John Arndt/Matt Maher/Stuart Garrard. "Makers of the Peace" from CCLI.

☼ Latty, Geraldine Agatha. "Lord You Hear the Cry (Lord Have Mercy)" from CCLI.

☼ Ligertwood, Brooke/Matt Crocker. "To Be Like You" from CCLI.

☼ McCracken, Sandra. "Send Out Your Light (Psalm 43)" from CCLI.

☼ Tai, Julie Kang/Esther Kim. "Kyrie" from *Revere/Restore*. jubalhouse.bandcamp.com. praise

☼ Rand, Lenora/Hannah Rand. "Forsaken" from *The Wilderness*. themany1.bandcamp.com.

Music for the Day
Choral

P♫ Bankson, Jeremy J. "Soli Deo Gloria." SATB, org, opt assembly, br qnt, timp. AFP 9780800678852.

P Chavarria, Vicente. "Be Thou My Vision," SATB, org. AFP 9781506421964.

♫ Haugen, Marty/arr. Lloyd Larson. "Gather Us In." SATB, pno, opt fl, gtr, perc. LO 10/4668L.

Pfautsch, Lloyd. "Seek to Serve" from *Easy Anthems for Classic Worship*, vol. 4. 2 pt mxd, kybd. HOP 8620.

Children's Choir

Bedford, Michael. "Jubilate Deo." U, kybd. CG CGA647.

P Burrows, Mark. "God's Hands" from *Again, I Say Rejoice!* U, pno or gtr. CG CGC56.

P Carter, John. "We Are Called to Be His Servants." U, pno. AFP 9780800675455.

Keyboard / Instrumental

♫ Biery, James. "Galliard on Gather Us In" from *Twentieth Century Hymn Tune Settings*. Org. MSM 10-863.

Marohnic, Chuck. "Lord, Whose Love through Humble Service" from *Piano Meditations: Reflections on Hymns and Biblical Stories in Jazz Style*. Pno. MSM 15-823.

P♫ Oines, Sylvia. "Precious Lord, Take My Hand" from *In Heaven Above: Piano Music for Funerals and Memorials*. Pno. AFP 9781451401912.

P♫ Powell, Robert J. "Lobe den Herren, o meine Seele" from *Augsburg Organ Library: Reformation*. Org. AFP 9781506413600.

Handbell

♫ Eithun, Sandra. "Glorify the Almighty." 3-6 oct hb, opt 3 oct hc, L3+. BP HB552.

♫ Lamb, Linda. "Precious Lord, Take My Hand." 3-5 oct hb, opt 3 oct hc, L3. Ring Out Press 3305.

♫ Moklebust, Cathy. "Jazz Waltz on Praise to the Lord." 3-7 oct hb, fl, DB, drm set, opt 3-5 oct hc, L5. CG CGB435. Inst parts, CGRP13.

Sunday, November 1
All Saints Day

The custom of commemorating all of the saints of the church on a single day goes back at least to the third century. All Saints celebrates the baptized people of God, living and dead, who make up the body of Christ. We remember all who have died in the faith and now serve God around the heavenly throne.

Tuesday, November 3
Martín de Porres, renewer of society, died 1639

Martín was the son of a Spanish knight and Ana Velázquez, a freed black slave from Panama. Martín apprenticed himself to a barber-surgeon in Lima, Peru, and was known for his work as a healer. Martín was a lay brother in the Order of Preachers (Dominicans) and engaged in many charitable works. He was a gardener as well as a counselor to those who sought him out. He was noted for his care of all the poor, regardless of race.

⊕ = global song   ♫ = relates to hymn of the day   + = semicontinuous psalm

☼ = praise song   P = available in Prelude Music Planner

His own religious community described him as the "father of charity." His work included the founding of an orphanage, a hospital, and a clinic for dogs and cats. He is recognized as an advocate for Christian charity and interracial justice.

Saturday, November 7

John Christian Frederick Heyer, died 1873; Bartholomaeus Ziegenbalg, died 1719; Ludwig Nommensen, died 1918; missionaries

Three missionaries are commemorated on this date. Heyer was the first missionary sent out by American Lutherans. Ordained in 1820, he established Sunday schools and taught at Gettysburg College and Seminary. Heyer became a missionary in the Andhra region of India. During a break in his mission work he received the M.D. degree from what would later be Johns Hopkins University.

Bartholomaeus Ziegenbalg (ZEEG-en-balg) was a missionary to the Tamils of Tranquebar on the southeast coast of India. The first convert to Christianity was baptized about ten months after Ziegenbalg began preaching. His missionary work was opposed by the local Hindus and also by Danish authorities in that area. Ziegenbalg was imprisoned for his work on a charge of converting the natives. Today the Tamil Evangelical Lutheran Church carries on his work.

Ludwig Ingwer Nommensen was born in Schleswig-Holstein, Germany. In the early 1860s he went to Sumatra to serve as a Lutheran missionary. His work was among the Batak people, who had previously not seen Christian missionaries. Though he encountered some initial difficulties, the missions began to succeed following the conversion of several tribal chiefs. Nommensen translated the scriptures into Batak while honoring much of the native culture.

November 8, 2020
Time after Pentecost — Lectionary 32

Today the prophet Amos calls for justice to roll down like waters. Paul urges us to encourage one another with the promised coming of the Lord. Jesus tells the parable of the wise and foolish bridesmaids. Surrounded by the faithful of every time and place, we celebrate Christ's coming in our midst in the word of life and the feast of victory—the marriage feast of the lamb.

Prayer of the Day

O God of justice and love, you illumine our way through life with the words of your Son. Give us the light we need, and awaken us to the needs of others, through Jesus Christ, our Savior and Lord.

Gospel Acclamation

Alleluia. Keep awake and be ready, for you do not know on what day your Lord is coming. *Alleluia.* (Matt. 24:42, 44)

Readings and Psalm
Amos 5:18-24

In the days of Amos, people thought that the day of the LORD would be a time of great victory, but Amos announced that it would be a day of darkness, not light. He said liturgy is no substitute for obedience. The LORD demands justice and righteousness in the community.

or Wisdom 6:12-16

Wisdom is part of the structure of the universe and is easily accessible to those who want to find her. Wisdom actually seeks people out. People who are wise are free from care.

Psalm 70

You are my helper and my deliverer; O LORD, do not tarry. (Ps. 70:5)

or Wisdom 6:17-20

The beginning of wisdom is the most sincere desire for instruction. (Wis. 6:17)

1 Thessalonians 4:13-18

Some of the Thessalonians are worried that dead Christians will be excluded from the resurrection to eternal life when Christ comes again. Paul reassures them with the word of hope that all Christians, living or dead, will be raised into everlasting life with Christ.

Matthew 25:1-13

Jesus tells a parable about his own second coming, emphasizing the need for readiness at all times.

Semicontinuous Reading and Psalm

Joshua 24:1-3a, 14-25

In the Near East, *covenant* means "agreement" or "alliance." It describes relationships and is the primary word used to characterize the relationship between God and Israel. By delivering Israel, God has already begun the relationship. Joshua calls upon the people to respond.

Psalm 78:1-7

We will recount to generations to come the power of the Lord. (Ps. 78:4)

Preface   Sundays

Color   Green

Prayers of Intercession

The prayers are prepared locally for each occasion. The following examples may be adapted or used as appropriate.

Longing for Christ's reign to come among us, we pray for the outpouring of God's power on the church, the world, and all in need.

A brief silence.

Holy God, rouse us to deep praise as we gather for worship. Enliven our worship with sincere and heartfelt song. Sustain the work of all church musicians and artists who lead us in praise and prayer (*especially*). Hear us, O God.

Your mercy is great.

Holy Creator, surprise and delight us with the beauty of the world you have made. Bless the work of landscapers, architects, and artists whose work invites us into harmonious living with your creation. Hear us, O God.

Your mercy is great.

Holy Judge, let justice roll down like waters over this world. Reign over the courtrooms of every land, in the hearts of those who guard the law and those who stand accused of crimes. Be present in cases where we long for both justice and mercy to prevail (*especially*). Hear us, O God.

Your mercy is great.

Holy Companion, console those who feel lonely or abandoned. Share the hours of those who live and eat alone. Comfort those who have few friends or who struggle with their identity and place in this world. Hear us, O God.

Your mercy is great.

Holy Protector, be with all observing Veterans Day. Guard the lives of active duty and retired military personnel. Comfort all who mourn those who have died in the line of duty. Heal the wounds, both physical and mental, experienced by service members. Hear us, O God.

Your mercy is great.

Here other intercessions may be offered.

Holy and Immortal One, we pray in thanksgiving for the lives of all who have died. Remind us of the frailty and shortness of our own lives and inspire us to use them for the building up of your kingdom. Hear us, O God.

Your mercy is great.

Receive our prayers in the name of Jesus Christ our Savior, until that day when you gather all creation around your throne where you will reign forever and ever.

Amen.

Ideas for the Day

- The reading from Amos contrasts religious rituals with righteous living and doing justice. The parable of the bridesmaids ends with the encouragement to keep awake. Connecting alertness with righteousness and justice is consistent with the practical preparation asked of the bridesmaids in the parable. This Sunday may be a good one to highlight a justice ministry in the congregation, synod, or community. The ELCA's website includes a section with resources related to a variety of justice issues (elca.org /Resources).

- In her book *Short Stories by Jesus: The Enigmatic Parables of a Controversial Rabbi* (New York: HarperCollins, 2014), Amy-Jill Levine cautions against allegorizing the parables of Jesus and assuming God is a character in them. It is easy to assume that the bridegroom represents Jesus in the parable of the bridesmaids. If, however, we do *not* assume the bridegroom is Jesus, how might this parable be reframed? In that reframing, what does each character in the parable contribute to our understanding of the kingdom of heaven?

- As the holiday shopping season approaches, Black Friday will draw some people to dedicate hours to standing in lines in the cold to get great deals. Others will spend Cyber Monday searching for low prices and gift options that can be delivered, saving them a trip to the store. Some shoppers spend months picking out gifts here and there so the season is not so stressful. There are also those last-minute shoppers who will rush into stores the day before the family Christmas gathering, hoping to find something meaningful. Are there any insights to be drawn from the preparations the bridesmaids in the parable make—or don't make—and the ways in which our society prepares to celebrate Christmas? How does the church's preparation for Christ's coming look like the parable? How does it look like the various shoppers?

- In the parable, only half of the lamps are still lit when the bridegroom arrives at the wedding banquet. Consider lighting only half of the candles in the worship space at the beginning of worship today, then refer to this situation in a children's message or the sermon. Alternatively, extinguish half of the candles just before or during the reading of the gospel. These changes to the normal worship environment can help people connect to the visual elements of the parable.

Connections with Creation

A landscape that has been shaped by the flowing water of rivers and streams is one that has been impacted by the slow, steady energy of water to cut ravines and valleys into the geography around it. Moving water also has the power to transport rocks and sediment, depositing them into floodplains and deltas. When God describes the most important kind of worship and religious observances, God speaks about "justice [rolling] down like waters, and righteousness like an ever-flowing stream" (Amos 5:24). God's vision for the world is one of human communities and societies that make possible the flourishing of every person and of the earth. This is the long and steady work of justice-making that we are called to do in our neighborhoods, cities, states, and nations.

Let the Children Come

The children could sing the first stanza of "Let justice flow like streams" (ELW 717) following the first reading; insert it before the reader closes by saying, "The word of the Lord" or "Word of God, word of life." The assembly responds, "Thanks be to God."

We are soon to begin the church year anew. Make note of the ways you have tried to welcome children into worship. What worked? What did not? What would you like to try in the year to come? Do not try something only once. Children learn by repetition and love to sing "by heart." Let the children come deeply into the worship of the church.

Assembly Song
Gathering

Lo! He comes with clouds descending ELW 435, LBW 27

O God, our help in ages past ELW 632, LBW 320

Praise to the Lord/Louez l'Eternel ELW 844

Psalmody and Acclamations

Mathis, William H. Refrain for "Psalm 70" from *After the Prelude: Year A*. U/cant, hb. CG CG CGB658 (digital version), CGB659 (print version). Use with ELW psalm tone 9 (in Dmin).

Raabe, Nancy. "Psalm 70" from PSCY.

Weidler, Scott C. "Wisdom 6:17-20" from PSCY.

Messner, Sally. "Wisdom 6:17-20" and (+) "Psalm 78:1-7" from PWA.

(GA) ELW 170 with verse for Lectionary 32.

Hymn of the Day

All who love and serve your city ELW 724 *NEW ORLEANS* LBW 436 *BIRABUS*

Rejoice, rejoice, believers ELW 244, LBW 25 *HAF TRONES LAMPA FÄRDIG*

Wake, awake, for night is flying ELW 436, LLC 276, LBW 31 *WACHET AUF*

Offering

In the singing ELW 466

Let us go now to the banquet/Vamos todos al banquete ELW 523, LLC 410

Communion

Drawn to the Light ELW 593

Soul, adorn yourself with gladness/Vengo a ti, Jesús amado ELW 488/489, LLC 388, LBW 224

Wait for the Lord ELW 262

Sending

Blessed assurance ELW 638, WOV 699, TFF 118

Lift every voice and sing ELW 841, TFF 296, LBW 562

Additional Assembly Songs

Let justice roll like a river W&P 85

People of the Lord GTG 632

Who will set us free? SP 44

⊕ Taizé Community. "Wait for the Lord" from *Songs and Prayers from Taizé*. SATB. GIA G-3719. Also ELW 262.

⊕ Thangaraj, M. Thomas. "Lord, We Pray/Let Justice Roll Down like Waters" from *Em Tua Graça*. WCC Publications 2825414492. Out of print. Hannelore.Schmid@wcc-coe .org.

☼ Assad, Audrey/Bryan Brown/Jason Petty. "River" from CCLI.

☼ Gresham, Judy. "Lift Up Your Eyes" from CCLI.

☼ Harris, Craig/Isaac Wardell. "We Labor unto Glory" from *Work Songs*. theportersgate.bandcamp.com.

☼ Massey, Micah. "Arrive" from CCLI.

☼ Tomlin, Chris/Jason Ingram/Jess Cates. "Even So Come" from CCLI.

☼ Tomlin, Chris/Jesse Reeves/Matt Redman. "Shout" from CCLI.

Music for the Day
Choral

Britten, Benjamin. "Deus in adjutorum meum." SATB, a cap. OXF 9790060014246.

ᴾ Crouch, Andraé/arr. Jack Schrader. "Soon and Very Soon." 2 pt mxd, pno. HOP C5825.

ᴾ ♫ Ferguson, John. "Rejoice, Rejoice, Believers." SAB, org. AFP 9781451401684.

⊕ = global song ♫ = relates to hymn of the day + = semicontinuous psalm
☼ = praise song ᴾ = available in Prelude Music Planner

P ♫ Gesius, Bartholomaeus. "Wake, Awake, for Night Is Flying" from *Augsburg Chorale Book*. SATB, opt kybd. AFP 9781506426303.

Children's Choir

P ♫ Bach, J. S. "Zion Hears the Watchmen Singing" from *Bach for All Seasons Choirbook*. AFP 9780800658540.

P Helgen, John. "Keep Your Lamps Trimmed and Burning." U, kybd, opt desc. AFP 9780800677497.

P Miller, Mark. "Let Justice Roll" from *Roll Down, Justice!* U, kybd. CG CGBK72.

Keyboard / Instrumental

♫ Miller, Aaron David. "Wachet auf" from *Oxford Hymn Settings for Organists: Advent and Christmas*. Org. OXF 9780193392335.

Miller, Dan. "Blessed Assurance" from *How Great Thou Art: Three Hymns for Organ*. Org. MSM 10-577.

P ♫ Organ, Anne Krentz. "Rejoice, Rejoice, Believers" from *Piano Plus: Hymns for Piano and Treble Instrument, Advent/Christmas*. Pno, C or B-flat inst. AFP 9780800638542.

Schrader, Jack. "Soon and Very Soon" from *I Have Heard You Calling in the Night: Piano Reflections for Memorial Services*. Pno. HOP 8598.

Handbell

♫ Boatright, Linda. "Rejoice, Rejoice, Believers." 5-6 oct, L4. FTT 20451.

♫ Page, Anna Laura. "Rejoice, Rejoice, Believers." 3-5 oct hb, opt 3 oct hc, L2. CG CGB642.

♫ Tucker, Sondra. "Wake, Awake." 3 oct, L2. CPH 977381.

Wednesday, November 11
Martin, Bishop of Tours, died 397

Martin's pagan father enlisted him in the army at age fifteen. One winter day a beggar approached Martin for aid, and he cut his cloak in half and gave a portion to the beggar. Later Martin understood that he had seen the presence of Christ in that beggar, and this ended his uncertainty about Christianity. He soon asked for his release from his military duties, but he was imprisoned instead. After his release from prison he began preaching, particularly against the Arians. In 371 he was elected bishop of Tours. As bishop he developed a reputation for intervening on behalf of prisoners and heretics who had been sentenced to death.

Wednesday, November 11
Søren Aabye Kierkegaard, teacher, died 1855

Kierkegaard (KEER-keh-gore), a nineteenth-century Danish theologian whose writings reflect his Lutheran heritage, was the founder of modern existentialism. Though he was engaged to a woman he deeply loved, he ended the relationship because he believed he was called to search the hidden side of life. Many of his works were published under a variety of names so that he could reply to arguments from his own previous works. Kierkegaard's work attacked the established church of his day—its complacency, its tendency to intellectualize faith, and its desire to be accepted by polite society.

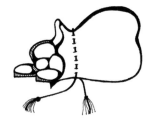

November 15, 2020
Time after Pentecost — Lectionary 33

Our readings during November speak of the end times. Zephaniah proclaims that the coming day of the Lord will be filled with wrath and distress. Paul says it will come like a thief in the night and urges us to be awake and sober. Jesus tells the parable of the talents, calling us to use our gifts, while we still have time, for the greater and common good. In a world filled with violence and despair, we gather around signs of hope—word, water, bread, and wine—eager to welcome the good news of Christ's coming among us.

Prayer of the Day

Righteous God, our merciful master, you own the earth and all its peoples, and you give us all that we have. Inspire us to serve you with justice and wisdom, and prepare us for the joy of the day of your coming, through Jesus Christ, our Savior and Lord.

Gospel Acclamation

Alleluia. Abide in me as I abide in you; those who abide in me bear much fruit. *Alleluia.* (John 15:4, 5)

Readings and Psalm

Zephaniah 1:7, 12-18

Zephaniah (like the prophet Amos in last week's first reading) presents the day of the Lord as one of judgment and wrath. Descriptions of the last day in the New Testament include details taken from Old Testament accounts of the day of the Lord.

Psalm 90:1-8 [9-11] 12

So teach us to number our days that we may apply our hearts to wisdom. (Ps. 90:12)

1 Thessalonians 5:1-11

Though we do not know and cannot calculate the day of Christ's return, we live faithfully in the here and now as we anticipate the day when we will be given eternal salvation through our Lord Jesus Christ.

Matthew 25:14-30

Jesus tells a parable about his second coming, indicating that it is not sufficient merely to maintain things as they are. Those who await his return should make good use of the gifts that God has provided them.

Semicontinuous Reading and Psalm

Judges 4:1-7

Deborah was a prophet and judge who, with her general, Barak, led a victorious holy war against a stronger Canaanite force from the north.

Psalm 123

Our eyes look to you, O God, until you show us your mercy. (Ps. 123:2)

Preface   Sundays

Color   Green

Prayers of Intercession

The prayers are prepared locally for each occasion. The following examples may be adapted or used as appropriate.

Longing for Christ's reign to come among us, we pray for the outpouring of God's power on the church, the world, and all in need.

A brief silence.

Lord of the church, ignite your people with the passion of your love. By the fire of your Holy Spirit, unify us across ministries, congregations, and denominations, and refine us to participate in your activity throughout the world. Hear us, O God.

Your mercy is great.

Lord of creation, we stand in awe at the works of your hands and praise you for the beauty of nature (*local places of natural beauty may be named*). Bless the earth for your glory and restore its integrity where exploitation has caused ruin. Hear us, O God.

Your mercy is great.

Lord of the nations, sound forth your justice in the ears of all leaders. Increase concern for those who are most vulnerable, especially as international leaders forge trade agreements and cooperate to end human rights abuses. Hear us, O God.

Your mercy is great.

Lord of all in need, search out all who cry to you in distress. Scatter the heavy clouds of depression, chronic illness, unemployment, and loneliness with your radiant light. Send us as encouragement and signs of your healing. Hear us, O God.

Your mercy is great.

Lord of the stranger, stir up holy restlessness in us to extend love to those at the margins. Release our desire for control and open us to learn from the perspectives of others. Hear us, O God.

Your mercy is great.

Here other intercessions may be offered.

Lord of the living and the dead, we give you thanks for all the saints at rest from their labors (*especially*). Rouse us to live by their example, that saints yet to come may also know your love. Hear us, O God.

Your mercy is great.

Receive our prayers in the name of Jesus Christ our Savior, until that day when you gather all creation around your throne where you will reign forever and ever.

Amen.

Ideas for the Day

- Depending on its age, a Monopoly game will include either $15,140 or $20,580. These totals are not far off a present-day laborer's annual earnings. A talent in biblical times represented fifteen years' wages for a laborer. It would take the money from seventy-five Monopoly games to represent the five talents given to the first servant in the parable of the talents. Two talents would require thirty games' worth of money. The final servant would get the money from fifteen games. Also, we might imagine what would happen if someone left the Monopoly game and another person played in their place for a while. If the substitute player buys no property and builds nothing, they just circle the board paying out rent and fees. The Monopoly illustration may be furthered by exploring Free Parking and Get Out of Jail Free as examples of grace.

- In today's parable, one slave, starting out with little, takes the careful approach and manages to hold on to what he has. The other two act almost brashly and obtain great returns on what they have. In the end, caution fails and daring is rewarded. Obviously, in parts of our lives prudence is justified, but faith is not one of them. We stand to lose much if we treat the gospel as something to be preserved rather than put to work. There is risk involved in exposing our faith and values to the glare of public examination, of course. But unless we are willing to put it all on the line, taking chances for the sake of increasing the gospel harvest, we will end up losing even what we had to start with. Staying alive isn't enough. Take a chance, for heaven's sake!

- At the heart of most romantic comedies is trust. Love blossoms and then trust is broken by a secret kept or an act of betrayal. Without this breach there is nothing to drive the plot. The drama in the parable of the talents comes from the servant who broke the master's trust. The others are called trustworthy. The romantic comedy ends with trust restored. Liturgy is an act of trust. Confession and forgiveness, the peace, communion, and baptism are all gifts from God, and through these words and actions we express renewed trust in God. Unlike the characters in the romantic comedy, however, God will never break our trust.

Connections with Creation

In this ecological age, many Christians are more worried about the cataclysmic destruction of the earth caused by climate change, pollution, and other human-caused forms of environmental degradation than they are concerned about the possibility of an end-times scenario like the ones described in various apocalyptic texts in the Bible. To be people of the light and "children of the day" (1 Thess. 5:5) means that even as we hope for God's salvation, we live faithfully by treating one another and the earth with kindness and compassion. Paul encourages people to build each other up; our current environmental situation also calls for us to build up the natural world by acting as restorers, stewards, and conservationists on this planet that gives us the gift of our embodied lives. We each have gifts to use in the urgent work of caring for creation.

Let the Children Come

In today's second reading, the apostle Paul says, "You are all children of light" (1 Thess. 5:5). Show children one of the candles that is given in your congregation to a newly baptized person. Remind them that the candle is presented with words of Jesus from the Bible: either "Jesus said, I am the light of the world. Whoever follows me will have the light of life" or "Let your light so shine before others that they may see your good works and glorify your Father in heaven" (John 8:12; Matt. 5:16; *ELW*, p. 231). Show the children the large paschal candle that is lit for baptisms, funerals, and during the Easter season. The gift of baptism is an Easter life in Jesus for our whole lives—lives that show Jesus' love and light in all we do.

Assembly Song
Gathering

> Let streams of living justice ELW 710
> O Zion, haste ELW 668, LBW 397
> Oh, happy day when we shall stand ELW 441, LBW 351

Psalmody and Acclamations

> Feeley, Ephrem. "Fill Us with Your Love." SATB, cant, assembly, kybd, gtr, C inst. GIA G-9632.
> Mathis, William H. Refrain for "Psalm 90" from *After the Prelude: Year A.* U/cant, hb. CG CGB658 (digital version), CGB659 (print version). Use with ELW psalm tone 1 or 6 (in C).
> + Gelineau, Joseph. "Psalm 123" from ACYG.
> (GA) ELW 170 with verse for Lectionary 33.

Hymn of the Day

> Lord our God, with praise we come ELW 730 *ROMEDAL*
>   LBW 244 *GUD ER GUD*
> O Christ the same ELW 760 *RED HILL ROAD* WOV 778
>   *LONDONDERRY AIR*

+ = semicontinuous psalm

When peace like a river ELW 785, TFF 194, LBW 346 *VILLE DU HAVRE*

Offering

God, whose giving knows no ending ELW 678, LBW 408

Let us talents and tongues employ ELW 674, WOV 754, TFF 232

Communion

Bread of life from heaven ELW 474

Come, ye thankful people, come ELW 693, LBW 407

Jesu, Jesu, fill us with your love ELW 708, WOV 765, TFF 83, LS 146

Sending

Build us up, Lord ELW 670

Thine the amen ELW 826, WOV 801

Additional Assembly Songs

For the troubles and the sufferings/Pelas dores deste mundo GTG 764

Heal us, Lord SP 14

I've just come from the fountain WOV 696, TFF 11

⊕ Red Crearte, Collective Creation. "Huapango del pan/A Chance to Earn Their Bread" from *Hosanna! Ecumenical Songs for Justice and Peace*. U. WCC Publications 9782825416679.

⊕ South African trad. "Freedom Is Coming" from *Freedom Is Coming: Songs of Protest and Praise from South Africa*. SATB. GIA WB528. Also TFF 46.

☼ Baloche, Paul. "My Reward" from CCLI.

☼ Breakey, Bryson. "Anywhere" from CCLI.

☼ Cates, Chad/Jason Walker/Moriah Peters. "Well Done" from CCLI.

☼ Cobb, Caroline. "Wake Up" from CCLI.

☼ Kensrue, Dustin. "Come Lord Jesus" from CCLI.

☼ Pardo, Jeff/Michael Fordinal/Tauren Wells. "Making Me New" from CCLI.

Music for the Day
Choral

P Carter, John. "Standin' in the Need of Prayer" from *Augsburg Choirbook for Men*. TTBB, a cap. AFP 9780800676834.

P ♫ Frahm, Frederick. "O Christ the Same." SATB, org, opt bsn, vc, cl. AFP 9781506426129.

Haydn, Johann Michael. "Angelis suis Deus mandavit." SATB, kybd. Various editions.

P Tsai, Yu-Shan. "It Is Well with My Soul." SATB, pno. AFP 9781451462371.

Children's Choir

P Anderson, Shari. "I Want to Walk as a Child of the Light" from *ChildrenSing in Worship*, vol. 2. U/2 pt, pno. AFP 9781451424126.

Bailey, Lynn Shaw/Becki Slagle Mayo. "Use Your Gifts." U/2 pt, pno. CG CGA1184.

P Taylor, Terry T. "Walk as Children of Light" from *Shine Your Light*. U/2 pt, pno. CG CGA1661.

Keyboard / Instrumental

P ♫ Farlee, Robert Buckley. "Lord Our God, with Praise We Come" from *Treasures Old and New: Hymn Preludes for Organ*. Org. AFP 9781451499094.

♫ Larkin, Michael. "When Peace, Like a River" from *A Mighty Fortress: Piano Mediations on Great Hymns of Faith*. Pno. MSM 15-750.

Phillips, Craig. "Forest Green" from *Joy to the World: Three Preludes for Christmas*. Org. SEL 160-815.

P ♫ Raabe, Nancy. "O Christ the Same" from *How Good It Is: Piano Settings of Carl Schalk Hymn Tunes*. Pno. AFP 9781451401165.

Handbell

Moklebust, Cathy. "Londonderry Air." 3-6 oct hb, opt 3-5 oct hc, ob, or C inst, L2+. CG CGB1041.

♫ Stephenson, Valerie. "It Is Well with My Soul." 3-5 oct hb or hc, L2-. Genesis Press 2029.

♫ Tucker, Margaret. "It Is Well with My Soul." 3-6 oct hb, opt 3 oct hc, L3. CG CGB511.

Tuesday, November 17
Elizabeth of Hungary, renewer of society, died 1231

This Hungarian princess lived her entire life in east-central Germany and is often called Elizabeth of Thuringia. Married to a duke, she gave large sums of money, including her dowry, for relief of the poor and sick. She founded hospitals, cared for orphans, and used the royal food supplies to feed the hungry. Though she had the support of her husband, her generosity and charity did not earn her friends within the royal court. At the death of her husband, she was driven out. She joined a Franciscan order and continued her charitable work, though she suffered abuse at the hands of her confessor and spiritual guide. Her lifetime of charity is particularly remarkable when one remembers that she died at the age of twenty-four. She founded two hospitals, and many more are named for her.

November 22, 2020
Christ the King
Last Sunday after Pentecost — Lectionary 34

On this final Sunday of the church year our gospel is Jesus' great story of judgment. In the end, the faithful are those who served Christ by ministering to those who are poor, hungry, naked, sick, or estranged. In the first reading God is the shepherd who seeks the lost, weak, and injured and feeds them with justice. We gather this day to celebrate the reign of Christ and his victory over death, yet we await the consummation of all things yet to come. Acknowledging Christ as our merciful ruler, we go forth that his reign may be known in our loving words and deeds.

Prayer of the Day

O God of power and might, your Son shows us the way of service, and in him we inherit the riches of your grace. Give us the wisdom to know what is right and the strength to serve the world you have made, through Jesus Christ, our Savior and Lord, who lives and reigns with you and the Holy Spirit, one God, now and forever.

Gospel Acclamation

Alleluia. Blessed is the one who comes in the name of the Lord. Blessed is the coming kingdom of our ancestor David. *Alleluia.* (Mark 11:9)

Readings and Psalm
Ezekiel 34:11-16, 20-24

Because Israel's kings proved to be bad shepherds, Ezekiel declares that the LORD will assume the role of shepherd in Israel. The LORD will also set over them a shepherd-messiah, "my servant David," who will feed and care for the people.

Psalm 95:1-7a

We are the people of God's pasture and the sheep of God's hand. (Ps. 95:7)

Ephesians 1:15-23

In this passage, God is praised for revealing ultimate divine power in raising Jesus from the dead. The resurrected, exalted Christ is Lord of both the church and the entire universe, now and in the age to come.

Matthew 25:31-46

Jesus compares himself to a king who moves among his subjects to see how he is treated: what is done for the least of those who belong to his family is truly done for him.

Semicontinuous Reading and Psalm
Ezekiel 34:11-16, 20-24

See above.

Psalm 100

We are God's people and the sheep of God's pasture. (Ps. 100:3)

Preface   Ascension *or* Sundays

Color   White *or* Green

Prayers of Intercession

The prayers are prepared locally for each occasion. The following examples may be adapted or used as appropriate.

Longing for Christ's reign to come among us, we pray for the outpouring of God's power on the church, the world, and all in need.

A brief silence.

Sovereign of all, train our ears to hear your cry in the needs of those around us. Bless all social ministries of the church through which we seek to serve others as we ourselves have been served. Hear us, O God.

Your mercy is great.

You cause rain to fall on the just and unjust alike. Direct our use of creation to provide for the needs of all people in ways that are sustainable for the earth. Hear us, O God.

Your mercy is great.

Bring peace to every place where conflict rages (*especially*). Grant opportunities for ending divisions among us and usher in your reign of unity and reconciliation. Hear us, O God.

Your mercy is great.

Heal the sinful divisions we erect between us and release us from systems of oppression and prejudice. Restore our capacity to see your image in those whose dignity we have stripped away (*especially*). Hear us, O God.

Your mercy is great.

Pour out the gifts of your Spirit on children and youth throughout the church. Sustain those who work in children's ministry, youth ministry, and campus ministry as they nurture the gifts of young people. Hear us, O God.

Your mercy is great.

Here other intercessions may be offered.

Thank you for saints now departed who fed the hungry, clothed the naked, and tended to the sick. Inspire us by their example,

that we may see your presence in those in need around us. Hear us, O God.
Your mercy is great.
Receive our prayers in the name of Jesus Christ our Savior, until that day when you gather all creation around your throne where you will reign forever and ever.
Amen.

Ideas for the Day

- The image of a king is far removed from the daily experiences of most twenty-first-century Christians. Consider what movies, TV shows, or books might be well known in your community and provide a meaningful model of kingship from them. As one example, the children's book *The Quiltmaker's Gift* (Jeff Brumbeau and Gail de Marcken [New York: Scholastic Press, 2000]) begins with a king who is harsh and unforgiving, "powerful and greedy . . . who liked nothing better than to receive presents." By the end of the book he embodies the same kind of kingship that Jesus models for us: generous and selfless, materially poor but spiritually rich. Perhaps your sermon, children's message, or this month's newsletter article could include a description of someone who embodies the role of a servant king.

- Ezekiel 34:16 states that God will seek out and care for those who have been oppressed and will feed the people justice. How does your faith community feed justice to the world? What organizations or causes do your people care about? This might be a good week to start an initiative like a giving tree, where folks can buy Christmas gifts for a family in need, or to advertise a fundraising campaign for one of the outreach ministries you support. Maybe you could put up a display in your gathering space, have a take-home bulletin insert, or ask someone to do a temple talk to teach worshipers about the importance of the justice ministries your community supports. God's caring for the oppressed often happens through the efforts of God's people, so encourage your people to take on the challenge!

- The title "king" evokes strong masculine imagery. Sometimes this imagery is helpful for people seeking to understand the nature of God. Other times, however, such language can be harmful. How would a person experiencing abuse at the hands of a strong male figure in their life hear the message that Jesus is one of those strong men? This might be a week to consider using expansive language for God (both masculine and feminine pronouns, for instance) or offering a variety of titles for God in the prayers. Be sure that the title you use for God does not cause harm to the worshipers in your community.

Connections with Creation

On Christ the King Sunday we are reminded that the highest and most holy form of power is not coercive and domineering but, rather, self-emptying and servant-like. Jesus is a king like no earthly king, and his ministry on earth revealed that God's reign operates with an ethic of care for the most vulnerable and most in need of compassion. Psalm 95 echoes the creation stories and acknowledges that God's reign includes care for the mountains, land, and seas, as well as for the earth's human inhabitants. The creation does not exist merely for our self-serving use at the expense of other creatures and their ecosystems. As God's appointed stewards of creation, we are called to exercise self-emptying and servant-like power in our relationship with the natural world. As we do unto the oceans, atmosphere, and soil, we do unto Christ. Let us learn anew to value the kind of power that Jesus demonstrated rather than the power of death and destruction.

Let the Children Come

"Jesus, remember me" (ELW 616), a refrain from the ecumenical Taizé Community in France, is an easy song for children to learn. Have the cantor sing it first, then the children. Next add higher voices, then lower voices, ending with children alone. This song could be used during a gospel procession on this feast day. If gospel processions are not part of your congregation's practice, this refrain could simply be sung before and after the reading of the gospel.

Assembly Song
Gathering

O God beyond all praising ELW 880, WOV 797
Oh, worship the King ELW 842, LBW 548
Shout to the Lord ELW 821, W&P 124

Psalmody and Acclamations

"Come, Let Us Sing to the Lord" from ELW Morning Prayer, pp. 300–301.
Oh, come, let us sing W&P 107
+ Lim, Swee Hong/arr. John Bell. "All People Living on the Earth." SATB, pno, gtr, assembly, C inst. GIA G-8011.
+ Organ, Anne Krentz. "Psalm 100." SAB, pno, opt assembly. AFP 9781451498813.
(GA) ELW 170 with verse for Christ the King.

Hymn of the Day

All hail the power of Jesus' name! ELW 634, LBW 328
  CORONATION TFF 267 *DIADEM* LBW 329 *MILES LANE*
Christ is the king! ELW 662, LBW 386 *BEVERLY*
Rejoice, for Christ is king! ELW 430, LBW 171 *LAUS REGIS*

Offering

The trumpets sound, the angels sing ELW 531, W&P 139
We give thee but thine own ELW 686, LBW 410

Communion

Beautiful Savior ELW 838, LS 174, LBW 518
We come to the hungry feast ELW 479, WOV 766, DATH 84
What feast of love ELW 487, WOV 701

Sending

Crown him with many crowns ELW 855, LBW 170
Soon and very soon ELW 439, WOV 744, TFF 38, W&P 128,
LS 2

Additional Assembly Songs

Come now, you blessed LS 141
Feed my lambs ASG 8
You, Lord, are both Lamb and Shepherd GTG 274
🌐 Matsikenyiri, Patrick. "Namatai (Shepherd God, to You We
Pray)" from *Njalo (Always)*. ABI 9780687498079.
🌐 Mozambique trad. "Nzamuranza" from *With Many Voices*.
SATB, cant. Binary Editions 9790900140104. Also
from *Africa Praise Songbook*. SATB, cant. GBGMusik
1890569070.
☼ Durham, Trenton. "Christ the King Is Risen" from *Weep +
Rejoice EP*. trentondurham.bandcamp.com.
☼ Hall, Mark/Matthew West. "Jesus Friend of Sinners" from
CCLI.
☼ Juby, Chris. "Come and Worship Christ the King" from CCLI.
☼ McDowell, William. "Sound of Heaven" from CCLI.
☼ Morton, Luke. "The Least of These" from *Let the Little Chil-
dren Come*. glkids.bandcamp.com.
☼ Rose, Danielle. "You Did It to Me" from *I Thirst*. daniellerose
.com.

Music for the Day
Choral

Handel, George, Frideric. "Awake the Trumpet's Lofty Sound"
from *Judas Maccabeus*. HAL 08596786.
℗ Niedman, Peter. "Lift Up Your Heads, Ye Mighty Gates"
from *The Augsburg Choirbook*. SATB, org. AFP
9780800656782.
℗ Shoenfeld, William M. "Oh, Come Let Us Sing!" from *Augsburg Easy Choirbook*, vol. 3. 2 pt trbl or mxd, kybd. AFP
9781506414041.
Williams, Ralph Vaughan/arr. Craig Courtney. "Let All the
World in Every Corner Sing." SATB, pno 4-hands. BP
CU1001.

Children's Choir

Bedford, Michael. "Te Deum." U, org, opt tpt, opt timp. CG
CGA1127.
℗ Burrows. Mark. "Make a Joyful Noise" from *Again, I Say
Rejoice!* U, pno or gtr. CG CGC56.
℗ Patterson, Mark. "Let All the World in Every Corner Sing" from
*ChildrenSing: Seven Anthems for Elementary Age Sing-
ers*. U, pno, tamb. AFP 9780800677695.

Keyboard / Instrumental

℗♫ Organ, Anne Krentz. "Christ Is the King!" from *Reflec-
tions on Hymn Tunes for the Fall Festivals*. Pno. AFP
9780800663834.
♫ Schelat, David. "Coronation" from *Oxford Hymn Settings for
Organists: Autumn Festivals*. OXF 9780193400689.
℗ Unke, Zach. "At the Name of Jesus" from *At the Name of Jesus:
Piano Settings*. Pno. AFP 9781506448046.
℗♫ Weber, Jacob B. "Rejoice, for Christ Is King!" from *Christ Is
King: Organ Hymn Preludes*. Pno. AFP 9781451486032.

Handbell

♫ Kinyon, Barbara. "All Hail the Power of Jesus' Name." 2-3 oct,
L3. HOP 1658.
McChesney, Kevin. "Blessing and Honor." 3-5 oct, L2. ALF
21854.
♫ Page, Anna Laura. "All Hail the Power." 3-6 oct hb, pno. L3. BP
HB453A. Full score/pno, HB453.

Monday, November 23
Clement, Bishop of Rome, died around 100

Clement was the third bishop of Rome and served at the end of
the first century. He is best remembered for a letter he wrote
to the Corinthian congregation, still having difficulty with
divisions in spite of Paul's canonical letters. Clement's writing
echoes Paul's. "Love . . . has no limits to its endurance, bears
everything patiently. Love is neither servile nor arrogant. It
does not provoke schisms or form cliques, but always acts in
harmony with others." Clement's letter is also a witness to early
understandings of church government and the way each office
in the church works for the good of the whole.

Monday, November 23
Miguel Agustín Pro, martyr, died 1927

Miguel Agustín Pro grew up among oppression in Mexico,
where revolutionaries accused the church of siding with the
rich. He was a Jesuit priest who served during a time of intense
anticlericalism, and therefore he carried out much of his ministry in private settings. He worked on behalf of the poor and

🌐 = global song   ♫ = relates to hymn of the day   + = semicontinuous psalm
☼ = praise song   ℗ = available in Prelude Music Planner

homeless. Miguel and his two brothers were arrested, falsely accused of throwing a bomb at the car of a government official, and executed by a firing squad. Just before the guns fired, he yelled, "¡Viva Cristo Rey!" which means "Long live Christ the king!"

Tuesday, November 24
Justus Falckner, died 1723; Jehu Jones, died 1852; William Passavant, died 1894; pastors in North America

A native of Saxony, Falckner was the son of a Lutheran pastor and, seeing the stresses his father endured, did not plan on becoming a pastor himself, though he studied theology in Halle. Instead, he joined with his brother in the real estate business in Pennsylvania. Through this business he became acquainted with a Swedish pastor in America, and finally he decided to become ordained. He served congregations in New York and New Jersey. Not only was he the first Lutheran ordained in North America, but he published a catechism that was the first Lutheran book published on the continent.

Jones was a native of Charleston, South Carolina. Ordained by the New York Ministerium in 1832, he became the Lutheran church's first African American pastor. Upon returning to South Carolina he was arrested under a law prohibiting free blacks from reentering the state, so he was unable to join the group of Charlestonians he had been commissioned to accompany to Liberia. For nearly twenty years Jones carried out missionary work in Philadelphia in the face of many difficulties. There he led in the formation of the first African American Lutheran congregation, St. Paul's, and the construction of its church building.

William Passavant created and nurtured a new level of organized social ministry in western Pennsylvania. It was the seed of the system of social services that is now known as Lutheran Services in America. Passavant and his legacy sought to serve the poorest of the poor, providing shelter, medicine, and living assistance.

Wednesday, November 25
Isaac Watts, hymnwriter, died 1748

Isaac Watts was born in England to a family of nonconformists, people who thought the Church of England had not carried its reforms far enough. As a youth, Watts complained to his father about the quality of hymnody in the metrical psalter of his day. That was the start of his hymnwriting career. He wrote about six hundred hymns, many in a two-year period beginning when he was twenty years old. Some of Watts's hymns are based on psalms, a nonconformist tradition. When criticized for writing hymns not taken from scripture, he responded that if we can pray prayers that are not from scripture but written by us, then surely we can sing hymns that we have made up ourselves. Ten of Watts's hymn texts are in *Evangelical Lutheran Worship*, including "O God, our help in ages past" (ELW 632).

November 26, 2020
Day of Thanksgiving (USA)

At harvest time we join the psalmist in offering thanksgiving to God: "You crown the year with your goodness, and your paths overflow with plenty." We are grateful for the abundance of the good things of God's creation. Paul reminds us that our thanksgiving overflows into generosity. As the body of Christ in the world, we give ourselves away as bread for the hungry.

Prayer of the Day

Almighty God our Father, your generous goodness comes to us new every day. By the work of your Spirit lead us to acknowledge your goodness, give thanks for your benefits, and serve you in willing obedience, through Jesus Christ, our Savior and Lord.

Gospel Acclamation

Alleluia. God is able to provide you with every blessing in abundance, so that by always having enough of everything, you may share abundantly in every good work. *Alleluia.* (2 Cor. 9:8)

Readings and Psalm

Deuteronomy 8:7-18

Times of abundance tempt us to forget God and rely on our own power and resources. But God is the one who took Israel out of Egypt, led and fed them in the wilderness, brought them into the land, and gave them power to be productive. To thank this God is to remember and proclaim God's deeds.

Psalm 65

You crown the year with your goodness, and your paths overflow with plenty. (Ps. 65:11)

2 Corinthians 9:6-15

Christian fellowship involves sharing with those in need. Here Paul is gathering a collection for the church in Jerusalem from all the Gentile churches he helped found. We can be extravagant in our giving because God is extravagant in providing for our lives.

Luke 17:11-19

A Samaritan leper becomes a model for thanksgiving. He does not take for granted the kindness shown to him but takes time to thank Jesus and to glorify God.

Preface   Weekdays

Color   of the season

Prayers of Intercession

The prayers are prepared locally for each occasion. The following examples may be adapted or used as appropriate.

Longing for Christ's reign to come among us, we pray for the outpouring of God's power on the church, the world, and all in need.

A brief silence.

Gracious God, you send from your abundance the people, talents, and resources needed for all the ministries of your church. We give thanks for the work you have accomplished through your people, and we pray for your continued blessings in our ministry together (*specific ministries could be named*). Hear us, O God.

Your mercy is great.

Bountiful God, you feed us through the richness of the land, water, sunlight, and ample crops. Bless all those who cultivate the land to bring forth its bounty, especially farmers and migrant workers. Hear us, O God.

Your mercy is great.

Merciful God, you order our lives by your providence. We give you thanks for laws, infrastructure, and leadership that structure and support our human endeavors. Align our purposes with your own, that all our undertakings might bring you glory. Hear us, O God.

Your mercy is great.

Loving God, you open our hearts in compassion for one another. We give you thanks for the care and healing received through the hands and feet of your servants. Send us to love those most in need of your mercy (*especially*). Hear us, O God.

Your mercy is great.

Hospitable God, you connect and strengthen us through meals and conversation with family and friends. In this time of thanksgiving, steer us from passive receiving to active response, from old quarrels to reconciliation, and from overconsumption to true gratitude. Hear us, O God.

Your mercy is great.

Here other intercessions may be offered.

Eternal God, we give thanks for the love and care we have received from saints who have gone before us. By their example, enrich the generosity of our witness to others. Hear us, O God.

Your mercy is great.

Receive our prayers in the name of Jesus Christ our Savior, until that day when you gather all creation around your throne where you will reign forever and ever.
Amen.

Ideas for the Day

- Most worshipers in North America are not familiar with crops of figs, pomegranates, and olives as described in Deuteronomy 8:8. What local produce can you celebrate in your worship service? If you have farmers or gardeners in your community, perhaps they could bring in some samples of their produce for tasting, a meal, or a farmers' market. This could happen before or after worship, or as an experiential part of worship as a way of giving thanks for the bounty of your own neighborhood.

- Following Thanksgiving festivities, thousands of folks around the country will head to work for their busiest weekend of the year. Retail workers often struggle to make ends meet, but once the Christmas shopping season begins, they may see an increase in their paychecks. Who in your congregation makes a living by working retail? Do you have any small-business owners? Consider offering a blessing for these folks during Thanksgiving worship as they enter the time of year that is usually the busiest and most stressful.

- Holidays are emotionally complicated for many people. People who are experiencing Thanksgiving without the presence of a loved one may not feel like celebrating. Approach this holiday with sensitivity to individuals glad to give thanks for the many blessings in their lives as well as those who struggle to find any blessing amid their suffering.

- As many parents teach their children, writing thank-you notes is important. This is also important into adulthood. Do church volunteers receive thank-you notes for their service to the congregation? Not all adults remember the craft of writing a good thank-you note. Perhaps you could set up a station in your gathering space or fellowship hall for thank-you note writing this weekend. Provide blank notecards and envelopes or postcards printed in-house on cardstock, and encourage folks to thank those people in their lives who have done something meaningful lately. Perhaps a child's schoolteacher, a healthcare provider, a neighbor, or a long-distance friend needs special recognition. If your budget allows, also offer to mail these notes for worshipers.

Connections with Creation

Although Thanksgiving is celebrated as a one-day holiday in the United States and Canada, Christians have at the heart of our worship life the sacramental practice of giving thanks for God's goodness and grace. In preparation for eating bread and drinking wine in holy communion, we give thanks for God's saving presence in our lives made known to us tangibly in the fruits of the earth. Participating in this meal of thanksgiving helps us cultivate an awareness of our daily reliance upon clean water, healthy soil, seeds, and sunlight. A deep and genuine expression of gratitude for the natural world emerges readily from an understanding of the truly dependent position we find ourselves in as earth creatures. This gratitude for the very gift of life inspires us to be generous in our love and care for the web of creation.

Let the Children Come

Parents and teachers are constantly reminding children, "Did you say 'thank you'?" Worship on this day is a time to remember that our thanks is always directed to someone, and ultimately, to God. Saying thanks is not merely a social duty; it draws us closer to the person we are thanking. Children can learn that the good feeling of receiving a gift is surpassed by the joy and fulfillment of a relationship in which thanks is naturally and freely expressed. Children can learn to say simple prayers of "Thank you, God" in the middle of their daily experiences. Children can learn to join with the whole assembly at the end of the liturgy: "Thanks be to God."

Assembly Song
Gathering

> For the beauty of the earth ELW 879, LBW 561
> Lord, your hands have formed ELW 554, WOV 727
> We praise you, O God ELW 870, LBW 241

Psalmody and Acclamations

> To bless the earth/Psalm 65 GTG 38
> Dudley-Smith, Timothy. "Every Heart Its Tribute Pays" (ST. GEORGE'S WINDSOR) from PAS 65E.
> Krentz, Michael. "Psalm 65" from PWA.
> Long, Larry J. "Psalm 65," Refrain 2, from PSCY.
> (GA) ELW 170 with verse for Day of Thanksgiving.

Hymn of the Day

> Now thank we all our God ELW 839/840, LBW 533/534
> NUN DANKET ALLE GOTT
> Sing to the Lord of harvest ELW 694, LBW 412 WIE LIEBLICH IST DER MAIEN
> We plow the fields and scatter ELW 680, LLC 492 SAN FERNANDO ELW 681, LS 102, LBW 362 WIR PFLÜGEN

Offering

> For the fruit of all creation ELW 679, WOV 760, LBW 563
> We Are an Offering ELW 692, W&P 146

Communion

As rain from the clouds   ELW 508
By your hand you feed your people   ELW 469
I am the Bread of life   ELW 485, WOV 702

Sending

Let all things now living   ELW 881, LBW 557
To God our thanks we give/Reamo leboga   ELW 682, GS2 8

Additional Assembly Songs

For the healing of creation   MSB2 S522, SP 12b
Give thanks   TFF 292, W&P 41
I am thanking Jesus   TFF 286
⊕ In the Lord I'll be ever thankful   SP 18, GTG 654
⊕ Tahiti. "Na oe" from *Em Tua Graça*. SATB. WCC Publications
2825414492. Out of print. Hannelore.Schmid@wcc-coe
.org.
☼ Brown, Chris/Matthew Ntlele/Stefan Green/Steven Furtick.
"Grateful" from CCLI.
☼ Cairns, Chelsea/Isak Peterssen/Jock James/Ryan Carins. "A
Thousand Times (Thank You)" from CCLI.
☼ Flanigan, Ryan. "General Thanksgiving" from CCLI.
☼ Hesler, Jonathan David. "Find Me" from CCLI.
☼ Leonard, David/Jason Ingram/Leslie Jordan. "We Give You
Thanks" from CCLI.
☼ Redman, Matt. "Thank You for Healing Me" from CCLI.

Music for the Day
Choral

P Betinis, Abbie. "Psalm 126: A Song of Ascents." SATB, a cap.
AFP 9780800677206.
P Cherwien, David. "Harvest Gold." 2 pt mxd, org. AFP
9781506425801.
P Cooman, Carson P. "Te Deum (We Praise Thee, O God)" 2 pt
mxd, org. SEL 410-930.
Farnell, Laura. "i thank You God for most this amazing day."
SSA, pno. Alliance Music Publications AMP1087.

Children's Choir

Bedford, Michael. "Let All the Peoples Praise You, O God." 2 pt,
pno, fl. CG CGA933.
Burkhardt, Michael. "From All That Dwell Below the Skies." U,
kybd. MSM 50-9415.
P♫ Patterson, Mark. "Now We Give Thanks" from *Young ChildrenSing*. U, kybd. AFP 9780800676803.

Keyboard / Instrumental

P♫ Hovland, Egil. "Nun danket alle Gott" from *A New Liturgical
Year*, vol. 1. Org. AFP 9780800656713.
P♫ Nelson, Ronald A. "We Plow the Fields and Scatter"
from *Easy Hymn Settings for Organ*, vol. 3. Org. AFP
9781451462562.
Palmer, Nicholas. "For the Fruit of All Creation" from *For the
Care of the Earth: Hymn Reflections for Piano*. Pno. MSM
15-751.
P♫ Sullivan, Christine. "Sing to the Lord of Harvest" from
*All Good Gifts Around Us: Piano Settings of Creation
Hymns*. Pno. AFP 9781451401899.

Handbell

♫ Helman, Michael. "We Plow the Fields and Scatter." 3-6 oct hb,
opt 3-5 oct hc, U vcs, L3. ALF 29956.
♫ Larson, Lloyd. "Raise the Songs of Harvest." 3-5 oct, L3-. BP
HB279.
♫ Waldrop, Tammy. "Calypso on Sing to the Lord of Harvest *with*
For the Fruit of All Creation." 3-5 oct hb, opt 3 oct hc, perc.
L3- HOP 2841. Full score, 2841D.

⊕ = global song   ♫ = relates to hymn of the day
☼ = praise song   P = available in Prelude Music Planner

New and Noteworthy from Augsburg Fortress

Preaching

§ Lathrop, Gordon. *Proclaiming the Living Word: A Handbook for Preachers*. By providing wise encouragement and concrete tools for ministry, this book will equip preachers for faithful preaching in their assemblies.

∞ The Preaching Module, an add-on subscription to sundaysandseasons.com, features content from *Sundays and Seasons: Preaching* and *New Proclamation*.

Communion Preparation and Formation

Daniel Erlander's *A Place for You* springs to life in a family of books and videos designed to help people of all ages gain a richer understanding of Jesus' invitation to his special meal. Augsburg Fortress, now the sole distributor for Daniel Erlander's publications, has a deep commitment to stewarding what he has created. Visit augsburgfortress.org to learn about the new interactive edition of *A Place for You*, a board book using simplified words and images from the original edition of *A Place for You*, a Leader Sourcebook, and a set of animated videos featuring a hand-drawn animation style that perfectly complements Daniel Erlander's illustrations.

Baptism Preparation and Formation

Come to the Water (available summer 2019) is a new family of resources based on Daniel Erlander's two baptism manuals (*Let the Children Come* and *Water Washed and Spirit Born*) designed to support baptismal preparation and ongoing baptismal education for people of all ages. Visit augsburgfortress.org to learn more.

Life Passages

Music Sourcebook for Life Passages: Healing, Funeral, and Marriage. Assists church musicians and leaders in planning for services of life passage, including marriage, funerals, and healing services. Contains music originating in different cultures and varying accompaniment styles. Includes reproducible pages, an appendix of additional resources, and a CD-ROM of files to assist in the creation of service folders.

∞ *In Sure and Certain Hope: A Funeral Sourcebook*. Melinda A. Quivik, ed. A collection of resources for planning and preaching funerals and memorial services. Includes practical advice for special circumstances, conducting the funeral, and working with the funeral home. Multiple contributors. CD-ROM with reproducible materials.

Peace at the Last: Visitation with the Dying. A beautifully illustrated liturgy that can be used by individuals or groups who visit those who are dying. Includes prayers, psalms, simple chants, and suggestions for ritual action, all accompanied by rich watercolor artwork.

§ Quivik, Melinda A. *Remembering God's Promises: A Funeral Planning Handbook*. Offers notes and commentary on the funeral service in *Evangelical Lutheran Worship*, lists of suggested scripture readings and hymns, and information on other planning options. Pastors can also use the handbook to encourage individuals to plan their own funerals in advance.

§ Walters, Paul E. *Love and Faithfulness: A Marriage Planning Handbook*. Provides couples with brief explanations and the entire text of the *Evangelical Lutheran Worship* marriage service, as well as more recent supplemental resources. Twelve reflections encourage couples to plan the marriage service and prepare for married life together.

Music

See augsburgfortress.org for the most current listings of newly released choral and instrumental music.

Augsburg Organ Library, Series II: Advent and Christmas. Organ music from the 20th century for worship and recital. This popular series of volumes is starting a second series in response to recent hymnal publications and continued interest in hymn-based organ literature.

Healing Leaves of Grace: A Thomas Pavlechko Hymnary. Forty new hymn tunes by Thomas Pavlechko, setting to music hymns by fifteen contemporary poets.

Singing in Community: Paperless Music for Worship. Reconnect with singing and leading music as generations before us have done, without printed music for each singer.

Young ChildrenSing, vol. 2. Ten pieces for young singers, each quoting a familiar hymn. Includes reproducible pages for singers and instrumentalists.

Devotional Resources

Families Celebrate Advent & Christmas 2019–2020. A deck of 56 cards full of rituals, prayers, reflections, and activities to celebrate the Advent and Christmas seasons. Dated for the first Sunday of Advent through the Day of Epiphany.

∞ electronic or Web resource
§ also available as an ebook

Hear My Voice: A Prison Prayer Book. Multiple contributors. A prayer resource to accompany those who are incarcerated and those who pray with them. Enhanced with beautiful artwork by Robyn Sand Anderson, it includes reflections for the church year, daily prayer material, and selected scripture passages.

Luther's Small Catechism with African Descent Reflections. Multiple contributors. Presents the current version of the Small Catechism widely used in the ELCA, along with reflections from a distinguished group of African descent Lutheran theologians.

§ *Wondrous Love: Devotions for Lent 2020*. Multiple contributors. Connects Jesus' journey to the cross with our baptismal journey, using texts from Matthew's gospel.

Online Worship Planning Tools

∞ www.sundaysandseasons.com. A subscription-based online worship planning tool. Browse, select, and download content for worship planning and worship folder preparation. Complements *Sundays and Seasons*. Add-on subscriptions to preaching and video content are also available. The Preaching Module features content from *Sundays and Seasons: Preaching* and *New Proclamation*. The Worship Videos Module features worship videos and loops by The Work of the People.

∞ www.preludemusicplanner.com. A subscription-based online music planning tool. Create comprehensive plans. Browse, preview, and download music from a multi-publisher library. Search music based on lectionary days, keywords, skill level, and more. Store your usage history. Upload and organize your own library.

Ongoing Worship Support

Evangelical Lutheran Worship. More than 150 resources for God's people, gathered in word and song around gifts of grace, sent with good news into the world. augsburgfortress.org/elw.

∞ *Leading Worship Matters: A Sourcebook for Preparing Worship Leaders* with accompanying DVD and CD-ROM. Practical, succinct, easy-to-use tools and resources to plan, execute, and evaluate worship leadership training. Covers assisting ministers, readers, altar guild/sacristans, intercessors, acolytes, ushers, greeters, communion ministers, and more.

§ Worship leader handbooks. Designed to train those who serve in various worship leadership roles. Topics include preachers, presiding ministers, assisting ministers, musicians, intercessors, readers, hospitality ministers, funeral planning, and marriage planning. See more at augsburgfortress.org.

Worship Matters: An Introduction to Worship. Multiple authors. A five-session adult course that illuminates the whys and hows of Christian worship so that worshipers might experience a deeper appreciation of their community's worship. Leader guide and participant book.

§ Worship Matters Series. Examine key worship issues in topical studies by pastors, musicians, and lay people from throughout the Evangelical Lutheran Church in America.

∞ www.elca.org/worship. Evangelical Lutheran Church in America. Monthly WorshipNews enewsletter.

Key to Psalm Collections

The suggestions in the "Psalmody and Acclamations" listing for each day all include singing by the gathered assembly. Within each day several options for singing the psalms are presented. The refrains included in the resources below may be reprinted with a OneLicense.net copyright license. Exceptions are *Psalms for All Seasons* and *Lift Up Your Hearts*, both of which contain psalm settings from a variety of publishers—some, but not all—of which are covered under the OneLicense.net license. In other cases (e.g. *Psalter for Worship* and *Psalm Settings for the Church Year*), permission to reproduce refrains is included with volume purchases. Psalm collections that follow the Roman Lectionary are indicated with [RL]. Although the psalms appointed for the Roman Lectionary and the Revised Common Lectionary (RCL) are not identical, there is sufficient overlap to make these volumes very useful to those who follow the RCL.

ACYG   *Arise, Come to Your God: Forty-Seven Gelineau Settings of the Revised Grail Psalms.* GIA G-8769. An excerpted and edited collection of the Gelineau psalm settings included in the Psalter section of *Worship*, Fourth Edition (2011). Many of the original Gelineau collections are now out of print, so this collection is a most welcome addition.

   ChildrenSing Psalms. Marilyn Comer, ed. Augsburg Fortress 9780800663872. This collection of 15 of the more well-known psalms is a must-have for anyone working with children's choirs. Reproducible singer pages and assembly refrains.

   Cry Out with Joy. GIA. This four-volume set includes individual volumes for years A, B, and C, as well as a separate volume for festivals. Verses are chanted rather than through-composed. Composers include David Haas, Kathleen Harmon, Stephen Pishner, Paul Tate, and Lori True. [RL]

DATH   *Dancing at the Harvest.* Ray Makeever. Augsburg Fortress. This collection of songs includes lyrical settings of selected psalms with refrains and through-composed verses. Melody line (9780800655938) and accompaniment (9780800655945) editions.

5GP   *The Five Graces Psalter: Lectionary Psalms.* Luke Mayernik. MorningStar MSM 80-416. This collection features refrains for assembly singing and 4 part chanted verses for choir or accompanied cantor. The refrains and choir harmonizations are beautiful, although some of the refrains may be challenging for assemblies hearing them for the first time. [RL]

GTG   *Glory to God.* This hymnal from the Presbyterian Church (USA) provides full settings of more than 100 psalms as metrical paraphrases set to new and well-known hymn tunes as well as responsorial versions. Metrical versions are especially helpful when neither choir nor cantor is available to assist in leading the psalm.

   Lift Up Your Hearts: Psalms, Hymns, and Spiritual Songs. Faith Alive Christian Resources 9781592555598. Includes all 150 psalms in a variety of settings for assembly singing.

TLP   *The Lyric Psalter.* Tony Alonzo and Marty Haugen. GIA. This set contains four editions, one for each of the three years of the lectionary and one for solemnities, feasts, and special occasions. Each has a companion volume of descants for C-instrument. Psalm verses are through-composed and can be sung by a cantor. [RL]

MSB1   *Music Sourcebook for Lent and the Three Days.* Augsburg Fortress 9780806670409. This volume and its companion volume for All Saints through Transfiguration contain a wealth of musical resources, including some psalm settings and gospel acclamations.

MSB2   *Music Sourcebook, vol. 2: All Saints through Transfiguration.* Augsburg Fortress 9781451424263.

   Psallite: Sacred Song for Liturgy and Life. Liturgical Press. This set of resources includes an accompaniment edition for each lectionary year and one volume for cantor/choir. In addition to lectionary psalms, provides biblically based songs that can be used at other times in the liturgy. [RL]

PATP   *Psalm Antiphons for a Time of Penitence.* Carl Schalk. CPH 984222. A collection of twenty antiphons set for 2, 3, and 4 part choir to be paired with commonly appointed psalm texts.

PSCY   *Psalm Settings for the Church Year.* 2 vols. Mark Mummert, ed. Augsburg Fortress 9780800678562. A collection of psalm settings in a wide variety of styles and structures. Includes all psalms appointed in the RCL.

PAS   *Psalms for All Seasons: A Complete Psalter for Worship.* Calvin Institute of Christian Worship, Faith Alive Christian Resources, and Brazos Press. In addition to each of the 150 psalms and several canticles presented in multiple sung settings, this volume contains extensive appendixes and indexes.

PWA   *Psalter for Worship: Year A.* Augsburg Fortress 9780806653822. The first of three volumes of psalm refrains by various composers with *Evangelical Lutheran Worship* psalm tones. Coordinates with Celebrate and Today's Readings inserts. Includes a CD-ROM with reproducible psalm texts, refrains, and tones.

Key to Hymn and Song Collections

All published by Augsburg Fortress unless otherwise indicated.

*Indicates resources whose hymns or psalm refrains are, at least in part, included in the online worship planning tool sundaysandseasons.com.

ASG*	As Sunshine to a Garden	H82	The Hymnal 1982 (Church Publishing)	NCH	The New Century Hymnal (Pilgrim Press)
CBM*	Come, Beloved of the Maker: Hymns of Susan Palo Cherwien (vol. 2)	LBW*	Lutheran Book of Worship	OBS*	O Blessed Spring: Hymns of Susan Palo Cherwien (vol. 1)
DATH*	Dancing at the Harvest	LLC	Libro de Liturgia y Cántico		
ELW*	Evangelical Lutheran Worship	LS*	LifeSongs	SC	Singing in Community
GS2*	Global Songs 2: Bread for the Journey	MSB1*	Music Sourcebook for Lent and the Three Days	SP*	Singing Our Prayer: A Companion to Holden Prayer Around the Cross
GS3	Global Songs 3: Pave the Way	MSB2*	Music Sourcebook for All Saints through Transfiguration	TFF*	This Far by Faith
GTG	Glory to God (Westminster John Knox)			W&P*	Worship & Praise
				WOV*	With One Voice

Key to Music for Worship

acc	accompaniment	fl	flute	oct	octave	tbn	trombone
bar	baritone	glock	glockenspiel	opt	optional	timp	timpani
bng	bongos	gtr	guitar	orch	orchestra	tpt	trumpet
br	brass	hb	handbells	org	organ	trbl	treble
bsn	bassoon	hc	handchimes	perc	percussion	tri	triangle
cant	cantor	hp	harp	picc	piccolo	U	unison
ch	chimes	hpd	harpsichord	pno	piano	UE	upper elementary
cl	clarinet	hrn	horn	pt	part	vc	violoncello
cont	continuo	inst	instrument	qnt	quintet	vcs	voices
cym	cymbal	kybd	keyboard	qrt	quartet	vla	viola
DB	double or string bass	LE	lower elementary	rec	recorder	vln	violin
dbl	double	M	medium	sax	saxophone	wch	windchimes
desc	descant	MH	medium high	sop	soprano	ww	woodwind
div	divisi	ML	medium low	str	strings	xyl	xylophone
drm	drum	mxd	mixed	synth	synthesizer		
eng hrn	English horn	narr	narrator	tamb	tambourine		
fc	finger cymbals	ob	oboe	tba	tuba		

Key to Music Publishers

ABI	Abingdon	FB	Fred Bock Music	MFS	Mark Foster (Shawnee)	SEL	Selah
AFP	Augsburg Fortress	FLG	Flagstaff Publications	MMP	Masters Music	SF	SoundForthPublications
AG	Agape (Hope)	FTT	From the Top Music		Publication	SHW	Shawnee
AGEHR	American Guild of	GIA	GIA Publications	MSM	MorningStar Music	SMP	Sacred Music Press
	English Handbell Ringers	HAL	Hal Leonard	NOV	Novello (Shawnee)		(Lorenz)
ALF	Alfred	HIN	Hinshaw Music Co.	OCP	Oregon Catholic Press	WAL	Walton
AUR	Aureole	HOP	Hope	OXF	Oxford University Press	WAR	Warner/Belwin
BAR	Bärenreiter	HWG	H.W. Gray (Warner)	PAR	Paraclete	WCC	World Council of
BP	Beckenhorst Press	INT	Integrity (Capitol CMG)	PET	C. F. Peters		Churches
CG	Choristers Guild	JEF	Jeffers	PRE	Presser	WJK	Westminster John Knox
CPH	Concordia	KJO	Kjos	RR	Red River Music	WLP	World Library
DUR	Durand (Presser)	LOR	Lorenz	RW	Ringing Word		Publications
EAR	EarthSongs	LP	The Liturgical Press		Publications	WRD	Word Music
ECS	E. C. Schirmer	MAR	Maranatha			WT	WorshipTogether.com
	(MorningStar)						

A Note on Music Listings

Please note that some choral and instrumental music in the day listings may be out of print. We are unable to research whether musical pieces from other publishers are still available. Why do we still list music if it is out of print? Primarily because many music planners may have that piece in their files and can consider it for use. If a planner wishes to use a piece that has gone out of print, that may still be possible. For Augsburg Fortress resources, call 800/421-0239 or email copyright@1517.media to inquire about onetime reprint rights or to see whether a piece may be available on preludemusicplanner.org, or by print on demand.